M

28 DAY BOO[K]

D0944749

4/12 2+6R

SURVIVORS

SURVIVORS

JEWISH SELF-HELP AND RESCUE IN NAZI-OCCUPIED WESTERN EUROPE

BOB MOORE

OXFORD
UNIVERSITY PRESS

OXFORD

UNIVERSITY PRESS

Great Clarendon Street, Oxford OX2 6DP

Oxford University Press is a department of the University of Oxford.
It furthers the University's objective of excellence in research, scholarship,
and education by publishing worldwide in

Oxford New York

Auckland Cape Town Dar es Salaam Hong Kong Karachi
Kuala Lumpur Madrid Melbourne Mexico City Nairobi
New Delhi Shanghai Taipei Toronto

With offices in

Argentina Austria Brazil Chile Czech Republic France Greece
Guatemala Hungary Italy Japan Poland Portugal Singapore
South Korea Switzerland Thailand Turkey Ukraine Vietnam

Oxford is a registered trade mark of Oxford University Press
in the UK and in certain other countries

Published in the United States
by Oxford University Press Inc., New York

British Library Cataloguing in Publication Data

Data available

Library of Congress Cataloging in Publication Data
Library of Congress Control Number: 2010925656

Typeset by Laserwords Private Limited, Chennai, India
Printed in Great Britain
on acid-free paper by
Clays Ltd, St Ives Plc

ISBN 978-0-19-920823-4

1 3 5 7 9 10 8 6 4 2

For the very special *onderduikster* who inspired the writing
of this book and so much more besides.

Preface

This study began as an investigation into the motivations of non-Jewish rescuers in the Netherlands during the Holocaust period. Hiding and survival
had formed a part of my analysis in *Victims and Survivors: The Persecution
of the Jews in the Nazi-Occupied Netherlands 1940–1945* (1997), but had left
many detailed questions about the help received by Jews unanswered. Some
of these issues have been addressed by the sociological literature that has
used non-Jewish rescuers across Europe as examples of altruistic behaviour,
but the very different research questions and methodology employed to
collect information mean that the historical and contextual perspective is
sometimes lost. Most of this sociological literature has drawn its examples
from a range of countries, but its focus is very much on the behaviour
of non-Jewish rescuers honoured by Yad Vashem. Yet for the historian,
even a cursory examination of the sources reveals that non-Jewish rescuers
are only one element of the story of Jewish survival during the Holocaust,
and that self-help was equally important in many instances. As a result, this
study has ventured beyond an examination of rescuers to look at Jewish
survival across Nazi-occupied Western Europe. In so doing, it represents
an attempt to compare and contrast modes of survival in France, Belgium,
Norway, Denmark, and the Netherlands.

Any project on this scale has to rely on the existing specialist scholarship
on individual countries. In that context, I am grateful to, among others,
Jacques Adler (Melbourne), Dan Michman (Jerusalem), and Lieven Saerens
(Brussels) for their work on the Holocaust in France and Belgium. I
also owe an enormous debt to the historians of particular countries who
have published works based on extensive oral histories. The studies by
Bert-Jan Flim (Netherlands) and Sylvain Brachfeld (Belgium) on the rescue
of Jewish children have been invaluable and, while their contributions
are fully referenced in the text, it is important to acknowledge just
how important their work in collecting material has been; likewise, the
many anonymous interviewers and recorders who have contributed to
the collections at the Wiener Library, Netherlands Institute for War

Documentation (NIOD), CEGES-SOMA and United States Holocaust Memorial Museum (USHMM).

My research on Denmark was aided by scholars at the Department for Holocaust and Genocide Studies within the Danish Institute for International Studies, Copenhagen, and help from Cecilie Banke, as well as welcome contact with former colleague Don Watts. My knowledge of the Holocaust in Norway was greatly enhanced by advice from Arnfinn Moland, who was kind enough to put some unpublished works at my disposal. In Belgium, I was greatly assisted by hospitality afforded by my friend and colleague Frank Caestecker (University of Ghent), who was then working at CEGES-SOMA, and by the Institute's director, Rudi van Doorslaer and his staff. In France, I was given able assistance at the library and archives of the Centre de Documentation Juive Contemporaine in Paris by Diane Afoumado, and in Israel I am delighted to acknowledge the help and hospitality provided by the staff at Yad Vashem in Jerusalem, particularly the Director of the International Institute for Holocaust Research, David Bankier, and Irena Steinfeldt, Director of the Righteous among the Nations Department. More specifically, my sincere thanks go to Eliot Nidam-Orvieto for his thoughts and advice on rescue in France, and to Nannie Braunstein-Beekman for all her help with the archives. My links with the Netherlands go back many years and it is important to acknowledge just how important the Institute for War Documentation in Amsterdam has been to this study. The hospitality afforded to me by directors, Hans Blom, and more recently, Marjan Schwegman has been exemplary, as has the co-operation from staff across the Institute. Its library and archives have provided a major resource base, and I am extremely grateful to its librarian, Dick van Galen Last, for assiduously and exhaustively keeping me up to date with scholarship in this field of study.

This work has been aided financially, both directly and indirectly, by a number of organizations and I am delighted to acknowledge their help here. In 2003, the Center for Advanced Holocaust Studies at the US Holocaust Memorial Museum in Washington DC granted me a Charles S. Revson Fellowship. In 2006, the British Arts and Humanities Research Council and the University of Sheffield provided me with funded study leave in 2006–7 to write the final chapters of this book, and I also received travel funds from the University's Arts Faculty Devolved Research Fund and from the History Department. In addition, I benefited greatly from fellowships at the National Europe Centre at the Australian National University in 2003 and the Université Libre de Bruxelles in 2005, and a Visiting Chair at Sciences Po Institut d'Études Politiques Paris. In this context my thanks go to Professor Pieter Lagrou and his colleagues in Bruxelles, and Professors Jacques Semelin and Claire Andrieu in Paris for acting as my hosts.

On a more personal level, I would like to thank friends and colleagues in the United States, where Professors John Delaney (Kutztown), Troy Paddock (Southern Massachussetts), Vicki Caron (Cornell), and Lenore Weitzman (George Mason), all let me try explaining some of my ideas to their colleagues and students. Likewise, I benefited enormously from the collegial environment of the Center for Advanced Holocaust Studies during my stay in 2003, and help and advice I received from, among others, Suzanne Heim, Holly Case, and Christopher Browning. I have also been fortunate in having friends and colleagues willing to read parts of this book in manuscript form, and here my heartfelt thanks go to Dick van Galen Last, Jacques Semelin, Sue Vice, Eliot Nidam-Orvieto, Megan Koreman and Barbara Hately-Broad. Their comments, corrections and insights have been invaluable in improving the text, but whatever errors and omissions remain are the responsibility of the author.

Sheffield
August 2009

Contents

List of Illustrations

List of Maps

I

Introduction

Only when the Allied armies began to drive back German forces from the territory they had occupied in Europe did the world become fully aware of the enormity of Nazi crimes. The rumours and reports of slave labour and extermination programmes were given substance by the gruesome discoveries of the Red Army as it reoccupied Soviet territory in 1943 and 1944 before advancing across Poland to the gates of Berlin. In tandem with this, the armies of the Western powers invaded France and then Belgium, reaching the southern Netherlands by early September 1944 before being halted until the early spring of 1945, when the final assault on Germany took place. The day of liberation, wherever and whenever it took place, was a new dawn for all, but perhaps most poignantly for the Jews who had managed to survive the occupation and, unlike so many of their co-religionists who had perished at the hands of the Nazi *Einsatzgruppen* or in the death camps of Eastern Europe, were able to come out from their hiding places into a new era where they were not constantly under threat of arrest and summary deportation. However, the liberation guaranteed them nothing, as the months and years that followed would demonstrate, save the fact that their parentage would no longer be a matter of life and death.

On emerging from their shadow existence, these survivors often only then discovered the full horror of what had befallen their communities and their families. Yet this knowledge begged a fundamental question for all of them: to what did they owe their own survival? Was it due to their own efforts and farsightedness? Was it a result of the inefficiencies of the system created to trap them? Was it down to the efforts of others who had helped and sheltered them—often at the risk of their own safety and well-being—or to their own particular, and essentially unique circumstances? The small numbers of returnees from the camps could also pose questions about their survival, albeit from a very different perspective. However, for the majority, there was little or no time for such reflections as there were other, more pressing battles to be fought—daily struggles for food and shelter, rebuilding shattered lives and families, reasserting rights to homes and property confiscated or stolen under the Nazi regime and planning for a future in Europe, Palestine or elsewhere in the world.

Jewish survival has, nevertheless, been a central concern of Holocaust scholarship, and this study examines this issue in a Western European context, comparing the situations in the Low Countries, France, Norway and Denmark. Ostensibly there are many similarities in these five case studies although, as will become apparent, it was often the minor variations in circumstances and structures that made material differences to survival rates. There is, inevitably, a temptation to make the comparison much wider and include all Nazi-occupied territories, but the experiences of the Jews from Poland, the Baltic States, and the Soviet Union who were rounded up in their hundreds of thousands and killed were materially different from their counterparts in the West. Many were murdered in their own towns and villages by *Einsatzgruppen* as the Germans advanced, in some cases betrayed by their neighbours. Millions of others were trapped in the ghettoes of the General Government from which there was little chance of escape before being deported to the death camps, where even short-term survival was exceptional. Yet even those who did manage to evade capture or escape faced a hostile environment where the vast majority of their Polish neighbours had little sympathy for their plight. Ingrained antisemitism played a major role here, as did the fact that many millions of Poles were also subject to radical Nazi race and resettlement policies. Any outside help for Jews was therefore a relative rarity, both in Poland and also in other occupied Eastern European territories, and studies suggest that what help there was tended to come from the more marginal members of society.[1] Their history and their fate led to the famous phrase invoked by Hannah Arendt, Raul Hilberg and others: that the Jews went to the gas chambers 'like lambs to the slaughter'.[2] More recent research has served to modify this rather sweeping generalization by focusing on examples of Jewish partisan resistance and the 'fighting' ghetto leaderships: the often ignored instances of Jewish self-help.[3] Nevertheless, the fact remains that the efficiency of the system of annihilation, coupled with the highly adverse circumstances experienced by Jews in Eastern Europe, meant that their ability to survive the onslaught was extremely limited.

The situation of Jews in Germany, who had been exposed to increasing levels of Nazi persecution since 1933, and their Austrian co-religionists who suffered the same fate in the aftermath of the *Anschluss* have also been excluded from direct comparison. Substantial numbers had contrived, or been forced, to emigrate before most borders were closed in September 1939.[4] Of those that remained, thousands were deported from the country in the early period of the war, leaving only a minority who were able to attempt evasion inside the Reich, either on their own or with help from outside.[5] Conditions for the Jews in Italy were also very different. The Fascist regime had never wholeheartedly embraced antisemitism, even allowing for the anti-Jewish legislation in 1938. Thus Italy remained relatively safe for Jews, even acting as a haven for escapees from occupied France, until the armistice of September 1943 brought German forces and the bureaucracy of persecution into the north.[6] While there were instances of wartime self-help and rescue in both countries, the circumstances in which they took place make direct comparisons with the rest of Western Europe difficult.

In contrast to Eastern Europe, most of the half million or so Jews in continental Western Europe proved to have a better chance of evading the 'final solution'. Unlike Poland, where the Jews represented around 10 per cent of the population, they were small minorities in the countries of the West, numbering less than 1 per cent. However, there were important variations in their origins. Of the 300–320,000 Jews in France in 1940, a sizeable minority were non-French nationals and, of the French Jews, a good many had acquired their citizenship through naturalization.[7] In October 1940, the German census of all Jews in Belgium over the age of 15 showed that there were around 42,652 adult Jews in the country as a whole, and by adding an assumed proportion of children, this gave a total of around 55,600, of whom almost 95 per cent were foreign nationals.[8] Almost the reverse was true in the Netherlands, where comparable figures enumerated approximately 118,500 indigenous Jews and a further 21,750 foreign Jews, most of whom were recent refugees from Germany or Austria—a total of *c.*140,000.[9] Neither Denmark nor Norway had played host to any appreciable numbers of refugees, and the Jews there numbered only around 8,000 and 2,000 respectively, and represented only a minuscule 0.18 per cent and 0.05 per cent of their national populations.[10]

Nazi perceptions of Scandinavia, the Low Countries and France were conditioned both by racial thinking and the more practical imperatives of the war. Indigenous populations here were treated 'correctly', and in the first two years of occupation, some attempts were made to convert them to the ideas of National Socialism. As a direct result, policies directed against the Jews were constrained and only introduced gradually in order to limit public disquiet and the possibilities of disruption. Jewish reactions to the increasing persecution were also conditioned by local factors: by the social, economic and national composition of their communities, and by their relationships with their non-Jewish neighbours. Although subjected to processes of identification, isolation, expropriation and deportation like their co-religionists in the East, the Jews trapped inside occupied Western Europe had considerably higher survival rates, albeit that the percentages varied enormously between countries. Around 60 per cent of the Jews in Belgium survived the war, as did about 75 per cent in France and well over 95 per cent in Denmark, the only exception being the Netherlands where the 75 per cent mortality figure was more comparable with Eastern Europe.[11] In the vast majority of cases, they owed their lives to avoiding the deportation processes altogether, as returnees from the camps in the East were uniformly small in number. While their survival encompassed a myriad of individual stories, these can be distilled down to just two basic narratives: escape into a neutral country, almost invariably Switzerland, Spain or Sweden, or hiding, either entirely within the realms of illegality or 'cloaked' in some form that disguised their Jewishness.

That said, the two best-known stories of Jewish escape and hiding in Western Europe are anything but typical. The mass escape of Jews from Denmark to neutral Sweden during and after October 1943 is often held up as an example of what might have been possible elsewhere, but the circumstances, the element of German collusion, and the timing of events, all make this an exceptional case and not really comparable with conditions in the rest of Western Europe. Likewise, by far the most famous example of Jews going into hiding comes from the Frank family in Amsterdam, brought to life by the chronicle of their experiences and her own life written by their daughter Anne. The impact of her diary in countries across the globe since its publication, together with the cornucopia of additional books, articles and commentaries, means that she has become an iconic figure who stands for all the six million murdered in the Holocaust. Yet her position as a victim, along with most of her family, has tended to obscure the unrepresentative nature of their experiences in hiding. Father Otto was able to use his resources to plan in advance of the deportations, and he was able to harness the help of his non-Jewish business partners to create a hiding place in their premises. The family, unlike most Jews in Eastern Europe, had not been ghettoized by the Germans and continued to live at home until the call up for 'labour service in the East' arrived. Their help came primarily from people they knew, and their hiding place remained the same until they were betrayed to the Gestapo in 1944.[12] All these factors are in stark contrast to the experiences of most of the Jews in occupied Europe and even those of other Jews in Amsterdam itself. The only typical element relates to their experiences as Jews in hiding—in the sense that they were discovered and deported—a fate that befell many others. Thus, as with Eastern Europe, where Oskar Schindler has become the most celebrated example of a non-Jewish rescuer, the most often cited examples of Jewish hiding and rescue are untypical of what befell the majority of Jews who survived the Holocaust.[13]

Only a very small minority of these survivors owed their salvation entirely to their own efforts, and most Jews in Western Europe were reliant at some point on help from others, either Gentiles or fellow Jews: 'rescuers' who took risks to save others from Nazi persecution. Until now, academic attention has been focused on this topic primarily from only one perspective, namely the 'righteousness' of the Gentile rescuers. This is evident in the recognition and memorialization awarded to non-Jewish rescuers by Yad Vashem, where, by April 2009, the award of 'Righteous among the Nations' has been made to more than 22,700 individuals, and the numbers continue to grow as more stories come to light.[14] While this has been the most important development in bringing non-Jewish help to the forefront of discussions on Jewish survival during the Holocaust, the very criteria used by its Commissions for the Designation of the Righteous have served to create anomalies in distribution.[15] For example, there remain far more 'righteous Gentiles' from the Netherlands than from neighbouring Belgium, yet Jewish survival rates in the latter country were much higher.[16] The main explanation for this seems to be in the quantity and quality of information and contemporary testimony available on rescues carried out in the two countries. In this respect, the Dutch government's decision to carry out immediate research on the occupation for a national official history[17] greatly aided the identification and honouring of rescuers in the Netherlands at an early stage. Moreover, it was in the interest of the Netherlands to play up its relationship with the newly created state of Israel at a time when the full scope of the tragedy that had befallen Dutch Jewry during the occupation was becoming increasingly manifest. The identification of rescuers in other countries had no such in-built advantages and has continued to rely mainly on the piecemeal, and sometimes serendipitous, survival of witnesses and documentation.

While this recognition can be seen as an important task in its own right, it has led to the collection and publication of narratives with little attention being paid to the geographical or political context in which the rescues took place, or any wider analysis for the explanations behind them save for some broad categorizations.[18] This trend has been compounded by the use of information on righteous rescuers as the basis for sociological studies on the origins of altruism,[19] and on the highlighting of Christian motivations behind acts of rescue and the behaviour of particular individuals.[20] More recent works have made great play with further in-depth interviews of surviving rescuers and non-rescuers, comparing and contrasting behaviour patterns in an attempt to draw overarching conclusions about the impact of Christian belief and moral values as well as analyses of altruism.[21] While such studies play a very important role within their own disciplines, their focus on particular rescuers cannot do justice to the wider aspects of understanding rescue and Jewish survival during the Holocaust. Four features are essentially missing. The first is the importance of the chronological, geographical and social context to acts of rescue by non-Jews; the second is the relationship between individual acts of rescue and the creation or existence of networks; the third relates to the structure and organization of the Jewish communities in Western Europe; and the fourth is the interrelationship between rescue by Gentiles and Jewish self-help.

It is widely acknowledged that help for the Jews during the occupation period had to have some form of social context, but it is only in recent years that the relationships between Jews and non-Jews in the interwar period and more generally have been subjected to closer scrutiny, not only in relation to questions of rescue, but in the wider framework of non-Jews as bystanders to the Holocaust.[22] This has led to new insights into the ways Jews were perceived by their neighbours and has undoubtedly helped to shape an understanding of popular reactions when the persecutions and deportations began. There is also the vexed question of the risks run by would-be rescuers. It is often implied that rescue was invariably a matter of life and death, both for the rescuer and the person, or persons, rescued, but this takes no account of the fact that the laws, decrees and regulations that prohibited helping Jews varied enormously from one country to another, and only developed into their final and most draconian forms relatively late in the occupation period.[23] While we should be most concerned with what the rescuers and rescued thought would happen to them if they were caught, this is difficult to ascertain at a distance, as the punishments dictated by such laws were often not rigorously implemented in practice.[24]

However, even national studies have a tendency to underplay or ignore regional variations and often fail to identify local features, such as the existence of rural traditions or the dynamics of border regions that had an important bearing on how Jews were perceived and treated. Furthermore, there is the question of individual and organized help given to the Jews by the Christian churches. In the immediate post-war era, all Christian denominations were keen to stress their opposition to Nazism during the occupation, but rescue activities were seldom given much prominence. In the Dutch case, authors focused almost exclusively on the public pronouncements of the Church leadership—whether on the persecution of the Jews or on the wider imposition of Nazi authority—while all-but ignoring the practical, but often very important, help provided by individual clergymen and parishes.[25] In fact, the differing attitudes of leading clergymen and the very organizational structures of their churches were to have a profound effect on the incidence of rescue across the entire region.

Because the sociological and social anthropological studies of rescue are primarily concerned with interrogating and understanding the role of the individuals—a tendency reinforced by the widespread collection of individual testimonies for the same purpose—the role played by organized networks has often been downplayed. Yet even the most cursory examination of the subject reveals that most participants were ultimately linked into, or became members of, wider organizations created or adapted to oppose the occupation, or more specifically, to meet the needs of Jews and others on the run from the Nazis. This, in turn, raises questions about how individuals became involved in rescue. Were they all motivated and drawn in by their own experiences or was their involvement prompted by others? Inevitably perhaps, the answer is complex. Many rescuers became involved through direct contact with victimized Jews or with the machinery of Nazi persecution. Some never graduated beyond being individual rescuers—albeit perhaps helped by a network later in the occupation—but there were others who expanded their commitment by drawing in other people, whether family members, neighbours, professional contacts or church congregations, to meet the needs of those on the run. It may come as some surprise, given the focus on righteousness and altruism, that many were drawn in, not by individual commitment, but by prompts from others. Indeed, they often did so with some misgivings and initial reticence, as is shown by the testimonies of network organizers. Knowing how these networks developed holds the key to understanding rescue activities, and why there could be both 'havens' and 'deserts' in specific areas when it came to helping fugitive Jews.

In the same way, the pre-war social, economic and organizational structures of the Jewish communities themselves have often been ignored as a factor in understanding their responses to persecution. As has been shown, the numbers of immigrant and refugee Jews varied enormously across Western Europe, and this had a major impact on how communities responded to the authority of the state and then to the impositions of the occupying Germans. Similarly, the distribution of wealth and material differences directly affected the ability of these communities to defend themselves at an individual and at a collective level, and there were also major variations in their organizational structures and leadership. This leads to the final factor that has to be considered in this context; that is, the existence and extent of Jewish self-help against the Nazis. Discussion of this often-ignored element has been heavily influenced by the assumption that the Jews were passive victims and divided among themselves, and that many community leaders were ineffective at best, and collaborationist at worst. This perspective has meant that steps taken by individual Jews and local organizations to avoid identification and deportation, either on their own or in collusion with non-Jewish help have often been ignored. Only recently, and perhaps in a belated response to this perception, have scholars begun to re-evaluate the importance of self-help in Jewish resistance and Jewish survival.[26]

In order to make a full evaluation of the incidence of rescue, it is therefore essential to write these aspects into the analysis, and to look, not at comparisons between individual rescuers, but at rescue in all its forms as an agent of Jewish survival, rather than as an end in itself. This allows a greater consideration of Jewish self-help, and also highlights rescues that were not motivated by philanthropic or altruistic motives and that would—by definition—be excluded from recognition by Yad Vashem. Put another way, it is important to recognize that not all manifestations of rescue were based on righteousness. In addition, in order to draw any worthwhile conclusions about the rescue and survival of Jews in Western Europe, it is essential to maintain a balance between the advantages of a comparative approach to the subject and an awareness of the various national contexts involved.

The comparative approach has become more popular among historians over the last twenty years as a means of understanding apparently similar phenomena in different countries, but its use remains problematic. The 'discovery' that Jewish mortality during the Holocaust varied enormously between Western European countries that had ostensibly similar experiences of German occupation during the Second World War prompted some of the earliest attempts at using comparative methods to investigate this apparent anomaly.[27] Yet two of the most respected historians and pioneers in this field, Robert Paxton and Michael Marrus, were forced to conclude that any generalizations broke apart on the 'stubborn particularities of each of [their] countries'.[28] Their comments were not intended to deter other researchers or preclude future work, but served to highlight the problems involved—namely, the vast array of changing circumstances and situations that existed within each national case study and how difficult it was to define a national picture, let alone draw parallels across national frontiers. More recent studies in the Netherlands have also suggested that the national model is much too broad to be meaningful and that regional and even local models may be more instructive.[29]

By the same token, it is also important to place rescue and the incidence of Jewish survival within the wider context of the Holocaust and the national historiographies of German occupation. Perhaps because the Netherlands had by far the highest Jewish mortality of the Western European states, it has also had the most extensive public debates on how this national disaster occurred. One simple, but nevertheless insightful observation based on a comparative approach was that, unlike her neighbours, the Netherlands had no 'favourable factor' that had served to prevent arrests and deportations or that had favoured hiding and rescue.[30] Further comparative analysis, while providing no definitive answers to the central question of why so many more Jews had fallen victim to Nazi persecution than in other states, did at least identify a series of issues for investigation under the three umbrella headings of persecutors, victims and 'circumstances'.[31] The key variables that marked out the Dutch case were perceived to be the relative cohesion of German rule in the Netherlands vis-à-vis the situation elsewhere and the influence of the SS; the relative compliance of both the Dutch public and bureaucracy to German measures against the Jews; and the relatively high level of integration of the Jewish community. More recent comparisons of Belgium and the Netherlands have identified contrasts in the German systems of rounding up and deporting the Jews, and also differences in the Jewish organizations created or adapted to represent the community. One final factor identified in this context and directly relevant to the question of rescue was that Belgium (and by implication France as well) presented more opportunities to go into hiding than the Netherlands.[32] Very few, if any of these factors can be compared empirically as we have neither the statistical evidence nor sufficient examples to make coherent judgements, but this should not act as a deterrent to drawing some conclusions.

To provide a comprehensive treatment of all the factors and issues raised here would be an impossible task, and what follows draws on suitable examples to demonstrate the many different ways in which the Jews of Western Europe managed to survive the Nazi occupation. The book begins with the first major attempts at escape from the Nazis, namely the exodus of millions of civilians that took place from the Netherlands, Belgium and France in front of the German advance. Relatively few Jews managed to escape anywhere that ultimately guaranteed their safety in this period, but the creation of vast numbers of refugees did provide the first of many organizations and relationships that would, in time, contribute to rescue and Jewish survival as the persecution increased, especially in southern France. The period between the arrival of the Germans and the first mass deportations in July 1942 also saw the nascence of attempts to escape from Nazi-held territory, and the following chapters examine this in the unoccupied zone of France and then in the rest of occupied Europe. This involves some celebrated cases such as Varian Fry in Marseilles, but also many other unsung individuals and groups who provided aid to those on the run, or were drawn into helping Jews through charitable and welfare work. Escape lines into Switzerland or Spain were to become central to the operations of many groups helping resisters, Allied servicemen and former POWs as well as Jews. If nothing else, this demonstrates that the rescue of Jews was far from being an activity isolated from other forms of opposition and resistance to the Germans—even in this early stage of the occupation, but it also highlights the involvement of all manner of people in these activities, and a huge range of motivations, from the purely philanthropic through the material and commercial to the downright exploitative. As will become apparent, the motives of the rescuers had no more than a tangential effect on the likely survival of those rescued, and even the most upright and law-abiding of rescuers could find themselves soliciting help from criminals and dubious elements within society.

The mixture of high moral motives with increasing recourse to illegal means was certainly evident within many of the organizations that tried to assist the Jews and other (foreign) refugees incarcerated in appalling conditions in the unoccupied zone of France by the Vichy regime. While there were individual actors here who have rightly been recognized and lauded for their work, the overwhelming impression is of organizational help, albeit at a very early stage in its development. For example, the Protestant CIMADE expanded its activities helping Spanish Republican refugees in the camps to include the foreign Jews and anti-Nazi activists. Its history also shows how the various relief agencies in the unoccupied zone of France were already working together: a feature of rescue in this region until the German and Italian armies occupied the whole country in November 1942. Highlighting rescue in Vichy France should not be allowed to obscure the fact that, although the unoccupied zone was the most obvious staging post for escape into Spain or Switzerland, there were other escape lines that began in the Netherlands or Belgium and helped both Jews and other fugitives to escape southwards. Further north there were the rescue organizations and individual escapes made by members of the small Norwegian Jewish community across the border into Sweden, as well as the much-vaunted escape of most Danish Jews to the same country in October 1943.

It is impossible to disaggregate escapes from wider forms of rescue where Jews were hidden inside occupied Europe as the two were never mutually exclusive, but the country-specific chapters that follow examine rescue activities by non-Jews and their relationship to Jewish self-help in a national context. This not only shows the extent and range of these activities, but also highlights the many regional and local differences within and between the different countries. Of major importance here is understanding how pre-war social and political structures affected the ways in which Jewish communities and the wider population responded to German occupation and to the initial measures against the Jews. Thus the analysis begins with an assessment of how Jewish self-help emerged, before showing how this was augmented by outside assistance.

One notable feature of the literature in the last twenty years has been an outpouring of books and articles on the saving of Jewish children.[33]

Treating them as a separate category, nevertheless, requires some further explanation. One very practical reason is that the child survivors lived further into the twentieth century, and often beyond, and could still identify and provide testamentary evidence on those who had sheltered them many years after the event. However, there is no doubt that Jewish children were a privileged group across Western Europe: widely perceived by their Gentile neighbours as 'innocents' in a way that their parents were not; easier to hide as family members or evacuees; and more acceptable and less threatening as house-guests. These are all positive features that figure heavily in the narratives, but it is important to show that there was also a negative side to the story that went unrecorded or was ignored in the search for the righteous, namely that children could be taken in to be exploited as cheap labour or worse, or in exchange for exorbitant charges for bed and board, or as targets for conversion. Such cases exist across Western Europe and are not peculiar to any particular social or religious milieu. Here again, the fact that the rescuers' motivations may have been far from pure was no bar to the rescue being 'successful' and the fugitive surviving the occupation. One further complication to an understanding of this topic is the acrimony caused across Western Europe in the post-war era by the fate of Jewish orphans. Three high profile cases in France, Belgium and the Netherlands all had similar features in that the children concerned had been successfully sheltered during the occupation but were then retained by their wartime foster parents in defiance of state authority and to the outrage of the residual Jewish communities. In each case, devout Christian rescuers claimed to see it as their duty to retain their charges within the Christian milieux in which they had been raised—not only as a religious obligation, but also to protect the immortal souls of the children concerned.[34]

Beyond the special case of children, there were also unlikely rescues carried out by the persecutors themselves. Even leading Nazis protected certain individuals in return for favours or services rendered. Lower level functionaries were likewise involved in protecting Jews, and even some in particular positions have been credited with trying to save entire groups, for example the 'racial expert' Hans-Georg Calmeyer, who used his executive position to protect the Sephardic Jews in the Netherlands. The term 'Nazi rescuer' seems inherently contradictory, but in practice highlights some of the problems of seeing rescue as a black and white issue.[35] At the other end of this scale there were Jews who were formally employed by the

German security services to track down and betray their co-religionists. Although small in number, it could be argued that this was just another form of self-help, albeit under duress, but one that could also be seen as a survival strategy. Finally, not all the Jewish victims of Nazi policies were themselves law-abiding citizens, and there are instances of survival through involvement with the underworld, and where discovery was often a function of criminal behaviour rather than pursuit or betrayal as a Jew.

Situating self-help and rescue in its wider context has been assisted by several recent historiographical trends. The shift towards social history from the late 1970s onwards in Western Europe has led to a more nuanced approach to how societies reacted to occupation: away from the simplistic resistance myths and narratives that had helped to bolster national cohesion and social reconstruction in the immediate post-war years. Black and white interpretations of behaviour during the occupation have been replaced by approaches that stress the shades of grey involved.[36] Indeed, in recent times, it has become almost impossible to discuss the role of any state, religious or private institution during the occupation without some reference—and often quite extensive reference—to antisemitism and the persecution of the Jews.[37] Likewise, the importance of Jewish self-help is now firmly recognized as a factor in resistance and survival.

Finally, the growth of interest in other genocides has also opened up new avenues for comparing rescue in Nazi-occupied Europe with examples of similar behaviour from other case studies.[38] Of greatest relevance here are the recent examples of Bosnia and Rwanda, where examples of civilian rescues have come to light, but perhaps as instructive, if less accessible, has been the role of rescuers in the Armenian genocide during the First World War.[39] For the most part, these studies have dealt with the rescue of civilians by other civilians, but the history of the First World War also provides us with other examples of rescue—in the help offered by civilians in German-occupied Europe to allied servicemen in hiding, escaping POWs, deserters, and draft-dodgers. Moreover, in the case of Belgium—overrun in 1914 and in 1940—there are clear linkages between resistance and rescue activities in both occupations. The crucial conclusion here is that 'rescue' was not unique to the Second World War except insofar as the Jews became the primary targets of the occupation regime. Yet even this requires some qualification. Jews were by no means the only victims of Nazi persecution, albeit they were the only ones for whom capture could almost automatically be equated with death, at least after the summer of 1942. Political opponents were the first targets, as they had been in Germany in 1933, and they were followed, not just by Jews, but also by many hundreds of thousands of others avoiding the imposition of German measures, most notably those related to forced labour. Thus, even when the plight of the Jews was at its height and the first mass deportations from Western Europe began in July 1942, they remained just one of the groups, albeit large in numbers, who were perceived as victim of the Nazis. This commonality of experience is again not often reflected in the available literature. Discussions of national resistance to Nazism often marginalize the help given to Jews and, likewise, texts on the fate of Jews and the incidence of rescue often have few reflections on the wider context of resistance. There are, of course, notable and honourable exceptions, but the division remains, and the wider social context of rescue is often lost in the many narratives that focus on the heroism of individuals. Without wishing to detract from the undoubted heroism of many rescuers and the bravery of the Jews who defied the Germans by refusing to allow themselves to be deported, this study is an attempt to place both self-help and rescue into a wider chronological and national context, in order to build a more objective picture of how some Jews in Western Europe managed to survive the Holocaust.

2

Escape in the First Months

The Chaos of May–June 1940

The rapidity with which the German armed forces overran all of Western Europe between April and June 1940 came as a massive shock. Norway was overrun during April in spite of British and French military assistance, and on 10 May, the full force of the Nazi war machine was unleashed on France and the Low Countries. People living close to the frontier awoke that morning to find the Germans already in control. In the days and weeks that followed, they were joined by most of their countrymen as the *Wehrmacht* continued its inexorable and apparently unstoppable advance into France. Many in Belgium and the Netherlands found it hard to credit that their carefully constructed and maintained political neutrality had been so comprehensively ignored, or in the case of the French, that their armies could so easily be brushed aside.

For civilians with time to react, there was the possibility of flight in advance of the German armies, either across the Channel to England or southwards away from the war. In the Netherlands, where the overt belief in the power of neutrality had perhaps been greatest, the shock of invasion was most strongly felt.[1] Almost from the first day of hostilities, people made plans to flee. Three days into the war, when it became apparent that the Dutch armies were unlikely to contain the German advance, there was a flood of refugees, including many Jews, towards the roads leading south, or to one of the North Sea ports. Ijmuiden, the closest to Amsterdam, was besieged with refugees attempting to reach whatever shipping they could find. Ultimately, the authorities closed the port as a precursor to the oil storage tanks being blown up, and this served to limit still further the numbers who were able to escape. One exception

was Truus Wijsmuller-Meier who persuaded the guards to let her through
with a group of children from the *kindertransporte*, who were thus able to
escape to England.[2] Less fortunate was the Amsterdam art dealer, Jacques
Goudstikker, who managed to find passage on a ship, only to die when he
fell down a hatchway.[3]

   The thousands heading south crossed into Belgium, but were soon joined
by Jews and many others from both Antwerp and Brussels as it became
clear that the German advance was unstoppable, and all headed for the
French border.[4] All Belgians had good reason to fear occupation, having
had direct experience of German hegemony in the years 1914 to 1918, but
members of the Jewish communities clearly saw even greater risks in Nazi
rule. Exactly how many chose to leave their homes will never be known
but their numbers were swelled by thousands of émigrés from Germany
and Austria who had found temporary refuge in Western Europe. In their
panic, many left their homes with little or no preparation; sometimes they
handed the house keys and their property to neighbours or people they
trusted.[5] Cars and other vehicles were just abandoned at ports, at breaks
in the road or when they ran out of petrol. Many paid exorbitantly high
prices for passages on ships attempting to leave—and in some cases even
bartered to buy small boats themselves. There were even some hardy souls
who succeeded in crossing the North Sea in a canoe. How many others
failed in such foolhardy attempts will probably never be known.[6] Equally
expensive were journeys overland, including one group that was charged
BFr.600 each for the journey from Antwerp into France.[7] It was estimated
that some 3 million refugee civilians were caught in Western Flanders when
the German advance to the Channel ports cut off their means of escape,
while the remainder fled as far south into France as possible, joined all the
time by further cohorts of frightened people, where they also effectively
became trapped, as further journeys were difficult if not impossible without
funds and proper documentation.[8]

   It is difficult to characterize the chaos that was France in the days and
weeks surrounding the armistice. In the short term, nothing was fixed.
Knowledge of the German advance and what was happening was largely
confined to rumour. The flow of Dutch and Belgians was augmented by
French civilians driven out of their homes by military action or fleeing
from the prospect of living under *les boches*. The towns and cities of the
north, remembering the occupation and conditions of the First World
War, emptied rapidly. It was estimated that the urban populations here

dropped by anything up to 90 per cent, but small communes were equally deserted. Overall, it has been estimated that between 6 and 8 million people in France left their homes and took to the road, usually without any clear idea of where they were going.[9] As the north emptied, so the south became filled with displaced people. The population of Bordeaux doubled to 600,000, helped no doubt by the evacuation of the government there, and further south in Pau there was a fivefold increase to 150,000.[10] Georges Friedmann, a philosopher in peacetime, who was a lieutenant in the French Army described what he saw:

> A whole country seems to have given itself up. Everything has collapsed, imploded. The 'refugees' (how few of them really deserve the name), the runaways, the panic-stricken, the pitiable herds of civilians are still in the village streets, the town squares and the roads, mixed in with the debris of the most powerful army—we were told—in Europe.[11]

Likewise, the memoirs of Gustave Folcher recounting the scene near Sedan:

> the refugees pass by in every kind of transport. I see poor old women coming from Luxemburg and Belgium, dragging with great difficulty, the poor things, little wagons, children's prams and some of them even wheelbarrows, often with a baby only a few months old sitting on top. And the endless file-past continues.[12]

Like other cities in the northern half of France, Paris was also depopulated as crowds descended on every form of available transport—or just walked—heading away from the German advance. In all three countries, many undoubtedly remained unaware of what Nazi occupation might bring, while others chose to ignore it or to seek other solutions, most notably in suicide. Lazare gives a very clear exposition of what happened in Paris.

> Tens of thousands of Parisian Jews had also chosen the route of exodus. Among those who had not fled were the families of prisoners, officials, owners of small stores, artisans, and the most poverty stricken proletariat. Ignorant of French and of France, of which they knew only a neighbourhood to which they had barely become acclimated, the recent immigrants had scarcely budged.[13]

In effect, the French Jews who had contacts elsewhere or knowledge of the country were more likely to have left, unless there were material or family reasons that encouraged them to stay put, whereas immigrants and recent refugees, with no access to contacts, knowledge or resources were trapped by their circumstances.[14]

Thus when the city was occupied on 14 June, there were reputedly only 800,000 of the normal 3 million people still in residence. Explanations for the sheer scale of exodus have been linked with wider questions about the speed and totality of French defeat in the summer of 1940, but the memory of the First World War certainly loomed large in many minds, with panic being increased by stories told by those arriving from the north.[15] By the time Pétain sued for a negotiated peace, the whole country was in complete political and administrative disarray. One indicator of the scale of disorganization and panic was that in the weeks and months following the armistice, the Red Cross reunited no less than 90,000 children who had been separated from their parents in the flight.[16]

The vast majority of the refugees on the road were fleeing from no more than a generalized fear of what German hegemony might bring, but for the Jewish and left-wing émigrés who had fled to France, and particularly Paris, in the 1930s, the threat was both real and well founded. Establishing their precise numbers is particularly difficult, not least because restrictive entry policies in the later 1930s meant that many refugees had entered these Western European states illegally, and were therefore unknown to the authorities. One estimate suggests a maximum number of around 60,000 German nationals at any given time, but to these need to be added 5–6,000 refugees from the Saarland and another 18,000 who arrived from Austria after the *Anschluss*.[17] These were all people who might have had some claim to German citizenship had it not been for Nazi policies. In the panic that followed the outbreak of war in September 1939, many males had been interned in camps by the French authorities, only to be released and sometimes then re-interned in May 1940. However, they were not the only refugee and émigré Jews in France, as the country had also provided a haven for many thousands of Eastern European Jews, fleeing persecution and economic disadvantage in their home countries, or having been driven out of Germany. Some had become naturalized French citizens during their stay, others had chosen not to, or had not been resident long enough to consider such an option.

In these first weeks and months after the exodus and the armistice, both the native Jews and foreign refugees had to re-orientate themselves to their changed circumstances and surroundings. Those not in any apparent danger chose, or were persuaded, to return to their homes, but the Jews who had fled from the north or who had already been incarcerated by the French authorities had no such option. For them, the only choices were whether to stay under Pétainist rule in the hope that this would provide adequate protection from the Nazis, or to seek refuge further afield. For foreigners in general, their first obvious point of contact would normally have been with their diplomatic representatives, but for German, Czech, Austrian and now Polish citizens this was no longer practical. Their identity documents, papers and rights to any form of citizenship were thus time-limited, if not already expired. A return to their country of origin was also impossible, and thus they, and many others, looked for avenues to escape via the diplomatic representatives of other (neutral) nations. These were largely unforthcoming, as the uncertain international status of the Vichy regime meant that diplomatic credentials were also in doubt once the armistice had been signed. In addition, the war had led to highly restrictive consular policies on the issue of visas, whether for immigration or just for transit purposes. Nonetheless, this chaotic situation did produce the first diplomatic rescuer of the occupation period: a previously unremarkable Portuguese consul named Aristide de Sousa Mendes.

Diplomats as Rescuers

Aristide de Sousa Mendes

Portugal under Salazar had not been considered as a preferred destination for refugees from Nazi Germany in the period after 1933 as there were much more welcoming prospects, politically and economically, elsewhere in the world. A German Embassy report from Lisbon in 1935 noted that there were only about 600 German and Austrian refugees in the country.[18] A number had come from the Hamburg Sephardic (Portuguese) Community, and it appears that the Portuguese consul in Berlin had been sympathetic to other would-be immigrants by granting them entry permits and facilitating the transport of their belongings, even though they had no possibility of earning a living officially.[19] However, the regime had become increasingly worried about the possibility of subversion through an influx of foreign refugees, a fear that had been accentuated by the Spanish Civil War. As a result, from 1935 onwards, visa applications were vetted by the International Section of the Polícia de Vigilancia e Defenza do Estado (State Security Police, PVDE).[20] This had prompted complaints from several Portuguese consuls that their discretion to issue visas was being overridden by the PVDE. In theory, German and Austrian visitors to Portugal did not need visas, but because passports for Jews and political opponents would become invalid once they left the Third Reich, the Portuguese government informed the Germans in October 1938 that all holders of passports with a 'J' stamp would henceforward require a visa.[21] They would not be allowed to settle in Portugal but could stay as tourists for 30 days.

The Portuguese ambassador to Berlin, Alberto da Veiga Simões, had tried to resist the increasing incursions of the PVDE and, in spite of his apparent indifference to the victims of Nazism in general, he was keen to help a limited number of Jews and others who were members of the *haute bourgeoisie* or connected to the diplomatic circle. He thus began issuing visas without reference to Lisbon, as did his subordinate in Hamburg.[22] In his case, the choice of beneficiaries was very specific and limited to people he knew, and who were considered worthy or had been of service to Portuguese interests. In that regard, his behaviour did not stray far from that demanded of a diplomat, and his issuance of visas in defiance of regulations was primarily connected with the battle for supremacy between the consular department and the PVDE.[23]

The same cannot be said of the Portuguese consul in Bordeaux, Aristide de Sousa Mendes. He was a career diplomat from an old aristocratic family who had held a number of previous postings around the globe, and had been in Antwerp for nine years before being sent to Bordeaux in September 1938.[24] On 13 November 1938, he received Circular 14 from the Foreign Ministry in Lisbon, which listed groups of people to whom visas should not be issued, including aliens of dubious or contested nationality, stateless or holders of Nansen Passports, aliens whom the consul judged had no valid reasons for entering Portugal or whose passports indicated that they would have difficulty returning to their country of origin, and Jews expelled from their countries of origin and stripped of their nationality.[25]

The instructions could not have been clearer. In the next few months, de Sousa Mendes did refer cases back to Lisbon but often issued the visas in advance, knowing that the time taken to get a reply would mean the applicants would miss their only chance to travel. On one occasion, a refugee arrived in Lisbon with a visa dated 1 March 1940 in spite of the fact that the Foreign Ministry had refused approval some days later. De Sousa Mendes was sent a sharp rebuke by his superiors,[26] but in a letter to his brother he indicated that he had 'no problems with his conscience' on this matter, and therefore presumably not with any other similar cases where he issued documents in defiance of Circular 14. At this stage, the numbers involved were small, and the authorities in Lisbon were dealing almost exclusively with people who did have genuine onward travel plans. Thus it was easier to send them on their way rather than to try and repatriate them.

After 10 May 1940, the city was flooded with French government officials and refugees of all nationalities.[27] Inevitably, it was the consulates of the neutral states that were besieged by thousands of desperate people. De Sousa Mendes' nephew vividly described the scene.

> Even the consulate offices were packed with refugees. They were dead tired, because they had spent days and nights in the streets, on the stairs and finally in the offices. They could no longer relieve themselves or eat or drink, for fear of losing their place in the queue. That sometimes happened and caused scuffles. The refugees consequently looked haggard, and were no longer able to wash, comb their hair, shave or change their clothes. In most cases, anyway, the clothes they were wearing were the only ones they had.[28]

De Sousa Mendes had informed Lisbon of the situation in Bordeaux in May and requested instructions on how to deal with the flood of refugees. The response was that he should enforce Circular 14. On 17 May, Lisbon issued Circular 17 that made it clear that 'in no cases whatsoever' could consuls grant visas in passports without prior authorization.[29] The Ministry also continued to refuse visa applications transmitted by de Sousa Mendes,[30] including ones for Rabbi Chaim Krüger and his family. They had escaped from Antwerp in advance of the German army and arrived in Bordeaux in May.[31] After a chance meeting, the two men had become close friends. The numbers of visas issued from the consulate increased during May and early June, ostensibly through cases sanctioned by the Lisbon authorities.[32] However, as the political and military situation deteriorated, de Sousa Mendes seems to have undergone some sort of illness or breakdown. With his consulate building full of refugees and being policed by armed guards, he took to his bed, seeing no one. This began on 14 June and lasted for a full three days until, on the fourth morning, he awoke and announced that he would give everyone visas. According to one of his sons,

> our Father told us that he had heard a voice, that of his conscience or of God, which dictated to him what course of action he should take, and that everything was clear in his mind.[33]

A different version of events has him receiving an unannounced visit from Fransisco de Calheiros, the Portuguese Minister-Plenipotentiary to Belgium, on 16 June, although there is no record of the conversation between them.[34]

Explaining his conduct remains difficult. It has been suggested that it was based on his dislike of the Germans and their invasion of Europe and also on his discontent with his superiors in Lisbon and the Salazar regime more generally.[35] One justification de Sousa Mendes gave for his decision was the principle embodied in the Portuguese constitution that neither religion nor political beliefs could be used as a pretext for refusing them permission to stay in Portugal. He also referred to recompense for the persecution of Jews meted out by the Inquisition in the fifteenth century.[36] Helped by his staff, two of his sons, his son-in-law, and by the rabbi, he began the process of issuing visas. His consular secretary and some of his children tried to stop him, but to no avail. The secretary did initially attempt to keep a record of the visas issued, but abandoned the idea as the process went on. Fees for the visa were also waived.[37] Large numbers of applicants were Jews, but there were also plenty of anti-Nazi politicians from various European countries and even some friends from earlier days, such as Albert de Vleeschauwer, the Belgian Minister for the Colonies, who was not only given a visa but also temporary accommodation at de Sousa Mendes' family estate in Portugal.[38] Other recipients included Archduke Otto von Habsburg, his family entourage, and several hundred Austrians who had been working in France.[39]

Inevitably, news that visas could be obtained from the Portuguese consulate sent thousands more to queue outside the building in the days that followed. By 20 June the demand had abated but the Germans were moving closer. De Sousa Mendes had already told the Portuguese Vice-Consul in Toulouse, Emile Gissot, to start issuing visas to refugees there and he left for Bayonne. Complaints about what was being done were reaching Lisbon. The British Embassy in Lisbon wrote to Salazar with a list of irregularities committed by de Sousa Mendes and claimed (erroneously) that he was charging extra fees for the visas.[40] By this stage, people with his visas were probably also appearing at Portuguese entry points in substantial numbers. De Sousa Mendes continued his work until the last minute—in Bayonne, although the Spaniards had closed their frontier on 20 June, and finally at Hendaye as the Germans closed in.[41] In the meantime, Franco had complained to Salazar about the numbers of people who had entered

Spain carrying Portuguese entry documents while Lisbon issued further restrictions on entry. Only four nationalities were now to be considered eligible for visas. British and American citizens were not to be hindered from entering, but French applicants had to be non-Jews and only Belgian 'notables' were to be considered. Others could only be considered if they had tickets for their final destination.[42] Against this background, de Sousa Mendes was issuing documentation on passports, identity cards, and even blank pieces of paper.[43]

It is unclear exactly how many visas de Sousa Mendes managed to issue, or how many people they served to save. The sometimes quoted figure of 30,000 is a wild exaggeration,[44] but the fact that one document would often cover an entire family makes accurate figures impossible to determine. An estimate of 10,000 may be more realistic, but the judgement of Yehuda Bauer is apposite in declaring that the actions of de Sousa Mendes were 'probably the most outstanding example of individual help during the Holocaust'.[45] However, there was no guarantee that the holders would actually be admitted to Portugal. Some, including de Sousa Mendes' friend Rabbi Krüger and his family, were held at the border and only admitted after the intervention of the Portuguese Committee of Assistance to Jewish Refugees (COMASSIS), HICEM and the American Joint Distribution Committee (JDC). In this respect the Portuguese authorities seem to have been tolerant when these organizations were prepared to provide the means and documentation for refugees to leave the country.[46] They were also unwilling to provoke a diplomatic crisis with neighbouring Spain by forcibly sending the refugees back across the frontier.[47]

In a last act of insubordination, de Sousa Mendes drove in front of a convoy of cars to a minor crossing point on the Franco-Spanish border and demanded the guard let them across. The guard, having no telephone and unaware that the border was officially closed, let them through. Later, back in what was by then German-occupied Bordeaux, but without the power to issue further visas, he nevertheless managed to save one or two people by issuing them with fake Portuguese passports.[48] However, without an official posting and with nothing left to achieve, he returned to Portugal on 8 July. Only at this point did his conduct catch up with him. Expecting to be able to justify his conduct to Salazar personally, he was indicted for his insubordination and faced fifteen separate charges. In his defence, de Sousa Mendes stressed the humanitarian origins of his actions and a desire to defend Portugal's good name. His accusers saw only disobedience, and after the disciplinary committee reported on 29 October 1940, he was 'sentenced' on the direct orders of Salazar to withdrawal from active service for a year on half-pay and then subject to forced resignation.[49] He died in 1954, more or less penniless, and his house had to be sold to pay his debts. In an ironic twist, while the world's press was extolling the virtues of Portugal and the Salazar regime in helping to save so many people from Nazi oppression, that same regime was punishing the very man and his family who had brought it about.[50]

Apart from Veiga Simões and de Sousa Mendes, other Portuguese consuls also issued visas without authorization. Diplomats in Toulouse and Bayonne were implicated. In October 1940, the consul in Luxemburg was relieved of his post for issuing transit visas, and the consul in Marseilles suffered the same fate a month later. In each case, the PVDE initiated the complaints, presumably on the basis of visas being presented to their men at the frontier.[51] In addition, two consuls in Italy, Giuseppe Agenore Magno in Milan and Alfredo Casanova in Genoa, were both disciplined for their stance on providing visas for refugees. Reports in 1941 indicated that the diplomats in Antwerp, Bucharest and Budapest had taken similar action.[52] Ostensibly, there was no political or ideological link in this collective behaviour. The diplomats involved came from many different social and political backgrounds. Casanova had issued visas to nuns caught up in the Spanish Civil War and justified issuing documents to refugees on humanitarian grounds. The rest seem to have been motivated by similar impulses, although this was sometimes limited to the well-known and the respectable elements. Only in the case of de Sousa Mendes did the beneficiaries come from the whole social spectrum. Beyond this, it is interesting to note that Jewish and political refugees who obtained Portuguese visas in this way may have been the beneficiaries of the bureaucratic battles between the diplomats, the security police, and the authorities in Lisbon.[53]

Vladimír Vochoč

Even before the armistice of June 1940, there were some diplomatic representatives in France whose status was already tenuous. One such was Vladimír Vochoč, a doctor of law originally appointed by his government as consul in Marseilles in 1938.[54] When Czechoslovakia was finally dismembered by the Germans in mid–March 1939, its government-in-exile continued to maintain representatives in various parts of the world to look after the interests of citizens of the former Czechoslovak Republic living abroad. Vochoč thus continued his work in the French port after the outbreak of war and, in the spring of 1940, had to deal with increasing numbers of former Czech citizens fleeing the German advance.[55] Faced with hundreds of demands for documentation and realizing that any 'delay would present an incontestable danger' he decided not to wait for the normal channels to operate but began issuing passports and other official papers on his own authority. Running out of suitable blank passports, Vochoč arranged to have others produced by a local printer.[56] However imperfect, when validated with suitable consular stamps, they served to provide the holders with a means of identification and some measure of protection.[57]

The situation changed again towards the end of autumn 1940 when residence permits for foreigners in France became that much more difficult to obtain. As Vochoč explained,

> People without papers, without the resources to support themselves for the months to come, and the Jews, were pursued relentlessly by the police and placed in concentration camps, or at least locked-up. These cruel police measures, previously unknown in France, were harshly ordered by the Minister of the Interior at Vichy and carried out by functionaries who were tired and hungry; the traditional French courtesy was a rarity.[58]

Unlike the unfortunate Polish soldiers who found themselves in Marseilles, Vochoč managed to keep the Czech soldiers out of the concentration camps and 'tolerated' by the police in the city. Indigent Czechs were protected by a plan to organize a group emigration scheme to Colombia with capital from China. Fiction or not, the existence of this plan was enough to convince the French police and keep those involved at liberty.[59] Further problems arose with getting people out of France. Even those with the necessary papers still needed an exit permit from the French. This was problematic for anyone whom the Nazis considered an enemy, as a secret clause in the armistice had insisted that the French hand over 'all Germans in France' on demand. A strict interpretation of this stipulation would also have included people from the former Czech territories, but using contacts through the daughter of the Secretary-General of the Foreign Ministry at Vichy, Vochoč was able to obtain an agreement that exit permits could be given to all Czechoslovak citizens except those from the Sudeten region.[60]

By his own testimony, Vochoč did everything legally possible to help Czech citizens in Vichy France, of whom there were anything up to 10,000.[61] His position was precarious, given that the Czechoslovak state existed only insofar as there was a government-in-exile in London. Nevertheless, he was also prepared to explore illegal methods of helping people escape from France without the necessary exit permits. He had three possible routes. The first was over the Franco-Spanish border. It appears that the Spanish consul in Marseilles was prepared to issue transit visas to anyone with a Portuguese visa that was not of military age, and Vochoč noted that the local Pyrenean guides did not ask much in payment.[62] A second method was the boats that were used to transport demobilized French soldiers from metropolitan France back to their homes in North Africa. These voyages were paid for by the French state, but the consul seems to have been able to use journeys in August and mid-September to smuggle out (former) members of the Czech armed forces. The final method was bribery. It became apparent that officials in a number of prefectures, including Grenoble, Toulouse, Clermont-Ferrand, and Nîmes, would provide exit visas in exchange for money. The method was simple: they merely neglected to pass the requests on to the authorities at Vichy and issued the documents without the appropriate permission. The cost varied, but increased steadily over time from 2,000 to around 10,000 francs for each visa. Probably unknown to these corrupt officials, their superiors in Vichy were also capable of being bribed, although the charges were much higher. Vochoč admitted purchasing exit visas through an intermediary, the cost regularly amounting to 25,000 francs, although he strongly advised Czech citizens to avoid trying this method, as it held the danger of being charged with corrupting government officials.[63]

Vochoč also worked to help the Czech nationals who were interned in camps: providing money, food, clothes and books. In this he was aided by his contacts with Donald Lowrie, the YMCA representative in Vichy and president of the Nîmes Committee that co-ordinated all the organizations helping the internees. Lowrie had worked with Czech aid organizations in Paris before the armistice, and in Marseilles created an American Friends of Czechoslovakia organization to help Vochoč's work and provide necessary funds.[64] The two men were also able to help German and former Austrian citizens held in French camps by providing them with Czech papers. These included former German government ministers such as Rudolf Breitscheid and Rudolf Hilferding,[65] and the daughter of former Social-Democrat Chancellor Herman Müller, as well as several well-known Austrian politicians, their families, and leading intellectuals.[66] Help also came from other consuls and diplomats resident in Marseilles, the Spanish and Portuguese consuls providing transit visas for some people, and the Chinese consul, Tcheng Tchung, providing both Chinese and Shanghai visas. The honorary consul of the Kingdom of Siam was also regarded as co-operative, as were the representatives of some Central and South American states. For example, the Panamanian honorary consul apparently issued some transit visas for Czech soldiers for $10 apiece, on the strict understanding that they would not be used for the purpose stated, and the Brazilian consul also provided a number of visas.[67] Last but not least, there was help from local US vice-consuls, Hiram Bingham IV and Miles Standish, in providing protection and papers for some well-known political opponents of Nazism.[68]

Vochoč seldom mentioned Jews specifically in his report, but it is clear that many of the Czech nationals in Vichy France who were subsequently interned were Jewish. In 1941, he was involved with other relief organizations in establishing a school-colony for the children of interned former Czech refugees in the village of Vence. The colony was run by Josef Fišera, a refugee student of history and evangelical Protestant who had come to France after September 1938 and had been demobilized from the Czechoslovak army in 1940, but had then been made responsible for the reception of refugees in Marseilles.[69] As one of the children later recalled

> The children were mainly Czech, but had quite varied backgrounds. Many of them were the children of coal miners, some of whom had worked in Belgium. There were also many Jewish children. We were told we were all in the same boat and had to be discreet about where we came from ... Once we gave a concert in Vence. One of the girls sang a solo in Yiddish, but the audience was told that the song was in Flemish.[70]

Later Fišera co-operated with the OSE in finding hiding places for Jewish children taken from the internment camps, and moved his charges from Vence to Saint Agnant (Creuse) when the Germans invaded the Italian zone. Arrested by the Germans in October 1943 he was severely tortured, but all his charges survived the war.

At face value, the Czech consul and his assistant had done everything in their power to help Czech nationals, and Vochoč had clearly gone further than almost any other diplomat in Marseilles to facilitate departures from

French soil. His involvement with the quasi-legal and illegal operations marks him out from most of his contemporaries. While he regarded the weekly meetings of the Marseilles *Corps Diplomatique* as useful in gleaning co-operation where possible, his work went way beyond what might be described as the job description for a consul, even in the extreme and unusual circumstances pertaining in wartime Marseilles.

Arie Sevenster and the *Offices Néerlandais*

Other diplomats whose credentials had become undermined as a result of the changing geopolitical situation could also be found providing unofficial help for their countrymen in unoccupied France. On 14 May 1940, just as the Dutch Armed Forces were preparing to surrender to the Germans, the Dutch representatives in Paris created a specific organization to help its nationals, the Association de secours aux réfugiés néerlandais, under the leadership of Consul-General Arie Sevenster.[71] Its main purpose was to help Dutch refugees in the city and Dutch nationals who were in financial difficulties as a result of the fall of the Netherlands, primarily those reliant on pensions paid from the Netherlands. At this stage, there was still contact with the Dutch government-in-exile in London and some arrangements could be made to help. Pensioners were given funds and the 600 or so known refugees in the city, many of them Jewish, were housed and clothed.[72] For Sevenster, the problem was that he had no idea exactly how many Dutch refugees there were in the rest of France or where they were located. At the time, estimates varied wildly, but a realistic figure was probably around 10,000, although this included at least 4,000 people evacuated from the southern city of Breda.[73] When the French sued for an armistice, Sevenster moved his centre of operations southwards, leaving a small staff in Paris, and created a series of Offices Néerlandais, essentially to replace the consular service.

Given that there was little chance of evacuating all the Dutch nationals trapped in France, the Netherlands government-in-exile in London decided on 20 June 1940 that repatriation should be the norm for all except those at risk from the Germans; namely Jews, anti-German publicists, and agents of the Allied Secret Services.[74] Soon it became apparent that the offices in Perpignan and Toulouse were not only providing aid to young men 'on the run', but also helping them to cross the Spanish frontier.[75] J. A. van Dobben, who was in charge of the office in Toulouse, was also involved in smuggling diamonds to the United States by using refugees as couriers. He was eventually apprehended by the Vichy police and held for some time, but his extra-curricular activities did not rebound on the Toulouse Office Néerlandais, and it remained in place as a focal point for all manner of activities. Once the initial repatriation programme was completed, there were around 2,000 Dutch refugees left whose repatriation would compromise their safety—most of them Jews.[76]

The Perpignan Office Néerlandais was run by Joseph Kolkman, a former Jesuit priest turned journalist from a well-connected Dutch family who had previously been the Paris correspondent of the Dutch daily newspaper *Algemeen Handelsblad*. He had been recruited in June 1940 to help with the refugees in the city, and took over as vice-consul in August 1940 when his major task was in trying to secure French exit visas and Spanish transit visas for Dutch nationals. This was made more difficult because every new French regulation or change in procedure (and there were many of these) invalidated the application process and meant starting again from scratch. The Spaniards would not grant transit visas without valid French documents and a valid visa for a destination elsewhere, and were in any case wary of granting papers to anyone of military age.[77] Early in 1941, Kolkman established a *centre d'accueil* in a villa seven kilometres from Perpignan for those without means of support. It accommodated both Jewish refugees on the run from the Nazis and young Dutchmen anxious to escape to Britain to continue the fight from there. Tensions were inevitable. As one former resident later described it, there were 'two groups, two [different] worlds'.[78] Kolkman visited the villa about three times a week to discuss the refugees' problems and how they might be solved. By April of 1941, food shortages and French demands that the Dutch stop subsidizing its charges above the levels provided by French local authorities forced a compromise where the residents were compulsorily employed in agriculture to prevent the centre's closure.

Those who encountered him described Kolkman as 'energetic' and 'very active'. A measure of his chutzpah and commitment to the task was that he always introduced himself as the Dutch consul in Perpignan, and he had a Corps Consulaire plate on his car well into 1942. This was in spite of the fact that he had never actually held such a position, and that there had been no Dutch consular representation in France since November 1940.[79] He benefited from good contacts with Sevenster and with the Dutch diplomats elsewhere in France and Spain, and from excellent relations with the civil servants in his local municipalities and prefectures. He also received enormous support from the commune in which the villa was situated.[80] Initially, most of his work was done through official channels and he was able to expedite the departure of groups of refugees over the French border on the pretext that they had entry visas for the Dutch East Indies. After the Japanese occupation, this excuse was obviously closed, but replaced by documents from the Governors of Surname and the Dutch Antilles (under some pressure from the Dutch government-in-exile in London). Here the boundaries of legality and illegality became blurred as some men of military age who were intent on getting to England were attached to these larger groups and their documents altered to raise or lower their ages. Kolkman was also known to have purchased a small number of Chinese visas. However, his increasing willingness to bend and then break the rules was matched by the ever-tightening controls created by the Vichy authorities under pressure from the Germans. Latterly, Kolkman and his colleagues concentrated their attention on evacuating pilots, people of military age and those wanting to go to England. For Kolkman, it was largely a question of money, as his resources were stretched in having to support those in his care in Perpignan, but he also had to find the considerable funds used to pay the 'passeurs' who would lead the groups over the Pyrenees.[81]

In the summer of 1942, the Laval regime ordered the closure of the Offices Néerlandais and the transfer of their diplomatic functions to the Swedish protecting power. By this stage, the acquisition of legitimate French exit visas had become virtually impossible. Thus, at the same moment that the Germans began to round up and deport the Jews from Western Europe, the few remaining routes of escape were rapidly being closed. Kolkman was kept busy as his remaining charges were subjected to Vichy police harassment and often imprisoned for document irregularities. Once the Germans occupied the Vichy zone, he could no longer protect any of his charges, and was subsequently arrested and imprisoned. He was later deported to Buchenwald, and then to rocket-building *Aussenkommado* Dora (Nordhausen). In January 1944 he was placed on a train to Lublin with other sick prisoners and died on the journey.[82]

In addition to the centres at Perpignan and Toulouse, the Dutch also established a camp at Lessac to house escapees from the occupied zone. Together they accommodated some 400 people, of whom 300 were Jews. When the Vichy authorities attempted to have all men of military age placed in work camps, Sevenster was able to negotiate their removal to two spa towns at the foot of the Pyrenees. Here they had to work and food was not plentiful, but the refugees were saved the horrors of the main Vichy camps. One camp, at Châteauneuf-les-Bains, was commanded by a French colonel with Jewish ancestry and his men proved easy to bribe, with the result that many inmates were able to escape. In some respects, it could be argued that Sevenster did no more than he was told to do by his masters in London: helping Dutch nationals in Vichy France in whatever way he could while adhering to the precepts set down by the government-in-exile. Nevertheless, his actions in protecting Jews among those unwilling to return to the Netherlands improved their chances of survival in the increasingly hostile environment of Pétain's France by giving them financial support and negotiating their conditions of internment. Keeping clear of the Vichy authorities, or being able to bribe their way out of captivity, allowed an indeterminate number to escape.[83] Though they received little thanks at the time, the roles of Sevenster and Kolkman were potentially crucial to this particular group of Dutch Jewish refugees.

Private Enterprise

Varian Fry and the Emergency Rescue Committee

Far better known than the diplomats was the work of Varian Fry, to date one of only three American citizens awarded the accolade of Righteous among the Nations by Yad Vashem. His story has been told many times, in his own words and by subsequent biographers and film makers, and need not be repeated in detail here.[84] Nevertheless, the origins and development of his network do highlight some crucial aspects of rescue in Vichy France.

Fry had been appointed by the Emergency Rescue Committee (ERC) to expedite the escape from France of a specific list of leading intellectuals and artists who had fled from Nazism and were at risk of immediate reprisals. The ERC had its origins in earlier refugee relief efforts in the US and had garnered some high-level support via contacts with Eleanor Roosevelt. Gaining support and finance to help the refugees was one thing, but it was recognized that it would need a representative on the ground in France to further its work. Fry, therefore, set off on 4 August from New York for Marseilles. His intention was to stay for a month and use the $3,000 he carried to expedite the departure from France of the people on his list.[85]

Figure 2.1. Queues outside the American Consulate in Marseilles, 1941
Source: USHMM

On arrival in Marseilles, Fry's learning curve was a steep one. He had
only the vaguest notion of what papers and guarantees individuals required
to leave the unoccupied zone of France, and no knowledge of local
conditions. His first experiences of dealing with the US consulate in the
city were entirely negative.[86] Working with Frank Bohn, the European
representative of the Jewish Labor Committee, Fry began the task of
locating the people on his list, but news of his arrival rapidly spread beyond
the confines of the city, and his room at the Hôtel Splendide soon became a
magnet for all those desperate to leave Vichy France. Although expediting
the departure of people remained his primary purpose, he soon realized
that this could not be done entirely legally, and he therefore created a front
organization, the Centre Américain de Secours which ostensibly provided
only ameliorative aid, but in fact acted as a cover for the 'not strictly kosher'
business of arranging emigrations.[87]

Fry slowly accumulated a circle of helpers. Some were expatriate Americans such as the Chicago heiress Mary Jayne Gold, who provided vast
sums of money to support refugees and to purchase documents.[88] Fry was
also able to enlist the help of another rich American, Peggy Guggenheim.

She had been collecting art in Paris, and had become enamoured of the surrealist painter Max Ernst, making generous financial contributions to the organization and ultimately expediting Ernst's emigration to the United States.[89] Other Americans on the 'staff' included Miriam Davenport whose fluency in French and German made her adept at interviewing refugee artists and intellectuals.[90] Charles (Charlie) Fawcett had travelled in Europe for a number of years, earning a living as a wrestler, movie star and trumpet player before enlisting with the American Volunteer Ambulance Corps before the armistice.[91] He was employed as doorman and reception clerk, where his ambulanceman's uniform served to maintain order in the ERC's offices and waiting room.[92] All professed the desire to do 'something' to help the refugees and were thus drawn to the Centre Américain de Secours.

However, the more important helpers came from among the refugees themselves: men and women with particular practical skills and with a detailed knowledge of the refugee community, both in Marseilles and elsewhere. They ranged from the former Spanish Republican and French soldier Albert Hirschmann, (christened 'Beamish' by Fry), through social democrats such as Bedrich Heine, to the Austrian aristocrat Franz von Hildebrand.[93] Each brought some specific expertise and knowledge to the work. Hirschmann was an expert through experience. A veteran of the Spanish Civil War and of the defeated French army, he was able to 'disappear' from the latter after the armistice. His local knowledge allowed Fry access to the Marseilles underworld and to additional sources of false documents and usable currency.[94] Politically, the Catholic aristo-crat von Hildebrand was the complete opposite of Hirschmann, having fought for the *Heimwehr* in the 1934 Austrian civil war. Austrian social-ists were unnerved to see him in the ERC offices, but he was a useful contact for advice on non-socialist refugees, had been involved with the Austrian relief committee in Paris, and crucially, possessed a Swiss passport.[95]

Leaving aside the difficulties of finding the money, Fry could only recommend the issue of US emergency visas. The process of issue was long and complicated, with applications going via the ERC to the President's Advisory Committee, then through the Justice and State Departments before the documents were issued by the local consul. Moreover, the final decision on issue remained with the consul, and many office holders in the unoccupied zone proved remarkably unwilling to agree to it, even when it was sanctioned by their masters in Washington. The emergency visas had been brought in to compensate for a much more rigorous application of rules introduced when the immigration service was transferred from the Ministry of Labor to the State Department in June 1940. Although designed to meet objections that the US was closing its doors altogether—even for those in the greatest need—the qualifying criteria were stringent, as a contemporary press release made clear.

> In exceptional circumstances, Visitor's Visas may be useful in saving persons of exceptional merit, those of superior intellectual attainment, of indomitable spirit, experienced in vigorous support of Liberal government and who [are] in danger of persecution of death at the hands of autocracy.[96]

This left Fry with the problem of how to choose the people his organization was supposed to help. It soon became apparent that his original list was inaccurate and woefully out of date. While most of the nominees would probably have qualified for an emergency visa, some had already left France, and others had fallen victim to the Nazis: imprisoned or murdered by the Gestapo, or died by their own hand. The question of selecting others to take their place was complicated by the sheer numbers who besieged his offices. The criteria used owed much to the need for security against police spies and agents provocateur. There was no means of gauging the precise danger any individual faced, but help was only offered to those known to people trusted by Fry and his co-workers.[97]

Inevitably, the refugee relief side of Fry's work brought him into contact with other relief organizations, such as the HIAS and the JDC, both based in New York, and the HICEM based in Lisbon. All three had been involved in ameliorative aid for Jews in Europe for some decades, especially in Eastern Europe, but their work had increased as the Nazi menace emerged, and changed focus as more energies and funds were expended on assisting refugees in the West. At the same time, Fry also encountered other non-Jewish humanitarian relief operations run by the Quakers (American Friends Service Committee) and Unitarians (Unitarian Service Committee, Boston), as well as Donald Lowrie of the YMCA.[98]

Whereas these links could be regarded as normal and legitimate, some of Fry's other contacts were less straightforward. In the first weeks after his arrival, it was apparent that some diplomats were still issuing transit visas without any close checks on final destinations,[99] but the amount of shipping active in the Mediterranean had rapidly diminished as Italy entered the war in June and relations between Britain and her erstwhile French ally deteriorated. Moreover, the Vichy regime's compliance with the armistice terms made it all-but impossible for those with known anti-Nazi backgrounds or foreign Jews to obtain permits. In the initial stages this requirement was not rigidly enforced or policed, but it still meant that departure was technically illegal. The dangers were clearly explained by Donald Lowrie:

> Some . . . paid boatmen to take them across to North Africa, or even just around the frontier line to a Spanish port, but the harbor was watched, of course. You might find a sympathetic harbor guard who would not look too closely at the documents a departing traveller carried, but you always risked being jailed and then, unless you could bribe your way out, the Nazis got you. And as for bribes, most of these people didn't have a sou. Some were even afraid to ask for relief, because this would reveal their address.

> In Pau I had heard that there were guides who could be hired to take people over the mountains to Spain at night. The professional smugglers now did a business in human cargo . . . Furthermore, one had to be sure that the frontier guards had been 'fixed'. And then there was the 80% chance the police on the Spanish side would put you in jail. It was fairly sure the Franco police had been supplied by the Germans with lists of men they were hunting.[100]

Finding a way of furnishing refugees with papers was by no means straightforward. Contact with Lowrie had put Fry in touch with Vochoč, who was prepared to provide Czech papers, suitably backdated to a time when his country was still independent.[101] These papers had a veneer of legitimacy, as did those that were purchased from unscrupulous diplomats who were prepared to issue identity documents in exchange for cash payments. Like Vochoč, Fry dealt with a particularly 'commercially active' Lithuanian consul who sold passports for $100 apiece, and also bought Chinese visas in Marseilles for Fr.100.[102] Other documents had to be forged, and this led Fry into the Marseilles underworld to find fixers and specialists to produce the documents he needed, but always at a price. Clearly there was money to be made from this system, and plenty of unscrupulous people to exploit it—and not just from among the criminal classes. Representatives of even the most reputable companies such as Thomas Cook could allegedly be found making money on the side by selling false transatlantic steamship tickets.[103]

With passages on ships at a premium, Fry began to explore the possibilities of smuggling 'his' people overland into Spain. His first 'guinea-pigs' were

Heinrich and Claire Ehrmann, two young anti-Nazi, Social Democrat activists, whose Jewish ancestry doubled the risks they took. Their first two attempts to cross the frontier ended in failure as the French customs and border guards apprehended them. Luckily, the authorities did no more than turn them back, as arrest and enquiry would have exposed their backgrounds and led to incarceration and even extradition into the hands of the Gestapo. However, with advice from the sympathetic socialist mayor of Banyuls-sur-Mer, Vincent Azéma, they attempted an old hiking trail across the Pyrenees.[104] This local knowledge proved invaluable as, by travelling at night, they were able to circumvent the French guards and make it across the mountains to the Spanish border post undetected. A small bribe at the frontier allowed them to pass through, and they ultimately sailed to the United States.[105] Their route had been used by Spanish Republicans to smuggle goods into the country during the civil war and was then used as an escape in 1939 when the Nationalist net closed in. However, these tracks across the mountains had been used for centuries before, for both legal and illegal reasons. The guides for this type of enterprise were often professional smugglers, or others who had good reason for avoiding the attentions of the authorities. The Ehrmanns' success gave Fry the information he required to organize further departures, and 250 other refugees successfully completed the journey over the next six weeks.[106] However, they had to be carefully chosen. The route was not easy and travellers required a robust constitution themselves and could not be hampered by too much baggage, ageing relatives or small children.

The route involved a train journey to Banyuls and then a journey to the mountains, ostensibly as French vineyard workers. The trick was to avoid the French border posts and then slip down to pass through the Spanish control points, thus making their entry legal.[107] To do this, the two border controls had to be far enough apart to prevent the one being observed by the other. Fry's experiences to some extent contradict the picture painted by Lowrie that the Spanish border guards were likely to return people arriving in this way, as most of his charges seem to have passed the frontiers unhindered—although changes of policy from Madrid had to be carefully monitored. On one occasion, Fry accompanied a party himself. It was an august group, including Heinrich Mann, his wife Nellie and nephew Golo, the novelist Lion Feuchtwanger and his wife, and the poet and dramatist Franz Werfel and his wife Alma. Fry travelled across the Spanish frontier by train, taking his charges' luggage with him, while they took the mountain route. He insisted that they destroy all unnecessary papers, but was horrified to find that Alma Werfel would not be parted from a satchel that contained the draft of her husband's latest novel, original scores of her former husband, Gustav Mahler, and the original score of Anton Bruckner's Third Symphony.[108] Stopped by a guard on the Spanish side and identified as Thomas Mann's son, Golo Mann expected to be sent back to the Gestapo but was instead told that the sentry was 'honoured to make the acquaintance of the son of so great a man'.[109]

During his time in Madrid, Fry made contact with Sir Samuel Hoare, the British Ambassador, and through him with MI6. His objective was to obtain British help in finding a sea route out of France. In fact, the British had not discovered a means of evacuating their own people in this way, and therefore tried to enlist Fry to help them. The British refused to use naval vessels for the purpose, but did suggest that if Fry helped get Allied servicemen out of France, then they would explore the possibility of using Spanish fishing vessels for the purpose. In the event, Fry delivered on his side of the bargain, but no shipping was ever forthcoming from the British, although subsequent contacts did bring further information on land crossings and the routes used by Catalan smugglers.[110]

By early September 1940, Fry's mission was becoming increasingly difficult. His work was dangerous, and the cover stories could only keep the Vichy police at bay temporarily. Some of his most important targets, such as Hilferding and Breitscheid, had been arrested and placed under house arrest by the police. Although the ERC did have powerful friends at home, the attitude of the State Department and the US Consul, Hugh Fullerton, became increasingly hostile, culminating in an instruction that Fry should leave the country by 23 September. Frank Bohn also proved something of a liability as his left-wing stance and lack of security consciousness brought greater levels of police attention and further disapproval from Washington. Fry's attempts to persuade the authorities that he had no direct association with Bohn and the JLC proved fruitless. Certainly, the US diplomats in France saw them as engaging in the same embarrassing work, as a despatch to the Secretary of State on 14 September made clear:

> As the matter is in danger of becoming a public scandal, I reluctantly feel that I must report the activities of Dr Bohn and Mr Fry in their well-meaning endeavors to help unfortunate aliens reach the United States. The Prefect at Marseille has taken occasion to tell Hurley of the 'difficulty and delicacy of

this position by reason of the certainty and inevitability of reprisals which would follow violation of the armistice regulations consequent on the illegal departure of emigrants of certain nationalities'.[111]

Even appeals from Eleanor Roosevelt were met with the response that consuls were doing everything within the laws of the United States and the countries in which they operated to expedite the issue of visas, but it was clear that the State Department was unwilling to be seen acting in ways that would embarrass countries with whom the US maintained 'friendly relations'.[112] The methods that had been used to evacuate people in August were also now becoming problematic. French surveillance of the border and of the refugees was tightening all the time. Internment in squalid camps was now a reality for many. Moreover, the authorities were also weeding out Fry's former associates. The Vichy police had charged Lowrie and Vochoč, and this effectively stopped the supply of Czech documents. Fry had to rely more and more on forgeries and forgers, thus adding to the risks involved. Even possession of all the right documentation was sometimes not enough as Spain and Portugal became increasingly nervous and began imposing greater restrictions, often at a moment's notice via instructions to their border posts. Thus there was no means of knowing in advance precisely what might be required for legal admission.[113]

Information on conditions at the border did filter back, often based on actual experiences of people who had either managed to negotiate the frontier safely or who had been turned back. Lisa Fittko had begun her work as a courier across the border before having much contact with Fry. She had been the leader of the ultimately ill-fated group including Walter Benjamin that had got to the Spanish Frontier, only to be told that they required French exit visas and would be returned.[114] Benjamin committed suicide as a result, but news that the route itself was sound got back to Marseilles and to Fry, who then recruited Fittko and her husband Hans as couriers.

There seem to have been an ever-increasing number of people with some access to documentation, either genuine or fraudulent, who were happy to make money from the plight of the displaced, the refugees, and the racial victims of the new regime, both in the metropolis and in the towns and villages nearer the Spanish border. Lisa Fittko describes some days at Perpignan on her way to Banyuls involving 'no contact at all with the bad guys'.[115] There were rumours of local guides and smugglers being hired at extortionate rates to guide people over the passes, only for them to rob their clients and/or then betray them to the authorities. How extensive this profiteering and deception was must remain conjecture, as hard evidence from those who may have survived such circumstances is perforce hard to find. A child with Romanian papers, in describing her family's escape across the Pyrenees to Andorra and Spain recalled that her father suspected their guide would try to kill them, 'because that is what a lot of the . . . guides did'.[116] Yet even the Fittkos had to collaborate with those earning money from the human traffic. A chance meeting with a Greek locomotive engineer high up on a mountain pass provided them with a contact to take people most of the way to Spain on a train, with them then having to walk only a few hundred yards from a tunnel to the safety of the frontier. This contact proved reliable, but expensive.[117]

A further complication was that some of Fry's earlier high-profile 'successes' had arrived in New York and lost no time in telling their escape stories. These were publicized by the ERC as a way of raising money, but inevitably betrayed the routes and methods being used to the French authorities, if not the names of the people involved.[118] Conditions in the unoccupied zone continued to worsen. In late November, Mayor Azéma of Banyuls was replaced by a Pétain loyalist.[119] Many more of the Jewish and non-Jewish refugees were now being interned, and were increasingly subject to scrutiny by the Kundt Commission, a group of Gestapo and German officials who combed the camp populations for particular individuals wanted in Germany.[120] Its existence also acted as a brake on emigration, even when the individual had all the necessary papers, as the French officials refused to allow anyone to leave until the Commission had screened them.[121]

Fry's work was essentially with the well known and the talented. Apart from the Feuchtwangers, Manns, Werfels, and other noted intellectuals who were helped to escape through Spain and Portugal to the US, his organization also came into contact with Marc Chagall, André Breton, André Masson, Jacques Lipschitz, Max Ernst, and Walter Benjamin. The case of Charlotte Brand is a good example of the ways in which the Centre Américain de Secours decided on whom to help. She was a German artist in her twenties who had arrived from Italy, having previously studied at the Bauhaus. She was supported with funds from the Centre, and her work was shown to consul Hiram Bingham '[to] see if she's worth a visa'.[122] In this instance, Bingham was suitably impressed and negotiated the necessary papers.

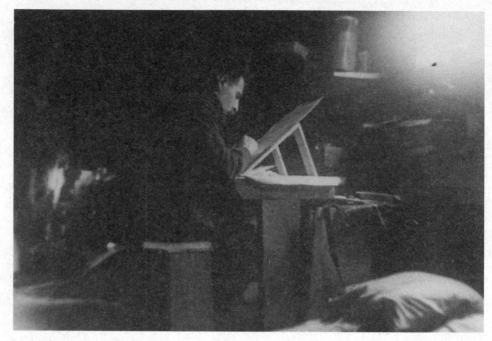

Figure 2.2. Bill Freier: refugee Viennese political cartoonist and forger
Source: USHMM

The focus on the great and the good did not prevent the Centre
Américain seeing more than 100 people each day in December 1940
and it had more than 500 people 'on its books'.[123] By this time, Fry's
organization had 'contacts' with several consuls—all potential sources of
visas, albeit at a price.[124] Further setbacks came when the organization's
forger, the refugee Viennese political cartoonist Bill Freier was arrested,
and French police raided the office of the Lithuanian consul. This gave the
authorities access to the names of all those refugees who had been sold that
country's passports.[125] As quickly as new possible means of escape were
found, so the various agencies involved found ways of closing them. Thus
the Spaniards suddenly discovered the need to insist on seeing the exit
visas of people arriving from France, a document that had been previously
of interest only to the French frontier authorities. Likewise, the US and
other consuls had become wise to the widespread currency of dubious
visas for South American and other exotic destinations, and soon insisted
on confirming their validity with the countries concerned before issuing
transit documents.[126]

Fry also had increasing contacts with the Marseilles criminal underworld including, for example, a smuggling network run by Carlos, a member of the CNT who charged Fr.15,000 per person for the journey into Spain. This did have some successes, but Fry was unimpressed by its leader, who he describes as 'an oily little creature who lied quite unashamedly and shifted nervously in his chair as he talked'.[127] The quality of many of the forged papers and visas they obtained also declined as 'real' sources dried up. This, combined with greater surveillance by the French and Spanish authorities, made crossing frontiers that much harder.

There are at least two debates that have emerged about Fry and his network. The first relates to the actual risks he was running. Certainly he developed two parallel organizations: an ostensibly legal welfare service and an illegal emigration operation, the one cloaking the other. Some of his activities were certainly in breach of Vichy laws and worked against German interests, but whether either country would have been prepared to countenance damaging relations with the US by giving him anything more than a hard time for a few days in prison is open to question. However, the one imponderable here is whether he might have been subject to assassination—an event that would be easily explained away by conditions in Marseilles at the time. More pertinent perhaps is the question of whom Fry was actually working against. One argument is that his main adversaries were not the French and Germans, but the countries surrounding Vichy France, and above all the US government itself.[128] Certainly, most of his efforts were directed towards circumventing increasingly draconian immigration restrictions, but it is also true that he worked to remove certain individuals whom the French and the Germans would have liked to retain. A second debate (and indeed charge) is that his operation was essentially elitist and was based on the US profiting from the 'fire sale' of 'brains' in Europe at that time. Certainly, Fry came to France with a list of the great and the good to rescue, although his network did ultimately help others as well. At the same time, his fundraisers in the ERC in the US needed these 'big name' arrivals to bring in the money that supported his work. The arrival of Mann, Werfel and Feuchtwanger had apparently brought in $35,000 but more high profile cases were reputedly needed to keep the cash flowing.[129]

Every aspect of rescue work required funding—something that caused headaches for all those involved. Even the diplomats like Sevenster and

Kolkman, working with backing from their governments in London, found it hard to finance all their activities, and Varian Fry was constantly looking for new ways of raising money. Indeed, one of his schemes probably led to the ultimate cessation of his activities in France when in desperation he became involved with the police and Gestapo informer, the Russian currency dealer Dimitriu.[130]

Quakers, YMCA and the Coordination Committee

The Centre Américain was not by any means the only international philanthropic organization or refugee welfare operation in the unoccupied zone, or indeed in the city of Marseilles itself. Most of the organizations that had been based in Paris, including the American Friends Service Committee (Quakers) and the Jewish Joint Distribution Committee (JDC), had moved their headquarters from Paris to Marseilles.[131] With little money at his disposal for the cultural work that the YMCA was permitted to do, Donald Lowrie had been actively encouraged by the Vichy Minister of the Interior to organize a Coordination Committee for Relief Work in Internment Camps, or the Nîmes Committee, as it was universally known.[132] The Committee provided a cloak for organizations that would otherwise have been banned by the Vichy authorities under pressure from the Germans, for example those emanating from territories that the Nazis deemed no longer existed, such as Poland, Czechoslovakia and Belgium. It also helped to protect Jewish organizations, and specific tasks could often be transferred to other (Christian) organizations if Vichy forbade the involvement of the former. As Lowrie was at pains to point out, an outstanding achievement of the Nîmes Committee was to have 'the complete and sympathetic collaboration of Christians and Jews'.[133] All of its affiliated organizations were able to operate lawfully, as their prime purpose was to provide aid for refugees or to arrange legal emigrations where possible. In practice, however, they all were ultimately forced to use more dubious methods to maintain their activities. This was especially true in relation to finance, where money had to be smuggled into the Vichy zone or converted into French francs illegally because the official exchange rate was so penal. Each of the organizations involved brought some expertise or contacts to the table. There were anonymous donors and couriers who brought French francs over the line of demarcation (at great risk to themselves) with details of where the equivalent in dollars was to be deposited. These included the secretary of a Reformed Church, an unnamed Venezuelan in Lyon and a Monsieur Bernard, who was later shot by the Germans.[134] Transfers expedited on behalf of individual refugees were, however, charged at the official rate so that there would be no evidence of the relief organizations acting outside the law.[135]

Lowrie and his YMCA organization were involved in the attempt to evacuate 600 Czechs on a Yugoslav freighter from Marseilles, but the failure of this operation ended large-scale emigration projects and illegal activities. From then on, he ostensibly adopted a policy of 'operating within the framework of existing law and in closest collaboration with all French authorities'.[136] Nevertheless, in association with Vochoč, agricultural and children's colonies were created to facilitate the release of children from the squalid internment camps created by Vichy to corral foreigners and especially Jews. He was able to use his 'frank relations' with Vichy's Chief of the National Police to expedite this. Thus, for example, some twenty Czech Jewish youngsters were moved from the camps to the Czech Children's Colony at Vence.[137] This would prove only a temporary respite, as five of the children were designated for deportation, re-arrested and put back in Rivesaltes camp with their parents. Ultimately, three were subsequently released by 'more-or-less' legal means, and the other two were smuggled out in a delivery truck, but no such help could be afforded to their parents.[138] By this stage, the Czech Aid organization had a full range of (forged) consular and police stamps that were used to expedite their countrymen's journeys out of France. On one occasion they had received a list from the US consul of thirty-two Czech citizens who had been granted entry visas. As none of these individuals were known to any of the relief agencies or apparently located in the internment camps, thirty-two other men were renamed and given appropriate papers—thus expediting their escape.[139]

While continuing to operate legally, it is clear that some within the Nîmes Committee also helped people cross the line of demarcation. As conditions worsened and the Vichy police began rounding up Jews outside the camps, this was extended to include moving people into neutral Switzerland. Technically, they could only leave if given exit permits by the Vichy authorities, and would only be allowed to enter Switzerland if in possession of valid documents for an end destination. To circumvent the need for exit visas, the fugitives had to avoid French border controls and were then given forged Cambodian, Portuguese and Mexican travel documents, thus proving that they could leave Swiss soil, although in fact most of the holders were Czechs destined for the United Kingdom. The alternative was to cross the border completely undetected, but the mountainous terrain between France and Switzerland made this a hazardous and difficult enterprise. Moreover, the Swiss authorities had no qualms about sending back those they caught, at least until the Germans occupied the southern zone.[140]

Lowrie likened the network established for this purpose to the 'underground railway' of the pre-civil war United States, with groups of refugees being conducted to the border by volunteers who took them by night from station to station. They were then handed over to smugglers who took them over the mountain passes. The Nîmes Committee paid the substantial fees demanded by these 'professionals', but eventually even the smugglers refused to make the crossings as the Vichy police became more proactive in apprehending them. This left the task to the amateurs, who were less well known to the authorities but were still occasionally arrested by the French border officials and given the statutory month in gaol for smuggling.[141] By the end of October 1942, 6,000 people were reported to have crossed the Swiss frontier, 2,000 having entered illegally during the first two weeks of that month. Crossing by train was only possible with all the necessary documentation, the only alternatives being the boatmen who plied their trade across Lake Geneva—at a price—or the mountain route.

Each of the men featured in this chapter was representative of a certain type of rescue activity taking place in unoccupied France during the first months of the Vichy regime. Their experiences have some common themes, the most important perhaps being their desire to do everything possible to help without coming into conflict with what was possible within the legal frameworks of their employment (for the diplomats) or their terms of reference. It was only a short step from looking for loopholes in the French regulatory regime to involvement in forgery and smuggling. For even the most upright citizen, the moral lines between the lawful and the unlawful became increasingly blurred. Brushes with illegality soon turned into a necessary, if not wholehearted, unholy alliance with underworld forgers and smugglers. Of note here is that the rescuers debated the reliability of those they 'employed' and the costs involved, rather than the illegality of what was being done or the dangers being run. The diplomats might have had some call on immunity, but this must have been tenuous in the case of

Vochoč, Sevenster and Kolkman. Fry and Lowrie could call on some help from the State Department as US, and therefore neutral, citizens, but this could not protect them altogether from criminal charges. As Lowrie later reflected: 'What with procuring false passports, smuggling people across boundaries, and helping others avoid police searches, I wondered if most of us would ever become law-abiding citizens again.'[142]

Their work also required the tacit or active co-operation of other groups of people. First, there were the French civil servants and other members of the diplomatic corps who turned a blind eye to what was happening or provided some element of (unattributable) assistance. One or two examples will have to suffice here. While it became apparent that some French civil servants could be bribed into providing exit visas or other documents, there were also elements within the administration who were sympathetic to the refugees' cause. One who stands out is Azéma, the socialist mayor of Banyuls. The frontier position of his commune made it a magnet for refugees, but he was proactive in requisitioning a large house to act as a hostel (*centre d'herbergement*). He was also free with advice for those trying to cross the frontier. Lisa Fittko recalled that he volunteered information on the living habits of the local population and on what *not* to do. This included precise instructions on how to approach the border crossing by dressing carefully, mixing with the vineyard workers and not carrying baggage. He also told her where the customs officials were likely to be stationed and where they might carry out checks.[143] Even some of the customs officials in the area offered advice to travellers on how not to look conspicuous.[144] Azéma could also be found providing ration stamps and identity documents for people such as the Fittkos, a moral lead that was followed by other members of the community, especially after Lisa had nearly died from jaundice. She was astounded when the local butcher offered her a pound of pork, way above what her ration stamps would buy, and the proprietor of the wool shop next door offered as much wool as she could use.[145] Azéma's sympathetic attitude was bound to attract the unwelcome attention of the Vichy executive, and it was not long before he was replaced.

Varian Fry also found some sympathy among the otherwise largely deaf American diplomatic corps, with the vice-consul in Marseilles, Hiram Bingham IV and his colleague Miles Standish being prepared to help in the issuance of visas to Jews and political opponents of Hitler's regime. Bingham also provided material aid to a number of people, including sheltering them in his home.[146] News of his activities spread quickly through the refugee community and also came to the notice of the French and German authorities. It is estimated that his documents were given to around 2,000 people during his tenure as vice consul. Some were already famous, such as Ernst, Chagall and Breton, but many others appear to have been 'ordinary' refugees who had found their way to Marseilles, but were then trapped. Bingham undoubtedly had to act with some circumspection. The unlimited issuance of visas would have provoked an uncontrollable rush of applicants, and US Assistant-Secretary of State Breckinridge Long was already keen to restrict visa issue still further.[147] Thus there is no indication of precisely how Bingham decided whom to help and whether it was based on the cases brought to him by men such as Fry and Frank Bohn but his conduct was undoubtedly exceptional, especially when compared with most of his contemporaries, and exactly how far he transgressed his official terms of reference remains a matter of debate.

It is impossible to do justice to the stories of spying, deceit and betrayal that emanate from the accounts of the rescuers in Marseilles and other towns and cities in southern France. Triumph and tragedy went side by side as those involved attempted to expedite the departure of their charges by any means possible. Upright citizens such as Varian Fry and the Dutch diplomats who were usually respectful of the law soon found themselves, much like the people they were helping, looking for loopholes to avoid or circumvent laws and regulations, and finally operating on the margins or outside the law altogether. To do this, they needed the specialist services offered by the local underworld of forgers, smugglers, and currency dealers. All these activities had long lineages often going back centuries, and it was primarily a matter of tapping into the available expertise. However, while the rescuers themselves were motivated by concern for the refugees (and in most cases paid by outside bodies), the systems they created relied heavily on those paid (and sometimes very handsomely paid) for their services. The traditions of smuggling and structures of criminality increasingly used by the rescuers and by those on the run long predated the Second World War. For the currency traders in Marseilles and the Pyrenean smugglers, the refugees and their helpers represented just another means of making a living. Yet by the same token, the rescuers highlighted here would have been far less successful without their help.

The same claim might be made for the consular officials who were prepared to issue visas to desperate people. As we have seen, there were some who acted from the purest and most upright motives in response to the plight of those in need, but for every de Sousa Mendes or Bingham, there were many others who were also prepared to act, but only at a price. The 'selling' of visas by their consuls in Berlin and Vienna had clearly been a problem for certain South and Central American countries before the outbreak of war, but in spite of the risks and the possibility of dismissal, the practices continued in other countries as the situation there worsened. This profiteering may have only been the tip of an iceberg, as complaints from other countries testify, but the issue of these documents was nevertheless instrumental in allowing a few more people to escape.[148]

Many refugees never came into the orbit of the now well-known rescue networks, but relied on their own resources and on making contact with specialists as and when they needed them. Their numbers are impossible to quantify, but comments suggest that border towns like Banyuls-sur-Mer were full of people prepared to offer assistance—at a price—with some more enterprising refugees also setting up on their own to help (and maybe to exploit) others. The dangers were immense. It was just as easy for the paid helpers to betray their charges as to carry them safely to the other side of the border—or have them picked up by the authorities once they had paid for the journey. Who would be any the wiser? Capture could be explained as a simple matter of bad luck or errors on the part of the fugitives. Another feature of these first escape networks is that they did not remain exclusively concerned with helping civilian refugees, even if this had been their primary aim.[149]

Perhaps the final point to make is that there was no more homogeneity among the rescued than among the rescuers. They were a complete cross-section of society united only by their persecution. Thus Jews were no more or less favoured than political opponents of Nazism, or those on the run from the German authorities for some other reason. Each one had his or her own foibles and requirements. Many of the well-known refugees were in later middle age, with medical problems to match. Thus they were not ideal candidates for crossing the Pyrenean Mountains. Perhaps it is not surprising then that the Fittkos could express relief when two men to be conducted over the mountains turned out to be young, healthy Austrians and not ageing Germans with heart conditions. These were people who had gone through the 'school of resistance' and therefore gave their helpers no trouble.[150] The same could not be said of some of the more high-profile people whom Fry and others tried to help. In the summer of

1940, Breitscheid and Hilferding had both been provided with false Czech passports, US visitors' visas and Spanish and Portuguese transit visas. Their only remaining step was to leave France illegally. This they refused to do on the grounds that they were so internationally important that Hitler would not dare request their extradition from France. In September 1940, they did agree to leave illegally, but the ship involved was sequestered. They were then given false Polish passports complete with exit visas, but again refused to leave. Soon they were placed under house arrest in Arles, and another attempt to get them aboard a ship bound for North Africa at the end of 1940 failed when they again refused to go at the last minute. In late January 1941, their desire to leave legally took another absurd turn. The plan was to travel to the French dependency of Martinique as a stepping-stone to the United States. They applied for, and received, exit visas from the French authorities, in spite of the fact that these were unnecessary for travel to another part of non-metropolitan France. To compound matters, Breitscheid then refused passage on the first ship he could have left on because there were no available cabins. In the meantime, the French—probably prompted by the unnecessary applications and realizing their mistake—revoked the exit permits and on 8 February arrested the men. Hilferding died three days later at the hands of the Gestapo in Paris, while Breitscheid was extradited and died in Buchenwald during 1944, ostensibly as a result of an air raid.[151] Their indecision and desire to behave within the law was ultimately fatal, but not unique. The Italian labour leader Guiseppe Modigliani also refused to leave in disguise with false papers, much to his wife's disgust, as this, he argued, would bring discredit on the movement he led.[152]

Not all the rescued were so intransigent or obsessed with ideas of legality and their own dignity, but they could still cause problems by making unreasonable demands of their helpers, or by insisting on transporting items of clothing or possessions that marked them out to the authorities as refugees or as illegal entrants. Thus, in these first months, no two rescue attempts were alike, and conditions for escape from the temporary haven of unoccupied France soon worsened as the Pétainist regime and their Nazi masters tightened their grip on the country. It was a situation that was not to improve in the following four years. Once the Germans imposed the labour draft in France, policing the borders became even more of a priority and they imposed a 50 kilometre exclusion zone along the Spanish frontier. Rumour had it that anyone caught in this area without a valid pass was likely to be shot, and the journeys became much more physically demanding—even for relatively fit young men—and there were many who died in the attempt.[153]

3

Fleeing the Captor: Escape from France and the Low Countries

Pilots and Prisoners of War

It is important to realize that rescue and resistance activities did not begin
with the Jews, nor even with the outbreak of war in September 1939, but in
many cases trace their origins to the First World War, or even further back
to long-standing local cultural traditions. The first clandestine organizations
in occupied Western Europe, therefore, emerged (or re-emerged) almost as
soon as the Germans arrived. At this stage, they were generally dedicated to
nationalist interests or to helping the Allied war effort and thereby opposing
Nazism and German occupation in the broadest sense, including helping
deserters, unwilling conscripts, escaped prisoners of war or downed pilots.
Many of the first groups were amateur and rather naïve constructions, based
on meeting an immediate need, and lacking the knowledge to build the
necessary safeguards to prevent infiltration and betrayal. Nevertheless, such
organizations were a feature of early resistance. Some of the first emerged
from groups of ex-servicemen or from within specific political groups, their
security resting on the bonds of trust between the original members. Long-
standing suspicions between different political organizations, especially on
the left, meant that communists were often excluded from wider alliances
and habitually organized by themselves. In this context, they were better
prepared than most—having had long experience of evading surveillance by
the police and security agencies in the 1920s and 1930s. Cell organization
and 'cut-out' techniques developed by the Comintern and indigenous

communist parties, designed to prevent infiltration, paid dividends when harassment by the police was supplemented by the attentions of the Gestapo.

Early resistance was both diffuse and unstructured, and rescue activities were initially, therefore, a question of self-help and protecting people on the run who had something to fear from the Germans. However, it was only a matter of days and weeks after the German invasion of North-Western Europe that this became more focused. Thus, for example, there were co-ordinated attempts to rescue the so-called *Malgré-Nous*, cohorts of men from Alsace whom the Germans attempted to conscript into the *Wehrmacht* after the summer of 1940, and when Belgian and French prisoners being moved across Dutch Limburg stopped at the border town of Eijsden, it provided an opportunity for the local population to assist a few men to escape custody.[1] Ultimately 768 Belgians and more than 71,000 Frenchmen found ways of escaping internment in Germany in the four years of occupation, and were given widespread support from civilian populations on their way home.[2]

The initial Allied response to helping their stranded servicemen inside occupied Europe was to recruit help from the existing networks known to the security services in London.[3] The most successful of these networks, Comète, was inspired by the charismatic 25-year-old Andrée de Jongh, who had approached the British consul in Bilbao in August 1941 with news of British servicemen hidden since Dunkirk. The network offered a string of safe houses from Belgium to the Spanish frontier, and the possibility of evacuating these men. After some distrust, because de Jongh was both a foreigner and a woman, further deliberation and checks reassured MI9 that she was genuine, and the network began the process of smuggling Allied soldiers and airmen to the safety of neutral Spain and Gibraltar.

Even in these early days, helping escaping prisoners of war was not viewed so severely by the Germans as helping pilots, which was seen as being of direct help to the ongoing war effort. It soon became clear that civilians could expect imprisonment and possible torture if caught, while most of their charges only had to show their service identity discs to be handed back to the military authorities.[4] Thus in August 1941, a British bomber was forced to make a landing near the village of Westmaas on the Island of Oud-Beyerland in Zeeland. The local population gave the crew food, money and some clothing, but all were captured within a short space of time. In the meantime, the entire male population of the village had been rounded up by the *Wehrmacht* and held in the main square while houses were searched. Nothing was found, but fourteen people were taken as hostages and tortured, three were subsequently imprisoned and five executed. The German commander General Christiansen refused to commute the sentences, as they were to serve as an example and a warning to others.[5]

The civilians who formed the backbone of these networks came from a wide variety of backgrounds. Many of the older generation in Belgium clearly remembered the occupation of 1914–1918 and needed no prompting to despise and hate the Germans. Indeed, there were some who had been engaged in illegal work in that conflict and saw the events of 1940 as a reason to resume their clandestine activities. While many early networks remained specialized, or moved into other forms of resistance such as clandestine newspapers or sabotage, there were some organizations that started out by helping pilots or servicemen but later extended their rescue activities to include Jews. In these cases, the penalties for discovery were equally shared between rescuers and rescued. This seems to have been the case in the Netherlands where early escape networks involving priests and local farmers began by helping escaping Belgian and French soldiers in areas near the German border. Similar groups and individuals near the southern border were able to expedite illegal frontier crossings into Belgium. Many of the problems of helping Allied airmen on the run—of appearance, language and lack of identity papers—were also to be evident in helping Jews later in the occupation. These first networks were often only concerned with a specific section of route, across a frontier or crossing point. They took the fugitives and transferred them onto the next group, having no idea how the pilots or escaped prisoners might ultimately be moved to safety in neutral Switzerland or Spain.

From the very beginning of the occupation, the rescue of Jews was, therefore, inextricably linked to other forms of escape activity. While certain networks deliberately retained a degree of specialization, the lessons learned by one group were nonetheless passed on to others, such as expertise in crossing frontiers, forging documents and 'cloaking' those who were clearly alien to the local environment. 'Specialist' services in the form of professional smugglers or forgers in a particular area were also evident here—and often used by several different groups—each with its own agenda, but often unaware that they were linked by this one activity or individual into a much wider, but nonetheless diffuse, network of resistance and escape organizations. Over time, accidental and deliberate links became more commonplace as networks expanded, amalgamating both horizontally and vertically, and forming geographical chains from the north to the south and east. What is also clear is that there was no chronological hierarchy of escape networks. Help for escaping prisoners seems to have been an initial prompt for many, but later there were groups that began by helping Jews and branched out into helping Allied aircrew.

For example, in the Netherlands, a group in Maastricht run by Jacques Vrij (the so-called Vrij-Groep) had some contact with a local government worker, J. J. van den Boogert, who had been helping Jews in hiding, and whose work had somehow come to the attention of MI9, who had recruited him as part of an escape network for pilots. Through him, they met Joop Piller, an Amsterdam Jew born in 1914 and married to a non-Jewish wife. Piller had been involved in sheltering German political refugees before the war. His communist contacts helped him to acquire a usable identity document in 1941 that allowed him to pass as an 'Aryan', but in 1942 this also brought his downfall when his communist cell was betrayed to the Germans. He was soon released and, leaving Amsterdam, hid in the village of Emst and went to work helping Jewish children to escape from Amsterdam. By 1943, this had brought van den Boogert's escape line for pilots in contact with the major assistance organization for those in hiding in the Netherlands, the Landelijk Organisatie (LO), which, in turn, also helped to shelter Allied aircrew.[6] For his part, Piller remained primarily involved in screening and helping pilots and later still, the Allied servicemen who managed to escape from the ill-fated attempts to bridge the Rhine at Arnhem in September 1944, but the story of this particular group shows how the various forms of escape activity could be interrelated and interdependent. Similarly, the Poels family who lived in a poor, former peat-cutting district near Venlo began by helping escaping prisoners, followed by Jews in hiding, and finally in assisting thirty-five to forty pilots and aircrew.[7] Its members continued their work until August of 1944 when some of them were arrested.[8] Having begun as a separate undertaking, this network soon established a chain of contacts to other organizations, including Comète, and to expedite the movement of people across the Belgian frontier.[9]

The contemporary recollections and post-war memoirs of those who worked in these networks suggest that there was no uniform perception as to the dangers involved in helping pilots and prisoners of war, and how this compared with helping Jews. One commentator described it thus: to bring a pilot to safety required many people, and all were in mortal danger the whole time. One could give a hiding place to a Jew, and if caught, one was likely to be given around a year in gaol—more or less.[10] However, it is likely that German priorities changed over time, and that the pursuit of these different 'crimes' also varied between areas, but the mere fact that there is no discernible pattern evident now makes it highly unlikely that contemporaries had any coherent view of the real risks they were running—and that this was then, as now, a matter of guesswork and conjecture.

For the most part, the help lines developed specifically by MI9 and the Allied security services for pilots, escaped prisoners of war or other political refugees never transferred themselves into helping Jews—or if they did do so, were usually too late to help most of them. Security was certainly one issue, especially when the extreme penalties for helping were publicized, but for those prepared to take the risks, the excitement of helping 'exotic' pilots on a temporary basis was often more appealing than helping Jews—who could not necessarily move on, and had to be sheltered for an indefinite period.

Smugglers and New Forms of Contraband

Histories of the Second World War tend to treat these networks as peculiar to that conflict, but there is plenty of evidence to suggest that 'illegal' border crossings and help for escaping service personnel and refugees had been a feature of frontier areas during the First World War, and that illegal activities during that conflict in both Flanders and Wallonia had some resonance with events in earlier times.[11] Differential taxation regimes and customs tariffs meant that there had always been scope for smugglers to make a living in border regions across Western Europe. This had been accentuated during the First World War when, because of the risks involved, substantial profits could be made smuggling goods and people across the border between occupied Belgium and the neutral Netherlands.[12]

The clandestine nature of these activities means that detailed examples are a rarity, but one newspaper account published in the 1970s gives a clear example of the continuities that could exist. Charel Willekens was a native of Neerpelt in the Kempen region of Belgium near the Dutch border. During the Second World War he was credited with having saved at least seventy-five Belgian and Allied servicemen by collecting them and then putting them in touch with an escape line, and he also reputedly assisted at least twenty-five Jewish families from the Netherlands to cross the frontier on their way southwards. As such, he was portrayed as a genuine hero of the resistance 'who would go out of his way [to further] the interests of the fatherland'.[13] His expertise as a *passeur* and illegal worker had been honed during the Great War when, by his own testimony, he had smuggled people, goods and mails across the Dutch frontier. The account gives no indication of Willekens' trade or profession save to record that he was illiterate during the First World War and could not read the mails he was delivering. This suggests that he came from a working-class agricultural background, but may also indicate that he was, in fact, a professional smuggler, whose expertise came into its own as a form of patriotic resistance during periods of occupation.

In the same vein, Maria Josepha (Miet) Cornelissen-Verhoeven was a Belgian woman who had been caught and sentenced to death by the Germans for smuggling people and information during the First World War, but reprieved by the armistice in 1918.[14] Decorated for her heroism by the Belgian state, she later married and went to live in the Belgian enclave of Baarle-Hertog where she ran a textile shop as well as raising a family of eight children. After the capitulation in 1940, she became involved in providing clothing and ration coupons for soldiers trying to escape internment. From here it was only a short step to a greater involvement—in smuggling people over the frontier, albeit this time in the opposite direction.[15] She was able to use her wider contacts outside the village, including traders and wholesalers elsewhere in Belgium as well as the smuggling community, eventually making contact with the Belgian resistance group *Witte Brigade*.[16] Trafficking goods was very much a way of life in this impoverished area and the authorities mostly turned a blind eye to the small-scale activities of the locals.[17] Even in 1940, her clientele included Jews as well as escaping prisoners and aircrew. The network lasted until 1944, but at some point, it was betrayed to the *Abwehr* in Antwerp who allowed it to continue functioning, but arrested the pilots when they arrived in the city. This ultimately stopped the network's operations with regard to aircrew, but the smuggling of arms and information continued. Only when the Allied advance moved into Belgium did the Germans act to round up the entire group.[18] Miet and two other members of the group were executed by firing squad on 10 September 1944.[19]

Policing of frontiers was inevitably haphazard. In many districts it was left to local policemen or depleted detachments of border police. Yet, as the First World War had demonstrated, the former were frequently compromised by their links to the community and unwilling to arrest people who were often friends and neighbours and subject them to the inflated penalties for 'crimes' that had previously been misdemeanours or overlooked altogether.[20] For their part, the understaffed border police were unable to mount an effective scrutiny of borders that ran for hundreds of miles through open country and unpopulated terrain. Only over time did controls become stricter and more assiduously enforced, but even later in the occupation, a Dutch network organizer was able to bribe the German patrol in a so-called 'smugglers' cafe' with drinks, and later described the Belgian guards as 'not bad chaps' (*geen kwade kerels*) who were co-operative if you put something (a few hundred francs) in their hands every so often.[21]

It was not only the traditional frontiers that presented barriers and potential threats to Jews on the run. The division of France into an occupied and an unoccupied zone instituted a new hurdle for travellers to cross—the line of demarcation—beset with the same official supervision and scrutiny as national boundaries. In the first weeks and months of the occupation, the Germans were content to allow Jews across the line and into the unoccupied zone, and the Vichy authorities to ban them from returning.[22] However, as time went on, the Germans continued to dump foreign Jews into the unoccupied zone and Vichy became increasingly worried about the numbers being foisted upon them, to the point where German and Vichy border officials would engage in retaliatory expulsions. Thus groups of Jews pushed into the southern zone could find themselves returned by the Vichy police, only to be put across the frontier again by the Germans.[23] This has to be seen in the context of much larger numbers of refugees returning home from exile in the unoccupied zone as German rule in the north stabilized. Estimates suggest that even allowing for the restrictions, some 10,000 non-French Jews had returned to the north by the autumn of 1940.[24] As controls increased, so those wishing to cross the line illegally had to find alternatives. Professional smugglers were reported by one refugee as charging between 3,000 and 5,000 francs for the journey from Paris to the Vichy zone, but contemporary police reports suggest much more exorbitant sums being involved.[25]

Both documentation and cover stories had to be believable if one was to have a chance of passing the controls unhindered. For this reason alone, the line of demarcation created its own border mentality and structures. Resistance groups had their own reasons for wanting untrammelled passage from one side to the other but there were individuals and other groups also involved. While some *passeurs* were described as 'greedy and treacherous' robbers, there were others who conducted people across the line of demarcation without asking for payment, and without regard for the risks to their own lives.[26] On the Vichy side, the Comité d'aide aux réfugiés and Amitié Chrétienne in Lyon created a *caisse noire* (black account) to fund help for people to cross the line, most of them being Jews.[27] A reception centre was created in Lyon to provide a small amount of money and an address for the fugitives. There were also examples of Jewish self-help, with a network composed of both Jews and Christians run by Rabbi Élie Bloch and Père Fleury, and also a commercial enterprise run by a Polish Jewish *passeur* who smuggled people in exchange for large amounts of money. Both appear to have fallen victim to a special *Abwehr* unit dedicated to uncovering the clandestine movement of Jews in France, some time between May 1942 and February 1943.[28]

Inevitably, conditions for crossing, therefore, varied enormously, depending on the topography of the region, the nature of the policing, and the attitude of the local authorities, as well as the motives of the groups and individuals involved.[29] The numbers of Jews who crossed the line after it had been established is impossible to estimate.[30] Certainly, the unoccupied zone continued to offer a haven for Jews in France and elsewhere until November 1942, but it is also clear from eyewitness testimonies that not all fugitive Jews used the services of third parties. Many relied just on their documentation, knowledge, and wits to cross into the southern zone. This became more difficult during the course of 1942 as controls were increased, and the Jews caught trying to cross were invariably handed to the German authorities. An estimate suggested that 75 per cent of the Jewish women in the Cherche-Midi prison in Paris in October 1942 had been arrested trying to cross into the unoccupied zone.[31] The line's existence represented just one more barrier for Jews attempting to escape Nazi persecution in the first months of the deportations, before all protection afforded by the southern zone disappeared when it was formally annexed in November.

Crossing frontiers was an essential but risky task for Jews attempting to escape from occupied Europe—whether it was into Switzerland or Spain, or just into another occupied state en route elsewhere. As time went on, the conditions in border regions and the control of frontiers became more and more rigorous. The Franco–Swiss border in the Haute-Savoie area was subject to much greater French surveillance after the end of 1942, and stringent road and railway controls were coupled with the identification and prosecution or internment of twenty-one known *passeurs*. After April 1943, the *zone pyrénéenne interdite* (exclusion zone) was declared on the Franco–Spanish frontier, and French customs officers and police were replaced by Germans. Only the Italian zone of occupation continued to provide some respite for Jews on the run, although this, too, was to be short-lived, as the Italian surrender in September 1943 introduced direct German rule there too.[32] At national frontiers, there were long-standing traditions of smuggling and illegal crossing—and people with the requisite knowledge who were prepared to use it, either altruistically or for profit. However, as the example of the line of demarcation in France shows, even where there had been no traditions or experienced practitioners, these soon emerged as the need and the opportunities arose.

Dutch-Paris

One good example of the way in which a complete international escape network was created, diversified, linked to other organizations, and reconstructed when damaged by denunciations and arrests was the so-called Dutch–Paris network created by Jean Weidner. Weidner was a Dutch textile merchant living in Paris, and the son of a Seventh Day Adventist minister who had spent years working in France. With his sister Gabriëlle, Weidner had been working for the church's organization in Paris when the Germans arrived in 1940.[33] His attempt to leave France for England in June 1940 failed,[34] but he moved to the unoccupied zone and re-established his textile business in Lyon with help from a friend, Gilbert Beaujolin.[35] There, he came into contact with refugees and in an attempt to help them, became involved with the welfare organization, Les Amitiés Chrétiennes.[36] He also came into contact with the Dutch diplomats, most notably Arie Sevenster, at the Offices Néerlandais.[37]

It was to Sevenster that Weidner initially offered his assistance and began the creation of an organization specifically to help Dutch refugees. At the beginning of July 1942, many of them were interned at Châteauneuf-des-Bains camp, near Vichy, and with help from the Dutch representatives, Weidner was able to gain access to the camp for 'social work', and the two men succeeded in getting many inmates released—either legally or by bribing the French guards.[38] This involved court actions, persuading French employers to hire men from the camps, and sometimes providing fugitives with travel documents of dubious validity. In this way, the religiously inspired honest philanthropic work began to be tinged with elements of illegality. Some of the money used for these activities came from Weidner's own pocket, or from the assets of his business.[39]

Getting people out of camps was one thing, but helping them escape was far more difficult. Sevenster was desperately short of funds and spent much of his time negotiating exit permits with the French authorities and entry visas to Spain for those who had some chance of escape.[40] His work was also complicated by the increasing numbers of Dutch men and women who managed to 'escape' into the unoccupied zone from the north. With limited resources, Sevenster attempted to concentrate the refugees in three centres: Perpignan, Lessac, and the largest, in Toulouse.[41] At this stage, he was aided by Salomon (Sally) Noach, a Dutch businessman who, like Weidner, had spent many years in France and had many business contacts there. Having fled Brussels in May 1940, Noach had been interned by the French near Toulouse but eventually found his way to Lyon, where he became cook and translator for Maurice Jacquet, the Dutch consul in Lyon. Noach quickly made contact with Dutch refugees in the city and was also active in raising funds for them—running a secret account within the Office Néerlandais. Money came from textile merchants in Lyon, dealings on the black market, and through contacts with the Dutch military attaché in Bern, General A. G. van Tricht. Noach tried and failed to arrange a route into Switzerland, but was successful in creating a network of contacts to provide false and forged papers for the refugees, and was also able to free people caught in raids by telling the French that their captives were not Jews. By September 1942, he was being sought by the French police and made his own escape over the border into Spain, and ultimately found his way to Britain.[42] Noach's career as a rescuer may have been relatively short, but it undoubtedly provided Sevenster and his colleagues with both knowledge and know-how. Yet the refugees were never going to be entirely free from the threat of internment, at the whim of the Vichy regime, nor could the limited resources of Arie Sevenster or Weidner's business support the work of helping these people indefinitely. Added urgency was given to their work when the deportations began in July 1942.[43]

Weidner, therefore, also explored the possibilities of using Switzerland as an alternative haven. In this respect, he was well placed. For many years, his father had taught at the Seventh Day Adventist seminary at Collognes, and Jean had spent a good deal of his youth in the area, very close to the Swiss border. He, therefore, knew many of the local guides, and was also personally acquainted with the roads, tracks, and passes that led across the border. Nevertheless, both the French and Swiss border police were on the lookout for refugees, and anyone in the border regions needed a special permit—issued only to residents and those who were considered economically important. Weidner circumvented this by establishing a subsidiary of his textile firm in Annecy and thus obtained a permit to travel in the border region.[44] His wife, who had previously been a secretary at the French consulate in Geneva, already possessed a permanent visa for the Franco-Swiss border. Weidner was, therefore, able to bring refugees to Annecy and then move them to the border near Collognes in the evenings or at night, either accompanying them across the frontier himself, or entrusting the work to others.[45] The network he created was made up of family, friends, staff from the Seventh Day Adventist College at Collognes, local farmers, and traders. The work was not without its dangers. Refugees caught by the French could expect to be incarcerated and possibly handed over to the Germans. Even on the Swiss side, capture could mean return to French hands. On at least one occasion, Weidner was arrested by the French police near Collognes and severely beaten.[46] He escaped only by getting a message to friends outside and then finally being released by a judge.

Initially, the network was essentially self-contained, taking people from camps or living in the unoccupied zone and conveying them across the border into Switzerland. Once there, it was known that Dutch nationals were not sent back across the border if caught, but interned in camps inside Switzerland. The work became far more difficult after November 1942 when the Axis forces occupied the southern zone, and the frontier area near Collognes was patrolled by Italian troops, themselves replaced by Germans after the Italian surrender in September 1943.[47] Initially, Weidner had been concerned solely with evacuating people who were already in France, but in October 1942, he had received a visit in Vichy France from B. M. (Benno) Nijkerk.[48] Nijkerk was a Dutchman resident in Brussels and a member of the so-called *Bolle-groep*, a network of Jews and non-Jews created by another Dutchman, Maurice Bolle,[49] dedicated to helping Allied pilots, as well as Jews and students from both Belgium and the Netherlands who were escaping from the Germans.[50] Bolle's entry into illegality and resistance was remarkable in a number of respects. Like Nijkerk, he was a businessman and had become involved with the clandestine Comité de Defense de Juifs (CDJ) in Belgium. He had been brought up in a very orthodox Jewish family but affected no religious convictions himself and was completely divorced from any Jewish communal life. However, he had actively opposed Nazism in Belgium before the war and was brought into the work of rescue in 1941 when one of his (Dutch) nephews arrived in Brussels illegally and wanted to move on to Switzerland with a companion, but had no papers or any idea of whom to approach for advice. Bolle was able to use an acquaintance in the refugee community with many years of clandestine experience to acquire suitable papers and contacts. Knowledge of this soon spread and his house was beset with other young visitors from the Netherlands who waited for him to return from work in the evenings. He later recalled that he had accommodated up to twenty of these fugitives under his roof at any one time.[51] Finance was a perennial problem, as was the fact that many smugglers were reputedly 'plundering' the refugees.[52] The group received some financial help from the pastor of the Dutch Reformed Community in Brussels, ds. A. G. B ten Kate and from Belgian sources, but they also needed help with hiding places. While pilots and other Allied servicemen could be moved on towards Switzerland or Spain, Jews were often unwilling to travel further and had to be hidden locally.[53] The group received assistance from Belgian civil servants and forgers, and had advantages in that Belgian identity papers were much easier to obtain, and to forge, than those used in the Netherlands. Nijkerk contacted Weidner to facilitate the movement of Jews into France, the idea being that those willing and able to move on from Belgium could be passed on to Weidner's network for onward travel to Switzerland or Spain.[54] This created a linkage between Weidner and the Bolle-groep in Brussels, reinforced when Edmond Salomon Chait was forced to flee to France and he became an important go-between for the two groups.[55]

Realizing that the route to Switzerland could only take a limited number of escapees, Nijkerk asked Weidner to create a separate route across the Pyrenees. To that end, Weidner had gone to Toulouse to meet two men he had recruited to help his work: the French doctor, Gabriel Nahas and a Dutchman, Aarts, who had taken over from J. C. A. M. Testers as director of the Office Néerlandais in the city.[56] In early 1943, when the mountains were impassable, Aarts brought the escapees to a hotel just outside Toulouse, Le Panier Fleuri. This became the jumping-off point for journeys across the Pyrenees. Among the many who were helped in this way were two survivors of the disastrous espionage campaign known by the Germans as the *Engelandspiel*: Pieter Dourlein and Johan Bernard Ubbink.[57] They had escaped to Switzerland, but to reach England, they had to leave the safety of the Confederation and travel across occupied France to reach the Spanish frontier. From there they could travel to Portugal and then to the United Kingdom.[58] Nahas was particularly important in being familiar with the area and knowing which of the mountain guides were reliable in getting people across the Spanish frontier.[59] His local network, made up of members of his family, brought the refugees to a railway station near the border. The involvement of the local stationmaster ensured that the Germans did not discover them. Later, the network was able to provide permits for the border region, suitably endorsed by sympathetic municipal civil servants.

Word of Weidner's work reached Willem Visser 't Hooft, the Secretary of the World Council of Churches in Geneva, and also the Dutch Minister in Bern, Johan Bosch van Rosenthal.[60] In March 1943, Weidner himself went to Switzerland illegally, using a freight train route across the frontier. Visiting Bosch van Rosenthal, and reporting on what Sevenster and he were doing, he was encouraged to continue the work. He also visited Visser 't Hooft and was given 200,000 French francs to help with the work being done in France. The money came from the church funds and had been collected from Dutch nationals in Switzerland.[61] Once Weidner had made direct personal contact with Dutch government representatives, there was an alternative and much more secure route. From September 1943, regular payments of around one million guilders were made via a Swedish diplomatic courier to Sevenster's successor, Janse. In order to deceive the Germans on the origins of the money, Janse convinced them that the money had come from other Dutch citizens in France rather than from the government-in-exile.[62]

The amount of German effort put into detecting these escape lines should not be underestimated. In July 1943, Bolle's activity came to an end when he was arrested, ostensibly sold-out (*vendre*) to the Germans by a double agent.[63] Paul van Cleeff took over the leadership of his group, helped by two other Dutch men, Henri Vleeschdrager and David Verloop.[64] Van Cleeff and Verloop concentrated on liaison with Dutch–Paris while other members of the group looked after the people 'permanently' in hiding in Belgium. In this way, responsibility for help for escapees and for those in hiding was divided. However, the attrition of the network continued. Jacquet was arrested in September 1943 and Aarts at the beginning of 1944.[65] The use of informers and infiltrators (*Vertrauensmänner*) was commonplace, and led to the downfall of many organizations. Although Dutch–Paris was relatively well insulated from such tactics by the personal and familial nature of the contacts within the group, the *V-männer* were by no means the only threat. Thus in February 1944, a large part of the network was 'blown' when one of the network's most diligent couriers, Suzy Kraay, was arrested in Paris with her parents, who had escaped from the Netherlands. The French police had no compunction about handing her over to the *Sicherheitsdienst*. This would have been bad enough, but it appears that she had committed the cardinal sin of carrying an address book. Although to some degree coded, Kraay allegedly gave up the real contents of the book when the Germans threatened the lives of her parents.[66] This allowed the SD to round up many network members in France, including one of its leaders, Herman Laatsman, Janse and even Weidner's sister Gabriëlle. In Belgium, nearly all the contact personnel in Brussels were also eventually arrested, including van Cleeff, Verloop, Vleeschdrager and ds. ten Kate.

By October 1943, Nijkerk had moved his centre of operations to Paris but was arrested under the pseudonym Bernard Smits at the home of the president of the Dutch Red Cross in March 1944.[67] He was imprisoned at Fresnes gaol on account of his involvement with the *Zwitserse Weg*, and was deported from Compiègne on one of the last trains to leave for Germany before the liberation.[68] Weidner kept the separate line to the Netherlands open and also continued to support those in hiding, but rebuilding the rest of the network was impossible. By this stage, the Brussels organization was being supported financially by the Dutch government with guarantees sent via Bern.[69] Finally, in May 1944, Weidner, Veerman, Rens and Nahas were also arrested in Toulouse by the French authorities. Nahas managed to escape almost immediately, and Veerman sometime later, but Weidner was severely mistreated by the *Milice*.[70] Eventually he and Rens were able to make good an escape with help from a sympathetic French policeman and they found their way to Switzerland. Later, in November 1944, Weidner was taken by aeroplane from occupied France to England.

The Dutch–Paris network is credited with saving around 1,000 people by organizing their escape from Nazi-held territory. Of these, around 600

Figure 3.1. Post-war gathering of the Dutch–Paris network
Source: (John Henry Weidner Foundation)

were Dutch, 200 French, 100 Belgian and other nationalities, and the
remaining 100 Allied aircrew.[71] They included the editor of the illegal *Het
Parool*, Gerrit Jan van Heuven Goedhart,[72] and one of only three escapees
from Stalag Luft III (Sagan) to reach England, Bob van der Stok.[73] The
network needed many hiding places and finding these was a great problem.
In evidence to the post-war government enquiry in 1949, Weidner noted,
'Now everyone says he helped the resistance, but at the time, it was
incredibly difficult to find people to help.'[74]

The Westerweel Group

A limited number of Jews did find some refuge in Switzerland or Spain
as a result of help from Dutch–Paris, but there were other escape lines
dedicated purely to helping Jewish fugitives. One such was the so-called
Westerweel group, named after its founder. Joop Westerweel had an
unusual background: brought up by parents who had converted to become

Plymouth Brethren (*Darbyistes*), he obtained his teaching qualifications largely through correspondence courses.[75] His first post in the Dutch East Indies had been terminated when he refused to be conscripted and he spent some time in gaol before being expelled.[76] Later, he and his wife became teachers at the progressive school run by the Quaker Kees Boeke at Bilthoven before he became the head of a Montessori Primary School in Rotterdam in 1940. Apart from teaching, he had also been involved in charitable work for children during the Spanish Civil War, and then for young Jewish refugees from Germany.[77] His personal ideology combined elements of socialism and anarchism with evangelical Christianity.

In August 1942, the leaders of the Zionist training farm at Loosdrecht had been tipped off that their remaining students were about to be arrested and deported. A Jewish schoolteacher and former colleague, Mirjam Waterman approached Westerweel for help to save them, aware that he had already begun sheltering a Jewish couple in his home.[78] The young Zionist trainees had already been targeted by the Germans and some had been taken as hostages in the summer of 1941 and deported to Mauthausen where all had died within a short time, thus speed was of the essence. Westerweel's first major achievement therefore was in finding shelter for all the forty-eight remaining students in the space of three days.[79] This began the work of hiding people inside the Netherlands, with Westerweel negotiating new hiding places across the country, with his Jewish co-workers acting as couriers, travelling with false papers and identities.[80] Westerweel continued to head the Montessori School in Rotterdam in spite of all his illegal activity. Even when he was not travelling, he was constantly dealing with problems. As a result he had little rest and reputedly slept mainly on trains and station platforms.

Although hiding children and students inside the Netherlands continued to be important, another solution had to be found—there were too many Jews needing hiding places and people were too afraid to take them in.[81] Westerweel's relationship with the two Zionist leaders, Joachim (Schuschu) Simon and Menachim Pinkhof, developed and, with the He-Halutz organization in Geneva, they attempted to create an escape line to Switzerland for the young Zionists who were threatened with immediate arrest and deportation.[82] Inevitably perhaps, some of the pioneers in hiding and waiting for their chance to escape were caught and ended up in the transit camp at Westerbork, but even here, steps were taken to prevent their

Figure 3.2. Hiding place on the heathland near Westerbork (Drenthe) used by
the Westerweel network
Source: Verzetsmuseum, Amsterdam

deportation by keeping their names off the transport lists.[83] Those involved
could also call on the services of a German Jewish refugee, Kurt Walter,
who had been put in charge of the light railway that brought supplies from
the nearest canal to the camp. A few people were smuggled out this way,
or were spirited away from the camp using false papers. The numbers were
never large, as the Germans carried out the threat to increase the numbers
deported by ten for every escapee.[84]

An initial party of eight pioneers was attached to a group of Jews
being taken to Switzerland by smugglers. They paid heavily for this help,
but were ostensibly betrayed to the Gestapo by the *passeurs* employed to
get them across the frontier. All eight ended up in the Mechelen transit
camp in Belgium and were transported to Auschwitz on 3 November

1942.[85] Abandoning this route, the network then pioneered a passage across the Pyrenees into Spain, and two later groups were successfully transferred to France using papers as Organization Todt workers as cover.[86] Here, they were in contact with the 'Nanno' group created by Kurt Reilinger. Reilinger was in a position to help with documents and even provided cover for Pinkhof as a military engineer that allowed him to cross frontiers and stay for free in military hotels.[87]

The dangers of the border crossing, especially between Belgium and the Netherlands proved to be well founded. Simon was arrested on his way back from taking a second group to the Spanish frontier and, realizing that he knew too much about the group's operations, committed suicide in Breda prison.[88] Westerweel continued the work, using around a dozen Jewish and non-Jewish helpers, but was forced underground when his wife was arrested in December 1943.[89] He was caught crossing the Belgian border in March 1944, using the papers of one of his couriers who was himself wanted for serious crimes, including the murder of a German.[90] Five months later, he was executed at Vught Concentration Camp.[91] Other members of the organization were also arrested as a result of betrayals. Menachim Pinkhof and Mirjam Waterman were to be sent as punishment cases to Auschwitz, but were saved when their names were added to a list of people with Palestinian passports by a member of the Jewish Council, and they were therefore sent instead to Bergen–Belsen where they both survived the war.[92]

In all, the Westerweel network helped around 200 young Jews, of whom 150 were smuggled across the border, 70 of them pioneers.[93] Most were kept in France where the French Zionists and the *Armée juive* helped to organize safe addresses. Some were passed off as workers for the Atlantic Wall project who, once in Paris, were able to find safer work with the Todt Organization,[94] but around eighty were taken to the Pyrenees and crossed into Spain. The organization even survived the arrest of Reilinger and the French Zionist leader Jacques Roitman, and continued its work until the liberation of Paris in August 1944. Westerweel's total commitment to the work of saving Jews can be understood through his apparent empathy with their plight and his apparent disregard for his own safety or for that of his children and wider family. His statements suggest that he saw rescue as God's work and therefore to be prioritized above love for family and friends.[95]

Escapee Stories

Accounts from those Jews who did make the journey from the Netherlands or Belgium to Switzerland provide a very different perspective from the organizational descriptions given above. Jenny Gans-Premsela gives a detailed account of her escape from the Netherlands to Switzerland in the summer of 1942. There is no mention here of networks, but only the contacts made during the journey she undertook with her husband, Mozes Heiman (Max) Gans. Galvanized into action by the first deportations, they discovered that the Jewish husband of a mixed marriage had found his way to Switzerland. Given the name of a contact near the Belgian border they removed their yellow stars and travelled using borrowed papers. Finding the right address was only the first stage: the 'removers' wanted more money—either cash or precious stones—than they had with them. More money was sent from home in Amsterdam, and they were then taken to a wooded area near the border and smuggled into Belgium by a *passeur*. In Antwerp, they were given a new contact and lodged in a café used by the Germans and thus unlikely to be searched for fugitives. They were given Belgian identity documents, but told that they would be sent to unoccupied France rather than direct to Switzerland as the border was impassable. They heard nothing from the network hiding them for some days, and had already decided they would not travel to unoccupied France when a *passeur* reappeared and demanded more money from them. Sufficiently suspicious to leave the café before the time appointed to meet the *passeur* again, they were horrified to see a raid taking place that rounded up a whole group of Jewish fugitives housed in the vicinity.[96]

In the meantime, through friends in the city, they had made contact with another man prepared to help them get to Switzerland. This turned into a party of six: Gans and his wife, their friends the Horodisch family, and two men from Rotterdam. Their guide made detailed plans to meet them in Brussels, but then failed to arrive at the appointed time. Returning to Antwerp to confront him, they were amazed to find that he had not come because he had failed to realize beforehand that it was the 13th of the month.[97] Superstitious and unreliable rather than untrustworthy, the following day he made good his promises and the group travelled via Brussels into occupied France. They travelled across the frontier by train, but the *passeur* soon made excuses and left, leaving them to find their own way to Nancy, where they spent the night in a hotel that charged for rooms by the hour, and then to Besançon. Here, they had a contact address given to them in Brussels. They had been told that this was part of a large French resistance network that had previously helped Belgian officers to escape to Spain, but were warned to say nothing and only give answers when asked. While the network would not fail to help Jews, they were not its prime consideration.

The contact address turned out to be a cottage—one of a row that backed onto a railway line. Having given the correct password, they were greeted by a railwayman and his wife, fed, and then amazed to be asked how much money they needed. Looking for an escape to Switzerland rather than money, they were offered a number of routes into Switzerland, ultimately choosing to go across the Jura mountains—a choice that was later vindicated when they discovered that some of their travelling companions who had opted for a longer route via the valleys were caught by a German control.[98]

This narrative demonstrates many of the contrasting aspects of those involved in helping refugees: the nervousness and unreliability of some couriers compared with the self-confidence and assurance of others, the diametric opposites of venality and extreme generosity among people engaged in essentially the same activity of people smuggling. However, this was a story of a successful escape where the survivors could reflect on their experiences. Their explanation for their own survival was a simple one. It was not a question of knowledge, money or skill: success or failure was down to good luck or bad luck.[99] One telling phrase also summed up their assessments of those who helped them: the trustworthy did not ask for money; the untrustworthy spoke of nothing else.[100]

Another young girl later recalled how she and her family had fled from the Netherlands to Belgium because they knew Maurice Bolle in Brussels and thought he would be able to help them get to Switzerland. They managed to cross the border with the help of a smuggler (probably without Bolle's help) and arrived in the Belgian capital where they initially stayed in Bolle's own house before being moved to a holiday hotel in the woods near the city. Here they met other people being helped by the network. Unlike them, they had certain advantages: knowing Bolle beforehand, knowing something of Brussels as a city, and having some access to funds. As she reflected:

Very few were so privileged. They had usually fled in a hurry, often without any Belgian currency, arriving in a situation and a country that was totally alien to them, dog-tired and with shattered nerves. That is why it was vitally important to know someone that you could go to. Without contacts it was virtually impossible to save yourself.[101]

It is, however, important to note that both Bolle, Nijkerk and many others who appear in the narratives of escape were also heavily involved in other aspects of resistance and helping Jews to survive inside occupied Belgium through their involvement with the Comité de Defense des Juifs.

Both the Dutch–Paris and Westerweel networks are now well-known examples of international networks created by motivated individuals who looked for routes to help Jews escape from Nazi persecution. They were built up through contacts with like-minded people and through association with other resistance groups, although how such links were initially made is sometimes clouded in mystery. Both were heavily dependent on the work of single individuals and, although both networks survived the occupation, they were far from intact, and most of their initiators had been arrested and/or executed, or gone to ground long before the liberation. The level of attrition involved here is testament both to the difficulties of maintaining security and to the assiduous nature of the German measures taken to apprehend these networks. While these are two high profile examples, they are not unique, and have to be seen against the background of other escape networks that dealt partly or exclusively with other fugitives such as Allied servicemen or labour draft evaders. Moreover, as will be seen in subsequent chapters, it is important to recognize that while these groups were designed exclusively to further escape to neutral states, many other networks came to organize their own escape routes as a means of reducing risks when hiding became too dangerous or impractical.

4

Swedish Havens

Escape from Norway

The Nazi persecution of the Jews in occupied Scandinavia provides us with contrasting images: the iconic story of rescue in Denmark during and after October 1943, and the almost unconsidered history of the, admittedly smaller, Norwegian community. Yet the escape of more than 50 per cent of the Jews from Norway to Sweden, fleeing from a German regime that had been far more hostile from the outset, and to a country that was less than welcoming in the first years of the war, is in some respects more remarkable than that of the better known Danish example.

The Jewish communities in Norway and Denmark had nothing like the profile of their co-religionists elsewhere in Western Europe. Modern Norwegian Jewry had its origins in the mid-nineteenth century, when the strictly enforced bans were lifted on Portuguese Jews (1844) and others (1851), but numbers remained very small, and in 1890 there were only 214 Jews in the country, with more than half being in Oslo (Christiana).[1] This grew to 1,359 in the 1930 census and was augmented by around 600 refugees, so that in April 1940 they numbered between 1,800 and 2,000 souls with 70 per cent concentrated in Oslo and the city of Trondheim, 500 kilometres to the north.[2] Occupationally, they consisted largely of an older generation of businessmen, coupled with a younger generation distributed in the free professions.[3] The community retained its own religious and secular organizations but it has been generally argued that the Jews were highly integrated into Norwegian society and suffered no social or political discrimination. However, this judgement requires some refinement. Jews and other dissenters (non-Lutherans) were often seen as outsiders and

Map 4.1 Norway, 1940–45

subject to a cultural prejudice.[4] Moreover, their small numbers and lack of visibility did not prevent antisemitic sentiments from being voiced by conservative politicians and even by the Nobel Prize winner Knut Hamsun. For them, the Jews were seen as negative influences on the economy and as the carriers of Bolshevism.[5] Antisemitic campaigns in the 1920s had prompted a ban of ritual slaughter in the country after a wave of public protest and acrimonious parliamentary debate, which meant that from 1930 onwards, orthodox Jews had to import kosher meat from Sweden.[6] The Norwegian National Socialist Party, the Nasjonal Samling, took up the cause of antisemitism, but was forced to engage in huge exaggerations of the numbers of Jews in the country to make their 'threat' seem credible. Its agitation is nonetheless credited with having limited the influx of refugees in the pre-war period.[7] In Norway the established Evangelical Lutheran Church had spoken out alongside the labour movement against Nazism in Germany, 'the motherland of Lutheranism', and condemned the concentration camps, use of torture and suppression of free speech.[8] A key leader was Bishop Eivind Berggrav who became bishop of Oslo in 1937 and who was later heavily involved in the resistance movement.

In Norway, as elsewhere in Western Europe, the Germans made few attempts at radical change in the first months of occupation, but first steps towards the Nazification of the Norwegian people in October 1940 led to the creation of a Christian Joint Council for the Norwegian Church. Their cause was aided by the resignation, en bloc, of judges of the Norwegian Supreme Court in protest at German actions.[9] As the state became increasingly Nazified under German and Norwegian national socialist control, so the church moved away from its relationship with authority, on the grounds that this was no longer used to uphold justice and righteousness in accordance with the word of God. This led to the dissemination of a critical pastoral letter across the country in February 1941, and by February 1942 all effective co-operation between Church and State had ended. This became apparent on 5 April 1942 when a declaration brought the resignation of 645 of the 699 ministers from their posts as civil servants, thus effectively creating the so-called 'Temporary Church Leadership' or 'Berggrav Church'.[10] It seems likely that this disobedience was treated leniently because the *Wehrmacht* did not want any additional trouble in Norway that would have used up scarce resources. Moreover, the pastors found it possible to go on working because they received both moral and material support from their parishioners. In this way, strong and very public protests against Nazi rule had been mounted before the major deportations of the Jews began.

The German invasion of Norway on 9 April 1940 had seen members of the Jewish community volunteering alongside their countrymen to fight in the armed forces. Although the campaign continued for sixty days, the rapid occupation of both Oslo and Trondheim by the German seaborne assault meant that few had the opportunity to escape. At the end of hostilities, Norwegian forces were interned, but like their Dutch and Flemish counterparts were soon repatriated and demobilized by the victorious Germans on ideological grounds. This included the Jewish servicemen.[11] Jewish community organizations had their first encounters with the Gestapo as early as May 1940. Synagogues and other Jewish organizations in Oslo and Trondheim were ordered to hand over their membership lists, and the Norwegian police were instructed to confiscate all radio sets held by Jews.[12] The Oslo community also received a request from the German Reichsvereinigung der Juden in Deutschland, doubtless prompted by the Nazi authorities, for details of all religious and racial Jews, categorized by age, profession, and membership of Jewish organizations. Some foreign refugees were arrested by the Gestapo in the summer of 1940, but most were subsequently released after enquiries into their backgrounds. There was a census of 'Jewish' businesses,[13] and antisemitic propaganda became more prevalent in the autumn of 1940, but the relative unpopularity of Vidkun Quisling's Nasjonal Samling limited its effects.

In the year following the German invasion, there were relatively few direct attacks on the Jews, although in Oslo, a leading Jewish musician was subjected to a public protest prompted by Quisling's party in January 1941. However in April, the Trondheim synagogue was vandalized and taken over by the Germans and in July of the same year, Jews were dismissed from public office, and those in the liberal professions had their licences to practise withdrawn. In the meantime, the German invasion of the USSR had prompted widespread arrests of both Norwegian and non-Norwegian Jews from northern cities, and their incarceration in a concentration camp at Sydspissen near Tromsø.[14] From there they were subsequently taken to Auschwitz-Birkenau where none survived the war.[15]

In Trondheim, stateless Jews were arrested and then released, and in Oslo, sixty Jews with Russian citizenship were arrested and tortured. At this stage, the rest of the Jewish community was left unmolested, but further actions in the northern cities during the autumn of 1941 saw arrests, confiscation of property and some summary executions.[16] Many were interned at the Grini concentration camp that ultimately held around 15,000 Norwegian and non-Norwegian prisoners. Here, the Jews were subjected to more severe punishments than other inmates and forced to wear the yellow star.[17] Four Jews were shot in Trondheim in March 1942, ostensibly for listening to the BBC and distributing illegal newspapers. In addition, the Germans began the seizure of Jewish businesses, and Norwegian policemen were used to round up Jews and to allocate and distribute special identity cards for Jews with the 'J' stamp appended.[18] This period also saw the first organized network to help Jews escape to Sweden. It was created by Wilhelm Rothkopf, an Austrian Jewish refugee who teamed up with Eger Ollum, whose sister was married to a Jew. Their initiative began in the autumn of 1941 and involved Rothkopf contacting Jews in Oslo and then taking them by train to the town of Flisa, near the border, before conducting them through the forests to safety.[19] By January 1942, the network had been unmasked and shut down by the police. It has been estimated that only around 150 Norwegian Jews managed to flee across the Swedish frontier before the summer of 1942. Perhaps surprisingly, given that Norway had been well informed about events in Germany since 1933, some early fugitives had actually returned during the course of the summer of 1940, thinking that the worst might already be over.[20]

The Jews of Norway were not included in the first stages of the Nazi plan to deport and exterminate the Jews of Europe.[21] Thus the underlying prompt for the major round-ups of male Jews on 25–26 October 1942 was probably Reichskommissar Josef Terboven's decree of 25 September that all people hostile to the state should be arrested, but the catalyst for action seems to have been the shooting of a Norwegian border policeman on a train near the Swedish border on 22 October 1942.[22] Karsten Løvestad, a member of the resistance and so-called 'border pilot' had attempted to take nine young Jews over the frontier to Sweden. This had misfired when the group was confronted by a frontier guard on a train who had asked for their papers. Knowing that the men had identity cards stamped with a 'J', Løvestad shot the guard and the group fled. This prompted a massive German search and all nine Jews were arrested. Some three days later, all male Jews over 16 were rounded up and their property confiscated. The only ones saved from these measures were those in mixed marriages, those with Swedish relatives (who were rapidly awarded Swedish nationality), and a few with foreign (neutral) nationalities. The arrests of the remaining Jews, primarily in Oslo, proceeded with great speed and were immeasurably helped by the co-operative attitude of the Norwegian police who carried out the round-up, returning several times to properties that had been empty when first visited. The speed of the operation and the relative period of calm that preceded it undoubtedly had an impact in its success. Neither the Jews nor most of the authorities realised it was about to happen.[23] Seven Lutheran bishops who had resigned their posts on 24 February 1942 in protest at attempts to Nazify or co-ordinate their churches spoke out against the arrest and deportation of the Jews, challenging the Quisling regime directly in an appeal on 10 November, and had the condemnations read from pulpits on both 6 and 13 November 1942.[24]

Subsequent attempts by the Norwegian government-in-exile to persuade the British to exchange the arrested Jews for wounded German POWs met with a refusal, based on the principle that such an exchange fell outside the terms of the Geneva Convention.[25] A month after the initial action, on 25–26 November, all the women and children were arrested and deported with their menfolk to Stettin by ship, and from there to Auschwitz.[26] The total deported in this, and one or two later transports, was 770 people, meaning that around 1,000 of the country's Jews either survived in hiding or escaped.[27]

The incidence of rescue in Norway, although small in comparison with other Western European states, nevertheless shows the same mixture of private initiatives and collective enterprise seen elsewhere, although nearly all the documented cases relate to escapes rather than to long-term hiding inside Norway. There is no doubt that information on the prospective raids did leak out from the police to the civil population and many immediate forms of help were organized to shelter Jews away from their homes, often by people already engaged in some form of resistance activity.

Hospitals such as Ullevål and Lovisenberg were used as hiding places, and doctors were known to have 'cloaked' patients in hospitals by refusing to discharge them, or by failing to notify the authorities of their discharge, thus giving them time to escape.[28] That said, flight from Norway was fraught with difficulties: the sea routes were closed, and Denmark was already under German control. The only real alternative was to seek sanctuary in neutral Sweden, and students, labour draftees, soldiers, and policemen were numbered amongst those who made the journey during the occupation. Explaining why more Jews did not make the attempt beyond the summer of 1940 and before October 1942 is complex, but has been attributed to a number of factors. Initially most seemed to believe that the Germans would not implement the policies used in Germany, Austria and, later, Poland and they therefore chose to stay put and resisted the pleas of friends and neighbours, as well as the nascent resistance organizations, to flee to Sweden. Later, fear of being caught trying to escape when they had otherwise done nothing wrong weighed heavily, as did the age of those involved and the perceived vicissitudes of the journey. Others were constrained by family members who could not travel, or by the possibility of reprisals against those left behind. Coupled with this was the continuing fear that Sweden might not be particularly safe and could also be overrun by the Germans in the foreseeable future.[29] However, as the pressures on the Jews mounted during the course of 1942, so increasing numbers looked for ways to cross this frontier. The terrain was inhospitable at any time of year and all-but impassable in the winter. Would-be escapers might get close to the border by train before identity cards were changed to identify Jews, but then they had to rely on penetrating thick forests and wilderness—and help from the local population—before using local guides to avoid German frontier patrols.[30]

A German decree of 12 October 1942 had stipulated the death penalty for anyone helping a Jew to escape, but the embryonic Norwegian resistance had already developed some networks to assist people crossing the frontier. Nonetheless, their capacity was overwhelmed by demand after the deportations began in November 1942. To avoid the controls on public transportation, scarce cars, fuel and their drivers were used in order to get people to the border. For example, Henriette Samuel and her three children, along with forty or so other Jews were taken close to the border hidden in trucks carrying potatoes in December 1942 before they were dropped off. They then crossed the frontier at night on foot in temperatures of −20°C.[31] In contrast, others were transported in trucks carrying produce or merchandise all the way into neutral Sweden. There is no indication if any of these fugitives were ever caught by German or Swedish border or customs controls. Another woman managed to ski across the frontier, carrying her 4-year-old daughter in a rucksack. Crossings could also be effected by boat, although these were affected by the stringency of German controls, and a few Jews even managed to find their way to Shetland and then Scotland via the so-called 'Shetland Bus'.[32]

In the initial stages, help usually began with individuals, but often came to involve many others. Thus, Herman Raskow and his wife, already in hiding in October 1942, were warned of impending raids by their neighbours and given temporary sanctuary with them. The neighbours used their wider family and their ties to the Pentecostal Church to find subsequent hiding places as the fugitives were sheltered for two months before finally making the journey into Sweden in January 1943.[33] There is no precise indication here that these rescuers had contacts with the established resistance movement, but others undoubtedly did. Gabriel Stiris fled his home in October 1942 and was initially sheltered by Hans Jacob Malm but was then taken by Pastor Per Faye Hansen to a number of hiding places before being brought to the border hidden in an ambulance.[34] Markus Rosenberg, a refugee German Jew who had left Oslo for the provinces, having rented a summer cottage in the countryside with his family in 1940, had continued to receive a salary from his employers where he was director of their paint manufacturing division. This was undoubtedly a fortunate situation, but improved still further in the summer of 1942 when his neighbour at the cottage, Einar Wellen, warned him about the persecution of the Jews in Oslo, and offered to help using his contacts with the resistance. Some four months later, on 14 January 1943, he returned and transported the whole Rosenberg family to Oslo—and then after one night's wait—to the frontier by truck, and then on foot into Sweden.[35]

When Henriette Samuel made her escape, the initial warning had come from a neighbour.[36] Unknown to her and almost by accident, Samuel found herself in the hands of a much larger organization. Likewise, Felix Adler and his wife were warned about the impending round-up and contacted

Per Faye Hansen whose contacts included Hans Christen Mamen, another member of the Norwegian church operating underground. He found them a hiding place with a different family while he arranged their escape to Sweden and travelled on the same bus as they did towards the border—although not acknowledging them. They survived a Norwegian police check, in spite of the fact that their identity cards were clearly stamped with a 'J', and ultimately crossed the frontier on foot.[37] Mamen expedited other border crossings with Jews, including one where he carried a 3-year-old boy into Sweden on his shoulders.[38] Another rescue involved two Norwegians who took a mother and baby 150 kilometres on skis from Leksvik to the Swedish border.[39]

Networks that helped the Jews were based mainly around existing resistance activity and personal links, including those forged through the Church. The 'export organization' created for crossing the frontier inevitably required numbers of people.[40] Several hundred fugitives were moved in November and December alone, but the nature of the journey meant that many had to stay in hiding for several months. Temporary accommodation and food from local populations were essential while escapes were organized. Some paid personally for the privilege with a set tariff of NKr.150 although the richer elements were invited to pay more, while others were apparently taken free of charge.[41] This suggests that the Norwegian resistance was already in control of the process and was setting 'fair' rates. The journey to Sweden had to be co-ordinated with the 'border pilots'. Their work involved the use of trains, where railway personnel could warn if train passengers were having papers checked by the authorities, safe houses near the border, and networks of informers to advise on the safety of specific routes where vehicles were used. Thus for example, local farmers became used to the habits of both the German and Swedish frontier guards and were in a good position to predict their movements and where the frontier was likely to be unguarded at any specific moment.[42] A survey in Stockholm suggested that by September 1944, there were 925 Jews from Norway who had managed to cross the frontier to safety.[43]

The escapes that took place in the aftermath of 25–6 October included many children and old people, some of whom actually crossed the border on stretchers.[44] One group, operating a crossing from a farm north of Ørje in Østfold, was run by a former policeman, Alf Tollef Pettersen.[45] It alone was credited with having smuggled over 1,000 people over the border, including several hundred Jews, between October 1942 and 14 January 1943, employing two trucks and working five nights a week.[46] Later he, his wife, and an accomplice also had to flee to Sweden to avoid capture.[47] Other routes used in the south were across the Iddefjorden and in the areas of Kongsvinger and Solør, while there were also routes as far north as Narvik.

Even these more organized and co-ordinated escapes were not without their hazards. Ole Jacob Malm was the secretary-general of the Coordination Committee of what became the civil resistance in Norway. Involved directly in the removal of Jews to Sweden, he had personally given shelter to a Jewish couple, the ageing Czech physician Wilhelm Jaroschy and his wife. Taken on foot to the border, it was doubtful that the doctor would be strong enough to make the trip, and when he blundered into a German patrol, he took a lethal dose of morphine, but was resuscitated by a young doctor at the behest of the Germans, only to be subsequently tortured to betray his helpers and hiding places. By the end of October 1942, it was well known that helping anyone to escape to Sweden was punishable by death.[48] This meant that any Jews captured inside Norway might be forced to give up the names of those who had helped them in the past. Thus Malm was forced into hiding and into relinquishing his responsibilities.[49]

Among other organizations involved in this work was a small group of Norwegian and foreign Quakers resident in the country. Its members had been helping refugees, and brought Jewish children from Czechoslovakia in 1939. During the occupation they continued their welfare work for both children and adult refugees.[50] Their shift into illegality and civilian resistance came at a relatively early stage in the occupation and they organized at least one clandestine escape to Sweden in the summer of 1941. At that time, moving near the border was relatively easy, although outsiders still needed a permit, but their first border pilots were a farmer's family who made regular shopping trips across the supposedly closed frontier to Sweden where goods were in plentiful supply.[51] On the night of 25 November 1942, Myrtle Wright, and Diderich and Sigrid Lund did their best to warn all the Jews they knew in Oslo about the impending danger of arrest. Nina Hasvold, the director of the home where refugee children had been housed, aided by Dr Caroline 'Nic' Waal and Gerda Tanberg found willing hosts to hide them all.[52] Those people unfortunate enough to be arrested were transported out of the country on the steamship 'Donau' the following day, but the Quaker group did manage to visit some of those brought in from outlying districts and held in prisons. This latter group were not sent away until 24 February 1943,[53] but most attention had to be given to those in hiding. This initially involved finding accommodation, bedding and food, but soon graduated to contacts with 'transport' or 'export' groups. Initially this seems to have been done individually, with fugitives given train tickets, papers and instructions on where to alight the trains and whom to meet. Later, reference was made to a *selskap* (party) where groups would be assembled in safe houses or other locations, including a side street in the centre of Oslo and a truck stop on the outskirts, before being conducted across the frontier.[54] One route involved using Frederikstad, a location that did not require a frontier pass, and then an arrangement with the Swedish authorities whereby people were brought to safety on Swedish customs boats.[55] Helping the Jews dominated the work of the Quakers in January and February 1943, and they were especially concerned with the nineteen Czech Jewish refugee children still in the country. Here they were helped by a number of pastors' families. To protect the foster parents, 'kidnappings' were staged so that they could have no knowledge of where the children had gone if the police came looking for them. Those evacuated included helpers whose cover had been blown as well as Jews, but the organization was beset by arrests and swamped by the need for others to use the escape lines and flee to Sweden.[56]

Some forty Jews also managed to survive in hiding inside Norway, either in hospitals, nursing homes or homes for the elderly. Two even remained unmolested in the Jewish old people's home, which unaccountably stayed open throughout the occupation.[57] Some also survived, albeit in appalling conditions, inside the concentration camps, where they were continually subjected to severe beatings and abuse by their guards—and by outsiders.[58] Although networks and escape lines had been established to evacuate resisters and other fugitives from Nazism before October 1942, they had been weakened by a series of betrayals and arrests, thus making their efforts to evacuate the Jews even more remarkable. They were aided by the fact that the time of greatest peril for the Jews did not coincide with the persecution of other non-Jewish groups such as students and Norwegian officers.[59]

Figure 4.1. The steamship 'Donau' on its way to collect Jews from Norway for deportation
Source: Hjemmefrontmuseum, Oslo

This picture of national heroism received only one major shock when, in 1947, it was revealed that two 'refugee pilots' who had acted as couriers for those on the run had killed a Jewish couple on their way to Sweden. Rakel and Jakob Feldmann, whose foster son had been arrested in October 1942, had sought shelter with the Løvestad family in order to escape to Sweden. They were helped by border pilots Peder Pederson and Håkon Løvestad who took them as far as the Skrikerud Pond and then ostensibly murdered them before stealing their money and valuables. The bodies were then weighed down and dumped in the pond, where they were not found until 1943. After the war, both men were tried for murder in 1947 but pleaded that they acted because the Feldmanns were too weak to reach the border, and if captured could have betrayed the routes into Sweden. Ultimately they were acquitted of murder and sentenced only for the thefts, with the result that the Sarpsborg Court's decision became

Figure 4.2. Refugees escaping across the Norwegian frontier into Sweden
Source: Hjemmefrontmuseum, Oslo

the most hotly debated issue in Norway's post-war reckoning with its occupation past.[60]

Although there were many successful escapes to Sweden, reaching Swedish soil was not always enough and those caught at the border were sometimes handed back by the authorities. It is also worth remembering that most of the networks involved did not specialize in helping the Jews, but dealt with them on the same basis as all others who were fleeing from Nazi persecution. In general, it seems that beyond the small numbers of dedicated individuals and networks, wider Norwegian public sympathy for the Jews was really only prompted by the final set of arrests and deportations, not least because earlier round-ups had taken place away from the capital and/or had involved foreigners rather than Norwegian nationals. Thus the radical change in opinion and switch to *holdningskamp* (literally battle of the

minds) by the majority of the Norwegian population really came too late
to save more of the Jews.

The Icon of Rescue: Escape from Denmark

The saving of Danish Jewry from under the noses of the Nazis in the
autumn of 1943 is the most celebrated example of collective rescue through
escape during the Holocaust era.[61] The successful removal of more than
7,000 people from the hands of the Nazis long after the 'final solution'
had begun in the camps in Poland was a major achievement, and the risks
taken by many people to ensure its success should not be underestimated.
As such, it has become the centrepiece in assessments of a heroic Danish
resistance to Nazism and therefore a very positive aspect of the country's
national narrative on the history of the Second World War. One eminent
historian has described the attitude of the Danish people as 'an exercise of
high moral and political responsibility, outstanding and exceptional for the
time in which it took place'.[62] It is also widely regarded as the consummate
example of what could be achieved in the face of Nazi persecution, and
thus as a damning criticism of what was not done for the Jews elsewhere
in Western Europe.[63] Yet, without undermining the undoubted heroism
of many Danes and others in carrying out this spectacular rescue under
the noses of the Germans, the context of place and time does serve
to show just how exceptional the circumstances were in allowing it to
happen.

Like their Norwegian counterparts, the Jews in Denmark were a small
and largely invisible element within Danish society. At least 50 per cent
of the Danish Jews were concentrated in Copenhagen, with the rest
mainly in Odense and Århus. Many were married to non-Jews, and the
community was highly assimilated. Numbering between 6,450 and 6,500,
plus those in mixed marriages, they represented only 0.18 per cent of
the population and comprised three distinct groups: an old-established
Danish-Jewish community of around 1,600 people, a larger group of
approximately 3,350 immigrants from Eastern Europe who had arrived
since the 1880s, and about 1,500–1,700 Jewish refugees from Germany,
Austria and Czechoslovakia.[64] Of those in the latter categories, about
2,200 did not hold Danish citizenship and included between 500 and

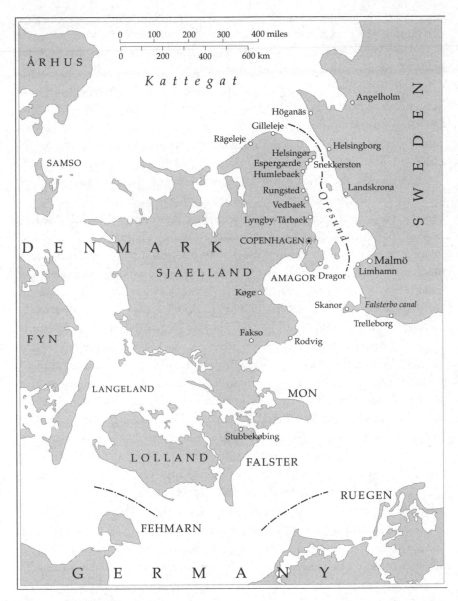

Map 4.2 Denmark, 1940–43

680 foreign agricultural students and *Alijah* trainees waiting for Palestine certificates.[65] The Danish state had not been particularly welcoming to refugees from Nazi Germany in the 1930s and this had limited the number of entrants. Jews were not subject to any specific legislation, although foreigners inevitably had to be registered with the police, and they were treated in exactly the same manner as all other Danish citizens. Only the communist refugees received special attention from the police, largely because they were considered as prima facie agents of the Soviet Union.[66]

In Denmark, the compromise reached between the German occupiers and the Danish state after April 1940 had allowed for the continued existence of sovereign, parliament, and institutions, albeit under a limited amount of supervision exercised via the German Foreign Office.[67] This suited the Germans as it dispensed with the need to provide anything more than a token occupation force, thus saving precious manpower and resources.[68] The profile of their armed forces was kept to a minimum and confined largely to coastal defence. Likewise the involvement of the German security police inside the country was limited to twenty-five men in Copenhagen until the summer of 1943.[69] In exchange for this 'freedom', the Danes were pressured to gear their agricultural production to the needs of the German war economy. This led rapidly to suggestions for a customs and economic union between the two countries, an idea that was widely opposed inside Denmark, but ultimately torpedoed by farming and industrial interests inside Germany.[70] The following three years saw a continuing accommodation with the Nazis as the government trod a tightrope of keeping the occupiers at arm's length while trying to keep a lid on increasing levels of civilian resistance. For their part, the Germans were also careful. Attempts to involve the Danish armed forces in the war against Bolshevik Russia were dropped in favour of a volunteer Danish Free Corps.[71] The compromise allowed Berlin to benefit from the agricultural production of its northern neighbour and also ultimately to recruit large numbers of the Danish unemployed for work inside the Reich.[72] The softer German approach taken to Denmark meant that resistance to occupation was limited in the initial phases of the occupation. The first year saw mainly patriotic and symbolic protests, with little in the way of organization. Worsening economic conditions did help to create a degree of alienation among the working classes, something that was exacerbated by the central involvement of the Social Democratic Party in the national government. Increasing economic impositions from Berlin also increased unrest, but this was largely reflected in the growth of the illegal press and occasional demonstrations. Organized resistance was limited to a few links with Allied agencies such as SOE, but this primarily to carry out sabotage actions and London had no interest in fomenting further civil resistance in Denmark.[73]

In this initial phase, the question of the Jews was never considered, and the Danish authorities were happy to claim that there was no 'Jewish problem' in Denmark.[74] In the same vein, the Jewish community leadership led by the supreme-court lawyer, C. B. Henriques, also encouraged the view that the Jews should put their trust in the institutions of the Danish state and not draw attention to themselves.[75] This attitude seemed to bear some fruit in the first months of occupation and it was not until early 1941 that the Germans turned their attention to Jewish refugee welfare organizations and demanded that they be shut down and the records handed over for scrutiny. It seems that the Jewish community was able to 'doctor' its books before surrendering them, and the Committee for Jewish Agricultural Students was able to avoid German measures by reinventing itself as a 'secretariat', thereby allowing its operations to continue.[76] Certainly, the Germans in Copenhagen realized that raising the 'Jewish question' was potentially dangerous to 'normal' German–Danish relations and would threaten the considerable strategic and economic benefits that had accrued. Thus they did not press the point.

The Jewish community nonetheless remained watchful, and registered with unease the arrests and internment of Danish communists in June 1941, in contravention of their legal rights, when war was declared on the Soviet Union.[77] However, the Danish authorities continued to defend the interests of the Jewish population and refused to countenance any legislative action against them. They sent signals to Berlin by taking action against the editors of *Kamptegnet*, an antisemitic magazine.[78] There were also public statements of support from politicians such as the Social Democrat Hans Hedtoft and Conservative leader Christmas Møller. Any attempt at discrimination against a specific group would have been against the principles of the Danish constitution, and all were convinced that if the Germans insisted on antisemitic legislation this would end all co-operation by the Danish regime. The German-sponsored Danish National Socialist Party (DNSAP) failed to break down the traditional political loyalties of the Danish people. Its membership had reputedly been responsible for an arson attack on the synagogue in Copenhagen on 20 December 1941. Later incidents led to night-time security patrols by young Jews in the autumn of 1942, but these were soon discontinued as the insurance costs were too high, and the building was closed for the winter when fuel ran out.[79]

In the autumn of 1942, after the deportations from other Western European countries were in full swing, there were changes in the German relationship with Denmark. This was prompted by the so-called 'cable crisis' where King Christian X had responded to Hitler's telegram on his birthday with a curt 'thank you very much' in reply.[80] Insulted by this, Hitler insisted on a new hard-line military commander, General Hermann von Hanneken, and SS-Gruppenführer Werner Best was appointed in October as Reich Plenipotentiary. This crisis in the relations between Copenhagen and Berlin led to the latter insisting on the appointment of a new, and more pro-German, Danish cabinet.[81] In practice, although it did enact some of the emergency legislation demanded by the Germans, this new administration under Erik Scavenius proved less malleable than Best and his Nazi masters had hoped. Attempts to maintain the co-operative attitude of the Danish people towards the occupation were increasingly hampered by greater repression by the military authorities against perceived resistance, worsening economic conditions, and the changes in the war situation. Nonetheless, in spite of increasing pressure, the Scavenius cabinet continued to fend off German attempts to introduce any actions against the Jews before the events of August 1943.

Although an SS man, and thus supposedly committed to the Nazi regime's ideological objectives, Best was there as representative of the German Foreign Office and of the Foreign Minister, Ribbentrop.[82] He was keen to maintain tolerable relations with the Danes in spite of the worsening war situation, and was able to counter the more radical anti-resistance measures advocated by General von Hanneken. The crucial change came in August 1943 when, in the light of the worsening economic conditions and Axis military failures in Russia and the Mediterranean, there were huge anti-collaborationist strikes and demonstrations in many provincial towns that led to clashes with German soldiers and many deaths. Government attempts to stop the disorder failed, and on 29 August the *Wehrmacht* declared a state of emergency, ostensibly because this might herald an Allied invasion.[83] The Danish army was demobilized and the government resigned, leaving Best as Reich Plenipotentiary to sort out the resulting vacuum.[84]

In effect, his policy of keeping the Danes pacified had finally failed. As a result, he had to try to recover his reputation with his masters in Berlin as quickly as possible. Understanding that the political changes in Denmark would undoubtedly lead to demands from the RSHA for the implementation of the 'final solution' in Denmark, he decided to pre-empt the move by suggesting it himself.[85] Thus on 8 September he cabled Berlin that 'the time has come to turn our attention to the solution to the Jewish question'. A week later he had permission from Hitler to deport the Danish Jews, and a German police battalion under the command of SS-Obersturmbannführer Dr Rudolf Mildner and specialists from Eichmann's Office at the RHSA were sent in to carry out the task. The arrests were ordered for the night of 1–2 October 1943: the short delay being to allow for the completion of the German–Danish economic agreements for 1944.[86]

In the meantime, Best followed a course that was apparently contra-dictory. Having instigated the move against the Jews, he then worked to undermine its execution. This is seen as problematic and somehow unbelievable by many historians, given Best's impeccable credentials as a committed antisemite and someone who had been involved in many actions against the Jews, including the expulsion of Polish Jews from the Reich in October 1938, ethnic-cleansing operations in Poland after September 1939, and actions against the Jews in France.[87] However, his most recent biographer has explained his actions as essentially pragmatic. Best's antisemitism can be seen as 'academic' in that he did not hate Jews per se, but saw them as alien and damaging to German interests. For him, 'solving' the Jewish question in Denmark could be achieved just as easily by removal as by physical destruction. This was undoubtedly his preferred option as the Jews were not a major problem in Denmark, but their persecution had the potential to inflame local opinion and preclude greater co-operation from the Danish administration—something that Best was very keen to avoid.[88]

His solution was to employ a German diplomat, Georg Ferdinand Duckwitz, to tip off his Danish contacts that imminent actions were being contemplated against the Jews, and also to approach the Swedes to open their borders for refugees from Denmark.[89] Duckwitz had been a Nazi Party member since 1932 and had joined the Party's Foreign Political Office (*Aussenpolitisches Amt*) run by Alfred Rosenberg. His knowledge of Danish saw him employed by the *Abwehr* as an agent in 1939 and finally took him to Copenhagen as a shipping expert (*schiffahrtssachverständige*) attached to the German ambassador. After Best's arrival in November 1942, Duckwitz became a central figure in his relations with Danish political and business elites.[90]

In the first three years of occupation, a small number of Jews had been spirited away from Denmark to Sweden in April 1940, and later it proved possible to send some eighty-seven children via Sweden, Finland, Russia and Turkey to Palestine.[91] Other attempts at escape had tragic consequences. Some Zionist pioneers attempted to escape by hiding under railway carriages. At least one group travelled as far as Sofia in Bulgaria, but their leader returned and was caught in Hamburg. Others attempted to escape by hiding in crates of machinery destined for neutral Turkey—all were caught and only one survived Auschwitz to tell the story. More successful were a small group trained as fishermen who managed to sail from Bornholm to Simrishamn in Sweden in March 1943. This was seldom attempted by anyone, as crossings of this nature were widely regarded as impossible due to the vagaries of the weather, minefields, and the Danish and German patrols.[92] The Jewish leadership, continuing its policy of maintaining a low profile, was worried when the Germans, aware that the escape had been successful, sent a warning that any further attempts would lead to reprisals. This led directly to the leadership warning the Zionists, and reminding them that there was no reason for such escapes.[93]

Beyond these examples of self-help, there were also some individual attempts at rescue that had their origins before the occupation in April 1940. Anna Christensen worked for the International League for Peace and Freedom and had been responsible for one group of young Youth Aliyah students sent to Denmark for training. Initially they were educated in local schools but after the Germans' arrival she organized a classroom in her cellar and later hiding places for all the children. Likewise, the Strassman family from Copenhagen were able to take shelter with Ester Handberg and her husband on the island of Fyn in October 1943, but their relationship had begun before the occupation when the couple had provided a holiday home for the Strassman's children. Ester Handberg made all the arrangements for the family to remain underground. Ultimately both groups were able to flee to Sweden.[94]

Until the summer of 1943 the Jews had been left largely unmolested. Scavenius had resisted the introduction of antisemitic legislation

Figure 4.3. Fugitives from Denmark on their way by sea to Sweden
Source: USHMM

but made it clear that he would not promote Jews to prominent positions in the administration where they were likely to be noticed by the Germans.[95] Confidence in this apparent protection and the inactivity of the Germans meant that Danish Jews were disinclined to attempt any form of escape themselves. As the vice-chairman of the Jewish community recalled

> There was unanimity that one should refrain from it. 6–7,000 people could not be hidden. Any action would demand help from non-Jewish countrymen, demands which one could not make, and could not be expected to be fulfilled. [. . .] All that one could achieve would be both to create panic and give the Germans an excuse. The question of rescuing the children received the same reply.[96]

This attitude began to change after 29 August. Although there was no formal announcement, it was widely feared that the end of civil government would precipitate action against the Jews, and on 31 August, the German authorities seized the records of the Jewish community in Copenhagen.[97] This was followed on 17 September by a German police raid on the Jewish community offices. However, it was not until 28 September that news reached the Jewish community of the impending round-up. It came from

Duckwitz via his friends in the Danish Social Democratic Party, Hans Hedtoft and H. C. Hansen. A day later, the Danish Foreign Office also became aware of the German plans. In the meantime, Duckwitz had also visited Sweden to meet Prime Minister Hansson to urge the Swedes to open their border.[98] This led to a message from the Swedish ambassador von Dardell to the Jewish community leaders that his country's borders would be open to Jewish refugees.[99] The last piece of the jigsaw also fell into place on 29 September when Eivind Larsen, head of the Danish Justice Department, informed Paul Kanstein, head of German Security, that with the fall of the government, the Danish coastguard patrols would no longer consider policing acts by Danish citizens against the occupying authorities as part of their duties. In other words, they would cease to police the waters around Denmark and essentially turned from gamekeepers into poachers by monitoring the activities of German sea patrols.[100] In apparent concert with this, German Naval vessels operating in Danish waters had been restricted to minesweeping duties from 1 October and also took no interest in civil traffic.[101] On the same day, the Danish Lutheran bishops issued a pastoral letter condemning the persecution of the Jews which was then read from pulpits the following Sunday.[102]

In the hours before the planned arrest of the Jews, news was spread via synagogues and also through countless individual contacts with friends, neighbours and business acquaintances. Some people just took the telephone directory and called people with Jewish-sounding surnames, warning them not to stay at home. This collective action by the Danes took place in spite of the fact that any genuine resistance organization was still in its infancy. The net result was that the vast majority of Jews took heed of the warnings and fled their homes—or at least contrived to be away from home on the night of 1–2 October. As a result, only 284 Jews were arrested, and these were because they refused to leave their homes for religious reasons, could not travel through ill health, or simply did not receive any warning. In the days and weeks that followed, a further 190 Jews were caught by the German authorities.[103] This meant that the vast majority had found some temporary shelter, but negotiating the journey to Sweden was another matter. There were no common denominators to the stories of escape, and no written records kept at the time. From those who escaped, it appears that they, or their hosts, found ways of making contacts that allowed for transit to the coast and then transfer across the sound to Sweden. There are numerous accounts of Danes providing hiding places—in their own homes or elsewhere. There seems to have been no question of payment, although it must have been assumed that any refuge inside the country was temporary.

Collection points were hastily set up to concentrate the Jews before organizing voyages. Some of these were near the coastal villages, but in Copenhagen the Bispebjerg Hospital became the focus of organization and 'cloaked' more than 2,000 Jews from the city as visitors or patients before sending them on.[104] Likewise, a group led by Mogens Staffeldt used his bookstore opposite the Gestapo headquarters as its operational headquarters. Taxis and ambulances were used extensively to move people from place to place, and there are no realistic estimates of how many Danes were involved in this work, either directly or indirectly. One or two of the individual stories do show elements of continuity between other forms of resistance activity and help for the Jews. Thus the innkeeper Henry Thomsen and his wife Grethe were honoured by Yad Vashem in 1968 for having operated a safe house for Jews on their way to Sweden and organizing voyages themselves. However, it is clear that this was merely an extension of their work with the resistance as they had already been involved in illegal cargo shipments to and from Sweden.[105]

Funding escapes was a different matter. The victims of persecution had no time to raise capital and often fled only with the clothes they had on and any money they had at home. Some benefited from gifts given by friends but the ad hoc organizations that emerged to help the Jews also raised money, largely from Danish organizations, businesses and donations from private individuals. This allowed them to provide money for travel to the coast and also to pay for the crossings to Sweden. This was the one area where money and profiteering seem to have been an issue. Fishing-boat owners were keen to stress the risks they thought they were running and charged high prices for each crossing. Some were accused of being 'ruthless in their greed' and amassing money in a 'distasteful way',[106] and some prices charged to individuals were undoubtedly extortionate.[107] One couple and their young son had been taken in by a farmer in 1939 where the husband worked as a labourer. In October 1943, the farmer took the family to Copenhagen and found a fisherman willing to take them and paid the DKr.3,000 demanded out of his own pocket.[108] However, the involvement of rescue organizations and the intervention of the Fishermen's Association did serve to limit such profiteering and also offset the costs for poorer people by having richer Jews pay more for their crossing.[109] There were several routes, some better known than others.[110] The most common form of transport was fishing boats, but Danish government vessels were also reportedly involved.[111] Dredgers and ferries were used, as were much smaller craft such as rowing boats and even kayaks. Estimates suggest that there were between 600 and 700 individual escape voyages, although some boats made several journeys.[112] In the first days, the system used was a simple one. Danish fishing boats would leave harbour ostensibly on fishing trips and have their papers examined by the Germans at a check point. Once clear of their scrutiny, they would head back to the coast and pick up their cargo. However, as the numbers of fugitives increased in these small fishing ports, so the level of German interest increased, and other methods had to be found. For example, the village of Gilleleje was a community of only 1,642 souls in 1940 and thus an appreciable number of arrivals was likely to be noticed.[113] The voyages were also complicated by the possibilities of German spies identifying boats docking in Swedish ports. Thus fugitives were often transferred to Swedish boats for the last section of their journey.[114]

Jews were transported from Copenhagen, but also from other ports along the coast. A group at Lyngby led by Aage Bertelsen involved a number of teachers and physicians, but lasted less than a month, as its activities were betrayed at the end of October 1943 by an informer posing as a fugitive.[115] Likewise, a group at Elsinore formed specifically to help the Jews included a reporter, a bookkeeper, a detective, a bookbinder, and a doctor among its leadership. Nicknamed the 'sewing club', they were prompted to action by seeing the arrival of the first Jewish fugitives in their town and were clearly keen to do something to oppose the German occupation of their country.[116] Mobilizing some elements of the local fishing fleet did not prove too difficult, but the sheer numbers of fugitives forced them to find alternative means. This came in the form of the railway ferries used to bring iron ore from Sweden. Because of the nature of the trade, the wagons used often returned to Sweden empty and could therefore be used to smuggle Jews on board prior to departure. The system worked well until the scheme was given unwanted publicity in the Swedish press and subsequent trains were all screened by the Germans.[117] This group expanded its activities to other fishing villages such as Gilleleje and even procured its own boats to expedite journeys across the sound. This network seems to have survived the period when Jews were its main cargo, but persisted thereafter in smuggling resisters and Allied aircrew out of the country, a policy that led to its downfall as German surveillance became more and more intense.[118] Not all networks originated from occupied territory. The 'Danish-Swedish Refugee Service' owed its inception to Ole Helweg, a Danish architect living in Sweden, who contacted the leader of the Danish resistance in Sweden, Ebbe Munch. They decided to use the longer route from Malmø to small ports south of Copenhagen on the grounds that those in the north were being targeted by the Germans. In spite of some initial Swedish surveillance, they were given permissions to sail, appropriate papers, and supplies of fuel by the Swedish Foreign Ministry. They also established safe houses to 'hold' those waiting for transit. This network is credited with having rescued over 700 Jews but like the 'sewing club' continued its shipping activities for the resistance—moving intelligence material, mail, Allied airmen, and resistance fighters out of the country and returning with arms and ammunition. The leaders were finally arrested during a voyage on 10 December 1944, but were released after intense questioning because they admitted that they had shipped Jews to Sweden for money. At this point the Gestapo tried to turn them by offering the chance to earn more money by bringing Jews—and information—to them. They were given permits to operate from any Danish port, but never made good on their promises to the occupiers.[119]

In addition to these organizations, Denmark also had its share of situational helpers. Thus, for example, the widow Mrs Nielsen, who hawked fish in Copenhagen to support her six children, was approached for help by two brothers who were local flower sellers. They wanted her contact with local fishermen and she agreed to take them in. Soon her help for these two became more widely known and she was approached by the resistance to help on a grander scale. Thus, at one point, she had thirty people hiding in her small house, waiting to be taken to the docks. After the Jews had been moved to safety, she continued her work by hiding resistance workers, but was captured in December 1944 and ultimately sent to Ravensbrück.[120]

Betrayals were few and far between and seem to have come almost exclusively from Danish Nazis. Ostensibly, not a single Jew was apprehended on the railway travelling to the northern ports, in spite of the fact that often there were at least as many Germans as Jews on the train.[121] One possible example occurred at Gilleleje from where more than 20 per cent of all escapes took place. On 5 October, a boat with fugitives had been forced to turn back by the Gestapo, and all further sailings had to be abandoned.

The local rescuers had to hide others already en route to the village, and accommodated them in the parish hall and the village church. The following day the church was raided by the Germans and eighty Jews and four helpers were arrested—a rare example of German success in stemming the flow of Jewish escapees to Sweden.[122] That said, the Germans did not seem to be particularly interested in punishing rescuers as those involved were released 'after a few days' in Vestre Prison.[123] However, it should not be assumed that the rescue of the Jews was a foregone conclusion. Fugitives were arrested by the Germans while waiting for transit and some boats were intercepted during the voyage, with dire consequences for the Jews and their would-be rescuers. The fears experienced by the Jews also have to be taken into consideration. For many, there was little doubt in their minds about what capture would mean for them, and even the slightest delay could cause panic. There were heartrending cases of suicide, including one young scientist and his wife who made a suicide pact—and when their boat was delayed, he killed his children and his wife with a razor, but was unable to inflict more than superficial wounds on himself. He therefore survived and was evacuated to Sweden.[124] In the same vein, because of the nature of their hiding and transport across the sound, families with young children were potential risks to themselves and to all the others travelling with them. Thus several narratives make reference to children being given sleeping pills and sometime stronger drugs to render them unconscious for the presumed duration of the journey.

Of the approximately 8,000 Jews in Denmark in April 1940, only 474 were caught and deported to Theresienstadt where 53 died before the liberation. Of the remainder, no more than 100 stayed hidden inside Denmark, while more than 7,000 found their way to Sweden, with only around 30 having died en route through accidents, drowning, or suicide.[125] Many different factors have been invoked to explain this overwhelming success. The changed attitude of the Swedes to the admission of refugees was undoubtedly critical as, without the possibility of a nearby safe-haven, few of the rescue voyages were likely to have been successfully completed. While the democratic–humanistic culture shared by the vast majority of the Danes and their opposition to German methods that framed their response to the crisis of October 1943 has to be a consideration,[126] there is also no doubt that the attitudes of some leading German functionaries and agencies played a crucial role.[127] Apart from the apparent ambivalence of Werner Best, neither the 1,500 German Ordnungspolizei stationed in the country nor the available *Wehrmacht* manpower were used to track down Jews after 2 October, and although there are escape narratives of boats being intercepted at the northern ports, this was almost exclusively done by the Gestapo. Indeed, the arrests that took place at Elsinore and Gilleleje were the work of just one particularly zealous SD officer and his staff, namely Kriminaloberassistent Hans Juhl—also known as Gestapo Juhl.[128]

If these were all positive factors, it should nonetheless be remembered that the rescue of the Jews in Denmark was essentially an improvised affair carried out by a society in which any form of organized resistance was still in its infancy, and where the potential for mistakes and failures was probably higher than in other countries with more developed and sophisticated networks that had learned their trade the hard way. By October 1943, the tide of war was beginning to turn and, having maintained a degree of independence, albeit within the parameters set by Berlin, the Danish government, civil service, and population at large were not willing to become subservient at this stage in the conflict. Thus the circumstances pertaining in Denmark in October 1943 were very different from those elsewhere in Western Europe fifteen months earlier when the deportations had begun, and comparisons using the Danes as an example to castigate the behaviour of bystanders in other countries cannot really be sustained.

In comparative terms, the story of rescue in both Norway and Denmark is one where, with very few exceptions, the Jewish populations were the passive recipients of aid from friends, motivated individuals and the organized resistance, rather than contributing much in the form of self-help. The explanations for this may well rest on the relative German inaction against indigenous Jews and then a rapid move to round them up in October 1942 and October 1943 respectively—both communities were thus taken by surprise and had limited scope for individual, let alone communal action. Nevertheless, around 50 per cent of the Jewish population of Norway survived through escape to Sweden, as did the vast majority of their Danish counterparts. However, there are clear differences between the two countries beyond the timing of the actions against the Jews. While there was a state of war between Norway and Germany from 9 April 1940, no such conflict existed with Denmark, and there was little in the way of a mobilized resistance before September/October 1943. In Norway, there was a full German occupation, whereas Denmark continued to run its own affairs. In Norway, there were more than 800 Gestapo men, whereas Denmark had only around forty. Unlike Denmark, where Nazi agencies worked to undermine the success of the deportation programme and the penalties for helping Jews were limited, no such considerations existed in Norway and helping Jews could, and did, lead to the death penalty for those who were caught.[129]

5

Rescue and Hiding in France

The collapse of the French war effort in June 1940 left the country in disarray, with a crisis of leadership, a paralysed administrative system, and chaos on an unimaginable scale, coupled with the displacement of millions of people through military action or fear. The Vichy regime that emerged from this defeat sought to rebuild French society in its own particular way, and to identify the causes and the people responsible for the country's defeat. In this regard, the Jews generally were very much at the top of the list, and in particular the foreign Jews who had made France their home after the persecutions in Eastern Europe and Germany. Almost as soon as Pétain's regime had taken charge, this malevolence began to make itself felt. Laws and decrees began to be promulgated. Investigations were carried out on the naturalizations of foreign Jews, and between October 1940 and 16 September 1941, the government published a total of fifty-seven pieces of legislation targeted at the Jewish community.[1] Traditionally portrayed as driven by the German occupiers, much of this legislation, in fact, had its origins in the minds of Vichy bureaucrats and politicians, thus serving Nazi interests without showing Berlin's hand.

Assessing how much public support there was for these measures is inevitably complicated. Traditional forms of (religious) antisemitism were still in evidence combined with fears of moral and material decadence that focused on the Jews as the progenitors of both these ills.[2] After 1918, antisemitism had lost its political edge and was carried forward only by groups such as Charles Maurras' Action Française. However, when the world economic recession hit France in the early 1930s, there were 2.8 million aliens in France[3] and attention was soon focused on those foreigners in work who might be displacing the French unemployed.[4] In this way, political antisemitism reappeared as part of a wider anti-foreign trend, and the absorption of large numbers of refugees from Nazi Germany became a central political issue, essentially because they were Jewish or left wing and recent arrivals. By contrast, the presence of 720,000 Italians in the country (some of whom were also political refugees from Mussolini's fascist regime) caused little or no comment.[5] The refugees were perceived to carry three distinct threats: to employment, to French culture, and as an unwelcome complication to France's international relations.[6] However, precisely how much of this anti-foreign sentiment was related to antisemitism is difficult to estimate. There were calls for a *numerus clausus* in the liberal professions and in commerce, and even a proposal from the *Rassemblement Antijuif* (Anti-Jewish League) of Louis Darquier de Pellepoix, whose membership of the Paris Municipal Council allowed him a public platform to expound his views, that all Jews should be considered as foreigners.[7] However, this remained the view of a small minority, and other movements of the radical right, such as Parti Populaire Français under Jacques Doriot, remained uninterested in generalized antisemitism as a political position at this time. In many French minds there remained a distinction between the Jewish refugee immigrants on the one hand, and the fully assimilated and acculturated French Jews on the other. Support for the rights of individuals as citizens remained, and even within Catholic circles, there was extensive condemnation of both racism and antisemitism. This in itself was important, as the level of nominal affiliation to the Church was high, with large numbers of people still having their children baptized and sending them to church schools, even if formal observance and attendance at Mass was in rapid decline.

French Catholicism had to deal with the particular fractures caused by the traumatic separation of Church and State under the Third Republic. All ninety-four dioceses in France, including Algeria and the colonies, were led by a bishop with a high degree of autonomy. There was an Assembly of Cardinals and Archbishops created in 1918 to issue collective statements, but it had no formal powers. It continued to meet as two separate groups after the armistice—albeit with some continuing links, and provided a degree of continuity and cohesion for French Catholicism during the occupation, as did the existence of a papal nunciature in Paris, a post held from 1936 onwards by Monsignor Valerio Valeri.[8] During the 1930s, leading churchmen had followed the papal line in condemning Nazi antisemitism, and Cardinals Jean Verdier (Paris), Achille Liénart (Lille), and Pierre-Marie Gerlier (Lyon) had all expressed their solidarity with the

Jewish community, both in 1933 and again after *Reichskristallnacht* in 1938.[9] Catholics could therefore be found expressing sympathy for the Jews, but condemning their role in alien ideologies such as capitalism or communism. Others were more outspokenly antisemitic and often focused on the alien identities of many Jews in France. This position undoubtedly reflected the ambivalence of leading French churchmen. Even Cardinal Gerlier, who was later to become a champion of persecuted Jewry was reputed to have 'an instinctive dislike for the Jews' based on their supposed role in the failure of the Union Générale bank that had led to the collapse of his family's fortunes. At the same time, he had good relations with the Jewish community leaders in Lyon and was viewed by them with respect.[10] Some French clerics were far more outspoken, with the bishops of Grenoble and Chambéry leading the way in welcoming the Vichy regime's first anti-Jewish measures.[11] What all this suggests is that attitudes could be, and probably were, largely determined by local considerations and local leaders. Moreover, like the French population at large, many Catholic leaders chose to make a distinction between the treatment meted out to foreign Jews, which they accepted as 'necessary', and the extension of the prejudicial legislation to French Jews, which they did not.

France also possessed a small, but nonetheless important, Protestant minority, numbering between 750,000 and 800,000 in 1940.[12] Traditionally, it had been strong in Alsace, which was soon to be overrun and annexed by the Germans, and in certain rural areas, but the flight to the towns had increased its adherents in Paris, Strasbourg and Lyon. Peasant Protestant communities remained, but a feature of the confession by 1940 was that it was overwhelmingly bourgeois and middle class.[13] The estimated 1,100 Protestant clergy were led by Pastor Marc Boegner, head of the Fédération Protestante de France, an organization that brought some degree of cohesion to an otherwise disparate group of believers through national, regional and local councils.[14] After the occupation, Protestantism was far more circumspect in its analysis of events and in its support for the new Pétainist regime, although there were probably as many convinced Pétainists among the Protestant clergy as in the country as a whole, and it certainly included a group of royalist–nationalists led by pastor Noël Nougat that was strongly collaborationist and antisemitic.[15] Even Boegner spoke of the duty to follow the Marshal and was considered by the new leader of France to be one of his best friends.[16] He later participated in the Conseil Nationale, the commission set up in January 1941 to draft a new constitution. In this way he strove to show his continuing loyalty to the new regime.[17] By contrast, the theologian Karl Barth had spoken directly to French Protestants in October 1940, warning of the evils of Nazism and exhorting them not to espouse neutralism or collaboration.[18]

In relation to the plight of the Jews in Germany, the French Protestants had been well informed through their links with German co-religionists.[19] Parallels were drawn between the contemporary persecution of the Jews and the persecution of French Protestants between 1680 and 1760, and the influence of Barthism made them more aware of the links between Christianity and Judaism through study of the Old Testament.[20] At a practical level, French Protestants also had strong links with their co-religionists in Switzerland, who had provided sanctuary for the persecuted in the sixteenth and seventeenth centuries, and it was these traditions, and even the routes they used to cross the border, that were to be rediscovered in the years after 1940.[21]

Jewish Resistance and Self-Help

In surveying Jewish resistance in France, Lucien Lazare has subdivided it into three separate categories. There were individuals and organizations wholly devoted to self-help through escape or hiding from their Vichy and German persecutors. These included the group known as the Rue Amelot Committee and the Oeuvre de secours aux enfants (OSE). A second category comprised those who had a double purpose—both as part of the Jewish resistance and as part of the 'armed' French resistance against Nazism and occupation. These included the Organisation Juive de Combat (OJC), Main d'Oeuvre Immigrée—Franc-Tireur et Partisans (MOI-FTP), and the Jewish scout movement, the Éclaireurs Israélites de France (EIF). Finally there were the communist armed resistance organizations that had no direct contacts with the Jewish community save that some of their members were Jewish.[22] Here we are concerned primarily with the first two categories and how their work of self-help and rescue operated and dovetailed with the activities of other non-Jewish agencies. Inevitably, Jewish resistance activities sprang from many different sections of the communities, but it is worth noting that many resistance leaders had, before 1940, been active in promoting Jewish interests and working against the general rejection of a specific Jewish identity.[23]

To understand this, it is necessary to look briefly at the pre-war structures of the various Jewish communities. By 1939, Paris was home to about two-thirds of the Jewish population, made up of indigenous French Jews, many of whom had fled from Alsace after 1870, an appreciable number of recently arrived refugees from Germany and Austria, and a larger group of immigrants from Eastern Europe who had come in increasing numbers since the 1880s.[24] For the French Jews, the arrival of these newcomers presented both advantages and disadvantages. On the one hand, they might serve to rejuvenate French Jewish institutions at a time when many were failing through a trend towards non-observance and secularism.[25] On the other hand, their presence had the potential to increase both political and social antisemitism at a time of crisis—something that would engulf both French Jews as well as their immigrant co-religionists. A Comité Nationale had been established to meet the welfare needs of the refugees unable to work in the country, but its funds were limited.[26] Moreover, the conservative elite of the Consistory also saw a threat from the Eastern Europeans and refugees, not only in their different religious observances, but also in their (left-wing and/or Zionist) political allegiances, factors that would inevitably retard assimilation. As Robert de Rothschild, the chairman of the Consistory commented: 'They are guests whom we receive with pleasure, but they must not break the china.'[27] Likewise the Chief Rabbi, Israël Lévi, opposed public demonstrations against Nazi antisemitism and was equally concerned about the number of Jews evident in such left-wing protests. The newly arrived refugees also provoked disapproval for being 'too noisy, too convinced of the superiority of German civilisation. In brief—veritable "Boches"'.[28] One French rabbi remarked that they did not seem to understand that they needed to conduct themselves with reserve and with discretion and 'not make a spectacle', and compared them unfavourably with the 'Pollaks' who had conducted themselves better.[29] In the meantime, the foreign Jews developed their own organizations; chief among them being the Main d'Oeuvre Immigrée (MOI), the Immigrant manual labour association organized by the communists. However, others were allied to the Bundists or the Zionists, who also had active branches in many provincial centres. Moreover, the immigrant communities continued to organize themselves according to their countries of origin and were large enough to sustain a thriving Yiddish press.[30]

Paris lost between 20 and 25 per cent of its Jewish population in the summer of 1940. Many of the French Jews, with family elsewhere and greater knowledge of the country, left in advance of the initial German onslaught and chose not to return to their homes after the armistice.[31] However, those without resources or knowledge of France outside the capital, and this included many of the foreign and recently arrived refugee Jews, had fewer choices. Compared with the estimated 200,000 who had been in the city in 1939, the census in the autumn of 1940 showed that there were only 113,462 adult Jews (over fifteen) in Paris, plus a further 34,557 children. Just over half the adults had French citizenship, but of these, 37.3 per cent were naturalized rather than French born. In contrast, most of the children had been born in France. Their occupational structure was also very different from their French counterparts, with 15–20 per cent in the commercial sector and 60 per cent in industry or artisanal work, including 50,000 described as home workers or *petit patrons*.[32]

This migration inevitably altered the structures of Jewish organizations in France, with most of them moving their centres of operation to Lyons, Vichy, or Marseilles. The Federation of Jewish Organizations formed an umbrella for immigrant groups in the south while the Amelot Committee was created to co-ordinate activities in Paris where only the Jewish Communist Party and the MOI had remained active, albeit underground, as both were actively pursued by the French and German police. Paradoxically, it was the foreign Jews in the unoccupied zone who had faced the larger threats when Vichy extended its internment programme.[33] The leaders of the Jewish community's Central Consistory also decided to stay in Vichy, helped by a German edict that prohibited Jews from returning to the occupied zone, but this effectively left the majority of the French Jewish community who remained in Paris without any obvious leaders. There was some discussion of 'defence committees' in the major towns and cities to counteract antisemitic propaganda, but the Consistory trod a careful line, not wishing to upset the new regime, and Jacques Heilbronner, its Vice-President, even went so far as to try and distance the French Jews from their foreign counterparts in both racial and social terms.[34]

The Amelot Committee was made up from three political groups (the Bund, and the left and right wings of Poale-Zion), and two other organizations, the Fédération des Sociétés Juives de France (FSJF) and the Colonie Scolaire, both of which had operated in the field of Jewish welfare before the occupation.[35] As with many other immigrant organizations, its leading lights had been politically active long before they arrived in France.

Maître Léo Glaeser had been sought by the Tsarist police after the 1905 uprising in Russia, Yéhuda Jacoubovitch was a Bundist from Poland who had been imprisoned for his opposition to Tsarism and arrived in France in 1913, and another of its leaders, David Rapoport, had been involved in both the 1905 and 1917 uprisings before coming to France in 1920.[36] However, their leftist backgrounds did not necessarily make them amenable to co-operation with the communists as there were inevitable objections from Bundists and the right wing of Poale-Zion. Moreover, collusion with the communists would open up the possibility of greater Gestapo surveillance, to which the latter were already subject. Thus the communists continued to operate separately under their own umbrella organization, Solidarité, founded in September 1940.

Formed on 15 June, the new organization took its name from the dispensary run by the Colonie Scolaire at 36 Rue Amelot in the eleventh arrondissement.[37] Glaeser became the treasurer, and Jacoubovitch its first secretary-general.[38] The new committee had an almost immediate impact. In three days, the various cantines run by the constituent organizations had re-opened with an agreement to pool resources. Likewise the Colonie Scolaire (also known as la Mère et l'Enfant) was open again within a week. This rebuilding of Jewish welfare was soon operating in tandem with the OSE, and having some contact with the Jewish communists, but the overriding problem was funds to support an increasingly destitute community. Ultimately, an envoy was sent to the unoccupied zone where the JDC representative in Marseilles, Herbert Katzki, provided a monthly subvention and used the Quakers as intermediaries to bring the money to Paris.[39] The committee functioned in a kind of semi-legality, ignoring most of the legislation on Jewish organizations imposed by Vichy. Its tasks were widened to include helping returning prisoners of war and the aged. By the autumn of 1940, it was regularly supporting at least 1,125 families, a number that continued to increase as 'aryanization' closed down many businesses, and Jews were thereby rendered unemployed.[40]

German measures to isolate the Jews in Paris from the rest of the community led to the forced creation of a co-ordinating committee (Comité de Coordination des Œuvres d'Assistance du Grand Paris, CCOJA) made up from the Paris Consistory, the Comité de bienfaisance israélite, Organisation reconstruction travail (ORT), OSE and the Rue Amelot Committee. Most of the organizations involved were wary of membership and their reticence proved well founded as the committee was soon exposed as no more than an agency for carrying out German wishes.[41] Many Jews likewise saw it merely as a tool of the Germans, but it was also the only source of material aid at a time when independent living was becoming increasingly difficult.

The Amelot Committee effectively formed the basis for the underground communal response to the plight of the immigrant and refugee Jews, although it formally excluded the communists. At this stage, it remained a legal organization and attempted to tread a path that would involve co-operation, both with the Consistory on the one hand, and the communists on the other. Although hotly debated, the Amelot Committee did join the Coordination Committee at the end of 1940, but the sudden arrest of 3,710 foreign Jews on 14 May 1941, coupled with increased German pressure, caused it to secede and effectively to go underground. Likewise, the communists who had stayed outside the system also found their institutions threatened, and shut them rather than comply with German demands.[42] Although Amelot came back into the open when no German reprisals ensued, the die had been cast, and the potential for a shift to illegality had been explored.[43]

The first mass arrests took place on 14 May 1941 when the French authorities ordered 6,500 former Polish, Czech and Austrian Jews to report to prefectures, ostensibly to discuss their status, and then deposited them in the camps at Pithiviers and nearby Beaune-la-Rolande, but a further action on 20 August saw an increased number of nationalities and some French Jews among 4,200 arrested and taken to the camp at Drancy. This provided tangible proof that further actions were inevitable. Protests were also raised against the camps themselves and the conditions suffered by the inmates.[44] By this stage, however, the Rue Amelot Committee had been forced to withdraw from the CCOJA again, rather than see its welfare organizations co-ordinated. This, in turn, removed their ability to operate inside the internment camps, but also drove them closer to the communists. This alliance foundered after the German attack on the Soviet Union in June 1941 when the communists attempted to dominate the other groups whose objectives were more narrowly based than the outright ideological and armed struggle against fascism. Nonetheless, both groups continued to support their respective workers and client groups with material aid. Moreover, knowledge of what was befalling the Jews in Eastern Europe after the attack on the Soviet Union in June 1941 was soon relayed to the MOI via what it regarded as a wholly reliable source, namely broadcasts in Yiddish from Radio Moscow. This information was reproduced in the 1 September 1941 edition of *Unzer Wort* for dissemination to the (immigrant) Jewish community at large.[45] In the interim, there had also been attacks on various synagogues. Thus, by the autumn of 1941, the communist MOI was increasingly directing its members towards armed struggle and economic sabotage, but both Solidarité and the Amelot Committee continued their ameliorative aid, both for those still held in internment camps and for immigrant Jews in the major cities. Peace between the two groups was not to last, as the increasing levels of armed resistance carried out by the communists threatened to undermine the welfare work. On 12 December 1941 there was a German reprisal raid against 'prominent French Jews' in which 743 male Jews were arrested, and 100 hostages were shot (including fifty-three Jews) in reprisal for communist attacks on French factories working for the German war effort. Amelot Committee representatives treated subsequent communist requests for money for the dependants of those killed with disdain, as they deplored the communists' commitment to armed conflict.[46]

It was not until late November 1941 that the German and Vichy authorities insisted on the creation of the Union Générale des Israélites de France (UGIF) as a national organization to represent the Jews in their dealings with both the Germans and Vichy.[47] Many French Jews were reassured by its existence—and doubly so if they themselves worked for the organization and were thus ostensibly protected from internment or deportation. Other categories were also protected. Citizens of 'friendly' or neutral states and those working for German war industries were the most notable and most numerous. However, by this time, most non-French Jews had drawn their own conclusions about the UGIF, even if they still relied on it for welfare, and there was opposition from within the Jewish community, including the Zionists and the EIF.[48] That said, the now largely illegal activities of the Rue Amelot were given some protection by members of the Council of UGIF-Nord. Thus, after the introduction of the yellow star and the beginnings of the round-ups, it was able to help in the rescue of Jewish children, left abandoned by the arrest of their parents. Its leaders also ultimately benefited by getting the identity cards issued to UGIF personnel which protected them from arrest. Under the overall control of Juliette Stern, the secretary of the Women's International Zionist Organization (WIZO), they became involved in helping to find shelter for these children, placing them in reception centres or with

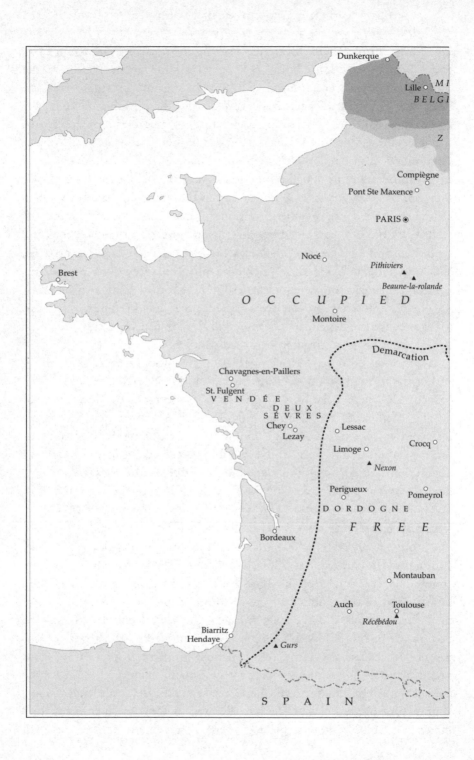

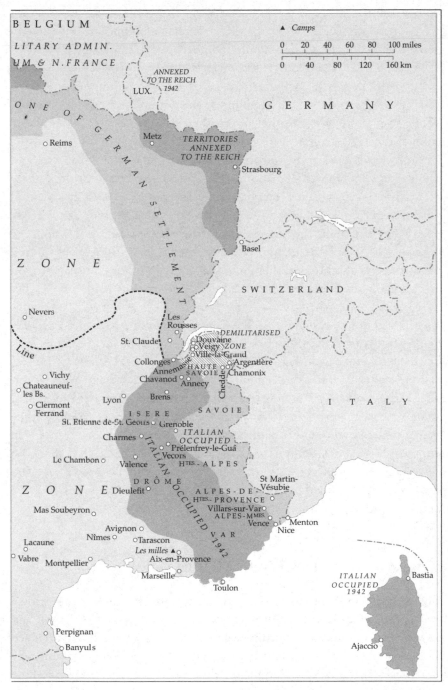

Map 5.1 France: showing the line of demarcation between the occupied and umoccupied zones prior to 1942

non-Jewish families—ostensibly under the supervision of the relevant government authorities. Nonetheless, it also helped others cross the line of demarcation illegally to join family members in the unoccupied zone, or to be taken in by reception centres there.[49]

Important here is the fact that there were Jewish organizations, both open and clandestine, operating to help those in need from the armistice onwards. While suspicious of each other, given their longstanding ideological and cultural differences, they were equally suspicious of both Vichy and the Germans, and acted as an essential counterweight to the collaborationist agenda forced on the UGIF. Another element to note here is the links these groups had to international Jewish charities, primarily the JDC, and to other Christian groups, such as the Quakers and the YMCA, who had already been active in helping the many refugees from the Spanish Civil War in the later 1930s.[50] The incarceration of many foreign Jews in the camps in the southern zone also brought them into contact with other Christian groups, most notably the Protestant Comité Inter-Mouvements Auprès d'Evacués (CIMADE), established in 1939 to help refugees evacuated to Haute-Vienne and the Dordogne from the frontier zones of Alsace and Lorraine. Led by Boegner, CIMADE consisted of five Protestant youth groups, plus the French branches of the YMCA/YWCA, the World Student Council, and the wider Scouting movements.[51] While the constituent parts of this welfare network were severely curtailed in what became the occupied zone, where independent youth movements were forced to close, they remained active in the unoccupied zone and formed the basis for the help provided by CIMADE after 1940.[52] The key here is that, even before the fall of France, there were well-established contacts with non-Jewish welfare networks to provide aid to all refugees and those held in camps, irrespective of their political or racial backgrounds.

The Era of Deportations

The path of the Rue Amelot Committee towards illegality was a gradual one, and its relationship with the Jewish communist movement MOI and its Solidarité organization remained fraught, but all were directly involved in ameliorative relief for a Jewish population that was being economically and socially marginalized from mainstream society. The beginning of June 1942 saw the introduction of the yellow star, a measure designed to further isolate the community from their Parisian neighbours, although it served to produce some gestures of solidarity through street protests and Gentiles deliberately wearing the stars.[53] The Protestant Federation protested on 5 June, and Father Dillard in Vichy preached against the measure in the very church where Pétain himself worshipped, but there were no formal protests from the Catholic Church hierarchy.[54] The leaders of both denominations saw the measure as an affront to the loyalty shown by their followers to Vichy in general, and to the Marshal in particular.[55] Exemptions from wearing the star were granted by the Judenreferat office in Paris, but only very sparingly. Several agencies and commercial concerns had 'their' Jews that they wished to protect, either because of their usefulness or prominent positions. The former included at least four Jews employed by the Commissariat Générale aux Questions Juives (CGQJ) as informers![56] Although the UGIF were given advance warning of planned deportations in July 1942, they saw no reason to spread panic by disseminating the information, and only gave a belated warning to the Amelot Committee on 13 July.[57] The Committee, albeit with no legal means of publishing, used word-of-mouth to get the message across, and Solidarité managed to issue a single tract that reached sections of the immigrant community. While knowledge of the impending round-ups may have been an impetus for some to consider going underground, the conditions experienced by the first victims held in the Vel d'Hiv made the dangers clear to both foreign and French Jews alike.[58]

Until the summer of 1942, Solidarité and the Amelot Committee had assumed that Jewish survival from Nazi oppression was only of concern to the Jews themselves, but it was after the major raids of 16 and 17 July and the incarceration of 12,000 non-French Jews in the Vel d'Hiv that they began to look for more outside help. The communist-inspired Mouvement Nationale Contre le Racisme (MNCR) responded to the first deportation convoys from the camps in June 1942 by identifying 200 Catholic and Protestant institutions likely to hide Jews, and the Amelot Committee began widening its contacts with non-Jewish social workers.[59] When the first mass round-ups took place in July, the communists distributed a special leaflet directed at the immigrant Jews.

> Do not passively wait in your homes . . . Take steps to hide your families with non-Jews. If arrested, resist the police by all possible means: barricade your apartment, call for help, fight, do whatever you can to escape.[60]

Thus the basis for an organized Jewish resistance to German measures had been laid.

The overt activities of the Rue Amelot Committee remained under constant German and French surveillance until 1 June 1943 when its dynamic leader, David Rapoport was arrested and the whole organization was dissolved by the authorities soon afterwards.[61] Faced with additional responsibilities for the welfare and feeding of Jews in the city, the UGIF soon saw the advantages of reconstituting many of the legal activities of the Committee, and these were carried on under new leadership. However, this also allowed the illegal work of placing and supporting children in hiding to continue. Instead of its clinic being used as a centre, parents were referred directly to social workers who had contacts with families hidden in the city and its suburbs. Its budget for such work was found courtesy of sympathetic local government officials. Its placements outside the city had effectively been in the hands of non-Jewish organizations during the six weeks when the Committee had been in dissolution, but its work paying the foster parents and finding material aid for families underground had to be rebuilt, using non-Jewish helpers as go-betweens.[62] This instigated a much wider co-operation between Jewish groups where the Organisation Juive de Combat (OJC) brought together the previously antagonistic Zionists and EIF, later the Union des Juifs pour la Résistance et l'Entraide (UJRE), and finally the Comité Général de Défense des Juifs (CGD) that eschewed armed resistance but therefore included the FSJF. This wider co-operation proved of great value, as the activities of the authorities became ever more intense as the occupation approached its fourth year.

One other group already mentioned that contributed to Jewish self-help, both in Paris and elsewhere, was the Jewish scout movement (EIF).[63] Given its social functions, it had long-standing ties with many different organizations, including, of course, the wider French scouting movement. Incorporated within the UGIF as the Service Sociale des Jeunes, it was subsequently banned by Darquier de Pellepoix of the CGQJ, but continued in clandestine form after July 1942 in helping those sought by the Gestapo and in developing contacts with other resistance organizations. Latterly, many of its members also became involved in aspects of armed resistance, although as one of its founders admitted, that had never been the original intention.[64] Although primarily an organization for young people, the EIF in Paris also developed a section to help adults, again finding places for them to shelter and false papers to hide their real identities. As an all-male organization, it did have to find women to do many tasks when men found it harder and harder to travel without arousing suspicion, for example in visiting those placed with families and paying the hosts where necessary. A group of women took responsibility for one or more *départements* and criss-crossed the countryside making sure contacts were maintained.[65] Unlike many of the other Jewish organizations operating in this period, the operations of the EIF represented a wholly new initiative and not one based on existing welfare activities, and it also extended its activities to help non-Jews.[66]

Rescue in Paris and the Occupied Zone

If the Vel d'Hiv action had the greatest impact on the Jewish community, this was also true of their non-Jewish neighbours. No advance preparations had been made by the authorities to receive those arrested and the brutality of the police made the experience hellish, even to the point of some parents being heard to say 'Run away child. Ask some good people to take you in.'[67] More compelling still was the inclusion of children and old people among those arrested, thus exposing the lie that the round-ups were being carried out purely to recruit a labour force.

It is clear from the available testimonies that many people attempted to avoid arrest by hiding in their own apartment blocks, or at the homes of neighbours or school friends. Neighbours on the same apartment block landing or in the near vicinity took in individuals or even whole Jewish families and sometimes kept them hidden until the liberation.[68] Local and community relations at a micro level were critical here, as these were individual relationships that sometimes represented only small steps from close friendships to direct help, but on other occasions involved offers of assistance from people with whom the beneficiaries had had little more than a previous nodding acquaintance. There could be no organization, and what emerged was a series of individual negotiations to take in children or sometimes whole families if time permitted. Attics and cellars were pressed into service as makeshift refuges from the police raids. More concerted attempts at help did emerge, even in these early days. For example, the owner of an apartment building agreed to rent rooms to Jews with false papers. The concierge was part of the conspiracy and checked the papers—but only to see if the forgeries were good ones.

The role of the concierge—that feature of Parisian everyday life—in the rescue of Jews demands some further attention. For example, Albert Grunberg, an assimilated Jew of Romanian origin who had been in France since before 1914 and lived in a well-to-do area of the city was sheltered by Madame Oudard, the concierge of his building, who fed him, looked after him, and kept him in contact with his relatives.[69] She was far from unique, and other concierges were recorded as performing similar roles.[70] This could include direct sheltering, but might be confined to warning potential victims of police raids, or delaying matters long enough for some form of escape to be organized. Here we can cite the example of Marie Chotel, a concierge in the eleventh arrondissement, who was able to delay the arrival of the police into her building long enough to warn Berthe Melszpajz and her daughter of the danger and then shelter them until she got rid of the police.[71] This 59-year-old woman had little or no education and had never learned to read and write, but with no children of her own, she had become attached to the daughter. Soon afterwards, the child was sent to an address in the village of Chavagnes-en-Paillers (Vendée), pre-arranged by her prisoner-of-war father, and when the mother also went underground, Chotel took on the responsibility for sending parcels to the father in captivity.[72] Concierges also had access to another invaluable resource, namely other unoccupied apartments in their block, and could therefore use these as short or longer-term shelters for those on the run.[73] This was certainly the case with Marie Chotel, who employed the Melszpajz's apartment in this way throughout the occupation, protecting it by suggesting—correctly—that it was rented by a prisoner of war who might well return. Moreover, even if they refused to be drawn into any form of direct action, the fact that they knew everything about the tenants, and who came and went in their building gave them enormous power that could be used for good or ill. Thus it was just as likely that they would use this power to inform the police about the political or racial backgrounds of people living in their buildings.[74] More directly, there were also instances of housekeepers and domestic servants in Jewish households providing the necessary contacts and help. There is no doubt that they could become the crucial bridge for middle-class families into the non-Jewish world, where children and sometimes adults were given shelter at the servants' parental homes or with other relatives. For example, Georgette Permanne had been employed by the same family since 1931 and fled with them from Paris to Marseilles in 1940. When the father was arrested and deported in

January 1943, the family fled again, eventually making their way back to Paris in a truck rented by Permanne, and then hidden with her relatives until the liberation.[75]

Individual rescuers were sometimes able to harness help from their business or employment to help those they had taken in. Thus, for example, the industrialist Édouard Marsat, attempted to help one of his employees and her family by providing funds and false papers for them.[76] In spite of opposition from his own family, who regarded the Jews as responsible for France's defeat, he continued his assistance and, when two sisters were betrayed crossing back into the occupied zone to visit their mother and were taken to Drancy, Marsat continued to do everything in his power to have them released.[77] Although unsuccessful, he continued to help the rest of the family even beyond the liberation.[78] Similarly, Abel Thibout, a railwayman from the eleventh arrondissement, had a Polish-Jewish family lodging with him, and when they were threatened with arrest, he contacted the resistance network of the SNCF and arranged for the children to be taken into the unoccupied zone, accompanying them as far as Lyon himself, where they were later joined by their mother who made the same journey on the footplate of an engine. The father remained with Thibout until the liberation.[79] These and other cases show how personal contacts and an ability to provide some specific service in the form of lodgings, money, or a secure route away from the capital created the basis for rescue.[80] Some scholars have stressed the prevalence of the 'quasi-familial' among many of these relationships but in these circumstances, generalizations are impossible beyond saying that in most cases of immediate rescue there was some pre-existing relationship between rescuers and rescued.[81] Likewise, it is impossible to provide any real quantitative measure of how widespread such help was, not least because every rescue of this nature relied on the tacit complicity of others. By the same token, neighbours could be the greatest danger to Jews in a particular community if their antisemitism, or even just their 'legalism' and propensity to inform the police about infractions of the law overrode any humanitarian or laissez-faire attitudes.

A different form of neighbourhood help in Paris came in the form of assistance from schoolteachers, of whom seven have been honoured by Yad Vashem. In almost every case, they helped an individual child, and sometimes the parents as well, by taking them into their own households and sheltering them—or finding alternative safer accommodation.[82] Social

workers were also prominent here. In theory they were neutral professionals, but their calling was to society and to the well-being of the family. Thus
when family units were threatened, some at least saw their role as helping,
even if this involved a shift into quasi- or outright illegality. It is also clear
that during the Vél d'Hiv round-ups, at least a few Parisian policemen chose
to leak their orders about forthcoming raids, either generally to people who
could then spread the word, or more specifically to individuals and families
they particularly wanted to protect. This was obviously premeditated and
could often give the intended victims twenty-four hours to make their
escape. A second form of help came in the actual raids themselves when
officers either allowed their victims time to escape, or gave them a few min-
utes' warning, or did not search apartments particularly thoroughly. Such
decisions were often apparently made at the last minute—on the basis of
a momentary acquaintance with the person they had come to arrest—and
the saving of one individual could only be masked by the arrests of many
others. Yad Vashem has honoured six detectives and one gendarme as
'Righteous among the Nations'. Some, but not all, had connections with
resistance organizations, but there were undoubtedly others who remain
unrecognized and even unnamed.[83] Nevertheless, they remain only a small
minority of the policemen employed to carry out raids against the Jews.

Critical to this analysis is the fact that Jewish organizations were also
involved from the outset. Solidarité began a more concerted campaign to
help those being pursued, sending children to farms in the countryside
in small batches and recruiting 'godmothers' to meet the costs of their
upkeep.[84] More ambitiously, the Amelot Committee used the services of
'Aryan' helpers and sometimes their spouses with legitimate papers to find
hiding places in the unoccupied zone and then conduct children across the
frontier. As the frequency and brutality of the police raids intensified, so
the Committee found more and more parents willing to hand over their
children. Outside the city there were also welcomes for escapees from
the round-ups. For example, the mayor and police in the commune of
Pont-Saint-Maxence (Oise) seem to have gone out of their way to help
Jewish families; finding ration cards and work for them, in spite of the fact
that the village was full of Germans.[85]

Between 8,000 and 9,000 of the 25,000 foreign Jews targeted in the initial
round-ups in Paris managed to evade capture, seeking shelter wherever they
could find it. The Vél d'Hiv roundup, or rather the manner in which it took
place, seems to have been the prompt for many spontaneous offers of help

from *personnes charitables*, friends and near neighbours, and from community organizations.[86] Arrests and persecution of Jews in the streets continued and had a profound effect on Parisian public opinion, not least because it was widely, but erroneously, believed that the measures were also being carried out against French Jews. As a result, this misapprehension served to mobilize help where it might not otherwise have been forthcoming. That said, the largely unassimilated immigrant population, whether working class or bourgeois, had to find assistance by knocking on the doors of strangers and asking for help to hide.[87] The fact that such help was often provided suggests that the Vél d'Hiv round-ups mobilized both Jews and non-Jews in Paris towards a realization of what real Nazi aims were, and how they might be successfully opposed through disobedience to the new laws.[88] This sentiment pervaded all sections of French society and served to mobilize non-Jewish opinion and grass-roots reaction long before their spiritual and community leaders had made any explicit statements.

Surveys of particular locations within Paris also demonstrate the gender distribution of both rescuers and rescued. Among the cases of rescue recorded in Paris, fifty-four involved families, but only two were childless couples; twenty-nine were children; nine were young women and there were a further thiry-one 'others' difficult to categorize. Likewise, a survey of the rescuers shows they were split between twenty-four couples, twenty-four (single) women and four (single) men.[89] From this it is clear that the involvement of children and young adults were undoubtedly the major factor in encouraging rescue, and that there was also a predominance of female participation in rescue itself. It also raises a wider question as to who made the decisions to help among the couples involved in rescue where both public and private sphere were directly involved. In relation to the round-ups, it is clear that decisions to help were often immediate and therefore taken without due consideration—thus one partner in a relationship may have returned home to find a fait-accompli. However, the general conclusion; reinforced by research from Germany and elsewhere, suggests that matriarchal nurturing impulses were a major feature in this predominance of female participation in the hiding of Jews.[90] Furthermore, it appears likely that this gender specificity existed in other forms, with women also involved in conducting fugitives to other parts of the country, especially because they would not be automatically suspect, and men being more involved in the provision of false or forged documents.[91]

Organized help from elements of both the Catholic and Protestant churches was also quickly mobilized. A controversial case is that of Emmanuel Suhard, the Catholic Cardinal Archbishop of Paris who had taken up his post on 18 May 1940. Like many of his ecclesiastical brethren, he refused to speak out publicly lest he draw attention to the Jews who had thus far been spared, and perhaps also because he did not want to cause rifts within his own confession or with the Germans by pursuing the issue too far. This led to post-war criticism[92], but it has also been argued that he used his position to help those interned in Drancy and Pithiviers during 1941—sometimes with success—and intervened directly with René Bousquet, the chief of the Paris police, against the Vél d'Hiv round-up. Moreover, it has been claimed that he was directly responsible for helping Jewish children find hiding places under false names in Catholic educational institutions and orphanages, and also organized social services for those in internment camps.

Other Catholic institutions were harnessed to the same end. An organization set up to help prisoners of war was easily adapted to help Jews, and was able to call on the help of Catholic secular organizations such as the Jeunesse Ouvrière Chrétienne (JOC) for support, as well as on religious foundations such as the Sisters of St Vincent de Paul and the Sisters of the Visitation, and also broadened its scope with contacts into the Red Cross and the Comité d'aide aux étudiants.[93] In these cases, the Catholic institutions seem to have become involved primarily at the prompting of ecclesiastical superiors, but a more immediate and autonomous form of intervention was led by Théomir Devaux, head of the Fathers of Notre-Dame-de-Sion. This foundation had been a centre for ecumenical discussion since his arrival in 1925 and had published La Question d'Israël, a revue that had a marked anti-Nazi tone.[94] As early as 1940 it was a target for the Gestapo, and their agents searched the building and confiscated the archives in order to stop any further publications. Nonetheless, in spite of being known as an opponent, Devaux became ever more involved in helping Jews, both adults and children. Thus, as early as 1941, he was engaged in finding false papers and hiding places for those in danger of deportation.[95] Using his contacts within the Church, he was able to place children in religious institutions across the country or with peasant families. Its sister institution, the Convent of the Sisters de Notre-Dame-de-Sion, had some of its building requisitioned by the Germans in 1940 and had been in danger of being closed as a reprisal for the singing of an anti-German hymn in praise of Joan of Arc in 1942. In the event, it was saved only by Suhard's direct intervention,[96] but became the headquarters for the publication of *Les Cahiers du Témoignage Chrétien*, an underground journal created by the Jesuit Father Pierre Chaillet that had not only actively condemned the antisemitism of the Vichy regime but also mounted a critique of the Catholic Church—and therefore of its hierarchy—for not having done more to help the refugees and those sought by the Germans.[97] This was in stark contrast to the line taken by Suhard, who was adamant that no illegal acts should be carried out to save Jews.[98] These and other religious institutions were mobilized by motivated individuals from an early stage in the occupation. They sometimes had clear anti-Nazi credentials or a history of ecumenical contact, both with the Jewish community and with other Christian and welfare groups. The foundations also had institutions outside the capital where Jews could be hidden. Moreover, their mobilization in many cases predated the major round-ups of July 1942 and shows how the early raids in Paris acted merely as a catalyst for further and more concerted action. At a secular level, the Service Sociale Internationale d'Aide aux Emigrants (SSAE) had been founded by Lucie Chevalley-Sabatier in 1920 to help transmigrants in France. During the occupation, the SSAE continued to help the families of foreigners placed in internment camps and sent social workers to work within the camps where, among other activities, they helped to effect releases whenever possible. Chevalley herself had an unrestricted permit to cross between the two zones and used this to good effect.[99] The all-important finance for its work came from rich individuals and from large companies, canvassed by various members of the group. The organization also benefited from contacts in the United States that remained able to provide funds inside France.[100] However, the SSAE was an officially recognized organization, and its members had to tread carefully, but nonetheless found its formal status a useful cover for the clandestine elements of its activities, embodied in the creation of L'Entraide Temporaire.[101] This had been created to provide aid to refugees at the outset of the war, but was recalled to action by one of its founders, Denise Milhaud, in February 1941, in response to the application of antisemitic laws to foreign Jews whom she knew.[102] She and her colleagues specialized in helping Jewish artists and workers who had lost their nationality as a result of their countries being removed from the map, such as Czechs and Poles, but their work included non-Jews as well. The organization presented itself as part of the Red Cross, but this was merely a camouflage. In 1942, both Denise Milhaud and her doctor husband Fred became employees of the UGIF. This had benefits in giving them access to the UGIF children's homes and the organization's clinics in the occupied zone.[103]

The much smaller Protestant community in the Paris region also became involved in the work of sheltering Jews. Pastor Paul Vergara had been ordained in 1909 and had served as a stretcher-bearer in the army during the First World War.[104] From 1922, he had been pastor of the Reformed Church at the Oratoire du Louvre in the heart of the city. During the Nazi period, his parish became a centre for non-violent resistance and at least thirty of his flock were mobilized to help Jews acquire false papers, false work permits and, of course, hiding places. Later still, as the staff of the UGIF lost their exemptions from deportation, one of his assistants, Marcelle Guillemot, helped find young women hiding places as domestic servants, again armed with suitable false papers. Eventually, Vergara was forced to go underground himself, but returned at the liberation to continue his ministry.

Another well-connected member of the parish was less fortunate. Suzanne Spaak, sister-in-law of the Belgian Foreign Minister-in-exile, Paul Henri Spaak, used her social connections to find hiding places. Not content with this, she also became involved with the Libération Nord resistance network, and her apartment became a centre for meetings between different networks as well as a mailbox for Leib Trepper, the leader of the 'Red Orchestra'. Like Guillemot, she also participated in the removal of children from the increasingly insecure UGIF institutions in February 1943, but she was arrested in September that year and executed two weeks before the liberation of Paris.[105] Pastor Henri Roser of Aubervilliers had Jewish friends whom he managed to shelter during the occupation, providing food and false identity cards, but he may also have been motivated to help by his strong pacifism, for which he had been imprisoned in 1939.[106] There was also the L'association des daiconesses at Neuilly-sur-Seine and the Béthanie clinic that acted as a refuge for children. The former also acted as a cover when the Salvation Army was closed by the Germans and the Vichy authorities.[107] Perhaps not surprisingly for such a relatively small community, the Protestant-inspired initiatives in and around the city seem to have had close relations with the church leadership and with each other. Indeed, the Béthanie clinic gave refuge to Marc Boegner and other leading personalities when they were ultimately also forced underground.[108]

The story of the rescue of Jews in Paris shows how the individuals and organizations were motivated—by self-preservation, religious conviction, humanitarian concerns or particular circumstances. Those involved in helping to hide Jews or conduct them across the line of demarcation knew they were running a risk, but precisely what risk? Those who helped Jews hide their property from the Germans were subject to the same penalties as the Jews themselves under a law of 22 July 1941, and a German circular of 6 June 1942 had indicated that anything that appeared to be a protest against the orders of the Military Governor (on the wearing of the Jewish star) would be severely punished. In practice, this seems to have involved anyone helping Jews receiving three months' internment in Tourelles prison, but no further ordinances existed. This did not mean that other laws could not be invoked to prosecute and imprison those involved, not least those that proscribed the provision or use of false papers, or illegally crossing the line of demarcation. Nor did it stop the Gestapo from using torture to obtain information from those it captured, but specific ordinances or legislation against the hiding of Jews per se did not exist.[109]

In the occupied zone away from the city, help for the Jews was tied up with wider issues of opposition and resistance to German aims. For example, the creation of the line of demarcation between the occupied and Vichy zones was widely resented by those whose economic and social lives it subsected. The Cher valley became a hotbed of evasion, and the canton of Bléré played a crucial role because of its position and the fact that the Germans did not have sufficient men to police the demarcation line there effectively. A number of priests became the instigators of rescue networks, helping all those in need. Their success was based on the fact that these local priests had been in post for some time and had met regularly in the years before 1939. Often, they had served in the army, been prisoners of war and then released back to their vocation. These networks of 'soutanes vertes' (country priests)[110] worked in tandem with their parishioners and often with local gendarmes to assist those crossing the line. One leader, Père Bernard de la Perraudière, had been a prisoner in 1940, but had returned to his parish to create an entire network helping those on the run. It is important to realize that the Jewish 'traffic' was in both directions, with some looking to escape from German hands before November 1942, while others chose to return north because their families or means of support remained in the occupied zone. Elsewhere, there were many other religious houses helping to shelter Jews, not just in ones and twos, but often in large numbers. Thus for example, the Franciscans of Notre-Dame-de-Pitié at Perrou (Orne) had Jewish families housed in the various pavilions of their retreat.[111] However, beyond the cloisters and convents, the French countryside in the occupied zone provided a haven for many Jews, both adults and children. These may have come through networks established after the occupation began or emanated from pre-war contacts of friends and acquaintances, the existence of second properties in the country or long-standing arrangements for children's holidays. However, each of these alternatives remained more accessible to the well-established French Jewish community than to the recent immigrants who had had little or no contact with France beyond the capital.

6

Survival in the Vichy Zone

The existence of an unoccupied zone after the division of France in the summer of 1940 provided a potential haven for both French and non-French Jews who saw themselves as threatened by the Germans. At first glance, this perception of the south as a haven may have been short-lived given the alacrity with which Vichy promulgated antisemitic legislation, but the reality was that Jews with French nationality were seldom pursued *as Jews* unless they were wanted for political or other judicial reasons—or they were on the lists compiled by the German occupiers. As we have already seen, it was the foreign Jews that were to bear the brunt of Vichy's malevolence.

The Nîmes Committee and its Organizations

Many non-Jewish philanthropic and charitable organizations in France came into the work of rescue through their activities in helping refugees, evacuees, and camp inmates prior to May 1940, including those from the Spanish Civil War and from frontier zones close to the German border at the beginning of the *drôle de guerre* in September 1939. They included both French organizations: the French Red Cross, Secours Nationale, the SSAE, CIMADE and the Amitié Chrétienne as well as many international ones, most notably the American Friends Service Committee (Quakers), Unitarian Service, Secours Suisse, and the YMCA. These groups were brought together by a directive from the Vichy Ministry of the Interior of 20 November 1940 that decreed the formation of a commission to co-ordinate assistance to those in internment camps. They were joined by representatives of both national and international Jewish organizations, including OSE and EIF as well as the HICEM and JDC.[1]

This co-ordinating body, usually referred to as the Nîmes Committee, was chaired by Donald Lowrie of the YMCA and was dedicated to alleviating the often appalling conditions in the camps. Co-ordination allowed resources to be carefully targeted and duplication of effort and waste minimized. Lowrie is widely credited with having obtained many concessions from Vichy, not least in improving material conditions inside the camps, including the provision of resident teams of social workers, chaplains, and doctors.[2] The work of the Nîmes Committee has been interpreted in different ways. Lowrie gained concessions from the Vichy authorities by pointing out the damage that stories about the camps were doing to the regime's international reputation, but it has also been argued that the committee's existence helped the Vichy regime cloak its neglect of the internees without making significant concessions. The motives of the Committee and its constituent organizations as a whole have also come in for severe criticism from certain quarters:

> The stultifying forbearance of confessional morality...chiefly regards the poor victim as an opportunity for the benefactor's self-perfection...no one, not a well meaning soul in that polite assistance organization...shouted out:...existence in the camps is not what should be improved—the existence of the camps [themselves] must be fought.[3]

This was levelled at the Jewish as well as the non-Jewish 'benefactors' who were accused of working for their own 'self-perfection'. However, questioning and opposing the existence of the camps would have precluded any co-operation with the Vichy authorities. One advantage from this collaboration came in the division of tasks between different groups. Thus the Unitarians were mainly concerned with education, while the Quakers and Secours Suisse dealt with food distribution, and the OSE with hygiene and medical matters.[4] Apart from ameliorating the often appalling conditions inside the camps, their main successes came in securing the release of various groups by championing the cause of potential emigrants, the elderly, military volunteers, veterans, and young mothers.[5] It was largely the elderly and the children who benefited, although Vichy did see the logic of reducing camp populations and had transferred jurisdiction over the camps from the police to the Ministry of Labour, at the same time transferring many able-bodied Jewish males into the Groupes de Travailleurs Etrangers (GTE) where conditions were somewhat better.

Amitié Chrétienne is widely credited with having been responsible for the first shifts from welfare to (illegal) rescue work among the organizations within the Nîmes Committee. It operated from Lyon as a coalition of Catholic and Protestant organizations, but backed by the 'moral auspices' of Cardinal Gerlier. One of its prime-movers, Father Alexandre Glasberg, conceived of reception centres for groups taken from the camps. His Direction de centres d'accueil (DCA) managed to persuade the Vichy authorities to sanction these centres and to allow certain adults to be moved there from the camps at Gurs and Rivesaltes. Cardinal Gerlier's backing for the project was crucial as his complete support for Marshal Pétain was well known and his name could be used as a talisman against uncooperative Vichy civil servants. Those selected by the social workers inside the camps had to prove an individual income of Fr.1,200 per month to qualify, and the first camp opened at La Roche-d'Ajoux (Rhône) on 25 November 1941 and four others followed. By the summer of 1942, the DCA was responsible for around 1,000 people who had been given this parole but were not to be released. When the deportations began, Glasberg realized that his charges could be recalled and then deported and thus he arranged for transfers between the camps where individuals were 'aryanized' with false papers and their files inside the camps 'lost' or 'mislaid' by the resident social workers. In this way, people could be spirited away, and the example was soon taken up by other Jewish organizations associated with Amitié Chrétienne such as the OSE and the FSJF, as well as the Rue Amelot committee in the occupied zone. Glasberg himself ultimately became too well known and was forced into hiding once the southern zone was occupied in November 1942.[6]

Although a relative newcomer among the welfare organizations operating in the Vichy zone, CIMADE began by helping French refugees from the potential war zones of Alsace-Lorraine who had been evacuated to Haute-Vienne and the Dordogne after September 1939, but soon extended its work to refugees in the camps of southern France. Getting into the camps was not easy. Led by Madeleine Barot, it had to contend with widespread bureaucratic obstruction. An initial visit to deliver nappies for the mothers of newly born children at the camp at Gurs convinced the organizers that their task was to provide whatever aid was possible to ameliorate conditions in the camp.[7] CIMADE members decided to make daily visits

Figure 6.1. Gurs internment camp
Source: USHMM

from a neighbouring village. The guards asked few questions and higher authorities remained in ignorance of their work. The arrival of 7,000 Jews from the Palatinate into a camp that was already full to overflowing meant that the new arrivals were held eighty to a barrack. Under these circumstances, the CIMADE took over a barrack for an office, meeting place and accommodation for its workers as, by this time, 'it was far too late [for the authorities] to evict them'.[8] Their presence was justified to the police on the basis that the camps contained a number of people who were registered or baptized as Protestants and this became the cover for a much wider welfare effort. Conditions were appalling and the provisions totally inadequate but the commanding officer claimed he had no resources to improve matters. He was, therefore, prepared to consider accepting the CIMADE offer to set up an infirmary inside the camp. This was cemented when Barot enlisted the help of Jeanne Merle d'Aubigné, a nursing major in the French Army, much to the amazement of the camp commandant.[9] The CIMADE presence at Gurs was followed by the Quakers, Secours

Suisse and Jewish welfare agencies, but in the meantime, CIMADE teams were installed into other internment camps that had sprung up: Rivesaltes, Brens, Récébédou and Nexon. Although no more than tolerated by the camp authorities, CIMADE was able to exert some powers. As more people in Gurs died through starvation, it became clear that money supposedly designated to feed them was being siphoned into other pockets. Merle d'Aubigné travelled to Vichy and denounced the camp commandant, who was then cashiered.[10] CIMADE was later able to negotiate the removal of certain sick and elderly people, as well as mothers with small children, on the basis that they were in the care of a recognized organization and under police surveillance. Refuges included the Coteau Fleuri near Chambon-sur-Lignon, Mas du Diable near Tarascon, Vabre (Tarn) and the Foyer Marie-Durand in Marseilles.[11] These were all financed by the Protestant ecumenical council and by money from Sweden,[12] as were other individual placements in various villages.

It is important to realize that at this stage, CIMADE did not see itself as a welfare and rescue organization either exclusively or even primarily for persecuted Jews. Barot was clear that its first forays into the camps were to protect the German refugees sought by the Nazis who had been arrested by the Vichy French authorities. As she said, 'no one spoke about Jews'[13] as those involved had all sought asylum in France after 1933 and included communists, social democrats, and others, whose only crime was not to support National Socialism. 'It was not a question of Jews at first, but the shame represented by article 19 of the armistice agreement, which was never published.'[14]

When the first arrests and deportations of foreign Jews began in the summer of 1942, CIMADE Pastor Henri Manen of Aix-en-Provence was alerted to the imminent deportation of people from the camp at Les Milles and rushed there in an attempt to save at least some of those at risk.[15] Appeals to free Protestant and Catholic 'converts' furnished with false baptismal certificates proved fruitless as the police chief explained that it was an ethnic rather than a religious matter. Manen then tried again using false papers and, by invoking the stipulation that children under 18 were exempt from deportation, persuading the parents to leave them behind to be accommodated in CIMADE homes. However, even those parents who agreed found themselves victims of harrowing scenes as their children were taken from the camp.[16] While the CIMADE workers could do little to help adults inside the camps beyond ameliorative aid, like their counterparts in

Amitié Chrétienne, they were often able to make those accommodated on licence outside the barbed wire disappear when the police came calling. The local pastors and the secretary of the CIMADE in Nîmes, Geneviève Priacel-Pittet, came up with a novel way of getting Jews out of the city who had avoided the round-up of 26 August. For many years, the Huguenot community had organized an annual meeting at the birthplace of the former Camisard leader, Rolland at Mas Soubeyran, then the home of the Musée du Désert. On the morning of 6 September, coaches arrived to take the faithful to the meeting, but instead they also conveyed around 100 Jews out of the city. Some Jewish teenagers were also brought out on foot, disguised and intermingled with local Scout troops.[17]

Once their charges had been removed from the camps or the homes, the CIMADE had to come to terms with helping them to live illegally. This inevitably involved providing false papers and ration cards. Again, this can be seen as a natural progression from legality to illegality, and certainly it seems to have been done without question or moral scruples in CIMADE circles. Its secretariat in Nîmes became a centre for the production of false identity papers and other documents, often recycling ration cards from those who had left the country. False stamps were made with potatoes, corks, and Indian ink. Later in Valence, they had a whole mix of youth movements exchanging plans, false papers and ration cards—in short a nest of gangsters. Some help came from the resistance in Lyon, which opened some doors in the border areas of Savoie, and there were also sympathetic government officials who provided certain services or at least did not ask too many questions.

Madeleine Barot has argued that the CIMADE shift into illegality took place only slowly.

> We looked to find routes over the Swiss and Spanish frontiers, organised escapes from the camps, produced false identity cards, all within the particular ethics of illegality with its extraordinary solidarity side by side with the Catholics, the communists and all those, who for one reason or another, worked within the resistance. None of this was decided, nor anticipated. Simply, there was no other solution.[18]

This post-war statement also shows that spiriting fugitives away from the camps or from centres known to the authorities soon had to be augmented by systems to help them escape from France altogether. Initially, Switzerland was more favoured than Spain, simply on the grounds that Pastor Marc Boegner and CIMADE had many more friends, contacts and co-religionists in Switzerland than in Catholic Spain.[19] However, involvement in certain illegal activities did not mean that the organization went entirely underground. Contact between representatives of the Reformed Synod and the Vichy authorities continued, with Boegner making protests and repeated appeals for help for those held in the camps.[20] Links with the Protestant Ecumenical Council and its refugee organization run by Pastor Adolf Freudenberg gave them good contacts with Swedish groups, the Bishop of Chichester, George Bell, in the United Kingdom, and Protestant resisters inside Germany, most notably Pastor Heinrich Grüber.[21] Switzerland also brought the organization into contact with Pastor Alphonse Kœchlin of Basle, the president of the Swiss Protestant federation, whose intercession and influence ultimately allowed them to broker a deal to protect refugees nominated by the CIMADE from expulsion if they arrived on Swiss soil.[22] Nevertheless, respecting the law and continuing to operate in a neutral and apolitical manner became increasingly difficult when the power of the State was directed against some sections of society. Creating and using false papers were considered perfectly acceptable under the exceptional circumstances, but collusion with armed groups was considered a step too far—partly because of the consequences if groups were caught, but also because there were certain methods incompatible with Christian witness.[23] Other limitations were also observed. After the United States had entered the war, money was received from the American Christian Committee for Refugees, but on the strict instruction that it could not be used in enemy or enemy-controlled territory. Thus it was used exclusively in Switzerland, while funds from the Swiss and the Swedes came without strings and could still be used for work inside occupied France.[24]

CIMADE moved its centre of operations to Valence at the beginning of 1943 in order to be nearer the Swiss border, and Pastor André Morel was sent by CIMADE specifically to survey possible routes across the frontier. In Chedde, he had made contact with Louis Audemard, an electrician and local leader of the Protestant Boy Scouts at Chamonix, who had already pioneered a route into Switzerland for British intelligence agents. He also enlisted the help of the Catholic bishop of Annecy who offered the monastery of Tamié and the convent at Chavanod as holding points for fugitives waiting to cross the border. However, the main assembly point in the city was the Protestant parsonage. This one building and its social hall often acted as a sanctuary to large numbers of people in transit. They were aided by a nearby restaurateur who regularly supplied food, and by the local *maquis* which provided false ration cards.[25]

Taken close to the border by train, fugitives were then taken by road to frontier areas. Like all other relief groups founded on principles of adherence to the law, organizing illegal frontier crossings was inevitably a matter of trial and error. The network was helped by pastors in border regions who would often become directly involved. Thus, for example, the Catholic Abbé Folliet, a chaplain to the JOC in Haute-Savoie, opened the doors of his cloisters in Annecy to shelter those on the run prior to their journey across the frontier, but also found hiding places for fugitives who could not make the journey, sometimes with his own family.[26] The Abbé Jean-Joseph Rosay, curé at Douvaine near the frontier was similarly active. Neither of these men survived the war as both were ultimately denounced. Rosay was arrested and died at Bergen-Belsen a few days before the camp was liberated, while Folliet was arrested on 10 June 1943 and served eight months in an Italian gaol before returning to join the resistance and was shot during a military engagement on 31 March 1945, dying nine days later.[27] Both were heavily involved in creating and developing networks, but these organizations also relied on other people who took part in the border crossings as '*conducteurs*'. Joseph Lançon, a small farmer who had brought up his seven children alone, and François Périllat, a day labourer from an impoverished family, organized the routes across the frontier through the barbed wire and away from the eyes of the Italian patrols. Usually they took families of three or four, but there were sometimes as many as ten or twelve in the party. Between October 1942 and the end of the Italian occupation in September 1943, they helped 810 people cross into Switzerland. Ultimately their work was disrupted when one of Lançon's sons was apprehended and questioned by the Germans after they had arrived to replace the Italians in their border village of Veigy.[28] Lançon and Périllat were arrested on 10 February 1944, interrogated, and sent via the prison at Compiègne to Auschwitz and then to a labour camp at Hersbruck where both died of hunger and disease.[29] In Annemasse, the missionaries of St François-de-Sales harboured around 2,000 Jews at one time or another who were trying to cross the Swiss frontier, and Monsignor Mondésert, the Auxiliary Bishop of Grenoble, spoke of the importance of the presbyteries of l'Ain as places of 'passage'.[30]

The first routes used by CIMADE went by way of Chamonix and Argentière, where they paid a guide Fr.500 per person to take people into Switzerland. However, it soon became apparent that he was extorting more money from the hapless travellers and then abandoning them to be arrested and deported back into France. Another route run from Chedde by students, pastors, an engineer, and his 12-year-old son was more difficult but safer. It, too, was abandoned when the snow came and one of the pastors was arrested.[31] Later, other routes were tried. Again, local pastors who knew the geography and topography of their border localities and the reliability of their parishioners were harnessed to negotiate temporary shelter and help with crossings. The guides were largely teenagers—too young to be liable for compulsory labour service (STO)—and who had been or still were members of the Scout movement. Later still, the organization used a much longer route through the Jura—involving a fifteen-mile walk from Saint-Claude to Les Rousses. Here they secured some unlikely assistance in the person of a communist pipe-cutter who acted as the headquarters on the French side. Those staying at his house overnight habitually had to share a bed with him, his wife, and two daughters, although when there were too many guests, a folding bed was found.[32]

Such journeys were sometimes unsuccessful and never routine. One group who went by way of Argentière in the summer of 1942 found its way successfully into Switzerland, only to be confronted by a change in Swiss policy that refused to admit any refugees. Consequently, all were dumped on the Swiss side of the frontier and forced to walk back into France where they were greeted by the pastor at Argentière who passed them on to Chedde. There they were sheltered in out-of-season mountain chalets until Pastor Boegner's appeal to the Swiss produced the agreement to allow CIMADE-sponsored refugees to enter. They were then moved via Annemasse and were able to cross the border with the apparent collusion of both French and Swiss gendarmes.[33] However, this system still required lists to be sent to the Swiss in advance for the visas to be issued, and these still had to be smuggled across the frontier by couriers. Thus Mireille Philip made several journeys as a courier on the footplate of a locomotive to expedite this. Moreover, if there was a delay, the fugitives had to be hidden in the vicinity until the requisite papers arrived.[34]

The stresses on the fugitives being taken over the frontier by the mountain route were enormous. Occasionally individuals would break psychologically. A pastor recalled two men who gave vent to a string of invectives against their helpers, claiming that they were only out to rob and then betray them, and that they would betray them first. In this case, the decision was made to exclude the two from the group. Others contented themselves with endless complaints against their guides and the severity of the conditions. For the CIMADE workers such accusations made no sense as their charges were never asked for money or gratitude for what they did. Their view was that they did what they had to do, as 'any man used to possessing others through money is no longer a man'.[35] Such journeys were not for the faint hearted and on more than one occasion, groups came to grief through their lack of stamina. For example, a small party that succumbed to the cold and the conditions near Buet were buried in a nearby cemetery without the local *Milice* suspecting anything. The locals attributed their deaths to a mixture of fear and alcohol, commenting that they were 'not people for the mountains'.[36]

Not all border crossings took place across the mountains. The frontier did run through some towns and villages such as Annemasse, where the local football field and the cemetery wall marked the boundary. This allowed at least one form of child-smuggling to take place, organized by Georges Loinger. A team of young boys in football kit played a game on the pitch while four or five of their number escaped across the wire into Switzerland where they were met on the other side. One or two days later, or when circumstances allowed, the same scenario was played out again.[37] The proximity of the cemetery also allowed the CIMADE workers to organize 'funerals' where *passeurs* and their charges arrived in full mourning clothing before being dropped over the wall using the gravedigger's ladder. This route later became impassable as the German and French police increased their surveillance in the area. On one occasion, a guide had jumped over the wall only to fall onto a passing German customs official. The man had to be 'gently' knocked out to get the fugitives safely across into Switzerland.[38] Annemasse also benefited from having a mayor who, although appointed by Vichy, was sympathetic to resistance ideals and later co-operated with the *maquis* in Haute-Savoie.[39] From August 1942 until December 1943, it was estimated that CIMADE evacuated around 400 people into Switzerland.

The proximity of the border and the ostensible need for the persecuted to pass into Switzerland undoubtedly created the circumstances where clergymen—both Catholic and Protestant—were more likely to help. Thus for example, Père Louis Favre, the head of the Saint-François de Sales secondary school in Ville-la-Grand, a commune close to Annemasse, helped those seeking entry to Switzerland. His work was ostensibly betrayed in February 1944 and he was arrested and then shot by the Germans. Other priests from his order were also involved in collecting information and occasionally also helping Jews on the run. As a result of his arrest, the priests dispersed and the school closed.[40] As with many of these network and way-stations, the survivors among those involved had only a vague idea of the numbers they had helped in some way or other. Hence estimates of the fugitives who passed through the Saint-François school varied between 1,000 and 2,000, although not all of them would have been Jews.[41] It is important to realize the peculiar circumstances that prevailed in these and other communes close to the Swiss border and to the city of Geneva. At Collognes-sous-Salève, where the Weidner network operated, its newly appointed priest, Marius Jolivet described his commune as a veritable tower of Babel, stuffed with agents of Germany, Italy, Britain, and the Free French and populated by people of diverse nationalities and religions, for the most part all searching for a trustworthy *passeur*.[42]

Hiding people while they waited to cross the border was just as taxing as organizing the crossings themselves, especially if arrangement had to be made at short notice. At Annecy, various cloisters were used, but also individual hiding places. One such was with the 92-year-old curé at Bout-du-Lac, at the far end of Lac d'Annecy. This could only be reached in rowing boats to avoid police controls, but his age meant that all negotiations had to take place with the 'grumbling old dragon' that was his housekeeper.[43] Another extreme solution was to use a bedroom of the Abbé Folliet's father.[44] In Valence, the organization had occasion to use a hotel requisitioned by the Gestapo. Although terrifying for the fugitives, it had one major advantage in that there were no checks on papers—thus making it one of the safest places in town.[45]

Hiding places could often become overcrowded when the weather in the mountain passes deteriorated, especially the small houses used as jumping off points for the border crossing itself. Reaching these isolated places had its own dangers, involving journeys on the mountain railways, avoiding major stations where there were likely to be police checks. This often meant leaving the trains at small halts and making much longer treks through the countryside. On the route from Chedde, CIMADE had enlisted the help of a woman whose husband was a prisoner of war. At one point, she and her children found themselves sheltering twelve people in their small chalet. She could no longer cope with the material and emotional pressure. All were moved out, either into the shepherds' huts or to Chamonix. Here, their lack of awareness of the dangers their behaviour could engender became all too apparent when their guides were warned by the head of the local gendarmerie that they should not be seen in the streets, especially given their strange clothing—and that they should not beg for tobacco, especially the women.[46] Such warnings were not uncommon from sympathetic bystanders.

Acting as a courier was undoubtedly a highly risky and fraught occupation. One woman acting as a 'conductor' was betrayed to the French police by her charges. This led to six weeks in gaol in the company of prostitutes, thieves and black marketers where she learned the rudiments of pick-pocketing.[47] Another recounted how she had met three panic-stricken women at Annecy station to give them tickets for their journey to the border. On the train, she distributed them in various compartments, but was shocked when one suddenly appeared in her compartment and in a loud voice said, 'Fraulein, I have lost the ticket you gave me.' This strange 'betrayal' caused stupefaction among the other passengers as the compartment was turned upside down to find the missing ticket. Ultimately, the courier had to buy another ticket from the conductor.[48] On other occasions, she moved children from Annecy to Douvaine and over the frontier. Travelling with these strangers, she was often viewed with suspicion by the authorities. Offered help and advice on where to cross by a French customs official, she was also warned by a passing woman to beware of the man as the Germans were offering bounties for *passeurs* and their clients. Arriving in Switzerland, she would then leave her charges to be found by the authorities, knowing that they would not be returned to occupied France. Later she discovered that the Swiss authorities had garnered a great deal of information about her activities.[49] She continued on, with these and subsequent groups of fugitives, but others were so affected by their experiences that they were transferred to different tasks by the organization or moved on altogether.[50] One woman courier decided at the end of December 1943 that it was time to give up—for personal reasons and because strange people had called at her sister's house looking for her. She left to join the FFL in North Africa via Spain.[51] Similarly, Mireille Philip of Lyon later gave up working for the CIMADE in order to join an information and communications network run by the maquis in the Vercors.[52] Her choice of engaging in more direct resistance may also have been influenced by her husband's activities as a socialist who had left France after the armistice to join General de Gaulle in London.[53]

Pastor Morel, who had been the conductor for the couple who died near Buet, also came unstuck as a result of a betrayal—albeit in a convoluted way. When the remaining monies and effects of the couple were conveyed to the man's brother in Switzerland, he insisted that his sibling would not have travelled without all his valuables and accused Morel and Audemard of having killed him and his wife in order to steal them. Morel and Audemard spent six days in Annecy gaol before the belongings were found in the mountains and the theft charges were dropped, although Morel was sentenced to one month for helping people to cross the border illegally.[54] He had also been accused of abducting the couple's children, although in fact they had not been considered strong enough to cross the mountain passes, and were still in CIMADE hands inside France. They were subsequently spirited into Switzerland with the help of the French police at Annemasse.[55]

CIMADE work was not confined to escape and illegality, and some of its efforts remained directed towards providing material help for those still in the camps or living elsewhere in the southern zone. Hiding places were not always just a staging post for a future escape and permanent refuges had to be found for some people.[56] Money and materials were essential for this work, and some undoubtedly came from unlikely quarters. Adolf Freudenberg, head of the refugee service of the World Council of Churches in Geneva, reported the German consulate in the city as being well disposed towards their work. As the service received ever-larger donations and packages of clothing it became increasingly difficult to transport these across the frontier, but help was provided by the German consul-general who provided a contact with the French consulate so that the packages could cross into France in the diplomatic bag. Another German diplomat acted as a courier to the Jura. Frontier crossings were carried out for any number of reasons, moving money and information as well as people to and from neutral Switzerland. All aspects of this work were illegal on both sides of the border and carried potentially severe punishments. Nonetheless, otherwise upright and honest citizens could be found smuggling huge sums of money into France to support CIMADE and other organizations.[57]

Even groups that did not join the Nîmes Commitee and remained strongly associated with the Vichy regime could still be found underwriting its activities financially, and some of their functionaries were directly involved in helping Jews in both occupied and unoccupied zones. Thus members of the Secours Nationale (SN) delegation in Orne reputedly hid 100 Jewish children by lodging them in the countryside under false names. In the Sarthe, its departmental delegate also helped hide Jewish children in collusion with the EIF, and children were also apparently hidden in SN homes in Limoges, Périgieux, and Nice. Likewise, the Maison d'Enfance at Sèvres reputedly sheltered fifty Jewish children after their parents had been deported or disappeared. The home was run by Roger and Yvonne Hagnauer, and it had been a home for war orphans from 1941 and Jewish children from 1942. It also employed people on the run from the authorities as pedagogues, including Marcel Mangel (Marcel Marceau), who was of Alsatian Jewish origin. Some of their charges were passed on by other SN groups via the OSE.[58] In similar vein, some elements of the national Assistance Publique adapted its work of caring for orphaned children and used its foster parents to shelter Jewish children in hiding. In this way, elements of some of Vichy's most high-profile welfare organizations were harnessed by individuals and groups within their staffs.[59]

The role of Marc Boegner in mobilizing Protestant communities to help Jews and other refugees in both the occupied and unoccupied zone is well known, but it could be argued that some of his Catholic counterparts were just as important in harnessing their much more numerous subordinates and congregations. In spite of the Church's continually professed loyalty to Vichy, this did not prevent some leading clerics from speaking out. For example, Jules-Géraud Saliège, Archbishop of Toulouse, promulgated a pastoral letter on 23 August 1942 affirming the position of the Jews as part of the human race. He was followed soon afterwards by Pierre-Marie Théas, Bishop of Montauban, and then by Cardinal Gerlier, who spoke for, if not with the authority of, all the Catholic clergy in France in condemning the deportations, while at the same time reaffirming loyalty to the Marshal and his regime.[60] These admittedly prominent Catholic clergymen were nevertheless a small minority and the Catholic Church was far from united on the issue. Ranged against the voices of Gerlier and Saliège was a powerful lobby from the Catholic right, still strongly supportive of all aspects of Vichy policy and maintaining the line of the Jews as aliens, as antithetical to Christianity and as agents of bolshevism. The influence of these leading clergymen was therefore largely limited to private advice to support Jews in hiding but this was of major importance at a regional and local level.[61] Thus, for example, Gerlier was able to threaten the Vichy authorities in Lyon that if the police attempted to take Jewish children from Catholic institutions, he could not be responsible for public order in the city.[62]

As with the occupied zone, the harnessing of the Catholic Church's resources was often a piecemeal affair because individual monasteries, convents, seminaries, welfare and educational institutions were not controlled by the diocese and archdiocese but directly from Rome or by the headquarters of the order concerned. However, the expressed wishes of individual prelates could count for a great deal in influencing the heads of such institutions, and this same moral authority can also be seen working at an individual level. For example, Jean Guillaud, a retired naval officer, and his wife had moved to the Vercors and in July 1943 had been approached to hide a 19-year-old German Jewish woman. She had been rescued from a camp by OSE, but the host family were asked to help 'in the name of Cardinal Gerlier'. Likewise, another German Jewess was taken in by Henriette Ogier and her husband in Lyon as a housemaid—again through a priest 'following the directives' of the Cardinal.[63] Both these examples were probably a direct result of the work done for Amitié Chrétienne in Lyon by Jean-Marie Soutou and Father Pierre Chaillet, both of whom operated under the auspices of the Cardinal and had no compunction about invoking his name. The Jesuit Chaillet is an important figure here as he had been at the forefront in criticizing the lack of Catholic help for the refugees. Arrested when the offices of Amitié Chrétienne were raided in February 1943, he escaped with a beating and continued his work underground thereafter.

Across the unoccupied zone, one can find examples of individual religious houses providing aid to fugitive Jews, although often alongside other activities. For example, the d'En Calcat monastery in Lacaune (Tarn) not only hid Jews, but helped others to flee, and also strongly supported the local maquis. At various times, at least thirty Jewish families were helped here as their names have survived, and the monastery played host to a number of well-known German émigrés, including Judge Laserstein from Berlin, who had lost his nationality in 1935 and come to France. In 1939 he had enlisted in a French regiment and had been demobilized in 1940, spending the next two years with the monks. Others also arrived and were accepted irrespective of their religion, race, or ideology, although the abbot did sometimes worry about infiltration by informers. However, the line taken by the clerics there after the occupation bears repetition. 'We did not aid the Jews because they were Jews, but because they were hunted. We

extended our activities to all those who were being sought.' Their response
to the idea of the monastery being recognized by Yad Vashem was equally
forthright. 'Monks don't look for honours.'[64]

As with the occupied zone, there were many instances of individual
help unconnected to networks. There are many recorded examples of
aid provided to friends, neighbours, and professional contacts, but many
thousands more have probably remained undocumented, and just a few
examples can be outlined here. In Toulouse, the Maurel family took in the
wife and child of a Jewish clothier who had supplied their son's priestly
garments. The father had fled to Spain, but ultimately returned. The wife
was later hidden in a Catholic convent, but the son remained with the
family, boarded out to school during the week and returning at weekends
when his mother would visit. They were also able to spend the holidays
together.[65] This was an example of previous business and commercial contacts forming the basis for help—and there were many others. However,
many of the Jews in the unoccupied zone were recent arrivals who had
fled in 1940, or only after the deportations began in July 1942, and who
therefore had no long-standing contacts with local communities. This did
not prevent relationships developing. For example, Marie-Louise Martin,
a widow in the village of Saint-Étienne-de-Saint-Geoirs (Isère) took in a
couple and their 5-year-old son as lodgers who had recently arrived in the
area looking for work. She had three grown-up sons but was clearly in
need of additional income and was prepared to accommodate the family, in
spite of the fact that the commune was equally divided between pro- and
anti-Vichy factions. Indeed her sons made no secret of their pro-German
feelings and the cafe owner across the street often voiced his disquiet
about his neighbour's sheltering Jews and what this might mean for the
village as a whole if they were caught.[66] Many widows and impoverished
peasants appear in the narratives as rescuers, and although seldom stated
explicitly, their motivation for helping Jews was in part the opportunity to
supplement their meagre earnings. In France as elsewhere, as the occupation progressed, instances of aid became more common, and distinctions
between resistance activities and helping Jews became more blurred as
more people looked for possible ways of opposing the hated 'boches' as the
tide of war turned.

The Quakers

Although often ignored in the narratives of rescue in France and elsewhere in Western Europe, the Quakers played a critical organizational and material role in helping Jews during the occupation. The number of French Quakers was extremely small, but they had strong links with both their British and American co-religionists before the outbreak of war.[67] Their combined activities included the establishment of a branch of the International Commission for the Assistance of Spanish Child Refugees at Perpignan in February 1939 to aid Republican refugees flooding across the French frontier,[68] and an ongoing commitment to helping refugees from Germany and Austria. As soon as hostilities commenced, their work was extended to include foreign 'enemy' internees in the camps and attempts to evacuate refugee children.[69] The organization also came into contact with the ORT-OSE and their children's colonies, overcrowded with children who arrived without their parents via Switzerland in the months before the war.[70] Early work was hampered by lack of funds, with so many cases that were 'heart-breaking', but funds were soon forthcoming from the American and British Friends Service Committees.[71] There were also close contacts with Pastor Boegner who recommended at least one woman to help with a Quaker children's colony at Charmes (Ardèche), and there were also reports of Quakers meeting the Protestant pastor at Nevers to discuss how to help camp inmates at Christmas.[72] This in turn led to links with the YMCA through discussions over how to arrange visits to those interned in camps.[73] A problem had arisen for the Quakers that the French would only allow French nationals to enter the camps. However, the YMCA had a privileged position, having been granted access under an old 'decret' of 1918 to engage in educational, recreational or 'moral welfare' purposes.[74]

In Toulouse, the Quakers were the only organization allowed to visit the camps and deportees, a dispensation granted by the German Military Governor who remembered their charitable work in a starving Germany at the end of the First World War when they fed an estimated 1.5 million children with so-called *Quaker-Speise*.[75] However, their work was not confined to victims of the war but also involved visiting and helping people in civil prisons.[76] This was more of a priority for the Quaker Office in Paris which concentrated on ameliorative aid for those held by the Germans or the Vichy authorities in some twenty nearby prisons and providing medical help and clothing for needy civilians.[77] Yet even the Quakers found difficulties in continuing their work, as their funds could help only the neediest of cases. Small subventions received from AFSC at the end of September allowed work to recommence, but this was stopped again at the end of October when the money ran out. The colony for refugee boys at Nocé had to be shut but the one for girls at Charmes remained open, and some arrangements for fostering remained in place. Some work in prisons also continued—including visits to interned British subjects—as did the canteen, but all activities were ultimately dependent on new funds from domestic or neutral overseas sources—effectively either from the AFSC or the JDC.[78] The British Quakers had been forced to leave in June 1940,[79] but their offices in London continued to work in tandem with the AFSC, not least in trying to persuade the British government to allow relief supplies into France—albeit without success.[80]

In the unoccupied zone, the work of the American Friends Service Committee was able to continue and its Marseilles office actually had six AFSC personnel led by Burns Chalmers, and the offices in Perpignan, Toulouse, Auch and Montauban one each. In addition, the centres numbered some thirty-five French and neutrals on their staff. Chalmers' main task had been to provide material and emotional support for 'the pathetic figures who have a childlike faith in the ability and will of the Quakers to help them.'[81] Initially, the focus of Quaker work with refugees had been to help those in the camps, but the organization had increasingly seen the need to protect the children of parents deported by the French to the occupied zone. By September 1941, the Toulouse centre reported that it was using funds to provide food for the camps at Gurs, Noë, Récébedou, Vernet and Rivesaltes. In the latter camp the daily death rate was 48—mainly children and babies—and here the Quakers instituted a feeding programme for 4,000 children.[82] Like their colleagues in CIMADE, the Quakers also sought to find places for children who could be released from camps. Finding French communities to take in such 'dangerous' guests was, according to Chalmers, extremely difficult, but a meeting with André Trocmé, the pastor of Le Chambon-sur-Lignon, provided an ideal opportunity to move children away from urban areas and into the relative safety of the French countryside.[83]

After the United States became a belligerent power, AFSC personnel took the decision to stay, and even received help from an unlikely quarter when Ambassador Winant in London allowed the British Quakers to use the diplomatic bag for correspondence on a mass evacuation scheme with their American counterparts in France.[84] In June 1942 there were still seven American Quakers in France, although there had been some turnover in personnel, and 'quite a large staff of other nationals'.[85] On November 14 they were still in post but applying for Swiss visas to expedite their departure if the Germans took over the southern zone. In the event, they were overtaken by events, arrested as enemy aliens and interned in a camp at Baden Baden, from where they were ultimately exchanged in 1944.[86] Thereafter, Quaker work was left entirely in the hands of a rump French Secours Quaker, but with no access to monies from the West. Insofar as was possible, the organization continued to help where it could, including supplying clothing for the children in the various children's homes run by the UGIF.[87] In the meantime, the Quaker representatives in the camps had had to deal with the deportations, attempting to save a few souls from the inflexible demands of the quotas, but realizing that for every one removed from the lists, someone else had to be included.[88] The AFSC and FSC continued to receive occasional reports and a post-war summary under the heading Urgent Help Service noted among other activities:

> Numerous board expenses for children were likewise paid; generally for Jewish children who were placed in the country thanks to the assistance of devoted friends living in the districts where these children were sent. On the whole, this aid was generally given to people who could either not procure help elsewhere for one reason or another, or who did not receive sufficient aid from other committees.[89]

After the liberation, Quaker activities re-formed and re-focused on prisons—now containing large numbers of collaborators.[90] Their activities were never directed exclusively or even mainly at Jews, but were determined by those in the greatest perceived need. No distinction was made between help for those in camps and those in prison, and a good deal of energy was also expended in helping conscientious objectors as well as direct relief work. The Quaker concept of service was meant to embody both the ideal of spiritual mission and practical relief work, but as one of the leaders pointed out, workers were chosen more for their experience and organizational skills—thus there was little space left for the spiritual.[91] This debate continued in the correspondence in the early 1940s that reflected on both elements, but it was generally accepted by all concerned that the two were intimately connected and 'one can hardly be considered without the other'.[92] The Quaker organizations in both occupied and unoccupied France continued to act within the law rather than outside it, although its workers were fully aware of clandestine activities carried out by others, and colluded with the 'disappearance' of the children at Le Chambon and elsewhere, even if they were not personally involved.

While Quaker organizations, both domestic and international, played an important role in the rescue of Jews, individual adherents were of crucial importance, and more likely to have acted outside the law. Perhaps the most notable example is of Gilbert Lesage, who had been on Quaker missions to many European countries in the pre-war period, including Germany. Returning to France, he was put in charge of the Service Sociale des Etrangers (SSE), a government organization created in January 1941 to oversee the welfare of men in the groupments de travaillevrs étrangers (GTE) and their families. This, of course, included many Jewish refugees and, after July 1942, it was Lesage and the SSE who were involved in selecting those arrested whom French law allowed to be handed to the Germans and those who should be allowed to stay. Lesage decided to disobey the orders he received from René Bousquet and informed both Jewish and non-Jewish rescue organizations about what was happening. In this way, many Jewish children were hidden and handed to rescue organizations.[93] Worried about the level of subversion being carried out against the police, Bousquet commissioned an inquiry into the activities of Lesage and the SSE, but in spite of evidence that they had been sabotaging the rounding up of Jews, the report was equivocal, suggesting that the SSE was not the principal source of the 'indiscretions' that had hampered the police and that it had been guilty only of a social and humanitarian approach to its work that was incompatible with administrative norms.[94]

Le Chambon-sur-Lignon and other Protestant Communities

Perhaps the most iconic figure associated with rescue in France during the occupation was the Protestant pastor André Trocmé who mobilized his

Figure 6.2. Postcard view of Le Chambon-sur-Lignon
Source: USHMM

parishioners in the isolated tourist commune of Le Chambon-sur-Lignon to shelter Jews from the Vichy authorities and later from the Germans themselves. His contribution, and that of his co-workers in the community remained largely unheralded until 'rediscovered' by Philip Hallie in the later 1970s. Hallie's approach was not to make the study an 'example of goodness or moral nobility',[95] but to try to understand what had happened in this particular community and, by extension, compare it with what had not happened in other apparently similar localities.[96]

Le Chambon was a very self-contained community that was economically dependent on a three-month summer tourist season. The population of around 3,000 contained only around 100 Catholics, with the rest either being Trocmé's Huguenot flock or adherents to a more radical form of Protestantism, the so-called Darbystes or Plymouth Brethren, who did not believe in the necessity of having either pastors or churches, and who were opposed to any form of oppressive state power. In this respect, Le Chambon was the classic example of an enclave of a religious minority likely to have empathy with others faced by persecution. One further factor that had a bearing on the later success of Le Chambon as a refuge was the legacy of Charles Guillon, who had been the pastor before Trocmé had arrived, and who had subsequently served as mayor before resigning his office on 23 June 1940 in protest at the creation of the Vichy regime. Nonetheless, his reputation and principled stand gave him an enduring political and religious influence in the whole Lignon-Vivarais area.[97]

Trocmé himself had a far from conventional upbringing. Born into a wealthy but strict household in St Quentin, he experienced the First World War and German occupation as a teenager, and was exiled as a refugee in Belgium for a period when conditions became intolerable in his home town. He studied theology at the University of Paris and worked with the poor in the Paris suburbs. Following his military service in the early 1920s he won a scholarship to the Union Theological Seminary in New York. Thus he was better travelled and had wider experiences than many of his contemporaries when he returned to France to begin his ministry. Arriving in Le Chambon in 1934, he knew his parish well before the defeat of 1940. Moreover, he had taken practical steps to broaden his mission and to benefit the local community by establishing the Cévenol School, dedicated to preparation for the *baccalauréat* in a spirit of non-violence, internationalism and peace, and crucially for many members of the local community—free from the strictures of the French public school system.[98] In creating the school he had the backing of his local presbyterial council and was able to bring in an old and trusted friend, Édouard Theis, as director. Although non-violence and pacifism were not particularly popular in the last years of peace, the school was saved by a small influx of German and Eastern European refugees—as pupils and as teachers.[99] Trocmé undoubtedly inherited a cohesive community when he arrived in 1934, but this was clearly strengthened in the years following, for example by his creation of a network of thirteen youth Bible study groups, each led by a '*responsable*'. They were designed to operate independently, but came into their own after 1940 when Trocmé was able to use them as conduits for continued Bible study and for clandestine activities where only he knew the full extent of the networks or people involved.[100] A fortuitous creation perhaps, but one that strangely paralleled, but was undoubtedly not based on, the communist cell networks of a similar vintage.

The first two years of Vichy rule were marked with various manifestations of disobedience, both by Trocmé and by the community as a whole. Trocmé and Theis refused to sign an oath of unconditional loyalty to

Marshal Pétain. They also resisted demands that they raise a French flag and require their students to salute it with the fascist salute. Finally, they refused to ring the church bells on 31 July 1941 to celebrate the foundation of the Legion Volontaire by the Marshal. In each case, these refusals or avoidances went unpunished by the authorities.[101] However, it was Trocmé's increasing reputation as a pacifist that was to provide the crucial link between his local initiatives in helping refugees and the wider cause of persecuted Jewry. He had initially approached the Quakers to offer his help to internees in southern France but, instead of being invited to join their work in the camps he was persuaded to mobilize his own community with the specific task of helping Jewish children.[102] In this way, geography, traditions, networks, structures, and contacts with the outside world all came together with the leadership qualities of a single individual to provide what must have been close to an ideal basis for rescue.

Trocmé's mobilization of his commune required its co-operation and approval. To that end, in the winter of 1941, he persuaded the presbyterial council that opening the village to the refugees from the camps was the right thing to do. Once he had the backing of his church—and by extension the community as well, the work of rescue began in earnest. Refugees arrived by train and were brought to the presbytery, where they were redistributed within the commune and the surrounding countryside.[103] Ultimately each of the thirteen *responsables* took full responsibility for looking after the refugees in their care, both adults but also, especially, children. This included feeding, clothing, protecting and educating the latter in the best way they could.[104] The refuges established during the occupation were externally funded by a number of international organizations, including the Quakers, American Congregationalists, and the Swiss and Swedish governments, and could have different functions. The so-called Farm School was the most secure because of its situation overlooking all the local roads and the presence of farm dogs that would sound the alert. Couteau Fleuri was used primarily as a temporary refuge for those being taken across the frontier to Switzerland and was funded by CIMADE.[105] Other properties also became central to the operation. The owners of more than a dozen *pensions* that accommodated the tourists in the summer and sometimes played hosts to students at the school were also mobilized to take in the refugees and others on the run from the authorities or from the Germans. This latter group included an increasing number of STO evaders. One such was owned by Madame Eyraud, who took in boys. Her task was made more difficult when the Germans arrived, both because her *pension* was on a main thoroughfare and also because her husband was heavily involved with the *maquis*, had a high-powered radio transmitter in the house and often played host to *maquisards* and occasionally to arms shipments.[106] Beyond these establishments in or near the village, there were many private individuals, including Darbyistes in outlying districts who provided hiding places.

The Cévenol School also played a role in cloaking the wider activities of Trocmé and his associates. Young Jews could be 'hidden' among the students, and adults could be invited to join the faculty as teachers. Perhaps not surprisingly, the work at Le Chambon became more insecure as time went on, as more and more people were sent to the commune by the relief and welfare groups organizing the evacuation of internees from the camps in the south, but amazingly, neither the school's main buildings nor its residences were ever raided, either by the Vichy police or the Germans. Apart from his *responsables*, Trocmé also collected some unlikely recruits to his illegal work. Alice Reynier arrived from Avignon to help in his house in January 1943. Although she came from a pious and very observant cloistered Protestant community, she was soon putting some of her skills to good use by forging signatures on identity and ration cards.[107] By and large, the relatively small number of practising Catholic families in the commune did not become involved in Trocmé's activities, primarily because their priest was himself uninterested in any form of ecumenical co-operation.[108] At the same time, the rescuers in Le Chambon had no qualms about sending refugees to Catholic-run refuges elsewhere.

Trocmé also had a somewhat uneasy relationship with the local *maquis*. He was often forced to intervene when the resistance 'sequestered' property from the village and could not prevent some of the pacificist Cévenol School pupils from joining its ranks. Even within his community there were inevitable tensions. Some objected to Trocmé's concentration on the foreigners at the expense of their spiritual needs, while other resented the arrival of so many different nationalities and languages—something that went beyond the tolerable intrusions of the tourists in the short summer season.[109] The leaders of the Reformed Church put Trocmé under pressure in January 1943 to give up his work, fearing discovery of his work might endanger the Protestant church as a whole.[110] Despite these pressures, Trocmé refused to back down and his networks went on growing. Estimates suggest that up to 2,500 refugees passed through the commune during the period, but this was the result of aggregation rather than advance planning.[111] One could point to the fact that there were no factors that prevented its further growth—such as a betrayal, a dearth of resources or a finite limit to the numbers of people who could be recruited to help. The people of Le Chambon have been described as inspired amateurs, but such a term could equally be applied to many other rescue networks. As a recognizable, religiously based community they could experience more of a sense of fellowship in doing something 'good' or 'of consequence', even though knowledge of who was doing what was limited. It was the framework of the community that provided the essential element to its success rather than any formal organization—which itself might have proved far more dangerous and liable to betrayal.[112] One last point that has never been fully explored in trying to explain the extraordinary events in the area round Le Chambon is that Trocmé and Guillon were unusual insofar as they had far more cosmopolitan backgrounds and experiences than most in their position (where cosmopolitanism was seen as a political insult).[113]

Even if Le Chambon is the best-known example of this type of col-lective rescue, it was not unique. The commune of Prélenfrey-du-Guâ in Vercors—later to become famous for its ill-fated *maquisard* insurrection in 1944—was dominated by a privately owned TB sanatorium, known as the preventorium, run by the Guidi-Lamorthe families, which became the hiding place for as many as twenty Jewish children and a further thirty-one adults.[114] The Jewish fugitives came from a number of sources. One who spent some time working at the sanatorium and who ultimately became a *maquisard* had arrived originally as part of a Boy Scout summer camp.[115] Many others, however, came as a result of the intercession of the OSE or of sympathetic doctors referring 'patients' to the sanatorium. The organizers of the Prélenfrey network did not confine their activities to sheltering Jews and were also involved in providing material help to the nearby *maquis*—a combination that led to a major German raid on the village on 22 July 1944. Attention was deflected away from the preventorium, and quick thinking by one of the nurses also convinced the Germans that their hostages were just local farmers and that the *maquisards* they sought had already left the district.[116]

The involvement of Protestant pastors in these and other communal rescues only tells part of the story. A survey of the Deux-Sèvres département, for example, reveals the existence of many pastors who were heavily influenced by Karl Barth and engaged in all manner of illegal activities, of which hiding Jews was only one. Thus when pastor Fouchier of Lezay was denounced to the German *Kommandantur* by an anonymous informant, he was accused of assisting STO evaders, but his role in helping Jews was not even mentioned.[117] Others were involved in finding hiding places for both Jews and STO evaders. Jean-Jacques Cremer at Chey had at least thirty such helpers among his parishioners. 'No one refused, and thanks to the local gendarmes who informed the villages of their intended visits, no one was captured.'[118] In explaining the propensity of Protestant pastors and their communities towards helping fugitives and opposing the dictates of Vichy and the Germans, rescuers' reminiscences time and again make reference to the centuries of persecution suffered by their community in France. As one put it; 'In the past, it was we who were the persecuted; today it is you.'[119]

Dieulefit

The links between Protestantism and help for the Jews have been made many times, both in France and elsewhere: the recognition of the persecuted minority, the more left-wing stance of many Protestants, the greater familiarity with the text of the Old Testament, a greater attachment to the ideas and values of the French Republic. These two examples both highlight the importance of isolated minority Protestant communes in an otherwise overwhelmingly Catholic environment, but it should be understood that such actions were not exclusive to one particular Christian denomination. Thus the commune of Dieulefit (Drôme) provides a good example of a similar mass rescue, but this time within a more Catholic milieu, although the Protestants comprised around one third of the population. The town itself comprised around 3,500 inhabitants and owed its existence to the textile industry, although this was in decline by the later 1930s, and to a certain amount of tourism.[120] In this case, one can talk of a collective reaction not defined by confession and one based on a *réflex ancestral* that had been reawakened in 1940.[121] In that year, the town received anything up to 1,500 'refugees' from all quarters. They included British and Americans, as well as the French and Belgians fleeing southwards from the German advance. They may have been drawn there by the Protestant community, or by the proximity of the Beauvallon school run by the famous pedagogue Marguerite Soubeyran.[122] This became a haven for Jewish children placed there by the OSE offices in Lyon and Marseilles. Sometime later, the local

Catholic school also became a haven, employing refugees as teachers and harbouring a number of Jewish children. The local pension also became a haven for intellectuals in hiding.[123] Their cause was helped by a town clerk, Jeanne Barnier, who had scruples about providing false papers until guided by her pastor.[124] After that, requests became easier to meet. The mayor in 1940 had been opposed to the Vichy settlement and was therefore replaced in February 1941. Luckily, his replacement turned a blind eye to what his subordinate was doing and thus acted as a suitable foil for any outside investigations.[125] As the numbers of refugees increased, so the town itself was mobilized to provide help, with both Catholic and Protestant families acting as hosts. This is remarkable in one respect, namely that these were ostensibly all individual acts and not sponsored by Catholic or Protestant organizations. By the same token, there was no opposition to what was happening, and while there were those in the village who remained loyal to Vichy, they, like the appointed mayor, Colonel Pizot, merely closed their eyes to what was happening.[126] Among the local clergy, there had been strong support for Pétain in the summer of 1940. The senior Protestant pastor, Henri Eberhard, expressed no great opposition to the new regime and took his line from Marc Boegner, as did his presbyterial council, nearly all of whom were from the 1914 generation. His shift was a gradual one, conditioned by events such as the attempted politicization of youth movements, and possibly also by the pronouncements of Karl Barth. Whatever the prompting, he attended the meeting that gave rise to the Pomeyrol theses, but did not sign them. He was not the only minister in the village, as he not only had a second pastor to assist him, but also three others who were themselves refugees from North-East France.[127] His Catholic counterpart, Joseph Constant, was equally wedded to the idea of Pétain and the national revolution.

After the summer of 1942, Eberhard never explicitly called upon his parishioners to help the Jews. Although many subsequently claimed to remember such an exhortation, he was more circumspect, and stated in a later sermon that he knew that only a minority would have the courage to take the risks involved and that others would refuse.[128] His successor in 1943 was even more conservative, even counselling Jeanne Barnier to give up her illegal activities. Likewise, Constant never made any public pronouncements, in spite of a more outspoken attitude from his ecclesiastical superior, Archbishop Saliège. Thus in the case of Dieulefit it was not the pastoral clergy who were the driving force behind either the rescue or the resistance work. However, one can point to others who were involved. Philippe Debû-Bridel was one of the refugee pastors from the north and was only accepted into the congregation in 1941 as someone who could provide services in outlying hamlets. Highly political, he became an active member of the resistance, acting as liaison for the maquis and supervising parachute drops. A nearby Catholic cleric, Abbé Magnet fulfilled a somewhat similar role, baptizing Jewish infants and helping to hide STO evaders. Denounced for his activities, he ultimately joined the resistance and was captured and killed by the Germans in August 1944.

However, it was in the years 1942 to 1944 that the town really became a lynchpin for helping Jews. It was left in no doubt about Vichy intentions after three Jewish boys and some others in the town were arrested by the French police in July 1942, and thereafter the rescuers took steps to cover their tracks and assure the hiding places of those they were helping. Indeed, Soubeyran and her colleagues went to extraordinary lengths to free the three boys from captivity, finally engineering their removal from a transport north at the last moment.[129] After the military occupation of France on 11 November, Dieulefit became part of the Italian zone. It also became much closer to the CIMADE headquarters now based in Valence (Drôme). The Italian presence meant that there was little direct pressure on those in hiding, but likewise they could do little to stop the activities of the French police acting on orders from Vichy and, indirectly, from Berlin.

Aside from being a refuge, Dieulefit also became a centre for resistance. In February 1943, it had a *maquis* made up from boys wanting to avoid STO, with the Beauvallon School acting as dormitory and refectory. This soon became an active resistance cell, being trained in military techniques and ultimately mounting raids on local railway lines. The area also became a hotbed of armed resistance involving units of the Armée Secrète and the FTP. In spite of its role, the village was ultimately saved from the punitive German measures handed out to so many other villages in the region for their pre-emptive actions by the arrival of the Allied forces in southern France and the deflection of the German forces to counteract them.[130] Although seen as somewhat miraculous at the time, its salvation probably owed more to Allied planning and German responses than to divine intervention.

The fact that so many communes in the French countryside had some contact with foreign Jews and other displaced people at a relatively early stage in the occupation was partly the direct result of Vichy government policy. A law of 3 November 1941 decreed that Jews who had arrived in France after 1 June 1936 and other undesirables were to be removed from major urban centres. This led to various communes with tourist facilities being selected to house these 'forced migrants'. Public responses to their arrival varied, according to whether the newcomers were seen as economically beneficial or as a financial or security threat.[131] However, such long-standing arrangements could have benefits. Thus a Belgian family of two couples and a young single adult were rented lodgings in the village of Lacaune (Tarn), where they had been assigned by the Vichy authorities, by a wine and spirit merchant, Roger Maraval. When there were rumours in August 1942 that the younger of the couples would be arrested, he arranged a hiding place for them and hid the son in his own house. The older couple, by virtue of their age, were supposedly protected and were never, in fact, hidden, although in many other areas no respect was paid to this supposed exemption, and many old and sick people were summarily handed over to the Germans.[132]

Protection in the Italian Zone

The towns and cities of the Eastern French Mediterranean coast had been a target for the Vichy government's antisemitic policies from the beginning of the persecution, with the police being harnessed to identify and then arrest those foreign Jews who had made their homes there, or who had found their way to the south since the outbreak of war. However, this victimization came to an abrupt halt after the occupation of the southern zone when Berlin handed to the Italians administrative control over eight *départements*: Alpes-Maritimes, Var, Hautes-Alpes, Basses-Alpes, Isère, Drôme, Savoie and Haute Savoie, an area that included some of the major southern French resort towns. A little over a month later, on 20 December, the *préfet* of Alpes-Maritimes, Marcel Ribière, decreed that all foreign Jews were to leave his *département* within 72 hours and move to areas of forced settlement, either Drôme or the Ardèche. As this latter *département* was occupied by the Germans, this was tantamount to handing them over to the Gestapo.[133] As a result of the intervention of the banker Angelo Donati via Alberto Calisse, the Italian consul-general in Nice, to his friend Count Vidau, a leading functionary within the Foreign Ministry in Rome, the Italian military authorities were given an order from Rome, and ostensibly from Mussolini himself, that no Jews were to be handed over in this way.[134] Moreover, the original proscription of removals from the Alpes-Maritimes was effectively extended to include all the territories under Italian military control.[135] Donati himself explained this by the fact that the majority of high-ranking Italian civil and military personnel had no strong antisemitic feelings, but were prepared to be moved by 'humanitarian considerations'.[136] In fact, there may also have been a strong feeling in Rome that Italy should assert its sovereignty over the territories concerned and distance itself from the actions of the Germans.[137] The protection afforded Jews in the Italian zone became a magnet for those being sought elsewhere, and the border became a hotbed of smuggling activity. By the same token it also became an issue of increasing friction between the Italians on the one side, and both the Vichy authorities and the Germans on the other.

There is no doubt that Berlin tried very hard to change Italian minds on this issue and to allow the French police free rein to carry out further antisemitic measures. The German Ambassador in Rome, von Mackensen, pushed hard, but found himself confronted with Italian officials increasingly keen to distance their country from the reports of atrocities and mass killings in Poland. A dossier submitted to Mussolini at the critical moment proved enough to make sure he did not give way.[138] Thus the German agreement with the Mussolini regime meant that there would be no change to existing practices, but that the Italians would not afford protection to anyone entering their zone after 26 March 1943. However, it proved impossible to determine precisely when someone had arrived as their only means of proof were the dates on hotel bills—and these were easy to ante-date. Thus the agreement proved unworkable and the Italians continued to turn a blind eye, even to new arrivals. In contrast, the local French police, prompted by the *préfet* Marcel Ribière, redoubled their controls around synagogues and 'micro-Palestine' in the area of the boulevard Dubouchage, checking papers at every opportunity.[139] Around 150 Jews were arrested and prosecuted for document irregularities. However, even this was not tolerated for long, and the Italians soon deployed *carabinieri* units to curtail excesses and arrest the French police if necessary to protect the Jews at the main synagogue in Nice from further harassment.[140] The situation improved still further in July 1943, when the hardline Ribière was replaced by the much more accommodating André Chaigneau, who proceeded to 'legalize' all the foreign Jews in his *département*.[141]

Estimates vary, but it can be argued that there were between 20,000 and 25,000 Jews who received some temporary protection from the occupying Italians. Worries about the future intentions of the Germans prompted an Italian scheme to remove the Jews from the region altogether. Even the collapse of the Mussolini regime did not prevent this going ahead, and Donati was charged by the Italian Foreign Ministry with negotiating the possible transfer of 20–30,000 Jews to North Africa. In the interim, plans went ahead to evacuate the Jews from the occupied zone into Italy, and special travel documents were produced to facilitate this. However events soon overtook the organizers when, in early August, the Badoglio regime decided to remove its troops from most of the area of occupation, save the city of Nice and its surrounding area. Thus there was a mass movement towards the city, a safe haven that became a trap in itself when Rome agreed to an armistice with the Allied powers, thus prompting an immediate German military occupation of the remaining elements of the Italian zone and of northern Italy itself.[142]

The specific role of Angelo Donati should not be ignored here. He had strong connections with France, having been a liaison officer during the First World War, and had become a respected banker in Paris during the interwar period. After 1933, he had also been involved in helping refugees from Nazism who had arrived in the French capital. After 1940 Donati continued his efforts in the unoccupied zone; working with Father Pierre-Marie Benoît of the Capuchin Monastery in Marseilles and using Father Benedetto as an intermediary with the Vatican. Without his energy and his contacts, it is unlikely that the Italian response would have been so positive. He was also instrumental in having the Italian Inspector-General of Police, Guido Lo Spinoso, who was charged with racial policy, and who had arrived in the city in March 1943, meet Father Benoît to persuade him to act with humanity towards the Jewish community and have no dealings with the Germans, something that Lo Spinoso was more than content to do.

The fact that Donati's activities failed to achieve all their objectives should not detract from the intention here, and it can also be argued that the period of peace was never seen as permanent and therefore encouraged all concerned—both rescuers and hunted—to find more permanent solutions. His association with Benoît is also worthy of comment. Like Donati, Pierre-Marie Benoît had been actively engaged in helping victims of persecution in and around Marseilles since the beginning of the war. Later, he became a regular visitor at Les Milles internment camp, acting as an intermediary between the inmates and the authorities. He was also quick to see the dangers posed by the *Statut des Juifs* for the foreign Jews held there. He used his position to obtain false papers and hiding places, even conspiring to help individuals escape the camps. His contacts were many and various, encompassing Catholic, Protestant and Jewish milieux in and around Marseilles. In essence, he became the lynch-pin in activities to help the Jews and others in this region—a function made more surprising by the fact that he had no ties to the area, having been caught there by the armistice on his way back to Rome where he taught philosophy. He was instrumental in helping all manner of fugitives, including Allied airmen, find places of safety, moving them to places less likely to be the targets of German or French raids. He also became involved with elements of the armed resistance in making contact with groups of smugglers to organize an escape route to North Africa via Spain, and instigated the far-fetched plan to transfer the Jews in Nice to North Africa via Italy, even discussing it with Pope Pius XII.[143] His other contacts included, among others, Joseph Bass, organizer of the André resistance group, and Jean Lemaire, the evangelical Protestant pastor in Marseilles, both of whom were similarly engaged in rescue activities in their own right.

Enclaves providing this sort of political protection for Jews, however temporary, were a comparative rarity. The relative peace of the Alpes-Maritimes did create an environment that facilitated rescue activities. For example, the OSE was active in finding places for Jewish children to be hidden in the areas round Nice, although other solutions were less successful. In order to reduce the refugee population in that city, many refugees were sent to nearby mountain resorts. Thus St Martin Vésubie played host to around 1,000 Jews. Hotel accommodation was paid for by the UGIF, and the ORT opened schools to cater for the children.[144] Thereafter, what had been something of a safe haven for the Jews became a trap, as large numbers of the Gestapo, Feldgendarmerie, *Milice*, and Doriotistes moved in, carrying out innumerable raids on the streets and in hotels, rounding up Jews of all ages and circumstances without exception. The Jew hunters were paid FFr.100 per head, and many leading personalities were quickly arrested. Thus work to save those who remained fell to members of the EIF, who produced enough false papers for around 2,000 people almost overnight.[145] In addition, a convoy of around 1,000 Jews left St Martin Vésubie and reached the Italian border, although many others who tried to escape were caught by checkpoints at stations and bus stops.[146] Others still found some way of hiding, either with unsolicited help from locals or through their own devices. One such story demonstrates how people could sometimes be 'persuaded' into helping. Rabbi Netter from Metz was assured by the local prefecture that French Jews were under the direct protection of the Marshal, but he nevertheless booked into a hotel under a false 'Aryan' name. The proprietess, the widow of a Catholic school headmaster, asked him to leave after two days because she suspected he was a Jew, with the implied threat that she would denounce him. Rather than leave, the rabbi contacted the local bishop's secretary (*chancelier*) who was aware of his true identity. Clearly, a word from the bishop's palace was enough to change the hotelier's attitude. Not only was the rabbi then allowed to stay, but also given some element of security.[147] Even in these straightened times, the persecuted could still sometimes exercise the right to pick and choose their helpers. One perhaps extreme example is of Rabbi Chneerson and his fifty yeshiva students. Offered the chance to shelter his entire group in a cloister, he refused on the grounds that 'since Torquemada, cloisters caused us much pain (*ne nous ont trop coûté*) and it is to the eternal father and not to the "curés" that he wished to entrust his charges'.[148]

Other groups were also active in the city. The André network run by Joseph Bass had links to various Catholic institutions and clergy, including the Abbé Alfred Daumas, until the latter was arrested and Bass was forced to flee the city, leaving the work to his assistants. Indeed the work of many groups was severely hampered by the arrests of large numbers of people from the Jewish organizations such as the UGIF and EIF and elsewhere—often just on suspicion of illegal activity. One man who managed to avoid this fate was Moussa Abadi of the local OSE branch. Unknown in the community, he was able to improvise the 'Marcel' rescue network with his assistant, Odette Rosenstock, and with the help of the Catholic diocese, to save between 300 and 500 children between September and the end of 1943.[149] At the end of 1942 Abadi had learned from a Jesuit priest who had been a chaplain with the Italian forces on the Eastern Front about the fate of the Jews, and in the spring of 1943, he approached the Bishop, Monsignor Paul Rémond, with a view to employing the many church institutions in his diocese to act as hiding places.[150] Abadi was already known to the bishop as an '*homme de théâtre*' who had given public-speaking lessons to seminarists in the diocese. Thus a pre-existing relationship helped to oil the wheels of co-operation.[151] Rémond agreed after being reassured that the work would not involve the use of arms, but also insisted that knowledge of the network should be restricted to him and his secretary, Mademoiselle Lagache.[152] At the same time, Abadi managed to recruit the help of local Protestant pastors, Gagnier and Edmond Evrard, and elicit funds, not only from OSE, but also from the Sixième, the JDC and the Quakers. The network benefited from an office within the diocesan administration where it was able to manufacture false identity cards and ration books. Abadi also benefited from being appointed *inspecteur de l'enseignement catholique* by the archbishop and was further armed with a laissez-passer signed by Rémond which gave him access to the Catholic schools and an effective authorization to ask for help from the heads of the institutions he visited.[153] In the interests of security, he tried to keep his network separate from others, although there was some overlap with that of Georges Garel, especially when it came to funding.[154] However, even his efforts were not without problems as the Germans began raiding OSE offices, on one occasion arresting a large number of people who had come to find hiding places for their children.[155]

As in many other parts of France, the role of the leading churchman in the region did not go uncriticized. Bishop Rémond of Nice never spoke out publicly against either the persecution of the Jews or the STO. His attitude seems to have been one of convinced anti-German feeling coupled with a sense of humanity that led him to advocate help for the Jews, in spite of having no particular sympathy for them.[156] It is also worthy of note that it was argued that there was a much greater sense of sympathy and help given by Protestant pastors at an earlier date here, than among the priests: testament perhaps to the importance of empathy with the persecuted and of the hierarchy in providing guidance—however unofficial or off the record—to its local representatives and thereby to its community. That said, Rémond was little different from many of his ecclesiastical colleagues.

The arrival of the Germans in September did prompt an immediate response from some Catholic institutions and individual parishes to Abadi's network. For example, Father Coeret in Villars-sur-Var gave sanctuary to Jews in his parish and created an alarm system to warn of German raids that involved the telephone at the station and the church clock.[157] Odette Rosenstock acted as intermediary, visiting the children regularly,

Figure 6.3. Group portrait of members of the Sixième/EIF
Source: USHMM

MOUSSA EN 1948

Figure 6.4. Moussa Abadi, Network organizer in Nice
Source: USHMM

distributing payments to foster parents and passing on information about them (but not their whereabouts) to the parents.[158] An assistant, Huguette Wahl, had been sent to them from the Garel network, but lasted only three weeks before she was arrested, tortured, and later deported and killed.[159] In April 1944, the network was rocked by the arrest of Rosenstock, which left Abadi isolated and without her knowledge of where all the children were hidden. He nevertheless continued to operate in spite of not knowing what Rosenstock might have revealed under torture and also used the expertise of the Garel network to expedite the removal of some children over the frontier to Switzerland.[160]

In spite of their commitment to the cause and the ferocity of their descent on the Italian zone, Alois Brunner and his German compatriots were not particularly successful in rounding up the estimated 25–30,000 Jews formerly sheltered by the Italians, even though they offered bounties that reached FFr.5,000 per head by December 1943.[161] This was in part a result of the widespread collusion of elements within the local Catholic Church organization and also that of the local authorities, not least in destroying records and in refusing to supply police help in organizing raids.[162] Moreover, the Gestapo went out of its way to trap Rémond and other Catholic institutions by using a 'false' Allied airman and a supposed anti-Nazi German. The archbishop was also subject to the attentions of 'Blond Alice', a Gestapo agent who arrived at his door with two Jewish children, asking that they be helped. Fortunately in this, and other cases, Rémond saw through the trap and refused to be involved.[163] Ultimately, even some of the more committed local antisemites lost heart. The local office of the CGQJ had become totally corrupt under the leadership of Darquier de Pellepoix, and the Germans failed to involve them or use their local knowledge. As one former activist was overheard speaking on the telephone: most people now expected an Anglo-Saxon victory and those who a few months before had greeted them, now chose to cross to the other side of the street.[164] This greater proximity of the Allied armies, although still only in southern Italy, seems to have increased the propensity for helping Jews in the community, as the survival of so many testifies. The fact that they were able to exist in the relative safety of the Italian zone until September 1943 did not, of itself, lead to their salvation, but the news of Allied progress and German defeats undoubtedly served to encourage many to help, in the knowledge that an end to the occupation was in sight.

'Other' Jews

Thus far, the discussion has been almost exclusively concerned with the Ashkenazi Jews in France, but it should be remembered that the country also had some 35,000 Spanish (Portuguese) Sephardic Jews in 1940. Some 3,000 of them were registered with the Spanish consulates, but the vast majority had come from Salonika in the early 1900s. The Franco regime pursued a self-serving line, agreeing that its citizens should not be exempt from racial laws but that aryanization should result in their property being handed over to Spanish commissioners. The Spanish consuls failed to save fourteen Spanish Jews rounded up in August 1941, but did intervene to help nationals on other occasions. Spain, however, only issued 250 visas for entry to Spain to the 2,000 Spanish Jews in Paris, and the ratio in the unoccupied zone was the same. It also insisted that this first group could not remain in the country and would have to leave Spain before the next batch of visas would be issued. A first group of eighty did not leave France until 10 August 1943, by which time some others had already been arrested and the Germans refused to release them. A few survived to be liberated in France, ostensibly because they possessed, though had not been able to use, the Spanish visas supplied by the consulates. In essence, the Spanish government was far more interested in the property of its 'nationals' than in ensuring their safety.[165] In addition, some 140 Sephardic Jews with Portuguese nationality were also safely removed from France in the summer of 1943 in two convoys, the first accompanied by Salazar's Consul-General as far as the frontier, but there is no clue as to what happened to the rest. These limited evacuations took place according to nationality rather than any reference to racial origins.[166] For their part, the Sephardic communities in France made only a token attempt to use their origins to gain exemptions. The discovery of a paper at the Pasteur Institute which suggested that Sephardim had a different blood from the Ashkenazim prompted the commissioning of a report from a professor at the Anthropological Institute that was submitted to the Racial Institute in Munich. It was prepared to agree the case but left the final decision with Laval, who was unwilling to grant better status to the Sephardim than to Alsatian Jews. Some leaders also objected to disavowing their Jewish origins and also worried that it might end up as a trap—thus the idea was dropped.[167]

Beyond the Sephardic Jews, there were other sects in occupied France with unusual origins: forty families of Gruzinians (Georgians), Jugutis (Afgan), and Karaites (Russia), all three of which had arrived after the revolution of 1917. The Georgian Jews were defended by Christian Georgians in Paris who were being courted by the Germans as a potential future government of a liberated Georgia. The argument was that these people were racially Georgian (of Chaldean origin) but had converted to Judaism. Berlin was content to accept this idea, but the French authorities continued to cause trouble, refusing to remove the word 'Jew' from their identity cards. Xavier Vallat was on record as arguing that, under the French legislation of 2 June 1941 that defined Jews, they were still Jews—as otherwise the French would have to reopen the cases of Jews in Provence and Alsace who also claimed to be converts descended from the Celts.[168] The Georgian leaders suggested that a commission be created to decide who should be granted status as 'Georgians of Mosaic faith' and this ultimately recognized some 243 families, encompassing around 1,000 people. As was admitted subsequently, this device was used to save others as well, with documents being forged and names changed to make the cases more acceptable. Even this did not provide complete protection as the Vichy Service d'Aryanisation Economique refused to recognize the new status and the debate continued. At the same time, German defeats in the Soviet Union meant that Berlin lost interest in the Georgians as a whole, and the Jews among them became easier targets for arrest and deportation, although most seem to have been able to survive the last year of occupation by going underground or with help from their Christian counterparts.[169]

The so-called Jugutis had been driven from Persia in the late nineteenth century, emigrating to Bukhara, Afghanistan and France. Thirty-eight such families registered as Jews in France in 1940, but others who failed to register remained untroubled through the whole occupation. One of the latter, Asaf Atchildi, became the representative for those registered, and succeeded in getting protection from the Afghan and Iranian representatives in Paris by arguing that these people were not, in fact, Jews. Helped by the Georgians, he was able to persuade Berlin, and a meeting with a Dr Weber on 5 October 1941 provided the necessary exemptions. Vallat and the French officials again opposed the German decision, refusing to give bureaucratic form to the directive from Berlin. Only in February 1942 were the Jugutis reluctantly provided with the necessary papers to live unhindered, and it was made clear to Atchildi that the French were distinctly unhappy but had been forced to comply, and that he would be responsible for the veracity of the list. Subsequently, he was also able to secure, albeit with considerable difficulty, the release of four men already arrested and held in camps.[170] Approached by many to be added to the list, he was aware that its usefulness would be governed by its selectivity, although some individuals close to the community were added, as were numbers of Iranian Jews whose names were supplied by their consul.

The Karaites were a Jewish sect founded in the eighth century and who had around 250 adherents in France in 1940. Their German counterparts had been granted an exemption from the Nazi racial laws in 1939. In occupied Poland, a commission of three scholars came to the same conclusion, thus exempting around 12,000 Karaites in all occupied territories. Once again, Vallat opposed the exemption from the French laws. He received a petition from the Karaite leaders indicating that they never allowed Jews into their community and rejected the idea that they were themselves Jews. They also refused to allow Jews to masquerade as Karaites in order to escape German persecution. With the support of the French 'racial expert', Georges Montandon, they were finally able to make their case and were thus protected from further persecution.[171]

Conclusion: Survival in France

The historiography on rescue and survival in France has undergone a huge change in recent decades. The 'Righteous among the Nations' from France recognized by Yad Vashem doubled between 1993 and 2001, and the number continues to grow year by year as more individual cases are uncovered.[172] There are also studies of individual *départements* that have added enormously to our knowledge of what took place in towns and villages across both the occupied and unoccupied zones. What then are the factors that had the greatest impact on Jewish survival? The first element is the division of France into occupied and unoccupied zones until November 1942. In theory, the unoccupied zone provided a safer haven for Jews while it existed, but as has often been pointed out, the antisemitic policies of the Vichy regime did much to undermine this safety, at least for the many foreign Jews who lived or had fled there in the aftermath of 1940. Nevertheless, this malevolence did have some positive effects in making Jewish organizations aware of the potential dangers at an early stage. The existence of various Jewish émigré organizations and their continuance after June 1940 meant that they were able to regroup and provide a focus for their communities. In some respects, their social and welfare work, with its links to non-Jewish agencies, was the most valuable of all, as it provided contacts that could be used when the deportations began in July 1942.

Another crucial factor to note is the level of co-operation between different Christian confessional welfare organizations as epitomized by the Nîmes Committee in the unoccupied zone but also evident elsewhere. This, in itself, was something deemed 'unthinkable before the war'.[173] This was also evident in the relationships forged between Jewish and non-Jewish agencies, even to the point of delegating tasks to prevent duplication of effort. The role of Catholic leaders who did get involved was undoubtedly of great importance in mobilizing help for the Jews—from the guidance given by Cardinals Gerlier and Saliège to their bishops—as well as the ways in which ordinary parish priests influenced their parishioners. Nevertheless, it is clear that their scope for action was limited by more conservative elements within the Church that were virulently pro-Vichy and even pro-German. In the same way, the leadership of Marc Boegner and the ideological influence of Karl Barth undoubtedly had a major impact on the Protestant minority, but like his Catholic counterparts, Boegner had to tread a very careful path in instigating and facilitating help for persecuted Jewry.

In looking at individual rescuers, it is interesting to note that some commentators have pointed out the prominence given to Protestant 'justes' who have been treated more sympathetically because their wives and immediate families were almost always involved, and this gave them entrée into the wider community. This was especially true in cases where whole villages were involved and where rescuers were in sufficient numbers to control or isolate pro-Pétain or antisemitic individuals in their midst. They also remain overrepresented among the 'justes', comprising 10 per cent of the total while being only 2 per cent of the population. Conversely, there has been greater criticism of the Catholic clergy highlighting the fact that for every Catholic 'juste' there was also another cleric who was silent or overtly pro-Pétain or overtly antisemitic, and for the most part the Catholic laity and peasantry have remained absent from the narrative.[174]

The stories of village rescues also raise another issue, namely why did particular communes come to play such an important role? One comparison has been made between Protestant Le Chambon and the nearby Catholic enclave of Sauges. Both had the same rock, the same winter snows, the same altitude, the same economy, the same isolation in the mountains and the same capacity for resistance. In the Protestant care from 1685 onwards, and in Catholic Sauges, to the Republican troops enforcing the inventarization of the churches.[175] One was a centre for rescue and the other was not. As we have seen, this has little or nothing to do with the ideologies of the different religions but everything to do with communal mobilization by religious or secular leaders. The mobilization of Catholic communities may not have been so common, but examples did exist. This, in turn, prompts another interesting possibility: of Catholic resistance being prompted in part by a spirit of opposition to the secular Third Republic and its traditions of anticlerical legislation after 1871.[176] However, this should be tempered for both creeds by the continuing loyalty shown by all Church leaders to Vichy as a bulwark against the perceived greater threat of communism.

The particularities of the French case also need to be stressed. French Jews were never sought by the authorities in the same way as their foreign counterparts, and many were able to disappear unseen and survived the occupation without further alarms. The existence of the Vichy zone and the absence of direct German influence before November 1942 inevitably aided both rescue and survival, although it is important not to understate the malevolence of Pétain's regime. There were many Vichy functionaries that outdid even the Germans in their pursuit of those it regarded as enemies. Even after the occupation of the entire country, the existence of the Italian zone before September 1943 proved a real bonus in sheltering appreciable numbers of Jews—and even facilitated their escape into Italy thereafter. Fluctuating political attitudes in Switzerland, while never entirely predictable, did nonetheless make the Alpine frontier a possible escape route, as did the Pyrenean frontier into Spain. Finally, France also threw up its fair share of exceptional cases. These were ethnic and religious groups that did not fit the Nazi stereotype of 'the Jew', and whose cases had to be referred back to the quasi-academic research institutes in Germany for resolution. For the most part, these groups seem to have retained their exceptional status and were thus exempted from deportation, albeit sometimes for blatantly political reasons, but it is worth pointing out that it was almost invariably the Vichy functionaries who pressed for their inclusion and the Germans who remained uncommitted.

In assessing the incidence of rescue in France it remains important to stress that it only ever involved a very small minority of the French population. Pre-existing personal or institutional links played a crucial part in instigating or facilitating the rescue through escape or hiding of Jews. That said, the majority of the population never came into contact with Jews, nor were they ever asked to help. Explaining this neutrality or indifference in any quantifiable terms is impossible, and there is every reason to suppose that some elements within society were more predisposed to help than others, but by the same token, this also created anomalies when it came to assessing their longer term role and place in the pantheon of the righteous. For example, eight families in the small village of Noirveau in the Bocage of the Vendee hid eight defectors and seven Jews, plus others who came for 'supplementary feeding'. Although subject to a German raid, the fugitives were spirited away and not betrayed by any of the locals arrested. However, at the liberation, the community gave shelter to a 'German-loving' colonel, two women with shaved heads, and a child from the local gaol.[177] In the same spirit and on a much wider scale, both CIMADE and the Quakers saw it as their moral duty to ameliorate the lot of collaborators after the war because they were now the ones in need.[178]

7

Jewish Self-Help in Belgium

The persecution of the Jews in Belgium is probably the least well-known episode of the Holocaust in Western Europe, at least for non-Francophone readers.[1] In total 24,906 Jews and 351 gypsies were deported from the transit camp at the Dossin-Kazerne in Mechelen in twenty-eight convoys and a further 218 were taken in five much smaller transports. This represented approximately 40–45 per cent of the total Jewish population. Of these only 1,337 returned.[2] Thus either through their own efforts, or those of Jewish or non-Jewish organizations, or a combination of all three, some 60 per cent of the Jews in Belgium at the beginning of the occupation survived the war, the vast majority inside the country. Hidden with neighbours and friends, or further afield in the houses of strangers, or in religious or secular institutions, they were supported by an unknown number of active rescuers and bystanders. As with France, the context may hold the key to the incidence of their survival.

The Jews of Belgium and their Christian Neighbours

Nineteenth-century Belgium had only a very small Jewish community and, although seen primarily as a transit land, it did absorb numbers of East European Jews between 1881 and the 1930s who chose, or were forced by lack of funds, to stop in Europe and not make the journey westwards to the New World. This immigration was largely made up of people from the lower-middle classes: shopkeepers, small businessmen, artisans, and traders, concentrated in the garment and luxury goods trades and in the diamond industry.[3] Their rather precarious existence was hard-hit by the economic depression of the early 1930s and this presaged an increased level of pauperization. The smaller, older established and generally more prosperous Belgian Jewish community was liberal, patriotic, and assimilationist, whereas Zionism, socialism, and communism were more prevalent among the majority immigrant elements, the latter giving rise to the foreign workers' organization, Main d'Oeuvre Étrangère (MOE).[4] The distribution of this population was also marked by its continued concentration in Brussels and Antwerp.[5] The differing nature of these two major Jewish communities meant that communism was more successful in Brussels than in Antwerp, where liberal Zionism had its strongholds.[6] The policies of the socialist political and trade union organizations towards the clothing and diamond trades also served to drive many Jewish workers towards communism.[7] It has been argued that the Jewish communists had become isolated by the late 1930s, condemned as communists by the wider Jewish community, and seen as 'foreign' by other political parties and the trade unions for retaining their ethnic identity. Nonetheless, they continued to play an important role within the Belgian Communist Party and learned the skills of clandestine activity,[8] skills that were to serve them well after the occupation began.

By 1 April 1942, on the eve of the first deportations, 52.6 per cent of the Jews were in Brussels and only 38.4 per cent were in Antwerp.[9] The Antwerp statistics also betray another feature of the Jewish population in Belgium, namely the overwhelmingly small number of Belgian citizens among them—a mere 8 per cent, while 54 per cent were formerly or actually Polish; 11 per cent Dutch; 6 per cent Romanian; 8 per cent Czechs; 4 per cent Russians; 4 per cent Germans and the rest 5 per cent.[10] The proportions in Brussels were different; mainly in terms of the German representation, where this was around 21 per cent and the Polish contingent was much the same at 58.5 per cent.[11] Most of the Eastern European Jews in Belgium had been resident for some considerable time, and it has often been suggested that their unwillingness to regularize their position and take out Belgian nationality was a result of an inherent fear of state bureaucracy, based largely on their experiences in Tsarist Russia. However, it is also true that Belgium did not make naturalization easy by insisting on proof of a 'bond' with the country, a ten-year residence period (after 1932), and by making the process increasingly costly.[12] In Brussels, the Jewish community was dispersed over a number of suburbs and therefore less visible than its counterpart in Antwerp, which was concentrated in one district near the

Map 7.1 Belgium, 1940–44

city centre.[13] Antwerp's community was also more wedded to its religious roots, with a thriving synagogue and religious school culture, something not shared by the more secular Jews of Brussels. There were also some differences in occupations, with Brussels being more associated with the leather trades and Antwerp with diamond cutting.[14]

In spite of the growth of radical nationalist and anti-democratic movements in the 1920s and 1930s, political or racial antisemitism was almost unknown in the country. Cultural antisemitism in religious and economic circles was more prevalent, and existed not only in right-wing milieux, but was also evident in labour organizations. Those in trades perceived to be most under pressure from 'Jewish' competition, the diamond workers in Antwerp and the textile workers in Brussels, demonstrated a virulent antisemitism during the depression years of the later 1930s.[15] This did not dissipate as the decade ended, but culminated on 25 August 1939 in the aftermath of the announcement of the Nazi-Soviet Pact, in anti-Jewish riots instigated by the Volksverwering[16] and other extremist groups. One telling assessment of the wider mood in the city was that even the Catholic *Gazet van Antwerpen* described the riots as 'spontaneous' and that 'the anger of the good citizens of Antwerp was justified'.[17] These manifestations of antisemitic sentiment were countered by a number of associations and leagues.[18] In Antwerp, Mayor Camille Huysmans complained to the prime minister in April 1938 about the Belgian security services targeting Jews in the city and expelling them. Huysmans' plea was prompted not by any regard for the Jews themselves, but by a fear that the diamond industry might be moved to South Africa, with disastrous results for the city and for the Belgian exchequer.[19]

The country was overwhelmingly Catholic, with 98 per cent of the population baptized and 80 per cent of weddings and funerals taking place according to Catholic rites.[20] Even though only just over 50 per cent of the population attended church on a regular basis, more than half of all children went to Catholic schools. These statistics do obscure one potentially important regional distinction within the country, namely that the Flemish-speaking areas were far more devout whereas secularism and socialism had made much greater inroads into the industrialized French-speaking areas. At the outbreak of war, Catholic spiritual needs were attended to by 9,700 priests, with a further 12,000 seminarists, 12,700 monks, and 49,600 nuns. In addition to its spiritual role, the Church played a major role in Belgian society, being heavily involved in all manner of charitable and secular work: controlling a network of schools and a whole array of charitable institutions, caring for the sick and elderly, organizing youth groups and ministering to the poor.

The Church had been led from 1926 onwards by Cardinal Archbishop of Mechelen, Jozef Ernst van Roey. His reaction to the persecution of the Jews inside Nazi Germany was therefore of crucial importance in determining popular attitudes inside Belgian society. In the pre-war period, he made no formal protests. This has been attributed to a traditional antisemitism and also to his belief in the possible links between Judaism, Bolshevism, and Freemasonry.[21] Nevertheless, questions about, and relations towards, the Jewish community continued to be a visible, but far from prominent part of Catholic concerns in the 1920s and 1930s. From the mid-1920s, a movement arose to organize 'prayer days' for the conversion of the Jews, an initiative supported by, among others Monsignor Kerkhofs, the Bishop of Liège and his counterpart Bishop Heylen of Namur, as well as priests from their dioceses.[22]

The short-lived Katholiek Bureau voor Israël served to demonstrate the limits of van Roey's action. Established by Catholic intellectuals in 1936 to improve communications between Catholics and Jews in Antwerp, its activities were largely in the form of lectures designed to undermine prejudices about Judaism and Freemasonry, and to combat racism.[23] Within two years, he was forced to order its dissolution, ostensibly because of the conflicts it was causing with radical Flemish nationalism, but more pertinently because its objectives were opposed by large sections of traditional Catholic opinion on the grounds that it was a doorway to clerical–masonic collusion or that it was becoming too heavily involved in work to counter antisemitism. Thereafter, the main aim of intervention to aid the Jews would be 'limited to saving souls'.[24] However, its contacts with the Jewish community did serve to create the basis for at least one rescue organization during the occupation.[25]

This suggests that even van Roey, as head of the Catholic Church in Belgium, could only steer a course that was approved of by the majority of his clergy and congregation—and many remained heavily influenced by traditional forms of antisemitism, accentuated by the economic depression of the 1930s and by anti-Jewish articles and commentaries that continued to appear in the Catholic press.[26] More pertinently, these newspapers and periodicals generally saw the 'obvious' solution to the Jewish problem in terms of conversion to Christianity.[27]

Van Roey nevertheless continued to wield substantial influence. Once the occupation had become a reality, he maintained his close links with the King and instructed the faithful to accept the German military victory and maintain their loyalty to the Crown.[28] As with many of his fellow bishops and archbishops, he saw his main task as protecting the spiritual and material well-being of the Church and was not inclined to engage in immediate conflicts with the occupying Germans. In this respect, he was sometimes compared unfavourably with his predecessor, Cardinal Mercier, who had been more outspoken during the Great War.[29] At the same time, and in contrast to Mercier, he was considered more even-handed in his dealings with the Flemish-speaking parts of the country, realizing that they had to be won over lest nationalism and separatism took root and threatened the unitary nature of the state. In the post-1918 world, it was Flanders that had become the economically vibrant region of the country and also returned forty-six of the eighty Catholic deputies to the Belgian second chamber in 1921.[30]

Important before the occupation, the Church's role became even more central as the Germans shut institutions down or 'co-ordinated' other more overtly political organizations. For pragmatic reasons and to avoid any unnecessary disruption to the running of Belgian public life, the German military government left the Church and its institutions alone.[31] Keeping the Church free from association with political groupings during the occupation undoubtedly paid dividends At the same time, van Roey did not make any public protests about the treatment of the Jews before the deportations began and his efforts were limited to the private sphere, with a limited number of specific interventions and some discreet help to those in need.[32]

Jewish Self-Help

The importance of Jewish self-help is even more marked in Belgium than in France. The German invasion of 10 May 1940 resulted in a flight south that included many Jewish community leaders and members of the elite including the Grand Rabbi, Joseph Wiener. Thus when the dust settled, the Jewish population was left with only the shells of its former structures and with many missing personalities. Only the Jewish military chaplain, Rabbi Salomon Ullmann, and the Rabbi of Antwerp, Markus Rottenberg remained in the country.[33] Consequently, the Secretary-General of the Justice Ministry asked Ullmann to take over the role of Chief Rabbi and re-form the Consistory with its remaining members. Ullmann later recalled that the impetus to create some form of representative body was deemed essential to maintain a 'presence' and so that the community had somewhere to turn in a time of crisis.[34] It maintained the central Jewish welfare organization in Brussels that catered for the increasing numbers of indigent Jews who looked for aid, and it also took over the running of various Jewish institutions such as old people's homes and orphanages.[35] From the very beginning, Ullmann was in close contact with the German authorities, and in the spring of 1941, the organization was formally constituted as a religious and lay Co-ordinating Committee for Jewish

Communities to represent Jewish interests, handing a tool to the Nazis that gave them enormous potential power. The Germans also insisted that the committee include a number of German Jewish refugees,[36] but it remained largely dominated by upper–middle-class Jewish 'notables' with little real contact with the Jewish proletariat.[37] The creation of this committee, and its close relationship with the occupying Germans provided plenty of warning signals for those prepared to read them.

As in France, the first Jewish victims of the Nazis in Belgium were members of the communist and socialist movements. In spite of the Nazi-Soviet pact, Gestapo attention was focused on the communists from the outset, and many activists were arrested and imprisoned, first at the prison of St Gilles and later at the infamous concentration camp at Fort Breendonck.[38] After the invasion of the Soviet Union, communists and other former Soviet citizens were removed from the country altogether and sent to camps inside Germany.[39] This repression served to show what to expect from German rule, but most middle-class citizens were prepared to believe that the communists were a special case—singled out by the Nazis for particular attention. In the meantime, the majority of apolitical Jews in Belgium had suffered the standard diet of Nazi antisemitic measures common to the rest of occupied Western Europe: registration of assets, bans on ritual slaughter, confiscations of radios, and the labelling of shops and businesses as 'Jewish enterprises'. In addition, Jews were also required to register as Jews on a special list held by the town halls. This was carried out with varying degrees of enthusiasm by every local authority in the country. In Antwerp, it was pursued with undisguised alacrity by the civil servants after the nomination of Leon Delwaide as mayor of the city on 8 December 1940. His appointment also gave rise to a series of antisemitic actions specific to that city carried out by the VNV leadership in April 1941. This included the breaking of Jewish shop windows, the plundering of diamond merchants, and an attack on Rabbi Rottenberg's house, with two synagogues also being set on fire—events which were enthusiastically filmed by the cameramen of the German *Propagandastaffel* IIIB.[40]

On 29 August 1941, Jews were placed under a curfew from 8 p.m. to 7 a.m. and had their residence limited to four major cities: Brussels, Antwerp, Liège and Charleroi. After 1 December 1941 they were excluded from all public and private non-Jewish premises, and at the very end of the year, Jewish children were excluded from the existing school system in expectation that special Jewish schools would be created.[41] In the meantime, on 25 November 1941, the *Sicherheitspolizei* had decreed that the presidents of the various Jewish communities across the country were to become the managing committee of a more formalized representative body, the Association des Juifs de Belgique (AJB). It effectively superseded the Coordination Committee, but the executive board created on 22 December 1940 was still led by the Chief Rabbi, with Nico Workum as his deputy and Maurice Benedictus as secretary. Essentially, it was Benedictus, who had had little contact with Judaism, who took on the day-to-day running of the organization.[42]

Based in Brussels, the organization had branches in other major cities and it suited the German purpose of isolating the Jews and also of separating their welfare needs from the rest of Belgian society.[43] It was supposedly compulsory for Jews to register, and the organization collected obligatory dues while providing welfare and schooling for children. In fact, there were a substantial number of Jews who took the decision not to register, not primarily because they had precognition of what was to come, but because of the dangers they already faced from the threat of forced labour.[44] The AJB oversaw the publication of German ordinances to the Jewish community and also advertised the punishments for non-compliance for individuals, their families, and the community at large, adopting a 'policy of presence' and a justification based on the idea that it was the 'lesser of two evils'.[45] Indeed, the interests of the whole organization were very much skewed towards those of the Belgian Jewish bourgeoisie and had little empathy with the majority of non-Belgian Jews in the country, even to the point where one of its leaders, Salomon Vandenberg, celebrated the fact that, after the intervention of King Leopold III, Belgian Jews had been exempted from labour service in Poland. On the same day, his diary recorded the shortages of fruit and vegetables, and later in the month the fact that the AJB had 'unfortunately' been required to distribute the call-up notices for forced labour.[46]

On 24 September 1942, six Jewish leaders, including Ullmann and Benedictus, were arrested and spent fifteen days in KZ Breendonck before being released in response to an appeal from Cardinal van Roey and pressure from the military administration.[47] After this, the credibility of the AJB was largely destroyed and its functions were reduced to educational and welfare work. For its functionaries in Brussels, there was still some degree of protection from special cards that indicated their status and exempted them from labour service. These cards were much sought after and served to protect those from the Belgian Jewish bourgeoisie who formed the basis of the AJB's staff, but were also clearly available for sale to those with money to buy them.[48]

Thus far, the Germans had only targeted non-Belgian Jews, in line with Himmler's assurances on 9 July 1942 that the Belgian Jews would not be liable for deportation 'for the time being'. However, this was undermined when raids targeted Belgian Jews on 3–4 September 1943.[49] By this stage, the AJB had been reduced to a single organization based in Brussels, and most of the Jews still living legally in the country were either its employees or housed in one of its welfare institutions. For reasons that remain unclear, these institutions managed to provide more-or-less permanent protection for some elements within the Jewish community. The best example is of the 600 children who lived legally in AJB orphanages and remained untouched by the Germans until the organization wound up its operations on 28 August 1944, at which point the children were ushered into hiding until Allied forces arrived in Brussels less than a week later.

A post-war assessment of the AJB's adherents by Pinkus Broder, the Secretary of the CDJ in Charleroi, identified four separate groups. There were the self-interested leaders who carried out the orders of the Germans to the letter and sold protection to other Jews. There were the rich Jews who bought the protection offered. There were also the ordinary Jews who had jobs as AJB functionaries because they saw it as a means of salvation, and finally among all the collaborators, there was also a group of honest people who were disgusted by the activities of the AJB but did not have the courage to go underground, but instead sought out the resistance to provide whatever help they could.[50] The post-war debate centred on whether the activities of this latter group had been of any real benefit and whether they outweighed the accusation of collaboration made against all aspects of the AJB's work. Certainly, even though the AJB was widely condemned at the time and subsequently for its slavish adherence to German orders, it was argued that it provided a haven and a cover for some aspects of Jewish resistance. Broder's report was sceptical, arguing that Jews working for the AJB and thus wearing stars on their clothing could bring nothing but trouble to Jews living illegally. They were often followed by the Gestapo and could easily be made to betray contacts. Nevertheless, the AJB did provide money for some Jews living illegally, and several high-ranking members and employees were able to have parallel existences as members of the resistance.[51] However, trust in the AJB's ability to protect the Jewish community had always been limited and its pretences had cut little ice in the face of increased German persecutions and deportations. This opened the door for others to act, and to assume de facto leadership roles, albeit in clandestine forms.

The co-operation between different welfare and resistance organizations in Belgium during the occupation, coupled with the willingness of Jewish and non-Jewish groups across the political spectrum to work together provided the basis for an organization unique in Western Europe. For a long time before the German invasion, there had been a number of secular organizations devoted to helping the Jews, many of which were oriented towards the extreme left. For example, the communist Main d'Oeuvre Étrangère (MOE) helped all immigrants, whereas Solidarité Juive had been created in 1939 specifically to help Jewish political refugees from Poland.[52] However, a greater degree of unity occurred only when the threat of mass deportation was on the horizon. The Comité de Défense des Juifs (CDJ) was formed as a national structure devoted exclusively to helping the Jews threatened by Nazi policies and opposed to the collaborationism of the AJB. It was an initiative that emerged from far-left Jewish circles more or less simultaneously in five major cities, albeit centred in Brussels, and in response to the first threats of deportation in July 1942.[53] However, its inception owed much to the elements within the Independence Front (FI),[54] a resistance movement founded on 15 March 1941 by the journalist Fernand Demany who brought together leaders from a number of different political strands.[55] Indeed, both the FI and the Belgian Communist Party had been instrumental in warning the Jewish population about potential dangers long before the CDJ was formed.[56]

Its inspiration and long-time leader was Hertz (Joseph/Ghert) Jospa, a communist of Romanian/Bessarabian origins, whose wife, Yvonne, was also to play a major role in the organization. He was joined in Brussels, by the left-wing, Catholic Emile Hambresin, former editor of the periodical *L'Avant Garde* and president of the Comité Belge contre le Racisme. Both men were engineers by profession and had known each other in the 1930s as members of the Ligue pour combattre l'Antisémitisme.[57] They were joined by six others, including Abusz (Abous) Werber of the left-wing Poale-Zion, and Israël (Maurice) Mandelbaum of Solidarité Juive. Whereas these three could be regarded as representatives of illegal groups, the intention was to create as broad a base as possible for the new organization. Thus the right-wing orientated Chaïm Perelman, Professor in the Faculty of

Philosophy and Letters at the Free University in Brussels was included. It was his credibility in the wider Jewish community that was credited with bringing bourgeois middle-class elements into the organization, and the early meetings in June and July 1942 were held at his house.[58] In addition to being involved with the CDJ, he was also one of the men associated with the collaborationist AJB.[59] The other representatives from 'legal' Jewry were the industrialist Benjamin (Benno) Nykerk and the secretary of the Brussels Jewish community, Edouard Rotkel,[60] both of whom were associated with mainstream Zionism, and Eugene Hellendael, another rich industrialist, who was invited to join in his capacity as a member of the Brussels branch of the AJB.[61] Although many of the bourgeois elements involved in the creation of the CDJ were wary of becoming involved with left-wing organizations and apostate Jewish communists like Jospa, they were prepared to stifle these fears in pursuit of an organization that would help the community as a whole.[62]

As the CDJ grew, it was subdivided into four sections: propaganda, finance, false papers and material aid.[63] The propaganda element was mainly directed against the collaborationist AJB, and in advising Jews not to co-operate with its directives and to resist German measures. This was done in many ways, but included production of the illegal newspapers in French, Flemish, and Yiddish— Le Flambeau, De Vrije Gedachte, Unser Kampf, Ounzer Wort and Notre Lutte (Charleroi)—specifically for the Jewish community.[64] This project was aided by individual contacts between Jews and non-Jews in various professions and the links made through membership of the FI. Print runs varied between 1,000 and 5,000 copies per issue.[65] The level of integration and co-operation between organizations is remarkable when compared with the situation elsewhere in Western Europe, but the scale of the CDJ operations in helping an estimated 15,000 people in hiding required huge amounts of money and resources. It was helped with food parcels provided by the Red Cross, ration stamps, and even by the German-inspired Secours d'Hiver (Winter Help). In this regard, aid came from Roger van Praag who had returned from military service and been offered a job working for the Secours d'Hiver as an alternative for government employees to working directly with the Germans. More remarkable was the fact that he was able to hide his Jewish origin, avoid registration and also to falsify an 'Aryan' background for his family.[66] Practical help also came from groups and organizations across the political spectrum, including the Secours Mutuel, Secours Populaire,

Secours Sioniste, and Solidarité Juive. Financing its work was inevitably a headache, and the CDJ began by making appeals to rich Jews for donations, as well as to banks and other organizations such as the Oeuvre Nationale de l'Enfance (ONE). Some small steps were taken to secure funds, for example by making richer Jews pay double for CDJ services in order to subsidize the rescue of poorer Jews. Money also came from non-Jewish sources, both institutional and private. Benno Nykerk was able to persuade the Banque de Bruxelles to provide a *prêt d'honneur* (unsecured loan) for the sum of BFr.3 million in instalments of BFr.250,000, and in May 1943 he travelled illegally to Switzerland for the first time to meet Saly Mayer, the JDC representative for Europe in Switzerland, who guaranteed a monthly subvention of SFr 20,000, raised progressively to SFr.100,000 per month, which was then smuggled into Belgium. At much the same time, David Ferdman, who later took charge of CDJ finances,[67] made contact with Georges Tehlin of the Save the Children Fund and obtained two subventions of BFr.500,000.[68] Some money also came from individuals in the form of letters of credit, but further substantial amounts came from the Société Belge de Banque (BFr. 5,000,000 during the occupation) and the Société Générale, with the latter providing BFr.1,100,000 between March 1944 and the liberation.[69] These were huge sums but had to be seen against the size of the CDJ operations. Around June 1943, the organization was spending BFr.300,000 per month just on help for adults in hiding, and the total budget during the occupation was estimated to have reached a staggering BFr.48 million.[70]

Practical actions were divided between three sub committees, one to deal with adults, one specifically for children, and a third for those engaged in resistance activity.[71] The work of the 'adult' committee involved finding or forging false papers for Jews in Belgium, Dutch Jews in transit southwards, and for labour draft evaders. Not content with this, the CDJ also tried to ensure that the new identities were included in the population registers of selected localities where there were sympathetic civil servants, to give them a greater veneer of legality, and security against German investigations. The CDJ also had systems for hiding Jews within the population, most notably as domestic servants. Its work with children was equally extensive. The organization benefited from the creation of Jewish schools by the AJB as these had only been in operation for a few months when they were subject to raids by the Gestapo. This led the director to shut the schools while at the same time seeing all the mothers individually to warn them to hide their children immediately and to offer assistance. The lists of Jewish students' names and addresses compiled by the schools proved invaluable to the CDJ in tracking down and helping the threatened children.[72] A whole sub-section (Section Enfance) was created and run by Maurice Heiber (Héber) and benefited from close co-operation with ONE led by Yvonne Nevéjean and with institutions of the Catholic Church. Also important was the work of Suzanne Moons-Lepetit (known as Brigitte) who was brought into the CDJ by Emile Hambresin and who was instrumental in finding placements for Jewish children.[73] It has been estimated that in total the CDJ directly saved 2,443 Jewish children and was instrumental in helping many more.[74]

The organization was further aided by some of its leaders continuing in roles at the AJB as a means of gaining information and subverting the latter's operations. An example was where mothers contacting the social service of the AJB were redirected to the offices of ONE or another organization capable of taking their child to safety. Full details were taken and then the mother was referred to another office. This allowed the information and the applicants to be checked before any formal steps were taken to help the child. On the assumption that the story checked out, the parents were then offered the opportunity to have their child go into hiding and the infant was then placed in the care of the Section Enfance.[75]

The cosmopolitan nature of the CDJ meant that the organization could cater for, and advise, representatives of all sections of the Jewish community in Belgium. The CDJ established 'distributors' in Brussels who acted as go-betweens—serving particular communities or groups. They were responsible for delivering ration cards, false identity papers, monthly payments of BFr.500 per person, and all the other materials needed by those in hiding.[76] Methods varied enormously as many hosts did not want regular visits by strangers or by people who 'looked Jewish' as many of the distributors reportedly did.[77] The organization had to work against the influence of the AJB and that of the Gestapo, who contrived to keep all Jewish institutions open after the deportations began, as a means of demonstrating that normal conditions still existed. At the same time, some 'distributors' benefited from AJB documentation that protected them from summary arrest and deportation.

The CDJ was able to contact non-Jewish organizations to find addresses and hiding places for around 12,000 adults, or almost a quarter of the entire Jewish population. While it had used Catholic institutions and welfare organizations for the placement of children, the same solutions could not be found for adults. Placing more than one or two adult Jews in convents or cloisters would soon be exposed by Gestapo raids, and it was believed that once one cache of people had been discovered, all other institutions would then immediately become targets, thus jeopardizing others in hiding, including many children. This caution was later vindicated by events in Rome, where Gestapo raids on convents discovered numbers of Jews in hiding, providing the excuse for other raids on Catholic institutions in the city and elsewhere.[78] Providing false papers was an essential element: papers that could also provide an alternative address where the individual was not known and had not been registered as a Jew. In this work, the CDJ was helped by its association with the FI, sympathetic local mayors and amenable civil servants who incorporated false identities into existing population records.[79] Indeed, this system seems to hold the key to understanding how so many adult Jews survived with the help of the CDJ, not so much by hiding 'underground' but by living false lives more or less in the open, while limiting their movements to reduce the risk of scrutiny of their papers.

In total, the CDJ may have helped up to 30,000 individuals with false papers, encompassing not only the Jews in Belgium, but also those passing through the country, and several thousand labour draft evaders. Its work in helping Jews avoid arrest and deportation did involve finding hiding places through its contacts with other institutions and organizations across the country, but it is clear that in many cases, 'rescue' did not involve non-Jewish rescuers as hosts, but was based on the idea that Jews could hide behind false identities that were difficult for the authorities to see through, and on the ability to move around within and between cities if suspicions were aroused, or the threat of discovery became too great.

Direct Action: The Twentieth Convoy

In addition to its welfare and charitable work, the CDJ also played an active resistance role. One of its key tasks was to subvert the work of the AJB, but its members were also actively involved in intercepting denunciations to the Gestapo or German military police, and in warning those betrayed. They also played a major role in the famous, and possibly unique, interception of a deportation train, the twentieth convoy, and the escape of several hundred Jewish deportees.[80] Up to that point, very few Jews had escaped from the trains that had left the holding centre at Mechelen en route to Poland: only the sixteenth and seventeenth convoys of 31 October 1942 had 'lost' any appreciable numbers of deportees by the time the trains reached the Belgian frontier—229 in a total of 1,937. However, most of the people on these two trains were men who had been taken from labour service with the Todt Organization to fill quotas for the deportations to the East.[81] Thus the social composition of these two trains was very different from other transports of the same period. Steinberg records an increasing level of resistance from the Jews being rounded up by the police and the German authorities in the last months of 1942.[82]

By the spring of 1943, knowledge of what was happening in the forests of Eastern Poland had become far more widespread. In March, the underground newspaper *Le Flambeau* published a report from a Belgian who had returned from Warsaw who talked of the liquidation of the ghetto and the extermination of the inhabitants. It had also passed on radio reports the previous month about the Nazis murdering Jews.[83] Within the CDJ leadership, there were plans to do something to stop the transports from Belgium. For this, Jospa needed the help of the Jewish elements within the armed partisans. His contact in the FI, Jean Terfve, refused to approve the plan, and it was eventually passed to Georges Livschitz via Maurice Bolle. Livschitz also failed to get help from resistance and partisan groups, so he decided to carry out the raid himself with the help of two non-Jewish friends, Jean Franklemon and Robert Maistriau.[84]

The twentieth convoy of 19 April 1943 became the target. It was more representative in terms of its victims, but was different from previous convoys in other ways. It was larger, containing a total of 1,639 people rather than the usual 900–1,000. For the first time, the transport was made up of 30–35 cattle wagons surrounded by barbed wire and not third-class passenger cars. The guard units were not Flemish guards and men from the Jewish Section of the SD but a special detachment of *Schutzpolizei*.[85] Various testimonies from those who escaped from this transport provide a picture of what took place. It is clear that some deportees had managed to smuggle tools onto the train with a view to escaping.[86] Once en route, the floorboards and bars were attacked and people in a number of wagons were able to jump or drop onto the permanent way below. Others took advantage of the raid carried out by Livschitz, Maistriau, and Franklemon. They were armed only with a small revolver and a lantern covered with red paper, but managed to stop the train by convincing the engine driver that there was an obstruction on the track. As the German guards at the front of the train did not leave their wagon, Maistriau was able to open one or two of the wagon doors, allowing perhaps fifteen prisoners to escape, and even giving them money provided by the CDJ to enable them to escape back to Brussels.[87] Their plans to empty the entire train were confounded by the presence of the strengthened guard unit and the difficulty of opening the wagon doors. However, other testimonies suggest that the doors that had been opened were not re-secured before the train continued its journey, thus allowing others to escape further down the line.[88]

Estimates suggest that 231 people attempted to escape from this one transport and that twenty-three were killed in the attempt.[89] Some of those injured during escape attempts were taken to the hospital at Tienen/Tirlemont.[90] Livschitz attempted to spirit them away, but his plan was undermined when one of the men used to provide transport, the Russian Count Pierre Romanovitch, turned out to be working for the Germans, and six of the injured were taken back into German custody.[91] Livschitz and Franklemon were betrayed to the Germans in the same way and held at KZ Breendonck. Livschitz was designated as a hostage and shot in February 1944 as a reprisal for other unrelated resistance actions. Maistriau continued working for the resistance Groupe G, but was eventually caught and deported to Buchenwald where he survived until the liberation.[92]

The work of the CDJ carried enormous dangers for its members, and its leadership structures had to be revised as the Gestapo tightened its net on both the Jews and the resistance organizations in Belgium. Hellendael and Rotkel were arrested and deported in September 1942. Heiber was caught in May 1943, followed by Jospa in June. Of these, only Jospa survived the war.[93] At this point, the whole organization had to be completely reorganized, with Roger van Praag and Maurice Bolle taking the lead, and bringing in Professor Allard of the Université Libre de Bruxelles to re-establish contact with London, and Jacques Pels to maintain contacts with the Belgian banks.[94]

To some extent, the CDJ provincial affiliates in Antwerp, Ghent, Liège and Charleroi/Namur operated separately from the centre. In Antwerp, the creation of a CDJ branch was complicated by the flight of many individuals who might have formed its core. German plans to put Jews to work on the Atlantic Wall in June 1942 persuaded the leadership of the communist MOE to move its members out of the city. Thus there was no obvious organizational structure to establish a branch of the CDJ in the city. Indeed, it was not until the end of 1943 that such an organization really existed. Instead, there developed three smaller and independent resistance and self-help groups. Two of these were run by Jews who had escaped from German forced labour on the Atlantic Wall: Josef Sterngold and Abraham Manaster. The third was organized by Leopold Flam, a Jew from a poor family of Russian origins who had become an atheist and had been a member of the Communist Party. He had become a naturalized Belgian before the war and worked as a teacher. Fleeing to France in 1940, he returned to Antwerp and established links with other left-wing individuals, both Jewish and non-Jewish. Flam created the basis of a resistance organization, but his early links to the CDJ in Brussels were limited to ideas about a Flemish-language newspaper for the Jews, and he was arrested on 12 May 1943.[95]

The development of his organization into a branch of the CDJ was largely the work of five or six women. These included Mathilde Castermans-Ruys, a Protestant and director of a crèche in the city who was one Flam's first co-workers, as well as the clerk Virginie Claassens-Mathieu, and the nurse Hubertina Peeters-Aretz—both from Catholic circles. Also involved was the trader Clementina van Beylen-van Damme. Her family background was unusual—and potentially more dangerous for a resistance organization—in that her brother had been a member of the National Socialist Flemish Workers Party before the war and had been interned and deported in May 1940 as a potential traitor. None of this prevented his sister from joining the Independence Front in early 1942 and becoming involved in Flam's network.[96] Peeters-Aretz' background was equally unusual, in that she was the daughter of a German father and Belgian mother, was born in Germany but fled to Belgium in 1936 because her strong Catholic sympathies and anti-Nazism had put her on German blacklists. Two of her brothers were NSDAP members but she retained her anti-Nazism and helped refugees in the later 1930s. In May 1940 she fled to France, only to return to work at the German military hospital in Antwerp in the autumn. Here she came into contact with Edward Salman, the curate of the Sint-Jozefkerk in the Jewish quarter of the city. The involvement of both women in the work of the CDJ and the left-wing Independence Front presented something of a contradiction as both were virulently anticommunist and objected strongly to the idea that their work might be funded by 'Russian' money. They had to be persuaded by Castermans-Ruys that it didn't matter if the money came from the Devil, it was needed to help people.[97] Claassens-Mathieu was a clerk in a metal company and married to a plumber. Ostensibly the couple's involvement had begun when the Jewish partner of Claassens' aunt had had to go underground in October and was hidden in their house.[98] Both subsequently became active in helping Jews, and at particular moments may have had eight to ten Jews in their own house, as well as brokering hiding places elsewhere. One of these was an empty house in nearby Mortsel where, with the full knowledge of the owner and the concierge, they accommodated seven Jews in hiding for twenty-two months until the liberation.[99] Claassens also enlisted help from non-Jewish bourgeois elements after they witnessed the brutal arrest of the Belgian Jews in the summer of 1943.[100]

There is no certainty about the degree of co-operation between these three organizations in Antwerp before the foundation of a unified CDJ in the summer of 1943, or any precision about the numbers of Jews they managed to help. The Manaster group reputedly found places for 175 Jewish children from Antwerp in private homes or in (Catholic) institutions, and a further sixty Jewish women were hidden as non-Jews, helped by the provision of false identity cards and ration stamps.[101] These came from an intriguing scheme created by Alfons Goethals. Each month, the rationing authorities sent a quantity of reserve stamps to each local authority to deal with emergencies and shortfalls. These had to be accounted for and returned each month, but Goethals hit on the idea of returning forged stamps and sending the real ones to the CDJ to support those in hiding.[102]

Flam was aware that his network was in danger as people talked too much, but felt there was little he could do except go on helping those in need, and his fears were finally realized on 15 March 1944 when nearly all its leaders were arrested by the notorious Jew-hunter Felix Lauterborn. Taken to the SD headquarters, both men and women were severely beaten by the Gestapo and SS-men who included one of Flam's own students.[103] Other arrests soon followed as the Gestapo and Jew-hunters continued to roll up the networks as the Allied armies approached from the south. Manaster was caught on 2 August 1944, and only Sterngold managed to stay one step ahead of his pursuers while still remaining active.

In Charleroi, the leading personalities were the communist former mineworker Pinkus Broder, the engineer Max Katz who was affiliated to Poale-Zion, and the tailor Sem Makowski. It was fortunate in having contacts with trustworthy elements within the local AJB, so that when the SD planned a raid to arrest the community, it was given fictitious

Figure 7.1. Identity Card of Felix Lauterborn, antisemite and wartime Jew hunter

Source: Ministerie van Justitie, Brussels

addresses, allowing the whole community, including the leadership, time to go underground.[104] In Liège, the leading group included the printer Albert Wolf, and Jeanne Otgen, his non-Jewish wife, as well as Abraham Federman.[105] Wolf, a Belgian national of Dutch Jewish origins who had been a member of the Comité de vigilance des intellectuals antifascistes (CVIA) in the 1930s, had joined the FI and had written and distributed resistance tracts after escaping from captivity as a prisoner of war in June 1940. He had been driven underground in 1941 and had come into contact with the CDJ through Jospa's sister, Liuba. His position within Liègeois society, being barely observant as a Jew and more at home in the majority Catholic milieux, gave him a wide range of contacts within the city.[106] This was reflected in the social make-up of the local CDJ itself that included both Jews and non-Jews from widely differing backgrounds. As with its sister organizations elsewhere, none of the members were paid for their work, and all the money raised went into helping those underground and into funding resistance against the occupying Germans. Its work was assisted by having one of its members remaining inside the AJB, and also by the Catholic authorities providing at least two suitable clandestine meeting places.

The various city committees were only brought together as a single organization in July 1943, but by this time, collective activities in Liège had grown to include every aspect of rescue. Federman had been forced to go underground at the end of August 1942, and had been 'hidden' as an employee under a false name by the head of the Hôpital des Anglais, Simone Verhoost. Using this position, Federman and a non-Jewish colleague, Alphonse Gaspar, were able to acquire the identity documents of patients who had died. The Liège branch also received ration cards from other sources, for example from a teacher, Paula Marchal, who was also sheltering a Jewish couple, and supplied between 150 and 300 cards of ration stamps each month.[107] It also arranged to get identity papers from a number of sources—some paid for and some free. Other branches had different sources of supply: Antwerp obtained at least fifty identity cards for children from a member of the city's criminal police and others from local distribution offices, Ghent had contacts with the local authorities in Ostend, and Charleroi developed contacts with no less than 126 local administrations, and pioneered a system where these offices produced new identity cards for people who had supposedly moved house. These were compiled with some faults so that they had to be reissued, with the faulty documents being passed on to people in hiding. In this way, the group managed to get its hands on at least 1,600 so-called 'false-real' documents.[108]

There is no doubt that the greater Jewish aversion to the German-inspired AJB and the concomitant creation of the CDJ were major contributory features in helping Jews to survive in hiding. Much of their work was designed to help adult Jews, while children were more likely to have been handed on to non-Jewish organizations as they could be kept more safely. Nonetheless, the CDJ was an integral and essential element in supporting those hiding from the authorities. The fact that from its very inception, the CDJ had links both to the wider Jewish and non-Jewish armed resistance movements was a major benefit when compared with the situation in both France and, especially, the Netherlands. Moreover, these links with non-Jewish agencies, both legal and clandestine, opened the door for brokering contacts and hiding places on a much broader scale than elsewhere. As a post-war report made clear, the organization had more than 300 people who took some direct role in the CDJ, and they came from almost every section of society: 'the religious and the free thinkers, bourgeois, workers and peasants'.[109]

This stress on organized Jewish self-help should not obscure the fact that individuals also took the initiative in trying to escape the Germans. From their arrival in the country, most foreign Jews habitually tried to stay below the radar of the authorities. One family, for example, had come from Germany to Brussels in 1939. In 1940, the father had fled southward and spent some time in a French internment camp before escaping. In the meantime, the mother kept on the move, never registering with the municipalities and renting new apartments every time the landlords or neighbours indicated that the authorities were asking questions about the tenants. Ultimately, they found refuge with a 'Belgian Christian' woman who did them 'countless favours' and this allowed them to stay in the same place for nearly a year.[110] Ignoring the requirement to wear the Jewish star to go outside was always a risk and food had to be bought on the black market as ration coupons could only be issued to those registered with the municipality, thus making access to considerable funds a necessity for long-term survival. Another family effectively went into hiding in 1940 when the father was called up in one of the earliest labour drafts for work inside Belgium. This took place in November 1940 when 'foreigners' were required to undertake essential war work in Limburg. He managed to persuade a doctor to give him an injection to induce heart arrhythmia and thus was exempted, but he suspected even at this stage that persecution would continue.[111] These two cases provide good examples of how many Jews in Belgium viewed the authorities even before more stringent measures were brought in. There was a natural predilection to avoid the scrutiny of the state machinery at all levels—a response based on previous experiences in Eastern Europe or more recently in Germany. Labour conscription continued to provide warnings to Jews in the big cities. One man and his family took the hint in May 1942 when ordered to report to the Central Station in Antwerp. Initially, they took shelter above the husband's shop but when the police raids and deportations began, they found refuge with a non-Jewish family where they stayed until the liberation. Again this seems to have been an entirely private arrangement between the families with no outside help.[112] The exact number of privately arranged rescues where Jews looked for shelter with neighbours or acquaintances is unknown, but given the numbers that survived, there must have been several thousand.

8

Non-Jewish Rescuers
in Belgium

Helping Hands

There is no doubt that the existence of the CDJ and other clandestine
Jewish organizations was central to the successful survival of many people,
but a great deal of their success rested on finding non-Jews willing and
able to help, either directly through the provision of hiding places, or
indirectly through supplying funds, ration cards, false identity papers, and
all the other essentials that those living clandestinely required. In Belgium,
the list of non-Jewish helpers begins at the very top of society. The fact
that the royal family had decided to stay after the Germans occupied the
country gave King Leopold and his mother Elisabeth some leverage with
the military government. In July 1942, he intervened to stop the arrest of
Belgian Jews, but it was the Queen Mother Elisabeth who was more active,
and during the occupation approached the German authorities on behalf of
several hundred Jews, primarily those of Belgian nationality. These included
Jews in mixed marriages, friends of the royal court, well-known Jewish
personalities, respected families, outstanding students, talented musicians,
and highly qualified engineers. How many of these interventions were
successful, either in the short or the long term, is difficult to ascertain, but
estimates suggest that only around 50 per cent fell victim to deportation.[1]
In the same vein, Leopold's cousin, Eugène, Prince de Ligne, became
involved in the Grynpas network through his contacts with the Jesuits.
Ostensibly completely separate from the mainstream Jewish and non-Jewish
organization, the network that bore his name was created by Benedikt
Grynpas. Of Eastern European origin, he had studied Semitic languages

and married a Jewess in 1929. Working at the University of Leuven, he was able to use contacts made with various elements of the Catholic Church to provide private and institutional placements for Jews, and it was estimated that the network helped around thirty people during the occupation. Among its contacts were a number of Jesuit priests, including Jean-Baptiste de Coster, head of the College of Saint-Jean Berchmans in Brussels.[2]

The Belgian Jewish elite also benefited from assistance from leading collaborationist civil servants such as Secretary of State for the Interior Ministry Gerard Romsée, suggesting that they adopted a similar line to their French counterparts in discriminating against 'foreign' elements.[3] The privileged position given to Belgian Jews did make them seem more secure, even to the point where some foreign Jews went through 'white' marriages with Belgians Jews in order to benefit from their protection, although in the end it only served to postpone their fate. A more effective variant of this was where Jews married Belgian Gentiles to create 'mixed marriages', often with money changing hands and with agreements drawn up by lawyers whereby either party could dissolve the marriage when the war was over.[4]

There were also earlier manifestations of collective protest against anti-Jewish measures by government agencies. This had its origins in the use of the Belgian police to arrest political opponents in June 1942, but led to the mayors in Brussels and Liège putting up some resistance to the introduction of the yellow star later in the month.[5] However, the major change in wider public perception took place after 6 October 1942 when the Germans introduced compulsory labour service in the Reich for Belgians. This placed Belgian administrators and police in a difficult position vis-à-vis the general population who had now become the targets of German measures.[6] This provides the clue to the Belgian reaction to the persecution and deportation of the Jews. Once the majority were also threatened with adverse measures, the question of what happened to the Jews became wrapped up with a wider anti-German sentiment. Even nationalists who had traditionally voiced antisemitic opinions now sought to show a united front against the occupier.[7] Most of the first help given to Jews trying to avoid round-ups and deportation, very much in line with elsewhere in Western Europe, came from family members (in the case of 'mixed' marriages), neighbours, friends, work-colleagues, or business partners. Also involved, albeit in smaller measure, were motivations based on pre-war antipathy to racism and antisemitism.[8] Some individual families seem to have taken burdens ostensibly way beyond their means, and yet managed to survive intact with their guests to the liberation. Thus near Charleroi, Camille D'Haeyer and his wife were persuaded by their daughter to take in her classmate, a sister, and parents in July 1942. Some two months later, they also took in another family of five. In spite of the problems of finding food for twelve people, the families survived together without being betrayed or raided until the liberation.[9] Similarly, the Lierszencweig and Wychina families, also from Charleroi, were helped by their neighbours, the Paquay family who took them to near relatives in the small village of Jauche. Here they were materially supported and looked after by the community, although in this case at least one of the rescuers was caught and tortured by the Gestapo, having herself been betrayed. This led to some of the children involved being placed in the hands of a network run by Father André from Namur and hidden elsewhere, again indicating how individual rescues could later be picked up by larger organizations in times of need.[10]

Other stories of rescue take different forms. A short and sober declaration compiled in 1965 told of a Jewish woman, Fanny Gluck-Weiser, who was admitted to the 'Lizzie Marsily' Sanatorium on 30 April 1941 suffering from progressive pulmonary tuberculosis. Her son Herman, who had developed the same illness, joined her on 2 November of the same year. This was long before the threat of deportation existed, but the sanatorium staff managed to prolong their stay for 'non-medical reasons' until just before 1946, on the grounds that as Jews they would have been subject to arrest by the Germans. A story of three and a half years in hiding encapsulated in a few lines, with no word of reflection on why the sanatorium had decided on this course of action, or why it had supported these particular people for so long, both during and for an extended period after the occupation.[11]

Once deportations became a reality, better-prepared families looked to sell off their property—presumably illegally—turning possessions into cash and hiding the rest with friends. Blank identity cards could be bought and filled in with false details or acquired from the legitimate holders, who then claimed they were 'lost'.[12] Some teachers were part of the networks looking to place young people with Gentile families.[13] Possession of these identity papers allowed those underground to live openly, but the risk of discovery remained. In theory, it was the local policemen who were responsible for making sure that all new arrivals in their district were registered with the local authority, but it is clear that some were deliberately negligent in carrying out this task.[14] However, travelling further afield and using public transport brought the dangers of street controls of identity papers and more stringent checks that might expose frauds and inconsistencies. Thus it remained important to limit travel and to know when and where such checks were most likely to occur. Others who looked to make good their escape were less fortunate. One man paid someone he assumed to be a representative of the Red Cross BFr.45,000 to arrange a clandestine passage to Switzerland, but when he was collected by a car, he immediately had a revolver pointed at him and he was handed over directly to the Gestapo.[15]

A woman in Liège described how her father approached his devoutly Catholic neighbours for help when he was called up. for transport, and via one of their sons who was a Trappist monk, they were able to move to the country where he had rented a house for them in his name. This particular arrangement did not last long as the family still had to return to Liège for their ration stamps, and this ultimately led to their discovery, although the woman herself had already been placed elsewhere into the home of a local doctor as a domestic servant.[16] Here it was a family connection that paved the way for access to a church-based network that provided some aid to the family later in the occupation, although individual decisions were still being made. By the same token, the woman also recorded that there was no real recognition of her family as Jews within the community before the occupation and thus no sense that they were in any way different from other Polish or Italian immigrants that had come to work in the mines.[17]

Such private arrangements could be both tenuous and tortuous. A woman from Antwerp whose husband had been deported in July 1942 under the false impression that his going would save his family, was herself later arrested with her infant daughter in a raid. Taken to the transit camp at Mechelen, she managed to persuade the Germans that she was Hungarian, but that her papers were still at home. Perhaps surprisingly, she was allowed to return with her daughter to fetch the papers unaccompanied, although this effectively meant she could escape. Back in Antwerp, she approached one of her husband's former employers who refused to take her in, but found a room for her in exchange for a sable coat. Another family staying at the same address was then caught by the Germans, and she was moved by the same employer, but only in exchange for several hours work each day. This arrangement also did not last as the location became dangerous and she moved to a warehouse. From a Jewish friend she acquired a Hungarian passport and it was only then that she came into contact with a rescue organization via two of her cousins. This resulted in her child being placed with a Catholic family in Flanders. Unusually, she visited the child and met the family she was fostered with. Later on, the family used its contacts to get her a job with a German photographer who provided false papers that allowed her to stay at liberty until the war's end.[18] This particular story shows clearly how individual initiatives were combined with limited contact with networks, individual rescuers—both philanthropic and materialistic—and a good deal of luck.

The Catholic Church

The role of the Catholic Church and its institutions are central to any understanding of the ways in which rescue developed in Belgium. Beyond neighbours and acquaintances, Christian leaders such as bishops and priests were often the first port of call for Jews who were forced to look for reliable help outside their own community. Initially this was often to obtain (false) baptismal certificates to exempt the holder from deportation, but later also encompassed requests for shelter, ration cards, or help to escape the country altogether. In several areas the network of organizations and institutions built up over centuries was harnessed to provide help for Jews in need. Moreover, local priests were also in a position to advise on trustworthy parishioners who could be relied upon to provide material and practical help.[19]

It is recorded that Cardinal Archbishop van Roey personally intervened on behalf of at least fifty-two people incarcerated at Mechelen or elsewhere, although all but seventeen were ultimately deported, and the remainder were either in mixed marriages or had some other special claim to protection.[20] He was more successful elsewhere, for example in protecting a small number of monks who were considered Jews by the Germans but who had converted to Catholicism. Three had been arrested in 1942, but released 'under certain conditions'. All three survived the war, although one was arrested again later and was ultimately rescued from a concentration camp by the Swedish Red Cross.[21] Van Roey remained opposed to public appeals to the Germans, even after the deportations had begun, preferring private interventions for individuals and small groups where he thought he might succeed. His reasoning was that previous appeals on other issues had achieved nothing, that the Germans had promised not to touch Jews with

Figure 8.1. Leaders of the Catholic Church in Belgium at the investiture of
Monsignor Charue as Bishop of Namur. Front Row from left to right, Mgr
Honoré-Joseph Coppieters (Bishop of Ghent), Mgr André Marie Charue,
Cardinal Archbishop of Mechelen Jozef Ernst van Roey, Mgr Louis-Joseph
Kerkhofs (Bishop of Liège), and Mgr Louis Delmotte (Bishop of Tournai)
Source: Rights Reserved, CEGES-SOMA, Brussels

Belgian nationality, and that any protest might bring adverse consequences
for Jewish children hidden in Catholic institutions.[22] There is no doubt that
van Roey knew exactly what was happening in the Catholic cloisters and
orphanages across the country and he had even privately sanctioned such
actions personally, no doubt being aware of the complicity of his secretary,
René Ceuppens, in this work.[23] He was also aware of the deportations
and wrote to the Vatican about the brutality and cruelty that revolted the
Belgian people.[24] Van Roey therefore trod the same tightrope as many
of his colleagues elsewhere in German-occupied Europe, balancing the
humanitarian and religious obligations of his office with the need to protect
the secular interests of his Church at a time of crisis.

Such overwhelming considerations did not have the same impact on
many of his subordinates, and it would be wrong to suggest that all this
was driven by initiatives or 'hints' from the Church leadership. There were

many cases of individual priests acting on their own or in concert with colleagues or the CDJ to provide assistance to Jews in various ways. This was especially true in Brussels in districts where there were higher than average Jewish populations, for example in Schaerbeek and Anderlecht. In Schaerbeek, the priest Georges Meunier, together with his curate, Armand Spruyt, had been 'specialists' in the baptism of Jews before the war, and during the occupation carried out at least 160 such ceremonies, almost exclusively as a means to cloak Jewish backgrounds and/or to diminish the chances of deportation.[25] In addition, in concert with a local schoolteacher, they found secure hiding places for twenty-two Jewish children. Beyond this, their position in their local communities made them the targets for innumerable requests from Jewish neighbours for some sort of help. This led to a wider involvement of Catholic cloisters, sanatoria and orphanages as well as lay-Catholic families in providing help and shelter. In addition, they also had contact with Edouard Froidure, a priest who led a movement promoting playing fields and had arranged summer holidays and food for Jewish children.[26]

What emerged in Belgium was a 'secret association' of priests dedicated to the well-being of the Jews. This included Meunier and Spruyt, but also Antoon De Breuker (Schaerbeek), Joseph André (Namur) and the Benedictine, Father Paul Démann from the Keizersberg Abbey in Leuven. Apart from the children and adults sent out of Brussels, some were retained in the city in Catholic institutions, for example in the convent of the Sisters of St Vincent de Paul in Schaerbeek itself. Another network was established in the Kuregem area of Anderlecht, where the priest Jan de Ridder and three curates at Our Lady of the Immaculate Conception (Onze-Lieve-Vrouw-Onbevlekt) used the community centre of the church as a refuge to find hiding places for Jews in Brussels and Mechelen. Here there seems to have been an unusual level of co-operation between the local population, the civic administration, and the clerics working to hide Jews from the Germans. This included the kidnap rescue of ten Jewish girls from the Convent of the Sisters of the Holy Saviour on 20 May 1943 to provide an alibi for the sisters after the children had been betrayed to the Gestapo.[27]

Away from the capital there was also co-operation between Catholic clerics and lay people and the organizations of the CDJ. In and around Leuven, there was the extensive work of Father Bruno Reynders, who became famous for helping children, but also worked to shelter many adult Jews during the occupation period. Not only did Reynders employ his institutional contacts within the Church but he also involved many of his family members (although in some cases these overlapped, as two of his sisters were themselves nuns).[28] Reynders also had contact with curates in Mechelen, including van Roey's secretary, Ceuppens, and his brother, who was a curate in the Leuven area. Again, these two brothers were central to the rescue of Jews in their respective areas. The region covered by the bishopric of Namur in the south-east of the country proved to be one of the most active centres for sheltering Jews. Its position near the border also meant that there had been greater opportunities to develop other types of resistance work, for example helping POWs and, later, forced labourers escaping from Germany, and also in helping Allied pilots through escape routes to the south.

In Namur itself, Father Joseph André was the prime mover. During the occupation he was *onderpastoor* of the parish of St Jean Baptiste in Namur and used his rectory (*parochiehuis*), as a shelter for Jews going into hiding. He began his work, like so many others, after a Jewish friend approached him to find a hiding place for a Jewish family from Antwerp as early as the winter of 1941–2. This led to other approaches and the beginning of an entire network and by the summer of 1942, his house was already functioning as a transit centre for Jews moving to hiding places found for them.[29] There also seems to have been greater community support here and links with both the Red Cross, and more surprisingly, the Winter Help. There is no doubt that André was working with the full knowledge of his bishop, Monsignor Charue, as the diocese provided financial aid for the work, as did the Socrates resistance network and innumerable members of the local community.[30]

His network formed part of a larger loose organization known as the *L'Aide Chrétienne aux Israélites* (ACI) that included many other groups associated in some way with the Catholic Church who were committed to the idea of saving Jewish children. There were often overlaps between groups and networks through personal contacts or organizational structures, so that defining the work of an individual group remains difficult, but it is also important to realize that there was no central leadership to the ACI from the Church hierarchy.[31] Nevertheless, the attitudes of the leading clergymen could make a substantive difference to the attitudes and actions of their subordinates. This was undoubtedly true in the Catholic diocese of Liège (Luik), where the bishop, Monsignor Louis-Joseph Kerkhofs was a prime-mover in instigating help for the Jews. He had initially been approached for help by the local rabbi, Joseph Lepkifker, whom he had hidden in his own house as his private secretary under an assumed identity. The rabbi's wife and youngest son were hidden in another Catholic institution run by the bishop's niece.[32] Kerkhofs also used other religious institutions in his diocese to harbour Jews, for example the College at Stoumont, established in the 1930s by the Abbé Marcel Stenne. This had initially been just a local school but Stenne developed its use as a permanent home for undernourished city children after 1940 and was first asked to accommodate four Jewish children in January 1942.[33] Kerkhofs took an active role in recruiting other members of the clergy into the work of saving Jews by holding meetings specifically to discuss the issue. As was recalled by one of his priests when he was made the award as 'Righteous among the Nations',

> I was one of a number of priests called to attend. The bishop did not compel anyone, given the dangers it exposed one to, but he desired that his priests should know how much pride he had in those who risked their life to save the lives of others.[34]

No other priests in the diocese recalled such meetings, but others spoke of letters from Kerkhofs encouraging them to aid and to hide the Jews.[35]

Together with a city lawyer, Albert van den Berg, Kerkhofs was instrumental in creating the so-called van den Berg network that saved several hundred Jewish children and a number of adults.[36] There is no doubting these individuals' humanitarian commitment. Kerkhofs provided the contacts and many of the hiding places through Catholic institutions in his diocese; van den Berg provided the money and the organization. Their acquaintance came via van den Berg's extensive secular work within the city parish of Saint-Christophe and the Catholic Church more generally.[37] Precisely how the two linked in this particular way remains unclear but it may be that van den Berg was an obvious choice for a bishop looking for a devout and well-connected organizer, or conversely that Kerkhofs was the obvious man to contact for a layman committed to helping the Jews.

Kerkhofs had been bishop of Liège since 1927 and had adopted a stronger stance than many of his ecclesiastical colleagues against both Rexism and racism, and after the capitulation, had taken a somewhat different position from that of Cardinal van Roey on the question of the new regime in Belgium. In spite of criticism, he continued to defend the interests of workers threatened with forced labour, civilians arrested by the authorities, and his priests. He intervened with the German military authorities on numerous occasions and had some success in obtaining the release of prisoners, but of the total of 109 clergy arrested in his diocese, 36 died in captivity.[38] His pastoral letters were also an opportunity to mobilize lay Catholics, although the language used was inevitably circumscribed. Nonetheless, he authorized his priests to issue backdated baptismal certificates and adjust parish registers.[39] In Liège, Kerkhofs worked closely with Abbé André Meunier, professor at the Catholic Grand Seminary in the city, who had been 'recruited' by Kerkhofs around the time of the first deportations and became the main contact with van den Berg in arranging the practical matters associated with hiding Jews: the identification of hiding places, and the provision of food, ration cards, and identity documents.[40] However, Meunier clearly had contacts of his own and was furnished with the names of Jews who needed to go underground by a certain Mrs Kleinberger, a Jewess from Antwerp.[41] It was also Meunier who seems to have been at the forefront of widening the network to include more and more Catholic institutions. Sanctioned by the bishop, he approached the directors of welfare institutions, rectors, and headmasters of schools, as well as the abbots and mother superiors of religious houses to provide aid and hiding places. In this regard, he even went beyond the diocese and, through contacts with Monsignor Louis De Gruyter, the former incumbent in the parish of Saint-Christophe, he was able to recruit other leading clergymen, including Emile Boufflette and Abbé André of Namur. Apart from encouraging others to take in Jews, Meunier also had some direct experience, hiding one Jewish boy in the basement of his seminary's library that was only accessible to the institution's professors.[42]

Perhaps surprisingly for a priest, Boufflette had been involved in clandestine activities from the very beginning of the occupation. As a member of the armed forces, he escaped from internment after the surrender. Soon he was organizing an illegal newspaper and quickly became associated with the armed resistance of the Mouvement Nationale Belge where, among other tasks, he helped numbers of French POWs on the run from internment. He had known van den Berg since 1937 and rapidly became involved with his network, having false papers as an agricultural worker as well as a priest in another name. His contacts included his parents and his brother, all of whom were directly involved in underground work. Among his achievements was to get communes to register people with false identities as residents. It was thought that the populations of the municipalities of Amay, Jupriller and Strée may have tripled as a result of his requests. Like other priests, he was also able to use his clerical friends and acquaintances to establish links with religious and secular Church institutions and is widely credited with helping around 1,000 Jews in hiding. Later, he also organized an escape line to Spain before being arrested in December 1943 and deported, dying in March 1945 at the age of 33.[43] Another example of a priest with a 'resistance' background before becoming involved in hiding Jews was Joseph Peeters, Curé of Comblain-au-Pont. He was secretary of the local Winter Help and heavily involved in distributing illegal newspapers and countless other illegal activities before the summer of 1942 when the first raids began. His precise links with the Catholic hierarchy and the CDJ are unclear, but at least one fugitive reported being sent to him via Monsignor Kerkhofs. Some 400 people were given false papers and lodged in local farms before Peeters was himself arrested in December 1942 and executed in Liège on 31 August 1943.[44] The rapid expansion and scale of these two clerics' operations can be explained in part by their pre-existing involvement in clandestine activity. Having existing contacts and networks meant that mobilization to meet the needs of Jews on the run could begin immediately. However, the same process could be seen on a smaller scale among those who had no previous contact with illegal work, but were brought in by their superiors. Thus for example, Joseph Dethier, Chaplain at Verleumont was recruited by André Meunier. Newly ordained in 1942, he was asked to provide temporary refuge to a Jewish boy of 10, but soon also found himself responsible for others.[45]

There are clues to Albert van den Berg's central involvement in this work from his family and personal background. Born in 1890, he was old enough to have served in the First World War as an ordinary soldier from 1914, one of four family members to have volunteered. Wounded in the early battles, he returned to the colours and spent four years fighting on the Yser front. Ultimately he was given a commission and participated in the liberation of his country where he was once again wounded. At the same time, many other members of his family at home in Liège were actively involved in the espionage network, La Dame Blanche, created by Walthère Dewé.[46] Thus a 'tradition' of resistance already existed in the family when the Germans once again overran the country in 1940, and it is clear that Albert van den Berg became associated with Dewé's Second World War 'Clarence' network, although there is some doubt about the level of his involvement. Several sources testify to his having organized missions for 'Clarence', but his brother-in-law Georges Fonsny, who took over the van den Berg network when Albert was arrested at the end of April 1943, insists that although he helped Jews and fugitives from labour service, he was never directly involved in armed resistance. These two positions may not be as contradictory as first appear. It is possible that van den Berg began his resistance activities attached to 'Clarence', but then specialized in the rescue of Jewish children and withdrew from other commitments, or alternatively that the deeply clandestine nature of 'Clarence' meant that Albert never revealed this other role to his brother-in-law.[47]

Van den Berg was the epitome of the practical, devout, and committed Catholic layman, involved in all aspects of the work of his parish, Saint-Christophe, and often referred to as the 'third vicar' alongside the two appointed clergymen, Boufflette and Louis Pluymers.[48] He sat on many institutional boards of governors, both in the city and in the wider diocese, including the Catholic *colonies scolaire*. These institutions had been expanded at the end of 1940 to take in those of all religions and political backgrounds 'on account of the current circumstances', and they were therefore prepared to meet the need to shelter Jewish children.[49] Thus it was that some far-sighted Jewish parents placed their children in his hands for safety as early as 1941 when the first major anti-Jewish measures were taken.[50]

Van den Berg's principled stand also led to his downfall. It has been suggested that he took much less care about his own security than that of his fellow resistance workers and the children and adults they helped hide, operating almost as though everything could be done legally: receiving those on the run at his offices and keeping compromising papers on the premises.[51] His lawyer's office was visited by all manner of people looking for a means of going underground, suggesting that he was well known in the city as someone who could help. One Jewish woman for whom he provided false identity papers was later arrested by the Gestapo. Her non-Jewish Belgian husband became a Gestapo informer to try to save his wife, and was used by them to trap van den Berg. The man asked the lawyer for a false identity card and then led the Germans to the handover. When van den Berg's offices were searched, various blank identity cards were found and he and his secretary were arrested on 30 April 1943. Charged with having the false papers and with helping Jews, the two men were only convicted on the first charge, with van den Berg receiving five months.[52] This relative leniency can be explained by two factors: first, that his secretary took sole responsibility for the false papers being in the office, and secondly, that the President of the Bar argued to the military tribunal that German legislation relating to Jews was not applicable in Belgium. The five-month sentence may have represented leniency on the part of the German authorities for the crimes they uncovered, but it is clear that they found out nothing about van den Berg's wider role in helping those underground, and had no idea of his real importance. To them, he was ostensibly a bourgeois lawyer engaged in some illegal activities rather than the leader of a major network.

With Albert van den Berg in gaol, his role was taken by his brother-in-law, Georges Fonsny, who led the network until the liberation. Van den Berg himself was not so fortunate. Ignoring the judgement of the military tribunal, the Gestapo had him transferred not to a Belgian prison, but to the concentration camp at Vught in the Netherlands, from where he was later evacuated to Neuengamme near Hamburg. Although not appearing on the list of those who died at that camp, van den Berg never returned to Belgium, and it is thought likely that he died when the refugee ship Cap Arcona was bombed by the Allies in Lübeck harbour on 3 May 1945. His secretary, Pierre Coune, did return, but died soon afterwards from tuberculosis contracted while in the camps.[53]

Apart from the connections with the local Catholic Church and the bishop, the network was very much a family affair. Even before its founder's arrest, Georges Fonsny had been an integral part of the network, as had his wife, who visited children in hiding, and his daughter, who worked in van den Berg's offices. His cousin, Berthe Vandenkieboom, was also involved. Another devout Catholic, she worked for the Bureau de l'Enfance au Grand Air, an organization that placed children weakened by tuberculosis or other diseases with families or institutions in the countryside. This again allowed the network access to other refuges and foster parents. She kept watch over the children she placed, visiting them to ensure their spiritual and material welfare, as well as sheltering children in her own home.[54]

Liège provides an outstanding example of how pre-existing social and professional contacts between Jewish and non-Jewish clandestine organizations with the Catholic Church provided huge advantages in mobilizing when the first arrests and deportations took place in 1942. However, mistakes were made and, as has been shown, the Sipo/SD targeted both the organizers and ordinary members of these networks. In this regard the Germans were heavily reliant on informers. While 'Big Jacques' in Brussels was the most famous of these agents, Liège had its own equivalent, and someone who was potentially just as dangerous. Oscar Evrard was a seminarist who also worked as an informer for the Sipo in the city. At the time, his role remained secret as he was never directly involved in raids or arrests. Thus he was able to insinuate himself into clerical circles and he was ultimately appointed by Monsignor Kerkhofs as an inspector of the various Catholic boarding schools in the diocese. Given that these were extensively used to hide Jewish children, this was a potentially lethal decision but throughout the occupation, his credentials as a patriot were never questioned, and it was only after the war that his role in the arrest of around forty people was exposed. Tried in a Belgian court, he claimed to have saved rather than betrayed people, but only one example could be produced: of a young widow whom he had provided with false papers and who had become his mistress.[55]

A different, but no less important example of this amalgamation of functions into a single organization can be seen in the Loubris Fonds. This was a fund created at the end of 1940 by Joseph Loubris, a police brigadier in Ghent. It was initially intended just to provide money for policemen hiding from the Germans and for their families and dependants. From these small beginnings, it was soon allied to the FI through other policemen, including the police commissioner for the 4 District of the city, Alphonse Dewalsche. During 1941, the narrow remit of the fund was extended to help all manner of other people on the run: escaped prisoners of war, allied aircrew, labour service evaders, and Jews. Helping people live underground was difficult, but the organization was well placed to raid trucks carrying ration stamps and to loot German supplies, which the police were supposed to be guarding. Loubris was ultimately arrested and deported to a concentration camp from which he did not return, but Dewalsche, in spite of being taken as a hostage four times, was ultimately always released. The fact that the organizers had compartmentalized the work being done from an early stage effectively prevented the Germans from rolling up the whole network when they caught one or two members. As with the CDJ, the members of the Loubris Fonds later gave credit to the co-operation they received, both from civil servants and from other non-police members of the FI.[56]

At local levels it is also possible to see how these networks operated. One example can be seen in Herve near Verviers where members of the local public assistance committee were active in hiding up to twenty Jews from May 1943 until the liberation. Some were sent there by the Abbé Meunier or by van den Berg, although one of those involved admitted that in some cases he could not say who had sent the people to him. Many were sheltered at the local hospice through an arrangement with the Mother Superior. Some seem to have paid for their keep while others were housed for free, although there was an assumption that their costs would be settled at the war's end. As they were ostensibly being supported by the public assistance, the men were required to work as road menders, thus partially offsetting any costs they might have incurred. While the local network leaders knew the major figures that sent them fugitives, there was no chain of command, and in this example, it is clear that those in hiding came via a number of different routes, both geographical and organizational.[57]

Penalties for those hiding Jews were unpredictable. A military government interdiction in 1942 had not been followed up with any formal legal proscription and those caught were often indicted for other crimes such as having false papers or black marketeering. One set of court documents shows that indictment purely for sheltering a single Jew from October 1943 produced a sentence of two months from the German military court, but the circumstances of this particular offence were not made clear. Another woman, held for the same offence of illegally hiding Jews, was ostensibly released by Office IVB3 of the Sipo in Brussels some six weeks later without trial, provided she continued to report there.[58] Given the propensity of the German security police to 'turn' those who had been caught into informers, her release can only be regarded as raising some suspicions.

Rescuers among the Demi-Monde

While not peculiar to Belgium, it is worth reflecting on the ways in which rescue intersected with criminality. Many networks harnessed petty criminal elements as well as the self-evidently righteous among their 'foot soldiers'. Thus Willem Bom from Liège made frequent trips to the Netherlands and post-war enquiries revealed that he had been arrested three times, once for helping manufacture false passports in Belgium, the second for helping Jews in the Netherlands, and the third for smuggling. All these offences were given short custodial sentences before a fourth arrest in August 1944 saw him sent to Upper Silesia. The fact that he was more harshly treated on this last occasion may have been due to the deteriorating war situation or the fact that the Germans had become bored with his habitual offending. He explained his deportation on the grounds that they had tried to turn him into an informer and that when he refused, he was arrested. Either way, they do not seem to have been aware that he had also been involved in smuggling allied pilots over the Dutch–Belgian frontier.[59]

Some escape networks could also betray a much deeper and long-standing involvement in criminal activity. One such was rolled up by the Germans in the autumn of 1942 and involved a number of people from the city of Brussels. Its activities had begun when Laurette Chainaye, a widowed tailoress, had been contacted in May 1942 by a Dutch Jewess who had left the Netherlands and was trying to get to Switzerland. In exchange for BFr.5,000 Chainaye took the woman to the Franco-Swiss border in early June and found three young men willing to smuggle her across the frontier. This plan misfired and the woman was arrested, but Chainaye returned to Brussels with the money. Soon afterwards, she took the woman's brother and two friends to the border. The two friends were arrested en route as their papers were not in order, but the brother made it safely to the border and Chainaye pocketed another BFr.5,000. Another brother was also taken to the frontier in July, as part of a much larger group. By this time, the fee had increased to BFr.10,000 per person.[60] She was only prepared to undertake further journeys if all her charges were in possession of Belgian identity cards so that they would not be apprehended by controls en route. To this end, she made the acquaintance of André Dumortier who brought her into contact with others who had some knowledge of forgery. They recruited a printer whose business was failing, to produce the cards while others procured or manufactured relevant official stamps for a number of municipalities.[61]

Soon the group was selling the false identity cards at BFr.5,000 each. Photographs were obtained from Jewish 'clients' and names chosen at random from the telephone book. At the same time, Chainaye was also increasing her charges for conducting people to the border. A group of six Jews were charged BFr.80,000 in advance for their passage, although the authorities claimed that she only paid the *passeur* employed to take them into Switzerland BFr. 10,000 and kept the remaining money. What had started as a favour for acquaintances had now become a business. Further journeys were made, including one with nine adults and five children that cost the fugitives BFr. 400,000 and netted BFr.110,000 for Dumortier and BFr.150,000 for Chainaye, with the rest going to the *passeur*. This operation was uncovered by the authorities in September 1942 when six Jews Chainaye was taking to the border were arrested because their papers were found to be forged and, by the time she had returned to Brussels, the others were already in custody. Further investigations suggested that there was little honour among this group of thieves. One of those involved in procuring the stamps, Berek Rothstein, claimed to have good contacts with the Geheime Feldpolizei and, when Chainaye's son was arrested, he offered to negotiate his release in exchange for BFr.50,000, of which he would keep BFr. 25,000. Dumortier made the offer to Chainaye and also demanded an intermediary's fee of BFr.30,000.[62]

In both these cases, the motives were undoubtedly financial and there was little concern for the plight of the victims, save that they were potential sources of wealth in exchange for services. Nevertheless, there were numbers of Jews in Belgium who owed their escape and survival in part or in full to the criminal classes. Similarly, it is important to remember that not all the potential Jewish victims of the Nazis were upstanding members of the community, and some owed their survival to their profession and to the strange workings of the judicial system. In this way, habitual criminals, although inevitably drawing the attention of the authorities and subject to the laws, could perversely find their convictions would save them from deportation. Take, for example, the case of Daniel Meyerson, a Dutch Catholic convert from Amsterdam who was living in Brussels with his Jewish wife and was arrested in November 1940 for stealing military supplies and foodstuffs (with assistance from some German soldiers) and hiding them at his house. His prisoner's file shows that he had no previous convictions but he was given a five-year sentence. His wife was sentenced to two years by the court and was back in Brussels by May 1944 when she was informed of her husband's death in custody in a German gaol. Both seem to have been dealt with by the judicial authorities and not transferred to the Sipo as Jews liable for deportation to Poland.[63] An even more colourful career was that of Israel Steinberg. This man had a police record dating back to 1930 when he had been arrested by the Viennese police as a pickpocket. He was subsequently tried for the same offences successively in Cracow, Halle, Brunn, and finally Brussels in 1937. Expelled from Belgium, he was again arrested by the Viennese police in 1938 and by the Brussels police in 1939. He was escorted to the border for a second time, but reappeared almost immediately in Liège where he was caught in the act of stealing. By this time, war in Europe had broken out so he was not taken to the border but sentenced to ten months in prison. His sentence was unfinished when Belgium came into the war and he was classed as an enemy alien and moved to an internment camp. Later the SD moved him to KZ Breendonk and then in February 1943 to Dossin Barracks in Mechelen where he was included on the 20th transport on 19 April 1943. Steinberg was one of the escapees and managed to return to Brussels. After these experiences, he adopted the unlikely alias of Alberto Ferrari, but could not give up his chosen 'profession', and he was twice arrested for pickpocketing by the Belgian authorities, in June and November 1943. He was then sentenced to six months in gaol for various offences and in this way survived the war without ever leaving Belgium.[64]

A Country Divided

In the Belgian case, it is noticeable that those identified as non-Jewish rescuers were not uniformly distributed across the country. The table below shows that the majority were to be found in the French-speaking Walloon region and in the city of Brussels, whereas the Flemish-speaking areas were under-represented, as was the city of Antwerp. Although Antwerp was half the size of Brussels, it had a substantial Jewish population, but contained only a fifth the number of identified non-Jewish rescuers. Similarly, the number of institutions and organizations known to have helped Jews were heavily concentrated in the Walloon region and in Brussels itself.[65]

Distribution of Rescuers in Belgium (by location)		%
Walloon Region	960	41.92
Brussels City	718	31.35
Brussels Region	102	4.45
Flemish Region	250	10.93
Antwerp Region	108	4.72
Antwerp City	152	6.63
Total	2290	100.00

Source: Saerens, 'Die Hilfe für Juden', 231–2

This is clearly mirrored in the deportation rates for these same regions. Thus 67 per cent of the Jews in Antwerp were arrested and deported, whereas the percentages for Brussels (37 per cent), Liège (35 per cent) and Charleroi (42 per cent) were appreciably lower. A substantial majority of the Jews saved by going into hiding, therefore, came from Wallonia or the Brussels district.[66] This can be attributed to a number of factors.[67] First, the Germans planned to incorporate Antwerp and the Flemish region into the Reich and therefore may have pursued more radical racial policies there. Secondly, the Jewish population of the city was much more heavily concentrated in a small area and more socially segregated than elsewhere. This made them easier to locate and more estranged from the rest of the population. Thirdly, it has been argued that antisemitism among the 'bystanders' was stronger in Antwerp than elsewhere, with attacks on Jews being more common. It was also true that there was a degree of ambivalence among sections of the population. To be anti-German was not to be pro-Jewish, as many who were opposed to the occupation also held antisemitic opinions. Even in the Antwerp underground press, the plight of the Jews received relatively little attention, with only one of the fifteen underground newspapers in the city reporting on the anti-Jewish measures of 1940–1 and only seven of the twenty-six that appeared during the whole war commented on the persecutions of the Jews.[68] Fourthly, there was the attitude of Mayor Leon Delwaide and his city government that did little to hinder the Nazis in their plans to isolate and deport the Jews, although this did undergo some changes after 6 October 1942.[69] Likewise, the city's Catholic Church also seemed less inclined to help Jews than elsewhere in the country. Finally, as has already been noted, it was also the case that organized Jewish self-help took longer to establish in Antwerp.[70]

This is not to say that the Jews in Antwerp received no help from their non-Jewish neighbours. A history of the Jews in the city, published in 1963, gives a list of ninety-nine 'real friends'.[71] Of those who were fully identified, a number had government functions in the rationing offices, including its chief Alfons Goethals, and the population registry. Others came from the judiciary or from the police. Priests were few in number, and only one actually operated in the city, but such an incomplete list cannot provide a full picture. A longer list of people active in the CDJ could also be seen as misleading, as again many of those recorded were actually relatives of rescuers and lived away from the city. There seems to have been little direct help given by the socialists to the Jews in the city, but a more positive reaction came from people who had been involved in the short-lived Katholiek Bureau voor Israël (KBI) before the war. Two of its members, Betsie Hollants and Professor Camille Van Deyck, helped Jews to get false papers and also to find hiding places. In this they were helped by their own experiences fleeing in front of the German advance in 1940 when they had taken refuge in the Benedictine Monastery in Menen. This provided a temporary haven for at least one family they helped to save.[72] Van Deyck was also later involved in the resistance 'Groupe G' and also in the Boerenhulp organization of the Catholic Workers' Youth Movement that acted as a front for the placement of Jewish children in the countryside. Hollants had been involved in helping refugee Jewish families before the war, and thus there was some continuity in her wartime work. A survey carried out almost forty years after the event covered responses from 300 priests in the Flemish province of Antwerp and the French and Flemish-speaking province of Brabant (including Brussels) revealed that 42.6 per cent of priests in Brabant had done something to help Jews, whereas the figure for Antwerp was only 12.8 per cent. This discrepancy probably owes much to the attitudes of the leading churchmen in the various parts of the country, but cannot be attributed to a crude split between Flemish and French-speaking clerics, not least because one of the most active rescuers—Kerkhofs—had a Flemish background. Nevertheless, the greater involvement of church leaders in particular dioceses may go a long way to explaining the greater mobilization of French speakers in the rescue of Jews.[73]

9

The Catastrophe of Dutch Jewry

Jewish Community Leadership

Perhaps not surprisingly, discussion about rescue and survival in the Netherlands has been subsumed into the wider debate on the disproportionate mortality of the Jews there when compared with the other countries of Western Europe. More than 107,000 of the 140,000 'full-Jews' of either Dutch or foreign nationality registered by the authorities in the autumn of 1940 were deported between 1941 and 1944, and only around 5,000 returned at the end of the war, having survived the horrors within the camp system and the death marches of early 1945.[1] Many factors have been put forward to explain the particular vulnerability of the Jews in the Netherlands and their apparent inability to avoid identification and deportation. A few of the most well known have included the relative isolation of the Jewish community, the 'collaboration' by the Amsterdam Jewish Council, the existence of tight population controls, the deference to principles of order and authority by both Jewish and Gentile populations alike, and the relative poverty of large sections of the Jewish community.[2]

In this debate, rescue plays only a small part, not least because it has been generally assumed that only a relatively small number of the Jews in the Netherlands sought refuge in illegality and escape when compared with their counterparts elsewhere. The raw statistics do give this impression. Working back from the number of Jews who survived inside the country (16,000+) and adding back those who were caught in hiding (c.8,000+) gives a total of 24,000 to 25,000 who apparently tried to evade capture

Map 9.1 The Netherlands, 1940–45

inside the country in some way.[3] At its most generous interpretation, this amounts to less than 18 per cent of the total number of Jews in the country and this percentage may be a good deal less as the survivors included many 'mischlinge' and Jews in mixed marriages, who were to some degree protected from summary deportation. Conversely, recent investigations suggest that the numbers caught by the Germans or their agents in hiding were larger than originally thought.[4] Moreover, the term 'hiding' also needs some qualification. After the first 'call up' in Amsterdam in July 1942, few Jews volunteered themselves for 'labour service' but waited to be fetched by the authorities—ostensibly because they believed they had no other course of action open to them. The nights spent waiting for the trucks to arrive in the street with the suitcase or rucksack packed, were commonly recounted by the few who survived the deportations. While there are occasional stories of benevolent policemen giving individuals the option of flight, there were few advance warnings and whole neighbourhoods would be in ignorance until the threat arrived at the door. More Jews may have wanted to escape into illegality but saw no means or opportunity to do so, lacking the resources or contacts, and took no active steps to save themselves, until the point when they were about to be arrested.

Help for Jews in hiding also appears in another element of the historiography on the occupied Netherlands, namely in the discussion of civil and armed resistance in all its forms. Yet here again, this particular activity is only seen as marginal to the more direct and more heroic aspects, such as sabotage and assassination, and even to the similar, but much more prevalent, hiding of people avoiding compulsory labour service in Germany. In many respects, rescue of the Jews in the Netherlands has been epitomized through the stories of a few well-known and famous cases, such as Corrie ten Boom, Marion Pritchard, Johannes Bogaard, Sara Walbeehm, Arend Smit and the Jolink sisters, all of whom were instrumental in sheltering large numbers of Jews at various stages in the occupation.[5] Some of them, such as ten Boom, have become internationally known as the epitome of religiously motivated rescuers, while others have been largely ignored, even by historians and commentators inside the Netherlands. Beyond these few individuals were many others who have now been identified and honoured by Yad Vashem, but in spite of the avid collection of survivor testimony over several decades, many have remained unidentified because, as with other countries, those who did survive in hiding did not know the names of those who helped them and had no knowledge of the contacts and networks that found them places to hide.[6]

In the Netherlands, organized Jewish self-help was rare. Apart from the social chasm between a well-off bourgeoisie and a far more numerous and impoverished proletariat, there were also divisions between long-established Ashkenazi and Sephardi communities, and between the indigenous orthodox Jews and refugee liberal newcomers.[7] There were points of contact, especially through secular community organizations, but these were primarily fund-raising and welfare bodies, with no political or representative role. Moreover, all the groups involved continued to eschew any involvement with political refugees and kept a distance from any communist or social democratic organizations.[8] As a result, they were more or less isolated from organizations likely to be early instigators of resistance to Nazi hegemony, and dominated by an elite leadership drawn almost exclusively from bourgeois circles.[9] Thus, when the Germans arrived in May 1940, the Jews as a group were singularly ill-equipped to respond to the realities of occupation. This pattern was exacerbated by the creation of the Amsterdam Jewish Council in the aftermath of the disturbances and strike in the city in February 1941. This was chaired by Professor David Cohen and Abraham Asscher, who had led Jewish refugee relief before the occupation—thus perpetuating the elite dominance of relations between the Jewish communities and the occupying Germans.[10]

Even when the first deportations began in July 1942, most Dutch Jews apparently continued to believe that they had nothing more to fear than a second-class status within society under the Germans, and thus were singularly ill prepared. One Amsterdam Jewish family were so frightened that they left their home on the first night and went to stay with non-Jewish friends. Reflecting on this, one of the women spoke of her feelings at the time as events turned so quickly.

> We were surprised by it and we were completely unprepared to make a decision. We had never thought that things would come to this. Malevolent tongues had in the past expressed suppositions in that direction, but the optimists among us did not see the future in such black terms. We were among that latter group and for us it was the same as for many others: the wish was the father of the thought.[11]

This view undoubtedly prevailed in many households, yet even for the Jews who were hostile and referred to the Jewish Council as the '*joodsche onraad*' (Jewish danger) or '*joodsche verraad*' (Jewish treason),[12] there were no obvious alternative sources of information or organized help in the first months of the deportations.[13] Wider resistance was still embryonic and confined to small groups of people. Making assumptions about collective or even individual mentalities here is difficult, not least because so few of those presented with these choices survived to give an account of their behaviour. Thus any assessment is bound to be somewhat subjective. By the summer of 1942, the German process of identification, isolation and pauperization was more or less complete. The creation of the Jewish Council had allowed just about all matters pertaining to the community to be handled through its offices rather than through normal (local) government channels. Restrictions and bans on employment had led to a financial crisis in many households where they had previously been self-sufficient, while large sections of the Jewish proletariat were reduced to penury. Even those with material assets were forced by decree to hand them to the Lippmann Rosenthal Bank, where they were subject to control and outright confiscation.[14] This is a critical factor as, certainly in 1942, any idea of going into hiding was an open-ended commitment. The war might last for many years—or result in an outright German victory. Without any means of earning additional money, the fugitive would have to rely on access to whatever existing savings and assets they had on going underground. This implies that the richer elements within society had an advantage, but this was only true if they had been prescient enough to keep some or all of their moveable assets out of the hands of Lippmann Rosenthal and the Germans.

Two major factors worked against this advantage of wealth. One was that the rich had more to leave behind if they went underground. A couple living in Amsterdam had found a cottage some twenty miles from the city where they could go underground, but at the last minute, the wife refused to go, as it would mean leaving her furniture behind.[15] Both were later deported and killed. The second factor was the availability of exemptions. These were placed in identity cards and were designed to protect the holder from being arrested and interned at Westerbork. Most had been brokered by the Jewish Council, ostensibly to help their employees stay in post and thus ensure the smooth running of its operations. The Council had originally asked for 35,000 of these stamps but been given only 17,500. Even then, they were used to protect many whose connections to the Council were tenuous, but whose middle-class status gave them some privileged access. Individual categories commanded different number sequences, although all were ultimately rescinded as the Germans strove to meet their quotas during 1943.[16] Belief in the protective power of these stamps undoubtedly persuaded many holders to ignore the threats around them. Only a small number seem to have consciously used the time these stamps provided to arrange an escape.[17]

A Jewish Council 'stamp' was by no means the only form of protection available. There were various other lists based on particular skills or attributes—or on an ability to pay. On 1 December 1942, a German list of all those who had been given some form of official protection totalled 32,655, a figure that had increased to 35,312 by the end of the year.[18] Included in these totals were the baptized Jews, although Nazi racial policy made no exception for them. Nevertheless, here, as elsewhere in Western Europe, they were not immediately subject to labour service or deportation. The numbers of genuine baptized Jews, cither Protestant or Catholic, was relatively small in spite of the churches' missionary activities, as conversions of indigenous Dutch Jews before 1940 had been rare, and only a few refugees from Germany and Austria during the 1930s had been added to the totals. However, evidence of baptism seems to have been harder to obtain than elsewhere in the West. Dutch churches were unwilling to countenance last-minute conversions. One post-war commentator on the Calvinist Church noted:

> we had to say to these people who came to the church for the first time that it was *now* too late for this and that the Church could not misuse its given power and had to uphold the holiness of God's kingdom only to give certificates to those whom we were certain had a right to them.[19]

This did not mean that all churches and all priests and pastors acted in the same way, as some Jews certainly did receive either genuine or forged baptismal certificates.[20] However, they proved to have only limited value in the longer term as the Germans refused to accept conversions that had taken place after their arrival and in the event, most Roman Catholic Jews were arrested after the protest of the Catholic Churches about the deportations was read from the pulpits on 26 July 1942 while the Dutch Reformed and Calvinist Jews stayed in the country for longer, albeit incarcerated at Westerbork, but 500 were eventually sent to Theresienstadt in September 1944.[21]

All these exemptions ultimately betrayed their holders, save for those who continued to be useful to elements within the Nazi hierarchy, either in the Netherlands, or in the corridors of power in Berlin. These included Jews employed directly or indirectly by the *Wehrmacht* (the so-called *Rüstungsjüden*), Jewish diamond dealers and a group of notables known as the Barneveld group. All three categories enjoyed a degree of protection beyond the point when the Jewish Council was wound up in September 1943—either because they remained economically useful or had potential as hostages as the war turned against Germany.[22] Local protection could also come in many strange forms, for example one or two members of the Jewish Council and custodians of various Jewish cemeteries were all apparently overlooked by the authorities, as were the two Jewish bicycle repairmen who were employed throughout the occupation by the German *Sicherheitspolizei*.[23]

Inclusion in one of these protected categories could in some cases be merely a matter of good luck or being in the right job at the right time. However, the existence of such lists did serve to suggest that an exemption from labour service was possible, even if it was only *bis auf weiteres* (until further notice) and fitted with a mentality that wanted to believe that some Jews would be allowed to stay in the Netherlands. The statements and actions of the Jewish Council leadership in Amsterdam heavily reinforced this thinking. Accommodation and compliance with German instructions remained the watchwords of the Council leaders, Cohen and Abraham Asscher, 'to avoid something worse'.[24] In this context, it is important to bear in mind that the 'something worse' did have a material form, namely deportation to Mauthausen. An initial group of 400 Jewish hostages had been sent there in the spring of 1941 and all were reported dead within a few weeks. Thus the penalties for being a *strafgeval* (punishment case) were well understood when compared with the indeterminate concept of 'labour service in the East'. The Council thus publicly condemned resistance and disobedience, and scope for subversion within the organization was limited as it provided at least temporary protection from deportation for its employees and their families. While there have been charges that the Jewish middle classes benefited from this temporary protection while their lower class co-religionists were sacrificed, it did not prevent the entire community from suffering the same ultimate fate. The only advantage that this temporary protection might afford was the time to arrange a hiding place and (although this could not be known at the time) a shorter period to survive in hiding.

Self-Help and Individual Rescuers

The Jewish Council in Amsterdam that came to represent all the Jews in the Netherlands was tied into a culture of accommodation and legalism that remained in place until almost the last Jews had been deported. Its structures, and those of Dutch society as a whole, provided no opportunities for organized opposition from within the community or links with state or non-Jewish social and political agencies. Thus, while the AJB and UGIF were paralleled by 'resistant' and illegal Jewish self-help organizations, no such development was evident in the Netherlands save for two exceptions. The first was the relatively small number of Jews who were involved in forms of illegal activity across the social and political spectrum. Only the communists had had any real experience of clandestine activity before the occupation, and their numbers remained small. Their cell organization was subject to increased attention from the authorities after May 1940, and it suffered grievous losses. Estimates suggest that the Germans ultimately caught half of the 2,000 who had been members at the beginning of the occupation.[25] The party made no distinction between Jews and other members, but continued to protest against all antisemitic measures in its newspaper *De Waarheid*. Some Jewish members of the communist party rank and file benefited from the cover provided by the organization, for example 'Harry', who was later shot by the Germans on Rotterdam Central Station, but who carried out leafleting raids for the party in the early years of the occupation;[26] likewise Meyer Lisser who was involved in helping to finance Dutch communists who wanted to go underground after the deportations had been announced.[27] Although less well organized in this early period, the Dutch Social Democratic Party (SDAP) also had many Jewish members among its illegal workers, and the first editorial group of the resistance newspaper *Het Parool*, included three Jews: Hans Warendorf, Maurits Kann, and Jaap Nunes Vaz. Kann had contacts with the military inspired resistance group, the *Orde Dienst* and was arrested by the Germans in the spring of 1941 for possessing a radio sender and was killed in Germany in March 1942. Nunes Vaz was arrested while in hiding in Wageningen in October 1942 and died in Sobibor in 1943, and only Warendorf survived the war.[28]

For these men, and others engaged in illegal activity, their Jewishness was often secondary to their political or nationalist commitment. Individual Jews could also be found in the ranks of later illegal organizations where their engagement alongside others in resistance activities was itself defence against Nazi anti-Jewish measures. Links to early manifestations of resistance may have helped them evade German persecution, but they were then tied to the fate of the group as a whole, and many of these early resistance groups were uncovered and 'blown' by the Germans, through betrayal, mistakes, naïvety or just bad luck. Exclusively Jewish resistance organizations were rare. One centred on the Palestine pioneers training in the Netherlands, some of whose number were involved in helping others go underground or escaping via the work of the Westerweel Group.[29] Many of the pioneers were themselves refugees, or at least had come from other countries in Europe before 1940 to complete their training on farms in the Netherlands. In addition, there were also the Jewish self-defence groups (*knokploegen*) in Amsterdam, created in response to national socialist provocations in Jewish neighbourhoods—provocations that culminated in the violence of February 1941.[30]

However, the most important manifestation of Jewish resistance came from the van Dien group. This had originated in the later 1930s among the German-Jewish refugees in Amsterdam who felt themselves isolated and excluded by the Dutch Jewish community. Some had been politically active in Germany and had escaped from, or fled, the threat of concentration camps and had been completely shunned by the Jewish refugee committee, as the Dutch government took a dim view of refugees engaging in any form of political activity. They gathered at Oosteinde 16, established in 1937 to act as a meeting place for the refugees. This soon became a centre for various forms of illicit activity, including help for refugees living in the country illegally. This was extended after the occupation to include distributing underground newspapers, forging documents, and helping people to go into hiding.[31] Initially independent, the group later allied with other resistance organizations and also sought to help those arrested and taken to the Westerbork transit camp.[32]

Thus although there were Jews in the Netherlands who, from the beginning, were prepared to engage in illegal activity to combat the Nazi menace, most came from those who had been politically active before the occupation, and their overall numbers should not be overestimated. It remains a matter of debate if Jews were proportionally more likely to have been numbered among the resisters than their non-Jewish fellow countrymen. In this context, the presence of non-Dutch Jews in many manifestations of resistance is also noteworthy. The van Dien group was a prime example of foreign Jewish political refugees having had better instincts about the true nature of Nazism, and being prepared to take direct action at an early stage.

The second exception to the general culture of co-operation can be seen in the actions of the provincial Jewish Council in Enschede. In contrast to groups elsewhere in the country, and in direct contradiction to the lead given from Amsterdam, its leadership actually encouraged the community to go underground, aided by warnings of imminent raids provided by a sympathetic police force and local authority which was not Nazified until the winter of 1942.[33] Although technically a branch of the Jewish Council in Amsterdam, the Council in Enschede was a very different body, made up of leading manufacturers and traders. Its creation had come about in October 1941, crucially after the first arrests of Jews in the area as reprisals for acts of sabotage. It was also a border area that had had first-hand experience of conditions in Germany through the refugees who had arrived during the 1930s. Thus the Council was more attuned to the threats posed by the Nazis and more willing to countenance illegal activity at an early stage, and its very different policies were to have a major impact on the fate of the Jews in its area.[34]

Self-help also played a role in the Netherlands, albeit at an individual rather than an organized level. For example, Lou Gompers had been a member of the Dutch Red Cross for more than twenty years and had been employed during the short-lived military campaign in May 1940. He had been dismissed as a 'non-Aryan' the same year, and in early 1942 decided to move out of Amsterdam to the small town of Doorn. Hiring a small house in the woods, he was helped by his brother-in-law, a local policeman, who warned of potential dangers. It soon became apparent that his house all-but backed onto the property of the local NSDAP 'Gauleiter' and former chauffeur of Kaiser Wilhelm II, and this prompted a move to nearby Zeist. Through contacts in the resistance, he acquired a job at a private commercial school and better papers. He was also offered employment by the local German authorities translating documents for the military courts after they had sequestered two typewriters from his school. This also gave him a permit to keep his bicycle—as he was carrying out work for the Germans—a prize possession later in the war when he collected and distributed food to the elderly and those underground.[35] Going underground 'in the open' was difficult in the Netherlands without the guarantee of proper identity papers, but some Jews did manage this trick. In some respects this was easier for foreign Jews, whose origins were not recorded by the Dutch authorities, and who could 'acquire' new or partially new identities after the occupation began.[36]

Others also found it possible to live openly. A family 'in hiding' from 1943 onwards had papers as a family evacuated from The Hague because their house had been demolished to make way for the Atlantic Wall. They were formally registered with the local authority and paid taxes. Moreover the children went to school 'as none of them looked particularly Jewish'.[37] Being an evacuee was a common cover for both Jews and others as it would explain their accent and presence in another part of the country. The destruction of Rotterdam city centre in May 1940 provided the obvious cover, but as is evident here, the clearance of coastal areas could also provide a suitable alibi. Another refugee Jewish family was also better prepared than most, having lost one son to the early deportations of young Jewish men in the summer of 1941. Thus, when the arrests began, they looked for help almost immediately and found it in the form of the younger son's college tutor who offered to take in the entire family, albeit that he had to accommodate some of them with his brother-in-law. Later they were moved to a farm in the south of Holland, although how this connection was made remains unclear. When their hiding place was betrayed, the mother and son made their way back to the tutor's apartment where they stayed for the next two and a half years, closeted in a single small room.[38]

Individual rescues play a disproportionately larger role in the Netherlands than in either Belgium or France simply because there was little or no pre-existing collusion between Jewish and non-Jewish organizations. These can be categorized under two headings: those that were the initiatives of the Jews themselves, and those prompted by concerned friends of acquaintances. Given the concentration of the Jews in the three largest cities of the Netherlands, and primarily in Amsterdam, it was there that the majority looked for immediate help. Surviving accounts suggest that initial individual contacts came in two different forms. The first involved asking friends, neighbours and workmates for help. This could initially be something as simple as helping to hide material assets from the registration of Jewish property, but could then develop into an offer of aid to 'disappear'. One man had been approached by a Jewish colleague in 1941 to help him and his wife go underground. This he did with the help of a friend involved in the distribution of ration and identity cards. Later he hid people in his house, but this was so small that it functioned more as a temporary refuge for those in the greatest need rather than a permanent home. He became part of a wider network in the city that helped Jews almost exclusively, but later in the occupation became associated with the Landelijke Organisatie (LO), the organization helping all those underground, when he began placing people in North Amsterdam, where people were accommodated for DFL25–35 per week, albeit only for proper lodgings.[39] It has been shown that the majority of Jews who went into hiding did so close to their former dwellings. This was hardly surprising, given that most arrangements were with friends and neighbours, but the fact that they remained in areas known to have been home to numbers of Jews made them easy targets for raids. This was especially true in Amsterdam, where the 'Jewish areas' of the city were well known. As a result, a high proportion of these private arrangements were ultimately unsuccessful. Those who did survive, often by sheer chance, owed their survival primarily to the fact that they eventually came into the care of one of the larger resistance organizations.[40]

As early as May 1940, the Arij and Riemke van der Meer family in Rotterdam tried to persuade their neighbours, the van Cleefs, to flee to England, but they refused to try, claiming that they had nothing to fear. However, some two years later, the van der Meers helped shelter them and their daughters—even arranging for false baptismal certificates for the daughters when they were taken to Westerbork—thus indirectly saving their lives.[41] Friendships formed at work could also be harnessed. More interestingly, there were examples of friendships created in the armed services. Leo Linssen was a sergeant in the Dutch army in 1939 and had offered Jacques Wallage his help should he ever need it. Thus three years later, when Wallage and his family needed to go into hiding they took up the offer. Linssen, by that time a baker in Venlo, knew enough trustworthy people to find suitable addresses for them.[42]

Individual rescues, and even some early networks, emerged from pre-existing relationships. Thus a woman in Utrecht who rented out part of her house had a refugee German rabbi, his mother, and his daughter as tenants—ostensibly before 1940. After the occupation began, they continued to live in the house until the mother was ordered to report for deportation in 1942, and the daughter was arrested in a raid, having been working at a local orphanage. Neither were heard from again, but the landlady then decided to help her remaining guest by applying for an exemption stamp for him from the Jewish Council. This protected him from arrest until April 1943 when he was required to report to the Vught concentration camp. She then attempted to exploit an exemption for Jews who had been of service to 'Aryans' by claiming that he had saved her from carbon-monoxide poisoning. In acceding to her request, the *Sicherheitspolizei* insisted that she become their agent and paid her Dfl.150 for the first month. It was at this point that she approached a local clergyman to find an alternative hiding place for her guest and was put in touch with a network that found another address for him. He returned to his hostess in August, after a hiding place had been built in her house, and was joined by a Dutch rabbi and his wife at the end of the year. All three survived the war, in spite of at least one major German raid in February 1945. While sheltering these three, the woman refused to take in any other fugitives, initially because of the unwanted attentions of the *Sipo*, and later because she felt three was the maximum number her house could shelter securely.[43]

A couple and their two children in The Hague were befriended by neighbours when the anti-Jewish legislation began to bite and the husband lost his job at a bank. Ways were found to support the family. In mid August 1942, the family received notice to present themselves at the station for deportation. Fearing the worst, they appealed to their neighbours for help, and at the last minute managed to see a locum doctor in order to persuade him that one of the children needed urgent hospital treatment—a fact that would temporarily exempt the whole family from the transport. The doctor was initially unsympathetic, but when he realized that 'the fate of four people was in his hands', he immediately referred the daughter to a local hospital where the consultant lost no time in admitting her.[44] Yet even with this co-operation, the ruse could be no more than a stay of execution, but in the meantime, the neighbours secured and hid most of the family's furniture from under the noses of the national socialists, and the family was put in contact with a resistance group that found the couple and the children individual hiding places where they stayed until the war's end.[45] Their story is unusual for a number of reasons, firstly because all four survived in hiding, but also because of the level of community co-operation deployed to help them. Few Jewish families were so lucky as to have such neighbours. Sometimes offers came completely unsolicited. One family recalled a note pushed through the letterbox, 'If you ever find yourself in difficulties, remember that you can always rely on us', and the hosts' first words as their guests arrived were: 'It is not going to happen. You are not going to Poland under any circumstances.'[46] This arrangement, as so many others were to be in the future, could only be temporary, as many neighbourhoods in Amsterdam were perceived as too dangerous as permanent places to hide.[47]

As was the situation in Paris, doctors and clergymen figure in many accounts of rescue. Doctors could be either instigators or intermediaries. They were often the first port of call for Jews looking for an exemption from the compulsory labour service in the Netherlands that preceded the deportations, and could be approached for the certification of illnesses that would make the holder exempt. Both clergymen and doctors also had strong links with the communities they served and with wider networks of trust, encompassing their own families, friends, and professional colleagues with whom they had trained or worked previously. In many accounts these links are assumed rather than explicitly revealed, but it is clear from more detailed explanations that many of the networks created away from the major population centres in the Eastern provinces were often the result of contacts between individuals with direct experience of the day-to-day persecution of the Jews in Amsterdam and their friends and contacts in 'safer' parts of the country.

Business relationships could also lead to later rescues. Albert Zefat, a chicken farmer in Valthe (Drenthe), offered sanctuary 'for as long as the war lasts' to Adolph From, a Jewish business acquaintance from the nearby town of Emmen, after the latter was told to report to Westerbork in August 1942. Zefat hid From and his family in chicken coops, and they were later joined by other families, often brought by the Warringa sisters from nearby Emmen, who also helped provide food. Ultimately there were eleven people sheltering there. This became too dangerous, even in the underpopulated regions of rural Drenthe, and the fugitives were moved to a specially dug underground shelter in the woods where they spent most of their time, but were fed each evening in the farmhouse. Rumours of Jews hiding in the countryside forced the group, by now numbering thirteen, to another shelter that had to be constructed by the fugitives themselves. Zefat was executed during a German raid on 27 July 1944 for refusing to betray the whereabouts of his charges.[48] His wife then arranged for those in the woods to be cared for by others in the community and all thirteen survived the war.[49] The devout Calvinism of Zefat and his family provide some of the answers for his willingness to help Jews in hiding, but the numbers he took in show how few alternatives there were until later in the occupation.

One family in Zwolle had provided a room where a Jewish radio repair engineer had continued his business after Jews were prohibited from owning radios or having them on their property. Intriguingly, most of his work was not radio repair, but adapting the sets to receive ultra short-wave signals, and thus the broadcasts from London. Thus later, when the first raids began and two young Jews needed a place to hide, 'there was no need for a long discussion' and one was offered a place to hide and was soon followed by the second—another person known to the family.[50] While some of these initial guests moved on, the family then discussed how many people they might be able to help. They decided on seven, not just on the basis of the size of their house, but also on the amount of food they could provide. To underwrite this, the husband acquired an allotment in order to grow more food for the potential new arrivals.[51]

A different form of help came from an unmarried German woman, Gertrude Markgraf, who ran a guesthouse in the seaside town of Scheveningen near The Hague. She had lived in the Netherlands since 1920 and was avowedly anti-Nazi. In spite of this (and perhaps because of her German origins) she had been forced to provided lodgings for a number of Gestapo/SD functionaries in the first years of the occupation, including the notorious collaborator Antonius van der Waals.[52] However, when the Jews were forcibly evacuated from the town on 22–23 August 1942, she became acquainted with a childless Jewish couple who soon after became her lodgers, living under false identities and paying Dfl.75- each per month. Her motivation was her anti-Nazi feelings and the desire to do something humanitarian and important. Her known 'connections' with the German security services made the house particularly safe from raids and served to protect her guests.[53] This fell through when both she and her guests were evacuated from the town and moved to Rotterdam. Shorn of her livelihood, with only limited recompense from the authorities, Markgraf was increasingly dependent on the rent from her lodgers, but the arrangement continued for thirty-two months until the liberation.[54]

The files at Yad Vashem record many other similar and gratuitous offers of help to Jews who were no more than casual acquaintances or even complete strangers. These arose from chance meetings or random conversations where the plight of the Jews was disclosed—either at the threat of being called up to report to Westerbork for transport to the East, or after the individual was already 'on the run'. For example, Laurens Mieloo was a window cleaner in Loosduinen, near The Hague and happened to be at the Jacobsen family house on the day they received their call-up. Without hesitation, he offered the couple shelter in his own house where they stayed in a small closet room for nearly three years until the liberation, avoiding detection during at least three German searches by hiding in the cesspool at the back of the house. His guests later reflected on their thousand days in captivity, noting how Mieloo had refused to shelter a non-Jewish industrialist who was offering a substantial sum because he was 'not interested in strangers or their money'. Moreover, although the house was isolated, there was a German couple living upstairs who were members of 'Die Partei' and thus noise had to be minimized at all times.[55]

Even more remarkable was the meeting between the farmer Jan Blok from Ijsselstein and Samuel Visser and his wife on the road. They had been offered sanctuary at the home of a man recommended by their neighbour, but he proved 'not to be a good man' and they left after ten days. With nowhere to go, they had cycled across the country and, having been refused help at a Catholic old people's home, arbitrarily knocked at the door of farmer Blok at IJsselstein and asked for help in hiding. Blok welcomed them in as God had sent them, and they remained in his care until the liberation.[56] Although adopting new identities, they still had to hide when visitors arrived—in this case in a 'bunker' no more than 40 cms high created under the kitchen cupboards—or in the cellar if guests arrived to stay for a period.[57] Accosting people on the road or knocking on the doors of strangers was fraught with dangers, and some Jews who survived in hiding claimed that no one would dare to go to a strange village or farm and ask to be taken in.[58] Yet in desperation, some Jews on the run did exactly that, having nowhere else to turn. There are many stories of people sheltering in barns overnight, with or without the owners' permission, and even being given some food the following day without any further offers of shelter being asked for or given. Sometimes, they would be presented with other addresses where the farmers knew, or suspected, that some form of clandestine activity was centred. For their part, the fugitives often looked to the manse or *pastorie* in a particular village, calculating that even if they received no help, it was also unlikely that the resident priest or pastor would betray them to the authorities.

This highlights a major complication for all clandestine activity in the Netherlands—the highly developed system of population registration overseen by the local authorities, backed up after 1940 by a system of individual identity cards.[59] Identity cards were initially difficult to forge, and adult Jews had the added, and potentially lethal, disadvantage that their cards were stamped with a large letter 'J'. Any journey, however short and by whatever means, could be subject to controls at checkpoints set up by Dutch or German police on street corners or at railway stations and tram stops. While forgeries or cards defaced or altered to 'aryanize'[60] them and to hide the true identity of their bearer might pass muster in the dark, or when scrutinized by disinterested or bored functionaries, they could not stand closer investigation, as the details could be checked back to a central register. Moreover, a common tactic used by the resistance of 'losing' cards—or indeed stealing them—nevertheless meant that the thefts and losses had to be reported so that the legal holder could gain a new one. The authorities thus had numerical lists of such cards that could be checked—the sole barrier to this was that over time the lists became longer and more unwieldy for functionaries 'on the beat' to use.[61] Only later in the occupation did various resistance organizations intervene to steal blank cards and attempt to destroy the central index.[62]

However, this means of cloaking was only viable if the holders were not likely to arouse suspicion as being too Jewish-looking. Hair dyes and haircuts could help in some cases, but more general dangers could also drive them underground, not least the Germans' continual search for more labour, so that any young man seen on the street during the day was immediately suspect. For others Jews in hiding, the dangers of their appearance remained and there were many who had to stay indoors permanently. The all-important ration stamps were also a perennial problem, as their issue was linked to the registered population and to the possession of identity documents, and these also had to be acquired illegally for those underground. This was done in many different ways, and later taken over on a massive scale by the organized resistance, but in the first stages stamps in many places could be acquired 'at the back door' of the distribution offices, provided by sympathetic civil servants or through traders not being too assiduous in insisting on stamps for all the goods they sold.[63]

This highly developed system of registration was obviously a direct threat to the Jews themselves before they went into hiding, but also proved a danger indirectly once they were underground as it also provided the basis for the Nazis campaign to call up Dutch workers for labour service in Germany. Thus if the hosts or their sons were called up in this way, the address automatically became unsafe, and liable to raids if those conscripted did not report. Moreover, if they themselves had to go underground, then the viability of the hiding place would in any case be brought into question, and their Jewish guests would have to move on.[64]

The First Networks

There are several well-known examples of help emanating from the committed work of individuals and their immediate families in the Netherlands. Although their stories and motivations have been examined many times, the background often provides clues to both their successes and failures, and is worthy of further detailed discussion. Perhaps the most internationally famous is that of the ten Boom family in Haarlem. While (Cornelia) Corrie ten Boom has become an icon through her experiences in a German concentration camp and post-war Christian witness, the whole family provides an example of selfless help to Jews from an early stage in the occupation. Devout and Bible-reading Protestants, the family was sustained by the father's watchmaking business in the old centre of Haarlem, and the house was a focus for all manner of philanthropy for decades before 1940. Food was provided for strangers as well as guests, often including beggars who arrived at the back door. Once his own children had grown, the father used the house to foster a total of eleven other children for shorter or longer periods of time. His shop was close to other businesses, some of them run by Jews, and many of his suppliers in Amsterdam were also Jews, with whom he had both professional and theological debates on his regular visits. The philanthropic ethic of the entire family is clearly discernible long before 1940, but it was the son, Willem, who was ostensibly the first family member to offer direct help. Having begun life as a pastor, his forthright manner had alienated many, and as a result he left the ministry to run a nursing home in Hilversum. He had found hiding places for the German Jewish residents of his home at the beginning of the occupation, and later for some of the Dutch Jews there as well, placing them with farmers in rural areas where there was less of a German presence and less surveillance of the population. His son, Kik, who had joined one of the embryonic resistance organizations, also became involved. When a Jewish furrier, a neighbour of the ten Boom's in Haarlem, had his shop looted by German soldiers in November 1941, it was Kik who found a hiding place for the man and his wife.[65]

Such was the reputation of ten Boom and his family that he was asked by the city's rabbi to hide the Torah scrolls and holy books from the synagogue, to prevent them from falling into German hands. Once word

got out that help could be found at ten Booms then the shop soon became
a transit point for Jews looking for shelter, as the family exploited their
extensive knowledge of the city and the many contacts they possessed
in every business and institution. It became a permanent home to seven
Jews in hiding: people who could not be found homes elsewhere because
they looked 'too Jewish' or had illnesses that posed a threat, such as an
elderly woman who suffered from chronic asthma.[66] The presence of these
fugitives in the house effectively forced Corrie and her family into illegality
on a scale that the god-fearing household could never have previously
imagined. The house was not large enough to hold them all, and was in
any case considered too overlooked and close to the police headquarters.[67]
The problem was passed to Willem, who provided advice but insisted that
the rest of the family run their own operation as he was being watched and
could not extend what he was doing without risking betrayal. His advice
on finding the all-important ration cards for fugitives was remarkable for
one who had been a minister—steal them! Corrie ten Boom attributed
her organization's success in finding the right people to God's guidance.
Others might just consider it to have been a case of good luck and knowing
the community.

    As their operations expanded, so did the risks. The innumerable visitors
did not help, and many of their placements went awry, especially when they
had to be done at short notice. One couple were taken to a woman who
already had eighteen Jews living in her attic. Even she complained about the
noise of her existing guests, but the whole group was finally betrayed when
some of them left the house—undisguised and unshaven—whereupon
the Gestapo soon picked them up and interrogated them. At this early
stage, many of the people involved had little or no idea about security—or
the risks they were running—and their approach was inevitably naïve.
Yet even the ten Boom network had its problems—being centred on a
single location that everyone knew. With more thought to the dangers
involved, the network might have been constructed differently, but this
was an organization that had grown in tandem with the problems it
confronted, and could not be changed or even adapted to meet new
dangers. Threats could come from many obtuse quarters. For example,
one of the grandchildren had become organist at the church in Velsen and
celebrated one service by playing the (banned) Dutch national anthem at
the end. Within a week he had been arrested and spent some time in gaol.
This had not led to any further repercussions, but the problem was there

for all to see. They were, however, aware of other risks. Thus, when a pilot was brought to the house, he was considered far too dangerous to keep, as sheltering airmen was known to carry the death penalty, as did being found with a gun. The pilot was swiftly handed over to the local resistance.[68]

Essentially the network was trapped. Ten Boom's memoirs recount her discovery that even the local police knew of her network and her resistance connections after they asked her for contacts to expedite the assassination of an informer within their own ranks. It was only a matter of time before someone, somewhere, informed the Gestapo, but there was no question of giving up, and Corrie ten Boom even kept a bag packed in her room, waiting for the moment when she would be arrested and taken to prison.[69] Her sister's house was raided and the two Jews caught along with her family, and eventually the expected raid on the family shop took place after a young courier had been arrested trying to move Jews from a hiding place that turned out to be a Gestapo trap. The morning of 28 February 1944 saw the whole family arrested, including some visitors.[70] Later it became apparent that part of the local resistance network had also been arrested in parallel raids across the city. Imprisoned in Scheveningen Gaol (the 'Orange Hotel'), she finally received news that her father had died soon after his arrest, but that most of her family and some of the resistance workers had been released—and that the Jews hiding in the house when the raid took place had also survived.[71] Only she and her sister Betsie remained in captivity and were later to be transferred to the Vught Concentration Camp and later still to Ravensbrück, where Betsie died. Corrie was released from the concentration camp in early 1945 because her sentence, for possessing false ration cards, had been served, and she returned to the Netherlands.[72] Had the Jews in the house been caught or her connection to the whole network been exposed, then the sentence would undoubtedly have been longer.

A similar individual initiative emerged from a single family in the farming community of Nieuw-Vennep on the Harlemmermeerpolder, south-west of Amsterdam. Johannes Bogaard Snr and his sons were devout members of the Orthodox Calvinist church (Gereformeerde Kerk) who owned three farms in the community and were clearly motivated by a strong anti-German feeling and seem to have disobeyed every possible German ordinance and decree from the beginning of the occupation. Thus, when the deportations began in July 1942, it was seen as natural for the family to help God's chosen people, and one of the sons who knew a Jewish family in Amsterdam collected them and brought them to the family farm, where they became the first guests of what was to become a major undertaking. From this one act, further contacts were made with other branches of the same Jewish family, and with others looking for a place to go underground. This was soon extended. (Geertuida) Truus de Swaan-Willems was married to a Jew who was himself acquainted with one of the first families helped by Bogaard. She then became a contact, persuading those called up by the Germans not to report, and then holding them at her home until Bogaard came to collect them, usually once or twice a week.[73] She also had contact with a Jewish orphanage in Amsterdam where children were removed on their way to school, with the director turning a blind eye. The network not only placed Jews in the Haarlemmermeer area, but also in Doorn and other places.[74] One estimate suggested that they helped around 300 Jews hidden on their property or in farms nearby between June 1942 and the end of 1943, without any outside help from other resistance organizations.[75]

Ration stamps were eventually obtained from a sympathetic civil servant and other hosts were paid up to Dfl.50- for each adult they sheltered and Dfl.30- for each child, but as the catchment became wider, so the need for more hiding places increased, yet the Bogaards found it very difficult to persuade their neighbours to help. As Johannes Jnr recalled after the liberation:

> it was impossible to find places for everyone. I still remember clearly visiting a farmer with a really large house (occupied by the man, his wife and one small child) and asking, it was only for a few days, to place a child there and the answer was: 'Not for a million, Bogaard, will I risk my family', and what he said was held by so many, but as a result *we* took far too many people.[76]

In contrast, another family contacted by the Bogaards managed to hide at least ten Jews in their house throughout the occupation. Sam Breijer and his wife lived in a day-labourer's cottage measuring no more than 6 metres by 4 metres that consisted of a single room with a small kitchen attached at the rear and an attic above. This normally housed the couple, their five sons and one daughter-in-law, plus their own disabled daughter, but was 'enlarged' by using the space under the floor to provide sleeping space for the Jews in hiding. In spite of several raids, at least once because of the link to the Bogaards, the fugitives were never found and all survived the war.[77]

It is clear that hiding Jews was discussed within the community. A meeting of the Calvinist Men's Association in the district had debated whether it was wise to take in Jews if you had children. The penalties were also discussed—a year in the 'political' prison at Amersfoort was seen as the norm, but some who had been caught had been sent to Buchenwald and had not returned, and there were rumours circulating that the Reich Commissioner had ordered the death penalty for those caught hiding Jews.[78] This open discussion indicates that there was a community of trust within the group, but although other hosts were found, the Bogaards' farms had to be made to hide many more people than could be comfortably accommodated—a function of the magnetic pull of their work and the fact that the family did not turn anyone away. There were so many children that a makeshift school was established to cater for them all and the farmhouses, outbuildings, and haystacks were all brought into service as hiding places.[79] There was no question of such a hiding place being kept secret. The fact that Bogaard and his sons approached others gave the game away, but knowledge was even more widely spread. One Jewish couple travelled to the Haarlemmermeerpolder by bus carry five large suitcases. Because the bus overshot the stop, the couple asked the driver for directions to Bogaard's farm, to which he replied, 'Oh, the Jew's farm', and then gave them precise instructions.[80]

Like the ten Boom's, this network operated from a single hub—and was centred on one or two individuals—and all the problems associated with keeping people in hiding came back to the same place. Thus every evening the farmhouse was filled with people bringing information or, more likely, their problems back to the network leader.[81] Proximity to Amsterdam made raids a real threat, and the farms were ultimately searched on five separate occasions. On the first occasion, the German discovered eleven Jews hiding on the farms and the second time three, yet the only actions against the owners were that Johannes Snr spent some time in custody. A third raid discovered no one, even though there were reportedly around 100 people hiding there at the time. As a hiding place known to the authorities, the farms could not have been considered safe for anyone, let alone Jews, yet the Bogaards continued their work, presumably because the need was still there, and because they considered that they had no choice and that God had called them to act as they did. Even exhortations from the resistance to ease up on the work did nothing to stop them. In fact, matters reached a head when the farms were raided for the fourth time when a policeman was shot by one of those in hiding, and a subsequent raid by *Ordnungspolizei* caught thirty-four people.[82] This led to a second arrest of Johannes Snr and a short period of incarceration in Vught. A fifth raid led to arrests of other members of the family and to Johannes Jnr having to go underground himself, but he continued to help those he had placed in hiding.[83] The conduct and persistence of this one family can only be explained by their unfaltering religious commitment, as they seem to have continued without any concern for their own safety. The same might have been said of the Jolink sisters in Varsseveld, two schoolteachers who sheltered both Jews and non-Jews in hiding. Their house had been raided in November 1942 but not before they had been warned by the local burgemeester. However, this should have made it clear that too many people knew what they were doing and that there were enough local people willing to betray them.[84] They saw it as their calling and thus paid little attention to their own safety, or to security in general. Thus in February 1944 they fell victim to a further German raid where six Jews and a Dutch merchant seaman working as a radio operator for a resistance group were discovered. The latter was killed during the raid and the Jews arrested and deported, but the sisters were again saved by the burgemeester, who intervened with the Germans to portray the sisters as simple souls who did not know what they were doing. As a result, they were freed and went to live with neighbours, only to be arrested again after the funeral of the merchant mariner for sending a wreath with a card that read, 'He died for the fatherland'. Both ended their lives in Ravensbrück.[85]

For the ten Booms, Jolinks and the Bogaards, the expansion of their work from small beginnings in a single location was to make a major contribution to their eventual downfall, yet the fact that they operated without much help from outside until late in the occupation made this more or less inevitable. Both networks were also known to a much wider circle of people than could ever be considered safe. They did expand geographically, using contacts and friends as potential helpers, and it was these contacts that largely determined the scope and physical extent of the hiding places used. Yet even among groups of friends and family, refusals were commonplace. Security and the perceived penalties for being caught were one important factor.[86] Many individuals who were ready to take the risk for themselves were not prepared to endanger their families. Beyond this, the reasons were many and varied. Hiding places had to have some element of security. Thus collaborationist family members or national socialist oriented neighbours could make any form of illegal activity impossible. Even benign but loquacious (*praatziek*) people living nearby could present an insurmountable obstacle, as could domestic servants and children whose silence could not be guaranteed.[87] As has already been said, the instigation of compulsory labour service in 1942 made many addresses insecure as those called up refused to report and were then sought by the authorities. Local changes could also make formerly secure addresses untenable, for example when new people who could not be trusted moved into the street or when properties were destroyed or rendered unsafe by military action or bombing. All of these factors were perfectly rational reasons for refusing to help. Whether they were sometimes no more than excuses to avoid a commitment or out of fear for the perceived punishments if caught can only be a matter for conjecture.

While these are merely some of the better-known cases of networks developing from the initiatives of certain committed individuals, there were others that were much less successful and were betrayed, or betrayed themselves, to the Germans at an early stage. There were networks where members' naïvety in being too open or insecure with their contacts overrode the element of luck that all such groups required. It has been argued that it took from the summer of 1942 to the spring of 1943 for the networks that did manage to survive intact to transform themselves from 'well-intentioned amateurs to trained professionals'.[88] Their learning curve was often a steep one and the penalties for failure catastrophic for both the organizers and those they sheltered. As one of the former put it, 'We were still decent people. We didn't have codenames. Unfortunately.'[89] A different spin on this same problem came from Jan Meulenbelt, writing in 1955, but having also been involved in helping rescue Jewish children:

> There were illegal workers, who were worryingly nonchalant in dealing with addresses and only a few were constantly aware that the lives of many were dependent on their carefulness.[90]

Yet even later in the occupation there were no guarantees, and betrayals, mistakes, and sheer bad luck continued to claim the lives of both rescuers and their charges. One feature of conditions in the Netherlands, and specifically in Amsterdam, was the existence of dedicated 'Jew hunters'. They are collectively estimated to have captured up to 8,500 Jews in hiding, primarily in the spring and summer of 1943.[91] The most infamous of these squads, the so-called 'Henneicke Colonne', named after its leader, operated largely on the basis of tip-offs and information gleaned from those they arrested. Although their 'official' status was somewhat unclear, their daytime employment was to search houses for Jewish assets, and hunting

Jews at night was merely an adjunct to that work. Although Jews on the run were sometimes caught in the street or at identity controls on trains or on stations, this was largely carried out by the SD, German Green police, or occasionally by their Dutch counterparts. In such cases, the names and addresses of hiding places and hosts might find their way into the hands of the SD, but there was no direct connection between the victim and a hiding place. The Jew-hunters operated in a different fashion, and raiding addresses became the norm for their operations. Their methods were often brutal and they were not beyond administering beatings to house-owners when the expected 'guests' were absent or did not materialize.

These squads would sometimes arrest suspected hosts to elicit information, but their powers of 'persuasion' were somewhat limited, and they often had to let their captives go after a short time.[92] Ostensibly much stranger was the behaviour of the Jew-hunters when they did find the victims they were looking for. Their reports, although often very brief and factual, would nevertheless indicate what they had done with the hosts involved:

We ... [...] arrested the Jewess Caroline ALTER.

She was walking in the street without a star and was in possession of a false identity card.

This Jewess was in hiding at the home of an Aryan woman, Jan Luikenstraat 21hs, Amsterdam.

The Aryan woman stated that she did not now that the woman was a Jewess and for that reason she was not arrested.[93]

Where it was obvious that the hosts were implicated, either by the circumstances of the raid or by the confessions of the Jews apprehended, then arrests were sometimes made, but members of the Colonne seem to have done everything possible to avoid taking non-Jews into custody. Thus in one case, the report made it clear that the hostess knew the people she was sheltering were Jews, but on account of her having six small children she was not arrested.[94] Similarly, the circumstances of the arrest of another Jewish couple left no doubt that the hosts knew of their guests' status 'but in consideration of the old age (78 years) of the Aryan family, their arrest was abandoned'.[95]

The sources shed little light on this, but the inference could be drawn that the Jew-hunters, interested only in Jews for whom they would receive a bounty, were uninterested in apprehending hosts, as they represented only additional paperwork with no monetary reward. Thus excuses, or assumptions, that hosts did not know their tenants were Jewish would be accepted without much question. In some cases, this may have been true as landlords would not necessarily be able to detect forged identity papers. It may also have been the case that leaving the hosts at large would provide the opportunity for the Jew-hunters to organize a further raid in the future. Even when hosts were arrested, they were often only held overnight and then released. Charges for a first offence seem to have been rare, although the leaders of the Colonne would often warn people off.[96] The activities of these squads, and their propensity not to arrest or report those found hiding Jews only served to complicate the popular perception of the precise penalties involved for those who were caught.

10

Too Little, Too Late, Organized Resistance and Rescue

Organized Help

It is widely accepted that organized civil resistance took longer to develop in the Netherlands than either Belgium or France, and that it came too late to help the majority of the Jewish community. In the years before the deportations began, and even for some time afterwards, the accommodation with the occupier that had been established in 1940 remained the primary response, although this was slowly undermined by ever-growing German economic demands as foodstuffs were increasingly diverted to Germany, fuel became scarce, and bicycles were confiscated.

As in France, the greatest impetus to civil disobedience and to wider resistance was the introduction of compulsory labour service. Thus when the Germans extended the obligation for labour service to all 18-year-old Dutchmen in September 1942, it prompted a Calvinist pastor and a devout Calvinist housewife from the East of the country to establish an organization, the Landelijke Organisatie voor Hulp aan Onderduikers (LO), that was to change the nature of resistance in the Netherlands and also provide some degree of incidental protection for the Jews already, or about to go, underground.[1] The pastor, Frits Slomp, was already known to the Germans as an outspoken critic and had been slated for arrest as a hostage in July 1942 for preaching against the Nazis.[2] Forewarned, he had gone to ground in the provincial town of Winterswijk. Here, he met Helena Theodora Kuipers-Rietberg, a woman who had been active in the Gereformeerde Vrouwenvereeniging (Calvinist Women's Association) and leading welfare work within her religious circle long before the occupation and who was later described as someone who 'resisted on principle'.[3] They recognized that helping workers go underground could not be done on a piecemeal basis and needed a proper organization. Thus they began the process of setting up a network of contacts across the Netherlands from their base in the East of the country.[4] In spite of being himself 'underground', Slomp, under the alias of Frits de Zwerver (Frits the Wanderer), undertook railway journeys to visit friends and acquaintances to persuade them to create local committees to help 'place' those wanting to go underground. His initial contacts came from Dutch Reformed and Calvinist economic organizations such as employers' associations.[5] Although some of his pleas fell on deaf ears, he did succeed in creating branches in many areas north of the main rivers and also integrated groups already engaged in this type of work elsewhere, including those specializing in help for Jews.[6] Essentially the idea was to create a type of local exchange (*beurs*) where offers of hiding places and work could be matched with the details of men and women who needed to go underground. Offers and requests that were not satisfied locally could be passed on to a provincial exchange, and ultimately to a national exchange.[7]

Kuipers-Rietberg had already had some contact with help for Jews wanting to go underground. A number of Jews from Rotterdam who were threatened with deportation had found their way to Driebergen, where the resistance had contacts with individuals in Winterswijk who were involved in the Gereformeerde Vrouwenvereeniging. Thus as early as the summer of 1942, and before the creation of the LO itself, there were Jews being hidden in the vicinity.[8] Over time, contacts were broadened as more groups were brought in until the summer of 1943 when the LO could really live up to its name as a 'national' organization.[9] Thus local meetings often included individuals who were already active in the resistance (primarily the *Ordedienst*), or who had already been involved in helping Jews to go underground, such as Johannes Post in Hoogeveen.[10] Slomp moved his centre of operations to Zwolle in Overijssel as Winterswijk was too isolated to facilitate contact with other parts of the country. Leaders of the various local and provincial groups met, usually in Zwolle, every Saturday to discuss the distribution of people who had not yet found places to hide.[11] Perhaps inevitably, those helped to go underground came from the same denominational groups as that of the local committees. Thus in its first stages, it tended to be the Dutch Reformed and Calvinists who were the main beneficiaries in the north. As more organizations were brought into the LO from Limburg and Noord-Brabant, so the Catholic element was better represented. Accounts of the placements speak of 'Dutch Reformed' bakers, 'Roman Catholic' smiths, and 'Calvinist' coachbuilders. In spite of Slomp's own insistence, there was no concerted co-ordination of help to Jews in hiding, but by the same token, they were not discriminated against—being treated the same as others on the run.[12] Local circumstances often dictated how Jews were treated. Thus in Zutphen there was a special group that had concerned itself with helping Jews, so that if any came into the hands of the local LO organization, they were handed over. Although separate, the LO still provided this group with supplies of ration cards for its work.[13]

It is also important to remember that the leaders and early members of the LO were all from Christian backgrounds and many were devout members of congregations.[14] Their move into illegal work was not done lightly and there was a good deal of discussion over many weeks about the rights and wrongs of their actions in relation to biblical teachings.[15] From its inception, the founders had a number of advantages, being part of a much broader Calvinist constituency at both a secular and spiritual level.[16] Thus contacts were often made through community leaders and elders of churches as well as through religious leaders themselves. A pastor who worked for the LO from 1943 onwards described his move into illegal work;

> At first I was not in the resistance, but was in principle against Germany. Around April 1943, I was ... [asked] ... about giving shelter to a German Jewess and her small daughter. I took the view that the person is the image of God, and this task of helping the Jews is the one that God has set us. Helping the Jews provided the opportunity to evangelise these people.[17]

This pastor then threw himself wholeheartedly into the work of helping Jews, escaped prisoners of war and students, and finding hiding places.

It seems that this particular cleric received very little guidance on how to organize his work, even though he had begun in 1943. He approached the hosts directly and there were no intermediaries used as cut-outs or as couriers. Only his fiancée was aware of what he was doing so that there could be continuity if he was arrested. Initially, he was careful not to make any written notes of records, but as the work expanded he was forced to commit things to paper, albeit in a secret code.[18] This pastor continued his work until October 1943 when the SD arrested him. He was tried and sentenced to seven months. He attributed his short sentence to the work of his advocate, but also to the Jewess who had been caught with him, as she had agreed to work for the SD in exchange for her freedom, but had never done so.[19] This pastor began his work with Jews, but many others were primarily concerned with people avoiding the labour draft, and Jews were only a minor part of their work—or entirely absent from it.

Other clergymen were more outspoken. The Calvinist pastor in Renkum was keen to help the Jews wherever possible, on the grounds that those who were sent to Germany because they had been in the armed forces, or a student, or a worker, were being sent to an uncertain future, but that was not so bad as the appalling fate of the Jews.[20] He made strident, if non-specific, statements from the pulpit about the proper attitude to be adopted towards the Germans and the organs of state under occupation and reputedly 'pressed his parishioners so hard to take in a displaced or wandering Jew or Jewess that they felt that there was no choice but to accept one . . .'.[21] Most of the Jews who lived locally had gone underground early and were thus able to survive the occupation, helped to some degree by a passive local police presence.[22] In the early stages of the LO, his statements were probably the exception rather than the rule, and the Jews were not considered a high priority.

Some LO workers nevertheless did become involved primarily because of their contacts with Jews. One man in Amsterdam married to a Jewess began by hiding his parents-in-law and a sister-in-law. Tragically, the parents-in-law decided to return a home a week before one of the great raids and were caught. Later he became involved with smuggling Jewish children out of the crèche at the Hollandsche Schouwburg holding camp and sending them to contacts in Friesland—and it was only through these contacts in the north-east of the country that he was put in touch with the LO in Amsterdam. By this stage, there were few Jews left in the city to hide, but as he had been sacked from his local government job because he was in a mixed marriage, he had the ability to work almost full time for the LO—looking after underground 'clients' in a particular district. In his case, of around 140 people, only twelve were Jews.[23] Although many LO workers had diverse responsibilities, there remained some whose induction into illegal work had come through helping Jews, and who were recognized and referred to by their LO colleagues as 'Jewish experts'.[24]

With hindsight, the historians of the organization summed up its role as follows:

> The LO had only a modest role in the hiding of Jews. In 1942, when the Jews had to go into hiding, this organisation had not yet developed. Also the working practices of the LO, geared to the wholesale help to large groups, lent itself less to the very special work [required] for the Jews. [. . .] Certainly many helpers of Jews later became members of the LO and their organisations became associated with the LO and the LO provided important help to Jews underground through the provision of ration cards and so forth.[25]

Likewise, one of the LO leaders, Henk van Riessen, spoke of the organization's links with help to Jews in responses to the post-war government enquiry:

> On work for Jews. Here and there it was linked to the LO, sometimes a [separate] branch, sometimes completely separate, sometimes just a connection to supply ration cards. An *onderduiker* could be dealt with on an assembly line basis. You can understand that, when there were 100 of these men to be dealt with at the exchange, and four were Jews, they never got a look-in. It was essential for the exchange to work quickly and it was very difficult to find places for them. Virtually no one took them. We also knew this and ourselves attempted to deal with the problem of the Jews, who were so much more difficult to hide and who people were so much more afraid [of helping], by using a separate channel or handing it over [to others].[26]

Contemporary wisdom suggested that LO networks might receive anything from five to ten offers of places for non-Jews for every one prepared to countenance giving shelter to Jews. In many areas it appears that any work to help the Jews was considered to be far too dangerous.[27] Was this just fear of the penalties for such action or something more sinister? Slomp, in a sermon at the beginning of 1944, was unequivocal. 'Anti-Semitism has increased dreadfully, and many Calvinists have been infected with this bacillus.'[28] This was also noted in the underground press where articles tried to combat this.[29] Herzberg subsequently described the help given to the Jews later in the occupation as an over-compensation for this antisemitism, as the fate of the Jews became clearer. He cited the motto that was often heard about the Jews: 'They are rotten people (*rotvolk*), but you have to help them.'[30]

However, even Slomp's actions in helping the Jews may have been tinged with an ulterior motive. While there were reports that he repeatedly stressed the importance of helping the Jews,[31] he and many of his fellow pastors saw no contradiction between the ideas of seeing help for the Jews as

God's work on the one hand, and an ideal opportunity to convert them on the other. While decrying the spread of antisemitism, he was also quoted in a sermon in early 1944 as saying that it was 'a wonderful time for a mission to the Jews. Many had come joyfully into the evangelical fold. In the last years, more Jews had been baptised than in decades before the war'.[32] This pressure to convert was undoubtedly substantial. Being taken to Church on a Sunday was seen primarily as a security measure to protect the cover story for many of those hidden in the countryside under false identities, but some hosts were far more direct—as, for example, the Frisian farmer who, after having sheltered a Jewish couple for fourteen days, insisted that they convert to Christianity or else live with his animals.[33] Hosts could also pressure conversion because they came to care for their charges, as one child recalled:

> Today Auntie asked me if I wanted to become a Calvinist. I won't do it, I won't let myself be baptised. Of course I'm glad that Auntie and Uncle have saved me, but that doesn't mean that I have to pray to the Christian God. Auntie doesn't understand it. She is afraid that I won't go to heaven if I don't become a Calvinist.[34]

While Slomp would have regarded his motives and purpose as unimpeachable, subsequent commentators have been more scathing and De Jong was at pains to point out that of the approximately 3,500 Jews sheltered in Calvinist households at some time during the occupation, only 126 were still members of the Church a few years after the war was over.[35]

Any thought that philanthropy or altruism underpinned all rescuers involved in the Netherlands needs to be qualified by many of the statements made by network leaders, and occasionally by the rescuers and rescued themselves. In the Blauwe Zand area of North Amsterdam, a popular place for Jews in hiding as it was north of the river and less subject to German raids, one LO worker noted that there was money to be earned in this work: money that many in the district could find useful. At the same time, the guests had all manner of complaints about their treatment, but it never came to open clashes and it was the organization's task to 'maintain harmony' between the families and their guests.[36] Later in the occupation, many of the Jews in this area were arrested, ostensibly through betrayal by two unnamed women, who later also helped in the breaking of another network in the east of the city.[37]

The development of the LO from the autumn of 1942 reinforced a trend that could already be seen among the rescue operations set up to help Jews, namely the increasing use of the relatively underpopulated and rural areas of the eastern Netherlands as a source of hiding places. These areas were well away from the major centres of population and—by extension—a long way from any substantial SD presence. Thus it is no surprise to find the three northern provinces of Friesland, Groningen and Drenthe featuring heavily in stories of rescue, alongside Overijssel and Limburg to the south. All were largely agricultural with scattered market towns and possessed only a few major centres of population. Large industrial activities were a rarity except for the textile manufacturing in the vicinity of Enschede and the extensive coal-mining and associated businesses in the far south of Limburg, close to the German border. Although relatively homogeneous in economic terms, these areas were very different in their confessional make-up. In the south, the vast majority of the population were Catholic, with only a sprinkling of Dutch Reformed and Calvinist believers—often brought to the area by the chance of work. Conversely, the Northern provinces were overwhelmingly Nonconformist; with a Dutch Reformed majority underpinned by a substantial orthodox Calvinist minority. Indeed, in some communities it was the Calvinists who were the majority group. This is an important distinction, as the supposed propensity of the Nonconformists, and Calvinists in particular, to help Jews has often been cited in works on the subject, although as will become evident here, rescue by Catholics was just as important in the Dutch context.

Friesland and Groningen

Jews had been small in number in both provinces.[38] As with other parts of the country, there was a certain cultural antisemitism, reinforced by the orthodox observances of the Jewish community, but among many Christians, attitudes towards the Jews remained ambivalent: seeing them both as the killers of Christ and as God's chosen people. They were also a minority group and, as such, gained empathy from Christians who also saw themselves as minorities, and even persecuted minorities, within Dutch society.[39] Most of the Frisian Jewish community fell victim to the deportation process in early October 1942, with some families reporting willingly to Westerbork in order to be reunited with husbands and fathers who had previously been employed in work camps. Ironically, public revulsion to the arrests in the city meant that, subsequently, hiding places were easier to find, and rescue organizations were able to place many Jews from the western cities in the neighbourhood.[40]

As in other parts of the country, there were examples of the police warning Jews of impending raids, or even of arranging hiding places, but these would sometimes fall apart when the beneficiaries refused to take the path into illegality, and the officers were left with no option but to take them to the collection points.[41] One particular order to arrest two sick Jews in the village of Grootegast led to one of the few collective protests by the police, where all eleven members of the Marechausee brigade stationed there refused to comply and were sent to Vught concentration camp and sentenced to death. Ultimately, only their leader Boonstra died in German captivity but the rest were freed only after the Allied liberation of the southern provinces in September 1944, or after the end of hostilities in May 1945.[42] Local historians have noted the unwillingness of some Jewish communities to consider going underground as an option and their commensurately high mortality rates. Explanations for this are wide ranging. Jews in towns and villages where the resistance was more active were more likely to have gone underground, as were those with wider non-Jewish families capable of sheltering them. Conversely, many highly orthodox Jews took the deterministic view that deportation to Poland had been ordained by God. Others were swayed by the threat of Mauthausen for those caught trying to hide. Even in 1943, many refused to believe the stories of what was happening in Poland. However, as with every other Jewish community in the country, the overriding determinant was a lack of resources and a reluctance to be dependent on others.[43]

The Frisians were highly praised by those involved in rescue work elsewhere. One LO worker in Amsterdam described their achievements as 'extraordinary' and noted that he could always go to them for help for the Jews. Indeed, in his case, they seem to have provided the impetus by sending telegrams when they had new places for people rather than waiting to be asked.[44] However, he was referring only to the small numbers actively engaged in helping Jews and not to the population at large. As with other provinces, the majority have elicited a great deal of moral condemnation as 'ostriches' unwilling to help the Jews they knew, or only at a price.[45] Most of the help that emerged from these two Northern provinces came too late to help the local Jewish communities, although there were some honourable exceptions, with small networks operating from the summer of 1942 onwards.[46] The towns of Heerenveen and Bontebok welcomed both adults and children, and 'always had more places'. By the autumn of 1942 there were rumoured to be up to 1,200 people in hiding there, albeit by no means all of them Jews.[47]

One example of a network will have to suffice here. Krijn van den Helm was a Mennonite and convinced antimilitarist who was 'converted' by his experiences in the army in 1940. As a tax official, he had been transferred to Leeuwarden in 1941 and as part of his work had come into contact with Jewish businesses, and in August 1942 offered his house keys to a man and his family 'if things became too dangerous'.[48] He had already conspired, with the permission of his superior, to help cloak money that the man had put aside from the company accounts, and it was in this way that the local tax office became the centre of a network for helping Jews underground.[49] Contacts with other parts of the country came about by more roundabout methods. Van den Helm was ostensibly recommended to networks in Amsterdam via the Mennonite pastors in Sneek and Leeuwarden, and it was in this way that Jews were brought from the west to hiding places in Friesland.[50] Soon other tax offices in the province were also mobilized to find further contacts and more addresses for both adults and children.[51] Van den Helm's own organization also grew. His links with other Mennonite businessmen, such as Sjoerd Wiersma, the director of a laundry business in Joure, led to the creation of another network. The latter was already involved in other resistance work and was thus himself already 'underground' having been involved with the Orde Dienst and distributing *Vrij Nederland*.[52] Wiersma was soon establishing his own contacts with organizations in Amsterdam to speed the supply of children into Friesland.[53] He saw the work as a mission from God, and was able to persuade others who were equally religious but saw the persecution of the Jews as a punishment from God that they should nonetheless help the persecuted. Yet even he was caught out, saying that in the end he had to hate the Jews for having crucified his saviour, leading to one of his contacts responding that if he had not known of his work smuggling Jews out of Amsterdam in lorries, he would have taken him for an antisemite.[54]

As a result of Wiersma's work, Joure became a centre for people in hiding. His contacts stretched across the country and included the ten Boom's in Haarlem. When in Amsterdam, he stayed with a director of a formerly Jewish textile wholesale business that was controlled by a German *Verwalter* and this gave him access to Jews looking for places to hide.[55] More widespread offers of help and greater mobilization of the public came only after the Germans attempted to re-intern the members of the Dutch army—to facilitate their use for labour purposes. This led to much greater levels of civil disobedience and strikes during April and May 1943, and was compounded by a German ordinance forbidding Jews from residing in all but the three western provinces. This served to force the issue for all parties and resulted in more coherent arrangements, backed up by the development of the LO. Ultimately, the network created by Krijn van den Helm was destroyed after one of its couriers, Esmé van Eegen, who had been sent to the area by the Amsterdam student organization, became attached to a German officer. This led to van den Helm and others leaving the area, but when van Eegen was herself betrayed and arrested, she gave away a series of names and addresses that allowed the Germans to round up and execute many of the network's leaders.[56]

Overijssel and Drenthe

Enschede was the major city in Overijssel and an estimated 49.5 per cent of all the 2,646 Jews in the province lived in this one town.[57] Much has been made of the very different survival rates of Jews from different communities within this region. Whereas perhaps 40 per cent of the Jews in Enschede survived the occupation, nearly all their co-religionists in the nearby towns of largely Catholic Oldenzaal and overwhelmingly Protestant Hardenberg were arrested and deported.[58] Levels of Jewish integration with the local community seem to have made no difference. The Jews in Oldenzaal were more isolated and subject to social and cultural antisemitism. In contrast, their co-religionists in Hardenberg were closely allied to their Christian neighbours, but nearly all reported for transport and refused offers of help to go underground. Attitudes of local officials and the police may also have played some role, but in spite of the extensive discussion of these case studies, the samples are really too small to draw concrete conclusions.[59]

In contrast to many other areas, Enschede had first-hand experience of German persecution of the Jews, not only from the arrival of refugees before 1940, but also in September 1941 when 105 Jews were taken as hostages after a series of sabotage actions in the neighbourhood and were sent to Mauthausen, where most perished within a few weeks. In contrast to the compliant attitudes of its sister organization in Amsterdam, and perhaps also because of this experience, the Enschede Jewish Council was prepared to countenance illegality from the beginnings of the deportation period, and actively encouraged its community to seek refuge underground. In this they were helped by Leendert Overduin, a Calvinist pastor who had already been involved in various forms of clandestine activity.[60] His involvement began with helping Jewish neighbours, and it was estimated that around thirty Jews spent some time living in his house during the occupation.[61]

Overduin was able to enlist the help of Friso van Hoorn, a local civil servant who had contacts with other branches of the resistance and was also able to warn Jews about impending raids and arrests.[62] These two men, coupled with Overduin's two sisters (Maartje and Corry) and a local baker and his daughters (Gerhard, Sara and Mijnie Voogd) formed the core of his organization.[63] In addition, they had contacts to distribute the necessary ration cards and money for people in hiding. Finding the money and ration cards was another matter, although Overduin benefited from his contacts with the resistance and later with the local branches of the LO, who delegated the work of hiding Jews to his organization as it was perceived as more dangerous than their other activities in supporting labour draft evaders. Money came from Jewish and non-Jewish industrialists in the vicinity, but later Overduin was able to use the resources provided by the Nationaal Steunfonds to support his work. His couriers also made regular journeys to Amsterdam to obtain funds for Jews in hiding held by their lawyers, or to sell gold and jewels on their behalf.[64] He also developed a system for moving those underground from place to place in relative safety by using the vehicles of Enschede's ambulance service as transports. The bodies of those who died could be moved, the sick could be taken to the doctor, and the healthy moved from one district to another—all without arousing the slightest suspicion.[65]

The network became geographically more diverse as more hiding places had to be found, both for local Jews and for an increasing number brought to it from other parts of the country. Thus its activities ultimately stretched from Friesland in the north to Limburg in the south as contacts were exploited to find suitable safe houses. One such was Pastor Moulijn in Blija (Friesland), who had already been involved in helping two allied pilots, but took time to decide to help, even after a personal visit from Overduin who left him with the words, 'in the end it is a question of belief'.[66] In early September 1943, Overduin was arrested, as was one of his sisters and Voogd, the baker. The latter were soon released, but Overduin spent nine months in prison, after which he went underground. In the meantime, his organization continued to function without him and carried on supporting its charges until the liberation. Assessing exactly how many Jews were assisted by this one network is difficult. There is a definitive list of 461 names that emerged at the liberation, but this was no more than a snapshot. More telling may be the fact that the organization was using between 1,100 and 1,200 ration cards every month at the height of its operations.[67] Although by far the largest operation of its type in the region, there was a similar rescue operation, albeit on a smaller scale, carried out by another pastor, F. W. Tjadens, who managed to save almost half the Jews in his Steenwijk community.[68]

There is no doubt that Overduin was a highly motivated individual who saw it as a Christian duty to help those in need. In this he was helped by his own forays into illegal work at an early stage in the occupation, some good contacts with the local bureaucracy, a co-operative police force prepared to warn Jews in danger of arrest, and also with a client group that did not conform to the national stereotype. While there was a Jewish proletariat within the community, there were also reputedly five millionaires among them, as well as many other families who were reasonably well-to-do.[69] If he was operating in a more favourable environment than many other rescuers, there were also some complaints that emerged after the liberation. It seems that he deliberately chose to place Jewish children in strongly Protestant homes where they would receive a Christian upbringing— thus completely ignoring their Jewish origins. In the same vein, and also inexplicable to many of his resistance colleagues, he later chose to help former Dutch national socialists on the run, again with a view to bringing them into the Christian fold.[70]

Drenthe was also the centre of one of the major independent networks that helped Jews in hiding. It was established by Johannes Post, a committed Calvinist who had a wife and eight children on the farm he ran in Nieuw-lande and who had also become an alderman on his local town council at the age of 29.[71] His farm became a well-known centre and might host anything up to 100 visitors a day to deal with all manner of illegal work. Perhaps not surprisingly, this level of visibility forced him and his family into hiding after July 1943, but his underground work went on until he was caught and executed after a raid on the Weteringschans prison in Amsterdam.[72]

His rescue work in Drenthe was taken over by Arnold Douwes in June 1943, a man who became one of the most famous Dutch rescue-network organizers. By profession he was a landscape gardener but came from a family of Dutch Reformed preachers. Already on the run from the authorities, he had found sanctuary with Post and his wife. He had first-hand experience of the persecution suffered by the Jews and was anxious to fight 'Satan' as he himself phrased it.[73] He realized that the area had enormous potential as a hiding place, and worked with (Max) Nico Léons to organize the removal of Jews from Amsterdam, rescuing perhaps 100 adults and 100 children as well as many non-Jews on the run.[74] He was also unique in maintaining a weekly diary that described the nature of his work.[75]

> We lied our way through life. We always said, "Yes, we have a hiding place," even if we didn't have a hiding place. We lied to the people who needed a refuge and we lied to the people who were to receive them. We lied everywhere and had arguments everywhere, with both the hosts and the guests. We had the most terrible arguments, but if we hadn't done this we would have achieved nothing.[76]

He was of the opinion that the most active resisters came from the extreme right-wing (conservative) and left-wing elements of the population, and that this was also true for those prepared to hide Jews.[77] Most of his contacts and 'hosts' were Calvinists and supporters of the Dutch Anti-Revolutionary party, but although not a majority in the areas where he operated, they were certainly not marginal in many of the individual communities involved. Here, as elsewhere, contacts often came through the local clergymen, meaning that a particular parish of a particular confessional group would become the source for many hiding places. These could be expanded outwards to other like-minded leaders of the same confession, or via family links to other parishes, but the effect was to create a very uneven spread across the country, with some communities sheltering tens, if not hundreds, of Jews, while others had none at all. For example, Nieuwlande itself is famous for the sheer numbers sheltered in that one community. Likewise, there were estimated to be around 300 Jews hiding in or around Ommen, mainly in local farmhouses, and the Overduin organization had placed many people in and around Enschede, yet only a few miles away, the town of Hengelo seems to have had few, if any, Jews in hiding. This pattern was also apparent elsewhere in the country with some localities playing host to many Jews in hiding with other, similar communities nearby having no involvement at all.

Douwes' diary shows that many of his contacts were with clergymen, in one case exchanging identity cards for hiding places,[78] but he also clearly used 'cold calling' methods to provide new addresses. However, approaches to religious institutions and ministers for help did not, as his diary recorded, always produce results:

> I visited a Catholic orphanage and spent several hours trying to persuade the mother superior to take in Jewish children, but she refused. I tried to work on her conscience and her Christian duty, but nothing worked. I also visited the dean who had a large rectory and could have taken in a dozen fugitives (*duikelaars*). But he claimed not to have any space[79]

He also visited a castle, the home of a baron, where he met a group of old women who were all as scared as rabbits. As he cynically observed, 'they had thirty rooms, possibly a couple more... but no room for fugitives.'[80] The maxim that 'anyone who helps a Jew will be treated like a Jew'[81] had a deep impact across the countryside, even though the actual penalties imposed were not well understood. It was only in September 1942 that the first notifications of people being punished for helping Jews by being sent to concentration camps were published in the press.[82] By October 1943, however it was widely held that being caught with Jews in your house would probably result in six months' imprisonment in a German camp, but executions and the burning of houses were not unknown as, while the fate of the Jews was clearly defined (Westerbork and deportation to the East), the treatment of the hosts was essentially subject to the moods and whims of those who apprehended them.

Douwes' testimony also made it clear that even when people had evinced some interest in helping the Jews, this did not necessarily translate into positive offers of help on the doorstep. Pledging assistance was one thing, but many would-be rescuers seem to have had cold feet when confronted with the reality of the situation on the doorstep. Supposedly 'good' Dutchmen would use the excuse that there were already too many Jews in the district or that Jews could not ultimately be trusted.[83] This became even more of a problem as the stated penalties for helping Jews were increased and more widely disseminated:

> Finding places for the varied Jewish fugitives was always an issue. First always 'temporary' places. People found it hard to say no if you said that the 'customer' would have to sleep in the open if they did not take him in. Of course, the result was an argument, but for the most part it turned out better than expected.[84]

This masked some rather more extreme tactics used by Douwes and others when they were under real pressure. It was not unknown for the courier to wait until the last possible moment before the nightly curfew came into force before knocking at the door of a potential host accompanied by the putative 'guest' and then more or less shove him (or her) through the door and run away, leaving the host with few choices.[85] Another ploy would be for the courier to stress the temporary nature of the arrangement and say that he or she would come back the following day—and then not return for two weeks while hosts and guests got to know each other.[86] The fact that these methods worked suggests that most hosts were unwilling to put their guests back out on the street lest they were caught, and thus made the best of the situation. However, this could happen, as Douwes also recorded:

> After a long conversation I had persuaded (a farmer and his wife) to take in a Jewish child, and had brought them a nine-year-old girl. Two days after I arrived with her luggage only to find that in the meantime they had thrown her out...I took her to another place that I had earmarked for a new arrival from Amsterdam.[87]

A countervailing element made apparent by Douwes was the level of 'rent' demanded by the hosts—either directly to their guests or to the network protecting them. While the existence of rescue networks helped to limit the more exorbitant demands made by people in private arrangements, there could be an element of negotiation on the precise level of remuneration, where some account was taken of the extent of the risk involved for the hosts, whether this was the result of a calculating mindset on the part of the hosts, or scaled more as a sweetener to persuade those who were wavering. However, given all of this it is hardly surprising that Douwes was constantly having arguments.

Hosts could also be contradictory when it came to their guests. One farmer who did shelter Jews was on record as saying, 'I think it's good that the Jews are plagued a little, because I don't like Jews. However, what is happening now is going too far.'[88] A different complaint came from another host who wanted rid of his guest, 'because ... the man is a German, also a Jew, but above all a German, and I don't like krauts (*moffen*)'.[89] That said, perhaps not surprisingly, there were many recorded instances where the cultural and social gap between hosts and guests was so great that it could not be bridged. This could happen when one party did not live up to the expectations of the other—or their behaviour created so much friction in an already tense situation that something had to give. Sometimes hosts did put their guests on the street, and guests sometimes walked away of their own volition. If informed, networks did try to remedy the situation by patching up differences or by finding alternative addresses, often at very short notice. By the same token, guests could also be problematic. Long after the war, Douwes reflected on one such case:

> 'Aunt' A was a very difficult person with all sorts of demands. As I was reading, I again saw how perfectly good hiding places were being ruined by her, 4 in a row! Hiding places were at a premium, it took hours of talk, often a lot of legerdemain, cunning, lying, trickery, to conquer a hiding place, and there she wasted one after another.[90]

The Douwes network also developed another important method when it came to finding hiding places, namely having codes that would identify the type of fugitive en route from the big cities. In the case of this organization, they employed an alphabetical and numerical system where 'A' indicated an adult male and a Roman suffix indicated the level of 'physical Jewishness' Thus 'I' was someone with very pronounced Jewish features whereas 'IV' indicated someone who, with good papers, could live openly and get a job. 'B' stood for male children and 'C' and 'D' for women and girls respectively.[91] Other networks had other and sometimes more sophisticated numerical codes while others referred, for example, to black, grey, and white rabbits in their communications.

Limburg

Catholic Limburg in the south-east exhibited different characteristics from areas to the north. Several towns had boasted Jewish refugee committees in the 1930s as a result of arrivals from Germany, and some municipalities had been more welcoming than the policy directives from The Hague had demanded.[92] The existence of many families with members on both sides of the border had fostered several networks that brought people safely across the frontier, and 'commercial' smuggling of people and goods also became more common as conditions for Jews in Germany worsened after November 1938.[93] However, the 1940 census showed that there were only 1,660 Jews in the whole province, a mere 0.27 per cent of the population.[94]

In the first years of occupation, the Roman Catholic Church took steps to protect the small number of children in its schools who were regarded by the Germans as Jewish, and also refused to have signs prohibiting Jews placed in Catholic public institutions when these were introduced at the beginning of 1942. Soon after the deportations began, the protest of the Catholic archbishop was read from every pulpit, prompting the Germans to arrest and deport most of the Catholic converts, including the philosopher Edith Stein and her sister from the Carmelite Convent at Echt.[95] Civil protests were also apparent. Signs prohibiting Jews were removed or defaced, but the removal of the Jews from the province was met with widespread popular indifference. Even the growth of civil and military resistance in the region did not necessarily bode well for the Jews as many of those involved continued to hold antisemitic opinions and could not see why others would endanger their lives to help an alien people.[96] Early assistance usually came in the form of helping Jews escape, and several individuals and families were credited with having operated more or less alone to expedite journeys across the frontier into neighbouring Belgium. How they were contacted by others, or how the Jewish fugitives came to know of their existence is unclear, and much of what we do know comes from police reports, as many of them were caught and spent time in German concentration camps for their pains.

Network organizers in the province often had backgrounds in illegal work, for example Arie van Mansum, a member of the small Calvinist denomination, had been involved in helping distribute illegal newspapers since 1940. In 1941 he was asked by one of his co-religionists to help a Jewish couple move to Apeldoorn.[97] This same individual had contact with several members of the Jewish business community in Maastricht, and also provided additional help in the form of contacts with a shopkeeper, who was able to provide food for those in hiding, and also a local police inspector who could warn of impending dangers from German raids.[98] Maastricht became the centre for helping individual adult Jews and a few families. Some were smuggled across the Belgian frontier, but the network as a whole may have sheltered up to 150 people at its height, of whom 50–60 were unaccompanied children.[99]

It has been estimated that the two small communities of Sevenum and Grubbenvorst played host to around 100 Jews between them. Although the numbers were not huge in comparison with 'rescue communities' elsewhere in Europe, they need to be seen in the context of the size of the villages involved—and also the nature of the surroundings. These were poor and isolated communes where the only available hiding places were in farms, barns and chicken houses—or *in extremis*—in makeshift shelters on the nearby heath and moorland. However, their tightly-knit sense of community limited the chances of betrayal and pastoral leadership provided the essential element of mobilization. In Sevenum, Eugénie Boutet was the central figure, helped by a close-knit community where 'houses, doors and hearts stood open'. Most of those who were sheltered there had very positive things to say about their hosts, save some comments about the fears of pressure to convert to Christianity.[100] Grubbenhorst had been mobilized by a son of the parish, the social democrat journalist Mathieu Smedts through its parish priest Henricus Vullinghs and his chaplain P. J. H.Slots. The village was again in an isolated part of the country, solidly Catholic but also very poor. Vullinghs had been born in the locality and studied for the priesthood in the still antisemitic environment of the University of Nijmegen at the end of the nineteenth century, before returning to minister in his home region. Apart from his pastoral duties, he also encouraged the brighter children to continue their education and often sponsored their studies. During the occupation, Vullinghs used his pulpit to mobilize his community to help those in need, and after being contacted by Smedts, used his position and influence to persuade many of his flock to shelter Jews sent by rescue networks.[101] Smedts had already been involved with the underground route into Switzerland,[102] but approached his friend and mentor Vullinghs with a view to finding hiding places inside the country.[103] Through Smedts they also came into contact with the Westerweel group and helped to shelter some of his Palestine pioneers and others who were later part of their activities.[104]

Although many of the groups operating in the province seem to have emerged from the Calvinist minority, these two examples show how Roman Catholic involvement was just as important in helping the Jews. Contacts were made across the confessional boundaries, and there was engagement with the work of helping children from among the Catholic majority. Nevertheless, the total numbers involved remained extremely small and a critical post-war report, probably written by someone within one of the organizations, reflected on the difficulties in hiding Jews in this particular province (although the same reasons probably held true almost anywhere in the Netherlands). There were perceived to be six special problems:

1. Most of the fugitives had never been to Limburg before and people feared, often without reason, their lack of adaptability to changed surroundings.

2. Very often it was not individuals but couples, sometimes with babies or older children, who needed to be hidden together.
3. The outward appearance of the fugitives, which was such a giveaway for many Jews.
4. The largely unsubstantiated stories of Jews being unreliable, especially if they were arrested.
5. The dangers for the rescuers if the Germans discovered them. These were undoubtedly greater than for sheltering 'ordinary' fugitives but not as great as for sheltering pilots.
6. Initially, the problems in finding good identity and ration cards for all the Jews who arrived in the province.[105]

The report was predicated not on outlining what had been done to help the Jews, but on what had gone wrong. It made much of the injustices committed against the Jews: of the people sheltered until they had been soaked of all their funds and were then betrayed to the Germans, of the huge amounts charged for largely worthless identity and ration cards, and of the fugitives offered the chance to go to Switzerland who were abandoned as soon as they had crossed the Dutch border.

In total, the province probably hid around 1,300 Jews, of whom 500 were children, spread between nine or so different organizations, but given that there were other organizations and private arrangements not covered by this total, and that fugitives were constantly moving in and out of the area, accurate figures are hard to divine. Cammaert estimates that between 2,500 and 3,500 may have been rescued in Limburg, of whom no more than 8 per cent fell victim to the Nazis while in hiding.[106] Thus in terms of those who were hidden, this was a successful outcome but took no account, as the morally-loaded post-war report had done, of what else might have been done for the Jews.

In the story of Dutch networks and organizations that sheltered Jews underground, the role of the local pastor or priest were often crucial to their success in obtaining help from local communities. They were the point of contact for the community as a whole—even in areas where religious belief was mixed—and acted as referees for suitable people to approach as potential helpers. However, most of the practical and day-to-day involvement came not from these men directly, but from their subordinates. As one Protestant network organizer explained,

Pastors are generally older people, and older people are more anxious people, and more a figurehead of the life of the Church. It was therefore tactical that this work, with all that involvement brought with it, was carried out by the chaplains.[107]

However, this did not mean that they were necessarily any less committed to the struggle against the German occupiers, and many could be found comparing National Socialism with Satan and justifying resistance on the basis that it was God's work.[108]

The 'Philips Jews'

While there are many examples across Europe of employers 'hiding' Jews in their workforces, the activities of the Philips electrical concern in Eindhoven represent an almost unique example of attempted 'corporate' rescue. That said, the firm's wartime role has been hotly debated in the Netherlands and remains the subject of controversy.[109] Early in the occupation, the company was designated as a *Luftwaffebetrieb* under a German *Verwalter*, and received at least Dfl.200 million of contracts. In addition, it was implicated in using concentration camp labour in order to fulfil these contracts. Against these manifestations of collaboration were the examples of apparent resistance from within the company: in providing radio equipment for the resistance, acting as a conduit for information between The Netherlands and England, and in protecting elements within its workforce. In addition, at least one member of the company's management had smuggled false South American papers for Jews into the country from Switzerland.

At the end of 1941, Philips' Jewish employees were designated as part of the so-called 'special commissions office' (SOBU) to protect them and their families from German measures that would have seen their dismissal from the main Philips concern. It was to indicate to the Germans that this was a highly specialized team of workers who could not be replaced.[110] They were nonetheless isolated in the factory, with a separate entrance and toilet facilities. Attempts to have the Jewish workers emigrate by paying a ransom to the Nazis was ruled out by the Allied powers, although the management did acquire around 180 of the most desirable '120,000' exemption stamps from the authorities that supposedly protected the holders from deportation.[111] As the deportation process continued into late 1942, the ability of the firm to protect its Jewish workers diminished, although the SOBU workers remained exempt.

At the same time, the Germans substantially increased their demands for skilled Dutch labour to work inside Germany. There is no doubt that Frits Philips saw it as a social obligation to protect his labour force, but the threat that the Germans would take over the concern altogether was ever present and thus limited his powers. This may also have been the case when the Germans more or less insisted that the company set up a subsidiary inside the Vught concentration camp.[112] This would allow the company to continue meeting its German contracts (and preclude a complete German takeover). At the time, Philips was equivocal on the issue, but after consultations with other directors and with the resistance (who thought it might be beneficial to have a presence inside the camp), he agreed to the plan.

The Vught *kommando* took time to grow. Established on 22 February 1943 it recruited no more than eighty male *Schutzhäftlinge* in the first two months and, although some of them may have been Jews, there was no question of employing *Ziviljuden* at this stage.[113] Thereafter the numbers increased but, although the work was meant to be a direct contribution and important to the wider German war effort, one employee later noted that what he did 'was a nothing job'. 'The work we did there was completely unimportant and had absolutely no significance, either for the firm, or for the Germans.'[114] Eventually it employed some 3,000 individuals for longer or shorter periods. These later came to include some *Ziviljuden*, primarily women who were recruited to do radio assembly work and who were thereby at least temporarily protected from the transports to Westerbork and the East. However, the vast majority of Jews from the camp had been deported by the summer of 1943 and no new Jewish workers were employed thereafter.[115]

At the same time, the firm did try to protect its remaining SOBU workers still employed at Eindhoven. In the spring of 1943, the province of Noord Barbant (which included Eindhoven) was gradually cleared of its remaining Jews as they were systematically arrested and taken to Vught. The province was formally declared *judenrein* on 12 April, and at the last minute, additional residence permits were acquired for some of the workforce, but the rest were compelled to report to Vught. The firm had a plan to evacuate the remainder to Spain or Portugal, but this ultimately came to nothing.[116] By mid-June, the remains of the rapidly diminishing workforce were approached by the management individually and told that the plan was moribund, and advised to disappear. Some had clearly already decided this was the best course of action, while others had to arrange whatever they could at short notice.[117] The authorities did make attempts to get them back by suggesting that emigration was once again an option. One woman later recalled her reasoning:

> My period in hiding lasted ten days. It bored me and as soon as I heard from my family that the plans were going forward again, I went back to Philips. I went happily back to work.[118]

Another had other motives. On her period in hiding, she recalled,

> In a moment, I was transported into a completely different world. A very simple way of life. No running water, you washed with a bucket by the pump. I was very young. The farmers wife, who had apparently had had a stroke or something, had a very lop-sided face. I was afraid of her. [...] The news, rumours or reports, reached the whole of Eindhoven and all the hiding places. Did I believe it? I wanted to believe it. I didn't like it on the farm; and how did you know how great the risks were? If you were caught in hiding, then there was the threat of Mauthausen. I gladly believed that it was safer at home and at the SOBU, and that we would be going to South America. Therefore I left and reported back for work.[119]

These two women survived their decision to reject being in hiding and to return to work at Philips, but their attitude may highlight another feature of going underground, namely that some fugitives saw being underground as worse than the presumed dangers of continuing to live openly—or perhaps just did not realize the extent of the danger. Few probably survived to tell this type of story. Most of the remaining Jews at Vught were deported to Auschwitz on 15 November 1943, but a small group, including elements from the *Philips-kommando* involved in radio assembly, were permitted to stay, and remained in the camp until 2 June 1944 when the remaining workers and their families—496 people in total—were also transported to Auschwitz. Even here, they were afforded some protection, being selected for work and given numbers. All but fifty were then sent on to a Telefunken plant at Reichenbach, where they remained until evacuated on 16 February 1945. After four days' march through the snow and cold, with those unable to walk being shot on the spot, the group was then transported across Germany before finally being found by the Danish Red Cross and taken to Sweden for recuperation. In total, 382 of this group survived to the liberation.[120]

Explaining the survival of members of this small group of Jews is not straightforward. The role of the Philips company in trying to protect elements of its Jewish workforce is irrefutable, as the creation of the SOBU and the emigration schemes attest. Its record in employing other Jews within the *kommando* inside Vught is less clear, not least because employment was initially restricted to *Schutzhäftlinge* and only later came to encompass the 'ordinary' Jews in the camp. Whether the Philips administration could have done more to provide work for other Jews in the camp is open to question.[121] Its powers were limited, and the survival of the *Philips-kommando* in the camp for so long may have been primarily the result of its administration by the SS-*Wirtschaftsverwaltungshauptamt* (Economic Administration Central Office, WVHA) in Berlin, rather than the Sipo and RSHA that controlled the other camps in the Netherlands and oversaw the deportation process. However, other businesses with *kommandos* inside the camp that also employed Jews were less fortunate. Thus the Menist (rag-sorting) and Escotex (clothing and fur) enterprises were both shut down in late 1943 and the last Jewish workers from the Escotex plant left with the transport of 15 November.

The charge that Philips actually made money from the enterprise also needs to be examined. Productivity of the *kommando* was only 40 per cent of normal (potentially a result of the poor conditions in the camp), and it was estimated that the firm made a loss of around Dfl.1 million on the project. At the same time, the protection afforded to the Philips Jews in Vught has to be seen in perspective. Their material and physical treatment differed little from that afforded to Jews in other camps, their only advantage being that they did receive some extra food paid for by the company,[122] and they were theoretically protected from deportation. By June 1944, any 'privilege' they might have been afforded had long-since vanished, as a contemporary description of their deportation from the camp makes clear:

> The Jews were driven like beasts, and had to stand for hours in the scantiest of clothes. Many of them were sick or infirm . . . some of them were pulling up tufts of grass [to eat], only to have them snatched out of their hands. They were treated brutally.[123]

While the conduct of the Philips enterprise during the occupation and its contribution to the German war effort will undoubtedly continue to provoke debate,[124] the role of Frits Philips personally in this has been extensively researched by Yad Vashem. Prompted by twelve former employees who had survived, it considered the evidence sufficiently compelling to warrant the award of the title 'Righteous among the Nations'.

Conclusions

The differences in the circumstances and context of rescue between the Netherlands and her southern neighbours are striking. The high proportion of indigenous Jews, their adherence to Dutch cultural values, including obedience to law and order, and the relative poverty of many, all militated against a more robust response to Nazi persecution. Their geographic position was also disadvantageous, with distances to safety across hostile territory being that much greater. Unlike both Belgium and France, most Jewish organizations were committed to legality and accommodation with the occupiers from 1940, and there was little leeway for any manner of resistant structures to grow within them. This was accentuated after the formation of the Amsterdam Jewish Council as its leadership continued to operate in accord with German wishes and slowly took control over all aspects of Jewish life. The relatively small numbers of refugee and foreign Jews in the country meant that they had few viable organizations of their own that might have provided an alternative focus for Jewish self-help. Thus there were none of the pre-existing immigrant and political organizations that featured so prominently in both France and Belgium, nor any viable links to the rest of society through welfare or social provision that such groups might have fostered in the 1920s and 1930s.

The focus on individual rescuers that is so apparent in the historiography of the Netherlands betrays another central theme that is evident from comparison with other countries, namely the relative absence of the Christian churches *as organizations* in providing an impetus to organize further rescue. Archbishop de Jong as a Catholic leader in the Netherlands seems to have been less vocal and less active than his colleagues, Cardinals Gerlier and Van Roey. The actual difference may have been little more than nuances, but they were enough to have a major impact in what happened 'on the ground' in individual parishes. That said, it is also important to recognize that the Dutch Catholic Church had less of an 'institutional' and welfare role than its counterparts in France and Belgium.

In contrast to the religious uniformity to the south, the Netherlands contained large Protestant congregations, both Dutch Reformed and Calvinist, They produced different responses to the plight of the Jews—often ones that were more firmly rooted in interpretations of the Bible, yet the federated nature of these churches and a lack of central leadership and guidance also militated against a more coherent organizational response. This is not to deny the fact that all the churches did mount protests in different forms (protests that were given a high profile after the liberation), but this seldom translated into any form of collective opposition or illegality. Again this should not obscure the role played by many individual churchmen in rescue. There are many who were at the forefront of networks, or who provided the green light for their subordinates to operate while themselves keeping a distance from the day-to-day work and concentrating on the spiritual aspects of ministry. It is perhaps surprising how little the organized churches made of these activities in their early published assessments of church opposition to the Nazis—leaving their roles to be 'discovered' by post-war historians and by Yad Vashem.

Another contrast to other countries was the creation of a national network to help those underground. At first glance this should have been advantageous to the Jews in hiding, and there are certainly many cases where aid was provided, but two factors served to limit its role. The first was its relatively late emergence, and the second was a combination of prejudice against Jews *as Jews* among many who were prepared to be involved in this type of resistance, coupled with a reluctance to help Jews because such work was perceived to carry greater punishments and greater chances of discovery. There were also claims voiced that the Jews could not be trusted or, more charitably, that they would be tortured to betray their former hosts if caught. Whatever the rationale, there is no doubt that the task of helping those Jews known to be living underground was often marginalized or hived off to separate organizations rather than being in the mainstream of LO activities.

The last ostensibly different manifestation of rescue in the Netherlands is the creation of the *Philips-kommando*. Only recently researched in detail, comparisons have been made with the activities of Oskar Schindler in saving a Jewish workforce from deportation and the gas chambers in Poland. There are, of course, examples of employers helping Jews who were part of their workforce, but few others, if any, on this scale have come to light. Comparisons are therefore difficult. In spite of its size and importance, the Philips company was still essentially a family concern in 1940 and decisions could therefore be made by individuals—as seems to have happened here. Whether other companies could have acted in similar fashion is open to some doubt, and perhaps the best comparison is with other Dutch employers who attempted to protect their workforces from the labour draft by keeping them 'employed' in so-called 'grey factories' that actually had no work for them. The logic here was to retain skilled workers and prevent their dispersal, in the hope that better trading conditions would emerge. Some Jews undoubtedly benefited from these schemes, but the mixture of employer self-interest and philanthropy involved here has continued to provoke debate.[125]

11

Suffer the Little Children . . .

Children as a special case

Throughout the world, in times of crisis, children are regarded as having a special status as innocents. While their parents can be condemned for their actions or beliefs, the offspring are exonerated until they reach an age when they are perceived to have a will of their own and can make informed choices. Although children had been direct or indirect victims of ethnic and religious persecutions at various moments in European history, they were seldom exposed to the same penalties as their parents and could be 'reformed' by religious conversion or by immersion in the culture of the victors. However, for the Nazis, Jewish children were just as dangerous to the *Volksgemeinschaft* as their parents. Indeed more so, as they represented the future of the race and had therefore to be pursued with equal vigour. There were no exceptions to be made for youth in the 'final solution'.

This gap between the inclusiveness of the Nazis' plans for the removal of the Jews on the one hand, and the perceptions of the occupied peoples of Europe on the other is clear to see, even among those who shared some antisemitic sentiments. Few could understand the need to make war on children, and their plight made them objects of sympathy, even in circles where the parents were somehow blamed for their own misfortunes. One extreme example of this sentiment can be found in the recollections of a meeting of rescuers in a network in the Netherlands where fugitives were being 'placed'. As always, it had been far more difficult to find people willing to take in Jews. Then, as one of the participants recalled,

> Everything was finished when one [of those present] said, 'I still have a number of Jewish babies', what should we do with them? It was a sort of Jews-market, on all sides, here two, here five, in the end there weren't

enough to go round. It was certainly wonderful that the whole problem was solved so completely. But no one would have an adult Jew.[1]

This one statement is indicative of the special place that Jewish children had in the consciousness, even among those who were already engaged in the work of helping those underground.[2] It begs the question why the children were seen as such objects of concern in comparison with their adult peers. Some of the answers are obvious. Given the nature of Nazi rule in Western Europe, children were easier to accommodate and easier to explain to friends and neighbours if brought into a community. Cover stories of evacuation or being orphaned were commonplace. Distant family connections could be implied without raising awkward questions about the precise relationship between guests and hosts. Likewise, such cover stories would help to stop too much questioning of the children lest they stir up painful memories. Children were also not subject to regulations on identity cards, although ration cards still needed to be arranged.[3] Foster parents were easier to find than hosts for adult Jews, but even in this more favourable environment, there were still distinctions made. Thus one Dutch rescuer recorded that children who did not 'look' Jewish were easier to place, whereas it was far more difficult to find homes for boys who had been circumcised and who did look Jewish.[4]

Yet even within this favoured group, there was still a hierarchy when it came to finding hiding places and foster parents. Nico Dohmen, who was directly involved in hiding Jewish children in and around Tienray in the southern Netherlands recalled after the occupation that most of the children they were sent caused few problems but that it was still difficult to find homes for boys between 10 and 15 years old but that there was an insatiable demand for babies. This developed to the point where one Amsterdam organization provided a 'reward' to the local network of one baby for every ten boys in that age group who were successfully placed.[5]

Whereas the rescue of adult Jews often took place within larger resistance and rescue organizations, France, Belgium and the Netherlands all saw groups devote themselves specifically to the rescue of Jewish children. However, the success or failure of such groups inevitably depended on a series of factors, not least the supply of children to be taken into their care. For Jewish parents, giving up one's child or children was only ever a last resort, an act of desperation when all other alternatives had been

exhausted. Generally speaking therefore, it was only when the deportation
to the East began that some of the persecuted began to look for ways
of saving their children from this unknown fate, even if they themselves
felt that they had no means of escape. Such sentiments prompted the first
approaches to non-Jewish friends and acquaintances, but were inevitably
constrained by the degree of contact that individual Jewish families had
with their non-Jewish neighbours. For some, there were obvious points
of contact, for others, none at all. At the same time, highly motivated
individuals began work in creating networks to facilitate the rescue of
Jewish children.

Perhaps because of the cultural and social value placed on saving Jewish
children by post-war Western society, the activities of these groups have
been better recorded and chronicled, and more intensely studied than many
other rescue operations, and many other resistance activities. That said, even
these studies leave many questions unasked or unanswered, preferring to
dwell on the heroic and charitable virtues that the stories embody. Yet
comparison between countries shows that, just as in the case of the wider
aspects of rescue, there were marked differences between countries, regions
and even localities that were determined by the prevailing social, political,
religious, and economic structures.

Saving Jewish Children: France

As with the wider comparison of rescue and resistance, the occupied
zone of France stands out as the case where the cloaking and hiding
of children began at an earlier stage than elsewhere in Western Europe.
During the exodus of June 1940 many Jewish families fled from Paris
taking their children with them. Some returned after the armistice, while
others chose to stay away—whether in the Vichy zone or the countryside
of the occupied areas. Even at this stage, some of the parents who did
return to Paris thought about making specific provisions for their children.
There was a strong tradition of parents sending their offspring to the
countryside during the summer holidays, and it was a natural step to
use these pre-war arrangements to provide temporary—and perhaps even
permanent—sanctuary for them at a time of crisis. While this form of
individual arrangement was largely the prerogative of the middle classes,
there were also opportunities for people in the poorer districts to benefit.

Charities there operated 'vacation colonies' for children to spend time in the countryside and these sometimes became the basis for children being removed from the city for extended periods. In 1940, such arrangements were often no more than plans and it was only as the Nazi net tightened round the foreign Jews in the occupied zone that more concerted steps were taken to shelter their children.

In the initial stages of the occupation, it was unusual for parents to be prepared to hand over their children, but when the first deportations of adult foreign Jews began, their children who were French born were not included and were often left behind, ostensibly to fend for themselves as the Germans proved unwilling to send anyone under 16 years of age on the transports, irrespective of nationality. The Vichy authorities had sought to have this stricture overturned so that foreign Jewish children could travel with their parents, but as of 16 July 1942, when the first major round-ups took place, they had not received a decision from Berlin. In cases where the police came to arrest a family, it was only the adults who were on their lists, although children were often taken into internment as well, only to be released later. Others were left on the street, with concierges, or with neighbours[6]—either by accident or design. This gave the Jewish charities operating in Paris both the obligation and the opportunity to find places for them. In theory, this became the responsibility of the UGIF, and many children did end up in its care, in orphanages and other institutions, but the understanding was that the authorities would always know where they were, and thus the children were under permanent threat of a change of policy that might see them designated for deportation.

Thus the Jewish groups working legally and illegally around the UGIF were faced with a twofold problem: how to look after those children already separated from their parents, and also how to help parents and children already on the run from the authorities, or likely to be targeted in the future. The organizations of the Amelot Committee were at the forefront of this work, although they were by no means the only agencies involved. Their approach was a considered and carefully organized one, using social workers to place children with foster parents or suitable institutions. Even at this stage, Amelot had a clear predilection for using secular institutions rather than religious ones, which meant that the risks of (forced) conversion were diminished and the children's welfare could be better monitored. It operated on the basis that parents should be asked to pay for their children's upkeep, but if they were arrested and deported then the children were subsidized. This element was run by Yéhuda Jacoubovitch with the help of three young female assistants and several social workers who acted as couriers and then supervised the children in hiding and liaised with any parents who were still in French camps.[7] Their level of organization and care for the children can be judged by their selection of refuges and the fact that their couriers would reject unsuitable places. Thus one report noted: 'Peasant house, very badly kept... Five people sleep on three beds, in a very dirty room, on grey bedclothes'.[8] Nevertheless, the social workers were able to find suitable placements across the occupied zone.[9] They were later dispersed to families when the Germans tried to regroup the children. The Amelot Committee has been estimated as helping 10.7 per cent of the 72,400 Jewish children under 18 who were not deported by the Nazis. Of these 30.5 per cent were orphans, a further 48.4 per cent had lost their father, and 7.2 per cent their mother, while only 13.8 per cent kept both parents.[10]

Its operations were linked with other Jewish groups involved in similar charitable work, such as the Womens International Zionist Organization (WIZO) and also several other non-Jewish organizations such as the L'Entraide Temporaire and SSAE. The WIZO developed its own networks that helped to place children in hiding well away from the capital. One particular example of its work also highlights instances of communities and individuals being mobilized to help the Jews. Chavagnes-en-Paillers (Vendée) was a community of some 2,900 souls, most of whom were agriculturalists, although the town also housed two seminaries and an Ursuline convent. It was a little away from the main roads, but nonetheless boasted a German *Kommandantur*.[11] The village received its first four Jewish children in April 1942, thus before the Vel d'Hiv round-ups, although two of them were soon taken back to Paris by their mother. However, these first children were exceptions as most of the later arrivals were delivered by Suzanne Mathieu, a courier working for the WIZO. As a non-Jew, she had had no direct connection with WIZO, except that she lived close to its headquarters in the Rue Bienfaisance and had been 'converted' to the idea of resistance by reading a copy of *Combat* at the Sorbonne.[12] She became the sole link between the WIZO and the village, collecting the children from others at the Gare d'Austerlitz and delivering them to Foucauld, the local doctor. He was the pivotal figure in the village, selecting and then approaching the households he thought would be able to look after the children, in each case making it clear that the children were Jewish.[13] At least three other people in the community were also central to the success of the rescue operation that ended up saving thirty children. The local priest, Père Crouzat, was described as the Stakhanovite of the Confessional who regarded Hitler as the new Satan, while the mayor, Gilbert de Guerry, was a Pétain loyalist. In contrast, Foucauld was a known 'Gaulliste', and the local aristocrat, Hélène de Suzannet, was connected to the Comète and Vanneau resistance organizations.[14] In spite of their very different ideological outlooks, they all co-operated in the work of hiding the children and keeping them secure.

It is not entirely clear exactly how the village became the centre of such an extensive rescue operation, as many communes housed only one or two Jewish children. Its extent may have been down to the influence of the doctor and his co-conspirators in negotiating new hiding places. The precise way in which the link to WIZO was made also remains unclear. It may have come via the first children brought to the town by their mother, or it may have been the result of earlier projects designed to provide holidays for children from the cities. Chavagnes had experience of at least two. One of the first children sheltered there had actually visited before, as part of a scheme run by a charity in the 20th arrondissement, Lumière et Santé, to give city children summer holidays in the country. A second was the scheme created by the Vichy organization, La Famille du Prisonnier to do much the same thing, but there were also schemes to remove children from areas subject to bombing. All these projects created possible links, but also provided cloaks for Jewish children in hiding. However, in the case of Chavagnes, there was yet another link, namely that of previous holidays before the occupation. In this way, four Jewish girls, including Odette Melszpajz, were sent to Auguste and (Moisette) Marie Raffin. Their fathers had been taken prisoner while in the French army but had left instructions for their daughters to be sent to the Raffins if they were in danger.[15] Thus, when the raids began, the children were saved and sent to the Vendée. For their part, the children had been versed by their now absent fathers to never admitting that they were Jewish. For her part, their foster mother Marie Raffin drilled them in the Lord's Prayer, the Hail Mary and the sign of the cross, and reinforced their cover story that their fathers were prisoners in Germany.[16] Later, Moisette Raffin's own connections with the nearby commune of St Fulgent provided shelter for Berthe Melszpajz and her daughter to live together. As an illegitimate child herself, she had been adopted by a local noble family, and it was to her foster parents that the Melszpajzs were sent.[17] The success of this particular devoutly Catholic commune in being a centre of rescue may therefore have as much to do with its history as a holiday destination, and as a historic centre of resistance in 1794, as with the conjuncture and collusion of ideologically motivated members of the community during the occupation.[18]

L'Entraide had close contacts with David Rapoport and the Amelot Committee, and was credited with helping at least 500 children, masking their records by incorporating them into old files of the Save the Children organization from 1941—altering dates and using place-name codes.[19] Children were taken to foster parents in the countryside. Interestingly, its organizer, Denise Milhaud, noted that none of the children caused any problems in leaving, except perhaps a moment's hesitation over their new names. The task of accompanying the children to their new homes and then subsequently visiting them was onerous, but also allowed for the identification of more foster parents, even though 'they had not always assessed the risks they were running'.[20]

> On behalf of the organisation, [the *convoyeuse*] discussed with the foster-parents the material problems of sheltering. She did not discuss with them the situation of the children's families and she also did not tell them that they were young Jews. Besides, they didn't ask. It was an era when one wasn't curious. Someone in the village nevertheless was in the know, usually the schoolteacher. The children went to mass with their foster parents.[21]

Other parts of occupied France also produced their share of village rescues. For example, Trôo (Loir-et-Cher) was a commune of 671 souls situated in the valley of the Loire. Both through individual actions and via aid organizations, twenty-eight or twenty-nine Jewish children were brought to the village and housed with foster families, attending the local public or private schools. Explained as 'little refugees from Brest', everyone in the village knew of their existence, but even though there was a local *Kommandantur*, 'no one said anything'.[22] The process had been set in train by the arrival of a doctor and a Red Cross social worker who had sought a list of potential foster families from the Mayor, Louis-Paul Pinchon, on behalf of the Rue Amelot Committee.[23] He was a veteran of the First World War, bailiff, and businessman. He had two sons held as prisoners by the Germans, and a third liable for labour service. Thus his anti-German sentiments should not have been in doubt. He nevertheless maintained a friendly relationship with the local Germans—too friendly for elements within the resistance who subsequently accused him of collaboration. His personal view of his administration was one of ignoring the demands of the occupier save where disobedience would bring down sanctions on the people. The outward collusion with the Germans was thus a front, both to protect the people of the commune and also the children hidden there. He was clearly an individual who had been in post long enough and knew his locality well enough to know whom to approach as potential foster parents, and to have the moral authority to persuade them. In this example, the origins of the children were known to all, in spite of the cover story, although there were other examples where this was not the case. Many of the houses were modest in the extreme, even for those times. Thus one young boy recalled that the house where he was sheltered had no electricity, just a paraffin lamp, 'but he was greeted like a son'.[24] Other children were also known to have been sheltered in nearby hamlets, whether at the behest of Pinchon or not it is impossible to say.

Similarly, Louis and Florentine Vaillant in the small hamlet of Fontaine near Pezou (Loir et Cher), played host to the children of the Zadjman family who had been coming for the summer holidays since 1932. Their house was little more than a single room and lacked electricity or running water and had to accommodate four members of the Vaillant family plus the five Jewish children. The fugitives did not attend the local boys' school as it had been requisitioned by the Germans, but were for a time given some lessons in the local girls' school. They were also given false identity cards in the surnames of their foster parents by the local Mairie. In summing up their attitude to their rescuers, one of the children subsequently recalled that they 'never made the slightest differentiation between their own child and us'.[25] The other young girls sheltered by the same family came to them via the Colonie Scolaire and the Amelot Committee in Paris.[26] Another widow in the same commune took in two other Jewish girls whose mother was hidden in Paris.[27]

As is evident from these few stories, the pattern of dispersal into the countryside at an early stage in the occupation was aided by pre-existing individual and organizational links, and by the continued existence of both Jewish and non-Jewish welfare organizations. In Paris, there were also some initiatives that emerged from Christian circles. Within the Catholic milieu, the *pensionnat* of the convent Notre-Dame-de-Sion led by Mère Francia became the centre of a rescue organization for children. The sisters had maintained a mission to the Jews in the Marais district since 1938 and the two nuns involved served as go-betweens with the parents, or if they had been deported, then with the Jewish organizations sheltering them. The organization also benefited from the fact that one of the nuns there from 1940 also spoke Yiddish and could thus communicate more easily with the foreign Jews who came to them for help.[28] Sympathetic policemen reputedly furnished papers and other documents. The organization showed another facet that was to be repeated elsewhere, namely that the head of the order, Mère Gonzalèz, was not aware of everything that was being done, and ostensibly did not want to know. In such a large institution, this was clearly possible, and Mère Francia was given a good deal of liberty by her superior.[29] The order was able to hide some children in its school at Grandbourg on the outskirts of Paris, and also had contacts with sister convents in Lyon and Grenoble that had been active in helping refugees since 1940 and 1941. The convent at Grenoble alone was credited with having provided aid, hiding places, false identity cards, or help in getting to Switzerland for at least 800 hunted families.[30]

This particular foundation, with its specific mission to the Jews was also unusual in another sense, namely that it engaged in the baptism of Jewish children during the occupation. In theory, this was only done with the parents' permission, but the vastly increased numbers in 1941, 1942, and 1943 testify to the perceived importance of such a step, even though baptism, of itself, was no defence against Nazi persecution. Inevitably, the existence of these baptisms has led to charges of 'rampant proselytism'[31] among the Christian churches, and it was certainly a worry voiced by the Amelot Committee about Catholic and Protestant rescue groups created in the capital after the German occupation. By the same token, knowledge of the Christian religion and its offices could be a major advantage in the hiding of children in both Catholic and Protestant milieu, and in the absence of detailed testimony, it is difficult to make hard and fast judgements.

Paris was also the base for a Protestant rescue organization created by Pastor Paul Vergara that is credited with sheltering nearly 500 Jewish children by spiriting them away from institutions controlled by the UGIF.[32] This work began gradually during 1941 and was linked to the social and welfare centre of the parish, La Clairière, founded by Wilfrid Monod in 1911, an organization that was itself involved in helping over 100 children in the immediate aftermath of the first arrests, by sheltering them in institutions and families in the countryside. Later, when the children in UGIF homes were under threat, Vergara's network discovered that there was a dispensation for people to take Jewish children for walks. Thus on 12 February 1943, Marcelle Guillemot of La Clairière stood outside the chapel after Sunday service distributing cards to those she could trust, encouraging them to come to the UGIF headquarters to take a Jewish child for a walk. In this way, and with the collusion of some UGIF workers, some sixty-three children between the ages of 3 and 18 were spirited away.[33] In the meantime, Vergara encouraged his flock to take in the children for a few days or longer.

In addition to Vergara and his network there were other pastors who helped Jews. Jean Jousselin in Montmartre had been charged by the Vichy authorities with providing a youth centre for bombed areas in the occupied zone. Using this as a cover, he organized hiding places and documentation for a number of poor Jews living in his area who were being sought by the authorities as well as for escaped prisoners of war. In May 1941, he was accused of being a philosemite and being sympathetic to de Gaulle and thus lost his post. However, he was then placed in charge of the Maison Verte, a youth organization created by the Mission Populaire Evangélique in the 18th arrondissement dedicated to providing opportunities for young people. In 1943 he decided with his colleagues to organize a summer holiday home for children from his arrondissement. He was thus able to remove some Jewish children with others out of the city, citing bombing and a lack of food as an excuse, to a property owned by the Scout movement, Cappy-Maison Verte near Verberie (Oise). Although only supposedly a temporary arrangement, he had the institution legally recognized as a children's home to assist with obtaining food, as their ration cards were no longer valid outside the capital. The decision to make the arrangement permanent was aided by the local mayor who allowed the children to be enrolled in the local school. A second home was opened at Gouvieux, but had to be closed in the summer of 1944 because it was too close to a V.1 launch site and was subject to frequent bombardments.[34] No distinction was made between children of parents who could pay for their upkeep and those who could not and between May 1943 and September 1944 this refuge received 135 children in total, including 87 Jews, in spite of being perennially short of both money and food.[35]

Jewish children in France also benefited from the existence of other long-standing welfare organizations, the most important being the Œuvre de secours aux enfants (OSE). This was a charity established in St Petersburg in 1912 by a group of doctors to help children and to provide medical aid to Jewish victims of Tsarist persecution.[36] Its headquarters moved to Berlin in 1923 and it became an international organization, moving to Paris in 1933 to avoid the attention of the national socialists. Its Paris section was founded by Professor Eugene Minkowski, and its initial work was in helping needy families in the Paris region by giving their children respite vacations at a purpose-built holiday home at Varenne.[37] However, after 1938, its work was directed primarily towards refugee aid, and particularly in helping Jewish children from Germany, Austria, and Czechoslovakia.[38] With the agreement of the French government, the organization was also allowed to bring Jewish children from Germany and Austria to France, on the understanding that it would pay for their upkeep, and this same arrangement was used to help children from the steamship St Louis in May 1939. The children were accommodated in homes and hostels (*foyers*) in Montmorency and elsewhere.[39] After the outbreak of war, it had also been involved in the evacuation of children from Paris and began the establishment of further children's homes.[40] Initially, these were three chateaux in the *département* of Creuse,[41] but by the spring of 1941 there were seven across the unoccupied zone housing 647 children—numbers that had grown to nine and 1,200 respectively by November of the same year. The organization was also by this time helping to finance a further four homes.[42]

It is important to recognize, as the OSE workers did, that their charges did not all share the same histories or circumstances, and thus had to be considered as separate categories if not as individuals. Religious upbringing and levels of observance were important factors, but cutting across this were questions of origins and circumstances. In 1941, five discrete groups could be identified. The first consisted of 310 refugees from Eastern Europe, who spoke no French and who had arrived in France from Belgium having lost contact with their parents. Then there were 165 orphans or semi-orphans, 202 children taken in after February 1941, 315 Polish children whose parents had disappeared or could not be contacted, and finally 117 infants whose parents could be found, but who were unable to support their offspring.[43] Each of the children's homes had its own character, functions, and individual leadership. The three in Creuse were dominated either by Russian Bundist or communist versions of Judaism.[44] Each also contained a mixture of children who needed not just shelter and food, but also education and training for a future in France or elsewhere. Many were candidates for emigration, and two cohorts totalling 162 children were successfully sent to the United States in June and September 1941.[45]

After June 1940, the headquarters of OSE had moved to Montpellier, although it retained an office in Paris. In spite of the increase in its work, the organization ultimately benefited from Vichy policies that dismissed Jews from state positions and thus provided a pool of qualified people to carry out social work tasks within the Jewish community.[46] From its new base it organized help for Jewish children across the country but concentrated on the internment camps where children were held in the south of France, its object being to improve conditions and medical care. To this end, its workers liaised with local *préfets* and succeeded in getting social workers permanently into the camps. Permission was sought to have the children examined by doctors and to have the sick removed to hospitals. Efforts were also directed towards getting children into foster homes, although it was apparent that in the xenophobic climate of France in 1940 and 1941, volunteers to take charge of foreign Jewish children, whether from Germany or Poland, were hardly thick on the ground.[47] One notable exception to this was the behaviour of the *Préfet* of Hérault and his colleagues who co-operated extensively with OSE to admit Jewish children to homes in their area. Once there, they could be transferred elsewhere as they were not required to have identity papers.[48] Thus OSE was able to get several hundred children removed from the camps with the aid of other groups, both Jewish and non-Jewish.[49] During 1941, it also saw the dangers inherent in the arrests of Jews and, like other agencies, began a shift towards clandestinity by the creation and distribution of (false) ration cards and the placement of children on farms or in laic and religious institutions. Previously, this had been done for shorter periods, but now the pressure was on to find permanent placements for an indeterminate period.[50]

The status of the organization was changed when it was forced to become part of the UGIF on 8 March 1942, although Joseph Weill claimed at the time that it made not one jot of difference to its work. Co-operation with the ORT and the EIF increased to provide training opportunities and to extend medical-social services. However, the liberation of children from camps and the collapse of many smaller charitable organizations placed enormous pressure on OSE facilities, and some children had to be sent home to their parents to make way for orphans with nowhere else to go.[51] Until July 1942, the work of OSE was largely directed towards ameliorative aid and its operations remained within the bounds of (Vichy designated) legality. Only at the margins were there the beginnings of a shift into illegality. Thus, for example, the Colonie Scolaire was reportedly placing children with so-called 'nourrices' (peasant women or families prepared to take in children) in 1941 and who were paid up to FFr.800 per month plus the provision of clothing and bedding.[52]

When the first transports from the southern zone began in August 1942, OSE workers were able to persuade a number of parents on the deportation lists to hand their children over, and in this way some seventy were given into the care of the organization, albeit not without some traumatic scenes.[53]

> While they [the children] were made to climb aboard the busses with their skimpy baggage, heart rending scenes occurred. The young children, who could not understand the reasons for this separation, clung to their parents and cried. The older children, who knew how great their parents' sorrow was, tried to control their pain and clenched their teeth. The women pressed up against the doors of the departing busses. The guards and policemen themselves could hardly hide their emotion. The impression was all the more hideous in that until then perfect calm had reigned in the camp.[54]

At the same time, OSE children's homes in the southern zone also came under threat and three were raided by gendarmes and *gardes mobiles*. As a result, 134 children were taken and deported, but approximately sixty were saved through local actions and the collusion of the local authorities.[55] At least one at Chabannes was purportedly requisitioned by the local authority (at the request of OSE!) so that the organization had an excuse to close and move the children elsewhere. On other occasions, children were even liberated from transports, for example when someone posing as a Red Cross delegate swept up twenty-five children about to be deported from Rivesaltes.[56]

Perhaps the most famous of these rescue attempts came after some 1,200 Jews were arrested in Lyon on 26 August and held at the camp at Vénissieux. This was a marshalling yard that had been turned into a holding-camp with the aid of fences and electrified barbed wire. Vichy had given an undertaking that children would not be sent with the adults. However, it soon became apparent that some *préfets*, including Maurice Papon in Bordeaux, had included children because he could not make up his demanded quota exclusively from adults. Pastor Boegner had thus gone to see Prime Minister Laval to appeal against their inclusion among the deportees, but was told that Laval considered it more humane if the children travelled with their parents. Boegner responded by insisting that the country's moral and spiritual authorities could not permit such an action to take place. Laval promised a response within twenty-four hours and in the meantime Boegner returned to Lyon and contacted local members of CIMADE and Père Pierre Chaillet of *Témoignage Chrétien*.[57]

Members of the OSE, and Abbé Glasberg and Jean-Marie Soutou of *Amitié Chrétienne* all tried their hardest to persuade parents to sign over their parental rights so that their children would remain in France, and they were promised that the children would be fostered with families and that there would be no attempts made to convert them, invoking the name of Cardinal Gerlier as a guarantee of good faith. While this took place, orders arrived that the children should also be deported, but they were suppressed by Glasberg and Soutou. In the interim, the resistance was commissioned to cut the power to the fence and a raid took place that managed to remove between 85 and 108 children who were taken to an EIF building using three police trucks.[58] By the time the police came looking for the children to ship them to the occupied zone, they had all disappeared—spirited away to secret destinations by OSE and the scouts. Amitié Chrétienne took responsibility for this and Cardinal Gerlier received strong protests from the authorities but without result. One leader of Amitié Chrétienne, Chaillet paid for his disobedience with three months' house arrest.[59] Thereafter, and in line with Laval's dictum, the Vichy authorities invariably included children in the deportations.[60]

This series of events marks the definitive shift of the OSE from welfare work to out-and-out rescue activity, and Georges Garel was commissioned to create a clandestine organization alongside OSE's legitimate functions.[61] A former cavalry officer, he insisted that his organization be completely separate from the legal elements of OSE and comprised people who were not typically Jewish in either outlook or appearance.[62] It was constructed as the Germans occupied the southern zone, and involved persuading parents to give their children into OSE hands, providing them with a false identity, placing them into a non-Jewish (and therefore safer) environment under proper supervision, and expediting the emigration of others to neutral states.[63] This work was aided by the co-operation of Monsignor Théas of Montauban and Monsignor Saliège, the Archbishop of Toulouse, who agreed to help with the saving of children and provided a letter of introduction to Catholic institutions in his archdiocese—thus opening the doors to many potential hiding places.[64] Children were often hidden under false names, but the network took care to send information on their true identities to Switzerland so that when the war ended, they could be 'recovered'.[65] Latterly, the organization was divided into four regions and employed a total of twenty-nine assistants who were also sheltered by religious or laic organizations. Estimates suggest that the Garel network was responsible for the placement of 1,500 children in the southern zone. A further 500 were hidden in the north, but when in January 1943, the Germans began to remove Jewish children from OSE homes around Paris, the provision of additional hiding places became even more imperative. This more virulent persecution placed some 2,000 legally registered Jewish children in the homes under threat, as well as a further 1,000 placed with (French) Jewish families.[66] Schemes to organize legal emigrations for the children in 1942 and 1943 had foundered, and OSE used the Bourgogne resistance network to provide contacts with *passeurs* and smugglers to expedite passages to Switzerland via the more 'liberal' Italian zone of occupation. Later escapes took place without the aid of *passeurs*, and between the autumn of 1943 and July 1944, OSE was credited with getting 1,069 children into Switzerland.[67] A much smaller number were taken over the much more difficult terrain into Spain between April and July 1944.[68] The primary candidates for evacuation were those children considered as '*aspécifiques*', namely those whose religious upbringing or observance made them difficult to place in Christian homes, or whose accent or physical appearance made them impossible to assimilate.[69] The methods used were carefully outlined by one OSE worker:

> Once the dispersion of children in a home had been decided, I went to visit the director and saw the children who had to go to Switzerland, above all the older boys who were of particularly Jewish appearance ... I became the so-called 'station master', meeting the children from the homes on their arrival. At Limoges this was difficult enough as the trains arrived and departed at night. It was therefore three or four times a week that I went to the station in the dark at about one in the morning to meet the children .... We prepared the transports [of 15–20 children] very carefully, and we told the children to leave all their papers, photographs of their families and so on, which would be dangerous if there were checks. They did not need anything except their false papers so close to the frontier, and on crossing, genuine documents. These were hidden in their clothing, under the arms as it was unlikely they would be searched there. In spite of our instructions, when we rummaged through their luggage we again found quantities of things that we needed to remove. We always chose one of the older ones from among the

children, a boy or a girl, who would be responsible for the others and told them; if you are arrested, you are unaware of any organisation. The name OSE should never be mentioned.[70]

However at the end of 1943 there were still 450 children in homes and many others under the supervision of the various *départements* in which they were located. Towards the end of the occupation, the organization suffered further setbacks, including the raid on the home at Izieu carried out by Klaus Barbie and the Lyon Gestapo that saw the arrest and deportation of forty-four children before they could be dispersed.[71] In spite of these disasters, the OSE was credited with helping more than 6,000 children, of whom 5,000 survived.[72]

One of its workers, Lucienne Clément, was a social worker with the Children's Section (no 5) of the UGIF, and from 1942 was responsible for the placement of children from Paris in the countryside or sent to live in more isolated areas within the occupied zone. She was particularly successful in the Sarthe *département* where she enlisted aid in more than thirty communes, and help from local officials who co-operated in the provision of papers and ration cards. In itself, this was not hiding the children, as the parents were supposedly still aware of where their children were. However, she also sought out foster parents for children who could then be hidden if the need arose. Thus in 1943, she was informed that a mother had been arrested in Paris and forced to give away the location of her son. Thus he and other children had to be swiftly removed from the commune where they had been living.[73]

This transformation from legality to clandestinity can be seen in many organizations during the occupation, and in that regard, OSE was no different from many others who were compelled by circumstances and the increasing Vichy and German demands to take steps to protect their charges. Crucial in this context was the early co-operation between Jewish and non-Jewish groups—highlighted by the dispersal of the children from Vénissieux. This had involved OSE and the EIF on the one hand, and Amitié Chrétienne and the church hierarchy on the other, in persuading desperate parents to give up rights to their children and then hiding them when the authorities came to round them up. This same co-operation was also central to finding shelter and food for the many who were hidden, through the goodwill of both church and secular organizations.[74] The concerted attack on the Jews in 1942–3 was met with a campaign in the clandestine press against racism and antisemitism. The widespread sympathy for the plight of the Jewish minors was summed up in a contemporary pamphlet that proclaimed, 'You shall not have the children'.[75]

In addition to the OSE, it is also worth reflecting on the role of the EIF in saving their co-religionists in concert with non-Jewish groups. It had been founded and was led by Roger Gamzon, who had rearranged its structure after the armistice so that it was organized by regions. The EIF took responsibility for children from the age of 13, often taking their care over from OSE. In Grenoble, there was extensive co-operation with Notre-Dame-de-Sion, which helped find places for girls with families. These were good hiding places as there was little contact with the outside world, but the families knew whom they were hiding. Boys presented a different problem as placing them with peasants was complicated by their strong accents marking them out as 'foreigners', thus attempts were made to place them with Compagnons de France, an organization created by Pétain and thus supposedly collaborationist, but with some local leaders who were clearly resistant. One of the women involved in placement noted after the war that she kept no written records of her work and did not know the real names of many children she helped hide.[76] Nevertheless, her main preoccupation was not to lose contact with those she had placed, and she was particularly careful with the girls at Notre-Dame-de-Sion, 'because the risk of conversion was always there'.[77]

The degree of collusion between Jewish and non-Jewish groups in France and the relatively early emergence of this co-operation undoubtedly helped in creating the means to save numbers of children from the Nazis, both by providing a haven when the deportations began in the summer of 1942, but also in providing a means for removing children from the horrors of the internment camps in the south—first legally, and then by spiriting them away to hiding places if the authorities came looking for them.

Saving Jewish Children: Belgium

The situation in Belgium has some parallels with France, the most obvious being the degree of integration, both personally and institutionally, between Jews and non-Jews in saving children, most notably with the formation of the CDJ and its children's section, and the greater involvement of churchmen and church institutions in helping to hide the children. As elsewhere in Europe, children were widely seen as a special case and innocent of any 'crimes'. Those directly involved often cited the heavy-handed and brutal nature of the first round-ups by the Gestapo and *Feldgendarmerie* alongside ideological, patriotic, or religious motives for their actions.[78] However, the first steps to hide children were taken by elements within the Brussels Jewish community itself, even before the deportations began. When the Germans ordered all Jewish children out of the city schools, the community created new schools called *Nos Petits*. The leading light in this movement was Fela Perelman, who used the children to contact their parents, with a view to sending their offspring into hiding with non-Jewish families. Thus if the adults were arrested, the children could be kept safe. At this stage, there was no real question of knowing that 'labour service in the East' was just a euphemism, but the motivation was that, even if this was the fate in store for the Jews, the children should be spared it if possible. In this way, some 325 Jewish children were placed with non-Jewish families.[79]

As with the rescue of adults in Belgium, the children benefited from the existence of the CDJ and its separate children's department led by Maurice Heiber. He already had experience with orphans, having been previously involved in the reform of the Jewish orphanage in Brussels. In that role he was then asked to join the AJB, but realizing that it was working for the Germans rather than for the good of the Jewish community, he transferred his allegiance to the CDJ, but remained inside the AJB to cover his illegal activities and to act as a source of information. The main day-to-day work was carried out by four professional social workers, Hava Jospa (Yvonne) and Ida Sterno (Jeanne) who were Jewish, and Andrée Geulen and Suzanne Moons-Lepetit (Brigitte) who were not. It was their task to find addresses and provide money, false papers, and ration cards.[80] These four women travelled the length and breadth of the country searching out addresses and permanent homes for the children. They looked to religious institutions, children's homes, and boarding schools, as well as to individuals for help. Contacts were made with the 'practical' Catholicism that created, little by little, what was termed, a 'chain of solidarity'.[81] They also had to provide new identities, papers, money and ration cards, as well as food and clothing for some of the children. Meetings between parents and their children in hiding were organized in a neutral venue so that the adults could not know where the children were sheltered, but this had many dangers, not least the possibility that the parents were being followed by the Gestapo.[82] While face-to-face meetings were a problem, the organization also facilitated other forms of communication, especially the transmission of letters.[83] It also held the view that separating parents from children not only represented the best possible chance for escape for the children, but also gave the parents more chance of survival through increased mobility.[84]

The problem for the CDJ was that it had to go looking for children to hide. Initially it was able to place children from the *Solidarité Juive* and the *Secours Mutuel*.[85] Later, they turned to the Œuvre National de l'Enfance (ONE). Contacting individual Jewish families was far more difficult. There were no central registers, and families who had already gone underground were, by definition, difficult to trace. Those without hiding places only had the AJB to rely on, but CDJ workers took steps to contact those who came to the AJB offices and to offer them help.[86] Other CDJ 'agents' were placed in organizations such as the Red Cross, Winterhelp, and ONE to intercept Jews looking for help.[87] The approach here was a subtle one. The 'agents' would talk to the parents about placements for children, but claim to know nothing except that another institution might be able to help. The net result was that the parents were sent from pillar to post so that when they were finally contacted by the CDJ, they could have no idea from whom the referral actually came.[88] However, persuading even those in the greatest danger to give up their children remained difficult. After the liberation, Estera Heiber recounted how in July 1942, the Jewish orphanage had been sent seven Jewish mothers with their young children who had been captured trying to escape to Switzerland. Although in imminent danger of deportation, only one of the mothers agreed to give up her child to be placed in a children's home, where he survived the war. All the others were deported.[89]

This was almost always the most painful element for the parents—and for the CDJ workers—visiting the home and taking away the children. Yvonne Jospa never made more than one or two 'visits' each day, as she herself described it—invading a Jewish family who knew nothing of her and had never seen her before, and taking away their child. She recalled the first time this happened. Visiting a house in the Brussels suburb of Anderlecht, she met the parents of a single, 5-year-old child. She told them that they could not know the child's false name, nor where he was being hidden. Then there was a long silence while the child, sitting at their feet, played unconcernedly. Then the mother began to cry and Jospa took the child out into the street. It was important for her that the child did not cry as this would invariably attract attention. In this case, he held her hand tightly and went with her to the station without protest. Her only problem arose in trying to convince him of the need for a new name that would conceal his Jewish identity, but even this proved a success with the aid of stories and a few sweets. The child was subsequently successfully placed with a foster family in the south-east of the country.[90]

In spite of the fact that contact between parents and children was deliberately broken when they were fostered through the CDJ, some problems remained. One girl in a group of fifteen who were hidden in a convent in Ghent sent word to her mother of her location—in direct contravention of the instructions she had been given. As a result, the mother attempted to sell some leather goods to pay for a journey to visit her daughter, but made the mistake of telling the buyer why she needed the money. The purchaser proved to be a collaborator whose daughter was being educated at the same convent, and he lost no time in passing on his 'indignation' to the Mother Superior. This meant that the CDJ had to expedite the immediate removal of all the girls hidden in that convent back to Brussels, where they were collected by ONE staff and hidden, at least temporarily, at the organization's headquarters.[91]

Apart from a 'recruitment' section, the CDJ also had a 'placement' section that matched children to potential homes and hosts, and a 'research' section geared to finding suitable hiding places. As a contemporary report put it, this latter section 'moved heaven and earth' to find suitable locations in religious institutions, charitable homes, boarding schools, and with private citizens.[92] CDJ workers were often confronted with potential foster parents who wanted to adopt children and were very clear what sort of child they wanted, not only in terms of gender and age, but also in terms of appearance. Yet even when they had specific details (insofar as they were prepared to deal in this way), their perception of a 'pretty and intelligent young girl' could still be very different from the potential hosts.[93] It is clear that the CDJ was prepared to countenance the adoption of children that had been orphaned or, as Maurice Heiber put it, 'had the greatest probability of being alone after the war'. To that end he claimed that the organization developed a special intuition about which children would be best suited to particular environments.[94]

One of the key associates of the CDJ was Yvonne Nevéjean, director of ONE. She made sure that all the orphanages under her supervision were primed to hide Jewish children and her wide range of friends and acquaintances among the directors of Catholic, Protestant and non-religious institutions ensured the widest network of contacts imaginable. Apart from finding placements, Nevéjean provided nursing, food, and other forms of care to children and also ensured that they were monitored and well looked after—all through the good offices of ONE. Her organization was also officially responsible for the AJB orphanages. These had been established to deal with the problems created by the German deportation programme. By inflating the figures for the actual number of children in these orphanages, she was able to siphon some ONE money into funds to help children underground.[95] The children's section of the CDJ is credited with having helped to hide around 3,000 Jewish children, and provided for 2,443 of them.[96] They were hidden in at least 138 institutions and with at least 700 individual families, the vast majority (c.95 per cent) in either Brussels or Wallonia. The placement process and security systems operated by the CDJ appear to have been highly successful, with betrayals being the exception rather than the rule. However, there were some disasters. Maurice Heiber recalled the case of a Jewish mother who had betrayed members of the organization in Antwerp. Arrested after placing two of her children with the CDJ, she was taken with her newborn infant to Mechelen and questioned about the whereabouts of her two remaining children. She was tortured but refused to give up any names, and it was only when the torturers began burning her baby with cigarette ends that she finally cracked.[97]

CDJ links with the armed resistance of the Independence Front also proved to have some advantages. Thus, in May 1943, some fifteen Jewish children placed by the children's section at the Convent of the Sisters of Très St Saveur in Anderlecht were discovered by the Jew-hunter Icek Glogowski, otherwise known as 'Gros Jacques', and the Gestapo. The Mother Superior, Marie-Aurelie, was ordered, 'on pain of death' to prepare them for evacuation to an unknown destination the following day when the authorities would supply a truck. Straightaway she informed Maurice Heiber who arranged for an immediate partisan night-raid on the convent to 'liberate' the children.[98] This served to remove the children successfully and also provided the Mother Superior and the nuns with an alibi. However, it also cost Heiber his liberty, as he was arrested the following day.

Nevéjean was undoubtedly a remarkable individual. She had been involved with the placement of children in Belgium after the *Anschluss* and was thus no stranger to the specific needs of Jewish children.[99] Forty years old when the German occupation began, she is reputed to have worked for Belgian National Security and also possibly for the British. In 1938, she had been to a Bund Deutscher Mädel congress in Berlin and made the acquaintance of Erich Hilgenfeld, who later became an SS–General and head of the German *Winterhilfe*. These contacts in high places may have given her a degree of protection, for example when the Gestapo in Brussels suspected her of hiding Jewish children. Certainly, she did not limit her activities to the rescue of children as she was also an active member of the *Services et Reseignements* resistance group.[100]

The CDJ also investigated the possibilities of trying to evacuate children to neutral countries. Indirectly, it sounded out the German authorities if this could be done officially, but although they received a positive answer, it was to be at the expense of major monetary payments (taxes)—something that the organization was unwilling to countenance. Contacts were made with an organization specializing in getting people to Portugal, but the journey was considered too onerous to be considered for most children to attempt, but some professional smugglers were employed who had managed to get children across the frontier into Switzerland. However, their first journey with CDJ-sponsored children saw them caught and taken to Drancy. This major dent in morale caused the abandonment of any further organized attempts to move children to safety abroad.[101]

The CDJ was probably responsible for the majority of rescues of Jewish children in Belgium, but there were also many private arrangements. For example, one girl and boy were taken by their father to the home of two women in Ottignes, initially for a summer holiday in 1942 that was turned into a permanent arrangement. Thus the parent had a direct contact with the foster mothers, something that may help to explain the rapid conversion of the children to Catholicism to match their cover as an evacuated niece and nephew. In this case, the introduction to the Catholic faith was a matter of convenience, both for the parents and for the foster mothers, who were described as 'wary of too much religion'.[102] Even though the children were baptized and went to the local Catholic Church, they were educated separately in a makeshift school for the Jewish children hidden locally. Nonetheless, their presence was well known to the local community but there was no question of betrayal. Ottignes was also the site of a school for disturbed children run by Renée Jacquemotte that, during 1942, slowly filled up with Jewish children as others were sent home. Again, this seems to have been a piece of private enterprise although the venture did receive support from the resistance.[103]

As we have already seen, the active role played by the Catholic Church *as an institution* was a feature of the rescue of Jewish children in Belgium. Thus Monsignor Kerkhofs in Liège was instrumental in mobilizing Catholic institutions around Banneux to help, and also in using three homes (*colonies*) originally established to house the mentally ill children of the middle classes.[104] These homes also sheltered a number of adult Jews as 'domestic servants', but they were primarily refuges for children. Their surnames were altered slightly to disguise their Jewish origins, thus 'Rappoport' became 'Rapport' and first names were Christianized where necessary, with Myryam becoming Maria. They would also sometimes be baptized as a further protection, but only in consultation with the parents.[105] The lawyer Albert van den Berg and his brother-in-law, Georges Fonsny, were both on the administrative council of the charity set up to run these homes, and once the war began, it was van den Berg who organized the work and collected the necessary funds. He was helped by the Capuchin Fathers from Verviers and by German Franciscans who had fled from Aachen and established themselves in Herstal. This latter group were a mixture of Germans, Eupenois, and Luxembourgeois, who were particularly active in helping the welfare of Jewish boys at l'Hospitalité. The other home, La Vierge des Pauvres, was based at the Château des Fawes and run by the Sisters of St Vincent de Paul. Here, van den Berg was able to hide dozens of Jewish children, although precise numbers are impossible to determine.[106] Children were also placed in boarding schools, sanatoria and other convents and abbeys.[107] Their education was something of a problem as the obvious schools for these children would be Catholic ones, designed specifically to provide a Catholic upbringing. The governors of the schools raised the matter and it was decided that the Jewish children hidden in the diocese of Liège would be incorporated into the religious instruction offered. This had two important advantages; namely, that it would not seem odd to the other children in the school, and also that there would be no awkward questions if the schools were subject to state inspection. For the children who had been handed over directly by their parents, it was made a condition that they signed a form indicating their willingness for the child to attend classes and also nominated a guardian. The children were only excused communion and confession.[108] For their part, the parents agreed to pay for their child's upkeep.[109] The fact that educational institutions were subject to state inspection did occasionally cause problems, although not always for the obvious reasons. Thus when the network placed some children in a home near Belleghem, the local schools' inspector deemed it illegal for francophone children to be registered at a Flemish school. The children were therefore moved on to a convent in Wallonia, but the Mother Superior, frightened when she discovered the children were Jewish, took steps to move them on again to another home in Linkebeek, unaware that this was controlled by the Gestapo. The network therefore intervened to save the children and move them elsewhere.[110] In total, it was estimated that the Van den Berg–Fonsny network helped at least four hundred children.[111] It is also worthy of note that van den Berg was far more than a distant organizer and took a personal interest in the children placed in his care. Thus one young girl later recalled:

> Mr van den Berg came to visit them regularly. He was for them like a father, talking to them and taking an interest in their joys and their sadnesses, in everything that made up their lives.[112]

The question of state supervision of education seems to have been a major problem for the rescuers insofar as it restricted the places where francophone children could be placed. In one example, a linguistic commission visited an institution near Namur, in the French-speaking part of the country. The commission was reportedly made up of individuals from the Vlaams Nationaal Verbond (VNV) 'and other blacks' (collaborators), and proceeded to interrogate the children. One was asked, 'Do you speak French?' 'Yes' came the reply. 'Do you speak Flemish?' Again the reply was in the affirmative. Floored by this, the commissioners then tried to elicit a definitive response. 'What language do you speak at home?' To this there was no reply. Frustrated, they tried another avenue, 'What language do you speak to your mother?' 'Yiddish,' replied the child to a stunned audience.[113] The linguistic commission and the VNV were primarily interested in preventing Flemish children being brought up as francophones, and were therefore not directly concerned with unearthing Jewish children in hiding. However, given the collaborationist nature of the VNV, the CDJ could not be certain that this episode would not be reported to the Gestapo, and all the children had to be moved from the home immediately.

Apart from the van den Berg–Fonsny network, there were many other organizations and individuals within Catholic milieux that later came together under the umbrella of L'Aide Chrétienne aux Israélites (ACI).[114] Among the most famous of these was Bruno Reynders who in 1942 had become almoner for a small home for the blind in Hodbomont-Thieux.[115]

He soon realized that the director, as well as some of the residents were Jews in hiding.[116] After a Gestapo raid removed all the adult Jews but left the children, van den Berg, as the home's supervisor, met Reynders for the first time.[117] In January 1943, they began the process of hiding these and other children, with Reynders doing most of the work of finding hiding places himself from among friends and acquaintances.[118] As we have already seen, these included his mother and brother as well as many Catholic institutions, including his own former school. He undertook most of this on a bicycle and at the end of the war, it was estimated he had travelled the equivalent of 40–50 times the distance of the cyclists' Tour of Belgium.[119] He also adopted a peripatetic lifestyle to stay out of the hands of the Gestapo and, with hindsight, can be seen as extremely fortunate not to have betrayed his entire network. Unlike most other illegal workers who understood the importance of secrecy, Reynders actually kept details of all his fellow workers and the people he had hidden in three notebooks.[120] The amount of detail recorded in them would have made it very easy for the Gestapo to have rounded up the entire network in a matter of hours. In the end, he also had to go underground after his base at the Mont César monastery was threatened by the Gestapo.[121] In spite of his apparent lack of personal security, Bruno Reynders refused to work closely with the CDJ because this would have meant sharing information about the location of children in his care.[122]

Reynders and van den Berg were involved in both finding and housing Jewish children. Thus sometimes Reynders would send children, or *colis* (parcels) as they became known, for van den Berg to hide, but on other occasions the 'trade' might be reversed.[123] Children had to be moved on for all sorts of reasons, although it was less likely for those in institutions when compared to those in private homes.[124] Thus, for example, two boys and a girl placed in a château that was subsequently requisitioned by the *Feldgendarmerie* had to be moved after the Germans had let it be known that they knew the children were Jewish. The lack of effective co-operation (and even active dislike) between the military and the Gestapo undoubtedly saved these particular children, but the fact that they did need to be moved helps to explain contemporary reminiscences of Banneux as a place of permanent comings and goings.[125]

There is no doubt that the network created by van den Berg and Reynders was overwhelmingly successful, not only in finding places for Jewish children to hide, but also in keeping them safe throughout the occupation. Inevitably, the work of the network organizers became more onerous as the number of their charges increased and the Gestapo devoted more energy to tracking down resistance networks of all types. Reynders was forced underground when his cloister came under suspicion, and van den Berg was arrested by the Gestapo. As a precaution, the children at the homes in Banneux were moved, but there is no indication that they were under threat or that the existence of the network supporting the children was betrayed in any way.

The network built by Joseph André in his parish of St-Jean-Baptiste in Namur owed much to the priest's friendship with Arthur Burak, a German Jewish refugee and his family who had come to live in his parish.[126] His rectory, known as Notre-Dame-de-Sion, or Hôme de l'Ange, became a transit point for several hundred Jewish children smuggled out of Antwerp and Brussels en route for hiding places in Wallonia in the two years between July 1942 and the summer of 1944. The building was close to the German *Kommandantur* but this did not prevent André from hiding both children and adults in the building—anything up to thirty-five were known to have been there at one time, although only a few were permanently resident and most moved on to other hiding places after a short stay.[127] These were either cloisters or families, although older children were sometimes placed with artisans or shopkeepers as apprentices.[128] Many of his helpers were also engaged in other forms of illegality, thus increasing the risks of accidental betrayal, and André instituted some elements of security, not least in insisting that the children never reveal their real names and that others did not speak about anything they were doing. The rectory was raided on a number of occasions but children were able to escape through an outhouse. Jews were sometimes taken by controls on the street and some were arrested in André's own house, leading to his abandonment of the rectory as a hiding place and his decision to go underground in May 1944.[129]

André kept much of the running of his network in his own hands, facilitating meetings of children and parents in hiding, and negotiating treatment for sick individuals in hospital under assumed identities. He also personally monitored the suitability of placements and moved any children he did not think were being properly cared for. His helpers came from many sections of society, including a neurologist who hid Jews in the contagious diseases ward of the St Camille Hospital in Namur. What was surprising about him was that his pre-war career had been as a 'mystic and a dreamer', rather than one schooled in the practicalities of day-to-day life under occupation. Yet his dynamism in the cause of helping Jewish children was second to none and surprised even his superiors.[130] At the beginning of 1943, he came into contact with Max Katz of the CDJ in Charleroi and this marked the start of a co-operation between André's network and the CDJ that was to last until the end of the occupation. Records show that he sheltered sixty-six people on CDJ books but refused any financial help as the CDJ would then insist on knowing all the details of the child and of the foster parents, and this, like Bruno Reynders, André refused to divulge.[131] His reasoning was partly to do with security, but also the fact that in some cases, parents had entrusted their children to him with the stipulation that they should not be placed in the hands of the CDJ. Again, this had echoes of the relationship between Bruno Reynders and the CDJ and some Dutch independent rescue groups' relationship with the LO in the Netherlands. This isolation meant that André had to find money from other sources, He was able to obtain help with ration cards and false papers from sympathizers within the city administration, and appears to have raised money primarily from his own resources, from his family, and from friends and acquaintances, as well as from the Socrates resistance group that catered primarily for *réfractaires*.[132] His helpers included schoolteachers, youth leaders, and members of the medical profession, as well as the local town clerk and some of his subordinates. Each contributed some essential element to the work but they were increasingly hampered by Gestapo raids that saw the arrests of local civil servants, ration office workers, and policemen. André reputedly made no attempt to convert any of his charges to Catholicism while they were under his care.

Beyond these two networks run by Reynders and André there were many other priests involved specifically in rescuing Jewish children. For example, there was Father Maurice Robinet who was reputed to have helped around 400 children, including twenty-nine whom he sheltered in the cellars of the Gesù Church in Brussels during the last months of the occupation.[133] Likewise, Abbot Bruylants lived in a quarter of the city that had a substantial Jewish population, and when the persecutions began, converted the parochial residence into a hiding place. He also brokered hiding places elsewhere in the city, including a Catholic school, and around Mechelen, saving around eighty people. He had contacts with the Jeunesses Ouvrière Chrétiennes (JOC) through Cardinal Jozef Cardijn, Queen Elisabeth, and Cardinal van Roey, but he was perpetually short of money for his activities and had no dealings with the resistance. Also in Brussels, Antoon de Breuker established an organization called l'Ami des Pauvres to help not only the poor, but also *réfractaires* and Jews on the run from the Germans, including an estimated 265 Jewish children.[134] Again, he used his parishioners and convents to help hide children and co-operated with the JOC, but as with both Robinet and Bruylants, his initial motivation had come from specific conditions in his particular locality rather than any promptings from his superiors.

Other help came from secular Catholic organizations such as the JOC. It had established the Entr'aide service in 1940 run by Father Capart, the self-confessed right-hand man of Cardinal Cardijn, who himself had established the Kristelijke Arbeidersjeugd (KAJ) in 1924 to help children in danger and also founded homes at Braine-l'Alleud, Schaltin, Banneux, Lauwe, Dworp, and Leffe-lez-Dinant.[135] Capart was subsequently approached by his father, the Egyptologist Jean Capart, who had in turn been asked by Queen Elisabeth to help provide assistance to the Jews. As a result, the first Jewish child was brought to a JOC home at the end of 1942. After March 1943, contact was established with the CDJ, but it was never the only source of children as others came from individual parishes and other institutions. Essentially, the JOC took full charge of the upbringing of the children held in its homes. It is impossible to say if there were any deliberate attempts to convert Jews hiding in this way, but at least three boys in its care whose mother had died were adopted by a priest responsible for education at Banneux and Leffe. One of them later entered holy orders and became a parish priest.[136]

Like the CDJ, the JOC was able to obtain documentation for those in hiding from sympathetic civil servants. Its headquarters in the Boulevard Poincaré was used as a temporary shelter and distribution point for children, a fact made all the more remarkable in that three-quarters of the building was occupied by the German army and police. One JOC home at Schaltin was raided by the Gestapo, resulting in three leaders, four Jewish children, and three other Jews being arrested and ultimately deported.[137] Unlike the networks created by the priests specifically to help Jewish children, the work of the JOC was far more wide ranging and had been more concerned with providing help to escaping prisoners of war and *réfractaires*. Thus, while the Jews, and Jewish children in particular, were not discriminated against, they were viewed by the JOC as just one of many categories of Belgian citizens in danger from German measures.[138] In total, it was estimated that the JOC had saved fifty-nine Jewish children during the occupation.[139]

Children whose parents or guardians still had access to funds could afford to send their children to boarding schools in the countryside where they were considered safer and could live using false papers and assumed identities. The directors and head teachers of these institutions almost invariably knew the origins of their new charges and sometimes even acted as couriers. However, such institutions would often shelter numbers of fugitives, both children and adults, with each one unaware of others in a similar predicament, or at least warned not to ask any questions. Realizing a possible compromising situation, one headmaster warned an older girl arriving at his school in late 1942 about another pupil who had been at her school in Brussels and that if she was recognized, another hiding place would have to be found for her.[140]

Hosts could and did ask for subsidies to support foster children. In February and March 1943, three farming families in South Hainaut asked for and received 10 francs a day (or 300 francs per month) for each child they sheltered. Other records from the van den Berg network show that Jewish parents were often responsible for the upkeep of their children. Thus a brother and sister were supported with 25 francs per day and a fund of 12,000 francs, and the foster parents of another boy received 300 francs per month.[141] These figures bear some relationship to what is known about other children in hiding where their upkeep was met from other sources. The surviving records show that children were fostered with sums ranging from 400 to 1,000 francs per month.[142] How these amounts were calculated seems impossible to reconstruct. There is no correlation according to age, and no indication of any special needs that individual children might have had. The differences may have just been a result of demands from the foster parents: a conclusion reinforced by one or two examples where children were apparently fostered without charge, or where it was made clear that they were taken in on an *au pair* basis.[143] However, the standard rate seems to have been 600 francs per month during the crucial period from the end of 1942 until the liberation, and the fact that there were accepted 'rates' probably reduced the possibilities for profiteering, except where arrangements were made privately and without reference to an aid organization. Charges did change over time and there were increases noted long after the liberation for children still being fostered. Thus for example, the foster parents of a fifteen-month-old child were paid 600 francs per month in December 1942, but this increased to 750 francs per month by October 1944.[144] These increases may simply have been to compensate for inflation, but there were also cases where additional payments were made because the child had, or developed, a critical illness.[145] It is also clear that not all charges were borne by the organizations involved, as some cards record the fact that part-payments were made by the parents, or that the individual case was 'free to us', indicating that all the charges were being paid or subsidized by third parties.[146] Food was also an issue, especially later in the occupation. Even with subsistence payments, children still needed ration cards, food stamps, and clothing. This was not so much of a problem if the local civil servants and merchants were sympathetic, but poor relations between hosts and these crucial members of the community could lead to difficulties. This was overcome in some measure by the system set up by van den Berg in Liège where network members presented their own papers to the communal authorities but with false addresses. This allowed them to receive duplicate ration stamps that could then be handed on to those in hiding.[147]

Beyond the Catholic institutions, there were also other networks and organizations that helped save substantial numbers of children. Pastors from the very small Protestant community in Belgium helped by providing baptismal and confirmation certificates, and by sheltering Jewish children in orphanages run by their churches. In numerical terms, the most important was the Foyer Protestant pour Enfants in Brussels that helped between eighty and ninety Jewish children for longer or shorter periods, usually referred to it by the CDJ. However, other pastors and parishes were also involved.[148] Beyond the confessional organizations there were other secular institutions involved, some at the prompting of the CDJ—others because it represented an extension of their existing resistance work. For example, the Ecole Nouvelle des Ardennes had been used by its director to hide arms and a radio, labour-service evaders, and resistance workers, as well as Jews. Soon the latter formed two-thirds of the residents. Ultimately, the whole operation was betrayed to the Germans by a local farmer and they were all arrested and deported.[149] Another haven was the children's homes run by the Œuvre Nationale de Service Social aux Familles de Militaires. Its director, Georges Rhodius, established contacts with the CDJ and created a clandestine organization, the Aide aux Abandonnés, that ultimately helped around 350 Jews, including 300 children.[150]

The total number of children saved by these major networks will probably never be accurately known, not least because children were sometimes transferred between networks or double-counted in some other

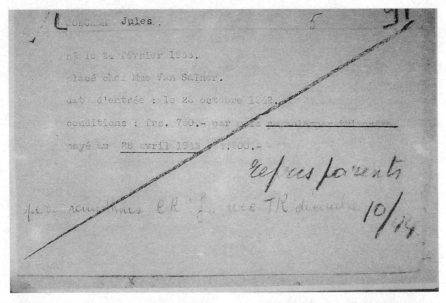

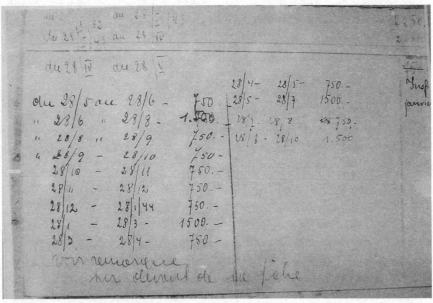

Figure 11.1. Index card showing the name and location of a hidden child in Belgium, together with the remuneration agreed and payments made to the foster parent

Source: USHMM/CEGES-SOMA

way. By the same token there were others who survived as a result of private arrangements that were never formally recorded.[151] For the children hidden in non-confessional environments, there were no problems of religious conformity, but in the many confessional hiding places, this was a major issue, both during and after the occupation. Both André and Reynders were adamant that there should be no pressure placed on Jewish children, either by force or persuasion, to be baptized in the Catholic faith, and that this should only take place with the express permission of the parents.[152] This was mirrored in the attitude of Kerkhofs who reserved all decisions on the baptism of Jewish children in his diocese, and only very rarely gave permission if the parents were absent.[153] Nonetheless, the very nature of the hiding places for many children—in Catholic religious or educational institutions—meant that exposure to Christian education and belief were almost inevitable— as any exclusions or exceptions would have immediately drawn attention to the children's presence.[154] Thus even before the occupation was over, claims and counter-claims were being traded and the post-war period saw increasing animosity between the CDJ on the one hand, and the various Catholic-based rescue organizations on the other.[155] While refusing to use the children as a source of converts during the occupation, Reynders nonetheless took the view after the war that orphan children who had been baptized in hiding should not then be returned to the Jewish organizations who claimed them.[156] Nevertheless, even before hostilities were over, he had accused the CDJ of trying to establish a monopoly over all the Jewish orphans created by the Holocaust, and used this as an explanation for the distance between the two groups.[157] For its part, the CDJ had a rather less charitable view of 'certain Catholic institutions' that obliged hidden children to say prayers, attend confession, and attempted to convert them. Some complained about this when the CDJ workers visited them, and they in turn raised it with the institutions' leaders. However, such charges were often met with incomprehension, and it was better to change the location of the children involved.[158] Other complications could arise where only some of an institution's staff knew that Jewish children were being sheltered there. Thus one small Jewish boy was removed from a kindergarten when it became clear that one of the nuns—presumably suspecting he was Jewish—had excluded him from the presents given on the feast of St Nicholas.[159]

It would be impossible to discuss the rescue of children in Belgium without reference to perhaps the strangest case of mass survival, namely the

Figure 11.2. Post-war portrait of Monsignor Louis-Joseph Kerkhofs, Bishop of Liège. Rights Reserved,
Source: CEGES-SOMA, Brussels

children who were transferred into homes controlled by the collaborationist AJB and with the full knowledge of the Gestapo, but who nonetheless survived the occupation. The AJB had been charged with finding placements for children and the elderly whose nearest relations had been, or were about to be, deported. For their own reasons, and perhaps because they wanted to maintain the fiction of deportation being for 'labour in the East' the young and the very old were excluded from the holding centre at Mechelen but needed to be found shelter elsewhere. Children became de facto orphans through any number of routes. Sometimes they were placed in the care of a Jewish orphanage by their parents before they themselves reported to Mechelen. Others arrived there because their parents were arrested in raids, or the people sheltering them took fright at the risks they were taking, or the money they received for the upkeep of their charges dried up.[160] Unlike their fellow Jews in hiding, these children retained their own identities and were able to talk openly about their families. Initially, their numbers were small and they were housed at the Jewish orphanages in Antwerp and Brussels. Ultimately, the numbers grew to around 500, although it was estimated that over 700 children had spent some time there.[161] All were under the control of the Gestapo, administered by the children's department of the AJB, and funded by the state organization for child welfare. In the post-war era, the directors of these homes and the members of the AJB were castigated for having collaborated with the Germans, but the fact remains that, although the homes' existence helped to bolster the image of the deportations that the Germans wanted to portray, until the last days of the occupation, they also provided an unlikely sanctuary for a large number of children. Although the CDJ did take over the care of some of the children in the AJB homes, there were never any plans to remove all of them. While the CDJ may have harboured genuine and well-founded fears for the safety of the children, the scale of the task in finding placements for all the other children at risk served to prevent any pre-emptive action.[162]

Beyond the orphanages in Antwerp and Brussels, other institutions were established during the occupation. The first of these was Ophem-Wezembeek, which opened in September 1942.[163] Soon afterwards, on 30 October, the home was subject to an SS-Gestapo raid and its staff members and eighty-five children were taken to Mechelen for deportation.[164] The camp commander was prepared to free the director, Marie Blum-Albert, on the grounds that she was a Belgian national, and also gave her charge of a 23-month-old child, to which was added another infant who had been taken in a raid on a hospital the same night. Two other boys with diphtheria were also released so as not to infect others in the camp. All were confined inside the camp while the deportation of the remainder was organized lest they raised the alarm. In fact, this was done by a member of staff left at the home, who telephoned the National Office for child welfare, where Yvonne Nevéjean lost no time in contacting the AJB. It was able to contact the Ministry of Justice, who in turn involved the Queen. So great was the protest against this action that the military command insisted that the staff and children not be deported and allowed to return to the home. Within twenty-four hours, this had been accomplished and only one or two foreign members of the staff were held and sent to Poland.[165]

As the Allied armies advanced across France in the late summer of 1944, the Germans finally took action against the 4,000 or so 'legal' Jews remaining in Belgium. An SS officer arrived at the orphanage in Brussels on 24 August and demanded full details of all the children there. The directors were warned that the Germans intended to clear all the orphanages, hospitals, and old people's homes within forty-eight hours. In this regard, the children at Wezembeek were a particular problem as the home's hairdresser had managed to infect many of them with head-lice, making it doubly difficult to find hiding places. Nevertheless, all the children in the AJB homes were spirited away at very short notice with the help of the CDJ and the resistance, and were doubtless saved from further pursuit by the arrival of Allied forces only a few days later.[166] Many of them ended up in the care of Sister Marie Beirens of the convent at Héverlée, but hiding places varied enormously. Some children were kept in groups while others were placed with local farmers.[167] Thus the children from the home at Aiche-en-Refail were taken to a school where local farmers came to choose those they would take—always preferring the strongest and best nourished of the candidates. Some proved unwilling to hand over their charges after the liberation and pressure had to be exerted so that all the children were returned to the care of the authorities.[168]

The rescue of Jewish children in Belgium was, therefore, a story of relative success, with co-ordination and co-operation between a range of Jewish and non-Jewish organizations, albeit not without some frictions. As with the rescue of adults, the creation of the CDJ as a counterweight to the later AJB gave Jews in Belgium some measure of choice over whom to trust, and the infiltration of the latter by CDJ activists had major advantages for the clandestine workers in knowing what the Germans had planned. The involvement of both Catholic clergy and laity is also worthy of note. The fact that some leading churchmen were proactive in encouraging help for Jews was undoubtedly important, as was their mobilization of secular organizations such as the van den Berg network. This greater integration was beneficial, although the case studies show that there was still some distrust and reluctance to share information and risks between different networks. That said, Belgium also provided a number of structural advantages for those involved. The most important one was probably the sheer number of religious institutions that could be used as hiding places, in addition to the houses of individual rescuers. The cause was also helped by the nature of the German occupation. The military governance of the country limited the scope of the SS and Gestapo, both in terms of influence and manpower. Thus the officials sent to Brussels from Department IVB4 in Berlin were never able to call on much help from the Belgian civil service or its police force to track down Jews in hiding, and they had to rely primarily on indigenous national socialists and informers to fulfil their tasks.

12

At the Eleventh Hour: Saving Jewish Children in the Netherlands

As has already been shown, in contrast to both France and Belgium, there was little in the way of Jewish self-help in the Netherlands, or any organized help from the rest of society much before the end of 1942. Ultimately there were a number of groups that specialized in sheltering Jewish children, but their origins were very different from those in the countries to the south and none of them predated the beginnings of the deportations. Nevertheless, there are also many parallels and the richness of the documentation allows us to highlight some common issues in more detail than is possible elsewhere.

Rescue Networks: The Role of Student Societies and Illegal Newspapers

In chronological terms, the first rescue network devoted exclusively to saving children was formed by university students in Utrecht, later known as the *Utrechtse Kindercomité*. It was founded by a student of social geography, Ad Groenendijk, and Cor Bastiaanse, a woman whose husband was held as a hostage by the Germans.[1] Their activity began when Bastiaanse was told by an 18-year-old Jewish girl, Beppie de Hont, about the first call-ups of Jewish families to the *Zentralstelle* in June 1942. Via this link, a number of those called-up asked if Bastiaanse could shelter their children, and so the first placements were made.[2] She collected the children from Amsterdam and hid them in her attic. Groenendijk and others then distributed them to other addresses. One of Groenendijk's contacts was with a fellow student of social geography, Jan Meulenbelt, and his mother provided one of the first foster homes for the group. Subsequently, Meulenbelt also telephoned other friends to find further addresses to take in Jewish children.[3] Precisely how Meuelenbelt chose his contacts, or how his mother intimated that she was able to provide permanent shelter for Jewish children remains unclear. At this stage, the fostering of children had a temporary character. Although the call-ups in June had been followed by the first major raid in Amsterdam on 14 July 1942, most of those arrested had subsequently been released. In the ensuing period of quiet, many parents of children taken in by the *Kindercomité* decided it was safe to have their children back. At this stage, the total numbers involved were very small, but the initial elements of a future network had nonetheless been established.

The role of universities in this process also requires some comment. Traditionally, student life had been essentially a-political, taken up with the business of learning, sport and student societies. This slowly began to change as German impositions began to restrict student life through curfews and Nazi provocations.[4] The societies in Utrecht were forced to disband in July 1941, but this did not preclude further clandestine organizations and an increasingly anti-German sentiment. One of the main societies, the *Utrechtsch Studenten Corps* (USC), became the source for many future members of the *Utrechtse Kindercomité*. As one of their number later recalled, National Socialist students were very thin on the ground and were shunned, but of the majority you could be 99 per cent certain.[5] This conclusion also held for the female equivalent of the USC, the *Utrechtsche Vrouwelijks Studenten Vereeniging* (UVSV). Unlike its male equivalent, the UVSV did not find itself disbanded in 1941, although its buildings were taken over by the *Wehrmacht* in July 1941. Thus it continued to have a legal existence, probably because the German authorities overlooked it. In addition to contributing contacts and personnel to the *Kindercomité*, the UVSV also provided the organization with two of its later leaders, Hetty Voûte and Olga Hudig. In the post-war era, Hudig described their situation:

> The desire to resist existed fiercely within us, but we had not yet found the way, we were not yet familiar with the meaning of illegality. One did not yet know the nature of German practices and therefore felt unsure about the weapons one had to wield.[6]

That said, her compatriot Hetty Voûte had already had some experience
of resistance activity before the question of Jewish foster children arose.
With her two brothers, she was responsible for the first illegal newspaper
in the city. Their mimeographed *Bulletin* was distributed every month
until September 1941. Other direct actions included the smearing of
German and NSB cyclists' saddles with an evil-smelling compound called
duivelsdrek (Devil's shit), or slashing their tyres.[7] Later, her group graduated
to espionage and resistance.

The role of the student societies was therefore crucial in broadening
networks of trust between disparate individuals and small groups. Jan
Meulenbelt was not a member of the USC, but he effectively led the
group through sheer force of personality and was able to recruit reliable
helpers, even from among the initially unwilling.[8] The majority of students
had gradually been driven from their a-political stance by the increasing
impositions and restrictions placed on them by the occupying Germans,
but most were unsure of what they might do to give practical vent to their
opposition, and helping Jews provided a possible outlet. The specialization
with children came about because Meulenbelt believed that this was not
seen as such a crime by the Germans, in spite of the fact that it still required
many actions that were in themselves illegal, such as finding false ration
cards. A further reason for limiting the activity to children was given by
another member of the organization:

> In July and August we had only a few female students and friends at our
> disposal. [. . . .] But with a handful of amateurs you could not really do much
> more than [help] children. Thus it was an essential restriction [. . . .] It was
> naturally also easier to find addresses. Indeed we did not believe that it was
> really illegal work. At least, that term was never used.[9]

Meulenbelt and his colleagues realized that they needed to reduce the risks
involved to a minimum, and to create a more rational organization if their
work was to be expanded. The first principle was that no hiding places
were to be used in Amsterdam itself. This was inherent logic as the city was
subject to German raids against the Jews and 'no one had the wish to snatch
children from the hands of the Germans more than once'.[10] Other leading
members included Frits Iordens, a classical musician, and his friend Anne
Maclaine Pont. Like most of their fellow students, they both came from
bourgeois backgrounds. Iordens' father was a bank director and Pont's, a
brush manufacturer. Both brought further contacts outside the city, Iordens

in his hometown of Arnhem, and Pont in the area around Zwolle where she had been at school. The latter was able to enlist well-placed friends and members of her extended family. A final 'affiliate' was established through Meulenbelt's contacts with anti-militarist circles in The Hague.[11]

Wanting to help Jewish children was one thing, but having a supply of suitable candidates was another. To that end, Meulenbelt enlisted the help of people in Amsterdam. Jur Haak, a 22-year-old student of mathematics became his primary contact. Like so many of the linkages established in this period, it is now impossible to determine how it was first made. Very much a born leader who played a major role in student life at the University of Amsterdam, Haak was able to enlist the *Amsterdamsch Studenten Corps* (ASC) to recruit more help, including the anti-militarist law student Piet Meerburg.[12] Meerburg later recalled how the arrest of a fellow ASC student who was Jewish had spurred him into action. He also explained the specialization in children rather than adults, as just helping the children was such a large undertaking in its own right. Haak's sister, Tieneke, and her boyfriend, Wouter van Zeytveld, joined them. These two were only 19 and 18 respectively in 1941.[13]

A third group, the so-called Naamloze Vennootschap (literally, limited liability company, NV) arose from a single Jewish family in need and a single Calvinist pastor. The Brauns were a Calvinist family from Austria who had come to the Netherlands as refugees on account of their Jewish ancestry. When the son and daughter were told to report for deportation in July 1942, their parents approached their local pastor, Constant Sikkel. He then used his next sermon, in a suitably circumspect way, to ask what might be done to help these people. Two brothers, Jaap and Gerard Musch, responded. As a result, the children, Marianne and Leo, were taken to addresses in Friesland and the parents to a farm in Gelderland. The addresses in Friesland came from the brothers, while the hiding place for the parents was provided through contacts made by Sikkel with another Calvinist pastor. The two brothers then enlisted a friend, Dick Groenewegen van Wijk, and the three became the NV. At this stage, they had no idea where to find either hiding places or a means of contacting Jews wanting to hide, but were driven by a desire to help their Jewish fellow citizens. Gerard Musch and Groenewegen van Wijk both went underground themselves in October 1942 when the latter was threatened with being sent for labour service in Germany.[14] These two had spent several fruitless weeks trying to find suitable hiding places in Groningen Province before Jaap Musch moved to a new job in South Limburg and discovered another Calvinist pastor, Gerard Pontier, who was prepared to seek out addresses in his parish in the southern town of Heerlen.[15] Again, precisely how this contact was made is unclear, although Musch went to their first meeting armed with a letter of introduction from Sikkel. Pontier thus became involved in the NV's work, providing the first addresses for the network when he gave shelter to one of the Braun children, with the other being placed with the family of Harmen Bockma, a virulently anti-German local mineworker. Pontier was a man imbued with missionary zeal. His dream had been to go to the Indies, but when he was instead sent to South Limburg, he embraced the challenge to minister to a flock in an area that was overwhelmingly Catholic. Jaap Musch also showed his commitment to the work by giving up his job at the University of Amsterdam and moving to Heerlen to work as a chemical analyst for the mining industry and taking up lodgings with the Bockma family. At the same time, he broke off his engagement when it became clear that his fiancée did not approve of him being involved in illegal work.[16]

The final example is of a rescue network that grew alongside a wider resistance organization. The founder of the so-called Trouw group in Amsterdam, Hester van Lennep, came from an old and respected Dutch family and, after the German invasion of the Netherlands, a number of men in her neighbourhood became involved in armed resistance, including her two nephews, Gideon and Jan Karl Boissevain. Karl later became the leader of the CS-6 (Corellistraat 6) resistance group.[17] At that time she owned an institute for skin care in the Keizersgracht, but it was through one of her acquaintances, a notary, that she was first asked to help a Jewish child in the latter half of 1942. Her first 'address' was that of her mother in Hilversum. Further children came her way through contacts with CS-6 and especially through the institute. It seems that it became known in Amsterdam Jewish circles through word-of-mouth that the institute was a place where hiding places could be found for Jewish children. As a result, there were an increasing number of Jewish visitors to the premises in the Keizersgracht.[18] This 'snowballing' of knowledge about the existence of an opportunity for Jewish children to disappear also worked for van Lennep in finding addresses for the children to hide. Visits home produced more contacts from among her mother's friends and acquaintances. Over time, more and more members of the extended Boissevain family became part of the network, together with their friends and acquaintances.[19] Children were transferred to their foster parents by van Lennep or by intermediaries. In some cases, van Lennep herself had little or no knowledge of the people she enrolled to help. They were always recruited on a temporary basis, but were almost invariably enthusiastic about a more permanent commitment.

Van Lennep seems to have been particularly well placed to carry out this work. Her association with her nephews in the resistance and her extended family facilitated further contacts and practical help when it was needed, and her institute provided invaluable cover for people visiting to solicit help. However, this individual enterprise was by no means the end of the story. Through her older sister, van Lennep met Gesina van der Molen, the editor of the illegal newspaper *Vrij Nederland*.[20] In conversation it emerged that there had already been discussions within the newspaper's circle about doing 'something' for Jewish children and a separate section of the group had been suggested. Van Lennep allowed van der Molen to prove herself by asking her to find a place for a single child. When that worked without difficulty, a second child was offered, and again successfully placed. The advantage was that this wider contact provided a much more extensive supply of potential hiding places among people trusted, or at least known, by an existing illegal organization.

Gesina van der Molen was a remarkable woman by any measure.[21] She had been born in the province of Groningen to orthodox Calvinist parents. Against their wishes, she set out to make herself economically independent, something almost unthinkable for an unmarried woman from such a background, and in 1924 at the age of 32 she began studying law at the Free University in Amsterdam.[22] In 1930, she set up house with her lifelong friend Mies Nolte and in 1937 became the first woman to have a *proefschrift* (doctorate) accepted by the Free University. Her role in *Vrij Nederland* from April 1941 led to her arrest and incarceration for a number of weeks in July and August 1942, but her credentials as someone opposed to Nazi racial policies were already well established.[23] Earlier, she had not only refused to sign the Aryan attestation demanded of all government employees, but had also sent in a detailed explanation as to why she was refusing to comply. She argued that this would be 'the first step to the persecution of the Jews, a shame on all Christian peoples and in particular completely at odds with the best traditions of the Dutch people'.[24] Although she had opposed the principles of her parents, she had clearly not abandoned her faith and had been a prominent member of the *Christelijke Vrouwenbond* (Christian Women's Union).[25]

After her release from custody, she went underground in Amsterdam and, having fallen out with the leadership of *Vrij Nederland*,[26] was approached by the leadership orthodox Calvinist Anti-revolutionary Party to found and edit a new underground paper representing their interests. The first edition of *Trouw* appeared in January 1943, and the newspaper developed close links with the LO. In this way, the Trouw group rescuing children had access to a ready supply of essential documents. They also had access to its wider network of safe houses and contacts that could be used to facilitate their work. This also applied to the recruitment of potential foster parents from among the Calvinist community, although the group also placed a small number of children in Catholic Limburg, probably through the agency of Mies Nolte.

The absence of independent Jewish welfare organizations and the lack of any wider mobilization to help the Jews before the call-ups and deportations began meant that the first children taken into hiding by all these groups came primarily from personal contacts of would-be rescuers with individual Jewish families. Thus the numbers involved were initially very small. Only as the threat posed by the deportations increased, did the attitudes of Jewish parents begin to change. How they learned about the networks is difficult to determine, but it is clear that supply and demand did not always match. In the case of the student organizations, it appears that it became widely known in the Jewish districts of Amsterdam that there were four young students working to shelter and hide Jewish children. The initial call-ups tended to be from those in the 16 to 40-year-old category (a smokescreen for the official line that deportation was for labour in the East). Because this included large numbers of young families with parents unwilling to be separated from their offspring, many children went with their parents on the transports to Westerbork and beyond. Only a minority saw the importance of leaving their children behind simply because there was an opportunity for them to be kept safe inside the Netherlands. At this stage there was no structure to the work being done, and contacts were loose and often occurred by pure chance.

Children were moved from Amsterdam to Utrecht by women as their travelling during the day would arouse no great suspicions and be perceived as perfectly normal.[27] Once in Utrecht, the children could not always be placed immediately. To provide temporary shelter, the students used a crèche run by another UVSV member, Truitje van Lier. This had been opened as early as October 1940 to help working women and unmarried mothers, but was also used to house children in council care.²⁸ Later, when Jews were increasingly concentrated into Amsterdam, it was developed into a transit point for many children as families were broken up as they tried to go into hiding.²⁹ To cloak the children, the institution possessed its own very inventive security systems. Children were given aliases, and van Lier 'acquired' blank registration cards from the Amsterdam Jewish Council offices that were then completed with the alias, false address, and the information that they were the product of a mixed marriage between a Jewish woman and a non-Jewish man. The latter deceit was designed to cover the fact that the children might well 'look' Jewish and needed a cover story that fitted the facts. Certainly, it was already understood that '*mischlinge*' were safer than children with two Jewish parents. Their presence in the crèche was explained by the mother being confined to a hospital or sanatorium and the father being away working in Germany.³⁰ A more daring procedure still was to use the existence of illegitimate offspring of Dutch women and German soldiers at the crèche—children who therefore came under the protection of the local military commander—as a means of cloaking other Jewish children and as a protection from SD raids. Van Lier was also active in finding hiding places herself, and even when those approached refused to take in a child, they were pressed to 'sponsor' one instead—thus helping her organization financially.³¹ Her crèche was not the creation of the *Kindercomité*, nor was it for their exclusive use, as both a communist and a Calvinist resistance group also placed children with her temporarily.³²

Rescue workers felt they were working against the clock and thus took children whenever they could, even if they had no permanent addresses for them. Making contact was problematic, but the student groups' 'recruitment' of Jewish children from Amsterdam was aided by contact with a paediatrician, Ph. H. Fiedeldij Dop. His practice had been greatly enlarged when two Jewish paediatricians in his locality had stopped work and effectively handed their patients over to him.³³ As a direct result of his work with Jewish patients he began to look for ways of finding hiding places for children and this, eventually, brought him into contact with Piet Meerburg. Fiedeldij Dop thus became a crucial point of contact between the Jewish community and the student rescue network in the city. Of those who were asked if they wanted a safe hiding place for their children, only a small minority accepted. A further appointment some days later would then be made for those who accepted help, when the child (or children) would be collected by one of the students.

It would be easy to suppose that there was only one student group in Amsterdam helping Jewish children, but the experiences of Fiedeldij Dop suggest otherwise. In his quest for help, he first heard of a group of students working out of a city hospital. When he arrived, he was greeted warmly by the students and told all about their operations. He quickly took the view that their complete lack of security consciousness would lead rapidly to disaster, and he therefore decided to look elsewhere for help. The indirect and careful approach from Meerburg inspired him with more confidence, and it is clear that his group had thought through its security systems. Parents were never told where their children were going, although some exchanges of letters and photographs were allowed through intermediaries. However, if the parents were deported then this stopped, and even if they went underground, contact was usually lost after they had moved addresses more than once or twice.[34]

Initially, the NV was committed to finding hiding places for both adults and children, but experiences with one of their first fugitives, who had left his hiding place and attempted to return to Amsterdam, convinced the group that it was better to specialize in dealing with children, as they usually did what they were told.[35] Like the other organizations, the NV found making contact with Jewish parents difficult, and this was only partially solved by enlisting the help of a half-Jewish acquaintance in Amsterdam, who, with his neighbour, visited Jewish households in their neighbourhood to persuade them to let their children go into hiding.

The Crèche at the Schouwburg

There is no doubt that the single most important source of children for all the networks helping the Jews was the crèche in the Plantage Middelaan attached to the Hollandsche Schouwburg. Popularly referred to as the 'Joodsche' Schouwburg, this Amsterdam theatre was used by the Germans as a holding centre for Jews from July 1942 onwards before their removal to the transit camp at Westerbork. The crèche had existed as an institution for Jewish and other children since 1906, but in 1941 had become a completely Jewish institution with the forced dismissal of its non-Jewish staff members.[36] After the establishment of the Schouwburg, the crèche became an obvious means to accommodate the large numbers of children arrested who could not easily be kept in the unsuitable theatre premises twenty-four hours a day. This became a formal arrangement soon after 3 October 1942, when the crèche was designated as an annex of the Schouwburg.

The Schouwburg was one of the few institutions staffed by personnel of the Amsterdam Jewish Council where some attempts at self-help and rescue were organized. This was extremely difficult as it was heavily guarded, but escape from the crèche became an extension of the work already being led by Walter Süskind to free adult Jews from captivity. German security measures meant that only three children's nurses were allowed to enter the Schouwburg to take children out or return them to their parents. Although Süskind and his colleagues had already given some thought as to how Jewish children might be rescued from the crèche, at that stage they had no knowledge of organizations or individuals capable of helping them 'on the outside'.

The crucial meeting that changed matters took place in January 1943 between Süskind and Joop Woortman of the NV. Having helpers on the outside, the crèche workers could now begin to find ways of spiriting the children away. The Germans did not consider the crèche to be a security risk and it was therefore easier to enter and leave than the main building on the other side of the street. Thus initially, babies could be smuggled out of the building and taken directly to the Central Station where members of the NV would meet them. An alternative was to use the tram that passed outside, both as cover and as a means of transport. As the tram arrived, the rescuers would grab a child and run alongside so that the guards (outside the Schouwburg on the other side of the street) could not see them. They then caught the tram at the stop round the corner. As two NV couriers later recalled,

> The whole tram began to laugh. They had seen everything and where we had come from, but no one betrayed us.
>
> Nine out of ten of the tram drivers were wonderful fellows (*geweldige kerels*). They knew exactly what was going on...[and] the anonymous people in those trams, it's unbelievable what help and common humanity (*medemenselijkheid*) you got from them.

Although it was the NV that began transferring children from the crèche, it was not long before the *Utrechtse Kindercomité* joined in and their first rescue was a form of retaliation. Three Jewish children placed by the *Utrechtse Kindercomité* had been captured by the Germans and taken to the crèche

Figure 12.1. The crèche opposite the Hollandsche Schouwburg holding centre in Amsterdam, from where Jewish children were smuggled out by rescue networks

Source: Verzetsmuseum, Amsterdam

prior to their deportation. In order to get them back, Pont and Iordens dressed in SS uniforms and demanded the children be handed over. The frightened crèche staff meekly complied and the children were spirited away.[37] At this stage, the only children taken from the crèche by the rescuers went with their parents' permission. This was inherently sensible, as only so many could be saved. It also prevented chaos on nights when transports took place as no children would have been taken without their parents' knowledge. The three children's nurses were given the task of contacting parents the night before the transports to see if they would agree to having their children rescued. As one recalled,

Then you went [to the Schouwburg] and had to try to speak to these people with all the others all around, and very carefully... 'Won't you leave your boy or your girl with us?... We'll make sure that they will go to people who will look after them until you return.' Most refused.[38]

There were two exceptions to the rule. The first was that children who had been caught in hiding were assumed to have had their parents' blessing to go underground and so could be rescued a second time. The German authorities treated them as orphans and punishment cases. Thus if a transport could not be filled from people in the Schouwburg, the orphans from the crèche were used to make up the numbers. The second exception was made where the rescuers found a home in a family for a particular type of child, for example to take the place of one who had died.[39] In such cases, it was important for the substitute to be approximately the same age, height and have the same colouring. It remains to be seen if potential foster parents were ever able to 'order' particular types of children to meet their personal preferences. Ultimately, all manner of means were used to smuggle children out of the building. Babies were put in rucksacks, boxes, bundles of washing, and even milk churns and potato sacks. Sometimes, children hidden in the crèche had to be handed over if the Germans asked for them specifically, or if the total numbers requested could not be made up from other sources or by falsifying the count. Similarly, parents had to leave on transports clutching their 'babies' that were in reality a doll or dressed-up cushion. They also had to act the part, being delighted to have their children returned to them and keeping up the pretence while not allowing anyone else to see the deception.

After May 1943, the number of children smuggled out of the crèche increased. This was a combination of the rescue networks being better organized, there being more doors open after the April–May strikes, and new and better ways being found to escape from the building.[40] Like the NV who used a pharmacy, the Trouw group used a grocery store as cover, and its couriers did not come to the crèche but were given pick-up points via the network's mail drop. It recruited some of its helpers from those initially drawn into the writing and distribution of their newspaper.

As the system around the Schouwburg and the crèche became better established, so the workers became more adept at creating escape routes beyond the opportunistic methods employed at the outset. In early 1943 the crèche had acquired a next-door house after its inhabitants had been deported. This gave the institution a common boundary with a Christian teacher-training college. As the numbers of people held in the Schouwburg increased, the crèche director, Henriëtte Pimentel, asked the college principal, Johan van Hulst, if some part of his establishment could be used as a playground for the children. This was agreed and then extended so that the children could also have their midday nap in the school buildings. This allowed the rescuers to 'visit' the college and remove children from its premises without being seen near the crèche. Van Hulst and the college caretaker were part of the conspiracy, but the director had some doubts about telling all the eighty-four trainee teachers there immediately. A visit from the state-appointed external examiners to the college in May 1943 also proved particularly fortuitous.[41] Van Hulst had to admit that he was allowing the college premises to be used every day by the crèche, as they could be clearly heard. However, it was the external assessor for history, Gesina van der Molen, then already deeply involved in resistance activity with the Trouw group, who was to prove the key link in this particular chain. On realizing the opportunity that her position afforded, she took no time in arranging for some children to be smuggled out to the Trouw group. Even before the final examinations had finished, she had already taken twelve.[42]

The system became so sophisticated that the workers in the crèche could tell the rescue groups what children they had available to go underground, and the groups could then consult their reception points in Friesland or Limburg to see which of the children could be placed. Communication between crèche and rescuers was in code; thus ersatz tea (*theesurrogaat*) described a blond child who would be better sent to the north and ersatz coffee (*koffiesurrogaat*) was a dark child who would be less conspicuous in Limburg.[43] The processes of smuggling children continued through into the summer of 1943 and allowed the escape of many hundreds into hiding. Yet, as the rescuers and the crèche staff both knew, the rescues they carried out could only take place if other children were there to act as cover. Many years later, van Hulst described the awful nature of the process.

> And then Virrie Cohen came to me and said. 'The crèche is full to over-flowing. Come with me and take a couple (of children) temporarily into the college and they can then perhaps be collected from there.' Now you have to imagine being there. 80, 90, perhaps 70 perhaps 100 children and you had to decide, which children . . . That was the most difficult day of my life. You knew for certain you could not take all the children. You also knew that the children you did not take were sentenced to death. Thus I took twelve. Afterwards I asked myself, why not thirteen?[44]

As the numbers of Jews living in the Netherlands legally dwindled in the summer of 1943, the Germans turned their attention to the remaining institutions and branches of the Jewish Council. On 26 July most of the crèche staff, including Pimentel, were slated for deportation. This temporarily closed the crèche's doors and all the children were also deported, but within hours it had to be reopened to deal with a fresh wave of arrests. Virrie Cohen, a fully qualified nurse who had been working in the crèche, became the new director, saved from the transport through the intervention of her father, David Cohen.[45] These last arrests and the removal of the remaining Jews in Amsterdam prompted increased activity by the rescue organizations. The crèche closed for the final time on 29 September 1943 when all the remaining Jews, including the leaders of the Jewish Council, were taken to Westerbork. The crèche had a few days' notice of its closure and the staff did what they could to spirit away as many children as possible. The last week became hectic with the NV collecting fourteen children on a single visit and Virrie Cohen herself smuggling out fifteen so that they could be picked up by rescuers.

Virrie Cohen was persuaded to go underground by Meerburg, mainly so that she could help identify the children after the war was over. Most of the remaining staff also managed to escape underground. Ultimately, the crèche alone provided 385 or around 35 per cent of all the children rescued by these four networks, but this was by no means the entire story. It has been estimated that a total of 600 children were smuggled out of the crèche between July 1942 and November 1943, indicating that the other 215 were taken out, either by individuals or by other rescue organizations. The tragedy was that

Figure 12.2. Virrie Cohen, daughter of Professor David Cohen, co-chairman of the Amsterdam Jewish Council, but herself heavily involved in the rescue and placement of Jewish children in hiding

Source: Verzetsmuseum, Amsterdam

the 'success' of the rescuers in spiriting these children out of German hands came only at the expense of the others. The escapees were estimated at around 10–12 per cent of the 5,000–6,000 children who passed through the crèche. These others were the smokescreen that cloaked the escapes. Only through their sacrifice to the German quotas could a select few be saved.[46]

However, none of this would have been possible without the additional work of falsifying the internal bureaucratic processes of the Schouwburg so that the Germans did not become aware of what was happening, literally under their noses. The most important element was the card index that was supposed to record all the people held in the Schouwburg and crèche at any given moment. Thus if children were to disappear then the card index would need to be 'amended' without the Germans or unreliable members of the Jewish Council staff realizing. This was the work of Süskind and his colleagues. Between them, they kept the records 'straight', while at the same time keeping the Germans at arm's length. In this, they were helped by the indolence of Ferdinand aus der Fünten and his liking for alcohol.[47] Süskind regularly plied the Austrian and his colleagues with drink acquired through black-market trading[48] while Halverstad was busy falsifying the card index and the figures. To a large extent, the numbers of children who could escape from the crèche was determined by how far the figures could be gerrymandered.

Widening Participation: The Networks in the Provinces

Beyond the four specialist networks, help did come from other elements of the resistance. For example, Eugénie Boutet in Sevenum was approached by contacts in Amsterdam about helping children, but as she was too involved in other activities, she directed them to her cousin, Hanna van der Voort, who had been helping escaped prisoners of war since the end of 1940.[49] She and Nico Dohmen created what was to become a major network helping Jewish children in the areas around Venray and Tienray. As a local nurse, she had an unrivalled excuse for travelling and knew, and was trusted, by a wide range of people, so when she approached them and said, 'You have to help this child because it is in great danger', the reply was, 'If you think that Hanna, then we will help.'[50] Couples with large families seem to have been especially amenable, seeing one more mouth to feed as less of a problem. In total, Hanna van der Voort and Nico Dohmen managed to find places for around 123 Jewish children between August 1943 and the middle of 1944, 75 per cent of whom were boys. Their cover story was invariably that they were evacuees from Rotterdam, and the foster parents were supplied with papers that identified them as such.[51] Those old enough to understand were well coached in the stories they had to tell: of their houses being destroyed and there being no accommodation or food in the city.[52] Foster parents were reputedly always told the truth about their charges, although at least one former hidden child has argued to the contrary. Flim suggests that van der Voort may have withheld the crucial piece of information that the children were Jewish, but also deems it possible that this piece of information actually meant very little to the overwhelmingly Catholic residents of this small Limburg town, whereas they all knew about the bombardment of Rotterdam and focused on that instead.[53] Certainly he quotes another rescuer in the same area implying that virtually no one actually believed the story about the evacuees, but that they all played along with the conceit.[54]

As a Catholic, Dohmen reputedly found it easier to elicit help from the local clergy and thus to have influence with their parishioners. He was also very much involved in the day-to-day care of his charges, visiting on a regular basis and dealing with 'all kinds of domestic quarrels' and playing the ersatz father to the children. As one of the rescued described it, his dedication was indescribable, and his own safety completely disregarded. 'He was available day and night and there was never any time of rest for him'.[55] Virrie Cohen was equally effusive:

> Nico Dohmen was a big help for Hanna to find places for all these children and older people, sometimes on farms far away. He was a father for these little children, they felt lonely, and he comforted them, and talked with them. He was a big help for all of us.[56]

One of those rescued later recalled the work of Nico Dohmen in finding new hiding places:

> Day and night he was at work to find placement with farmers who had many children of their own and who were willing to feed one more mouth. Nico usually had to speak to the local priest who in turn convinced the farming family that it was a good deed to save a child.[57]

Wherever possible, the older children and adults were expected to contribute to their upkeep by working on farms or in houses, but the supervision exercised by Dohmen and van der Voort limited any exploitation or abuse. Such arrangements could still cause trouble, as with an observant Jew who wanted to work Sundays, when his hosts went to church, rather than Saturdays, and who would not eat meat. Dohmen apparently persuaded the young man to soften his demands and took him to a more isolated farm where he could hold on to 'some elements of Judaism.[58] As a young male student, Dohmen took enormous risks in making these journeys, not least because his mere presence on the street in the latter stages of the occupation would have been remarkable when the Germans were scouring the country for workers. The Germans failed to find more than a small number of these hidden children through informers and betrayals, but a raid on 30 July 1944 saw the arrest of Hanna van der Voort and a few of her charges. In spite of this, she managed to claim that she did not know the children found with her were Jewish and was thus released and able to resume her work, which continued until the area was liberated on 25 November 1944.[59]

Most of the major networks expanded their activities numerically and geographically over time, benefiting from increased levels of resistance to German measures. However, the key figures in each group remained the cornerstones. For the NV, Jaap Musch was working legally in Heerlen, while his brother and Dick Groenewegen van Wijk were also living underground there, both furnished with false papers that identified them as mineworkers, although 'neither had ever set foot in a mine'.[60] Soon these two moved to other nearby municipalities to find new addresses. They continued to pay return visits to foster parents in order to provide the necessary ration cards, and occasionally also acted as couriers for children being moved from Amsterdam. Pontier's position in Heerlen remained crucial, as did that of Jaap Musch, whose lodgings with the Bockma family provided a centre for operations and a distribution centre for children coming from Amsterdam. Harmen Bockma was also deeply committed to the work of his lodger. Although working as an engine-driver in the mines, he had previously had a milk round, and used his contacts with his former customers to elicit new addresses. In order to make more time for the work of saving children, he cut off part of his little finger in order to get sick leave from his job. His house was always full of people in hiding, up to ten adults plus children at any one time. He also engaged in other forms of illegal activity, including helping pilots and sabotage. This mixing of activities increased the risks for Bockma, his family, and those he sheltered.

To counter this, he instituted a strict regime. As the Calvinists were a small minority in this overwhelmingly Catholic area, it was easier to insist that the children did not bring friends from school to the house. This led to a sense of isolation from the outside world that was made worse by a rumour that the family were members of the NSB, something that Bockma did nothing to counter. This was further embellished when the disappearance of an elder son was coupled with a rumour that he had joined the SS, when in fact he had escaped to England.[61]

Equally important was Joop Woortman in Amsterdam, whose contacts with the resistance also provided much needed access to funds and forged ration cards. However, this dependence was potentially a great weakness, and Jaap Musch arranged for an alternative illegal supply of food through a local bakers' co-operative that supplied bread, clothing, and occasionally money for the NV.[62] In the first months of 1943, Woortman began to receive more requests for help through his contacts in the Jewish districts, and also made direct contact with Walter Süskind at the Schouwburg.[63] In this way, the scope of the NV's activities was increased and, by April 1943, the network was sheltering around eighty children. Usually, the foster parents received only ration cards as compensation for their actions, but in some cases where the hosts were poor mineworkers' families, the network paid an additional thirty guilders per month.[64]

By September 1943, the number of children sheltered by the network had increased to around 225. Inevitably, more hiding places had to be found and this was again done through the good offices of Calvinist pastors in the district who provided lists of trustworthy parishioners. Many were described as primarily anti-German and this may have been a particularity of this border region, but the measure of their trustworthiness was probably primarily their devotion to their religion and their ability to keep secrets. After September 1943, the NV extended its activities and also became merged into the LO. This had certain benefits, for example in making the provision of funds and ration cards easier, although the group continued to carry on with its specialist work and did not extend its activities.

The removal of the last Jews living legally in the Netherlands meant that there were few new children to be rescued. Contact between different parts of the country also became more difficult as German controls on trains increased, and even female couriers began to be at risk as the German demand for Dutch labour extended beyond just the male population. Some members of the group then transferred themselves to other forms of illegality, including Joop Woortman who threw himself into armed resistance, and Anne Maclaine Pont and Frits Iordens created a network to help Allied pilots escape from the Netherlands that became linked to the Dutch–Paris network. This form of resistance 'fitted better with their taste for action'.[65] This brought its own dangers as it increased the chances of capture and the possibility that contacts and perhaps whole networks could be compromised.[66] However, there was also the all-too-frequent occurrence of Dutch rescuers who became liable for labour service. If they went underground, their home addresses became prime targets for raids by the Gestapo, SD, or even the Dutch police, and therefore unsafe for any form of clandestine activity.

Similar patterns were evident in Limburg in the last eighteen months of the occupation. The Bockma family became increasingly involved in more direct forms of resistance but continued to provide for the Jewish children hidden in their district, and also relocated them when there were problems. This part of the network also provided one or two addresses for the Overduin network from Enschede. It also became more common to move children out of Limburg altogether as new addresses became more and more difficult to find. Even if there was a spirit of greater public co-operation towards the resistance, many people still took the view that it was better just to keep away from dangerous activities. Moreover, the NV was also competing with other networks for hiding places, not only for Jews, but also for potentially huge numbers of Dutch men and women avoiding labour service.[67] As a result, the Musch brothers, Groenewegen van Wijk and their fellow workers sought addresses in the Betuwe and Twente areas to the north. By April 1944, the NV had moved some 140 children into these areas and was sheltering a total of 231 altogether.[68] Many of their contacts came initially from local pastors, and in one case from a local stationmaster. Nonetheless, using these districts brought other problems not previously experienced in Limburg, arising from the greater number of blond people the further north one travelled. Thus many requests for help were refused initially because the Jewish children looked so different from the local population.

On 6 November 1943, Pastor Pontier was arrested as a result of his address appearing in a letter intercepted by the Gestapo. Although briefly forewarned, he decided to allow himself to be taken so that the Germans would not search his house and discover the Jewish couple hidden in the top storey.[69] His arrest and warnings from a sympathetic policeman about impending raids prompted the NV to remove twenty-five children from their foster parents and hide them in a local swimming pool, a cellar and a pumping station. When the danger had receded, they were taken back to their hiding places, but the effect of the raid had been to put fear into some foster parents to the point where they refused to continue their work. As a result forty new addresses had to be found, and some of the children had to remain in the cellar and pumping station for nearly three months. Both hiding places had been carefully selected. The cellar belonged to a family with German relations and was therefore considered above suspicion. The pumping station was vital to the coal industry and was thus guarded by the Germans—albeit badly. The rescuers were able to ferry food to the children there apparently without hindrance and their medical needs, including an outbreak of scabies, were catered for by a local nun.[70] One further scare for the network in August 1944 provides some further insight into the availability of hiding places, albeit very late in the occupation period when the Allied armies were already moving rapidly northwards through France and Belgium, and into the southern Netherlands. A German raid in the centre of Tienray had caught some of those in hiding and prompted fears for the remaining 123 children lodged in the district. Again through the mediation of local Calvinist pastors, some seventy families were found who were willing to shelter Jewish children—all in the space of forty-eight hours.

In the late summer of 1942 Piet Meerburg had attempted to make contacts in Friesland, but these had come to nothing. A second attempt was more successful after a chance meeting with a cousin who worked as an assistant pastor for a Calvinist community in Sneek. One of her tasks was to provide religious education in the state schools of the area.[71] She provided the linkage into the 1,750 strong Vrijzinnig Hervormde community via Kapelaan Jansen. He, in turn, recruited the local Mennonite (*doopsgezinde*) pastor Willem Mesdag, and between them they attempted to persuade their parishioners to shelter Jewish children. Mesdag then approached other younger Mennonite pastors in the locality—again widening the network.[72] Sneek itself may have housed between sixty and eighty Jewish children, but further contacts were also made in other communities of the north-eastern Netherlands using the knowledge of other pastors about the trustworthiness of potential helpers.[73] Mesdag's house in Sneek became a centre for the students' work, with many Jewish children being accompanied on the train journey by female members of the group. Meerburg also recruited the help of Krijn van den Helm in Leeuwarden.[74] Through his contacts, new addresses were found for children, both in the city and in other parts of Friesland. These often developed into sub-networks of like-minded families, spread across rural areas. As with the networks rescuing adult Jews, these networks also used the good offices of local clerics to aid the work of finding reliable and trustworthy people to shelter children.

Again, a single example will have to suffice. Pieter Miedema was a recently ordained pastor in Friesland who had spoken out against the persecution of the Jews, at least in private. From his own account it is clear that he and his colleagues had discussed what they should do 'when a Jewish refugee knocks on our door', albeit that they had not made any decisions. He also speaks of what would happen, 'when the Jews reach us'. In other words, he was not in a position to be proactive but was committed to the cause in an abstract form and responded when a request came from his superior in the Church. By this stage, he had already been interrogated by the local SD for having made anti-Hitler utterances, suggesting that he was already under suspicion. Miedema became connected to the work of hiding Jewish children in April 1943 after being asked to find a home in a hurry for a young Jewish boy. He tried the home of the chairman of the local agrarian association, who turned out to be an NSB sympathizer, and even his own father-in-law refused to help. Both these men would have been parishioners, yet there was no question of appealing to their religious beliefs. In the last resort, the boy was hidden in the pastor's own house. The clash of cultures between the simple rural Nonconformist minister's family and that of an adolescent urbanized Jewish boy could not have been more marked, and the boy was soon moved on to a farm where he could be more gainfully employed. He was replaced by his brother, who was equally unsuited to a rural existence and who made all sorts of unreasonable demands. His stay was also curtailed when the local police chief hinted that it was known the pastor had a Jew under his roof. The same day he left, Miedema was confronted with a request for fourteen new hiding places. These were found, in spite of the fact that they were for Jewish children from a TB sanatorium. He used the technique of veiled hints in sermons that led to individual parishioners contacting him. These were not always positive encounters as he recalled at least one individual who knew of his work demanding two thousand guilders for each child transported and a further two thousand guilders for each hiding place. Such demands were far from unique, as earlier arrivals in his parish had been moved because their hosts were charging three thousand guilders for false papers and a further fifteen hundred for room and board. Similarly, Jewish parents joining their children on a peasant farm in Friesland found their offspring starving and in rags, having paid the farmer three thousand guilders. He offered to take in the parents for a further five thousand guilders. Ultimately, the family were 'rescued' through the intervention of Miedema. As his wife reflected, 'we had our share of leeches', although it was almost unbelievable that Frisian Christians could act in this way.[75] Miedema and his wife were finally betrayed and spent the last year of the occupation on the run and in hiding, returning to their family home only after the liberation.[76]

Finding Homes

Although it has been widely acknowledged that finding people to help Jewish children was easier than finding anyone prepared to help adults, safe places for children with reliable foster-parents were still at a premium in the summer of 1942 and, while changes in attitude did take place over time, addresses were hard to find, even for children. Hetty Voûte recorded some of her early experiences.

> In Noordwijkerhout, I usually went from farm to farm; to look around if someone would finally say 'yes'. [..] The farmer with the splendid farm . . . And then he said, 'If it is God's will that these children are picked up, then it is God's will.' Then I said, 'If it is God's will that your farmhouse burns down tonight, is that also God's will? And then, of course, your neighbours would not come and help.'[77]

This continued to be a pattern for the rescuers. Tieneke Haak was involved in finding addresses from among her school friends' parents during 1943, but was always surprised and alarmed when they refused.[78]

A rather different experience occurred some time later in a town in Friesland when a beautiful young girl with wonderful curly hair was placed with a local family. The activists were then inundated with requests from others, 'Can I have a girl like that?' However, a second child proved to be an emaciated skeleton who had just had chicken pox. The intended hostess then responded by claiming that this was not the child she had ordered. The local network organizer then had to put her firmly in her place, as she later recalled:

[I said to her] 'You don't order anything here. You have a human being to save here. And this one has just had chicken pox. If you don't want to do it, OK. I have addresses enough. I'll come to collect the child before the day is out.' But the child stayed there, and it went well.[79]

In Limburg, networks had mixed fortunes. Pastor Pontier found addresses hard to come by in Heerlen and he had taken some children from local Jewish families into his own house with the result that one of his daughters had to sleep at a neighbour's house.

Interrogating the motives of 'rank and file' rescuers is in some ways more problematic. One Calvinist family in Groningen sheltered a number of Jewish adults and children. Their experience of Jews was somewhat unusual. The elder sisters had in the past acted as 'shabbat goyim' for a (presumably orthodox) Jewish family by going to turn their lights on and off on the Sabbath. Just before the occupation, a Jewish family moved in next door to them, but there had been little contact beyond saying 'hello'. In 1941, the family had sheltered a young Roman Catholic convert for a few days, but in 1942 'someone' asked them if they would look after a little 6-year-old girl. Later, they also had her 10-year-old sister. Both were eventually moved on to older siblings of the family who had separate households.[80] Another couple in The Hague took in a Polish Jewish girl in 1942. At the time, it was 'not as much of a dilemma as . . . it seemed more of a sport back then'. Only in 1943 was the reality of the situation brought home to them. By that stage, they had asked the Jewish girl to leave as she was incredibly spoiled and difficult, and deliberately seemed to compromise her safety, and that of her hosts. They give no indication of how they came to host this girl but did know that she survived the war as she returned to thank them and to apologize for her behaviour. As the couple reflected, 'the guardian angels must have worked overtime to save her'.[81]

It is apparent that the families who took in children were not necessarily making conscious choices, either about the nature of their guests, or about specific requests for help. Many were brought in by members of their own families, or through the intervention of their local pastor or priest. Others moved into the work gradually, as one rescuer recalled:

[One] did not set out on some quest to help Jews or those being hurt. Instead, it usually happened that they were asked to take care of some personal belongings while a person was 'gone'. Later it became a child that they were asked to take care of. Then one day a couple came to them because there was nowhere else to go.[82]

Another rescuer, Johan DeVries, a coalminer who had moved from Friesland to Limburg in 1929, began his family's involvement when asked to take in a young boy evacuated from Rotterdam in 1940. He stayed more than a year, but the DeVries family clearly had a reputation as 'a lady' came to ask them if they would take another boy, this time a Jewish boy. The wife insisted on talking it over with her husband but decided 'if you closed the door on children like that now, and they were taken away, how would you feel for the rest of your life?' Some time later, they realized that the boy had a sister in hiding nearby. Having 'sniffled (sic) around', DeVries found where the 18-month-old girl was staying and, discovering that her hostess was finding her difficult to cope with, offered to reunite the two under his own roof. By his own admission, 'They'd shoot me for one, they might as well shoot me for two'.[83] They were able to allow the children they sheltered to go out and play, but adults had to remain indoors. They also benefited from a sympathetic local policeman who warned them about impending raids. Their house was thus much better protected than many other hiding places.[84]

A more tragic story came from the same province, where the rabbi of Roermond's only son was in hiding in a village. After a short time, he was taken ill and transferred to hospital where, in spite of the best care, he died a few days later. The parents were in hiding elsewhere but made it clear that they would report to the Germans if anything happened to their son. For their hosts, the only course of action was to hide the death of the boy from his parents, and they therefore continued to write to the rabbi and his wife about what the boy was doing in hiding. This kept up the morale of the parents for more than a year, and it was only at the liberation when the rescuers were forced to tell the parents the truth—something they described as the most difficult task they had undertaken of all their illegal work.[85]

Persuading people to help clearly took many different forms. The fact that individuals could be told they had been recommended by their local priest or pastor might be enough to underwrite the religious obligation involved. This may well have been backed up by suitably veiled hints in recent sermons. Others required more prompting, and the degree or persuasion may have depended on the level of desperation. One child remembered his putative foster father being told that his adoption would ensure the family a place in heaven:

This was basically a kind of religious bribery, if you wish. So they agreed to do it on that basis. Plus the fact that they saw we were tired and discouraged. And I think they also were interested in getting someone to help them with their farm.[86]

Having a child in the household had its advantages for the hosts, not least in terms of another pair of hands to help with housework or on the farm. Such expectations were not unreasonable, but there were clearly occasions when the relationship became more than just a way of paying back the costs of upkeep and drifted into the realms of exploitation. Thus the placement of foster children with otherwise childless couples was very much an act of faith, whereas larger families gave some indication that the parents knew how to treat children—even if they sometimes discriminated against their guests in comparison with their own children.

By its very nature, the recruitment process had none of the checks usually associated with finding suitable foster homes for children. There was no time to make anything more than cursory enquiries and there were no criteria for such foster parents. As one rescuer made clear, 'we were far too happy that we had found an address' to impose any criteria.[87] The fact that people were related to, or were friends of, rescue workers was enough in the beginning. Later, the recommendations from local pastors and parish priests served the same function. This lack of control, while perfectly understandable given the circumstances, nonetheless created problems where supervision of the arrangements made was often limited or non-existent.

Once placed, it appears that the *Kindercomité* left responsibility for the children with the foster parents. Obviously, an eye was kept on the general health and well-being of the child from a distance, with a few words being exchanged when the ration coupons were delivered, but further monitoring was considered unnecessary. As Hetty Voûte explained,

If people were prepared to take on the responsibility of a child, then they had to be given the freedom to do this in their own way [...] You noted how the children were received. I do not believe that I ever felt uneasy. These were people who were very conscious of what they were undertaking.[88]

The lack of knowledge about Judaism and the huge cultural gulfs between the foster parents and their charges could lead to problems. People would agree to take in a Jewish child with no real understanding of his or her background or upbringing. This was exacerbated by the networks' inability to provide such information at short notice. Thus Jewish children could be confronted with food that they had been taught was forbidden, such as pork, or other practices that infringed on their dietary laws. The fact that many children were ostensibly evacuees meant that they had the papers to make them legal, and the younger ones could thus attend the local schools. Head teachers and their staff were usually aware of the new arrivals' real status, but knowledge was kept to a minimum, and even where two or three 'hidden' children were in the same class, they were not made aware of each other.

The experiences of the NV workers were very similar. They visited most of their charges on a fortnightly basis and, although they set few rules for the foster parents, they objected to Christian baptisms. However, as Dick Groenewegen van Wijk recalled:

> it was a huge change for the children. They came into a completely different environment. They had come from the Jewish quarter of Amsterdam [and were placed] with either Protestant or Catholic families who sometimes had the feeling, 'hey, here is another opportunity to save a soul'. I still have a baptismal certificate of one of the Jewish children baptised by the Catholic Church . . . Certainly people were prepared to go to these lengths.[89]

A very small number of newborn babies were hidden in a rather different way. Instead of just giving them to a foster family, they were, by prior agreement, left outside the house of the potential hosts and then 'discovered' on the doorstep. The foster parents were then able to register the children as foundlings with the municipality. This meant they were issued with ration cards in the name of the foster family. To all intents and purposes, the children had thus been 'aryanized'. The numbers who could be placed in this way remained small, not least because there were few given up so early in their lives, but also because the number of foundlings could not be seen to increase greatly without attracting the attention of the authorities. In spite of this caution, suspicions were aroused and an Amsterdam police decree of 12 December 1942 insisted that all foundlings were to be handed over to the municipal alms-house for their racial origins to be examined.[90]

Another way in which children could be disguised was if a woman was prepared to admit that a baby was her own—born out of wedlock. The shame and social stigmatization this carried would have deterred all but the most committed of rescuers, but there were examples of it taking place. Perhaps the most famous is of Marion van Binsbergen, who managed to register three illegitimate children as her own with the authorities, two in the space of only five months. The lawyer Lau Mazirel also used the same technique, passing off a Jewish baby as her own every year. Only in the last year did she consider the possibility of 'twins'.[91]

Individual rescuers and networks could only function if they had access to money and resources to support their charges. The *Utrechtse Kindercomité* had undertaken to provide both money and ration cards for children sheltered by foster parents. In the early stages, the students encouraged Jewish parents to provide money for upkeep of their offspring and this sum, usually fl.50.- per month, was sent via the network to the foster parents. This was not payment for the placement per se, but more that the students encouraged those who could pay to make such a contribution. Thus in recruiting foster parents, the networks could say the children came with ration coupons, clothing and a 'subsidy' payment, making it impossible for the surrogate families to make objections to helping on material grounds.[92] As the scheme grew, more money was raised from carefully selected private individuals, the student corps itself, and from the Catholic Church. The Archbishop of Utrecht, Johannes de Jong, circulated what was for that time an extremely candid letter to the four Catholic bishops outlining the work being done and suggesting that they each contributed fl.2,500 from their special needs funds.[93] With a similar donation from the archbishopric, this provided fl.12,500 for the *Kindercomité*.[94] The circular gave no indication of the motivation for supporting this illegal work so generously, but the deportation of Catholic Jews from the Netherlands the previous month may have been fresh in the mind of the archbishop and his colleagues.[95]

What had been seen as barely illegal or as a sport in 1942 would ultimately cost some of the rescuers their lives. For example, Groenewegen van Wijk and Gerard Musch were arrested on 9 May 1944. Musch's identity as a mineworker was checked by two *landwachters* and found to be false. He was also in possession of five false identity cards intended for use in Haarlem. This had nothing to do with his work with children and suggests that he also had branched out into other areas of illegal work. Jaap Musch was caught by chance on 8 September when a group from a local punishment labour camp came into the woods looking for hidden petrol and discovered his cottage. The Jewish children living with him scattered into the woods, but he was arrested, tortured and shot some two days later.[96] Other participants found themselves arrested and often spent time in prisons or concentration camps before the liberation.

The Darker Side of Rescue

Although the rescue of children is often seen as the height of philanthropic
and altruistic behaviour during the Holocaust, and thus the subject of
many historical, sociological, and philosophical texts, there are less edifying
aspects to the story of child rescue across Western Europe. Some non-
Jewish rescuers saw it as part of their task of saving Jewish children, not
only in physical, but also in spiritual terms. Elements within the Christian
churches had seen conversion as a part of their religious duty long before
the advent of Nazism. Indeed, some had even set up specific missions
for the purpose, and we have seen how these organizations were part
and parcel of the response to the plight of persecuted Jewry. Not only
organizations, but also individuals, whether encouraged by their spiritual
leaders or merely interpreting their religion in their own way, sought
to convert the children—and sometimes also the adults—in their care.
The relationship was inevitably an unequal one, with the foster parents
having unparalleled control of their charges, given the everyday dangers
of the situation. The stories of attempted or actual conversions would
inevitably emerge at the war's end, but came into sharper focus during
the vitriolic battles between former foster parents, the post-war Jewish
communities, and the state over the fate of Jewish orphans. It was only at
this point that some of the network leaders had to take a position—and
this was sometimes at odds with their perceived altruistic role during the
occupation. Thus for example, the paragon of child rescue in Belgium,
Bruno Reynders did not see why children who had been brought up with
Catholic foster parents should be returned to the faith of their fathers.
Likewise, Gesina van der Molen was unequivocal that 'children who had
the good fortune to end up with a Christian family should not be returned
to Jewish non-belief after the war'.[97] This attitude provoked widespread
anger among the post-war Jewish communities who were struggling to
rebuild their shattered existences, but was perfectly logical to someone
who believed that any individual who, having once been exposed to the
'true' teachings of Christianity, endangered their immortal soul if they then
abandoned the faith. These conflicts were immutable and the post-war
custody battles were fought out in the press and the courts for years after
the liberation.

Such statements that relate directly to the motivation behind the rescue of children tend to detract from the purity of the motive. However, the stories of rescued children being forced to learn the Lord's Prayer or the catechism need to be taken in context. Given the cover stories were that they were evacuees distantly related to the family, the children would be expected to share the religion of their hosts. As they were too young to be left at home alone, they would need to be taken to church and would therefore have to 'conform', at least outwardly. Some basic grounding in the rituals was an essential attribute. The fact that children were moved around could involve transfer between religions as well as between neighbourhoods, with the result that they might be 'converted' on more than one occasion.

The fact that children were being offered by desperate parents or help organizations to willing foster parents also opened up other avenues. While this is not to impugn the integrity of the vast majority of rescuers who took children into their homes for the best of reasons, there were nonetheless some whose motives were less than pure. As we have seen, some foster parents were looking for 'designer' babies that they could not possibly hope to obtain through normal adoption channels—but where the exigencies of war created opportunities. This in itself is a fairly mild aberration, but could often turn into something more sinister, especially if the foster child did not meet the expectations of their putative 'parents'. Beyond this, there were the arrangements where the child or adolescent was expected to work for his or her keep. For girls this was almost invariably housework, whereas for boys it could be farm work—although this was limited by the need to maintain their invisibility. Thus it is no surprise that teenage boys were the most difficult to place. Whether this was 'fair' is difficult to determine—especially if the children could not be sent out to school. The fact that many rescue organizations paid for the fostering of children also complicates the issue, as it was accepted that the costs of upkeep had to be offset. In some rural communities, this additional money seems to have been a major bonus and sought after as an additional source of revenue—thereby implying that the risks involved were not an insuperable deterrent. The existence of organizations with set, and therefore reasonably negotiated, rates helped also to curb excessive demands of private arrangements—at least over time and when they became known. That said, examples of extreme exploitation, either physical or financial, often came to light only after the liberation and, while the children had survived, this was often

at some cost, and helps to explain why some of these rescuers have been
ignored by Yad Vashem.

   One last element can also be alluded to here—namely the sexual
exploitation of children and young people by their hosts. Not surprisingly,
such cases are seldom recorded and only the faintest traces remain in the
archival record, but there are accounts from Jewish women in hiding that
they were sometimes, and perhaps often, subjected to various forms of
sexual harassment by those supposedly sheltering them. A Jewish family
with three daughters tried to find hiding places for their girls. The eldest,
aged around 20, was given an address of a farm where she could lodge
in exchange for keeping house. The farmer turned out to be a widower
and after a couple of days in residence, it became clear to the girl that he
had 'very different plans for her'. As a result she fled back to her former
home and was subsequently helped to another, and safer, address.[98] A more
complex story comes from a Jewish family in Belgium where the mother
was approached by a woman who said she could find a safe place for the
daughter at a farm in the countryside. Taking up the offer, the daughter was
then propositioned by the farmer, and when she refused, was denounced
to the Germans. How the farmer managed to do this without implicating
himself is unclear, but the mother came to hear of her daughter's arrest
and deportation—and then made trouble for the woman—who promptly
denounced both her and her son. It is possible that the woman was just
procuring for the farmer, but their use of denunciation suggests that they
were working hand in glove with the Germans while at the same time
engaging in a little exploitation of their own on the side.[99] The most
extreme example of the perils faced by Jewish women in hiding came from
the Netherlands: a married woman who had been in hiding since 1942
and had been at twenty-three addresses before arriving at the house of a
teacher in Groningen claimed that it was the first place where the man of
the house had not tried to 'touch' her.[100] This suggests that such behaviour
by males in the household was endemic across the country, but explaining
it requires more care. It would have been unthinkable for 'ordinary' female
guests in bourgeois households to be subjected to sexual advances of this
nature, which suggests that the Jews in hiding had a status more akin to
that of live-in servants, where in some cultures and quarters they would
have been seen as fair game by the men in the house. In other cases, it may
have been no more than prolonged proximity, as in the case of a young
Jewish girl who had worked as a dentist's receptionist for some time before

her employer made advances. This particular case was complicated by her living in the family home and having some responsibility for the couple's children.[101]

Guests were not always the innocent parties. One young Jew in hiding with his parents on a farm in South Holland described the pleasant conditions he enjoyed there until another Jewish couple arrived. The husband was 'a very nice, lovely person', but ordinary in every way. His wife, by contrast, was beautiful and a tremendous flirt who soon began an affair with the farmer. In 'desperation' the farmer's wife then informed the authorities that there were Jews in her house, leading to the arrest of the farmer and the two Jewish men. Ironically, it was the woman who had caused the trouble who escaped through the woods, while the boy and his mother hid successfully in the house before making their escape when the Gestapo left.[102] A young woman sheltered in Overijssel provided a rather different problem for her hosts. She sometimes threatened them that 'if she went, they would go too', but this was in part attributed to her youth and the fact that the rest of her family had all been deported.[103] However, the threat came from a relationship she began with an underground worker who was being actively pursued by the authorities—thus increasing the danger of discovery.[104]

A rather different gloss on the question of sleeping arrangements comes from a well-known Dutch rescuer, Marion van Binsbergen, who pointed out that if a house was raided, the number of beds being used had to tally with the number of people supposedly resident there: 'if you had two Jewish people and a family of five, you had to make sure when the Germans arrived that there were not seven beds being slept in'. Thus guests often had to sleep with their hosts, 'which sometimes led to all sorts of abuse of the Jews'.[105] Cases of 'abuse' were not confined to the hosts. In one household there were two Jews in hiding, one a female painter and the other a gay male ballet dancer who shared a room. The painter decided that she was going to make the ballet dancer sexually straight but after two weeks he pleaded that he would rather go to a concentration camp than be subjected to the painter's attentions. He was thus moved to a shed in the garden.[106]

A different, and in many respects far more dangerous, aspect of the subject was where Jewish women in hiding began relationships with the occupying Germans. There were at least three documented cases in the eastern part of the Netherlands, but there may have been many others. The NV in

Limburg had to deal with an older Jewish girl in hiding who had dyed her hair red and began dating German soldiers. She was warned about this but to no avail, and the group eventually decided that she had to be liquidated as a security risk. Ultimately the two men sent to do this found she had disappeared, but had also obviously not said anything untoward as there were no German repercussions on the network.[107] A similar case arose in a village in Overijssel where a 'divinely beautiful' girl was suspected of having sex with Germans. This came to the notice of the local policeman, who considered having her 'liquidated', but on this occasion, the farmer sheltering the girl took her into the cellar and made it clear that this would be her grave if she continued to behave in the same manner. By all accounts, she became a reformed character and survived the war.[108] The final example was of a woman whom her host subsequently described as 'Rachel the whore' who habitually slept with German soldiers.[109]

Although not directly addressed here, the enormous stresses placed on hidden children should not be underestimated. Mental illness among people cooped up for months, or even years, was not uncommon among those hidden during the occupation, and this was not confined to adults. Children too could succumb to psychological illnesses, brought about by the tensions of everyday life in hiding, or the difficulties of maintaining a false identity. Even if their conditions were relatively benign, the months and years of pretence could take their toll, leaving their hosts with problems of security and looking for outside help to find a solution that would maintain the safety of the unfortunate child and his or her previous hiding place.[110]

Here again lies the importance of the trained social work element in the hiding of children, with couriers making regular visits to the children they had placed to ensure their continuing welfare and to minimize the possibility of abuse or exploitation. Yet this behaviour was not confined to those who were trained, as can be seen from the roles of men such as Albert van den Berg and Nico Dohmen who also attempted to make sure that the children they placed were well looked after. That said, these were the best of the arrangements and some others clearly did not meet such standards, as the emergence of survivors in the post-war world was to prove.

In all the countries concerned in this study, children were considered as a special case, both by the legal and illegal Jewish organizations, and by the non-Jewish rescuers who helped them. While the perceived innocence of the young was a major factor in this, it is clear that other considerations were also important—for Jewish organizations in trying to protect a future generation and for certain Christian groups in fulfilling their evangelical mission. Likewise, at an individual level, children were clearly more desirable than adults in the minds of most rescuers, and their motives in offering help remained many and various.

13

Nazi Rescuers and Jewish Traitors

As we have already seen, rescue and survival were not always dependent on unrewarded assistance, philanthropy, or altruism on the part of bystanders, or even on self-help on the part of the victims. Indeed, there were an appreciable number of instances where survival came about from factors within the Nazi system itself, or from individuals working within that system. Such aid and assistance might only be temporary, but could nevertheless contribute to long-term survival beyond the occupation. The majority of the examples cited here come from the Netherlands, and in some cases relate to specific circumstances in that country, but there are good grounds for suggesting that many of the features highlighted could be found to a greater or lesser extent across German-occupied Western Europe.

Nazis as Rescuers

The title itself may seem a contradiction in terms. How could the German functionaries of the occupation regime, and members of a movement ostensibly devoted to carrying out the will of its leader and committed to the idea of antisemitism and a solution to the 'Jewish question' play any part in saving Jews from deportation and death? The answer lies in the multiplicity of organizations involved, the changing imperatives of the Nazi regime over time, and the sheer diversity and quality of personnel actually involved in the process of identifying, arresting, guarding, and then deporting the Jews from Western Europe. Motivations also varied. There were cases of corruption where victims or their accomplices were able to bribe guards and officials to turn a blind eye in order to expedite an escape from captivity. Even German policemen were known to have allowed children arrested during house-searches to 'escape'. These had to be spontaneous acts as colleagues and senior officers were invariably nearby. Others were undoubtedly swayed by the offer of bribes in the form of money, valuables, or even sexual favours, although these transactions were potentially dangerous both for the pursued and the pursuers, if they were discovered. Thus for example, Max Bauer, a German refugee interned in the Belgian transit camp at Mechelen, managed to buy his freedom by bribing the commandant and members of the SS with BFr.1.5 million—a huge sum. Unfortunately for the Germans involved, Bauer then bragged about his abilities to bribe his way to freedom.[1] Police and officials were under strict instructions to hand over any Jewish assets to the authorities, and the penalties for profiteering in this way were severe. For the pursued, there was no guarantee that the same men would not return later to arrest them or to attempt to elicit a further bribe to assure their continuing silence. The sexual dimension is also interesting in that there were cases of Nazis and German functionaries taking Jewish mistresses (albeit always illicitly) in direct contravention of the miscegenation laws. Thus in these cases, the Jewish partner would sometimes be able to exert some leverage and undermine an otherwise one-sided power relationship.

However, Nazi 'rescuers' could also be found at much higher levels. A very different form of rescue came about as a result of the Nazis' love of fine art. In 1939, Hitler appointed the then director of the Staatliche Gemäldegalerie in Dresden, Dr Hans Posse, as head of the Sonderauftrag Linz, the project to create a new art gallery in Hitler's home town.[2] Posse was charged with identifying and locating collections and individual works of art suitable for inclusion in this new institution, and all Party and government departments had Hitler's instruction to co-operate with his work.[3] Among the collections identified by Posse was that owned by the widow of Otto Lanz, some of which was on exhibition in the Amsterdam Rijksmuseum. The transaction was complicated by the fact that the purchase had to be made partially in Swiss francs, but also by Lanz's widow insisting that Nathan Katz, one of the Netherlands' leading art dealers, act as the intermediary between herself and Posse. Thus in addition to negotiating the necessary foreign currency, Posse also had to acquire an exit visa for Katz to travel to Switzerland. Leaving in late 1941, Katz avoided any further difficulties over his Jewish origin by staying in

Switzerland for the duration of the war. Moreover, he was able to negotiate a further twenty-five exit visas for his family in exchange for a Rembrandt painting he owned that was housed in Basel. In this way, the Nazis' desire to acquire works of art allowed at least one family to escape from the occupied Netherlands. However, it was Katz's track record in having brokered many art deals for leading Nazis or their representatives before his departure that undoubtedly protected him, a function that he continued from exile in Switzerland.[4]

Economic considerations also helped to save some Jews from summary deportation. The struggles between agencies in occupied Eastern Europe over the fate of Jewish workers are well known, but in the Netherlands, the Germans recognized from the beginning the wider economic importance of the diamond industry in Amsterdam. This included not only the diamond dealers, whose international contacts made them invaluable, but also the industry's skilled cutters and polishers. They were treated as a special case and given a certain degree of protection, even when many of them were transferred to the Vught concentration camp in 1943. Himmler's intention was to use their expertise to train disabled SS-men until they could replace their Jewish teachers. Likewise, diamond dealers were to be used to broker deals to buy more diamonds for the German war economy. On this basis, some Jews were even released from the camp in order to carry out this work although there was no intention that either dealers or workers be allowed to leave the country. Because the training programme was never completed, and the German war economy continued to need diamonds, many of the Jews were protected until the last year of the occupation.[5]

In the Netherlands, the German leadership, and particularly those charged with the implementation of the deportation process had proved remarkably successful at meeting the targets set by their masters in Berlin. The fact that fully-laden transports left from the Westerbork transit camp on a regular basis meant that Seyss-Inquart and his colleagues could afford to make temporary exceptions in order to ensure smooth relations with indigenous interest groups. As has already been shown, by far the biggest of these schemes was the one attached to the Amsterdam Jewish Council, but some categories of Jews were exempted from deportation through other means. To avoid a clash with the major Dutch churches, the small numbers of Jews baptized into the Christian faith—both Protestant and Catholic—were initially protected. In addition there was a group of so-called *Verdienstjuden* (deserving Jews) nominated by two of the

Dutch Secretaries-General K. J. Fredericks (Interior) and J. van Dam (Education).[6] These included former government ministers, members of parliament, former governor-generals, retired general staff officers and university professors. Once approved on the list, the individuals and their families were given stamps in their identity cards to protect them from deportation. The Germans wanted no more than 500 people to be protected in this way, but by the beginning of 1943, the Fredericks and van Dam lists together contained 585 names. These two Dutch ministers were reputedly not particularly sympathetic to the plight of the Jews and had been party to the implementation of the 'aryan attestation' for civil servants in late 1940. Fredericks was on record as saying that he would have been unhappy if his son or daughter had married a Jew, and van Dam thought that the Germans, as occupiers, had every right to send the Jews to the East—something he thought was perfectly understandable. Nevertheless, both were prepared to see the need to protect some Jews because they had made an important contribution to Dutch cultural or intellectual life.[7] All the people on the lists were interned at Kasteel de Schaffelaar at Barneveld.

There were also references in Zentralstelle correspondence in 1942 to prominent Jews being under the personal protection of Generalkommissar Schmidt in the Netherlands, and thus exempted from deportation.[8] Even the rabidly antisemitic Erich Rajakowitsch,[9] of the Zentralstelle itself, was ostensibly prepared to countenance the emigration to Switzerland of Professor Eduard M. Meijers from Leiden and his family in exchange for a payment of 150,000 Swiss francs.[10] This proved impossible to organize, and the Meijers family were added to the Barneveld group. The reasons for the German authorities allowing these exceptions are complex. Ostensibly, it was a way of making short-term concessions to the Secretaries-General in order to ensure their continued co-operation without any long-term guarantees.[11] This certainly made sense, although it has also been argued that the scheme was championed by Generalkommissar Fritz Schmidt simply because his colleague and security police chief, Generalkommissar Hanns Albin Rauter, opposed it. In other words, the protection of these Jews was just one element in the wider internal competition between Nazi satraps in the Netherlands.

This privileged status was not to protect the internees indefinitely. By the spring of 1943, both Rauter and the functionaries of Referat IVB4 in the Netherlands were pressing for the Barneveld group to be deported. Making the Netherlands fully *judenrein* remained the prime consideration among the Nazi leaders, and Seyss-Inquart was keen that the exceptional cases should sooner or later be deported, albeit to the 'model' camp at Theresienstadt rather than to an extermination centre.[12] In July of that year, Schmidt died in France and the Barneveld group were removed on 29 September, the same day that the Jewish Council in Amsterdam was wound up. On that day, the inmates were taken to Westerbork, where they retained their separate status before being sent on to Theresienstadt. Before this a small number were able to escape when the camp commander unaccountably left the perimeter fence unguarded.[13]

Other groups of Dutch Jews also found themselves sent to Theresienstadt rather than directly to Auschwitz or Sobibor. They included German Jews who had received military honours during the First World War, Sephardic Jews, and the leadership of the Amsterdam Jewish Council.[14] This was far from a guarantee of safety. Of almost 5,000 people sent from the Netherlands to Theresienstadt, more than 3,000 were sent on to Auschwitz to be gassed in September 1944. This included many of the Amsterdam Jewish Council employees who had previously been protected by exemption stamps. Only the Barneveld group and the baptized Protestant Jews were excluded from this mass evacuation (the baptized Catholic Jews having been deported in 1943 as a reprisal for church protests against Nazi antisemitic policies).[15] The leaders of the Jewish Council also survived, albeit in different ways. David Cohen and his family went from Westerbork to Theresienstadt, while Abraham Asscher was sent to Bergen-Belsen, in all probability because his position as a leading diamond merchant made him a suitable candidate for 'exchange' rather than because of his role in the Jewish Council.[16] Both survived the war.

Sending Jews to Theresienstadt and Bergen-Belsen may have been no more than a stay of execution if one assumes that the Nazis' ultimate aim was to exterminate all the Jews under their control. However, it is clear that political and economic factors played some role in the process. Offering alternatives to 'labour service in the East', the Germans could ensure levels of co-operation among the elite and facilitate the deportation of the rest of the Jewish population. Moreover, it seems that at certain times some German agencies sought to promote exchanges and thus important or well-known Jews could be segregated and held as human capital. Finally, there was also the financial imperative. Nazi policies had always been directed towards exploiting every possible source of Jewish wealth. This included the widespread looting of assets left by those deported from the

West. However, in the never-ending quest for foreign currency to keep the German war effort going, the imperatives of the final solution could also be sacrificed, if wealth could be obtained through ransoming rich Jews or by exploiting their contacts in the outside world. Thus even the highest-ranking Nazis were prepared to preserve the lives of Jews who had some presumed utility for the German war effort—or for their own personal gain.

The idea of using Jews as negotiating instruments had been a feature of Nazi plans since 1933, with the Ha'avara Agreements and later Schacht-Rublee talks designed to expedite mass emigration.[17] However, the outbreak of war and the move to a policy of extermination during 1941 should have brought an end to such thinking, especially when Himmler prohibited further emigration from Eastern Europe in October 1941, ostensibly to protect the secrecy of what was taking place there. Nonetheless, the commodification of Jews continued—both as a labour force and as a negotiating instrument. While the use of Jewish labour was only meant as a temporary measure, it was clear from a Himmler memorandum on 10 December 1942, he was already thinking of the Jews in a different light:

> I have asked the Führer with regard to letting the Jews go in return for ransom. He gave me full powers [*Vollmacht*] to approve cases like that, if they really bring in foreign currency in appreciable quantities from abroad.[18]

This led directly to Himmler ordering the head of the Gestapo, Heinrich Müller, to segregate French, Hungarian and Rumanian Jews who had important connections abroad. Whether this would be in exchange for gold, currency, German POWs or civilians remained unclear. A limited exchange of Palestinian nationals in occupied Europe for German Templars had been effected through Istanbul in December 1941 and November 1942 as a result of Anglo-German discussions.[19] This encouraged Ribbentrop and the German Foreign Office, who were anxious to expedite the return of German nationals abroad, to consider the possibility of keeping back around 30,000 Jews from Norway, Belgium or the Netherlands who might have some exchange value.[20]

This led directly to the creation of the special 'civilian internment camp' at Bergen-Belsen in the spring of 1943, where 20–30,000 so-called *austauschjuden* (exchange Jews) could be held pending emigration.[21] Conditions in the camp were initially much better than in other concentration camps, not least because the number of inmates was small.[22] The first arrivals were in July and consisted of approximately 2,500 Jews from Poland who possessed some claim to Latin American or neutral citizenship. Later in the summer they were joined by 367 Spanish and 74 Greek Jews—all brought from Salonika. They were supplemented by further small cohorts of Spanish, Portuguese, Argentinian and Turkish Jews. Beginning in January 1944 they were joined by 3,751 people brought from the Netherlands. These included individuals and families with Latin American papers or Palestine certificates, and a group of diamond workers.[23] Later they were joined by other disparate groups: the wives and children of French-Jewish POWs who were mainly of Polish origin, Jews from North Africa with British papers, Jews who had held important positions or had important connections, for example the nephew of Leon Trotsky, and half-Jews who had been convicted of *Judenbegünstigung* (assisting Jews).[24]

Knowledge of the exchanges in 1941 and 1942 (that had included a dozen women from the Netherlands) encouraged the Jewish Council in Amsterdam to think that anyone with relatives in Palestine might be eligible for an immigration certificate, although in fact the British authorities would only countenance applications from minors with parents already in Palestine. In early 1943, the British accepted the idea that any such children might be accompanied by a number of Zionist 'veterans'. Certificates for these people were issued by the British authorities in August 1943, and they included a large number of Jews from the Netherlands as a result of pressure from Miriam de Leeuw.[25] In addition, both the Jewish Agency representative in Switzerland, Chaim Pozner, and later the Agency in Palestine itself began receiving requests to be placed on the exchange scheme, in spite of the fact that no such list existed and the applicants had no grounds for being included on an immigration list. Both ended up issuing letters explaining that the recipient had been added to an 'exchange' list—and even adding a spurious registration number.[26] These had the effect of affording some protection from immediate deportation to the holders, but it soon became clear that it was better to be on a 'veteran' list and many more requested such a status.

Ultimately, there was no exchange of minors, but the planned transport went ahead. The few Palestinian Jews in German hands, including those held in the French camp at Vittel, were exchanged through Istanbul in early July 1944. Because the Germans could not find sufficient numbers of qualifying Jews, they were permitted to substitute people from the 'veterans' list. At that time, Belsen contained some 1,297 people who might qualify for such a transport, but the Germans were unwilling to allow men of military age to be included.[27] Moreover, having compiled an initial list of 272 people, mainly women and children, this number was then cut when genuine Palestinian citizens were located elsewhere. One of those removed from the list was the well-known Zionist, jurist and later historian of the Holocaust in the Netherlands, Abel Herzberg. At the time, he was understandably vitriolic about the selection:

> A group of Jews is going to Palestine who, for the most part have nothing to do with Palestine, and will have nothing to do with it. They are using the exchange to escape from the misery. Once they have escaped, they will begin abusing the Zionists again, insofar as they don't already. And among those who are going, the majority are completely useless. Old, sick, infirm. A troop of half-corpses is being exchanged.[28]

Ultimately 222 Jews (110 Dutch, 101 German and 11 with Latin American papers)[29] were transported from Belsen to Vienna as 'veterans', where they were joined by 50 Palestinians from Vittel and a further 10 from the camp at Laufen. Their inclusion allowed the exchange to go ahead although the British were at pains to point out that they had not been part of the exchange itself, but merely filling vacant places.[30] A further exchange of 136 people with South or Central American papers took place via Switzerland in January 1945.[31] The Nazis continued to send Jewish notables to the camp, but conditions deteriorated rapidly as more prisoners were brought in from other camps as the Third Reich collapsed. Whatever privileges the remaining exchange-Jews may have had were lost as the camp became the charnel house discovered by British forces in April 1945. Only a very few survived the war.[32]

Some Jews were also protected by the Germans within the transit camp at Westerbork. It seems that the Nazis favoured German Jews among the camp population in choosing an internal administration. For example, two of the prominent *dienstleiter* (service leaders) within the camp were Germans, Kurt Schlesinger (administration) and Dr Fritz Spanier (medical), and the third, Arthur Pisk (*Ordnungsdienst*, order service), an Austrian.[33] All three had been refugees who had come to the Netherlands in the 1930s and had been taken to Westerbork in 1939 when it functioned as a refugee camp.[34] They had become the camp elite—having been there the longest—and their position was unassailable for as long as the commandant, Gemmeker, protected them. For his part, Gemmeker was happy to leave the existing administration of the camp in place. Each used his position to protect family members and those within his circle, leading to widespread resentment from the Dutch Jews, not only because of this, but also because their overbearing attitude was seen as indistinguishable from that of the Nazis.[35] For their part, the German Jews responded by criticizing their Dutch counterparts for not having helped them before 1940. Schlesinger in particular had a pivotal role, in that Gemmeker effectively charged him with making up the transport lists, merely indicating the numbers involved. Spanier also possessed life-and-death powers as anyone he deemed unable to travel was also automatically protected—at least in the short term. His power was described as 'mysterious' and evidenced by the fact that he did not get up from his chair when the commandant entered his office.[36] While their powers of patronage declined as the numbers of Jews in the Netherlands and the camp population was steadily reduced, these men and their families were nonetheless held back from the transports by the Nazis long enough so that they were still in the camp after the last trains were able to leave for the East in November 1944. Thus they were still there in April 1945 when the Allied armies finally liberated the northern Netherlands.[37]

One far more complicated example was the case of SS-Scharführer Alfons Zündler who, after being wounded on the Russian Front in 1941 and discharged from active service, had been posted to Amsterdam. He was employed at the Hollandse Schouwburg as head of the guard unit and reputedly turned a blind eye to individual Jews being allowed to escape, on one occasion even lending his uniform to assist an escapee.[38] His duties also extended to the nearby crèche and here he was implicated in allowing children to be smuggled out of the building by Walter Süskind and his associates. In the post-war era, at least twenty-three people came forward to say that they felt they owed their lives to Zündler.[39] Some admitted that they had approached him directly, although Zündler himself claimed that no selection process was involved and that he operated as circumstances permitted. If his colleagues were absent or drunk, an opportunity might present itself for an individual to escape.[40] He was also drafted into units sent with Dutch police to round up Jews from addresses in and around Amsterdam. Here he was also able to expedite some rescues.[41] On one occasion, the father of the family was absent when the raid took place and Zündler contrived to drive him away from the house with the words 'We have no need of curious Gentiles. Get out of here!', removing his yellow star in the process.[42] Nor did his benevolence for this family end there.

Having failed to persuade the·mother and children to escape from the truck in which they were being transported, he was nevertheless able to prevent them from being registered at the Schouwburg and ultimately contrived to smuggle them out of a back door.

In May 1943, the German authorities finally discovered his activities. It is possible that he had been caught *in flagrante* with one of his female Jewish conquests, or that a Jewess who had been helped to escape was later recaptured and implicated him. He, and those of his subordinates who had also benefited from bribes and sexual favours, were brought before an SS court martial in The Hague. Among the charges was one where a Jewish woman had been forced to dance naked in front of the SS guards and had then been sexually assaulted. He was tried for *Rassenschande* (racial defilement) and *Judenbegünstigung* (helping Jews) and sentenced to death. This was later commuted to ten years in a special punitive section of Dachau concentration camp, on account of his war service and wounds. It was widely assumed that he had died there,[43] but in fact he had been conscripted back into an SS unit, the notorious Dirlewanger Brigade, in February 1945 to help stem the Allied advance. Having survived the war, he then retired in Munich.[44]

His willingness to turn a blind eye to certain irregularities and even become directly complicit in some escapes undoubtedly helped the underground organizations working in the crèche and Schouwburg. Their task would have been much harder without him. For those he saved, Zündler was a hero and very different from the other SS men they had encountered, as he showed compassion for their plight and effected escapes where possible. He himself estimated that he had assisted in the escape of around 400 Jews from the crèche or the Schouwburg during the time he was stationed there—or around one for each day of service—and his motivation was just that he 'felt sorry' for the Jews. When his story became public knowledge in the early 1990s, it appeared to be the first, and perhaps the only case of an altruistic SS man within the Nazi system who had been actively engaged in rescue activities. There was talk of him being a possible recipient of the title 'Righteous among the Nations' and a detailed investigation began.[45] This revealed a more complicated truth behind Zündler's activities. Even his status as a member of the SS was also somewhat confused. He had been born Alfons Cislowski and brought up in Danzig, where he had changed his name to the more Germanic-sounding Zündler. Conscripted into the city militia in 1939, his unit was eventually transformed into an

SS police division and ultimately incorporated into the Waffen–SS. During that time, he was not given the opportunity to leave.[46] However, the image of innocent victim was somewhat undermined by his later decisions when, while recovering from his wounds, he had volunteered to join the SD.[47]

Even those who spoke in his favour were at pains to mention his penchant for young Jewish women. Some claimed to have obtained help from him without offering, or being asked for, sexual favours. However, stories of his licentious behaviour with Jewish women in the Schouwburg were legion. Described as young and handsome, and as 'a beautiful man, a Don Juan', it was widely reported that he had an obsession with feminine beauty.[48] Some women apparently offered him sexual favours willingly, in the hope of escaping deportation, but with others it was a question of sleeping with him in exchange for a specific favour. He was also known as one who could be bribed with alcohol, sweets or other gifts. This undermined the claim that he had acted altruistically and it was his sexual activities that ultimately led to his downfall. Nonetheless, his role in helping Süskind and the other rescuers working in and around the Schouwburg cannot be denied, even though his motives were less than pure.[49] In the face of such a detailed examination of his conduct, Zündler could not meet the criteria for a righteous Gentile. Yet whether motivated by altruism or sexual desire, or a combination of the two, it cannot be denied that he was instrumental in effecting or assisting in the rescue of many hundreds of Jews in the Netherlands who would otherwise more readily have fallen victim to the deportation process.

Other rich Jews found that some German officials were willing to 'sell' security in the form of special stamps on identity cards to protect the holders from deportation 'bis auf weiteres' (until further notice). Those with assets could purchase specially numbered stamps for the equivalent of 20,000 guilders.[50] To distance the German authorities from the selling of exemptions, intermediaries were used to acquire such stamps, the two most important being Erich Puttkammer and J. J. Weismann. Puttkammer was a banker of German origin who had been involved in negotiating emigration permits for Jews since 1941. He did not ask for a fee save for a small contribution to expenses or a contribution to the German Red Cross. Weismann, however, was far less respectable, being a member of the Dutch National Socialist Party (NSNAP) and a former convicted bank robber. He demanded the payment of 1,000 guilders for his services, and

NAZI RESCUERS AND JEWISH TRAITORS 341

confessed after the war to having accumulated 125,000 guilders through these transactions.[51] In the end, none of the exemption stamps brokered by either Weismann or Puttkammer were of any lasting benefit as all were rescinded in late September 1943 and the holders arrested.[52] Although it is unclear if either man knew that the stamps were useless, there were others involved in the process whose motives were entirely mercenary. Two Dutch crooks, N. J. Ros and P. C. Docter, charged a commission of 10 per cent for their services, but rarely ever delivered any stamps. A Swiss businessman in Amsterdam, Walter Buchli, also became involved in this trade, mediating between rich Jewish families anxious to emigrate to Switzerland and the Sicherheitspolizei. In exchange for large sums, the families were given exit visas but then arrested on their way through Germany and sent to concentration camps. Not surprisingly, Buchli made a substantial amount from each transaction.[53]

The German system for deciding who was covered by the antisemitic legislation included the provision that all those with 'one Jewish grandparent by race' were required to register as Jews, although race was actually defined in terms of membership of a Jewish religious community. In the Netherlands, any doubtful cases had to be referred to Reichskommissar Seyss-Inquart for a final decision. Although most people with Jewish ancestry had registered with the authorities in 1940, the increasing restriction placed on Jews thereafter encouraged those whose backgrounds were contentious to use this bureaucratic channel to challenge their status. A flood of petitions began which were handed down to the Generalkommissar for Administration and Justice, Dr Friedrich Wimmer, and from him to a specialist, the head of the Referat Innere Verwaltung, Dr Hans-Georg Calmeyer.[54] It was Calmeyer's office, and in practice Calmeyer himself, who made the final decision on whether one or more of the applicants' grandparents were Jewish. This might have the effect of downgrading a 'full-Jew' to the status of a 'mischling', or even remove a 'mischling' from the list altogether. His office included a handful of German bureaucrats, typists and two Dutch lawyers. One of these, Jaap van Proosdij, came to Calmeyer's office via the firm of van Krimpen that had a significant number of Portuguese-Jewish clients, and had been recommended to Calmeyer specifically to deal with the status of Portuguese Jews.[55] The Amsterdam Sephardic community presented problems to the Germans as they did not conform to the stereotypical Ashkenazi image of 'the Jew' as understood by Nazi ideology, but this in turn created opportunities for the lawyers and the Sephardic Jews themselves to plead their immunity from arrest and deportation.

Van Proosdij was able to take the list of Portuguese Jews submitted to Calmeyer's office and was trusted to make decisions based on the case files. In fact, he used information from the Amsterdam Jewish Council to 'sacrifice' those who were already dead or who had left the country, in order to have many others exempted. Even after the war, when confronted with the truth of what had happened, Calmeyer refused to believe that van Proosdij had been anything less than honest in his evaluations.[56] Calmeyer had refused to deal with the Sephardim as a group and referred the question of principle to the Reichssippenamt in Berlin. However, he did legislate on individual cases and granted some exemptions where the applicants' families had not intermarried with Ashkenazi families and were overwhelmingly 'Portuguese'. Ultimately Calmeyer's involvement in this case made no difference, and even those granted exemptions were arrested and deported in 1943 and 1944 on orders from Berlin.

Van Proosdij was later employed in investigating other cases where the parentage or origins of individual Dutch Jews were in question. Here he was able to 'verify' people as the products of mixed marriages or the result of illicit liaisons between Jews and non-Jews.[57] The mere act of entering a petition was enough to have the individual placed on the so-called Calmeyer List and be given an exemption stamp in their identity card. The petitioners used every possible device to 'prove' that their grandparents or parents were not Jewish, or that they themselves were illegitimate. Falsified information and certificates were smuggled into state records. Blood test results were submitted to prove illegitimacy. Letters were falsified using old paper and archaic handwriting to validate claims to Christian forebears, as were baptismal records. After the status of the Portuguese Jews had been settled, it was these individual cases that took up most of van Proosdij's time and energy, investigating claims and preparing dossiers. Where possible, he did not enquire too closely into the provenance of documents presented in support of individual cases. Dubious baptismal certificates, divorce papers and letters disputing parentage were often accepted with minimal scrutiny. Likewise where claims involved records that were supposedly in Germany, or in the Dutch colonies, they were almost impossible to disprove.[58]

This was the evidence that Calmeyer had to weigh. He was widely regarded as 'highly intelligent, extremely conscientious and totally incorruptible'.[59] He was neither a Nazi committed to the party's racial theories nor a non-Nazi, but it was his attitude to his work that was to prove the crucial factor in saving a small number of Dutch Jews.[60] Evidence suggests that Calmeyer was known to have gone further than this, by actually looking for loopholes that would strengthen cases still further and by going to inordinate lengths to verify documentation that supported certain claims, for example where 'Jewish' grandparents had supposedly attended Christian churches. Certainly, some of those who encountered him personally were convinced of his good intentions. Marion van Binsbergen noted long after the war that he 'did his damndest to help everybody he possibly could'.[61] He also operated in collusion with the Dutch Ministry of the Interior, advising them of the appropriate advice to give to Jews. Pressures increased on his office after the deportations began in July 1942, when the system was inundated with a fresh wave of appeals. However, most of these were so transparently false that there was little he, van Proosdij, or any other members of his staff could do. Seyss-Inquart had insisted that all decisions be made by December 1942 and that thereafter, questions would be sent to the German authorities. Thus Calmeyer's role was gradually wound down towards the end of that year. At the same time, van Proosdij used his position in Calmeyer's office, even after September 1943, by travelling to the Westerbork camp every fortnight to carry out enquiries and prepare dossiers that served to save others on the point of deportation. His network of helpers expanded to include the amateur genealogist Cornelis Teutscher, who turned his hand to falsifying records and forging signatures and official letterheads. The group even invented an entirely fictitious church with an impressive crest and motto, whose stamp was used to authenticate baptismal certificates and other documentation. So trusted did this imprimatur become that even the Jewish Council enquired about the location of the church because the Germans refused to accept documents that did not bear its stamps.[62]

There is no doubt that Calmeyer's decisions saved a number of Jews who would otherwise have been deported and killed. Van Proosdij indicated that his decision-making was unpredictable, agreeing to sign off some cases and categorically refusing others. He also seems to have allowed some files to 'disappear'.[63] However, it has been suggested that his powers were not unlimited and his decisions were based on what he could justify to the watching SD. Having the supposedly 'easy-going' Friedrich Wimmer as his boss helped, but there were others who took a much closer interest in his work and constantly challenged his decisions, most notably the officials in *Referat IVB4*, and the specially appointed *Judenreferat* appointed by Rauter, the fanatically antisemitic Lodo(vicus) ten Cate.[64] In spite of this 'supervision', Calmeyer's office certified 2,026 half-Jews and 873 quarter-Jews, a total of 2,899 people—thus removing them from any immediate danger of deportation. Against this should be weighed the 500 cases where Jewish ancestry was discovered and the rejection of at least 25 per cent of the appeals made. More recent estimates suggest that Calmeyer's office probably saved around 3,700 individuals.[65]

In conclusion, it seems that Calmeyer probably was working at the margins of what was possible, and it would be difficult to condemn him for not having done more. He and his staff would also try to ameliorate the decisions made—by warning those who were unsuccessful. Nevertheless, explaining his motivation is difficult. As a bureaucrat within the German administrative system, he made few friends by granting Jewish appeals that served to frustrate those who saw the Jewish question in black and white terms, and who were anxious to deport as many Jews as possible. Commentators have tried to rationalize this by suggesting that he enjoyed being contrary for its own sake, rather than acting out of any commitment to helping the victims of Nazi persecution.[66] There may also have been some idea that he continued the work of adjudication for as long as possible to inflate his own importance within the system, and also thereby keep him in the Netherlands rather than being sent elsewhere.[67] A great deal rests on how much he really knew about the fraudulent nature of the cases put before him. If he was aware that the wool was being pulled over his eyes, then his reputation as a rescuer—or at least someone working within the system of deportation in order to undermine it—is secure: a bureaucratic rescuer among bureaucratic murderers. If he was unaware, then the role of rescuers transfers entirely to those, such as van Proosdij, who worked within his office to prepare the dossiers that he then adjudicated.[68]

Calmeyer's position was perhaps exceptional, but there were many other German functionaries across occupied Western Europe who were recorded as having offered a helping hand or advice that bordered on help for Jews. Thus, for example, Alexandra Brodsky recalls a visit to a Major von Hahn at the Brussels *Kommandantur* of the German military administration in Belgium to enquire about her imprisoned father. He offered his help, and although admitting that it was not in his power to help her and her family get to Switzerland, did suggest that they travel under an assumed name to another town in Belgium where they were not known, and that the fact that they did not look Jewish would help them.[69] A far more bizarre story concerned Theodor (Teddy) Auer, the head of the German Economic Office in Morocco in 1940 who also claimed to be in charge of the Gestapo there. A notorious and flagrant homosexual at a time when this was punishable in the Third Reich, Auer seems to have been well protected by friends in high places, but this also allowed him to offer one of his lovers, an Austrian Jew named Franz Duschnitz, help with transit and residence permits from the local police.[70]

A very different, but nonetheless very pertinent example of how jurisdictional conflicts and the career aspirations of German functionaries could sometimes assist individual Jews and their helpers can also be found in the Netherlands. Kriminalkommissar Walter Julius Horak led Sonderkommando 5, which was charged with tracking down black market and ration card frauds. In October 1942, he was in hot pursuit of a network led by Theo Dobbe that had carried out raids on distribution offices in Friesland. Horak threw all his resources into finding those responsible. While making arrests, his men found two Jewish families in hiding. Procedure required that they should be handed over to IVB4 and that, because of the political elements involved, the whole case should be handed over to the Sipo/SD, but in order to avoid this, Horak not only allowed the rescuers to walk free, but also conspired to facilitate the Jews' emigration to Switzerland. Among those who benefited from his 'generosity' was none other than Pastor Leen Overduin who had been apprehended with false identity documents in his case and with a list of hiding addresses. Yet within four days he had been released.[71] In his single-minded pursuit of Dobbe, Horak was prepared to make almost any sacrifice, and was also committed to keeping the case out of the hands of other German agencies by maintaining its economic focus and effectively denying the political element—even to the point of releasing those whose arrest would complicate matters. In this way, his actions served to help some of the Jews who were inadvertently caught by his police raids.

Self-Help: Salvation Through Treason

Across Nazi-occupied Western Europe, there were a small number of Jews who acted in collusion with the German authorities, either voluntarily or under duress, in order to save themselves or their families from arrest and deportation. Sometimes, this 'employment' as an agent was to carry out a specific task, but more often was directed at the Jewish community itself—to identify and locate Jews in hiding, or to extract further information from those already captured. Documented examples are relatively rare, not least because many of those involved did not survive. However, testimony from Jewish survivors and their former persecutors allows us to glimpse the wartime careers of a few of these Jewish collaborators.

In Belgium, the *Sicherheitspolizei*/SD proved adept at 'turning' some Jews to help them catch those underground. Icek Glogowski, or 'Gros Jacques', was perhaps the most famous. Operating in Brussels for the Security Police headquarters in the Avenue Louise, he claimed that he could 'smell' Jews at a distance.[72] Although originally arrested with his wife and three children in September 1942, he seems to have had no qualms about working for the Gestapo, in spite of the fact that his family were deported to Auschwitz the following month.[73] Touring around in an unmarked police vehicle, his technique was certainly successful, and he was credited with having been responsible for 50 per cent of the Gestapo arrests of Jews on the streets in Brussels and was considered sufficiently dangerous to warrant an assassination attempt by a Jewish resistance group led by Charles (Alter) Pasternak in June 1944. The group lost six men in the subsequent gunfight with German police.[74]

Another target of this group was Erich Adler. He had come to Belgium with a non-Jewish wife in 1938 but fled to France in May 1940 where the French interned him in the camp at St Cyprien. Returning to Belgium in the late summer, he was arrested by the Germans and sent to the concentration camp at Breendonck. Here he claimed to have been imprisoned for giving blood to a Belgian soldier. In December 1940 he was released because of his decorated war service in the German army during the Great War. Arrested again on 5 May 1943 for stealing furniture from a house requisitioned by the Germans, he was 'forced' to catch Jews for the Juden Abteilung of the military government.[75] Living in the Place Flagey in Ixcelles and described as having a deformed right eye,[76] he spent several months working for the Germans and was paid Bfr.100 for each Jew arrested as a result of his information. Technically, he was used by the Germans from May 1943 until August 1944, but spent part of this time in gaol, again for stealing furniture owned by Jews and destined for redistribution by the Ostministerium. Adler was also known to have associated with Gros Jacques in the course of 1944. Resistance attempts to assassinate him failed and he was ultimately arrested and tried by the Belgian authorities after the war and sentenced to fifteen years' imprisonment.[77] How many Jews he was responsible for betraying will probably never be known. A sample list was put forward at his trial, but it was only representative of a much more extensive series of crimes. Another Jew who became a Gestapo agent was Jacques Levine-Kantorevitch, a homosexual Polish Jew and hotel worker in Ostend. He was employed, like Glogowski, for his expertise in Jewish physiognomy and paid BFr.500 for each arrest. Among others, he was responsible for the arrest of Bruno Reynders in June 1944.[78] In addition, there were others known to have been employed by the Gestapo in Brussels and elsewhere. Léon Landera was, like Glogowski, a Pole.[79] There was also a Hungarian woman who operated as a prostitute and worked alone or with Erich Adler, and also a Turkish Sephardic Jew employed to unmask other Jews in order to save his parents.[80]

Other people of Jewish origin could also be found operating in the shadowy areas between the Gestapo and the Jewish organizations in Belgium. Steinberg notes people who were arrested by the Gestapo and then turned: working for the security services until the deportations were over and then transferring to other agencies such as the customs.[81] One example was Madame Sorokine, a woman who was employed by the AJB but acted as the liaison between it and the Winter Help and the Red Cross, jealously guarding her monopolistic role and reputedly benefiting from the clearances of houses owned or rented by Jews who had been arrested and deported. Her role was reinforced through her 'intimate' association with a leading member of the VNV, an exemption from wearing the yellow star, and possession of a safe conduct that allowed her to travel during the curfew.[82] Other charges were levied against some protected Jewish fur dealers who were reputedly manufacturing jackets for the German army while at the same time milking the welfare payments made to their Jewish workforces.[83]

Such stories are not peculiar to Belgium. The Gestapo in the Netherlands also used individual Jews to betray their co-religionists. Perhaps the most extreme and well-known example is of Ans (Anna) van Dijk. Born in 1905 into a (lower) middle-class Jewish family, her early life was uneventful. Married in 1927, and living in respectable parts of the city, she became the co-owner of a millinery shop in the centre of Amsterdam. Her marriage foundered in the late 1930s, ostensibly because she discovered her lesbianism, and by 1940 she was living above the shop with one of the assistants. Such conduct was not particularly remarkable as Dutch society had not really accepted the existence of adult lesbianism. The only legal proscription was for same sex-activity between adults and minors (under 21) passed in 1911, but only four women had ever fallen foul of this before 1933. Women sharing accommodation were seen as acting for economic rather than sexual motives, an increasingly valid excuse as the depression struck the Netherlands. When the Germans arrived in 1940, penalties were brought in for homosexual acts between adult males but women were not mentioned.[84] The millinery shop was included in the registration of Jewish businesses, but van Dijk did not register herself as a Jew, and thus avoided the telltale stamps on her identity papers. By so doing, she faced possible sanctions as her true status could be checked in the population registry, but this was apparently never done. Her move into this form of illegality may have also been aided by her experience of 'clandestinity' as a lesbian.[85] In effect, and alongside an estimated 7,000 others, she had managed to step outside the machinery designed to trap her. On 1 November 1941, her shop was closed as a Jewish business and she was forced to move. Her companion had also moved out and was later able to flee to Switzerland, reputedly with the aid of a German officer.[86]

Although not registered as a Jew, her position was nonetheless precarious and she lived a shadow existence, essentially underground, but at the same time becoming involved in helping other Jews find hiding places and securing some Jews' possessions before the Germans stripped their houses after their arrest. In April 1943, two women whom she had placed were arrested, and two days later she was arrested, as was the family that had sheltered her, and several other people whom she had helped to hide. All fell into the hands of the Jewish Affairs Bureau of the Amsterdam Police. According to one testimony, she was asked by an arresting officer if she would work for the SD, an offer apparently made to many arrested Jews. Unlike most others, albeit under severe duress and threats that she would be treated as a punishment case, she appears to have agreed and became, in the policemen's own words, 'the best of the ten who worked for me'.[87] Such agents were especially valuable if they could move in, or had knowledge of, the Jewish community. They could provide information gleaned from the street, but could also be used as stoolpigeons, and put into holding cells to extract further information from those already captured.[88]

To prove their usefulness, new agents were expected to produce early results, and in this it seems that van Dijk excelled. Thus in her first weeks, she managed to betray at least nine Jewish friends and acquaintances whom she knew were living underground. She also betrayed others who assumed she was still involved in illegal work and had not been 'turned'.[89] Indeed, this became her method of operation, trading on her resistance credentials. Later still, she was paired with another arrested Jewess, Branca Simons, and the two of them created a false safe-house, luring Jews looking for hiding places and then informing their police 'handlers'.[90] Eventually, the duo became a threesome with Rosalie Roozendaal, another Jewess coerced into helping in order to save herself and her mother.[91] Apart from the spurious safe-house, the women also travelled to other parts of the country, either collectively or individually, again ostensibly at the behest of their handlers, to worm their way into underground and Jewish circles in order to effect betrayals. They also continued to recruit others to help them, including Simon van Hoorn, who provided information in exchange for the release of his mother who had been arrested for helping Jews. Needless to say, the mother was never released and the son was also later betrayed by van Dijk as a *mischling*. At the end of July 1944, the van Dijk group took a short holiday in Zeist, but continued their work of informing their bosses about Jews in hiding. Moreover, even when no information was forthcoming they provided intelligence on other resistance activities—for example, the existence of an illegal radio sender, the source of its batteries, and the place where illegal pamphlets were being printed.[92]

In total, the whole group betrayed at least 145 people, of whom 107 were Jews and 38 non-Jews. Their activities were halted after the arrival of Allied troops in the southern Netherlands, when most members of the Jewish Affairs Department took flight or went underground. This left Ans van Dijk and her partner with no means of support, and they moved to The Hague where they survived through black-market dealings. Only after the liberation did her name begin to appear in the testimonies of Jews who had either survived underground or returned from the camps. Confronted with the accusations, van Dijk accused many of her former associates and tried to minimize her own role.[93] In spite of this, she was tried and convicted on 10 March 1947 and after unsuccessful appeals, executed by firing squad on 14 January 1948, the only Dutch woman to be executed for crimes committed during the occupation.[94] Branca Simons was also sentenced to death, but this was commuted to life imprisonment soon afterwards and she was released in 1959.[95] Roozendaal's case was more complicated. As a 19-year-old girl, she was considered young and naïve and helped the

Gestapo on and off to keep herself and her mother off the transports. However, after four months, both women contrived to go underground, and Rosalie was credited with helping the resistance in the last year of the occupation. As a result, she was sentenced to only two and half years in gaol.[96] Explaining van Dijk's collaboration with the police is not straightforward. She was certainly not the only Jew to be 'turned', but other 'volunteers' may have outlived their usefulness, or have known too little of others underground to justify their being kept as informers. Van Dijk seems to have been both assiduous and successful in carrying out her given tasks, thus impressing her police 'handlers' until their own activities were cut short. She achieved at least one of her own objectives—to be spared deportation to the East—but at huge cost to her family, friends and many others. Probably betrayed herself, she seems to have switched easily from genuine resistance in helping Jews to using it merely as a cover after her own arrest. Explaining her post-war treatment is also complicated. Certainly she was portrayed as a she-devil and a mass murderess, but was it her being a woman that so appalled society—or worse still a lesbian? Was it the fact that she was Jewish? Or that she had betrayed other Jews? Had the Netherlands actually become more antisemitic as a result of the German occupation, even though most of the Jewish community had been destroyed? Was it because she was considered to be the centre of a web that had ensnared so many Jews in hiding? Thus, while Branca Simons could have her sentence commuted, pleas for leniency for Anna van Dijk fell on deaf ears.[97]

The group collected around van Dijk were not the only Jews to be employed by the Gestapo. Bernhard Joseph was a German Jew who had arrived in the Netherlands with his parents as a refugee in 1937, but had gone to work for the Amsterdam *Sicherheitspolizei* as an agent in 1940, on the grounds that he saw himself as German and not in any sense as a Jew. Initially, he was used to write *Stimmungsberichte* but in 1942 began hunting Jews in hiding. Latterly, he was helped by both his father and sister, and as a result the family were not deported. Together they were responsible for the arrest of tens of Jews, including some children and even one member of their own family. At least two other Jews worked for the *Sicherheitspolizei* and *Abwehr* in Rotterdam. These, and others, were also used as stoolpigeons; placed in holding cells with other arrested Jews to see what further information might be gleaned from casual conversations among those who all appeared to be in the same situation.[98]

Figure 13.1. Ans van Dijk at her trial in 1947. She was executed by firing squad on 13 January 1948

Source: NIOD, Amsterdam

There are also cases of Jews trying to help themselves under cover of helping others. In the Netherlands, the case of Friedrich Weinreb is by far the most famous. An economist living near The Hague, he hatched the idea of persuading the *Wehrmacht* to allow some Jews to be sent to the unoccupied zone of France (later this was altered to Spain). This allowed him to compile a list of selected people who would then be protected from immediate deportation by a special stamp in their identity cards. At a time when many other Jews were receiving such stamps as working for the Jewish Council or for the German war effort, this did not appear to be an unreasonable tactic—even if the scheme itself was far-fetched in the extreme.[99] As part of the process, Weinreb insisted on a welter of documentation and even on conducting personal intimate medical examinations on some women and children (although he had no medical qualifications).[100] Those Jews 'selected' by Weinreb would be allowed on the list on payment of 100 guilders. He was arrested for the first time in September and from that point onwards was probably working for the *Sicherheitspolizei*. The fact that his arrest lasted only three days, rather than setting alarm bells ringing among Weinreb's clients, was finessed into an idea that even the security police were in on the scheme. What started as a scheme to save thirty individuals was soon expanded to thirty families and finally to thirty *groups*, an expansion that brought huge amounts of money into Weinreb's hands as his clients were asked to pay to get on the list and for the costs of travel in advance. It has been estimated that the scheme garnered in excess of 300,000 guilders. However, by the end of 1942, Weinreb was in trouble as the *Sicherheitspolizei* wanted to know more about his contacts with the *Wehrmacht*. As these were purely fictitious, he even went to the extent of paying someone to impersonate one of the supposed intermediaries. All were arrested in January 1943 and many of those on his emigration lists immediately lost their exemptions and were deported to Auschwitz.[101] Weinreb tried to save himself and his family by going to work for the *Sicherheitspolizei* again, tipping them off about Sara Walbeehm who was hiding twenty-five Jews in a flat in The Hague. She survived an eighteen-month incarceration in Vught concentration camp, but all twenty-five of her charges were deported and died in the East. Weinreb spent some time in Westerbork with his family and was kept from the transports by the *Sicherheitspolizei*, who thought he might still be useful, and brought him back to act as a stoolpigeon in the detention cells in The Hague. As the Germans found it harder and harder to find Jews in hiding, he and his family were re-housed in the city so that he could start a variant of his earlier emigration scheme—this time to Portugal. He was able to go out without the telltale star on his clothing and recruit candidates for emigration on payment of a fee, which went straight to the *Sicherheitspolizei*. Those inside Westerbork who went on the list were protected from deportation. This held good until the beginning of February 1944 when all the exemptions were cancelled and many of the 800–900 people involved were summarily deported to Auschwitz. Ostensibly, they were sacrificed because Weinreb's plan had failed to uncover many Jews still in hiding.

Although he was estimated to have betrayed at least 150 Jewish families, he and his family survived the war after he escaped from the *Sicherheitspolizei* and went underground in Gelderland. Back in The Hague in June 1945, he was arrested and underwent two trials that led to a six-year sentence, commuted in December 1948.[102] His defence of his conduct after the war was over, led to a huge public debate that stretched into the 1960s and as far as the United States, where a pro-Weinreb committee in the United States tried to portray him as a Dutch Dreyfus.[103] A further official enquiry into his conduct produced damning conclusions and finally laid the debate to rest:

> [Weinreb] carried out much greater crimes than the judicial authorities in 1947 and 1948 were able to establish. His first list was no more than a great swindle, the second a function of his work as a V-man for the *Sicherheitspolizei*.[104]

France was not immune to similar examples of Jews being 'turned' or blackmailed by the Gestapo into becoming informers and betraying their co-religionists underground. However, many cases were far from straight-forward. Pastor Pierre-Charles Toureille's papers tell of one German Jewish merchant married to a Protestant who had established themselves in Brussels before the war, and had presumably fled to France in May 1940. Interned in the Gurs internment camp, the wife had become a barrack leader and helped the Protestant relief effort in the camp. The man became secretary of the local foreign forced labour battalion (GTE) and remained in France until the liberation. Only then was his wife accused of spying inside the camp, and he was also arrested and accused of being 'a sinister individual who had sold himself to the Gestapo', a charge repeated and embellished by the local newspaper. His mere survival in the GTE was considered enough to condemn him, although his German origins had also given him a prominent role as an interpreter, thus making him doubly suspect. Most of his GTE comrades who might have spoken in his defence had been deported, and when faced with the summary justice meted out in post-war French courts, he was sentenced to death, although subsequently reprieved.[105] His survival may have had more to do with his usefulness to the Germans as an interpreter than anything he might have done to catch Jews, and may also have been a result of being in a 'mixed' marriage. While the truth of the accusations are impossible to verify so long after the event, the fact remains that Jews could find themselves accused of crimes merely for having, through luck or good fortune, been able to survive the Nazi occupation.

The distrust shown towards many surviving foreign Jews in the immediate aftermath of the occupation did have a rationale, as almost from 1933 onwards, the Nazis had used refugees as a cover for espionage. What could be more appropriate than for agents to pass themselves off as Jewish or political refugees in order to identify or flush out opponents resident in other countries? It appears that the same cover was used after the occupation began, and for the same ends. Thus for example, the Vichy counterespionage services were well aware of this type of subterfuge but found it hard to unmask such agents when there were so many refugees who had washed up in Vichy as a result of the exodus and who had been trapped there by the armistice.[106]

Absolute portrayals of the Nazis as persecutors and the Jews as victims undoubtedly requires some qualification. Stories of German functionaries turning a blind eye to Jews are legion, and there were many employed in the administration of Western Europe who did not share the fanaticism of the leadership in Berlin. However, even among high-ranking Nazis and committed antisemites there are examples of exceptions being made where individual Jews could be useful in some other capacity: brokering deals in the outside world, as hostages, as sources of wealth, or as informers. Thus we can see how even the Nazis themselves protected Jews who were prepared to work for them.[107] It is also not difficult to see how the *Sicherheitspolizei* and the Gestapo were able to recruit informers from the Jewish community. Once arrested, there was a minority who were prepared to try to assure their own safety by working for the enemy. This is often portrayed as treason by Jews against Jews—and condemned as such, but perhaps the surprising element is not so much that it took place, but that it was relatively rare. Jews captured by the authorities and taken to holding cells in the middle of the night, often unsure of what had happened to family and friends and unsure about their own fate, were clearly in a position to be threatened and, either willingly or unwillingly, succumb to the offer of protection. We will never know how much information was extracted from Jews held in the police cells by stoolpigeons, nor the full extent of the betrayals made deliberately. Suffice to say that Jews did survive the Nazi occupation in this way—as is shown by their discovery, denunciation and trial by post-war courts where they were forced to answer for their conduct.

14
CONCLUSIONS

In surveying the many different ways in which Jews in Western Europe managed to survive the Holocaust, this study has had to be selective in its coverage, highlighting different aspects of escape or hiding, while making clear the sometimes stark contrasts between different countries and regions. The need to incorporate the prevailing social and political circumstances within each national case study necessitated a country-by-country approach, but most of the main comparative conclusions to be drawn from this study are evident in the body of the text. Nevertheless, it is worth reiterating some of the issues raised here that contradict or modify the existing explanations of Jewish survival in Western Europe during the Nazi occupation.

Turning first to the Jewish communities in Western Europe, it has often been argued that they were largely passive in the face of the Nazi threat and did little to help themselves. In fact, this was anything but the truth, and perhaps one of the most important conclusions to emerge from this study is that it is impossible to understand rescue and survival by seeing the Jews purely as passive victims and non-Jewish benefactors as the sole active participants in the process. The flight of Dutch Jews to the ports provides stark testimony to the fears engendered by the invasion in May 1940—and the propensity of many members of this most conformist community to do something to save themselves. Belgian and French Jews similarly took to the roads in huge numbers, but were likewise swept up in much larger refugee movements, most of which lost all momentum once they reached southern France. For many French Jews, their flight from Paris did nevertheless provide the basis for their long-term survival. Although they could not have known it at the time, the more bourgeois elements among French Jewry who had the resources to sustain themselves outside the capital benefited from the Vichy government's unwillingness to pursue them. Thus many thousands were able to live unmolested by the authorities and with little chance of discovery, even after the southern zone was occupied in November 1942.

In contrast, their foreign co-religionists who had come as migrants, or as refugees after 1933, and who had not acquired citizenship had no such advantages. The outbreak of war in 1939 saw France choosing to treat all Germans, whether Nazi or anti-Nazis, as enemy aliens and resorting to the use of internment camps. Not only did the appalling conditions in these camps and the attitudes of the French authorities serve to act as a warning to the refugee community of what might be in store, but also brought about the mobilization and initial co-operation of Jewish and non-Jewish welfare organizations even before the occupation began. In a perverse way, therefore, the poor treatment meted out by the French authorities in the final months of the Third Republic helped in the process of prompting assistance and orientating the Jews to the dangers they faced once the armistice had been signed. This situation was peculiar to France, as the only one of the five states actually at war before 10 May 1940, and the similar actions of Belgian, Dutch and Norwegian regimes against their German nationals were of such short duration as to have had little effect.

Some studies have highlighted the more established position of the Jews in the Netherlands when compared with their Belgian and most French counterparts, yet their apparent integration was into a vertically organized social (and political) system that gave Jews full civil rights but effectively separated them from other confessional or ideological groups. Their emancipated and undifferentiated political position may have masked a more isolated social position in which many Jews had few non-Jewish friends or even contacts outside their own milieu. Assimilation was essentially impossible, but the political equality, tempered by only a degree of cultural antisemitism in the Netherlands lulled its Jewish citizens into a false sense of security when compared with their Belgian and French counterparts. In Belgium, the overwhelming majority of Jews were recent immigrants whose citizenship was often in doubt, and whose attitude to state bureaucracy was framed by earlier experiences in Eastern Europe. Levels of integration were also affected by local factors. Most of the Jewish population was to be found either in Brussels or in Antwerp, but antisemitism was much more virulent and obvious in the latter. France likewise had high proportions of recent Jewish immigrants, including many refugees, and they were heavily concentrated in Paris. In both Belgium and France immigrant Jews had had little time to become either integrated or assimilated and were still dependent on social and organizational structures that prevented their assimilation into mainstream society—even if they had wished to do so. Thus in all three countries, albeit for different reasons, the ability of Jews to call on non-Jewish help after 1940 was severely limited.

It is nonetheless important to note that Jews did participate in more active forms of resistance against the Nazis. In one sense, their propensity for direct action against the occupiers increased their vulnerability, but involvement in organized resistance also had the potential to cloak their Jewish origins. Here there are contrasts between Belgium and France, where there were specific armed Jewish resistance groups as well as marked Jewish involvement in left-wing organizations, and the Netherlands where this was restricted to a very small number operating within the ranks of the social democrats, communists and some right-wing underground groups.

While the image of passivity may have some veracity in the cases of Norway, Denmark and the Netherlands, even the most cursory examination of events in France and Belgium shows just how important Jewish organizations were in warning their communities about the dangers they faced and then mobilizing help. Surviving or sidestepping Nazi attempts at co-ordination in the first years of occupation, they were able to function in quasi-legal and later in illegal forms, both on their own and in concert with other welfare and clandestine groups; a feature that proved to be of enormous value in organizing help to the Jewish community even before the deportations began.

Some of this was undoubtedly the result of foreign Jews being at the centre of key organizations like MOI and MOE: individuals whose political commitments and natural scepticism about both the state apparatus under German rule and the wider intentions of the Nazis served to galvanize them into direct action. Many had some prior experience of clandestine organizations, including men and women who had experienced the Tsarist state in Russia, and also those of the radical left who formed the backbone of the communist parties that operated on the margins of legality during the interwar period, and who were more actively persecuted for their political beliefs once the Germans had arrived. In Belgium, the development of the

CDJ saw left-wing and bourgeois elements working together in a common cause of self-defence. Likewise, the Rue Amelot Committee in Paris was an amalgamation of many different groups. In both cases, they were aided by the Germans' tardiness in creating their own representative bodies for the Jews that could be used as agencies to ensure the smooth running of their plans. Thus the advent of the UGIF and AJB came towards the end of 1941, whereas in the Netherlands, the Amsterdam Jewish Council dated from March of that year. Its bourgeois Jewish leadership had refused to have any dealings with overtly political (left-wing) organizations—a throwback to the pre-war era where the same people had been responsible for the organization of refugee relief and fostering a relationship with the Dutch government. However, it did mean that the bureaucracy and structures used to provide refugee relief were incorporated wholesale into the new organization, whereas in both France and Belgium, they remained independent. These differing structures also affected the speed with which communities and individuals reacted when the deportations began. With a more sceptical and resistant leadership, Jews in the major cities of Belgium and France had more options than their counterparts elsewhere, and did not have to rely entirely on the information or support available from the collaborationist UGIF or AJB. This again contrasts with the comprehensive dominance of the Jewish Council in Amsterdam that came to control every aspect of Jewish life in the city.

Investigations into the motivations and actions of non-Jewish rescuers have been heavily centred on individuals—as epitomized by the work of Yad Vashem—and attempts by sociologists to find patterns of altruism within the incidence of rescue. Both these approaches have yielded vast quantities of narrative and quantitative data that constitute a major resource for the historian, but they have also served to underplay the role of social, political and religious networks in facilitating the survival of Jews. Many people who were subsequently recognized as 'Righteous among the Nations' became involved through direct contact with the victims of Nazi persecution. Most limited their actions to helping a few individuals whom they knew, but there were also highly motivated individuals who were the instigators of wider networks by mobilizing their friends, relations, neighbours or parishioners, and approaching those whom they thought could be trusted to help in their work. For lay members of the community, family members were often the first port of call, followed by business or professional contacts whereas parish priests and pastors had the opportunity to use their contacts within the church to find assistance among their peers and to influence entire congregations. Their role was undoubtedly crucial in driving the expansion of rescue activities and probably does more than anything else to explain the very uneven distribution of hidden Jews—with some communities becoming hotbeds of activity while other nearby and apparently geographically, sociologically, religiously and politically identical communities were not involved at all.

However, even the picture of individual communities united in a desire to help the Jews needs some modification. While the story of Le Chambon apparently shows the mobilization of an entire community, the more down-to-earth comments of the Dutch network organizer, Arnold Douwes, suggests some widespread reticence towards providing assistance, even in places where priests, pastors or community leaders had given a clear lead. Thus it can be argued that in all countries, there were many people who were never drawn into rescue simply because they were never asked. Conversely, there were others who were asked and were offered the opportunity and who, for whatever reason, refused their help. As we have seen, analysing refusals remains problematic. No two hiding places were the same. Even discounting the fears for personal safety and the potential penalties for being caught sometimes quoted by those approached, there were other salient factors. Committed national socialists or collaborators living next door, small children who were likely not to keep secrets, inquisitive and talkative relatives, houses made unsafe by being the homes of labour draft evaders: all of these could be cited as reasons for refusals to help—and all of them with a degree of validity. This makes any moral judgements both problematic and inadvisable. The frustrations of network organizers in not finding enough suitable hiding places were often recorded, but to use this to castigate or condemn entire communities for their failure to help seems to fly in the face of rational examination of a highly complex issue.

It is clear that people in Belgium and France were quicker off the mark when it came to organizing escape and hiding for fugitives from the Germans. This can be attributed to a number of factors. Belgium and northern France had had first-hand experience of German rule during World War I, and all elements within society had developed strategies for dealing with it, ranging from collaboration through compliance and indifference to opposition and resistance. State and local governments charged with continuing their roles under foreign control thus had models on which to draw. In the same way, early forms of organized resistance activity often came from people and groups who had been active in 1914–18. Networks were re-formed to carry out intelligence-gathering and sabotage work, while others resumed helping Allied soldiers and prisoners of war on the run. Neither resistance nor 'rescue' work should therefore be seen as something developed exclusively in response to the events of 1940 or to the plight of the Jews. Even Denmark, Norway, the Netherlands and the rest of France that had not undergone these experiences directly had nonetheless seen the effects second-hand—through the privations wrought by four years of warfare.

Thus it was the immediate needs of the war and occupation that led to the first mobilization or refocusing of welfare and relief agencies and, although it is possible to identify very specific initiatives and organizations that were solely concerned with the plight of the Jews, there were many overlaps in terms of origins, personnel and purpose with other clandestine organizations. In other words, organized rescue was never a singular activity, but tied into other forms of resistance, if only at the level of sharing some of its basic tools—access to hiding places, ration cards, and identity papers. However, we also need to note that many important distinctions remained. Lucien Lazare makes the point that, while the armed resistance saw things in military terms and focused their attention on sabotage and destruction that would hamstring the German occupation, actions against the deportation of the Jews did not feature on their radar, as such actions would invite just as many reprisals, but with no perceptible measurable gain of weakening the occupier, politically, economically, or militarily. The rescuers were in some respects the exact opposite of the armed resistance, in that their objective was to save lives rather than take them (in relation to Germans).[1] However, this assumes a rather narrow definition of resistance, and rescuers should still rightly be seen as part of the resistance, as they were preventing the Germans from carrying out their ideological aims of deporting the Jews, and it is certainly true that the Germans saw them in that light.

The focus in this study has been very much on the role of rescue networks and the ways in which they were created. This is not to downplay or underestimate the role of decision-making for individual rescues—carried out by single hosts and unconnected to any wider organizations—at least at the outset. Large numbers of rescues began through the agency of neighbours, workmates, schoolmates, and teachers. Thus the more contact that Jews had with non-Jewish neighbours, the better placed they were likely to be. Again, this cannot be a hard and fast rule, but proximity and awareness undoubtedly facilitated requests and offers of help. More complicated to unravel is the possibility that some major urban areas had greater degrees of community solidarity, for example where working-class interests overrode any religious or racial distinctions. This may well have been the case in Paris and Brussels, but was possibly less evident in Antwerp and Amsterdam. The extensive historiography on the individual rescuer and his or her motivation shows how hard it is to provide concrete conclusions. Motivation was seldom, if ever, singular, and often related to a series of contextual and contingent factors peculiar to the individual at the moment when he or she had to make a decision. For most of those involved, this was the point of no return (although as we have seen, some would-be rescuers thought better of their decisions and attempted to reverse them, again for a multiplicity of reasons). In this context it is useful to reflect on the concept of 'banalité de bien', the banality of goodness.[2] Derived from the banality of evil thesis postulated by Hannah Arendt, it seems at first to be just a way of dismissing the possibility of understanding motivation at all, but it does provide a way of suggesting that the decisions taken by some people to help Jews in need were often predicated on combinations of factors that included both the rational and the irrational. In other words, they cannot be easily categorized, or indeed understood, beyond the time and place when they were made.

Local cultures may also have played a crucial role in the incidence of rescue. Much has been made of the Christian milieux, both Catholic and Protestant, in many areas closely associated with collective activities. Claims have been made about minority religious groups having a greater empathy with the plight of the Jews, seeing this as an enhanced version of their own situation. In this regard, one can point to the Calvinists in the Netherlands and Huguenots in France, although the larger Catholic population in the Netherlands also shared this sense of inferiority. This also raises another salient issue, namely the community and religious leadership of individual pastors and priests and their role in fostering help for the Jews in their particular parishes. More important still were their contacts within their own confession and the attitudes of their church superiors. As with the civil servants, the inevitably nuanced statements of church leaders had a major impact on the behaviour of rank-and-file parish incumbents. This was of course more evident in the hierarchical Catholic Church than in the federal or autonomous Nonconformist religions. In the Netherlands, this religious leadership seems to have been generally more conservative than in Belgium and France. While there were statements critical of the treatment of the Jews, there was no hint or call for practical action.[3] In the latter countries, one can point to the statements and actions of Cardinal Archbishops Gerlier (Lyon) and van Roey (Liège) that, while guarded, were nonetheless nuanced in particular ways. The precise lead given from the top had the potential to mobilize (or immobilize) help across an entire diocese. In areas dominated by Catholicism there were also many more spiritual and temporal institutions, from cloisters and nunneries to orphanages and old-people's homes that were under the influence, if not the control, of leading churchmen. While not a definitive guide, a word or a hint from a religious superior could do much to influence the behaviour of abbots and abbesses, as well as directors and managers of secular charitable foundations, into providing hiding places for Jews. One other intriguing factor, specific to France, is that local Catholic behaviour could be conditioned by an anti-State attitude fostered by the anticlericalism associated with the Third Republic.

This, in turn, raises a wider question, namely the degree to which state authority during the occupation was seen as legitimate and therefore to be obeyed, or conversely as illegitimate and to be resisted. Perspectives on this undoubtedly changed over time as German economic and ideological demands increased, but it is important to remember that the relationship between individuals, communities and the state were not forged when the occupation began, but stretched back decennia if not centuries, and undoubtedly varied between one country and another, and between different localities. This suggests that the propensity to resist (in all forms) was dependent both on the severity of the occupation and on potentially long-standing traditions of resistance to state authority. In general, this seems to have been greater in France than in the Netherlands where respect for constituted authority (*gezagsgetrouwheid*) was more ingrained. Whether these generalizations would stand close empirical scrutiny is another matter. One specific possible exception of direct relevance to the history of rescue can be found in border regions where long-standing traditions of smuggling and avoidance of state regulation of trade and the non-payment of duties and taxes were often endemic. This can be seen in the Pyrenees, where both Spanish and French mountain guides were able to make money by conducting people over the frontier in secret. However, similar traditions—albeit across less challenging terrain—can also be found further north along the frontiers of Belgium, Germany and the Netherlands. The adaptation of these traditions to exceptional circumstances had in many cases had precedents in the Great War and there are examples of people whose experiences as smugglers (*passeurs*) spanned both periods. In these areas, the notion of what was legal and acceptable behaviour may have been somewhat different from that in other parts of the country.

However, there are other features of local cultures that played a role in motivating help, both for Jews and others on the run from the occupying power. The first of these is peculiar to isolated rural areas and involves long-standing traditions of helping neighbours and travellers in need on the basis that there was no other help available. In more isolated parts of the eastern Netherlands, this was called the '*noaberplicht*', but is manifest in other places under different names.[4] Its application to those on the run from the Germans was a natural extension of an existing cultural norm, especially where the ideological/racial imperatives of the occupier were seen to go beyond any acceptable demands that properly constituted state authority could make.

Although the perpetrators do not loom large in the analysis here, leading Nazis did conspire to protect some Jewish 'notables', either for their own benefit or because they were perceived to be useful to German interests. The positions taken by individual Nazi leaders as well as the very different structures of occupation regimes across Western Europe clearly did have some marked effects, most notably in Denmark, where the lack of direct German control followed by the ambivalent attitude of the Reich Plenipotentiary Werner Best towards the Jews after the summer of 1943 undoubtedly contributed to the successful rescue of Danish Jewry by facilitating, if not conspiring with, the mass exodus to Sweden. In this case, advance warnings, coupled with popular antagonism towards the Germans, and a willing country of refuge, all came together to provide an opportunity for mass escape. The major structural differences elsewhere were largely the result of competition between the Nazi Party and RSHA/SS on the one hand, and the military authorities on the other. In the Netherlands, this struggle was largely resolved in favour of the former under the civilian leadership of *Reichskommissar* Arthur Seyss-Inquart, whereas in both Belgium and France, the military authorities maintained a large element of control, and saw the anti-Jewish policies desired by the RSHA and party in Berlin as counterproductive to the interests of a stable and uncomplicated occupation regime. In France, the military raised no objections to Himmler's demands for deportations, while the Vichy regime was an active accomplice, but was unwilling to use too many coercive measures when the supply of non-French Jews for deportation had been exhausted, for fear of compromising existing working relationships. This is even more evident in the Belgian case, where the military governor Alexander von Falkenhausen prized the contribution of the Belgian Secretaries-General far too highly to force their compliance in the face of objections and a potential withdrawal of bureaucratic co-operation in all other fields. Belgium also provides an example of how German ideological precepts had the potential to affect the nature of the occupation and the responses of the general population. Distinctions made between Flemish and French-speaking areas—epitomized by the return of Flemish prisoners of war in 1940—reflected the perceived status of the former as part of the 'aryan' community.[5] While Flemish nationalism had gained little from the German occupation of 1914–18, the re-occupation in 1940 did allow a militant collaborationist nationalism to flower in the north and west of the country. This may be a contributory factor in explaining the relative absence of rescue activities in these areas when compared with the French-speaking areas, in spite of the existence of an equally collaborationist Rexist movement there.

The rescue and survival of Jews was to an extent dependent on the degree of direct control the Germans managed to exert on the executive apparatus they needed to carry out their programme against them, primarily the police agencies. In key cities such as Amsterdam, the Nazis were able to elicit a high level of co-operation, although the motivation may have had more to do with maintaining the competences of the Dutch police than any commitment to antisemitism. Likewise, in Paris, René Bousquet was a willing collaborator in rounding up foreign Jews, but less keen to pursue French citizens, arguing that his men would become 'unco-operative' if asked to perform such tasks. In Belgium, with few exceptions, the SS were unable to use the local police for anti-Jewish measures and had to rely on German police and various collaborationists to carry out their work. The numbers and commitment of such collaborationists was also an issue and, where numbers could be mustered, they could inflict a good deal of damage. Allied to this was the contribution of Jews who were 'turned' into informers by the Gestapo and bribed with their own freedom and that of their immediate families. Icek Glogowski and Ans van Dijk are two of the most high profile cases, but there were undoubtedly others.

The testimonies of Jews who fell into German hands but who nevertheless survived the occupation provide compelling evidence of exactly how prevalent such offers were. Perhaps the surprising element is how few of the disorientated and frightened individuals who fell into German hands actually succumbed to these Gestapo blandishments. By the same token, some areas had German agencies that were far more committed to rounding up the Jews than others. Places where the Gestapo or *SS-Aussenstelle* were less assiduous in carrying out the ideological aims of the regime may have increased the chances of Jews avoiding deportation, but conversely may also have reduced the imperative for local populations to engage in rescue activity because the threat involved was not seen to be so great.

A different, but no less important element of German rule was the steps taken to outlaw the help given to Jews by non-Jews. It was, and is, often assumed that the penalties and their enforcement were much the same in every occupied country. Assessing this is complicated by the parallel operation of indigenous and German legal codes, as well as arbitrary acts carried out by the Nazi occupiers beyond any legislative norms. While there seem to have been clear penalties for helping Jews in the Netherlands, their imposition was by no means uniform or consistent—and it was only in the autumn of 1943 that there was a general understanding, via the underground press, that being caught helping Jews was likely to result in six months in a concentration camp. Yet even this was undermined by the experiences of rescuers, who were often left at liberty even after they had been caught harbouring Jews. In some cases this may have been the result of the Germans assuming that the suspects would continue their work—leading to another haul of fugitives in the future, or because the hosts were already in collusion with the pursuers, or more prosaically because there was no pecuniary or personal advantage in handing over rescuers to the relevant authorities. This can be contrasted with both France and Belgium where this precise 'crime' was never formally punishable under any specific legislation. Thus Albert van den Berg could still claim in 1943 that he had done nothing wrong under Belgian law when he was arrested. This did not mean that such activities went unpunished as there were always other decrees that could be used for arrests—not least possession of stolen or forged identity papers or ration cards, but it made it far more difficult for the public at large to understand the precise perils involved. This is not to decry the heroism of people who did engage in rescue, as their behaviour would have been conditioned by what they *thought* the risks involved were, but it nonetheless shows once again the uncoordinated and piecemeal way in which the Germans chose or were forced to approach the task of carrying out the removal of Jews from occupied territories.

In conclusion, it is important that the rescue of Jews during the Holocaust period is not analysed in isolation, lest it ignores the wider social context and local traditions that framed the nature of rescues and the behaviour patterns of rescuers. It is also important to find a balance between the national generalizations about rescue that fall apart when exposed to detailed empirical scrutiny, and giving in to the 'stubborn particularities' identified by Marrus and Paxton, a course that ultimately reduces us to describing individual rescues and destroying any possibility of a meaningful comparison. Glib categorizations of religious or humanitarian motivations or the stereotyping of national reactions towards the persecution of the Jews and their plight during the Nazi era have dominated the popular literature on the subject for too long, as have unsustainable moral and value judgements about behaviour. As we have seen, the processes that led to the rescue and survival of Jews were far more complex, and conditioned by both national and local circumstances and social structures. However, the fact that they *were* complex and defy simple explanations should not prevent us from trying to understand them.

Notes

CHAPTER I

1. In this context, see especially Nechama Tec, *When Light Pierced the Darkness: Christian Rescue of Jews in Nazi-Occupied Poland* (New York/Oxford: Oxford University Press, 1986), 184–193. Although the behavioural explanations in the text are fully nuanced, she uses the term 'Christians' to categorize all non-Jews. While Christian (Catholic) affiliation may have been almost uniform in Poland, the idea that all rescuers are in some senses Christian undermines the possibility of humanistic or atheistic motives. Yet, even if this is tenable for Poland, it certainly cannot be made to apply to other Western European countries where rescues took place. See also L. Smilovitsky, 'Righteous Gentiles, The Partisans and Jewish Survival in Belorussia 1941–44', *Holocaust and Genocide Studies* XI/3 (1997), Nechama Tec, 'Helping Behaviour and Rescue During the Holocaust', in Peter Hayes (ed.), *Lessons and Legacies: The Memory of the Holocaust in a Changing World* (Evanston IL: Northwestern University Press, 1991), and Perry London, 'The Rescuers: Motivational Hypotheses About Christians Who Saved Jews from the Nazis', in J. Macauley and L. Berkowitz, (eds), *Altruism and Helping Behavior* (New York: Academic Press, 1970).

2. Hannah Arendt, *Eichmann in Jerusalem: A Report on the Banality of Evil* (London: Faber and Faber, 1963). Raul Hilberg, *The Destruction of the European Jews* (New York: Holmes and Meier, 1985), 293–305, but the term itself had been culled from contemporary testimonies, for example, see Emmanuel Ringelblum, *Notes from the Warsaw Ghetto: The Journal of Emmanuel Ringelblum*, ed. Jacob Sloan (New York: McGraw Hill 1958), 316, and Abraham Lewin, *A Cup of Tears: A Diary of the Warsaw Ghetto*, ed. Anthony Polonsky (Oxford: Blackwell, 1988), 151.

3. See, for example, James M. Glass, *Jewish Resistance during the Holocaust: Moral Uses of Violence and Will* (Basingstoke: Palgrave, 2004). Israel Gutman, *Resistance: The Warsaw Ghetto Uprising* (Boston: Houghton Mifflin, 1994). Isaiah Trunk, 'Attitudes of the Judenrats to the Problem of Armed Resistance against the Nazis', in Y. Gutman and L. Rothkirchen (eds), *The Catastrophe*

of European Jewry (Jerusalem: Yad Vashem, 1976).Yuri Suhl, *They Fought Back: The Story of Jewish Resistance in Nazi Europe* (New York: Schocken, 1975). Reuben Ainsztein, *Jewish Resistance in Nazi Occupied Eastern Europe* (New York: Barnes and Noble, 1975). D. Levin, 'The Fighting Leadership of the Judenräte in the Small Communities of Poland', in Michael Marrus (ed.), *Jewish Resistance to the Holocaust* (London Meckler, 1989), 73–89. In addition, there has been renewed popular interest in the subject of Jewish partisans following the release of the film feature 'Defiance' (2008) based on the book by Nechama Tec, *Defiance: The Bielski Partisans* (Oxford: Oxford University Press, 1993, reprinted with new foreword and introduction 2008). See also, Peter Duffy, *The Bielski Brothers: The True Story of Three Men who Defied the Nazis, Built a Village in the Forest and Saved 1200 Jews* (New York: HarperCollins, 2003).

4. Herbert A. Strauss, 'Jewish Emigration from Germany: Nazi Policies and Jewish Responses', *Leo Baeck Institute Yearbook*, XV (1980), 318–61 and XXVI (1981), 343–409.

5. See especially Wolfgang Benz (ed.), *Überleben im Dritten Reich: Juden im Untergrund und ihre Helfer* (München: C. H. Beck, 2003), and Mark Roseman, *The Past in Hiding* (London: Allen Lane, 2000).

6. Susan Zuccotti, *The Italians and the Holocaust: Persecution, Rescue and Survival* (London: Peter Halban, 1987), xvi–xvii argues that it is more important to examine why any Jews were deported from Italy. See also Alexander Stille, *Benevolence and Betrayal: Five Italian Jewish Families under Fascism* (London: Penguin, 1993).

7. Jacques Adler, *The Jews of Paris and the Final Solution: Communal Responses and Internal Conflicts, 1940–1944* (New York: Oxford University Press, 1987), 8–9. In Paris there were 55,854 adult Foreign Jews out of a total of 113,467, and 21,314 of the 57,110 French Jews had acquired citizenship through naturalization.

8. Lieven Saerens, *Vreemdelingen in een Wereldstad: Een geschiedenis van Antwerpen en zijn joodse bevolking (1880–1940)* (Tielt: Lannoo, 2000) 546. This tallies with the Sipo card index that contained 55,670 cards. Lucien Steinberg, *Le Comité de Défense des Juifs en Belgique* (Bruxelles: Editions de l'Université de Bruxelles, 1973), 15.

9. Gerhard Hirschfeld, 'Niederlande', in W. Benz, (ed.), *Dimension der Völkermords: Die Zahl der jüdischen Opfer des Nationalsozialismus* (Munich, R. Oldenbourg, 1991), 137. Abel Herzberg, *Kroniek der Jodenvervolging 1940–1945* (Amsterdam: Querido, 1985), 66–7, 317. Bob Moore, *Victims and Survivors: The Nazi Persecution of the Jews in the Netherlands, 1940–1945* (London: Arnold, 1997), 259.

10. Jørgen Hæstrup, 'The Danish Jews and the German Occupation', in Leo Goldberger (ed.), *The Rescue of the Danish Jews: Moral Courage under Stress* (New York: New York University Press, 1987), 19–20, cites a survey by Julius Margolinsky, Librarian of the Danish Jewish Community. Finding precise figures for the number of refugees is complicated by the problems of illegal immigration. Danish police reports suggested that before *Kristallnacht*, there were 727 refugees in the country on 1 October 1938. See Lone Rünitz, 'The Politics of Asylum in Denmark in the Wake of the *Kristallnacht*—A Case Study', in Mette Bastholm Jensen and Steven L. B. Jensen (eds), *Denmark and the Holocaust* (Copenhagen: Institute for International Studies—Department for Holocaust and Genocide Studies, 2003), 17. Christhard Hoffmann, 'Fluchthilfe als Widerstand: Verfolgung und Retuung der Juden in Norwegen', in Wolfgang Benz and Juliane Wetzel (eds), *Solidarität und Hilfe für Juden während der NS-Zeit,* Vol. 2 (Berlin: Metropol, 1998), 205. Abrahamsen, *Norway's Response to the Holocaust: A Historical Perspective* (New York: Holocaust Library, 1991), 35. Hugo Valentin, 'Rescue and Relief Activities on Behalf of Jewish Victims of Nazism in Scandinavia', *YIVO Annual of Jewish Social Science* VIII (1953), 231. Thus they represented only between 0.05% and 0.067% of the total Norwegian population.

11. J. C. H. Blom, 'The Persecution of the Jews in the Netherlands: A Comparative Western European Perspective', *European History Quarterly*, XIX (1989), 333–351. Pim Griffioen and Ron Zeller, 'Anti-Jewish Policy and Organisation of the Deportations in France and the Netherlands, 1940–1944: A Comparative Study', *Holocaust and Genocide Studies* XX (2006), 437–473. Griffioen and Zeller, 'A Comparative Analysis of the Persecution of the Jews in the Netherlands and Belgium during the Second World War', *Netherlands Journal of Social Sciences*, XXXIV (1998), 126–164. Marnix Croes, 'The Holocaust in the Netherlands and the Rate of Jewish Survival', *Holocaust and Genocide Studies* XX (2006), 474–499.

12. See especially David Barnouw and Gerrold van der Stroom, *The Diary of Anne Frank: The Critical Edition* (London: Viking, 1989). Miep Gies (with Alison Leslie Gold) *Anne Frank Remembered. The Story of the Woman who helped to hide the Frank Family* (New York: Simon and Schuster, 1987).

13. The story of Schindler, a German businessman who arrived looking to make money from the occupied territories and ended up trying to save members of his (Jewish) workforce is neither typical of rescues in Poland, nor without its complications in terms of interpretation. See for example, David Crowe, *Oskar Schindler: The Untold Story of His Life, Wartime Activities and the True Story behind the List* (New York: Basic Books, 2004). Emilie Schindler, *Where Light and Shadows Meet: A Memoir* (New York: W. W. Norton, 1997).

14. For publications associated with the work of Yad Vashem, see especially
    Mordecai Paldiel, *The Path of the Righteous: Gentile Rescuers of the Jews during
    the Holocaust* (Hoboken NJ: KTAV, 1993); *Sheltering the Jews: Stories of
    Holocaust Rescuers* (Minneapolis MN: Fortress Press, 1996); *Saving the Jews:
    Amazing Stories of Men and Women Who Defied the 'Final Solution'* (Rockville
    MD: Schreiber, 2000), Israel Gutman, Sara Bender, Jozeph Michman and
    Bert-Jan Flim (eds), *Encyclopedia of the Righteous* (Jerusalem: Yad Vashem,
    2003). See also, Lucien Lazare, *Dictionnaire des Justes de France* (Jerusalem/Paris:
    Yad Vashem/Fayard, 2003). For a detailed discussion of the criteria used by
    the Commission and the difficulties involved, see Mordecai Paldiel, 'To the
    Righteous among the Nations Who Risked Their Lives to Rescue Jews',
    Yad Vashem Studies XIX (1988), 403–425.

15. Paldiel, *Sheltering the Jews*, 203. Since 1962, this specialist commission has been
    responsible for deciding on the award. Paldiel, 'To the Righteous among the
    Nations', 403–425.

16. Paldiel, *Sheltering the Jews*, 206. Paldiel makes the important point that
    although these anomalies exist and mortality was much higher in Poland
    and the Netherlands, rescue was also more difficult and dangerous in these
    countries and therefore more worthy of honour.

17. See, Louis de Jong, *Het Koninkrijk der Nederlanden in de Tweede Wereldoorlog*,
    13 vols ('s-Gravenhage: Staatsuitgeverij, 1969–1988).

18. See, for example, Limore Yagil, *Chrétiens et Juifs sous Vichy (1940–1944):
    Sauvetage et Disobéssance Civile* (Paris: Cerf, 2005). Martin Gilbert, *The Righ-
    teous: The Unsung Heroes of the Holocaust* (London/New York: Doubleday,
    2002). André Stein, *Quiet Heroes. True Stories of the Rescue of Jews by Christians
    in Nazi-occupied Holland* (Toronto: Lester and Orpen Dennys, 1988).

19. See especially Samuel P. Oliner and Pearl M. Oliner, *The Altruistic Personality:
    Rescuers of Jews in Nazi Europe* (New York: Free Press, 1988), Samuel
    P. Oliner, 'Heroic Altruism: Heroic and Moral Behaviour in a Variety of
    Settings', in John K. Roth and Elisabeth Maxwell (eds), *Remembering for
    the Future. Vol.2 The Holocaust in an Age of Genocide* (Basingstoke: Palgrave,
    2001), 322, and Mordecai Paldiel, 'The Face of the Other: Reflections
    on the Motivations of Gentile Rescuers of Jews', in Roth and Maxwell
    (eds), *Remembering for the Future. Vol.2*, 334, 340–1. It has also generated
    a series of theoretical sociological studies, see Kirsten Monroe, Michael
    C. Barton and Ute Klingemann, 'Altuism and the Theory of Rational
    Action', *Ethics* CI (1990), 103–122. Kirsten Monroe, *The Heart of Altruism:
    Perception of a Common Humanity* (Princeton NJ: Princeton University Press,
    1996). Frederico Varese and Meir Yaish, 'The Importance of Being Asked:
    The Rescue of Jews in Nazi Europe', *Rationality and Society*, XII (2000),

307–334. Varese and Yaish, 'Resolute Heroes: The Rescue of Jews During the Nazi Occupation of Europe', *Archives Européenes de Sociologie*, XLVI (2005), 153–168.

20. See, for example, Douglas Huneke, 'A Study of Christians who saved Jews during the Nazi Era', *Humboldt Journal of Social Relations* IX/I (1981–82) 144–150. Perry London, 'The Rescuers: Motivational Hypothesis about Christians Who Saved Jews from the Nazis', in J Macaulay and L. Berkowitz (eds), *Altruism and Helping Behavior* (New York: Academic Press, 1970), and Samuel P. Oliner, 'The Unsung Heroes in Nazi-Occupied Europe: The Antidote for Evil', *Nationalities Papers* XII/I (1984), 129–136, and most recently Jeannine (Levana) Frenck, 'Righteous among the Nations in France and Belgium: A Silent Resistance', *Search and Research*, XII (2008), International Institute for Holocaust Research.

21. See most recently, Pearl M. Oliner, *Saving the Forsaken. Religious Culture and the Rescue of Jews in Nazi Europe* (New Haven CT: Yale University Press, 2004). Kristen R. Monroe, *The Hand of Compassion: Portraits of Moral Choice During the Holocaust* (Princeton NJ: Princeton University Press, 2004), and Mark Klempner, *The Heart Has Reasons: Holocaust Rescuers and their Stories of Courage* (Cleveland OH: Pilgrim Press, 2006).

22. Vicki Caron, *Uneasy Asylum: France and the Jewish Refugee Crisis, 1933–1942* (Stanford CA: Stanford University Press, 1999). Vicki Caron, 'French Public Opinion and the "Jewish Question", 1930–1942: The Role of Middle Class Professional Organisations', in David Bankier and Israel Gutman (eds), *Nazi Europe and the Final Solution* (Jerusalem: Yad Vashem, 2003). Vicki Caron, 'The Path to Vichy: Anti-Semitism in France in the 1930s', J. B. and Maurice Shapiro Annual Lecture, USHMM, 20 April 2005 (Washington, 2005). Lieven Saerens, *Vreemdelingen in een Wereldstad. Een geschiedenis van Antwerpen en zijn joodse bevolking (1880–1940)* (Tielt: Lannoo, 2000). Lieven Saerens, 'Antwerp's Attitude to the Jews from 1914–1940 and Its Implications for the Period of the Occupation' and Saerens, 'The Attitude of the Belgian Roman Catholic Clergy Towards the Jews Prior to the Occupation', both in Dan Michman (ed.), *Belgium and the Holocaust: Jews, Belgians, Germans* (Jerusalem: Yad Vashem, 1998). Frank Caestecker, *Ongewenste Gaste:. Joodse vluchtelingen en migranten in de dertiger jaren* (Brussel: VUB, 1993). Mark van den Wijngaert, 'The Belgian Catholics and the Jews during the German Occupation 1940–1944', in: Dan Michman (ed.), *Belgium and the Holocaust*. J. C. H. Blom and J. J. Cahen, 'Joodse Nederlanders, Nederlandse joden en joden in Nederland (1870–1940), in J. C. H. Blom et al. (eds), *Geschiedenis van de Joden in Nederland* (Amsterdam: Balans, 1995).

23. Oliner, *The Altruistic Personality*, chapter 1, 'Why Risk One's Life', 1–12.

24. This has become increasingly apparent in more critical studies of rescuers where the precise level of risk to the rescuers is questioned. See, for example, Pierre Sauvage, 'Varian Fry in Marseille', in Roth and Maxwell, *Remembering for the Future*, Vol.2, here, 349–350.

25. H. C. Touw, *Het Verzet der Hervormde Kerk* (The Hague: Boekcentrum, 1946). J. J. Buskes, *Waar Stond de Kerk?* (Amsterdam: De Volkpaedagogische Bibliotheek, 1947). Th. Delleman (ed.), *Opdat wij niet vergeten* (Kampen, n.p., 1949). S. Stokman, *Het verzet van de Nederlandsche Bisschoppen tegen Nationaal-Socialisme en Duitse Tyrannie* (Utrecht: Het Spectrum, 1945). E. Leclef, *Le Cardinal van Roey et l'occupation allemande en Belgique* (Bruxelles: Goemaere, 1945). More recent studies have been more comprehensive. See, for example, Michèle Cointet, *L'Eglise sous Vichy, 1940–1945 la repentence en question* (Paris: Perrin,1995). Lieve Gevers and Jan Bank, (eds), *Religion under Siege, I, The Roman Catholic Church in Occupied Europe (1939–1950)* (Leuven: Peeters, 2007), Gevers and Bank, *Religion under Siege, II, Protestant, Orthodox and Muslim Communities in Occupied Europe (1939–1950)* (Leuven: Peeters, 2007).

26. For example on France, see the books by Lucien Lazare, *La Résistance juive en France* (Paris: Stock, 1987); *Le Livres des Justes: Histoire du sauvetage des juifs par des non-juifs en France, 1940–1944* (Paris: JC Lattès, 1995); *L'Abbé Glasberg* (Paris: Le Cerf, 1990). Likewise, Renée Poznanski, *Les juifs en France pendant la Seconde Guerre Mondiale* (Paris: Hachette, 1994), Jacques Ravine, *La Résistance Organisée des Juifs en France, 1940–1944* (Paris: Julliard, 1973), and Adam Rayski, *The Choice of the Jews under Vichy: Between Submission and Resistance* (Notre Dame IN: University of Notre Dame Press, 2005). On Belgium, Lucien Steinberg, *Le Comité de Défense des Juifs en Belgique* (Bruxelles: Université de Bruxelles, 1973), Sylvain Brachfeld, *Ze hebben het overleefd* (Brussel: VUB, 1997). On the Netherlands, Ben Braber, *Zelfs als wij zullen verliezen: Joden in Verzet en Illegaliteit 1940–1945* (Amsterdam: Balans, 1990). Braber, *Passage naar de vrijheid: Joodse verzet in Nederland, 1940–1945* (Amsterdam: Balans, 1987).

27. Cornelis J. Lammers, 'Persecution in the Netherlands during World War Two: An Introduction', *The Netherlands' Journal of Social Sciences* XXXIV/2 (1998), 111–125, here 111. This 'discovery' is often attributed to the publication of Helen Fein, *Accounting for Genocide: National Responses and Jewish Victimisation during the Holocaust* (New York: Free Press, 1979), but the raw statistics were known long before then and had been reproduced, albeit inaccurately, in Lucy Dawidowicz, *The War Against the Jews, 1933–1945* (New York: Holt, Reinhard and Winston, 1975).

28. M. R. Marrus and R. O. Paxton, 'The Nazis and the Jews in Occupied Western Europe 1940–1944', *Journal of Modern History* LIV (1982), 687–714, here 713.

29. See, Marnix Croes and Peter Tammes, *'Gif laten wij niet voortbestaan': Een onderzoek naar de overlevingskansen van joden in de Nederlandse gemeenten, 1940–1945* (Amsterdam: Aksant, 2004). J. C. H. Blom, 'Gescheidenis, sociale wetenschappen, bezettingstijd en jodenvervolging: Een besprekingsartikel', *Bijdragen en Mededelingen betreffende de Geschiedenis der Nederlanden, BMGN* CXX (2005), 562–580. Marnix Croes, 'De zesde fase? Holocaust en geschiedschriving', *BMGN CXXI* (2006), 292–301. Marjolein J. Schenkel, *De Twentse Paradox: De lotgevallen van de joodse bevolking van Hengelo en Enschede tijdens de Tweede Wereldoorlog* (Zutphen: Walburg Pers, 2003).

30. A. J. van der Leeuw, 'Meer slachtoffers dan elders in West-Europa', *Nieuw Israëlitisch Weekblad*, 15 November 1985.

31. J. C. H. Blom, *Crisis, Bezetting en Herste: Tien Studies over Nederland 1930–1950* (Rotterdam: Universitaire, 1989), 134–150. Griffioen and Zeller, 'The Persecution of the Jews'. See also Griffieon and Zeller, *'Jodenvervolging in Nederland en België tijdens de Tweede Wereldoorlog : een vergelijkende analyse'*, *Oorlogsdocumentatie '40–'45*, VIII (1997), 10–63.

32. Lammers, 'Persecution in the Netherlands during World War Two', 112. Griffioen and Zeller, 'The Persecution of the Jews', 152–3.

33. See in general, Deborah Dwork, *Children with a Star: Jewish Youth in Nazi Germany* (New Haven CT: Yale University Press, 1991). Anita Brostoff (ed.), *Flares of Memory: Stories of Childhood during the Holocaust* (Oxford: Oxford University Press, 1998), and on rescue, Sylvain Brachfeld, *Ils Ont Survecu: Le Sauvetage des Juifs en Belgique Occupee* (Bruxelles: Racine, 2001). Suzanne Vromen, *Hidden Children of the Holocaust:. Belgian Nuns and their Daring Rescue of Young Jews from the Nazis* (New York: Oxford, 2008). Martine Lemalet, (ed.), *Au secours des enfants du siècle* (Paris: Nil, 1993). Hillel J. Kieval, 'From Social Work to Resistance: Relief and Rescue of Jewish Children in Vichy France', (BA Harvard University, 1973). Donald A Lowrie, *The Hunted Children* (New York: W. W. Norton, 1963).

34. J. S. Fishman, 'Jewish War Orphans in the Netherlands: The Guardianship Issue, 1945–1950', *Wiener Library Bulletin* New Series 30/31 (1973–74), 31–6. J. S. Fishman, 'The Anneke Beekman Affair and the Dutch News Media', *Jewish Social Studies* XL/1, 3–24. J. S. Fishman, 'The War Orphan Controversy in the Netherlands: Majority–Minority Relations', in J. Michman and T. Levie, *Dutch Jewish History* I (Jerusalem, 1984). J. Michman, 'The Problems of the Jewish War Orphans in Holland', *She'erit Hapletah* (Jerusalem 1990), 189–209. Elma Verheij, *Om het Joodse Kind* (Amsterdam:

Nijgh en van Ditmar, 1991). Nederlands-Israëlitisch Kerkgenootschap and Portugees-Israëlitisch Kerkgenootschap, *De Verdwijning van Anneke Beekman en Rebecca Meljado: Witboek* (Amsterdam, 1954).

35. See, for example, the case of Karl Plagge, a German army major credited with saving 250 in Vilna who was designated a 'Righteous Gentile' in April 2005. Michael Good, *The Search for Major Plagge: The Nazi Who Saved Jews* (New York: Fordham University Press, 2006). There is also the concept of the 'Jewish non-Jewish rescuer'—someone honoured by Yad Vashem who subsequently is identified as having Jewish ancestry.

36. See on the Netherlands, J. C. H. Blom, 'In de ban van goed en fout', in Blom, *Crisis Bezetting en Herstel,* (Rotterdam: Universitaire, 1989). Chris van der Heijden, *Grijs Verleden. Nederland en de Tweede Wereldoorlog* (Amsterdam: Contact, 2001). Bob Moore, ' "Goed en Fout" or "Grijs Verleden":
Competing Perspectives on the History of the Netherlands under German Occupation', *Dutch Crossing* XXVII (2006), 155–168. On France, see Henry Rousso, *The Vichy Syndrome: History and Memory in France since 1944* (Cambridge MS: Harvard University Press, 1991).

37. To quote just one example, Cointet, *l'Église sous Vichy* devotes more than a quarter of his book to the question of antisemitism and the persecution of the Jews.

38. See, for example, Jaques Semelin, Claire Andrieu and Sarah Gensberger (eds), *La Résistance aux genocide. De la pluralité des actes de sauvetage* (Paris: Sciences Po, 2008).

39. See Raymond Kévorkian, 'L'opposition de fonctionnaires ottomans au génocide des Arméniens', and Ugur Ümit Üngör, 'Stratégies de survie au cours du genocide des Arméniens', both in Semelin et al. (eds), *La Résistance aux genocides,* 205–220 and 221–234. Raymond Kévorkian, 'Pour une typologie des 'Justes' dans l'Empire ottoman face au genocide des Arméniens', Conference paper, *Si può sempre dire un sì o un no: I Giusti contro I genocidi degli Armeni e degli Ebrei* (University of Padova, 30 November 2000). Richard G. Hovanissian, 'Intervention and Shades of Altruism during the Armenian Genocide', in Richard G. Hovanissian (ed.), *The Armenian Genocide: History, Politics, Ethics* (New York: St Martin's Press, 1992) 173–207.

CHAPTER 2

1. H. W. von der Dunk, 'The Shock of 1940', *Journal of Contemporary History* II (1967), 169–82. Joel Blatt (ed.), *The French Defeat of 1940: Reassessments* (Providence RI: Berghahn, 2000).

2. Truus Wijsmuller-Meijer, *Geen Tijd voor Tranen* (Amsterdam: n.p., 1961).

3. Jacob Presser, *Ondergang: De Vervolging en Verdelging van het Nederlandse Jodendom, 1940–1945*, ('s-Gravenhage: Staatsuitgeverij, 1977), Vol. I, 13.

4. Susanne Loebl, *At the Mercy of Strangers: Growing up on the Edge of the Holocaust* (Pacifica CA: Pacifica Press, 1997), 32. Israel J. Rosengarten, *Survival: The Story of a Sixteen-Year-Old Jewish Boy* (Syracuse NY: Syracuse University Press, 1999), 20–5. Marcel Liebman, *Né juif: Une famille juive pendant la guerre* (Paris/Gembloux: Duculot, 1977), 20–2.

5. It has been estimated that up to 20,000 Belgian Jews fled the country in 1940 and did not return, or failed to register with the German authorities when ordered to do so. Steinberg, *Le Comité de Défense des Juifs*, 15.

6. Jacob Presser, *Ondergang* I, 13.

7. Lieven Saerens, 'Die Hilfe für Juden in Belgien', in Wolfgang Benz and Juliane Wetzel, (eds), *Solidarität und Hilfe für Juden während der NS-Zeit, Vol. 2* (Berlin: Metropol, 1998), 205.

8. Robert W. Allen, *Churchill's Guests: Britain and the Belgian Exiles during World War II* (Westport CT: Praeger, 2003), 14.

9. Julian Jackson, *The Fall of France: The Nazi Invasion of 1940* (Oxford: Oxford University Press, 2003), 174.

10. Ian Ousby, *Occupation: The Ordeal of France 1940–1944* (New York: St Martin's, 1998), 45. Jackson, *The Fall of France*, 174. Renate Hess, 'Was Portugal getan hat, hat kein anderes Land getan', in Wolfgang Benz and Juliane Wetzel, *Solidarität und Hilfe für Jüden*, 187, suggests the population of Bordeaux may have reached 1 million.

11. Georges Friedmann, *Journal de guerre* (Paris, 1987), 305, cited in Jackson, *The Fall of France*, 144.

12. Gustave Folcher, *Marching to Captivity: The War Diaries of a French Peasant, 1939–45* (London: Brassey's, 1996), 58.

13. Lucien Lazare, *Rescue as Resistance: How Jewish Organisations Fought the Holocaust in France* (New York: Columbia University Press, 1996), 36.

14. See, for example, Hanna Diamond, *Fleeing Hitler: France 1940*, (Oxford: Oxford University Press, 2007).

15. Ousby, *Occupation*, 43.

16. Ibid. 47.

17. Walter F. Peterson, *The Berlin Liberal Press in Exile: A History of the Pariser Tageblatt—Pariser Tageszeitung* (Tübingen: Niemeyer, 1987), 56–7.

18. Hess, 'Was Portugal getan hat', 175–6. See also Rui Afonso, 'Le "Wallenberg Portugais": Aristides de Sousa Mendes', *Revue d'Histoire de la Shoah*, 165 (January–April 1999), 7–28. This latter account is based on the files of the disciplinary action taken against de Sousa Mendes by his government.

19. Hess, 'Was Portugal getan hat', 177 notes the case of a dentist whose qualifications would not be recognized in Portugal, but whose application was approved on the basis that he was going into partnership with a Portuguese dentist.

20. Avraham Milgram, 'Portugal, The Consuls, and the Jewish Refugees, 1938–1941', *Yad Vashem Studies* XXVII (1999), 130–2.

21. Hess, 'Was Portugal getan hat', 180. Milgram, 'Portugal, The Consuls', 132–3.

22. Milgram, 'Portugal, The Consuls', 139–141.

23. Ibid. 141.

24. Afonso, 'Le "Wallenberg Portugais"', 11. Hess, 'Was Portugal getan hat', 185.

25. Instituto Diplomatico, *Spared Lives: The Actions of Three Portuguese Diplomats in World* War II/ *Vidas Poupadas: A accão de três diplomatas portugueses na Guerra Mundial II* (Lisbon: Ministério dos Negócios Etrangeiros, 2000), 18. Milgram, 'Portugal, The Consuls', 128. Fralon, *A Good Man in Evil Times: The Heroic Story of Aristide de Sousa Mendes* (New York: Basic Books, 2001), 46–7.

26. Afonso, 'Le "Wallenberg Portugais"', 10. Milgram, 'Portugal, The Consuls', 142–3. Jose-Alain Fralon and Peter Graham, *A Good Man*, 48.

27. Hess, 'Was Portugal getan hat', 187.

28. Fralon, *A Good Man*, 53–4, cites testimony from César de Sousa Mendes.

29. Instituto Diplomatico, *Spared Lives*, 19. Milgram, 'Portugal, The Consuls', 142–3.

30. Fralon, *A Good Man*, 56.

31. Hess, 'Was Portugal getan hat', 187.

32. Instituto Diplomatico, *Spared Lives*, 19.

33. Fralon, *A Good Man*, 60. See also, Milgram, 'Portugal, The Consuls', 144–5.

34. Afonso, 'Le "Wallenberg Portugais"', 15. He dates the visit to 16 June, thus two days after de Sousa Mendes had 'taken to his bed'.

35. Afonso, 'Le "Wallenberg Portugais"', 16.

36. Hess, 'Was Portugal getan hat', 187–8.

37. Fralon, *A Good Man*, 69.

38. Fralon, *A Good Man*, 68–9. Other beneficiaries included four members of the Rothschild family. Afonso, 'Le "Wallenberg Portugais"', 19–20.

39. Afonso, 'Le "Wallenberg Portugais"', 19. Hitler wanted von Habsburg extradited from Portugal. Salazar refused but asked von Habsburg to leave as soon as possible. Arriving in the US he asked for permits for his countrymen and was told by a senior Washington diplomat, 'There are enough Jews here already. Let Hitler keep the rest.' Von Habsburg had more luck with the

Central Americans, where General Rafael Trujillo Molina of the Dominican Republic granted 3,000 visas.

40. Fralon, *A Good Man*, 80–1. Milgram, 'Portugal, The Consuls', 149. Instituto Diplomatico, *Spared Lives*, 20.

41. Fralon, *A Good Man*, 86–7. He claimed this was to accompany refugees to the border, but another testimony has it that it was to sign visas for Belgian diamond merchants trapped at the border. Afonso, 'Le "Wallenberg Portugais"', 21–2.

42. Hess, 'Was Portugal getan hat', 181.

43. Fralon, *A Good Man*, 90–1.

44. Milgram, 'Portugal, The Consuls', 145, gives the source for this as Harry Ezratty, 'The Portuguese Consul and the 10,000 Jews', *Jewish Life*, Sept–Oct 1964, 17–19. See also Lazare, *Le Livre des Justes*, 42.

45. Yehuda Bauer, *American Jewry and the Holocaust: The American Jewish Joint Distribution Committee, 1939–1945* (Jerusalem: Hebrew University, 1981), 45, cited in Hess, 'Was Portugal getan hat', 189.

46. Milgram, 'Portugal, The Consuls', 147–8.

47. Instituto Diplomatico, *Spared Lives*, 21.

48. Afonso, 'Le "Wallenberg Portugais"', 25.

49. Fralon, *A Good Man*, 114–115. Hess, 'Was Portugal getan hat', 188, notes that de Sousa Mendes had only a small pension that was totally insufficient for his large family. He was supported by the JDC until his death in 1954. Two of his sons asked the Quakers to get them into the US as early as 1 October 1943 on the basis of their father's help for refugees—an application that he underwrote. Sutters, *American Friends*, Vol. 2 Part.2, 457 8. Louis Phillipe and Jean Paul de Sousa Mendes to AFSC Lisbon, 1 October 1943.

50. Afonso, 'Le "Wallenberg Portugais"', 27–8.

51. Hess, 'Was Portugal getan hat', 189–190.

52. Milgram, 'Portugal, The Consuls', 152–4.

53. Milgram, 'Portugal, The Consuls', 154–5.

54. Varian Fry, *Surrender on Demand* (Boulder CO: Johnson Books, 1997), 18. Vochoč had been a professor at the University of Prague and Chief of the European Personnel Division of the Czech Foreign Office before the fall of Prague.

55. Vladimír Vochoč, 'Compte Rendu' (London 1941), 18. Coll. Archiv Joseph Fisera, USHMM RG–43.028 1999 A 0069.

56. Andy Marino, *A Quiet American: The Secret War of Varian Fry* (New York: St Martins, 2000), 107, 119. Fry, *Surrender on Demand*, 19. The passports were actually printed in Bordeaux, inside the occupied zone.

57. Vochoč, 'Compte Rendu', 18–19.

58. Ibid. 19.
59. Ibid. 20.
60. Ibid. 21–2.
61. Letter, Donald A Lowrie (YMCA) to Mr. J. Lavicka, 31 July 1942 Coll. Archiv Joseph Fisera [Frame 1341] USHMM RG-43.028 1999 A 0069.
62. Vochoč, 'Compte Rendu', 23.
63. Ibid. 24–5.
64. Lowrie, *The Hunted Children*, 104.
65. Wolfgang Benz and Walter Pehle, *Encyclopedia of the German Resistance to the Nazi Movement* (New York: Continuum, 1997), 264, 284. Both men were later captured and deported back to Germany. Breitscheid was reportedly killed in an air raid at Buchenwald (1944) and Hilferding died in Gestapo custody (1941). See also, Simon Kitson, *The Hunt for Nazi Spies: Fighting Espionage in Vichy France* (Chicago: University of Chicago Press, 2007), 21.
66. Vochoč, 'Compte Rendu', 41–2.
67. This was Luis Martins de Souza Dantas, Brazilian ambassador to France for many years before the occupation who is credited with saving at least 425 people by issuing both diplomatic and ordinary visas to a range of people after being specifically told not to by his government at the end of 1940. See Interview with Fabio Koifman in *Folha Judaica* and www.raoul-wallenberg.org.ar/english/souzadantas.htm
68. Vochoč, 'Compte Rendu', 56.
69. Tela Zasloff, *A Rescuer's Story: Pastor Pierre-Charles Toureille in Vichy France* (Madison WI: University of Wisconsin Press, 2003), 112, 115. Lazare, *Righteous among the Nations: France*, 239.
70. Zasloff, *A Rescuer's Story*, 114, cites a letter written to her in 2001.
71. Sevenster was an agricultural engineer who had been resident in Paris since 1921 and had been a commercial attaché and commercial councillor before being appointed consul-general in 1939.
72. L. De Jong, *Het Koninkrijk der Nederlanden in de Tweede Wereldoorlog*, 13 vols ('s-Gravenhage: Staatsuitgeverij, 1969–1988), Vol. 9, 23–4.
73. Ibid. 544.
74. Ibid. 24.
75. Sierk Plantinga, 'Joseph Willem Kolkman (1896–1944) en de Engeland-vaarders: De hulp aan Nederlandse vluchtelingen in Vichy-Frankrijk', *Oorlogsdocumentatie* IX (1998), 10–36, here 15–16.
76. De Jong, *Het Koninkrijk*, Vol. 9, 547.
77. Plantinga, 'Joseph Willem Kolkman', 16–17.
78. Ibid. 17.
79. Ibid. 17. See also Herman Grishaver, correspondence with the author, May–September 2006.

80. Plantinga, 'Joseph Willem Kolkman', 20.

81. Ibid. 23.

82. Ibid. 29–30, 34.

83. De Jong, *Het Koninkrijk*, Vol. 9, 552, makes the point that there are few details on those who did manage to escape from the camps in this way.

84. Fry, *Surrender on Demand* (Boulder CO: Johnson Books, 1997). Sheila Isenberg, *A Hero of Our Own: The Story of Varian Fry* (New York: Random House, 2001).

85. Cynthia Jaffee McCabe, '"Wanted by the Gestapo: Saved by America"—Varian Fry and the Emergency Rescue Committee', in Jarrell C. Jackman and Carla M. Borden, *The Muses Flee Hitler: Cultural Transfer and Adaptation* (Washington DC: Smithsonian Institute, 1983), 79–94, here 80–1.

86. Isenberg, *A Hero of Our Own*, 13–14.

87. Ibid. 20–1, 31.

88. Sauvage, 'Varian Fry in Marseille', 354.

89. Isenberg, *A Hero of Our Own*, 136–9. Ernst's first wife was not so fortunate. Having been deserted by her husband in 1922, she had carved out her own career as a journalist and critic, but her Jewish ancestry caused her to leave Germany and she was in Marseilles in 1940. She refused to remarry Ernst to travel with him to the US and, in spite of Fry's best efforts, she remained trapped in France and was finally deported to Auschwitz via Drancy.

90. Fry, *Surrender on Demand* (Boulder CO: Johnson Books, 1997), 38, 117. McCabe, '"Wanted by the Gestapo"', 84. She later left France to marry a Slovene art student she had met before the war. Miriam Davenport Ebel, 'An Unsentimental Education' (1999), www.chambon.org

91. Sauvage, 'Varian Fry in Marseille', 354. Marino, *A Quiet American*, 86–8.

92. Fry, *Surrender on Demand*, 37.

93. Isenberg, *A Hero of Our Own*, 29–30. Marino, *A Quiet American*, 122.

94. Marino, *A Quiet American*, 128–9.

95. Fry, *Surrender on Demand*, 26–7.

96. McCabe, '"Wanted by the Gestapo"', 80.

97. Fry, *Surrender on Demand*, 31.

98. Isenberg, *A Hero of Our Own*, 25, 40.

99. Ibid. 26.

100. Lowrie, *The Hunted Children*, 48.

101. Varian Fry, *Surrender on Demand*, 18–19. Once he ran out of official Czech passports, he contrived to have new ones produced by a printer in Bordeaux, in the occupied zone. These had pink covers rather than the traditional green, and were intended for stateless émigrés, but this distinction was unclear to

most other consular officials. See also, Lisa Fittko, *Escape Through the Pyrenees* (Evanston IL: Northwestern University Press, 2000), 95.

102. Marino, *A Quiet American*, 119. Fittko, *Escape Through the Pyrenees*, 95. It was rumoured that the text of the visas actually said: 'It is strictly forbidden for the bearer of this document, under any circumstances, and at any time, to set foot on Chinese soil.'

103. Fittko, *Escape Through the Pyrenees*, 95.

104. Ibid. 101.

105. See also Isenberg, *A Hero of Our Own*, 45.

106. Ibid. 29.

107. Marino, *A Quiet American*, 118.

108. Isenberg, *A Hero of Our Own*, 15–17, 78.

109. Aaron Levenstein, *Escape to Freedom: The Story of the International Rescue Committee* (Westport CT: Greenwood,1983), 15–16.

110. Levenstein, *Escape*, 22–3. McCabe, ' "Wanted by the Gestapo" ', 86. Isenberg, *A Hero of Our Own*, 79–80. Marino, *A Quiet American*, 182, 218.

111. USHMM Rescue Folder: Matthews (Vichy) to Secretary of State, 14 September 1940. NARA RG59 811.111 Refugees/298 Section 2. Marino, *A Quiet American*, 109, 116.

112. USHMM Rescue Folder: Sumner Welles to Eleanor Roosevelt, 12 September 1940. NARA RG59. 811.111 Refugees/322 Section 2.

113. Fittko, *Escape Through the Pyrenees*, 96, 113. Isenberg, *A Hero of Our Own*, 92.

114. Fittko, *Escape Through the Pyrenees*, 113.

115. Ibid. 122.

116. USHMM RG50.030.302 Barac, 22.

117. Fittko, *Escape Through the Pyrenees*, 125, 129–30.

118. McCabe, ' "Wanted by the Gestapo" ', 85–6. Isenberg, *A Hero of Our Own*, 103.

119. Isenberg, *A Hero of Our Own*, 115. Fittko, *Escape Through the Pyrenees*, 133.

120. Michael R. Marrus and Robert O. Paxton, *Vichy France and the Jews* (Stanford CA: Stanford University Press, 1995), 69–70. Marino, *A Quiet American*, 109. Isenberg, *A Hero of Our Own*, 94, 108.

121. Lowrie, *The Hunted Children*, 96–7.

122. Isenberg, *A Hero of Our Own*, 125.

123. Ibid. 146.

124. The Panamanian consul in Marseilles was still illicitly selling visas in 1941, provided that the purchaser made no attempt to enter Panama—in exchange for salami. Fittko, *Escape Through the Pyrenees*, 165.

125. Isenberg, *A Hero of Our Own*, 144–5. Freier was eventually deported to Auschwitz but survived the war.

126. Fittko, *Escape Through the Pyrenees*, 167.

127. Fry, *Surrender on Demand*, 199–201.

128. Sauvage, 'Varian Fry in Marseille', 362.

129. Ibid. 359, 366.

130. Fry, *Surrender on Demand*, 45, 47, 168–9, 209–212.

131. Lowrie, *The Hunted Children*, p51. Fittko, *Escape Through the Pyrenees*, 187, refers to about fifteen separate organizations.

132. Lowrie, *The Hunted Children*, 83–4. It included among its 25 member organizations the American Friends of Czechoslovakia, the JDC, the American Friends Service Committee, the 'Belgian' Office, French and Polish Red Cross, International Migration Office, French, Polish and World Alliance of YMCA/YWCA, French Student Christian Association, Unitarian Service Committee, French Committee in Aid of Refugees (ORT), European Student Relief, the Central Jewish Committee of Relief Organisations, the French Protestant Federation, CIMADE, HICEM and the Catholic Centre d'Accueil.

133. Lowrie, *The Hunted Children*, 85.

134. Ibid. 91.

135. Ibid. 89–94.

136. Ibid. 110.

137. Ibid. 144–145.

138. Ibid. 188.

139. Ibid. 175–6

140. Ibid. 158.

141. Ibid. 160.

142. Ibid. 191.

143. Fittko, *Escape Through the Pyrenees*, 120–2.

144. Ibid. 143–4.

145. Ibid. 142.

146. Fry, *Surrender on Demand*, 12. David S. Wyman, *Paper Wall:. America and the Refugee Crisis 1938–1941* (University of Massuchusetts, 1968), 168.

147. Wyman, *Paper Walls*, 167, 174–5. Bat-Ami Zucker, *In Search of Refuge: Jews and US Consuls in Nazi Germany 1933–1941* (London: Vallentine Mitchell, 2001),165–7. Bingham was not the only consul with a more liberal attitude as investigations centred on the consulate in Vienna. The consul in Oslo also sheltered some Jews before their departure for Sweden.

148. Dalia Ofer, *Escaping the Holocaust* (New York: Oxford University Press, 1990), 134–5, 168, 354 n. 13 cites British protests to Bolivia, Uruguay, and Chile about the issue of visas and the reported dismissal of a Paraguayan consul.

149. Fittko, *Escape Through the Pyrenees*, 142, 157–8.

150. Fittko, 141.

151. Sauvage, 'Varian Fry in Marseille', 357. Levenstein, *Escape*, 17. Fittko, *Escape Through the Pyrenees*, 145–7.

152. Fry, *Surrender on Demand*, 22–3, McCabe, ' "Wanted by the Gestapo" ', 89. Modigliani was the brother of the painter Amedeo Modigliani. He ultimately escaped to Switzerland with his family.

153. USHMM RG50.030.306 Einhorn, Tape 2, n.p.

CHAPTER 3

1. Bob de Graaff, *Schakels naar de Vrijheid. Pilotenhulp in Nederland tijdens de Tweede Wereldoorlog* ('s-Gravenhage: SDU, 1995), 91.

2. De Jong, *Het Koninkrijk*, V/2, 755–6.

3. De Jong, *Het Koninkrijk*, V/2, 756 notes London using Willem Lenglet as a contact man for RAF personnel. He expedited the escape of thirteen airmen to Belgium before his arrest in 1941.

4. M. R. D. Foot and J. M. Langley, *MI9 Escape and Evasion 1939–1945* (London: Bodley Head, 1979), 83.

5. J. Meulenbelt, 'Bezetting en Verzet', in J. J. Bolhuis et al. (eds), *Onderdrukking en Verzet: Nederland in Oorlogstijd*, 4 vols (Arnhem: van Loghum Slaterus 1949–53) III, 580. De Jong, *Het Koninkrijk*, V/2, 758–9.

6. De Jong, *Het Koninkrijk*, VII/2, 912–913.

7. Mathieu Smedts, *Waarheid en leugen in het verzet* (Maasbree: Corrie Zelen, 1978), 198.

8. De Graaff, *Schakels naar de Vrijheid*, 97–8.

9. It is clear that care needs to be taken with this, as with all other rescue stories. Most of it is based on the book written by Bert Poels, *Mémoires. Vriend en Vijand* (Venlo: Van Spijk, 1977). In it he inflates the numbers of pilots and others helped by his network and hidden on his farm. Others have suggested that the network was much wider and that many of the claims made by Poels should be attributed to others in the district. See Smedts, *Waarheid en leugen*. Smedts was at one time (post-war) editor of *Vrij Nederland*.

10. Smedts, *Waarheid en leugen*, 198.

11. See, for example, Helen McPhail, *The Long Silence:. Civilian Life under the German Occupation of Northern France, 1914–1918* (London/New York: I. B. Taurus, 2001), 116–136.

12. Paul Moeyes, *Buiten Schot: Nederland tijdens de Eerste Wereldoorlog, 1914–1918* (Amsterdam: Arbeiderspers, 2001), 121–132.

13. *Het Volk* (Belgium), 16 June 1972.

14. Els Hofke, *Vrouw in Verzet; Miet Pauw en de bezetting in Baarle* (Baarle-Nassau: De Jong, 1989), 9–10.

15. Hofke, *Vrouw in Verzet*, 23–7.

16. Ibid. 29–30, 35, 39.

17. Ibid. 12. Smugglers were known locally as '*pungelaars*'.

18. De Graaff, *Schakels naar de Vrijheid*, 106–7. Hofke, *Vrouw in Verzet*, 50. This seems to have happened after the arrest of a man waving a Dutch flag during Dolle Dinsdag. In the days thereafter a series of raids led to the arrest of most of the network's members. Unusually, her husband had taken no interest in his wife's work and knew little of what was happening.

19. Hofke, *Vrouw in Verzet*, 52–62.

20. Moeyes, *Buiten Schot*, 123.

21. Smedts, *Waarheid en leugen*, 84.

22. Eric Alary, *La Ligne de Démarcation, 1940–1944* (Paris: Perrin, 2003), 183.

23. Alary, *La Ligne de Démarcation*, 186.

24. Ibid.

25. Ibid. 187. Cites the testimony of Léon Poliakov, *L'auberge des musiciens* (Paris:Mazarine, 1981), 82–4.

26. Yagil, *Chrétiens et Juifs*, 546.

27. Alary, *La Ligne de Démarcation*, 209.

28. Ibid. 207.

29. Ibid. 204–5. Some local *préfets* were convinced antisemites, but others objected to the rich Jews bringing money to poor areas near the line of demarcation, thus raising local prices.

30. Ibid. 213.

31. Ibid. 201.

32. Ibid. 212–213.

33. De Jong, *Het Koninkrijk*, VII/2, 895.

34. Herbert Ford, *Flee the Captor* (London: Pan, 1999), 45–8.

35. Ibid. 51.

36. De Jong, *Het Koninkrijk*, VII/2, 894.

37. Ibid. 544–5, 550.

38. Ford, *Flee the Captor*, 59 De Jong, *Het Koninkrijk*, IX/1, 552. Most notably Maurice Jacquet in Lyon.

39. Ford, *Flee the Captor*, 60.

40. De Jong, *Het Koninkrijk*, IX/1, 543.

41. Ibid. 549.

42. Ibid. 552–4.

43. Weidner's biographer dates the decision to use Swizerland as 'early 1942' but de Jong sees it as contingent on the beginnings of the deportations in summer 1942. Ford, *Flee the Captor*, 60. De Jong, *Het Koninkrijk*, VII/2, 896

44. Ford, *Flee the Captor*, 68–9.

45. For the story of one Dutch Jewess who escaped via this route, see Bep Turksma, *Vraag me niet waarom* (Baarn: Het Wereldvenster, 1971), 165–179.

46. De Jong, *Het Koninkrijk*, VII/2, 896. Ford, *Flee the Captor*, 139–50.

47. Ford, *Flee the Captor*, 75.

48. De Jong, *Het Koninkrijk*, VII/2, 897. Nijkerk was the partner in a Dutch wholesale metal concern resident in Belgium. Moore, *Victims and Survivors*, 170. Nijkerk's widow dates their meeting in the spring of 1942. CEGES-SOMA AA1915 Heiber Dossier 18. Steinberg, *Le Comité de Défense des Juifs*, 48–9.

49. De Jong, *Het Koninkrijk* IX/1, 561. CEGES-SOMA R706 238.777 Testimony of Maurice Bolle, 7 September 1990.

50. Lucien Steinberg, *Le Comité de Défense des Juifs en Belgique, 1942–1944* (Bruxelles: Université de Bruxelles, 1973), 123–4. CEGES-SOMA AB1491 N. Hamme, 'Een Hollander in België ondergedoken', 1. NIOD 251a LO-BP2 Verslag W. Klaassens, LO-Amsterdam Oost, 4 April 1946, 2.

51. Steinberg, *Le Comité de Défense des Juifs*, 125–6.

52. CEGES-SOMA AA1915 Heiber Dossier 18.

53. Coen Hilbrink, *De Ondergrondse: Illegaliteit in Overijssel* ('s-Gravenhage: SDU, 1988), 170, records that the brother-in-law of Lotte Simon from Deventer was one of those helped by Dutch–Paris into Switzerland. Simon was of German Jewish origin but remained active in helping hide Jews in and around the city.

54. De Jong, *Het Koninkrijk*, VII/2, 897. At more or less the same moment, in the border region, suitably endorsed by sympathetic municipal civil servants, one of the *Bolle-groep*'s members, Edmond Salomon Chait, arrived in an internment camp in the unoccupied zone, having been forced to flee from Belgium.

55. Steinberg, *Le Comité de Défense des Juifs*, 50,124. De Jong, *Het Koninkrijk*, VII/2, 897.

56. De Jong, *Het Koninkrijk*, VII/2, 897, Ford, *Flee the Captor*, 156. Testers had been working alongside Kolkman from Perpignan. Their work had been broken up by the Germans in December. Testers and Kolkman both later died in concentration camps.

57. M. R. D. Foot, *SOE in The Low Countries* (London: St Ermin's Press, 2001), 187–8. They had escaped from Haaren gaol and found their way into France.

58. De Jong, *Het Koninkrijk*, IX/2, 1015–6.

59. Ibid. 897.

60. Ford, *Flee the Captor*, 79–80. Weidner also had links via the French consul in Geneva (probably through his wife's former employment) and corresponded with him in code.

61. De Jong, *Het Koninkrijk*, IX/1, 557.

62. Ibid. 558. Nijkerk also visited Switzerland in May 1943 to obtain funds for the Comité de Defence des Juifs. CEGES-SOMA AA1915 Heiber Dossier 18.

63. Steinberg, *Le Comité de Défense des Juifs*, 126. By this stage the numbers of refugee Jews from the Netherlands had all but dried up as most had either been deported or were living underground inside the Netherlands.

64. De Jong, *Het Koninkrijk* IX/1, 561. Bolle was arrested in July 1943 and sent to Buchenwald but survived the war.

65. De Jong, *Het Koninkrijk* IX/1, 556–7. Jacquet survived the war, but Aarts died in gaol in Toulouse of a heart attack on 6 June 1944, having just heard of the Allied invasion.

66. De Jong, *Het Koninkrijk*, VII/2, 898. This is different from the story in Ford, *Flee the Captor*, 245–64 that suggests the initial interrogations were carried out by the French police, and that threats were made against her parents who were still in the Netherlands and not accompanying her.

67. Steinberg, *Le Comité de Défense des Juifs*, 124–5.

68. He probably died in a satellite *kommando* of KZ Neuengamme, although his widow claims that he was killed by Allied bombing when prisoners were moved to ships in Lübeck harbour. Smits was one of those listed as missing. CEGES-SOMA AA1915 Heiber Dossier 18.

69. De Jong, *Het Koninkrijk* IX/1, 562. This was expedited by E. van Hasselt, a Dutch Jew in a mixed marriage, who had provided help to Jews underground from the summer of 1942 onwards.

70. Ford, *Flee the Captor*, 284–94.

71. Jean H. Weidner 'De Weg naar de Vrijheid', in Bolhuis, *Onderdrukking en Verzet* III, 737, gives the totals as approximately 1,000 people, of whom 200 were French, 118 Americans, and 100 other foreigners (The assumption being that the rest were either Dutch or Belgian).

72. Van Heuven Goedhart was made Minister of Justice in 1944 before returning to editorship of *Het Parool* 1947–1950 and a subsequent career in politics.

73. Ford, *Flee the Captor*, 302.

74. De Jong, *Het Koninkrijk*, VII/2, 898.

75. YV M31/32 Joop Westerweel. VPRO Broadcast 8 May 1960 W. G. van Maanen. The parents had converted and turned the thriving family printing business into an organization for printing religious tracts. Westerweel had serious ideological conflicts with his father through his espousal of Christian socialism that created in him a lifelong hatred of authority.

76. Yehudi Lindeman, 'All or Nothing: The Rescue Mission of Joop Westerweel' in Scrase et al. (eds), *Making a Difference: Rescue and Assistance during the*

Holocaust (Burlington VT: Center for Holocaust Studies at the University of Vermont, 2004), 242. De Jong, *Het Koninkrijk*, VI, 340. Paldiel, *The Path of the Righteous*, 144. Lindeman, 'All or Nothing', 259.

77. Ineke Brasz et al. (eds), *De jeugdalijah van het Pavilioen Loosdrechtse Rade, 1939–1945* (Hilversum: Verloren, 1987), 61–3. YV M31/32 Joop Westerweel. VPRO Broadcast 8 May 1960 W. G. van Maanen.

78. Lindeman, 'All or Nothing', 262. They had been placed there overnight by a friend who had then been captured before he could move them on. Rather than upset the arrangement, Westerweel left them in the apartment and rented somewhere else for his family.

79. Brasz, *De jeugdalijah*, 70–1. YV M31/32 Joop Westerweel. VPRO Broadcast 8 May 1960 W. G. van Maanen, gives the number as 49.

80. Brasz, *De jeugdalijah*, 72. An offshoot of the network was created by Chiel Salomé who established contacts with the village of Sevenum in Limburg, where many children were eventually sheltered.

81. Brasz, *De jeugdalijah*, 79.

82. W. Westerweel, *Verzet zonder geweld. Ter herinneringen van Joop Westerweel* (n.p.,n.d.), mimeograph NIOD, 43–6. Lindeman, 'All or Nothing', 241.

83. Lindeman, 'All or Nothing', 255. It is not clear, though likely, that the deletion of pioneers from the lists would have required the substitution of other names to make up the quota.

84. Jac. Van der Kar, *Joods Verzet: Terugblik op de Periode Rond de Tweede Wereldoorlog* (Amsterdam: Stadsdrukkerij, 1981), 89, 92. Lindeman, 'All or Nothing', 255. Brasz, *De jeugdalijah*, 127–8.

85. Brasz, *De jeugdalijah*, 85.

86. Lindeman, 'All or Nothing', 252–3. Paldiel, *The Path of the Righteous*, 145.

87. Brasz, *De jeugdalijah*, 97.

88. Ibid. 96.

89. Paldiel, *The Path of the Righteous*, 145.

90. Westerweel, *Verzet zonder geweld*, 71–2. Lindeman, 'All or Nothing', 257.

91. Ben Sijes, *Studies over Jodenvervolging* (Assen: van Gorcum, 1974), 148 Brasz, *De jeugdalijah*, 106–7.

92. Brasz, *De jeugdalijah*, 107.

93. Joel S. Fishman, 'On Jewish Survival during the Occupation: The Vision of Jacob van Amerongen' *Studia Rosenthaliana* XXXIII/2 (1999), 160–173, here 163. Among those saved was Jacob (Jaap) van Amerongen, later Ja'akov Arnon, a prominent Dutch Zionist leader and later a senior Israeli civil servant. De Jong, *Het Koninkrijk*, 342. Paldiel, *The Path of the Righteous*, 145. The remainder were hidden in the Netherlands. See for example YV M31/32

Joop Westerweel. Note on Piet Wildschut whose brickworks was used as a hiding place.

94. H. Avni, 'Zionist Underground in Holland and France and the Escape to Spain', in Y. Gutman and E. Zuroff (eds), *Rescue Attempts during the Holocaust* (Jerusalem: Yad Vashem, 1977), 567, 570. Lindeman, 'All or Nothing', 253–4, notes that Westerweel's staunch antimilitarism had caused him to object to any use of documents involving the *Wehrmacht*, but he was overruled. See also WL-PIIId/229 and WL-PIIId/230. Reilinger survived the war but was killed in a car accident in 1945. Brasz, *De jeugdalijah*, 116–117.

95. Lindeman, 'All or Nothing', 263. Paldiel, *The Path of the Righteous*, 145. He reportedly quoted Matthew 10: 37–9 as his justification.

96. Jenny Gans-Premsela, *Vluchtweg. Aan de bezetter ontsnapt* (Baarn: Bosch en Koning, 1990), 30–1.

97. Gans-Premsela, *Vluchtweg*, 33–4.

98. Ibid. 35–42.

99. Ibid. 42.

100. Ibid. 'De beste helpers wilden geen geld, de onbetrouwbaren eisten alles van waarde'.

101. CEGES-SOMA AB1491 N. Hamme, 'Een Hollander in België ondergedoken', 1.

CHAPTER 4

1. Abrahamsen, *Norway's Response,* 30–4. Full citizenship rights for all were only established by a constitutional amendment in 1964, 36.

2. Hoffmann, 'Fluchthilfe als Widerstand, 205. Abrahamsen, *Norway's Response,* 35. Valentin, 'Rescue and Relief Activities', 231.

3. This is contested by Kathleen Stokker, *Folklore Fights the Nazis: Humor in Occupied Norway 1940–1945* (London: Associated University Presses, 1995), 48–9, 213, who argues that the absence of jokes about the Jewish question in 'resistance humour' shows an indifference to the Jews who lacked cultural and social integration into the non-pluralistic society, 49. Hoffmann, 'Fluchthilfe als Widerstand', 205.

4. Abrahamsen, *Norway's Response*, 40.

5. Ibid. 41–2.

6. Hoffmann, 'Fluchthilfe als Widerstand', 206. Abrahamsen, *Norway's Response,* 42–3.

7. Hoffmann, 'Fluchthilfe als Widerstand', 207. Quisling's organization put the number of Jews in Norway at c.10,000. Abrahamsen, *Norway's Response,* 52.

8. Samuel Abrahamsen, 'The Relationship of Church and State during the German Occupation of Norway, 1940–1945, in Jack Fischel and Sanford Pinsker (eds), *Holocaust Studies Annual*, Vol. 2, *The Churches' Response to the Holocaust*, (Greenwood FLA: Penkevill, 1986), 2–22, here 3. There had been consternation that some Lutherans in Germany actually supported Nazism, but a broad welcome for Niemoeller's *Bekenntniskirche*.

9. Abrahamsen, 'The Relationship of Church and State', 5–6.

10. Ibid. 10.

11. Abrahamsen, *Norway's Response*, 109 They were also reassured by a statement from Reichskommissar Terboven on 25 September 1940 that protection would be given to all religious denominations. Paldiel, *The Path of the Righteous*, 365, puts the number at around 150. See also the story of Bjørg Fjellberg whose family were helped to escape northwards to Finland/Sweden by Markus Rotvold in June 1940 but returned in January 1941, only for the Jewish father to be arrested on 18 June 1941 and later deported. YV M31/10764, 18 September 2004. François Kersaudy, *Norway 1940* (London: Arrow, 1991), 82, 107–8.

12. Abrahamsen, *Norway's Response*, 79–80.

13. Ibid. 81.

14. Oskar Mendelsohn, *The Norwegian Rescue of Jews* (New York: Thanks to Scandinavia, n.d.), 1.

15. Abrahamsen, *Norway's Response*, 83.

16. Arnfinn Moland, 'The Norwegian Holocaust and the Resistance', 4. Text courtesy of the author. Mendelsohn, *The Norwegian Rescue*, 2.

17. Abrahamsen, *Norway's Response*, 84–5.

18. Ibid. 96–7.

19. Ragnar Ulstein, 'The Rescue of c.1000 Jews in Norway during the Second World War' (1985), 3. Ollum escaped to Sweden, but Rothkopf 'disappeared' and his fate is uncertain.

20. Mendelsohn, *The Norwegian Rescue*, 3. Maynard M. Cohen, *A Stand Against Tyranny: Norway's Physicians and the Nazis* (Detroit: Wayne State, 1997), 138, notes that some even returned to Norway after hostilities ceased.

21. Moland, 'The Norwegian Holocaust', 7 cites the Wannsee Protocol.

22. Mendelsohn, *The Norwegian Rescue*, 2.

23. Moland, 'The Norwegian Holocaust', 8. This also included Berlin, which had made no transport provision for those arrested.

24. Abrahamsen, 'The Relationship of Church and State', 16 He also notes that even some NS pastors had qualms about the treatment of the Jews. Mendelsohn, *The Norwegian Rescue*, 3.

25. Samuel Abrahamsen, *Norway's Response*, 112. In truth, although this demon-strates the concern of the Norwegian government-in-exile, the British had had so little success in negotiating any forms of exchange with the Germans that such a scheme would have seemed far too far-fetched for the British Foreign Office to pursue, and might have set all manner of precedents.

26. Valentin, 'Rescue and Relief Activities', 232. Abrahamsen, 'The Relationship of Church and State', 14.

27. Arnfinn Moland, 'Norway', in Bob Moore (ed.), *Resistance in Western Europe* (Oxford: Berg, 2000), 244. Wartime and post-war statistics suggest that a total of 740 people were deported (410 men, 268 women and 62 children), although Yad Vashem gives 761, of whom 24 survived to return. Moland, 'The Norwegian Holocaust', 12 cites Kristian Ottosen, *I slik en natt* (Oslo: Aschehoug, 1994).

28. Ragnar Ulstein, 'The Rescue of c.1000 Jews', 7. Mendelsohn, *The Persecution of the Norwegian Jews in WW11* (Oslo: Norges Hjemmefrontmuseum, 1991), 29. Mendelsohn, *The Norwegian Rescue*, 3.

29. Mendelsohn, *The Persecution of the Norwegian Jews*, 28–9.

30. Ibid. 30.

31. YV M31/616 Norwegian Underground Movement. Paldiel, *The Path of the Righteous*, 365. Henriette Samuel was the wife of the Chief Rabbi of Norway, Julius Isak Samuel, who had refused to go into hiding and had been arrested in October and deported.

32. Moland, 'Norway', 225. Ragnar Ulstein, 'The Rescue of c.1000 Jews', 10. David Howarth, *The Shetland Bus* (Shetland: Shetland Times, 1998). Paldiel, *The Path of the Righteous*, 366. Mendelsohn, *The Persecution of the Norwegian Jews*, 30, also suggests that people managed to escape by boat across the North Sea.

33. YV M31/8611 Einar Follestad and others.

34. YV M31/11021 Testimony of Gabriel Stiris, 2 February 2006.

35. YV M31/6846 Einar Wellen. Testimony of Margrit Stenge, 21 September 1994.

36. The Rabbi's wife attributed this to Ingebjørg Sletten. YV M31/70 Ingebjørg Sletten. Letter from Henriette Samuels, 5 April 1967, but subsequent testi-monies show that the neighbour was Sigrid Lund. See Sigrid Helliesen Lund, *Always on the Way* (London: 2000), 66. Israel Gutman (ed.), *The Encyclopedia of the Righteous among the Nations: Rescuers of Jews during the Holocaust. Europe (Part I) and other Countries* (Jerusalem: Yad Vashem, 2007), 420–1, credits Slet-ten with involvement in saving thirteen children from the Jewish orphanage, but six other people, including the orphanage director were also subsequently honoured by Yad Vashem for the escape. See YV M31/10816 Nina Hasvold.

Moreover, her role in this—although not in other escapes—has been denied. YV M31/10856 Sigrid Helliesen Lund.

37. Paldiel, *The Path of the Righteous*, 368. This was not an isolated example, and suggests that the Norwegian police were less than assiduous in carrying out such checks.

38. YV M31/1248 Hans Christen Mamen. Testimony of Edith Adler, 18 February 1972 and Hans Christen Mamen, July 1961. He also later fled to Sweden while his sister was arrested and spent several years in gaol.

39. Ragnar Ulstein, 'The Rescue of c.1000 Jews', 9–10.

40. Mendelsohn, *The Norwegian Rescue*, 3, estimates that it took 15–20 people to expedite the journey of each group of Jews across the frontier.

41. Valentin, 'Rescue and Relief Activities', 233. Ragnar Ulstein, 'The Rescue of c.1000 Jews', 13.

42. YV M31/10565 Oscar and Frieda Sjølie. Testimony of Berit Demborg, 31 August 2004.

43. Mendelsohn, *The Persecution of the Norwegian Jews,* 28. Valentin, 'Rescue and Relief Activities', 234. For a sociological analysis of resistance based on experiences in Norway, see Vilhelm Aubert, *The Hidden Society* (New Brunswick NJ: Transaction Books, 1965), 288–310. Mendelsohn, *The Norwegian Rescue*, 7.

44. Mendelsohn, *The Persecution of the Norwegian Jews*, 29.

45. Very few Norwegian policemen were recorded as helping Jews but Pettersen had been dismissed for his anti-Nazi sentiments. Ulstein,'The Rescue of c.1000 Jews', 4–5. See YV M31/10565 Oscar and Frieda Sjølie. Testimony of Irene Levin, 27 March 2007.

46. This may have been Westgård's route run by Åge Bjerring. Interview of Sigrid Helliesen Lund by Ragnar Ulstein, 3 December 1970 YV M31/10856 Sigrid Helliesen Lund, 7.

47. Mendelsohn, *The Norwegian Rescue*, 7.

48. Myrtle Wright, *Norwegian Diary 1940–1945* (London: Friends Peace International Relations Committee, 1974), 111. Diary entry for 30 October 1942.

49. Cohen, *A Stand Against Tyranny*, 142–3. His father was arrested and succeeded in committing suicide while in gaol.

50. Lund had been the Chair of the Childrens' Committee for the Nansen Organisation. YV M31/10856 Sigrid Helliesen Lund. Interview of Sigrid Helliesen Lund by Ragnar Ulstein, 3 December 1970, 1. Cohen, *A Stand Against Tyranny*, 135.

51. Wright, *Norwegian Diary*, 61.

52. Paldiel, *The Path of the Righteous*, 366. He suggests that all were soon transferred across to Sweden. Wright, *Norwegian Diary*, 46–7, 100–3. Kevin

Sim, *Women of Courage* (London: Corgi, 1983), 136–8. Mendelsohn, *The Norwegian Rescue*, 6–7. Ragnar Ulstein, 'The Rescue of c.1000 Jews', 8. Cohen, *A Stand Against Tyranny*, 143.

53. YV M31/10856 Sigrid Helliesen Lund. Interview of Sigrid Helliesen Lund by Ragnar Ulstein, 3 December 1970, 3–4.

54. Mendelsohn, *The Norwegian Rescue*, 5.

55. Wright, *Norwegian Diary*, 102.

56. Cohen, *A Stand Against Tyranny*, 135. Wright, *Norwegian Diary*, 126–7.

57. Mendelsohn, *The Persecution of the Norwegian Jews*, 30.

58. Moland, 'The Norwegian Holocaust', 12. Mendelsohn, *The Persecution of the Norwegian Jews*, 24. This included the infamous Stalingrad-night at Grini when drunken guards 'avenged' the German defeat on their hapless Jewish prisoners.

59. Labour conscription was announced only in February 1943. This is later than other countries—but did act as the same prompt for more widespread civil disobedience and resistance. However, the opposition of the Church did help mobilize public opinion at an earlier stage which in turn helped the Jews in later 1942. In this context one should also note the importance of the attack on the Rjukan Heavy Water plant although this was after most Jews had escaped—late February/early March 1943.

60. Arnfinn Moland, *Over grensen? Hjemmefrontens likvidasjoner under den tyske okkupasjonen av Norge 1940–1945* (Oslo, 1999), 307. Mendelsohn, *The Persecution of the Norwegian Jews*, 30. Abrahamsen, *Norway's Response*, 102–3. Moland, 'Norway', 244. Håkon Løvestad was the brother of Karsten Løvestad who had killed the Gestapo agent on the train on 22 October 1942. He later escaped to Britain and joined the airforce. Pedersen was arrested by the Germans in 1943 and survived the war in Sachsenhausen.

61. It is also asserted by some historians that it has been used to cloak the les savoury aspects of Denmark's wartime history, including the treatment of Jewish refugees and the participation of Danish SS men in mass killings. See, for example Vilhjálmur Örn Vilhjámsson, and Bent Blüdnikow, 'Rescue, Expulsion and Collaboration: Denmark's Difficulties with its World War II Past', *Jewish Political Studies Review* XVIII/3–4 (2006), and Vilhjálmur Örn Vilhjámsson, *Medaljens Bagside: Joediske flygtningskaebner i Danmark 1933–1945* (Copenhagen: Forlaget Vandkunsten, 2005). On the refugee question see Rünitz, 'The Politics of Asylum in Denmark', 14–32.

62. Gilbert, *The Righteous,* 223.

63. The Danish case as a comparative has been an integral part of the scholarly debate on rescue, see for example, Leni Yahil, 'Methods of Persecution: A Comparison of the Final Solution in Holland and Denmark', *Scripta*

Hierosolymitana, XIII (1972), 279–300. Leni Yahil, *The Rescue of Danish Jewry: Test of a Democracy* (Philadelphia: Jewish Publication Society, 1969). Helen Fein, *Accounting for Genocide: National Responses and Jewish Victimization during the Holocaust* (New York: Free Press, 1979), and J. C. H. Blom, 'The Persecution of the Jews in the Netherlands: A Comparative Western European Perspective', *European History Quarterly*, XIX (1989), 333–351.

64. Jørgen Hæstrup, 'The Danish Jews and the German Occupation', 19–20, cites a survey by Julius Margolinsky, Librarian of the Danish Jewish Community. Finding precise figures for the number of refugees is complicated by the problems of illegal immigration. Danish police reports suggested that before *Kristallnacht*, there were 727 refugees in the country on 1 October 1938. See also Rünitz, 'The Politics of Asylum in Denmark', 17.

65. Jørgen Hæstrup, *Passage to Palestine: Young Jews in Denmark* (Odense: Odense University Press, 1983), 196–7. Therkel Stræde, *October 1943: The Rescue of the Danish Jews from Annihilation* (Copenhagen: Danish Ministry of Foreign Affairs, 1993), 19. The estimate of 1,400 agricultural trainees quoted in David Lampe, *The Savage Canary: The Story of Resistance in Denmark* (London: Cassell, 1957), 67, and reprinted in Ruby Rohrlich (ed.), *Resisting the Holocaust* (Oxford: Berg, 1998), 220, seems an overestimate. Margolinsky gives the figures as 350 Zionist trainees and 270 Aliyah children, while 'Die Rettung der Juden in Dänemark', 18, suggests 380 trainees and 265 Alijah children.

66. Hermann Weiss, 'Die Rettung der Juden in Dänemark während der deutschen Besetzung 1940–1945', in Wolfgang Benz and Juliane Wetzel (eds), *Solidarität und Hilfe für Juden während der NS-Zeit*, Vol. 2 (Berlin: Metropol, 1998), 21.

67. Hans Kirchhoff, 'Denmark', in Bob Moore (ed.), *Resistance in Western Europe* (Oxford: Berg, 2000), 95.

68. Hermann Weiss, 'Die Rettung der Juden in Dänemark', 13.

69. Ibid. 16.

70. W. Glyn Jones, *Denmark: A Modern History* (Beckenham: Croome Helm, 1986), 153–7.

71. The Danes did, however, sign the Anti-Comintern Pact, but with the reservation that they would only operate against Bolshevism within their own frontiers. See Jones, *Denmark*, 159–60.

72. Weiss, 'Die Rettung der Juden in Dänemark', 14–15. Germany received 10% of its total meat and butter requirements from Denmark, and 18% of its fish.

73. Kirchhoff, 'Denmark', 103–105.

74. This was the response given to Himmler on a visit to Copenhagen by the Danish Chief of Police, Thune Jacobsen in April 1941. Hæstrup, 'The Danish Jews', 28. See also Michael Mogensen, 'October 1943—The Rescue of the Danish Jews', in Mette Basthom Jensen and Steven L. B. Jensen, *Denmark and the Holocaust* (Copenhagen: Institute for International Studies, 2003), 35.

75. Hæstrup, 'The Danish Jews', 23–4.

76. Ibid. 26.

77. Weiss, 'Die Rettung der Juden in Dänemark', 29–30. Hæstrup, 'The Danish Jews', 29.

78. Hæstrup, 'The Danish Jews', 32, 53. *Kamptegnet* was a weekly newspaper subsidized by the Germans with a maximum circulation of 12,000.

79. Weiss, 'Die Rettung der Juden in Dänemark', 31. Hæstrup, 'The Danish Jews', 30, 32.

80. Jones, *Denmark*, 160. Weiss, 'Die Rettung der Juden in Dänemark', 35–6.

81. Weiss, 'Die Rettung der Juden in Dänemark', 36–7.

82. Kirchhoff, 'Denmark', 96. Best's position was made easier by Himmler's support for his conciliatory policies in Denmark.

83. Kirchhoff, 'Denmark', 105. Jones, *Denmark*, 163.

84. In theory, Best and von Hanneken were regarded as having equal powers in Denmark, but Berlin had made it clear that it was Best's will that should prevail in cases of dispute. Kirchhoff, 'Denmark', 95. This was thrown into question after 29 August, when von Hanneken seemed to have the upper hand in the power struggle, but Best's pre-eminent political position was confirmed by Hitler in early September. Stræde, *October 1943,* 11.

85. Hans Kirchhoff, 'SS-*Gruppenführer* Werner Best and the Action Against the Danish Jews—October 1943', *Yad Vashem Studies* XXIV (1994), 196.

86. Stræde, *October 1943*, 11.

87. Kirchhoff, 'SS-*Gruppenführer* Werner Best', 212.

88. Mogensen, 'October 1943—The Rescue of the Danish Jews', 37–8. Kirchhoff, 'SS-*Gruppenführer* Werner Best', 213. See also Martha Loeffler, *Boats in the Night* (Blair NE: Lur, 2000), 34.

89. This interpretation is certainly contested. Thus, for example, Jørgen H. Barfod and Max Nielsen, *Escape from Nazi Terror: A short history of the Jews in Denmark and Norway and the Danish underground refugee service* (Copenhagen: Forlaget for Faglitteratur, 1968), 11, speaks of Best 'happening to mention' the coming action. Conversely, Gerd Stolz, '1943—Georg Ferdinand Duckwitz und die Rettung der Juden aus Dänemark', *Grenzfriedenshefte* I (1993), 50, and relying heavily on Jonannes Dost, *Georg Ferdinand Duckwitz in Dänemark* (Bonn: Auswärtiges Amt, 1987) merely notes that the information came via the German Foreign Office and makes no mention of Best's involvement.

90. Tatiana Brustin-Berenstein, 'The Historiographic Treatment of the Abortive Attempt to Deport the Danish Jews', *Yad Vashem Studies* XVII (1986), 182–5.

91. Stolz, '1943—Georg Ferdinand Duckwitz', 55. Hæstrup, 'The Danish Jews', 21–22.

92. Hæstrup, 'The Danish Jews', 40–1. Stolz, '1943—Georg Ferdinand Duckwitz', 55.

93. Hæstrup, 'The Danish Jews', 42. He cites a statement by Karl Lachmann, Vice-Chairman of the Jewish Community Board.

94. YV M31/226 Anna Christensen. YV M31/6145 Ester Handberg.

95. Jones, *Denmark*, 161.

96. Hæstrup, *Passage to Palestine*, 192, cites Karl Lachmann, Vice-Chairman of the Mosaic Religious Community. Hæstrup, 'The Danish Jews and the German Occupation', 42.

97. Raul Hilberg, *The Destruction of European Jewry*, 359. Rohrlich, *Resisting the Holocaust*, 228. Jørgen Hæstrup, 'The Danish Jews', 43.

98. Kirchhoff, 'SS-*Gruppenführer* Werner Best', 211. Brustin-Berenstein, 'The Historiographic Treatment', 206.

99. Hæstrup, 'The Danish Jews', 49. Harold Flender, *Rescue in Denmark* (New York: Simon and Schuster, 1963), 76–7. Loeffler, *Boats in the Night*, 54, notes that Sweden's change of policy was broadcast on the radio and featured on the front pages of daily newspapers. This ostensibly came about because Niels Bohr, the Danish physicist who had escaped to Sweden in September put pressure on King Gustav V by refusing to leave to help the Allies until Swedish borders were opened.

100. Hæstrup, 'The Danish Jews', 49.

101. Mogensen, 'October 1943', 52.

102. Loeffler, *Boats in the Night*, 50–1.

103. Hæstrup, 'The Danish Jews', 51.

104. Stræde, *October 1943*, 13–14. Flender, *Rescue in Denmark*, 116–124.

105. YV M31/471 Henry and Grethe Thomsen. Henry Thomsen was later arrested and died in KZ Neuengamme on 4 December 1944.

106. Mogensen, 'October 1943', 47. Stræde, *October 1943*, 15.

107. Flender, *Rescue in Denmark*, 133, recounts the story of 30 Polish Jews being charged $5,000 for passage to Sweden whereas later voyages might have cost them $1,800 (30 x $60).

108. YV M31/4602 Harald Petersen. For comparison, Mogensen, 'October 1943', 48, notes that unskilled wages at the time were around DKr.2 per hour.

109. Flender, *Rescue in Denmark*, 106, 109. Loeffler, *Boats in the Night*, 56, 71 suggests that what emerged was a standard rate, but that no refugee was turned down for lack of money.

110. See, for example, Barfod and Nielsen, *Escape from Nazi Terror,* 38.

111. Hæstrup, *Passage to Palestine,* 207.

112. Loeffler, *Boats in the Night,* 73.

113. Barfod and Nielsen, *Escape from Nazi Terror,* 17, 19.

114. Ibid. 27.

115. Flender, *Rescue in Denmark,* 145–9.

116. Ibid. 152–3.

117. Ibid. 155.

118. Ibid. 160.

119. Ibid. 173–6. There were also other routes, such as the Bornholm Ferries, that passed through Swedish waters and were able to unload fugitives (illegally) en route. Barfod and Nielsen, *Escape from Nazi Terror,* 39.

120. Flender, *Rescue in Denmark,* 183–4. Here, because of her supposed help for Jewish children, she was given the task of taking those too small or weak to walk to the gas chambers and then from there to the crematorium. She was ultimately saved by the Bernadotte mission.

121. Yahil, *The Rescue of Danish Jewry: Test of a Democracy* (Philadelphia, Jewish Publication Society, 1969), 267.

122. Stræde, *October 1943,* 16.

123. Barfod and Nielsen, *Escape from Nazi Terror,* 23–4.

124. Flender, *Rescue in Denmark,* 156.

125. Mogensen, 'October 1943'; Yagil, Rescue of Danish Jewry, 276, suggests that there may have been as many as 30 suicides.

126. Gutman, *The Encyclopedia of the Righteous Europe (Part I) and other Countries,* li.

127. See for example, Emmy E. Werner, *A Conspiracy of Decency: The Rescue of Danish Jews during World War II* (Boulder CO: Westview, 2002), 68, 72, whose stories of the rescued often contain references to Germans 'looking the other way'.

128. Mogensen, 'October 1943', 53–5. The changed attitude of the Swedes to the admission of refugees was undoubtedly also critical.

129. Moland, 'The Norwegian Holocaust', 18–19.

CHAPTER 5

1. Adam Rayski, *The Choice of the Jews under Vichy,* 13. This came in the form of 26 laws, 24 decrees, six orders and one regulation.

2. Vicki Caron, 'The Path to Vichy', 3–4. Marrus and Paxton, *Vichy France and the Jews,* 29. Adler, *The Jews of Paris,* 4.

3. Caron, 'The Path to Vichy, 4, gives the figure as 2.7 million. See also Caron, *Uneasy Asylum,* 4.

4. Marrus and Paxton, *Vichy France and the Jews*, 34–5.

5. Caron, *Uneasy Asylum*, 2.

6. Marrus and Paxton, *Vichy France and the Jews*, 36.

7. Ibid. 44.

8. W. D. Halls, *Politics, Society and Christianity in Vichy France* (Oxford: Berg, 1995), 9–12.

9. Ibid. 97.

10. Ibid. 99, 106. He was also a friend of Heilbronner, the chairman of the Consistoire Israélite de France, with whom he had studied law.

11. Halls, *Politics, Society and Christianity*, 103.

12. Uta Gerdes, *Ökumenische Solidarität mit christlichen und jüdischen Verfolgten. Die CIMADE in Vichy-Frankreich 1940–1944* (Göttingen: Vandenhoeck und Ruprecht, 2005), 44. Lazare, *Le Livre des Justes*, 54. It consisted of about 2% of the French population, or about twice that of the Jewish population.

13. Halls, *Politics, Society and Christianity*, 11.

14. Halls, Ibid. 11, 13. Around 20% of these pastors were in Alsace, a region annexed by the Germans in 1940. Some smaller groups remained outside the Federation.

15. Lazare, *Le Livre des Justes*, 55. Its views were disseminated in the periodical, *Sully*.

16. Gerdes, *Ökumenische Solidarität*, 47. Halls, *Politics, Society and Christianity*, 49, 60, 69.

17. Halls, *Politics, Society and Christianity*, 72–3. Boegner sat on the commission concerned with youth.

18. Halls, *Politics, Society and Christianity*, 38.

19. Victoria Barnett, *For the Soul of the People: Protestant Protest against Hitler* (New York: Oxford University Press, 1992), 160.

20. Halls, *Politics, Society and Christianity*, 98.

21. Gerdes, *Ökumenische Solidarität*, 44–5.

22. Lazare, *Rescue as Resistance*, 26.

23. Ibid. 31.

24. Eugen Weber, 'Reflections on the Jews in France', in Frances Malino and Bernard Wasserstein (eds), *The Jews in Modern France* (Hanover NH: Brandeis University Press, 1985), 18–19. Adler, *The Jews of Paris*, 4–5. Paul Webster, *Pétain's Crime: The Full Story of French Collaboration in the Holocaust* (London: Macmillan, 1990), 28. It was estimated that anything up to 100,000 Jews had arrived from the East in the 1930s. Michel Abitbol, 'The Encounter between French Jewry and the Jews of North Africa: Analysis of a Discourse (1830–1914)', in Malino and Wasserstein (eds), *The Jews in Modern France*, 35–8.

25. Caron, *Uneasy Asylum,* 96. Webster, *Pétain's Crime,* 27, notes that the Paris Consistory had only 6,000 registered families.

26. Originally founded as the Comité d'Aide et d'Acceuil aux Victimes de l' Antisemitisme en Allemagne, it was soon renamed and reorganized as the Comité Nationale Français de Secours aux Réfugiés Allemands. Caron, *Uneasy Asylum,* 22, 96–7. The de Rothschilds alone contributed one-third of the Committee's funds in 1933, but many patriotic elements within middle-class French Jewry were reluctant to provide money for Germans, and rich German Jewish refugees already in France were also castigated for not providing more assistance.

27. Webster, *Pétain's Crime,* 28.

28. Martin, 'Ce qui se passé chez nous: Les Emigrés d'Allemagne en France et la question juive', *La Terre Retrouvée,* 25 March 1936, 10 cited in Caron, *Uneasy Asylum,* 99.

29. Ernest Ginsberger, 'Tribune des lecteurs', *Univers israélite,* 3 November 1933, 218–219, cited in Caron, *Uneasy Asylum,* 99.

30. Lucien Lazare, *Rescue as Resistance,* 17–18. Camille Ménager, 'Le Sauvetage des Juifs à Paris 1940–1945 Histoire et mémoire' (Unpublished Masters Thesis, Institut d'Études Politiques de Paris, 2005), 7 cites David Weinberg, *Les Juifs à Paris de 1933 à 1939* (Paris: Calman-Levy, 1974), 8.

31. Adler, *The Jews of Paris,* 33.

32. Ménager, 'Le Sauvetage des Juifs', 7.

33. Adler, *The Jews of Paris,* 33. This included the Alliance Israélite Universelle, the Comité de Bienfaisance and the Fédération des Sociétés as well as the Consistory itself. Yagil, *Chrétiens et Juifs,* 511. Rayski, *The Choice of the Jews,* 17–19.

34. Ibid. 28.

35. Béatrice le Douairon, 'Le Comité "Rue Amelot"', 1940–1944 à Paris. Assistance aux Juifs et Sauvetage des Enfants' (Maitrise, Paris 1—Sorbonne, 1994), 1–2, 8.

36. Le Douairon, 'Le Comité "Rue Amelot"', 10, 25.

37. The Colonie Scolaire had been founded in 1926 to provide medical help for Jewish children and also specialized in sending city children to the seaside for holidays. The FSJF had also been founded in 1926 and had united a plethora of institutions and associations that served the foreign Jewish community.

38. Le Douairon, 'Le Comité "Rue Amelot"', 10.

39. Lazare, *Rescue as Resistance,* 48, 259. This was done on the orders of Joseph Schwartz, the AJDC's European Director.

40. Le Douairon, 'Le Comité "Rue Amelot"', 15–16.

41. Adler, *The Jews of Paris*, 38.Rayski, *The Choice of the Jews*, 43–4. Le Douairon, 'Le Comité "Rue Amelot", 27–8.

42. Adler, *The Jews of Paris*, 175–6.

43. Ibid. 178.

44. Rayski, *The Choice of the Jews*, 49–51.

45. Ibid. 55.

46. Le Douairon, 'Le Comité "Rue Amelot"', 39–44.

47. For a detailed history of the UGIF, see Adler, *The Jews of Paris*, chapters 5 to 7, 81–161.

48. Rayski, *The Choice of the Jews*, 58–9.

49. Le Douairon, 'Le Comité "Rue Amelot"', 51, 64.

50. Asher Cohen, 'Rescuing Jews: Jews and Christians in Vichy France', *British Journal of Holocaust Education* III/1 (1994), 8–9.

51. Gerdes, *Ökumenische Solidarität*, 52–3.Yagil, *Chrétiens et Juifs*, 113. Halls, *Politics, Society and Christianity*, 102.

52. Madeleine Barot, 'La Cimade: une présence, une communauté, une action', in Emile C. Fabre et al. (eds), *Les Clandestins de Dieu: CIMADE 1938–1945* (Paris: Fayard, 1968), 28.

53. Ménager, 'Le Sauvetage des Juifs', 33–4. Around 92,600 stars were actually issued for 46,542 French adult Jews, 15,322 children, 46,322 Foreign adult Jews and 2,106 children. The reason for the discrepancy in the numbers of children was due to French-born children to foreign parents.

54. On Père Victor Dillard, see Charles Molette, *Prêtres, Religieux et Religieuses dans la Résistance au Nazisme, 1940–1945* (Paris: Fayard, 1995), 42.

55. Rayski, *The Choice of the Jews*, 75–6.

56. Ibid. 78.

57. Adler, *The Jews of Paris*, 123.

58. Ménager, 'Le Sauvetage des Juifs', 60, argues that the perception of the danger was clear among the immigrant groups but only spread to the French Jews after the Vel d'Hiv round-ups.

59. Adler, *The Jews of Paris*, 193.

60. Ibid. 194 cites *Dos Vort fun Vidershtant un Zieg*, a collection of illegal Yiddish publications 1940–1944, Mimeographed (Paris: Centre de Documentation de l'Union des Juifs pour la Résistance et l'Entre'aide, 1949), 105–6.

61. Jacqueline Baldran, and Claude Bochurberg, *David Rapoport* (Paris: Montorguiel, 1994), 192–3, 213–217. The precise nature of the denunciation and arrest remain unclear, not least since the Paris police prefecture destroyed much of its archives on Jewish affairs in 1948–9. Le Douairon, 'Le Comité "Rue Amelot"', 77.

62. Baldran and Bochurberg, *David Rapoport*, 200–1. Le Douairon, 'Le Comité "Rue Amelot" ', 81–2. This was expedited by Juliette Stern (WIZO) at the rue Bienfaisance which had escaped the attentions of Gestapo and CGQJ agents.

63. The organization and operations of the EIF deserve much wider study. See CDJC CCXVII-9, 'Rapport sur l'activité des mouvement EIF de 1939 au lendemain de la libération'. This suggests it had *c.*700 Scouts in the Seine region, *c.*200 in Lyon/Marseilles, 300–400 in Alsace-Lorraine and 500–600 in North Africa, see above, 3.

64. Ménager, 'Le Sauvetage des Juifs à Paris', 156–7, 159, 202, cites the memoirs of Emmanuel Lefschetz, Weill family archive.

65. Ménager, 'Le Sauvetage des Juifs à Paris', 162–3.

66. Ibid. 165.

67. Rayski, *The Choice of the Jews*, 90.

68. Limore Yagil, *Chrétiens et Juifs*, 533–4.

69. Ménager, 'Le Sauvetage des Juifs à Paris', 72–4, cites Albert Grunberg, *Journal d'un coiffeur juif à Paris sous l'Occupation* (Paris: Les Éditions de l'Atelier, 2001), 75, 136, 326, 328.

70. See, for example, Frenk, 'Righteous among the Nations', 34.

71. YV M31/3125 Marie Chotel and Henri Briard. Testimony of Berthe Miller (Melszpajz), 29 November 1984 suggests that she had been involved in the resistance even before the raid on her apartment, as had Chotel.

72. See YV M31/5063 (Raffin) Lazare, *Dictionnaire des Justes de France*, 172–3. Odette Meyers, *Doors to Madame Marie* (Washington: University of Washington, 1998), 88–93, and YV M31/3125 Marie Chotel and Henri Briard. Testimony of Odette Meyers, 1978 suggests that this was not an isolated example and that both were also more involved in resistance activity, noting that their apartment was 'a headquarter for transmitting messages and mails for Jews and Resistants. Idem. Testimony of George Miller (Melszpajz), 29 November 1984 that confirms that these parcels saved his life.

73. Ménager, 'Le Sauvetage des Juifs à Paris', 102, cites examples of other concierges, all women, who provided help in this way. For a similar example of a male concierge hiding his tenants see, YV M31/1027 Henri Roser.

74. Ménager, 'Le Sauvetage des Juifs à Paris', 103. Lazare, *Righteous among the Nations: France*, 373 cites one example of a family who had hidden in their attic but been driven out by the concierge. See also, Sutters, *Archives of the Holocaust. Vol. 2 Pt.2, American Friends Service Committee, Philadephia 1940–1945* (New York: Garland, 1990), 345. Elizabeth E. Blenke, Report of Nazi-Europe Information, 1 October 1942, 3, notes rumours that 'janitors

have informed the authorities where Jews have hidden themselves or where they have stored some valuables'.

75. Lazare, *Righteous among the Nations: France*, 433–4.

76. Ibid. 376. Marsat was managing director of a large metals company and honorary president of Gaz de France—a public utility.

77. YV M31/6793 (Marsat).

78. YV M31/6793. Marsat. Testimony of Suzanne Topeza-Gryntuch, 29 March 1994.

79. YV M31/6956 (Thibout).

80. Yagil, *Chrétiens et Juifs*, 535–6. Ménager, 'Le Sauvetage des Juifs à Paris', 122.

81. Ménager, 'Le Sauvetage des Juifs à Paris', 119. See also, Lazare, *Rescue as Resistance*.

82. Ménager, 'Le Sauvetage des Juifs à Paris', 107.

83. Ibid. 105.

84. Rayski, *The Choice of the Jews*, 95. The organization paid between Ffr.600 and Ffr.700 per month for the upkeep of each child.

85. Rayski, *The Choice of the Jews*, 92–3, cites written testimonies, Paris 1964 CDJC DLXXVII—7b and 7c.

86. Ménager, 'Le Sauvetage des Juifs à Paris', 72, cites a report from the Joint 'Situation au 25 août 1942', CDJC XCVI-31, 25 August 1942.

87. Rayski, *The Choice of the Jews*, 98.

88. Ibid. 99, cites Henri Michel, Jerusalem, April 1968.

89. Ménager, 'Le Sauvetage des Juifs à Paris', 120–1.

90. Beate Kosmala, 'Verbotene Hilfe: Rettung für Juden in Deutschland, 1941–1945', cited in Ménager, 'Le Sauvetage des Juifs à Paris', 121.

91. Ménager, 'Le Sauvetage des Juifs à Paris', 121.

92. See in this context, Yehuda Bauer, *A History of the Holocaust* (Danbury CT: Franklin Watts, 1982), 305, 313.

93. Yagil, *Chrétiens et Juifs*, 518–21. Michèle Cointet, *L'Eglise sous Vichy*, 293–8.

94. Madeleine Comte, *Sauvetages et baptêmes. Les religieuses de Notre-Dame de Sion face à la persecution des juifs en France (1940–1944)* (Paris: l'Harmattan, 2001), 87.

95. YV M31/7245 (Devaux).

96. Comte, *Sauvetages et baptêmes*, 63.

97. YV M31/1770 Pierre Chaillet. *Cahiers du Témoignage Chrétien* and its successor *Courrier français du témoignage chrétien* issued between spring 1943 and the liberation had a circulation of close to 100,000. *La Croix*, 24 May 2000.

98. Lazare, *Righteous among the Nations: France*, 132–3.

99. YV M31/5891 (Chevalley-Sabatier).

100. L'Entraide Temporaire. Sauvetage d'Enfants Juifs sous l'Occupation', 3. Ménager, 'Le Sauvetage des Juifs à Paris', 168.

101. Ménager, 'Le Sauvetage des Juifs à Paris', 166. Yagil, *Chrétiens et Juifs*, 531–2.

102. 'L'Entraide Temporaire', 1 (1984) records the case of Mme Burstein *orienteuse professionelle* and the wife of a psychiatrist who had lost her job on account of the racial laws.

103. 'L'Entraide Temporaire', 4.

104. Paul Vergara, *Le Pasteur Paul Vergara* (Nancy: Berger-Levrault, 1966), 7.

105. YV M31/62 (Spaak). Ménager, 'Le Sauvetage des Juifs à Paris', 170. Yagil, *Chrétiens et Juifs*, 528–9.

106. YV M31/1027 (Roser). Yagil, *Chrétiens et Juifs*, 529–30.

107. Yagil, *Chrétiens et Juifs sous Vichy*, 529 As a organization begun in Britain, the Salvation Army was particularly suspect by the Germans and Vichy who regarded it as a potential refuge for Gaullists.

108. Yagil, *Chrétiens et Juifs*, 526.

109. Ménager, 'Le Sauvetage des Juifs à Paris', 174, points out that an edition of *France Libre* of 27 September 1942 carried a story that anyone harbouring foreign Jews who had been called up and were being sought by the police would be given 2–5 months in prison, but there is no other evidence for the existence of such a law.

110. Yagil, *Chrétiens et Juifs*, 552. A term used in a radio broadcast by Maurice Schumann to discriminate between country priests and urban priests (*soutanes noires*).

111. Molette, *Prêtres, Religieux et Religieuses*, 78.

CHAPTER 6

1. Lazare, *Rescue as Resistance*, 90–1.

2. Ibid. 49–50, 91.

3. Ibid. 92, cites Nina Gourfinkel, *L'Autre Patrie* (Paris: Editions du Seuil, 1953), 210, 222, 225.

4. Lemalet, *Au secours des enfants du siècle*, 61. Provision of food was also divided, with the Quakers responsible for rice and dry vegetables, the Secours Suisse for milk and the OSE for flour, fresh vegetables, jams, and fruit.

5. Lazare, *Rescue as Resistance*, 92.

6. Ibid. 94–5.

7. YV M31/3830 (Barot). Lazare, *Le Livre des Justes*, 53. Barot, 'La Cimade', 28–9.

8. Barot, 'La Cimade', 30–31.

9. Raphaël Delpard, *Les Enfants Cachés* (Paris: JC Lattès, 1993), 158–60.

10. Raphaël Delpard, 159–160.

11. Lazare, *Le Livre des Justes*, 54.

12. Delpard, *Les Enfants Cachés*, 160. Princess Bernadotte of Sweden was a friend of Madeleine Barot and a director of the International Committee of the Red Cross who spent a day at the camp at Gurs.

13. Delpard, *Les Enfants Cachés*, 156. Madeleine Barot was a brilliant intellectual and had been archivist at the École Française before Italy joined the war and had then returned to France penniless. A meeting with Pastor Boegner brought her to Nîmes at the beginning of September 1940.

14. Delpard, *Les Enfants Cachés*, 157. This stipulated that Vichy would hand over to the Germans any individuals wanted by Berlin.

15. YV M31/3369 Henri Manen. See his account 'Au fond de l'abime'.

16. YV M31/3369 Henri Manen. Henri Manen, 'Diary Notes from the Milles Camp', in D'Aubigné and Mouchon, *God's Underground*, 111. Rayski, *The Choice of the Jews*, 108–9. The children were placed in the care of Pastor Marc Donadille in the Cevennes.

17. Lazare, *Le Livre des Justes*, 72–3.

18. Barot, 'La Cimade', 34–5. Delpard, *Les Enfants Cachés*, 156.

19. Delpard, *Les Enfants Cachés*, 161–2.

20. YV M31/2698 (Boegner). Rayski, *The Choice of the Jews*, 115.

21. Adolf Freudenberg, 'Au-delà des frontiers: L'action du Conseil œcuménique des Églises' in: D'Aubigné et al. (eds), *Les Clandestins de Dieu*, 41.

22. Ibid. 45, 57. Delpard, *Les Enfants Cachés*, 162.

23. Barot, 'La Cimade', 37.

24. Freudenberg, 'Au-delà des frontiers', 48–9. See also Lazare, *Rescue as Resistance*, 27.

25. André Morel, 'The Witness to the Drama Speaks', in D'Aubigné and Mouchon, *God's Underground*, 181–2.

26. YV M31/4872 Camille Folliet, Testimony of Herbert Herz, 2 June 1990.

27. Cohen, *Persécutions et sauvetages*, 441. Lazare, *Le Livre des Justes*, 96–7, 101. Suzanne Loiseau-Chevalley, 'Sur la frontière', in D'Aubigné et al. (eds), *Les Clandestins de Dieu*, 148. Molette, *Prêtres, Religieux et Religieuses*, 83. *Le Courrier Savoyard*, 16 March 1990, 20. YV M31/4845b (Rosay). Lazare, *Righteous among the Nations: France*, 242, 480.

28. Lazare, *Le Livre des Justes*, 97–8.

29. Ibid. 101.

30. Molette, *Prêtres, Religieux et Religieuses*, 83.

31. Geneviève Priacel-Pittet, 'Passages de frontières' in: D'Aubigné et al. (eds), *Les Clandestins de Dieu*, 116–117.

32. Ibid. 121.

33. Marthe Besag et al., 'The Victims of the Drama Speak', in D'Aubigné and Mouchon, *God's Underground*, 189.

34. Lazare, *Righteous among the Nations: France*, 439.

35. E. C. Fabre, 'A la recherché de l'équipe qui ne revient pas', in D'Aubigné et al. (eds), *Les Clandestins de Dieu*, 173.

36. E. C. Fabre, 'The Search for the Team That Did Not Return', in D'Aubigné and Mouchon, *God's Underground*, 179.

37. Delpard, *Les enfants cachés*, 181–2.

38. Priacel-Pittet, 'Passages de frontières', 119–120.

39. Delpard, *Les enfants cachés*, 184–5.

40. Lazare, *Le Livre des Justes*, 94.

41. Ibid. 94–5.

42. Ibid. 102.

43. Cohen, *Persécutions et sauvetages*, 442.

44. YV M31/4872 (Folliet). Priacel-Pittet, 'Passages de frontières', 119.

45. Priacel-Pittet, 'Passages de frontières', 120.

46. E. C. Fabre, 'Order out of Disorder', in D'Aubigné and Mouchon, *God's Underground*, 168–9.

47. Priacel-Pittet, 'Passages de frontières', 118–119.

48. Suzanne Loiseau-Chevalley, 'Brens: de la cellule vide aux cris des enfants', in D'Aubigné et al. (eds), *Les Clandestins de Dieu*, 148–9.

49. Loiseau-Chevalley, 'Sur la frontière', 152–3. Lazare, *Le Livre des Justes*, 100.

50. Loiseau-Chevalley, 'Sur la frontière', 134.

51. Priacel-Pittet, 'Passages de frontières' 121. This was autobiographical.

52. Adolf Freudenberg, 'Across the Border: The Activities of the World Council of Churches', in D'Aubigné and Mouchon, *God's Underground*, 46. Loiseau-Chevalley, 'Sur la frontière', 147–8. Delpard, *Les Enfants Cachés*, 162. Lazare, *Le Livre des Justes*, 82, 99. She was replaced by Suzanne Loiseau-Chevalley.

53. YV M31/1026 (Philip).

54. André Morel, 'The Witness to the Drama Speaks', 184. Lazare, *Righteous among the Nations: France*, 402, suggests that Morel was fined Fr.1000 by the French authorities for smuggling Jews into Switzerland and this substantial fine was actually paid by local Jews.

55. E. C. Fabre, '. . . And the Children of the Dead', D'Aubigné and Mouchon, *God's Underground*, 187.

56. E. C. Fabre, 'The Bridge of Manne-en-Royans', in D'Aubigné and Mouchon, *God's Underground*, 165.

57. The upright citizens included Charles Guillon, the mayor of Le Chambon-sur-Lignon, who was a member of the World Committee of the YMCA and thus had a legitimate reason for travelling to and from Switzerland.

58. Jan Sigurd Kulok, 'Trait d'Union: The History of the French Relief Organisation *Secours national/Entr'aide française* under the Third Republic, the Vichy regime and the early Fourth Republic, 1939–1949' (Unpublished Oxford DPhil, 2002), 208–212.

59. Frenk, Righteous among the Nations', 68–9.

60. Francis R. Nicosia (ed.), *Archives of the Holocaust. Vol. 4 Central Zionist Archives 1939–1945* (New York: Garland, 1990), 161–6 shows that these pastoral letters were widely distributed and known outside France. Rayski, *The Choice of the Jews*, 118–119.

61. Frenk, ' Righteous among the Nations', 55.

62. Sutters, *American Friends* Vol. 2 Part.2, 367. AFSC Lisbon, Confidential Memorandum, 19 September 1942, 3.

63. YV M31/7529 Pierre and Henriette Ogier. Testimony of Maurice Ogier, 16 August 1996. Like many others, her poor French accent was explained by her being from Alsace. Lazare, *Righteous among the Nations: France*, 289–290, 413–414.

64. Pierre Mathieu, 'Des chrétiens au secours des Juifs dans le Tarn de 1942 à 1944: Des catholiques face au drame des Juifs', in Jacques Fijalkow (ed.), *Vichy, Les Juifs et les Justes: L'exemple du Tarn* (Toulouse: Privat, 2003), 237–42. The seminary at Pratlong near Vabre (Tarn) also became a centre for a local Jewish *maquis* and played host to young men avoiding the STO and to evaders and escaped prisoners of war.

65. Mathieu, 'Des chrétiens au secours des Juifs dans le Tarn', 251.

66. Lazare, *Dictionnaire des Justes*, 397.

67. FSC/AFSC/10 (1939) Sturge (FSC) to Jones (AFSC), 23 September 1939.

68. FSC/FSC/F/4 Religious Society of Friends, XVth Annual Assembly, General Report 1938–1939, 7. Roger C. Wilson, *Quaker Relief: An Account of the Relief Work of the Society of Friends* (London: Allen and Unwin, 1952), 127.

69. FSC/FSC/F/4 Henry van (Centre Quaker, Paris) to Sturge, 12 September 1939.

70. FSC/FSC/F/4 Henry van Etten to Sturge, 29 September 1939.

71. FSC/FSC/F/4 Henry van Etten to Mary Hoxie Jones (AFSC), 12 October 1939.

72. FSC/FSC/F/4 Marguerite Czarnecki to Edith Pye and Fred Tritton (FSC) 2 November 1939. FSC/FSC/F/4 Report of Visit to Two Refugee Camps, Helen Kirkwood, 11 December 1939.

73. FSC/FSC/F/4 Helen Kirkwood (Delegate of the FSC in Paris) to Jones (AFSC), 10 January 1940, Kirkwood to Tritton, 25 January 1940.

74. FSC/FSC/F/4 Helen Kirkwood (Centre Quaker, Paris) to Tritton (FSC), 10 November 1939; Kirkwood to Tritton, 19 November 1939. FSC/FSC/F/4

Report 'Changes in the Conditions in the Refugee Internment Camps', Helen Kirkwood, 30 January 1940.

75. *L'action du Secours Quaker*, 5. Philip Hallie, *Lest Innocent Blood be Shed*, (London: Michael Joseph, 1979), 130.

76. FSC/FSC/F/4 Religious Society of Friends, XVth Annual Assembly, General Report 1938–1939, 7.

77. FSC/AFSC/11 (1941–44) Jones (AFSC) to Sturge (FSC), 5 December 1941 indicated this was still continuing in Paris on a small scale—with visits to families as well as prisoners. See also *L'action du Secours Quaker*, 10–12.

78. FSC/FSC/F/4 Paris Quaker Centre, General Report, June-November 1940, Henry van Etten, 4 November 1940.

79. Wilson, *Quaker Relief*, 127. At least one, Mary Elmes, who had an Irish passport decided to stay on. FSC/FSC/R/SP/3/4 Emily Hughes (FSC) to Mrs E. T. Elmes, 3 July 1940.

80. See, for example, FSC/AFSC/10 (1940–41) F. J. Tritton (FSC) to Pickett (AFSC), 5 August 1940. See also Lawson to Jones, 25 September 1941 suggesting that some progress was finally being made with the British authorities.

81. FSC/AFSC/11 (1940–41) Howard E. Kershner, 'AFSC in France', 1–2.

82. *L'action du Secours Quaker*, 5. FSC/AFSC/11 (1940–41) Extract of letter from Margaret E. Jones to Bertha Bracey (GEC), 25 September 1941.

83. Hallie, *Lest Innocent Blood be Shed*, 135–7.

84. CDJC CMXXI-12 Meeting at AFSC Marseilles, 27 October 1942. FSC/AFSC/10 (1940–41) Bracey and others to Pickett, 8 December 1941.

85. FSC/AFSC/11 (1941–44) Jones (AFSC) to Sturge (FSC), 13 January 1942 and 10 June 1942. By this stage the Kershners had returned to the US, and the personnel in Marseilles had been entirely changed. No mention of other centres in France FSC/AFSC/11 (1941–44) 'Delegates to Europe—Their Families', 11 July 1942.

86. Wilson, *Quaker Relief*, 128. FSC/AFSC/11 (1941–44) Pickett (AFSC) to Sturge (FSC), 21 November 1944.

87. USHMM YIVO-UGIF RG43.005M Roll 74.98.7 Secours Quaker to UGIF Direction Santé, Marseille, 27 January, 22 July 1943.

88. Rayski, *The Choice of the Jews*, 112.

89. FSC/FSC/F/4 Société Religieuse des Amis, General report 1940–1944, 5.

90. FSC/FSC/F/4 Notes on a talk with Clarence E. Pickett by Tritton, 6 December 1944. Noted 60,000 Jews in Paris of whom 35,000 needed relief. Synagogues turned into reception centres.

91. FSC/AFSC/11 (1940–41) Fred J. Tritton to Dorothy Bonnell (AFSC Marseilles) 5 September 1941.

92. FSC/FSC/F/4 Van Etten to Lawson (FSC), 5 January 1940. Van Etten was a member of the Paris Committee of the International Quaker Commission.

93. Lazare, *Le Livre des Justes*, 59–61.

94. Ibid. 62–3.

95. Hallie, *Lest Innocent Blood be Shed*, 4.

96. Ibid. 46. He explicitly raises the question of why nothing was done in the nearby and equally Protestant village of Le Mazet.

97. Lazare, *Le Livre des Justes*, 55–6.

98. Hallie, *Lest Innocent Blood be Shed*, 82

99. Ibid. 144. In 1939 Trocmé had submitted his resignation to the commune and to the Reformed Church because it regarded his conscientious objection to violence as damaging to the Church. While the Church accepted his resignation, the commune did not and he continued his ministry.

100. Hallie, *Lest Innocent Blood be Shed*, 17, 173.

101. Ibid. 89, 93, 95.

102. Ibid. 129–138.

103. Ibid. 167–8.

104. Ibid. 168, 173.

105. Ibid. 176.

106. Ibid. 178, 185. Unusually in this community, Mme Eyraud had been raised as a Catholic but claimed not to have a religious affiliation.

107. Hallie, *Lest Innocent Blood be Shed*, 150–2.

108. Ibid. 186.

109. Ibid. 174, 184.

110. Ibid. 142–3.

111. CDJC DCXI-98 Collection Anny Latour, Témoignage de Trocmé, 7. Hallie, *Lest Innocent Blood be Shed*, 196.

112. Hallie, *Lest Innocent Blood be Shed*, 198–9.

113. Lazare, *Le Livre des Justes*, 58–9.

114. David Klugman, *The Conspiracy of the Righteous. The Silence of the Village of Prélenfrey-du-Guâ Saved Jewish Children and Adults in 1944* (Nîmes: C. Lacour, 1994) 56.

115. Ibid. 66.

116. See also, Lazare, *Righteous among the Nations: France*, 288–9. Yagil, *Chrétiens et Juifs*, 207–8.

117. Pouplain, *Les Enfants Cachés de la Résistance* (La Crèche: Geste,1998), 33–4. The letter was intercepted and handed to the pastor on the day of the liberation.

118. Pouplain, *Les Enfants Cachés*, 34–5.

119. Besag et al., 'The Victims of the Drama Speak', 189.

120. Sandrine Suchon, 'Dieulefit 1940–1944. Résistance et Liberté' (Grenoble, 1989), 10–12.

121. Ibid. 26.

122. Ibid. 28.

123. Ibid. 36–7.

124. Denise Levy, 'Les EI et la Sixième en Zone Sud pendant la guerre', *Revue d'histoire de la Shoah*, No.161 Sept–Dec 1997, 67–72, here 68.

125. J. P. Richardot, *Le peuple protestant français aujourd'hui* (Paris: Laffont, 1980), 131. Suchon, 'Dieulefit 1940–1944', 42. Lazare, *Righteous among the Nations: France*, 56.

126. Suchon, 'Dieulefit 1940–1944', 46.

127. Ibid. 65–6.

128. Ibid. 101.

129. Ibid. 74.

130. Ibid. 118–120.

131. François Boulet, 'Les juifs en Isère, Savoie et Haute-Savoie (1940–1944): De la touristophobie aux montagnes-refugies', *Revue d'Histoire de la Shoah*, 172 (May–Aug 2001), 184–6.

132. Lucien Lazare, Les Justes dans le Tarn', in Jacques Fijalkow (ed.), *Vichy, Les Juifs et les Justes: L'exemple du Tarn* (Toulouse: Privat, 2003), 211.

133. Leon Poliakov and Jacques Sabille, *Jews under the Italian Occupation* (Paris: Éditions du Centre, 1955), 21–3.

134. CDJC CCXVIII-66. Angelo Donati, 1. Yagil, *Chrétiens et Juifs*, 193, 274 David Konopnicki, 'Le Reseau Abadi: Histoire d'un réseau de sauvetage d'enfants dans les Alpes-Maritimes Durant la Seconde Guerre Mondiale' (Université Pierre Mendes-France, Grenoble, 2001), 77–8

135. Poliakov and Sabille, *Jews under the Italian Occupation*, 26.

136. CDJC CCXVIII-66. Angelo Donati, 1.

137. Yagil, *Chrétiens et Juifs*, 257.

138. Poliakov and Sabille, *Jews under the Italian Occupation*, 35.

139. Jean-Louis Panicacci, 'Les juifs et la Question juive dans les Alpes-Maritimes de 1939 à 1945' *Bulletin Trimestral ADAM* (1983), 262–3, cites P. Erlanger, *La Frances sans étoile*: Souvenir de l'avant guerre et du temps de l'occupation (Paris: Plon, 1974), 256.

140. CDJC CCXVIII-66. Angelo Donati, 2–3. Poliakov and Sabille, *Jews under the Italian Occupation*, 28.

141. Poliakov and Sabille, *Jews under the Italian Occupation*, 30,31,144. Circular from Chaigneau to Divisional Commissioner Chief of the Regional Office for Public Security, Nice, 23 July 1943. He was also later to frustrate the Germans by denying them access to official records of the Jews in his area.

Konopnicki, 'Le Reseau Abadi', 80, Chaigneau was later deported by the Germans for his contacts with the resistance.

142. Poliakov and Sabille, *Jews under the Italian Occupation*, 39–42. Gitta Amipaz-Silber, *Sephardi Jews in Occupied France: Under the Tyrant's Heel, 1940–1945* (Jerusalem: Rubin Mass, 1995), 327–332.

143. Lazare, *Righteous among the Nations: France*, 69–70.

144. Poliakov and Sabille, *Jews under the Italian Occupation*, 28.

145. Cohen, *Persécutions et sauvetages*, 452.

146. For a detailed description of their escape into Italy, see Alberto Cavaglion, *Les Juifs de St-Martin-Vésubie, Septembre–Novembre 1943* (Nice: Serre, 1995), 55–71. Cohen, *Persécutions et sauvetages*, 454–5.

147. Cohen, *Persécutions et sauvetages*, 455–6.

148. Ibid. 456–7, cites Leon Poliakov, *L'Auberge des musiciens*, 128–135.

149. Amipaz-Silber, *Sephardi Jews in Occupied France*, 332–3. Cohen, *Persécutions et sauvetages*, 458.

150. Konopnicki, 'Le Reseau Abadi', 87–9

151. Cohen, *Persécutions et sauvetages*, 392.

152. Konopnicki, 'Le Reseau Abadi', 92.

153. Ibid. 94.

154. Abadi had to some extent based the organization of his network on that of Garel. Konopnicki, 'Le Reseau Abadi', 97.

155. CDJC CCXVIII-106 cited in Kieval, 'From Social Work to Resistance', 76.

156. Cohen, *Persécutions et sauvetages*, 200, 459. On this controversy, see also Panicacci, 'Les Juifs et la Question juive dans les Alpes-Maritimes', 254, and Ralph Schor, *Monseigneur Paul Rémond, un évêque dans le siècle* (Nice: Serre, 1984), 117–122.

157. Konopnicki, 'Le Reseau Abadi', 112.

158. Ibid. 126–7.

159. Ibid. 128.

160. Ibid. 141–2.

161. They included a number of Austrians and at least two white Russians, Mojaroff and Karakaieff, who operated as 'veritable Jew hunters'. Konopnicki, 'Le Reseau Abadi', 104–105.

162. Konopnicki, 'Le Reseau Abadi', 108. This was also true of Lo Spinoso who destroyed records before escaping from the Nazis.

163. Konopnicki, 'Le Reseau Abadi', 136.

164. Cohen, *Persécutions et sauvetages*, 461.

165. Amipaz-Silber, *Sephardi Jews in Occupied France*, 261–3.

166. Amipaz-Silber, *Sephardi Jews in Occupied France*, 264–5.

167. Amipaz-Silber, *Sephardi Jews in Occupied France*, 290. See also Henri Amour-eux, *La vie des Français sous l'Occupation* (Paris, 1961), 416–417, and Claude Lévy and Paul Tillard, *La Grande rafle du Vel d'Hiv* (Paris: Laffont, 1967), 227, from where this story is taken. The professor was paid FFr.1m for his work.

168. Amipaz-Silber, *Sephardi Jews in Occupied France*, 272.

169. Ibid. 276–7.

170. Ibid. 281–2. Three were released almost immediately but a fourth remained in captivity for six months and was only released after a visit to the Gestapo.

171. Amipaz-Silber, *Sephardi Jews in Occupied France*, 289–290.

172. Patrick Cabanel, 'Des justes catholiques et protestants: un essai d'approche comparée', in Jacques Fijalkow (ed.), *Vichy, Les Juifs et les Justes: L'exemple du Tarn* (Toulouse: Privat, 2003), 199–200.

173. Sutters, *American Friends*, Vol. 2 Part 2, 365. AFSC Lisbon, Confidential Memorandum, 19 September 1942, 1.

174. Cabanel, 'Des justes', 198–200, 202–3.

175. Ibid. 203.

176. Eliot Nidam Orvieto, 'Catholic Religious and the Hiding of Jewish Children within their Convents and Institutions in France' (MA, Hebrew University of Jerusalem, 2002), 17–21

177. Georges Casalis, 'At the Side of the Road', in D'Aubigné and Mouchon, *God's Underground*, 205–6.

178. Barot, 'La Cimade', 38.

CHAPTER 7

1. The most important works that deal with the subject are Dan Michman (ed.), *Belgium and the Holocaust: Jews, Belgians, Germans*, (Jerusalem: Yad Vashem, 1998), Brachfeld, *Ze hebben het overleefd* (Brussel: VUB, 1997), Viviane Teitelbaum-Hirsch, *Enfants cachés: Les larmes sous le masque* (Bruxelles: Labor, 1994) and, Suzanne Vromen, *Hidden Children of the Holocaust: Belgian Nuns and their Daring Rescue of Young Jews from the Nazis* (New York: Oxford, 2008).

2. Jan de Volder and Lieve Wouters, *Van binnen weent mijn hart: De vervolging van de Antwerpse joden* (Brussel: Standaard, 1999), 72–3.

3. Caestecker, *Ongewenste Gasten*, 147.

4. Van Doorslaer, 'Jewish Immigration and Communism in Belgium', in Dan Michman, (ed.), *Belgium and the Holocaust: Jews Belgians Germans* (Jerusalem: Yad Vashem, 1998), 68–81, also suggests that the trade unions opposed the Jewish workers because they were communists, and sought to exclude

them from leading positions. Policies towards diamond workers also alienated many. Frank Caestecker, *Alien Policy in Belgium, 1840–1940. The Creation of Guest Workers, Refugees and Illegal Aliens,* (New York/Oxford: Berghahn, 2000), 210–213. Caestecker, *Ongewenste Gasten,* 149–160.

5. In Antwerp 52.9%, in Brussels 40.0%, in Liège 3.1%, and the remaining 4% spread across the rest of the country. For a complete breakdown, see Steinberg, *Le Comité de Défense des Juifs,* 32.

6. Van Doorslaer, 'Jewish Immigration and Communism in Belgium', 75.

7. Ibid.76 also suggests that the trade unions opposed the Jewish workers because they were communists, and sought to exclude them from leading positions. Policies towards diamond workers also alienated many, see 78–9.

8. Van Doorslaer, 'Jewish Immigration and Communism in Belgium', 80–81.

9. Saerens, *Vreemdelingen in een Wereldstad,* 547.

10. Ibid. 551. Some still had papers from their former domiciles but others had been rendered stateless. The small number of Germans was a result of many German Jews already having left or been moved from the city.

11. Saerens, *Vreemdelingen in een Wereldstad,* 552.

12. Frank Caestecker, 'The Reintegration of Jewish Survivors into Belgian Society, 1943–1947', in David Bankier, *The Jews are Coming Back: The Return of the Jews to their Countries of Origin after World War II* (New York/Jerusalem: Berghahn/Yad Vashem, 2005), 73–4. Rosengarten, *Survival,* 20–1.

13. Lieven Saerens, 'Antwerp's Attitude to the Jews', 159–198, here 161, cites W. E. Coolen, *Israël, Mon Voisin* (Brussels, 1938) 71.

14. Saerens, 'Antwerp's Attitude to the Jews', 160–2.

15. Ibid. 166–188. Saerens, 'Die Hilfe für Juden', 196–7.

16. The first political organization to be based exclusively on adherence to antisemitism.

17. Saerens, 'Antwerp's Attitude to the Jews', 187–8, cites *Gazet van Antwerpen.*

18. In the French-speaking areas the *Ligue pour combattre l'Anti-Semitisme* included both Jews and non-Jews, while the *Comité de Vigilance des Intellectuels Antifascistes* was essentially communist.

19. Saerens, 'Antwerp's Attitude to the Jews', 182.

20. Lieven Saerens, 'The Attitude of the Belgian Roman Catholic Clergy', 117.

21. Saerens, 'Die Hilfe für Juden', 199.

22. Saerens, 'The Attitude of the Belgian Roman Catholic Clergy', 134–7.

23. Ibid. 142–4.

24. Ibid. 142–7, especially 147. Saerens, 'Die Hilfe für Juden', 200. See also, Lieven Saerens, 'Het Katholiek Bureau voor Israel (1936–1938), *Onze Alma Mater* XL/1 (1986), 67–87. Saerens, 'Antwerp's Attitude to the Jews', 181–2.

25. Saerens, 'Die Hilfe für Juden', 197–8.

26. Saerens, 'Het Katholiek Bureau voor Israel', 81–6.

27. Saerens, 'The Attitude of the Belgian Roman Catholic Clergy', 153.

28. See especially his pastoral letter of 2 June 1940. Reprinted in Emile Cammaerts, *The Prisoner at Laeken* (London: Cresset, 1941), 267–8. See also Roger Keyes, *Outrageous Fortune: The Tragedy of Leopold III of the Belgians, 1901–1941* (London: Secker and Warburg, 1984) 464.

29. Cardinal Désiré Joseph Mercier was very much a war hero, but during the Peace Negotiations of 1919 had advised King Albert against pressing for annexations from the Dutch as it would merely strengthen the Flemish element within the country, a group for whom he had 'a profound contempt'. Sally Marks, *Innocent Abroad: Belgium at the Paris Peace Conference of 1919* (Chapel Hill NC: University of North Carolina Press, 1981), 82.

30. E. H. Kossmann, *The Low Countries 1780–1940* (Oxford: Clarendon, 1978), 634–5.

31. Van den Wijngaert, 'The Belgian Catholics and the Jews', 225–6.

32. Ibid. 228. It has been argued that his protests were in any case misdirected, as he communicated with the military government when measures against the Jews were effectively dictated by the RSHA in Berlin.

33. Maxime Steinberg, *L'Etoile et le Fusil: 1942 Les Cent Jours de la Déportation* (Bruxelles: Vie Ouvriere, 1984) 31. Ullmann had been made a prisoner of war but was returned to Belgium on 12 June 1940. Maxime Steinberg, 'The Trap of Legality: The Association of the Jews of Belgium', in Y. Gutman and C. J. Haft (eds), *Patterns of Jewish Leadership in Nazi Europe, 1933–1945. Proceedings of the Third International Historical Conference* (Jerusalem: Yad Vashem, 1979), 799.

34. Maxime Steinberg, 'The Jews in the Years 1940–1944: Three Strategies for Coping with a Tragedy', in Michman (ed.), *Belgium and the Holocaust*, 354. CEGES-SOMA MVDO 497.245.218 'La Question Juive en Belgique', 1–2. Steinberg, 'The Trap of Legality', 800.

35. Steinberg, *1942 Les Cent Jours de la Déportation*, 34–6.

36. Ibid. 41–2. This gave them a representation out of proportion to their (numerical) importance, but provides an example of the German Jews being more acceptable to the Nazis than other Jews.

37. Steinberg, 'The Jews in the Years 1940–1944', 355. Steinberg, 'The Trap of Legality', 800–1.

38. Steinberg, *1942 Les Cent Jours de la Déportation*, 50–56. The camp was ' cleaned up' on orders from the military administration in the autumn of 1941 to prevent further abuses of prisoners held there by the SS.

39. The so-called 'summer solstice' action. Steinberg, *1942 Les Cent Jours de la Déportation*, 57–9.

40. CEGES-SOMA MVDO 497.245.218 'La Question Juive en Belgique', 1–2. Saerens, *Vreemdelingen in een Wereldstad*, 559. Rosengarten, *Survival*, 28.

41. CEGES-SOMA AB2167 René De Lathower, *Comité de Defense des Juifs: Temoignages et Documents* (1951) 11.

42. For a detailed examination of the organization and workings of the AJB see, Rudi van Doorslaer and Jean-Philippe Schreiber (eds), *De Curatoren van het Ghetto: De vereniging van de joden in België tijdens de nazi-bezetting* (Brussels: Lannoo, 2004).

43. CEGES-SOMA AB2167 De Lathower, *Comité de Defense des Juifs*, 5. CEGES-SOMA MVDO 497.245.218 'La Question Juive en Belgique', 5–6.

44. Steinberg, 'The Trap of Legality', 800, 802.

45. Ibid. 801.

46. CEGES-SOMA AB 207 Memoirs Salomon vandenberg, 47–8 Entries for 16 and 31 July 1942. Saerens, 'Die Hilfe für Juden', 239.

47. CEGES-SOMA MVDO 497.245.218 'La Question Juive en Belgique', 11. CEGES-SOMA AB 207 Memoirs Salomon Vandenberg, 57–9, 23–24 September 1942.

48. Steinberg, 'The Trap of Legality', 816.

49. This was the so-called Operation Iltis. Steinberg, 'The Trap of Legality', 816.

50. CEGES-SOMA AA1915 Doos 13 CDJ Letter from Pinkas Broder to Maurice Heiber, 22 June 1966, 2. Broder was also highly critical of the rich Jews who refused to provide money to help their poor co-religionists, but nevertheless pumped 'millions' into the AJB coffers in return for 'cartes de protection', 5.

51. CEGES-SOMA AA1915 Doos 13 CDJ Letter from Pinkas Broder to Maurice Heiber, 22 June 1966, 4.

52. CEGES-SOMA R123 232.159 *8 Ans au Service du Peuple*, 4. Steinberg, *1942 Les Cent Jours de la Déportation*, 60–1.

53. Steinberg, *Le Comité de Défense des Juifs*, 39. CEGES-SOMA AB2167 De Lathower, *Comité de Defense des* Juifs, 2. Saerens, 'Die Hilfe für Juden', 250.

54. Front Independence (French) Onafhankelijksfront (Flemish).

55. CEGES-SOMA AB2167 De Lathower, *Comité de Defense des Juifs,* Introduction. He records that many of the records of CDJ activities remained in private hands or had been lost in the post-war era. Steinberg, *Le Comité de Défense des Juifs*, 36.

56. José Gotovitch, 'Resistance Movements and the "Jewish Question"', in Dan Michman (ed.), *Belgium and the Holocaust: Jews, Belgians, Germans* (Jerusalem: Yad Vashem, 1998), 281–2. Communist views on the Jews nonetheless remained equivocal within its class analysis where the 'poor deported Jews' were contrasted with the 'spared Israelite capitalists'.

57. Maxime Steinberg, *L'Etoile et le Fusil: La Traque des Juifs*, I (Bruxelles: Vie Ouvriere,1986) 66.

58. CEGES-SOMA AB2167 De Lathower, *Comité de Defense des Juifs*, 17. Testimony by Ghert Jospa. Steinberg, *Le Comité de Défense des Juifs*, 31, 69. Perelman just refused to co-operate with German ordinances and was supposedly dismissed by the University of Brussels, but he continued to work for it unofficially until the liberation. Saerens, 'Die Hilfe für Juden', 251.

59. Saerens, *Vreemdelingen*, 695–6. Jospa was arrested in Brussels on 21 June 1943 and Hambresin on the night of 20–21 July 1943, Saerens, *Vreemdelingen*, 705.

60. His name is also given as Rotgel and Rotkehl in various books and contemporary reports.

61. CEGES-SOMA AB2167 De Lathower, *Comité de Defense des Juifs*, 22–3. Lucien Steinberg, 'Jewish Rescue Activities in Belgium and France', 603–4, notes that the only major Jewish organization not represented was the Bund. Steinberg, *La Traque des Juifs*, I, 67–9. Betty Garfinkels, *Les Belges face à la persecution raciale 1940–1944* (Bruxelles: ULB) 88–89.

62. Steinberg, *Le Comité de Défense des Juifs*, 68.

63. Ibid. 74–5.CEGES-SOMA AB2167 De Lathower, *Comité de Defense des Juifs*, 2.

64. CEGES-SOMA AA1915 Heiber: Dossier 13 CDJ. Ofipresse No.23, 12 October 1945. CEGES-SOMA AB2167 De Lathower, *Comité de Defense des Juifs*, 9, 19. Jospa makes no mention of *Unzer Kampf*. Steinberg, *Le Comité de Défense des Juifs*, 77–82. CEGES-SOMA R123 232.159 *8 Ans au Service du Peuple*, 10.

65. Saerens, *Vreemdelingen*, 703. CEGES-SOMA AB2167 De Lathower, *Comité de Defense des Juifs*, 19.

66. Stcinberg, *Le Comité de Défense des Juifs*, 29–30.

67. Ibid. 75.

68. CEGES-SOMA AB2167 De Lathower, *Comité de Defense des Juifs*, 41. Garfinkels, *Les Belges*, 89–90, also records subventions from the Belgian banks, from the Ministries of Justice and Finance, and diversions of funds by Blum and Vandenberg from AJB funds. Steinberg, *Le Comité de Défense des Juifs*, 114–115.

69. Saerens, 'Die Hilfe für Juden', 254. Steinberg, *Le Comité de Défense des Juifs*, 115.

70. CEGES-SOMA AB2167 De Lathower, *Comité de Defense des Juifs*, 10, 29. CEGES-SOMA AA1915 Heiber: Dossier 13 CDJ. Ofipresse No.23, 12 October 1945. Steinberg, *Le Comité de Défense des Juifs*, 116.

71. CEGES-SOMA AB2167 De Lathower, *Comité de Defense des Juifs*, 2.

72. Ibid. 11.

73. YV M31/7474 Comite de Defense Juifs. Attestation: Suzanne Moons-Lepetit.

74. Saerens, *Vreemdelingen*,695–6. Other sources suggest up to 3,000.

75. Steinberg, *Le Comité de Défense des Juifs*, 67.

76. CEGES-SOMA AA1915 Heiber: Dossier 13 CDJ. Ofipresse No.23, 12 October 1945, 3, estimates that around 10,000 people were helped financially in this way. CEGES-SOMA AB2167 Comité de Defense des Juifs: Temoignages et Documents, 13.

77. Steinberg, *Le Comité de Défense des Juifs*, 112.

78. Ibid. 110.

79. CEGES-SOMA AB2167 Comité de Defense des Juifs: Temoignages et Documents, 15.

80. CEGES-SOMA AA1915 Heiber: Dossier 13 CDJ. Ofipresse No.23, 12 October 1945.

81. Maxime Steinberg, *Dossier Brussel-Auschwitz. De SS politie en het uitroeien van de Joden* (Brussels: Steuncomité bij de burgelijke partij in het process tegen de SS-officieren, 1981) 128–9.

82. Steinberg, *La Traque des Juifs*, II, 63–4.

83. Steinberg, *Dossier Brussel-Auschwitz*. 112–114.

84. CEGES-SOMA R497 246.139 Report: Actions en vue de provoquer l'evasion des juifs appartenant au XXème convoi, 31 August 1972. Saerens, 'Die Hilfe für Juden', 254–5. Steinberg, *Dossier Brussel-Auschwitz*, 121.

85. Steinberg, *La Traque des Juifs*, II, 69.

86. Ibid. 75–6.

87. CEGES-SOMA R497 246.139 Report: Actions en vue de provoquer l'evasion des juifs appartenant au XXème convoi, 31 August 1972. Idem R497 247.056, 7 November 1972. Steinberg, *Dossier Brussel-Auschwitz*, 121.

88. CEGES-SOMA R497 264.530 Report: Goldsteinas, Mendelis et son épouse...evades du XXème convoi des Israélites déportés le 19.4.1943, 4 June 1976. Steinberg, *La Traque des Juifs*, II, 100–101. Steinberg, *Le Comité de Défense des Juifs*, 130–8.

89. Steinberg, *La Traque des Juifs*, II, 103. Steinberg, *Dossier Brussel-Auschwitz*, 126.

90. Steinberg, *La Traque des Juifs*, II, 120.

91. Steinberg, *Le Comité de Défense des Juifs*, 138–141. Steinberg, *Dossier Brussel-Auschwitz*, 124. Romanovitch and his associates had been 'turned' by the Gestapo, having been arrested on smuggling charges and had become agents. He and three others were later tried and condemned by a post-war Belgian court, with two of them receiving death sentences. *Le Drapeau Rouge*, 20

February, 4 March and 19 March 1947. CEGES-SOMA AA1915 Heiber Box 31–34. Neither sentence was carried out and both were ultimately released. Romanovitch died later in Brussels. CEGES-SOMA R497 248.246 Report: Personnes ayant saboté l'action des Résistants pour provoquer l'evasion des juifs appartenant au XXème convoi, 30 January 1972. See also, Lucien Steinberg, 'Un aspect peu connu de la résistance juive: le sauvetage à main armée', Le Monde Juif LII (1968), 4–11.

92. CEGES-SOMA BD KD 1410 Le Soir, 23 June 1995. Steinberg, Dossier Brussel-Auschwitz, 125. For a more detailed reconstruction of the attack and its background, see Marion Schrieber, The Twentieth Train: The True Story of the Ambush of the Death Train to Auschwitz (New York: Grove, 2003).

93. Steinberg, Le Comité de Défense des Juifs, 70.

94. YV M31/7474 Andree Geulen to Sylvain Brachfeld, 31 March 1999. Allard was recognized as 'Righteous among the Nations', but Pels was excluded because he was a Jew.

95. Saerens, Vreemdelingen, 704–5 A victim of 'Big' Jacques. He was arrested on the street in Brussels. His Belgian nationality saved him from immediate deportation and he was released through the intervention of an unknown 'rijkaard' (rich) Catholic convert.

96. Saerens, Vreemdelingen, 705.

97. Ibid. 706.

98. YV M31/5176 Virginie and Alphonse Claassens, Testimony of Meilech and Anna Book, 26 June 1989.

99. YV M31/5176 Virginie and Alphonse Claassens, testimony of Jenny Kalsner, 29 June 1989. The concierge or maid was paid to do the shopping and provide food for those in hiding. Claassens was reputedly a member of the Witte Brigade resistance group.

100. Saerens, Vreemdelingen, 707.

101. Ibid. 708–9.

102. CEGES-SOMA AB2167 Comité de Defense des Juifs: Temoignages et Documents, 13.Saerens, Vreemdelingen, 709.

103. Saerens, Vreemdelingen, 709, records that although the student took no part in the beatings, he did comment to Flam that 'any methods are good if they bring out the truth'.

104. Saerens, 'Die Hilfe für Juden', 255–6.

105. CEGES-SOMA AA1915 Heiber: Dossier 13 CDJ. Ofipresse No.23, 12 October 1945. Florence Matteazzi, 'L'attitude du clergé face à la Shoa dans le diocese de Liège', in Maerten et al. (eds), Entre la peste et le choléra: vie et attitude des Catholiques belges sous l'occupation (Gerpinnes, 1964), 190.

106. Florence Matteazzi, 'L'attitude du clergé', 192.

107. Ibid. 194.

108. Saerens, 'Die Hilfe für Juden', 257. In other words, the documents were themselves real, but contained false information.

109. CEGES-SOMA AA1915 Heiber: Dossier 13 CDJ. Ofipresse No.23, 12 October 1945, 3.

110. Beatrice Meschman, *Never to be forgotten:. A Young Girl's Holocaust Memoir* (Hoboken NJ: KTAV, 1997), 29, 54.

111. Helene Moszkiewicz, *Inside the Gestapo: A Jewish Woman's Secret War* (New York: Dell, 1985), 22–3. Rosengarten, *Survival*, 27. On the deportations from Antwerp see, Walter de Maesschalk, *Gardes in de oorlog: De Antwerpse politie in WO II* (Antwerpen/Rotterdam: C. de Vries-Brouwers, 2004), 295–300.

112. USHMM Roll 867/16222 Samson Hofstäter to Ministère de la Santé Publique et de la Famille, 2 September 1956.

CHAPTER 8

1. Steinberg, *La Traque des Juifs*, II, 217, 220. Liebman, *Né juif*, 56–7. See also, for example, Dan Michman, *The Encyclopedia of the Righteous Among the Nation. Rescue of Jews during the Holocaust: Belgium* (Jerusalem: Yad Vashem, 2005), 95 Armand Deprez.

2. Michman, *Encyclopedia of the Righteous: Belgium*, 82, 132, Jean-Baptiste de Coster, Benedykt Grynpas.

3. Saerens, 'Die Hilfe für Juden', 246.

4. Alexandra Fanny Brodsky, *A Fragile Identity: Survival in Nazi-occupied Belgium* (London/New York: Radcliffe, 1998), 34. Moszkiewicz, *Inside the Gestapo: A Jewish Woman's Secret War* (New York: Dell, 1985), 65. Loebl, *At the Mercy of Strangers*, 67.

5. Rudi van Doorslaer et al. (eds), *Gewillig België. Overheid en Jodenvervolging tijdens de Tweede Wereldoorlog* (Brussels: Meulenhoff/Manteau-SOMA, 2007), 545–551. Saerens, *Die Hilfe für Juden*, 220–1.

6. Van Doorslaer et al. (eds), *Gewillig België,* 604–5. There had been no similar protests in March 1942 when the Germans had introduced compulsory labour service inside Belgium. Saerens, 'Die Hilfe für Juden', 235.

7. Saerens, 'Die Hilfe für Juden', 226.

8. Ibid. 228–9.

9. Michman, *Encyclopedia of the Righteous: Belgium*, 102 Camille D'Haeyer.

10. Gabriel Kierszencweig, *Exode de Juifs de Charleroi à Jauche* (n.p.,n.d.), Yad Vashem Library.

11. Declaration by Dr J Ferrant, 7 July 1965 CEGES-SOMA MVDO 497.233. 430.

12. Loebl, *At the Mercy of Strangers*, 67–8.
13. Ibid. 68.
14. Ibid. 71.
15. De Maesschalk, *Gardes in de oorlog*, 314.
16. USHMM RG50.030.242 Wallenstein, 11–14.
17. Ibid. 28–9.
18. USHMM RG02.002 Salomon, 1–3.
19. Saerens, 'Die Hilfe für Juden', 258, cites Lieven Saerens, 'L'aide des catholiques dans l'archevêché de Malines', in Fabrice Maerten et al. (eds), *Entre la peste et le choléra*, 208–240 and idem, The attitude of the Belgian Catholic Church regarding the Persecution of the Jews', in J. Th. M. Bank and Lieve Gevers (eds), *Churches and Religion in Occupied Europe: Politics and Theology* (Leuven: Peeters, 2007).
20. Saerens, 'Die Hilfe für Juden', 245–6, 269–70.
21. CEGES-SOMA R497 272.194 Report: Moines Juifs, 16 August 1979.
22. Van den Wijngaert, 'The Belgian Catholics and the Jews', 121. Brachfeld, *Ze hebben het overleefd*, 72–3. Lieve Gevers, 'Catholicism in the Low Countries During the Second World War. Belgium and the Netherlands: a Comparative Approach', in Lieve Gevers and Jan Bank (eds), *Religion under Siege, I, The Roman Catholic Church in Occupied Europe* (1939–1950) (Leuven: Peeters, 2007), 222.
23. Gevers, 'Catholicism in the Low Countries', 222.
24. Leon Papeleux, 'Un Liégeois qui sauva des centaines de Juifs (1940–1944)', *La Vie Wallonie* 1980, 283. Van den Wijngaert, 'Les Catholiques Belges et les Juifs', 123. He also wrote a private letter to Cardinal Gerlier in Lyon condemning the deportation of the Jews.
25. Brachfeld, *Ze hebben het overleefd*, 113. He gives a figure of 175 Jewish baptisms.
26. Saerens, 'Die Hilfe für Juden', 261.
27. USHMM A001019 1995 A287 Ministerie de la Santé Publique, Attestation, Soeur Claire d'Assise (Yvonne Vernant), 10 January 1949. Saerens, 'Die Hilfe für Juden', 262–3.
28. Saerens, 'Die Hilfe für Juden', 264–5.
29. CEGES-SOMA AA1593/M43 Vicaire Robert Barbier, 5. Paldiel, *The Path of the Righteous*, 68. Brachfeld, *Ze hebben het overleefd*, 75. YV M31/486 Joseph Andre, *Vers L'Avenir*, 5–6 February 1983 notes that the friend in question was Arthur Burak, a Jew who had left Germany in 1933.
30. CEGES-SOMA AA1593/M43 Vicaire Robert Barbier, 3. Thyange, 'L'Abbé Joseph André', 268.

31. Brachfeld, *Ze hebben het overleefd*, 77.

32. CEGES-SOMA AA1148-9 Doc. Enquête Kerk-Eglise: 85 Lepkifker, 2. Saerens, 'Die Hilfe für Juden', 272–3. Matteazzi, 'L'attitude du clergé, 180. She refers to Sister Lutgarde as the bishop's cousin. Gevers, 'Catholicism in the Low Countries', 223.

33. Matteazzi, 'L'attitude du clergé', 181. One of them recorded that he not only sang in the church choir but also became its soloist, accompanying the curé to other churches in the vicinity. Testimony David Herszlikovicz, 19 December 1988 YV M31/3708a Marcel Stenne. He spoke of 'natural pressures to convert' but excused the Abbé on the grounds that it was his job to save your soul. A lot of boys were baptized, but the end of the war nullified that and only one boy has remained Roman Catholic. *Jewish Chronicle*, 31 August 1990, 2.

34. Matteazzi, 'L'attitude du clergé', 182. Deposition of Abbé Louis Célis.

35. Ibid. 183.

36. YV M31/6678 Albert van den Berg. CEGES-SOMA R497.191.141. Report of Dumonceau de Bergendal, 7 October 1964.

37. Leon Papeleux, 'Le Réseau Van Den Berg', *La Vie Wallonie* (1981). *Resistance: Père Bruno Reynders*, 140.

38. CEGES-SOMA BD K1037 *La Cité*, 21 November 1984 claims that 120 priests were arrested in the diocese, of whom 20 met a violent death.

39. Matteazzi, 'L'attitude du clergé', 184.

40. Thierry Rozenblum, 'Une cité si ardente. L'administration communale de Liège et la persecution des Juifs, 1940–1942', *Revue d'Histoire de le Shoah*, no.179 (septembre–décembre 2003) 9–73. Matteazzi, 'L'attitude du clergé', 185.

41. YV M31/594 André Meunier.

42. Matteazzi, 'L'attitude du clergé', 186.

43. Ibid. 198–200.

44. L. Lombard, *L'héroïque curé de Comblain-au-Pont* (Liège, n.d.) cited in Matteazzi, 'L'attitude du clergé', 203. YV M31/1362a Joseph Peeters.

45. Matteazzi, 'L'attitude du clergé', 201.

46. Papeleux, 'Un Liégeois', 282. Papeleux, 'Le Réseau Van Den Berg', 139–140.

47. Papeleux, 'Le Réseau Van Den Berg', 141.

48. Boufflette's story shows how he also became involved in sheltering Jews and others (including escaped pilots). He was arrested in 1944 and died at KZ Dora in 1945. His parents were also involved in sheltering Jewish children.

YV M31/1361 Emile Boufflette. Testimony of Harriette Manela and others 1975.

49. Matteazzi, 'L'attitude du clergé', 187. It is not clear whether the specific impetus to shelter Jewish children came from Van den Berg or as a result of the Jewish community or CDJ discovering the existence of these institutions.

50. Michel Reynders, *Père Bruno Reynders, Héros de la Résistance* (Bruxelles: Carrefours de la Cité, 1992), 81.

51. Papeleux, 'Un Liégeois', 288.

52. Matteazzi, 'L'attitude du clergé', 188. This in spite of the fact that the military governor had published an interdiction on institutions sheltering Jewish children in August 1942. Van den Berg was probably the victim of a certain Joseph Kean, who informed on him in exchange for the freedom of his Jewish wife.

53. Papeleux, 'Un Liégeois' 288–9.

54. CEGES-SOMA R497 272.264 Report: Enfants juifs caches pendant la guerre 1940–1945, 17 December 1980. Matteazzi, 'L'attitude du clergé', 189–90.

55. Matteazzi, 'L'attitude du clergé', 205–6. He was sentenced to death by a Belgian court in 1947.

56. CEGES-SOMA MVDO 497.237.074 Het Loubris Fonds 1–2.

57. CEGES-SOMA AA1914 Gendarmerie Verviers, Brigade de Herve. Reports, 14 June 1950, 26 June 1950 and Commisariat de Police, Liège, 28 June and 6 July 1950.

58. USHMM Roll 7 No.4316 CEGES SOMA 65.001M Strafverfügung Albert Emil Lorriaux, 13 October 1943. USHMM Roll 2026 No.27460 CEGES-SOMA 45.001M Einlieferungsschein Andrée Ovart, 15 June 1943.

59. USHMM Roll 1296 No.20493 Commissariat de Police, Liège No.4517/174 Testimony of Willem Bom, 16 November 1950. He was liberated by the Russians in 1945 and returned to Belgium.

60. USHMM Roll 1411 No.21673 Dossier Dumortier 25.3.17, 5–6. The third brother was only charged BFr.5,000 on the basis of the commercial relationship that his family had with Chainaye.

61. USHMM Roll 1411 No.21673 Dossier Dumortier 25.3.17, 7–8.

62. Ibid. 11–14.

63. USHMM Roll 272 No.7335 Zuchthaus Rheinbach: Personal Akten Daniel Meyerson 355/41.

64. Rapport par M.Dumonceau, 11–14 October 1976: Israel Steinberg CEGES-SOMA MVDO 497.266.018. This unlikely survivor failed to mend his ways. Finally released in 1946 and supposedly repatriated to Vilna where he claimed to have left a wife and five children, he continued to attract the attention of the

police and was convicted by the Belgians again in 1954 and 1956, after which he disappeared from the judicial records. By this stage he was 76 years old.

65. Saerens, 'Die Hilfe für Juden', 231.

66. De Volder and Wouters, *Van binnen weent mijn hart*, 73.

67. For a recent discussion, see Herman.van Goethem, 'La convention de La Haye, la collaboration administrative en Belgique et la persecution des Juifs à Anvers, 1940–1942', *Cahiers d'Histoire du Temps Présent* XVII (2006), 117–197.

68. Saerens, *Vreemdelingen in een Wereldstad*, 672.

69. Van Doorslaer et al. (eds), *Gewillig België*, 604–9. Van Goethem, 'La convention de La Haye', argues that the role of Mayor Delwaide of Antwerp was crucial in affecting the attitudes of the local government officials and contrasted with the earlier alienation from German policies in Brussels under its mayor, van de Meulebroek.

70. De Volder en Wouters, *Van binnen weent mijn hart*, 73–4. For a partial critique of this standpoint, see Dan Michman, 'Why Did So Many of the Jews in Antwerp Perish in the Holocaust?' *Yad Vashem Studies* XXX (2002), 465–481.

71. Saerens, *Vreemdelingen in een Wereldstad*, 684, cites Ephraím Schmidt, *Geschiedenis van de Joden in Antwerpen* (Antwerpen, 1963), 222–4, 228–9 and 233, but points out that four came from outside the city and one had a Jewish background. Saerens, 'Die Hilfe für Juden', 268, cites the figure as 97 rather than 99.

72. YV M31/9654 Elisabeth Maria Hollants, Testimony of George S.Gourary, 24 August 1999. Saerens, *Vreemdelingen in een Wereldstad*, 689. See also Saerens, 'Het Katholiek Bureau', 67–87.

73. Saerens, 'Die Hilfe für Juden', 259–60. Among the small group of 24 Protestant clerics, many of whom were non-Belgians, the percentage was 62.5%. See C. Jacquemart, 'Les Justes et les Sauveurs de l'Holocaust au regard de l'opinion publique belge' (Magister Thesis, Université de Bruxelles Libre, 1996).

CHAPTER 9

1. The German census of autumn 1940 enumerated 160,820 Jews in the country, but of these 15,549 were designated as 'mischlinge' (half-Jews), and a further 5,719 as quarter-Jews, giving a total of 139,552, a figure that needs to be adjusted upwards to include those who avoided being registered. See Moore, *Victims and Survivors*, 259–60 and Ad van Liempt, *Hitler's Bounty Hunters: The Betrayal of the Jews* (Oxford: Berg, 2005), 11. The post-war Jewish

Co-ordination Committee registered 4,532 returnees and estimated that there were no more than 5,450 in total. No account is taken of Jews from the Netherlands who may have survived but chose not to return there after the war. See Hirschfeld, 'Niederlande', in Wolfgang Benz (ed.), *Dimension des Volkermords: Die Zahl der jüdishen Opfer des Nationalsozialismus* (Munich: Oldenbourg, 1991).

2. In this context see, J. C. H. Blom, 'The Persecution of the Jews in the Netherlands: A Comparative Western European Perspective', *European History Quarterly* XIX (1989), 333–351, and Pim Griffioen and Ron Zeller, 'Jodenvervolging in Nederland en België tijdens de Tweede Werelkoorlog: Een Vergelijkende Analyse', *Ooorlogsdocumentatie '40—'45* VIII (1997).

3. Bert Jan Flim, 'Opportunities for Dutch Jews to Hide from the Nazis, 1942–1945', in Chaya Brasz and Yosef Kaplan (eds), *Dutch Jews as Perceived by Themselves and by Others: Proceedings of the Eighth International Symposium on the History of the Jews in the Netherlands* (Leiden: Brill, 2001), 289. De Jong, *Het Koninkrijk*, VII, 443. In an earlier study, Sijes, *Studies over Jodenvervolging*, 145, suggested that the total was no more than 16,000 to 19,000.

4. Van Liempt, *Hitler's Bounty Hunters*, 18.

5. De Jong, *Het Koninkrijk*, VII, 444.

6. See Jozef Michman and Bert-Jan Flim (eds), *The Encyclopedia of the Righteous among the Nation. Rescuers of Jews during the Holocaust: The Netherlands*, 2 vols (Jerusalem: Yad Vashem, 2004). It could also be noted that some relationships were 'soured' at the war's end by claims of profiteering, attempted conversion and retention of orphaned children.

7. Ben Braber, *Zelfs als wij zullen verliezen. Joden in verzet en illegaliteit 1940–1945* (Amsterdam: Balans, 1990), 49. Moore, *Refugees from Nazi Germany in the Netherlands, 1933–1940* (Nijhoff: Dordrecht, 1986), 28–32.

8 Moore, *Victims and Survivors*, 34–5.

9. De Jong, *Het Koninkrijk*, I, 463.

10. The debate about the role of the Amsterdam Jewish Council in facilitating the deportation process has remained in the forefront of Dutch discussion of the holocaust. For some of the more contentious texts see, Hans Knoop, *De Joodsche Raad: Het Drama van Abraham Asscher en David Cohen* (Amsterdam: Elsevier, 1983), and Nanda van der Zee, *'Om erger te voorkomen'* (Amsterdam: Meulenhoff, 1997), but see also Presser, *Ondergang*, I, 78–83. One exception to the elite collusion came from Lodewijk Visser, President of the High Court. See, De Jong, *Het Koninkrijk*, IV, 708–710 and J. Michman, '*The Controversial Stand of the Joodse Raad in the Netherlands. Lodewijk E. Visser's Struggle*', Yad Vashem Studies, X (1974), 9–68.

11. NIOD Doc II/364b Nathalie L. van Neerland, n.d., 9.

12. Moore, *Victims and Survivors*, 87.

13. NIOD Doc II/364c 'De Mogelijkheid van Onderduiken' 2. This also sought to undermine the idea that thousands more Jews would have been saved by going underground if there had not been a Jewish Council.

14. Gerard Aalders, *Nazi Looting. The Plunder of Dutch Jewry during the Second World War* (Oxford: Berg, 2004) 3–4, 127–146.

15. W. Emanuel, 'Underground in Holland' (Amsterdam: c.1979) Mimeograph NIOD, 16.

16. Moore, *Victims and Survivors*, 118–119.

17. Some have argued that the stamps may have served to delay the deportation and therefore aided the survival of as many as 9,000 Jews, but this re-interpretation of the Jewish Council's role is not widely accepted. NIOD Doc II/364c 'De Mogelijkheid van Onderduiken' (Unsigned, no date).

18. NIOD HSSpF 111/181a Report: Pol. Angestellte Slottke, Rückstellungsjuden, 2 December 1942. A different set of figures can be found in the HSSpF files. NIOD HSSpF 20/37 Sonderbericht—Jahresbericht 1942, 29. For a wider discussion of these various forms of 'protection' see Presser, *Ondergang*, II, 50–110 and Moore, *Victims and Survivors*, 116–145.

19. Delleman, *Opdat wij niet vergeten*, 159.

20. See, for example, Touw, *Het verzet der Hervormde Kerk*, 410, where he contrasts one pastor arrested by the SD for issuing false baptismal certificates with another who refused to carry out perfectly legal baptisms lest he was placed in danger.

21. Moore, *Victims and Survivors*, 127–9. Many converts were protected not by their own status but as partners in mixed marriages to Christians. Delleman, *Opdat wij niet vergeten*, 170. Touw, *Het verzet der Hervormde Kerk*, 423–33.

22. NIOD HSSpF 111/181a Report: Abtransport jüdischer Rückstellungsgruppen nach dem Aufenthaltslager Bergen-Belsen, 21 September 1943.

23. H. Wielek, *De Oorlog Hitler Won* (Amsterdam: Amsterdam Boek-en Courantmaatschappij, 1947), 256–7. Presser, *Ondergang* II, 231–2. Bart van der Boom, *Den Haag in de Tweede Wereldoorlog* (The Hague, SeaPress, 1995), 167. Moore, *Victims and Survivors*, 118.

24. This phrase was used to excuse and explain Jewish Council policies at the time. In the post-war era, Cohen claimed he had no direct knowledge of the death camps and the fate of deported Jews at the time, thus making compliance seem more understandable. This has been widely criticized, not least by Knoop and van der Zee. The term also spawned some gallows humour in 1943: Cohen and Asscher are the only two Jews left and the

Germans demand that one of them is deported. Cohen says to Asscher, 'In the interests of the Jewish Community, it had better be you lest something worse befall.' Presser, *Ondergang* I, 525.

25. Braber, *Zelfs als wij zullen verliezen.*, 106.

26. Frits Reuter, *Communistische Partij van Nederland in oorlogstijd. Herrineringen* (Amsterdam: van Gennep, 1978) 59.

27. Meijer Lisser, '*Boekhouden 1940–1943*' (Alkmaar: Falstaff, 2008), 156.

28. Braber, *Zelfs als wij zullen verliezen*, 50, 103–6. Richter Roegholt and Jacob Zwaan, *Het verzet 1940–1945* (Weesp: Unieboek, 1985), 23–7.

29. Braber, *Zelfs als wij zullen verliezen*, 84–5.

30. De Jong, *Het Koninkrijk*, IV, 816–820. Van der Kar, *Joodse Verzet*, 37–40.

31. Braber, *Passage naar de vrijheid*, 88–9.

32. Ibid. 39. See also, Braber, 'De rol van het joodse verzet in de tweede weredoorlog', *TerHerKenning*, XIII (1985), 227–237. There were also other groups, for example one centred within the 400 Jewish workers at the Hollandia-Kattenburg clothing company.

33. Presser, *Ondergang*, 406–7. Schenkel, *De Twentse Paradox*, 82, 89–92.

34. Schenkel, *De Twentse Paradox*, 138–141.

35. NIOD Doc II/364b Lou Gompers, 1–3.

36. For example, one German Jewish refugee woman managed to survive the war as a domestic servant in a sanatorium for three years as she had papers that did not identify her as a Jew. Interview Annie Hoek-Wallach with the author, 16 September 1987. Transcript at the Wiener Library, London.

37. NIOD Doc II/364b (Rooseveltlaan 12.) This family was eventually arrested by the SD in January 1945 but then helped to escape from the police station by the local resistance.

38. USHMM RG50.030.241 Gerd von Halle, 20.

39. NIOD 251a LO-LKP, LO-BP2, Verslag J. W. J. Hamerling, Amsterdam (n.d.), 1–2. This was also true of other groups that helped form the beginnings of the LO. For example, see the origin of the Groep-Coops in NIOD 251a BG-1, LO Org3 Interview with drs. D Mulder, 9 December 1946, 2.

40. Flim, 'Opportunities for Dutch Jews', 296.

41. *Encyclopedia of the Righteous among the Nations. Netherlands II*, 507. The baptismal certificates meant that they were not sent to Auschwitz but to Theresienstadt where they became part of the September 1944 exchange.

42. *Encyclopedia of the Righteous among the Nations. Netherlands II*, 482. Leonardus Linssen.

43. NIOD 251a LO-LKP, LO-BP2, Interview No.2 Utrecht: Mevr. M. F. Meulemeester, (n.d.), 1–2.

44. W. C. Klein and P. de Grient Dreux (eds), *Pittige verhalen uit onveilige tijden: Scetsen van illegale werkers, hongerlijders enz. uit alle rangen en standen* ('s-Gravenhage: van Stockum, 1947), 77–9.

45. Klein and de Grient Dreux, *Pittige verhalen*, 81–3. The husband was also welcomed back to his old job in the bank.

46. NIOD Doc II/364b Nathalie L. van Neerland, n.d., 10.

47. Ibid. 12.

48. NIOD 245/195 Opgave voor de erelijst: Albertus Zefat.

49. YV M31/731 Albert Zefat. Testimony of Leo Kropveld, 26 February 1972. Ab van Dien, *Opgejaagden. Herinneringen van een joodse onderduiker in het Valther bos* (Valthe: Welzijnswerk, 1982), 9, 13–16. Paldiel, *The Path of the Righteous*, 133–4.

50. NIOD Doc II/364b Zwolle, 4–5.

51. NIOD Doc II/364b Zwolle, 6.

52. Frank Visser, *De pensionhoudster en de onderduiker* (Baarn: Bosch en Keuning, 1980), 10, 12.

53. Visser, *De pensionhoudster*, 56–7, 152–3.

54. Visser, *De pensionhoudster*, 168.

55. YV M31/855 Laurens Mieloo. Testimony of Johan Jacobson, 6 August 1973 and Flora Jacobson, 23 August 1973.

56. YV M31/1605. Testimony of Samuel Visser, 23 December 1976, 2–3. Blok also reputedly subscribed to the national socialist newspaper, *Volk en Vaderland*, to act as a cover. Paldiel, *The Path of the Righteous*, 101, 102–3.

57. YV M31/1605. Testimony of Samuel Visser, 23 December 1976, 3.

58. Maurice Ferares, *Violinist in het verzet* (Amsterdam: De Bataafsche Leeuw, 1991), 135.

59. Bob Moore, 'Nazi Masters and Accommodating Dutch Bureaucrats: Working towards the Führer in the Occupied Netherlands, 1940–1945', in Tim Kirk and Tony Mc Elligott (eds), *Working Towards the Führer* (Manchester: Manchester University Press 2003), 195.

60. NIOD Doc II/364c André Theun, 9.

61. P. Wijbenga, *Bezettingstijd in Friesland*, I (Leeuwarden: De Tille, 1995), 235.

62. Moore, 'Nazi masters and accommodating Dutch bureaucrats', 196.

63. P. Wijbenga, *Bezettingstijd in Friesland*, I, 235–6.

64. See, for example, E. Casutto, *The Last Jew in Rotterdam* (Monroeville PA: Whitaker House, 1974), 66.

65. Corrie ten Boom, *The Hiding Place* (New York: Chosen Books, 1971), 69.

66. Ten Boom, *The Hiding Place*, 102. Ten Boom, *Gevangene en toch . . . Herinneringen uit Scheveningen, Vught en Ravensbrück* (Amsterdam: W. ten Have, 1945), 12, notes that up to 80 people may have been given shelter

in the house at one time or another and the maximum number for a single night was twelve. One of the longer term non-Jewish residents published a memoir of his time in hiding, Han Poley, *Return to the Hiding Place* (Elgin IL: LifeJourney Books, 1993).

67. Corrie ten Boom, *Gevangene en toch . . .*, 10.

68. Poley, *Return to the Hiding Place*, 107.

69. Ten Boom, *The Hiding Place*, 113–114.

70. De Jong, *Het Koninkrijk*, VI, 334. Ten Boom, *Gevangene en toch . . .*, 14–19. It was later discovered that the house had been betrayed by a certain H. van Vogel. He was sentenced to death after the liberation and received a letter from Corrie ten Boom forgiving him. Guus Hartendorf, *Noodklokken luiden bij Ten Boom* (Haarlem: Corrie ten Boomhuis, 1994), 25.

71. Ten Boom, *The Hiding Place*, 142–4. Ten Boom, *Gevangene en toch . . .*, 23–4.

72. Ten Boom, *The Hiding Place*, 200–207.

73. Michman and Flim, *Encyclopedia of the Righteous: The Netherlands I*, Johannes Bogaard, 128–9. YV M31/876 Anthenius and Willem Bogaard. Testimony of D. Busnach et al., 15 April 1972.

74. YV M31/28 Johannes Bogaard. Letter Louis de Jong to Israeli Ambassador, 27 September 1963.

75. Cor van Stam, *Wacht binnen de dijken. Verzet in en om de Harlemmermeer* (Haarlem: De Toorts, 1986), 88–9. YV M31/4361 Geertruida de Swann-Willems. It is evident that at least two testimonials came from people in her building or who had business dealings with her husband. See also the feature in *Het Parool*, 3 October 1963, 19.

76. De Jong, *Het Koninkrijk*, VI, 336. English translation from Moore, *Victims and Survivors*, 180.

77. Van Stam, *Wacht binnen de dijken*, 92–4.

78. Ibid. 77.

79. De Jong, *Het Koninkrijk*, VI, 336.

80. Van Stam, *Wacht binnen de dijken*, 78.

81. Ibid. 89.

82. Ibid. 68–73.

83. De Jong, *Het Koninkrijk*, VI, 337. Three members of the family died as a result of imprisonment or maltreatment, including Johannes Snr, who might have survived but insisted on complaining to the SD that the police had confiscated his harmonium. As a result he was arrested again and died at Sachsenhausen. See *Trouw*, 12 February 1974. Van Stam, *Wacht binnen de dijken*, 83–7, gives a slightly different chronology for the raids and the victims, suggesting that the second raid caught eleven fugitives. YV M31/28 Johannes

Bogaard. Testimony of J. M. Snoek, 16 February 1964 on later attempts to acquire ration and identity cards whilst in hiding.

84. Jan Hof, *Vrouwen in het Verzet*, (Baarn: La Rivière en Voorhoeve, 1995), 202.
85. Paldiel, *The Path of the Righteous*, 128–9. John Breukelaar, *Halte Varsseveld: Verhalen over het onderduiken bij de dames Jolink en hun geestverwanten* (Aalten: Fagus, 2005). De Jong, *Het Koninkrijk*, VI, 334. Hof, *Vrouwen*, 206.
86. Coen van Tricht, *Onderduikers en Knokploegen: Het verzet van de Landelijke Organisatie voor Hulp aan Onderduikers en de Landelijke Knokploegen* (Amsterdam: De Bataafsche Leeuw, 1991), 18.
87. Van Tricht, *Onderduikers en Knokploegen*, 19.
88. Flim, 'Opportunities for Dutch Jews', 297.
89. NIOD 251a LO-LKP, LO-BP2. 'LO-werk. Oorlog 1940–1945 Het Gooi.
90. Jan Meulenbelt, *De duitse tijd. Vijf jaar vaderlandse geschiedenis* (Amsterdam: J. H. de Bussy, 1965), 127.
91. Ad van Liempt, *Kopgeld. Nederlandse premiejagers op zoek naar joden 1943* (Amsterdam: Balans, 2002), 53–5.
92. Van Liempt, *Kopgeld*, 177.
93. NIOD HSSpF 166/263H, Bericht: Alter, 10 August 1943.
94. Ibid. Bericht: Frank,
95. Ibid. Bericht: van Bergen, 1 September 1943.
96. Van Liempt, *Kopgeld*, 181.

CHAPTER 10

1. De Jong, *Het Koninkrijk*, VI, 119. To some extent, they were going against the teachings of their religion, whose leaders had voiced opposition to the idea of deliberately avoiding the draft.
2. NIOD 251a BG-1 LO-Org3, Onderhoud 1946 met Ds. F. Slomp. This had included preaching against National Socialism on the German side of the border Jan Hof, *Frits de Zwerver: Twaalf jaar strijd tegen de nazi-terreur* ('s-Gravenhage: Omniboek, 1976). Hof, *Vrouwen*, 26–7.
3. Hof, *Vrouwen*, 20–6. *Het Grote Gebod* I, 8–9. De Jong, *Het Koninkrijk*, VII, 708. Eppo Kuipers, *Er was zoveel werk nog te doen. Tante Riek en Oom Piet in de jaren '40–'45*, (Winterswijk: Het Museum, 1988), 30.
4. The first meeting took place in Zwolle because of its better train connections, and this was where the basis for the organization was laid. Kuipers, *Er was zoveel werk nog te doen...*, 41–2.
5. NIOD 251a BG-1 LO-Org3, Onderhoud 1946 met Ds. F. Slomp.
6. *Het Grote Gebod* I, 9–10. The organization became known as the Commissie van Zanten and Slomp as Ouderling (Elder) van Zanten.

7. J. M. Snoek, *De Nederlandse kerken en de Joden, 1940–1945*. (Kampen: Kok, 1990), 144. Jan Bank, 'Protestantism in the Second World War: The Case of The Netherlands and France', in Gevers and Bank (eds), *Religion under Siege, II*, 258.

8. NIOD 251a BG-1 LO-Org3, Verslag Oom Jan, Aalten, 1.

9. De Jong, *Het Koninkrijk*, VII, 711.

10. *Het Grote Gebod* I, 12. Bank, 'Protestantism in the Second World War: The Case of The Netherlands and France', in Liev Gevers and Jan Bank (eds), *Religion under Siege, II, Protestant, Orthodox and Muslim Communities in Occupied Europe* (1939–1950) (Leuven: Peeters, 2007), 259.

11. *Het Grote Gebod* I, 14, 20. De Jong, *Het Koninkrijk*, VII, 709, 711.

12. De Jong, *Het Koninkrijk*, VI, 123. NIOD 251a BG-1 LO-Org3, LO Verslag Zwolle District, 1.

13. NIOD 251a BG-3 LO-Org3, Verslag L. Rietberg, Zutphen, n.d., 2.

14. Snoek, *De Nederlandse kerken en de Joden*, 148. The LO and LKP together had around 15,000 members, of whom most were church members and around 1,600 lost their lives.

15. *Het Grote Gebod* I, 20.

16. Kuipers, *Er was zoveel werk nog te doen . . .*, 34 notes the role of Piet Kuipers, the husband of Helena in establishing contacts and working for the movement.

17. NIOD 251a LO-LKP, LO-BP2, Ds. K. Feenstra, 'Algemeen Overzicht Verzetsgeschiedenis'.

18. Ibid. 3.

19. Ibid.

20. Snoek, *De Nederlandse kerken en de Joden*, 146.

21. NIOD 251a BG-1, LO Org3, Fr. v/d Have, Vervolg Verslag Zuid-Veluwe en de Betuwe, 5. He was estimated to have had upwards of 100 Jews in his care.

22. NIOD 251a BG-1, LO Org3, Fr. v/d Have, Vervolg Verslag Zuid-Veluwe en de Betuwe, 18, 21.

23. NIOD 251a LO-LKP, LO-BP2, Interview met Dhr. T. van Leeuwen, LO District Centrum, (n.d.), 1–2.

24. See, for example, NIOD 251a BG-1, LO Org3, Interview with drs. D Mulder, 9 December 1946, 18. and Fr. v/d Have, Vervolg Verslag Zuid-Veluwe en de Betuwe, 4.

25. *Het Grote Gebod* II, 12.

26. Snoek, *De Nederlandse kerken en de Joden*, 146–7, cites *Enquêtecommissie Regeringsbeleid 1940–1945* ('s-Gravenhage, 1949–1956) Vol. 7c, 262.

27. Snoek, *De Nederlandse kerken en de Joden*, 147. De Jong, *Het Koninkrijk*, VII, 444.

28. De Jong, *Het Koninkrijk*, VII, 444.

29. Herzberg, *Kroniek der Jodenvervolging*, 324, cites articles in *Vrij Nederland*, 21 October 1943, *Trouw*, April 1944, *Ons Volk*, July 1944, etc.

30. De Jong, *Het Koninkrijk*, VII, 444.

31. See, for example, NIOD 251a BG-2, LO Org3, Interview with D. Buwalda, 5 March 1947, 2.

32. De Jong, *Het Koninkrijk*, VII, 444.

33. Moore, *Victims and Survivors*, 166, cites NIOD Doc II 364a, Letter Tusveld.

34. H. Wolf, *De Gespijkerde God* (Nijmegen: SUN, 1995), 79.

35. De Jong, *Het Koninkrijk*, VII, 445.

36. NIOD 251a LO-LKP, LO-BP2 Interview with J. Thijssen (Amsterdam).

37. Ibid.

38. Wijbenga, *Bezettingstijd in Friesland*, I, 201.

39. Ibid. 207–8.

40. Flim, 'Opportunities for Dutch Jews', 291.

41. Wijbenga, *Bezettingstijd in Friesland*, I, 218.

42. Ibid. 219–221. Several had been taken to Germany as forced labourers or sent to Dachau. In Vught they had been incarcerated with policemen from other districts who had also refused to round up Jews. Stichting Geschiedschrijving Philips-Kommando, *Licht in het Donker: Het Philips-Kommando in Kamp Vught* (Vught: Stichting Nationaal Monument Kamp Vught, n.d.), 29–30.

43. Wijbenga, *Bezettingstijd in Friesland*, I, 223.

44. NIOD 251a LO-LKP, LO-BP2, Interview met Dhr. T. van Leeuwen, LO District Centrum, (n.d.), 2.

45. Wijbenga, *Bezettingstijd in Friesland*, I, 225.

46. De Jong, *Het Koninkrijk*, VI, 333.

47. NIOD 251a LO-LKP, LO-BP3 Heeerenveen.

48. Wijbenga, *Bezettingstijd in Friesland*, I, 228.

49. Geale de Vries, *Verzetswijk* (Leeuwarden, 1968), 5–6.

50. De Vries, *Verzetswijk*, 6. Flim, 'Opportunities for Dutch Jews', 297.

51. Wijbenga, *Bezettingstijd in Friesland*, I, 227–9. He notes the specific work done in this regard by the tax offices in Dokkum and Drachten.

52. YV M31/8865 Sjoerd Wiersma. Report from Stichting Sneek 1940–1945, 17 April 1967.

53. Wijbenga, *Bezettingstijd in Friesland*, I, 230.

54. YV M31/8865 Sjoerd Wiersma. Wijbenga, *Bezettingstijd in Friesland*, I, 231–2.

55. YV M31/8865 Sjoerd Wiersma. Letter from L. Hogerzeil-Speerstra, January 1990.

56. De Vries, *Verzetswijk*, 7.

57. Coen Hilbrink, *De Illegalen: Illegaliteit in Twente en het aangrenzende Salland 1940–1945* ('s-Gravenhage: SDU, 1989), 26–7, 109. See also, A. H. Bornebroek, *De Illegaliteit in Twente* (Hengelo: Witkam, 1985), 36–40. T. Wiegman, 'Ds Overduin helpt onderduikers', *Sliepsteen* III (Autumn, 1985), 7; IV (Winter 1985), 15; V (1986), 7. They numbered only 0.84% of the province's population in 1942.

58. Hilbrink, *De Ondergrondse*, 30–1.

59. Ibid. 31–56. The Jewish community in Hardenberg consisted of 37 souls and that of Oldenzaal 70.

60. A. Bekkenkamp, *Leendert Overduin: Het levensverhaal van een pastor pimpernel 1900–1976* (Enschede: Van de Berg, 2000), 66. De Jong, *Het Koninkrijk*, VI, 113. Hilbrink, *De Illegalen*, 109–110. Hilbrink, *De Ondergrondse*, 57, 61.

61. Bekkenkamp, *Leendert Overduin*, 65.

62. Ibid. 69.

63. For all the members of the network, see Bekkenkamp, *Leendert Overduin*, 71–4.

64. Hilbrink, *De Illegalen*, 112.

65. Bekkenkamp, *Leendert Overduin*, 79–80.

66. Ibid. 77.

67. Ibid. 159–160.

68. Hilbrink, *De Ondergrondse*, 57.

69. Hilbrink, *De Illegalen*, 114.

70. Ibid. 113.

71. For a comprehensive biography of Post, see G. C. Hovingh, *Johannes Post: Exponent van het verzet* (Kampen: Kok, 1995).

72. De Jong, *Het Koninkrijk*, VII, 720–1, 753–66.

73. Arnold Douwes, *Belevenissen van een verzetsman in de periode 1940–1945* (Heiloo: Stegeman, 2002), 42. Max Léons and Arnold Douwes, *Mitswa en christenplicht: Bescheiden helden uit de illegaliteit* ('s-Gravenhage: BZZTôH, 2000), 38–40.

74. YV M31/56 Arnold Douwes.

75. De Jong, *Het Koninkrijk*, VII, 443. Douwes had originally been employed at a tree nursery and had been arrested for anti-German sentiments in September 1941 and had later worn a yellow star as a protest in the summer of 1942. NIOD Doc.II 364c. LO-BO4 'Dagboek van Arnold Douwes', 7. On the diary see YV M31/28 Arnold Douwes. Arnold Douwes to Dept of the Righteous, 4 August 1975.

76. Arnold Douwes in an interview for a television programme *Een tragisch ingrijpen* (May 1997) cited in Hilbrink, *De Ondergrondse*, 69–70. See also USHMM RG50.012.021 Arnold Douwes and Siene Otten.

77. NIOD LO-LKP 251a LO-BO4 Dagboek van Arnold Douwes, 3 November 1943, 54. See also, Frank Bovenkerk, 'The Other Side of the Anne Frank Story: The Dutch Role in the Persecution of the Jews in World War Two', *Crime, Law and Social Change*, XXXIV (2000), 237–258, here 249.

78. NIOD LO-LKP 251a LO-BO4 Dagboek van Arnold Douwes, 10 July 1943, 14. Douwes was the master in acquiring identity cards. He would ask people to 'lose' them, approach workers in the street and 'buy' them for DFl.10, or just steal them. Hospitals were good for this and he had networks of nurses working for him across the country. See, Léons and Douwes, *Mitswa en christenplicht*, 41–3.

79. De Jong, *Het Koninkrijk*, VII, 448. NIOD LO-LKP 251a LO-BO4, Dagboek van Arnold Douwes, 3 November 1943.

80. NIOD LO-LKP 251a LO-BO4, Dagboek van Arnold Douwes, 13 December 1943, 67.

81. Hilbrink, *De Ondergrondse*, 70.

82. Meulenbelt, *De duitse tijd.*, 125.

83. NIOD LO-LKP 251a LO-BO4, Dagboek van Arnold Douwes, 23 November 1943, 57.

84. Moore, *Victims and Survivors*, 175, cites NIOD LO-LKP 251a LO-BO4, Dagboek van Arnold Douwes, 3 November 1943, 54.

85. Van Stam, *Wacht binnen de dijken*, 77–8, notes that this was also used by hosts to rid themselves of their guests.

86. For one detailed example taken from Douwes' diary see De Jong, *Het Koninkrijk*, VI, 330–1.

87. De Jong, *Het Koninkrijk*, VII, 448. Diary entry, Wednesday 3 November 1943.

88. Hilbrink, *De Ondergrondse*, 70, cites L. Wijler, *Herinneringen*, 142.

89. NIOD LO-LKP 251a LO-BO4, Dagboek van Arnold Douwes, 17 March 1944, 120.

90. YV M31/28 Arnold Douwes. Arnold Douwes to Dept of the Righteous, 4 August 1975. The letter was written in English.

91. YV M31/28 Arnold Douwes. Arnold Douwes to Dept of the Righteous, 22 January 1989.

92. A. P. M. Cammaert, *Het Verborgen Front. Geschiedenis van de georaniseerde illegaliteit in de provincie Limburg tijdens de tweede wereldoorlog*, Vol. 1 (Leeuwarden/Mechelen: Eisma, 1994), 370–84.

93. Cammaert, *Het Verborgen Front*, 375, 383. This included contacts forged through the International Esperanto organization.

94. Cammaert, *Het Verborgen Front*, 386.

95. Robert M. W. Kempner, *Twee uit honderduizend. Anne Frank en Edith Stein* (Bilthoven: Nelissen, 1969), 102–110. Cammaert, *Het Verborgen Front*, 388–9.

96. Cammaert, *Het Verborgen Front*, 395–6.

97. Janet Keith, *A Friend Among Enemies. The Incredible Story of Arie Van Mansum in the Holocaust* (Richmond Hill: Fitzhenry and Whiteside, 1991), 41, places this event and thus his first direct involvement in the summer of 1942.

98. Cammaert, *Het Verborgen Front*, 402–3.

99. Cammaert, *Het Verborgen Front*, 404. According to Cammaert, only three of the Jews sheltered were betrayed to the Germans and failed to survive the war.

100. Cammaert, *Het Verborgen Front*, 425. The term used was '*bekeringsijver*', literally zeal for baptism. For one story of a fugitive in this area, see Paldiel, *The Path of the Righteous*, 123–4.

101. YV M31/8339a Henricus Vullinghs. Letter, Michael Lachman to B. Visser, 13 February 1994, 4.

102. Smedts, *Waarheid en leugen*, 83–6.

103. Smedts came from a poor farming family in the village and had been sponsored by Vullinghs—first in his studies for the priesthood and latterly in journalism. He was later arrested but survived in spite of spending more than a year as a '*nacht und nebel*' prisoner. YV M31/8339a Henricus Vullinghs. Letter, Michael Lachman to B. Visser, 13 February 1994, 4.

104. See, for example, YV M31/8339a Henricus Vullinghs. Letter, Avraham Perlmutter to Mordechai Paldiel, 4 May 1994, 3. They also seem to have acquired some Jews initially helped by the NV. See YV M31/8339a Henricus Vullinghs. Letter, B. Visser to Yad Vashem, n.d.

105. NIOD 251a LO-LKP, LO-BP3, 'Jodenverzorging in Limburg', 1.

106. Cammaert, *Het Verborgen Front*, 445–7.

107. NIOD 251a BG-2 LO Org3, Onderhoud met P. Verburg, n.d., 15.

108. NIOD 251a ES-4 Letter from R. W. Klein, October 1945 on Ds. H. de Jong.

109. See especially, P. W. Klein and Justus van de Kamp, *Het Philips-kommando in Kamp Vught* (Amsterdam: Contact, 2003).

110. Klein and van de Kamp, *Het Philips-kommando*, 76.

111. NIOD HSSpF 147/235 Zentralstelle für judische Auswanderung. Klein and van de Kamp, *Het Philips-kommando*, 77.

112. Klein and van de Kamp, *Het Philips-kommando*, 277.

113. Ibid. 86.

114. Ibid. 99.

115. Ibid. 141.

116. Philips had the money but needed Allied permission for the currency transfers and this was not forthcoming. YV M31/6720 Frits Philips. Testimony of Ir. Max Cahen, 4 April 1995.

117. Klein and van de Kamp, *Het Philips-kommando*, 148–9.

118. Ibid. 149 cites R. Froehling-Grunwald in Miriam Visser, 'Frits Philips heft "al het mogelijke gedaan"', *Nieuw Israelitisch Weekblad*, 12 January 1969.

119. Klein and van de Kamp, *Het Philips-kommando*, 149–150, cites interview with Juliette Cronheim-Cohen.

120. The fifty left behind in Auschwitz were older women or women with children, all of whom perished. Joop Citroen was one of the survivors of Reichenbach, see S. Citroen, *Duet Pathétique. Belevenissen van een Joods Gezin in Oorlogstijd, 1940–1945* (Utrecht: Veen, 1988). Gutman (ed.), *The Encyclopedia of the Righteous among the Nations: The Netherlands*, 597. YV M31/6720 Letter Betti Frank-Koppel, 28 February 1995 gives the full breakdown. 325 women arrived in Sweden and 10 children plus at least 40 men survived, plus a further 11 women who returned from Hamburg or Auschwitz. Frits Philips, *Vijfenveertig Jaar met Philips* (Rotterdam, 1976), 244, attributes this to the Swedish Red Cross finding them in Hamburg.

121. This raises the vexed question of selections and how they were carried out. Inevitably many were not selected and therefore became liable for immediate deportation. *Het Parool*, 12 January 1996.

122. YV M31/6720 Frits Philips. Testimony of Ir. Max Cahen, 4 April 1995. Annotation by his wife.

123. Presser, Ondergang II, 403, cites the description of the transport by Professor Cleveringa, then an inmate of the camp.

124. See, for example, Professor A. W. M. Teulings, who suggested that the award was an attempt by the Dutch to acquire 'their own Schindler', *Algemeen Dagblad*, 11 January 1996, and the charge that the Philips factory police worked hand in hand with the Gestapo made by Frans Dekkers, *Eindhoven 1933–1945: Kroniek van Nederlands Lichstad in de schaduw van het Derde Rijk* (Haarlem: Onze Tijd, 1982), a charge that led to the courts ordering the book to be withdrawn from sale. *De Volkskrant*, 6 January 1996.

125. See, for example, Joggli Meihuizen, *Noodzakelijk kwaad: de bestraffing van economische collaboratie in Nederland na de Tweede Wereldoorlog* (Amsterdam: Boom, 2003), and Dirk Luyten (ed.), *Penalization of economic collaboration in Western Europe after the Second World War* (Brussels: VUB, 1996).

CHAPTER 11

1. NIOD LO-LKP LO/BP2 Het Gooi, LO-werk Ooorlog 1940 -1945, interview with Mr Pos. Moore, *Victims and Survivors*, 178.

2. Elisabeth Maxwell, 'The Rescue of Jews in France and Belgium During the Holocaust', *Journal of Holocaust Education*, VII/1–2 (1998), 10.

3. This obviously varied from country to country and over time, but in general, children under 15 were not required to have identity cards.

4. Verhey, *Om het Joodse Kind*, 37.

5. NIOD 471/14f Aantekening uit het plakboek van Tienray, 6.

6. CDJC CCXVII-9 'La WIZO sous l'Occupation 1943–4', 1. See also Sutters (ed.), *Archives of the Holocaust. Vol.2 Pt.2* , 340. Joseph Hyman AJJDC to Clarence E. Pickett, 16 November 1942.This also reports the deaths of 200 children locked up in a school without food for several days.

7. Le Douairon, 'Le Comité "Rue Amelot" ', 68–9.

8. Le Douairon, 'Le Comité "Rue Amelot" ', 70.

9. See, for example, Férrand, Loir-et-Cher, 119, and the case of Raymonde Piédallu who sheltered two sisters of 12 and 1 from 1942 until the liberation.

10. Le Douairon, 'Le Comité "Rue Amelot" ', 94.

11. Jean Rousseau, *Des enfants juifs en Vendée. Chavagnes 1942–1944* (La Roche-sur-Yon: Centre Vendéen de recherché historique, 2004), 58. The town was more cosmopolitan in terms of new arrivals than many, even boasting a black baker married to the priest's sister.

12. Rousseau, *Des enfants juifs en Vendée*, 102.

13. Ibid. 110–111.

14. Ibid. 67–8, 114. It is also possible that she had links to Notre-Dame-de-Sion and may have been educated at one of its convents.

15. YV M31/5063 Raffin. Lazare, *Dictionnaire des Justes de France*, 476–7. Meyers, *Doors to Madame Marie*, 93. YV M31/3125 Marie Chotel and Henri Briard. Testimony of Berthe Miller, 29 November 1984 has a different version—namely that it was a friend of Chotel who, for a fee, took the children to Chavanges where the parents continued to pay for their bed and board.

16. Meyers, *Doors to Madame Marie*, 100–101.

17. YV M31/5063 Auguste and Moisette Raffin. Testimony of Odette Meyers, 5 July 1991. This was not without its problems as they were denounced by a temporary priest in the village who was avowedly pro-Pétain and antisemitic.

18. There were many cases of Jews from Paris and elsewhere using their own holiday homes as refuges or prolonging rental agreements with owners. See, for example, the Marx family and their hosts the Dussart family in Fointainebleau. Lazare, *Righteous among the Nations: France*, 222.

19. Ménager, 'Le Sauvetage des Juifs à Paris', 169.

20. 'L'Entraide Temporaire', 9.

21. 'L'Entraide Temporaire', 9.

22. Gérrard Ferrand, *Enfants Cachés, Enfants Sauvés: L'Exemple du Loir-et-Cher* (Saint-Cyr-sur-Loire: Sutton, 2005), 85–8.

23. Ibid. 90–1.

24. Ibid. 92.

25. YV M31/7637 Testimony of Simon Zajdman, 16 November 1995 and Albert Laurent, 20 November 1995.

26. YV M31/7637 Testimony of Henriette Bagès-Mandelcwajg, n.d.

27. Ferrand, *Enfants Cachés*, 95–7.

28. Yagil, *Chrétiens et Juifs*, 522–4. Comte, *Sauvetages et baptêmes*, 78–86.

29. Comte, *Sauvetages et baptêmes*, 75.

30. Molette, *Prêtres, Religieux et Religieuses*, 79. Comte, *Sauvetages et baptêmes*, 113, 121–2.

31. Comte, *Sauvetages et baptêmes*, 171–184. Ménager, 'Le Sauvetage des Juifs à Paris', 154–5. Renée Poznanski, *Etre juif en France pendant la seconde guerre mondiale* (Paris: Hachette, 1994), 600–1.

32. Paul Vergara, *Le Pasteur Paul Vergara* (Nancy: Berger-Levrault, 1966), 7. Yagil, *Chrétiens et Juifs*, 527. Any idea of accurate figures is rendered problematic by the co-operation between organizations and the dual memberships of some of their functionaries. Thus some children may well have been double-counted.

33. YV M31/3980 (Vergara); Dossier 4392 (Guillemot). Ménager, 'Le Sauvetage des Juifs à Paris', 143. She suggests the origins of this action are contested. Suzanne Spaak is credited with the idea by her husband's testimony, see Gilles Perrault, 'Suzanne Spaak, du sauvetage d'enfants à l'Orchestre Rouge de Trepper', in *La Lettre des résistants et déportés juifs* No. 46, December 1999, 12, but Katy Hazan, *Les Orphelins de la Shoah: Les Maisons de l'espoir* (Paris: Les Belles Lettres, 2000), 37 ff suggests the idea came from the Solidarité group and from Sophie Swarc.

34. YV M31/1670 Jean Joussellin. Testimony of Jean Jousscllin, n.d.

35. YV M31/1670 Jean Joussellin. Testimony of R. Joussellin, 10 November 1980. Testimony of Jeannine Lajzerowicz, 19 March 1973. Cohen, *Persécutions et sauvetages*, 437. Jacques Poujol, *Protestants dans la France en guerre 1939–1945* (Paris: Les Éditions de Paris, 2000), 112–114. Yagil, *Chrétiens et Juifs*, 530. Some give the total as 134 or 137.

36. Renée Poznanski, 'De l'action philanthropique à la résistance humanitaire', in Martine Lemalet (ed.), *Au secours des enfants du siècle* (Paris: Nil, 1993), 58. Sabine Zeitoun, 'L'OSE au secours des enfants juifs', in, Association pour la recherché et la sauvetage de la vérité historique sur la résistance en Creuse, *Le Sauvetage des Enfants Juifs de France* (Guéret, 1996), 95. Pierre Fayol, *Les*

Deux France, 1936–1945 (Paris: Harmattan, 1994), 123. OSE was preceded by a Société pour la protection sanitaire des populations juives.

37. Ferrand, *Enfants Cachés*, 127. Zeitoun, 'L'OSE au secours des enfants juifs', 96. Hillel J. Kieval, 'From Social Work to Resistance: Relief and Rescue of Jewish Children in Vichy France' (BA Harvard University, 1973), 3.

38. Laurence Rosengart, 'Les maisons de l'OSE: parcours d'une enfance fragmentée', in Martine Lemalet (ed.), *Au secours des enfants du siècle* (Paris: Nil, 1993), 83.

39. Rosengart, 'Les maisons de l'OSE', 84.

40. One example will have to suffice here, of Énéa Averbouh, a social worker who had arrived from Russia in 1929 under the auspices of the baroness Germaine de Rothschild. During the phoney war she was in charge of evacuating children to the Gironde. Returning to Paris in 1941, she began working for the OSE helping to identify and organize hiding places for children. Ménager, 'Le Sauvetage des Juifs à Paris', 128–9.

41. Rosengart, 'Les maisons de l'OSE', 84.

42. Poznanski, 'De l'action philanthropique', 59. Rosengart, 'Les maisons de l'OSE', 87, suggests there were between 1,000 and 1,200 in the unoccupied zone at the beginning of 1941 but confirms the totals for November, 88. Kieval, 'From Social Work to Resistance', 13.

43. Rosengart, 'Les maisons de l'OSE', 89.

44. Zeitoun, 'L'OSE au secours des enfants juifs', 102.

45. Rosengart, 'Les maisons de l'OSE', 90.

46. Kieval, 'From Social Work to Resistance', 13.

47. Fayol, *Les Deux France, 1936–1945*, 124.

48. Kieval, 'From Social Work to Resistance', 43.

49. Zeitoun, 'L'OSE au secours des enfants juifs', 99. Rosengart, 'Les maisons de l'OSE', 91.

50. Zeitoun, 'L'OSE au secours des enfants juifs', 98. Ménager, 'Le Sauvetage des Juifs à Paris', 81.

51. Kieval, 'From Social Work to Resistance', 33–5.

52. Ibid. 47.

53. Poznanski, 'De l'action philanthropique', 67.

54. CDJD CCXIII-114, cited in Kieval, 'From Social Work to Resistance', 60.

55. Rosengart, 'Les maisons de l'OSE', 100. Zeitoun, 'L'OSE au secours des enfants juifs', 104.

56. Kieval, 'From Social Work to Resistance', 60–1.

57. Delpard, *Les enfants cachés*, 163.

58. There is no certainty about the numbers involved as estimates vary. Poznanski, 'De l'action philanthropique', 68. Zeitoun, 'L'OSE au secours des enfants

juifs', 100, suggests 108 children and 60 adults were liberated through the actions of the commission. Delpard, *Les enfants cachés*, 164. It was argued that the name of Gerlier was used rather than Boegner because the former was much better known at that time.

59. YV M31/1770 Pierre Chaillet. Testimony of Maurice Moch, 25 July 1979. Poznanski, 'De l'action philanthropique', 69.

60. Delpard, *Les enfants cachés*, 165.

61. Fayol, *Les Deux France, 1936–1945*, 125.

62. Georges Loinger, 'Les circuits clandestins: l'exemple du réseau Garel', in Association pour la recherché et la sauvetage de la vérité historique sur la résistance en Creuse, *Le Sauvetage des Enfants Juifs de France* (Guéret, 1996), 122.

63. Zeitoun, 'L'OSE au secours des enfants juifs', 100.

64. Loinger, 'Les circuits clandestins', 122. Poznanski, 'De l'action philanthropique', 71.

65. Poznanski, 'De l'action philanthropique', 71.

66. Ibid. 72.

67. Ibid. 73.

68. Ibid. 74. Estimates range from 85 to 134. Rosengart, 'Les maisons de l'OSE', 103.

69. Zeitoun, 'L'OSE au secours des enfants juifs', 100. Poznanski, 'De l'action philanthropique', 73.

70. Rosengart, 'Les maisons de l'OSE', 103 cites Mme Germaine Masour-Ratner.

71. Poznanski, 'De l'action philanthropique', 74–5.

72. Precision here is impossible. Poznanski, 'De l'action philanthropique', 74 says that the organization looked after 6,000 children while Fayol, *Les Deux France, 1936–1945*, 126 talks of 5,000 being saved.

73. Lazare, *Le Livre des Justes*, 34–6.

74. Poznanski, 'De l'action philanthropique', 75. Among the better known of these people and organizations were the Amitié Chrétienne, CIMADE, l'Œuvre Sainte-Germain (Toulouse), Pastor Monod in Lyon, Secours Nationale in Limoges and Périgieux, and the Caisse de Compensation et d'Allocations Familiales in Grenoble.

75. Poznanski, 'De l'action philanthropique', 70.

76. Testimony of Liliane Klein. Delpard, *Les enfants cachés*, 168–9.

77. Delpard, *Les enfants cachés*, 170.

78. CEGES-SOMA AA1915 Heiber, Dossier 17, 'Les Enfants', 1. Brachfeld, *Ze hebben het overleefd*, 63.

79. Brachfeld, *Ze hebben het overleefd*, 64.

80. Saerens, 'Die Hilfe für Juden', 252. Brachfeld, *Ze hebben het overleefd*, 65–6. Moons was a member of the Catholic Workers' Organization and Geulen, who had been involved with the *kindertransporte* in 1939, was an administrator with the Brussels noviciate-residence that sheltered many young Jewish girls. Their co-workers also included Claire Murdoch who was a neighbour of Ida Sterno. YV M31/7474 Comité de Défense Juifs. Attestation by Andrée Geulen and letter Sylvain Brachfeld to Mordechai Paldiel, 19 November 1995. Vromen, *Hidden Children*, 98–9.

81. Testimony of Yvonne Jospa, Delpard, *Les enfants cachés*, 172. For example see, Michman, *Encyclopedia of the Righteous: Belgium*, 119–120, Constant and Simone Fooz who were asked to take Jewish children into their boarding school.

82. Brachfeld, *Ze hebben het overleefd*, 68.

83. USHMM RG 65.001 Roll 1901 File 26386, 'Les Enfants', written by Maurice Heiber in Tombeek Sanatorium, November 1944, 4.

84. USHMM RG 65.001 Roll 1901 File 26386, 'Les Enfants', 2.

85. Shlomo Kless, 'The Rescue of Jewish Children in Belgium during the Holocaust', *Holocaust and Genocide Studies*, III/3, 275–287, here 281–2 suggest that there was friction between the Zionists and Communists within the organization.

86. Betty Garfinkels, *Les Belges face à la persécution raciale 1940–1944* (Bruxelles: Editions de l'Institut de Sociologie de l'Université Libre de Bruxelles, n.d.), 91.

87. USHMM RG 65.001 Roll 1901 File 26386, 'Les Enfants', 2.

88. USHMM RG 65.001 Roll 1901/26386, 'Les Enfants', 2–3. Brachfeld, *Ze hebben het overleefd*, 67.

89. CEGES-SOMA AA1915 Heiber Dossier 13 CDJ, Letter from Capt. L. J. Eschelbacher to Messrs. Eschelbacher and Wachenheim, 26 September 1945.

90. Delpard, *Les enfants cachés*, 173–5. This child was left orphaned at the end of the war and was subject to disputes about his guardianship between a surviving uncle and the foster family. For similar stories recounted by Andrée Geulen, see Vromen, *Hidden Children*, 93–5.

91. Garfinkels, *Les Belges face à la persécution raciale*, 91–2. USHMM RG 65.001 Roll 1901 File 26386 'Les Enfants', 5.

92. USHMM RG 65.001 Roll 1901 File 26386, 'Les Enfants', 3. Kless, 'The Rescue of Jewish Children', 279–280.

93. USHMM RG 65.001 Roll 1901 File 26386, 'Les Enfants', 8.

94. GEGES-SOMA AA1915 Heiber, Dossier 17, 'Les Enfants', 9.

95. Brachfeld, *Ze hebben het overleefd*, 71. She was also involved in funding the work of the CDJ itself and used her contacts to approach the Société Général for money. It provided a monthly sum, and funds later also came via the Belgian government-in-exile.

96. CEGES-SOMA AA1915 Heiber, Roger van Praag to M. Denis, Premier commissaire d'Etat, 12 August 1952.

97. USHMM RG 65.001 Roll 1901 File 26386, 'Les Enfants', 11.

98. CEGES-SOMA AA1915 Heiber, Dossier 11, Attestation of Yvonne Vernant (Sister Claire d'Assise) 10 January 1948. See also *La Libre Belgique*, 3 August 1947, which gives her name as Sister Marie-Amélie AA1915 Heiber, Dossiers 31–34. CEGES-SOMA AA1915 Heiber, Roger van Praag to M. Denis, Premier commissaire d'Etat, 12 August 1952.

99. Saerens, 'Die Hilfe für Juden', 252–3.

100. Brachfeld, *Ze hebben het overleefd*, 71–2. See also CEGES-SOMA BD KD 765, *Le Soir*, 28 August 1987.

101. USHMM RG 65.001 Roll 1901 File 26386, 'Les Enfants', 9.

102. Meschman, *Never to be forgotten*, 69, 78.

103. Michman, *Encyclopedia of the Righteous: Belgium*, 146. Renée Jacquemotte.

104. Papeleux, 'Un Liégeois' 283. These were l'Hospitalité and the Home de la Vierge des Pauvres.

105. YV M31/6678 Undated note on the conduct of Curé Louis Jamin at Banneaux. Papeleux, 'Un Liégeois', 283.

106. Papeleux, 'Un Liégeois', 284.

107. Leon Papeleux, 'Le Réseau Van Den Berg', *La Vie Wallonie* (1981). *Resistance: Père Bruno Reynders*, 142. This refers to twenty convents being involved through the agency of Kerkhofs.

108. Papeleux, 'Un Liégeois', 284.

109. Leon Papeleux, 'Le Réseau Van Den Berg', *La Vie Wallonie* (1981). *Resistance: Père Bruno Reynders*, 144. Papeleux, 'Un Liégeois', 287.

110. Papeleux, 'Un Liégeois', 287.

111. Saerens, 'Die Hilfe für Juden', 272–3.

112. YV M31/6678 Albert van den Berg. Letter Hanna Kleinberger to Department of the Righteous, 21 May 1995.

113. USHMM RG 65.001 Roll 1901 File 26386, 'Les Enfants', 6.

114. Geneviève Thyange, 'L'Abbé Joseph André et l'Aide aux Juifs à Namur', in Maerten et al. (eds), *Entre la peste et le choléra*, 272-3. The ACI was refused post-war recognition by the Belgian state as civil resistance organization on the grounds that it was only officially founded after the war, although it was indisputable that it had existed in all but name during the occupation. Recognition of the ACI may in itself have been a ploy to prevent the CDJ having a monopoly on the fates of the children saved in hiding.

115. *Resistance: Père Bruno Reynders. Juste des Nations* (Brussels: Les Carrefours de la Cité, 1993), 16.

116. Teitelbaum-Hirsch, *Enfants caches*, 73–4. This gives a different story where Reynders is charged by the abbot of his monastery with the task of saving Jewish children from deportation and looking after their security and well-being. See also, Reynders, *Père Bruno Reynders*, 6, and his testimony in English YV M31/84 'Father Bruno (Henry) Reynders', 3.

117. Leon Papeleux, 'Le Réseau Van Den Berg', *La Vie Wallonie* (1981). *Resistance: Père Bruno Reynders*, 156.

118. *Resistance: Père Bruno Reynders*, 17. Brachfeld, *Ze hebben het overleefd*, 78. Van den Berg provided funds for the work carried out by Reynders. Van den Wijngaert, 'Les Catholiques Belges et les Juifs', 125. Teitelbaum-Hirsch, *Enfants caches*, 73–4.

119. *Resistance: Père Bruno Reynders*, 17.

120. Brachfeld, *Ze hebben het overleefd*, 79. Saerens, 'Die Hilfe für Juden', 265–6 gives details of where the children were hidden.

121. Paldiel, *Sheltering the Jews*, 108.

122. Teitelbaum-Hirsch, *Enfants caches*, 73.

123. Papeleux, 'Un Liégeois', 286.

124. Vromen, *Hidden Children*, 11.

125. Leon Papeleux, 'Le Réseau Van Den Berg' *La Vie Wallonie* (1981). *Resistance: Père Bruno Reynders*, 157. Papeleux, 'Un Liégeois', 284.

126. The city had a Jewish community of only 31 souls prior to the summer of 1942.

127. YV M31/186 Joseph Andre, *Vers L'Avenir*, 5–6 February 1983 Thyange, 'L'Abbé Joseph André', 263.

128. Brachfeld, *Ze hebben het overleefd*, 75.

129. Ibid. 77. Thyange, 'L'Abbé Joseph André', 270–1.

130. Delpard, *Les enfants cachés*, 177. Paldiel, *The Path of the Righteous*, 70–1.

131. Thyange, 'L'Abbé Joseph André', 265–6. See also CEGES R497.235.825. Bruno Reynders 'Notes sur le situation légale des enfants israélites', 9 January 1944, 3–4.

132. Brachfeld, *Ze hebben het overleefd*, 75. Thyange, 'L'Abbé Joseph André', 266–7.

133. CEGES-SOMA Doc. Enquête Kerk-Eglise AA1448-9/110 Rommens. Rommens to Navorsings en Studiecentrum, 8 October 1980.

134. CEGES R497.235.348. Report by M. Dumonceau de Bergendal, 'Aide aux Israélites pendant la guerre, 1940–1945, 6 April 1970. The information came from Bruylandts himself and from De Breucker's sister, who had also been heavily involved in the work of hiding Jews and others hunted by the

Germans. Thyange, 'L'Abbé Joseph André', 269. Brachfeld, *Ze hebben het overleefd*, 87. YV M31/7474 Letter Sylvain Brachfeld to Mordechai Paldiel, 19 November 1995.

135. Brachfeld, *Ze hebben het overleefd*, 82.

136. CEGES R497.234.655. Report by M. Dumonceau de Bergendal, 'Aide de la JOC: Declaration du R. P. Pierre Capart, 4 February 1970.

137. CEGES R497.238.395. Ofipresse No.21, 28 September 1945, 1–2. Jean Brück, 'L'Aide aux Refractaires, aux Juifs, aux Prisonniers de Guerre', in Emilie Arnoud et al. (eds), *La Résistance dans la Mouvement Jociste (JOC, JOCF, KAJ, VKAJ) pendant la guerre 1940–1945*, 28. CEGES R497.234.449. Report by M. Dumonceau de Bergendal, 'Aide de la JOC. Declaration de M. Bouton, 27 January 1970.

138. Brück, 'L'Aide aux Refractaires, aux Juifs, aux Prisonniers de Guerre', 29.

139. CEGES R497.234.449. Report by M. Dumonceau de Bergendal, 'Aide de la JOC. Declaration de M. Bouton, 27 January 1970.

140. Brodsky, *A Fragile Identity*, 85.

141. Leon Papeleux, 'Le Réseau Van Den Berg', *La Vie Wallonie* (1981). *Resistance: Père Bruno Reynders*, 157–8.

142. USHMM CEGES-SOMA Roll 1850, File 25843 Service Social Juif to Inspecteur Géneral, Ministère de la Santé Publique, 6 December 1962. Roll 2028, File 27481 Card Index.

143. USHMM CEGES-SOMA Roll 2028/27481. Index card for Mathilde Stevens.

144. Ibid. Index card for Annie Legros.

145. See, for example, USHMM CEGES-SOMA Roll 2028/27481. Index card for Pierre de Bonnaires where he was described as bronchial and nervous.

146. USHMM CEGES-SOMA Roll 2028/27481. Index card for Suzanne Demoulin.

147. Papeleux, 'Un Liégeois', 286.

148. Brachfeld, *Ze hebben het overleefd*, 88–9. Kless, 'The Rescue of Jewish Children', 284–5.

149. Brachfeld, *Ze hebben het overleefd*, 86–7, 89. Eight of the Jews managed to escape during the raid. Four of the five staff failed to return from captivity in Germany and only two of the deported Jews.

150. Brachfeld, *Ze hebben het overleefd*, 88–9.

151. CEGES R497.235.825. Bruno Reynders 'Notes sur le situation légale des enfants israélites', 9 January 1944, 4.

152. Brachfeld, *Ze hebben het overleefd*, 82.

153. Papeleux, 'Un Liégeois', 285.

154. CEGES R497.235.825. Bruno Reynders 'Notes sur le situation légale des enfants israélites', 9 January 1944, 5. For a wider discussion, see Vromen, *Hidden Children*, 14–15 and Luc Dequecker 'Baptism and Conversion of Jews in Belgium', in Michman, *Belgium and the Holocaust*, 235–271.

155. Kless, 'The Rescue of Jewish Children', 285, notes that the Protestant Ecumenical Council insisted that all Jewish children sheltered by its churches be returned to the Jewish community.

156. Brachfeld, *Ze hebben het overleefd*, 82.

157. CEGES R497.235.825. Bruno Reynders 'Notes sur le situation légale des enfants israélites', 9 January 1944, 3–4.

158. Delpard, *Les enfants cachés*, 177.

159. *Encyclopedia of the Righteous: Belgium*, 70–1 Ferdinand Collin.

160. Brachfeld, *Ze hebben het overleefd*, 108.

161. Ibid. 154.

162. Ibid. 156.

163. Thierry Delplancq and Catherine Massange, 'L'Hospice de Scheut (1943–1944)', *Bijdragen tot de eigentijdse Herinnering/Les Cahiers de la Mémoire contemporaine*, 5 (2003–4), 13–14.

164. Brachfeld, *Ze hebben het overleefd*, 218–219.

165. GEGES-SOMA AA1915 Heiber, Dossier 17, 'Les Enfants', 13. Brachfeld, *Ze hebben het overleefd*, 219–221.

166. Brachfeld, *Ze hebben het overleefd*, 200–201, 224–5.

167. YV M31/7474 Comité de Defense Juifs, Letter Andrée Geulen to Sylvain Brachfeld, 31 March 1999. CEGES-SOMA BD KD 765 *Le Soir*, 28 August 1987. Vromen, *Hidden Children*, 62–6.

168. Brachfeld, *Ze hebben het overleefd*, 231–2.

CHAPTER 12

1. Bert Jan Flim, *Omdat Hun Hart Sprak: Geschiedenis van de georganiseerde hulp aan Joodse kinderen in Nederland* (Kampen: Kok, 1996), 31.

2. In a more recent interview Hetty Voûte claimed that the inspiration came from seeing children in the Amsterdam streets after their parents had been taken away in the first raids. See Mark Klempner, *The Heart has Reasons: Holocaust Rescuers and their Stories of Courage* (Cleveland OH: Pilgrim Press, 2006), 22.

3. De Jong, *Het Koninkrijk* VI, 48–9. Flim, *Omdat Hun Hart Sprak*, 32.

4. See Gerard Hirschfeld and Presser.

5. Flim, *Omdat Hun Hart Sprak*, 35.

6. Flim, *Omdat Hun Hart Sprak*, 35, cites UVSV, *Almanak der Utrechtsche Vrouwelijke Studenten Vereeniging* 1946 (Utrecht, 1946), 102.

7. Flim, *Omdat Hun Hart Sprak*, 36. Klempner, *The Heart has Reasons*, 21.

8. Klempner, *The Heart has Reasons*, 23–4. Flim, *Omdat Hun Hart Sprak*, 38.

9. Flim, *Omdat Hun Hart Sprak*, 41, cites his interviews with Rut Matthijsen, 1 August 1990 and 16 May 1991.

10. Flim, *Omdat Hun Hart Sprak*, 41.

11. Cammaert, *Het Verborgen Front*, 398. Flim, *Omdat Hun Hart Sprak*, 49–51.

12. USHMM RG50.030.154 Pieter Meerburg, 12 October 1990, 11.

13. Cammaert, *Het Verborgen Front*, 398, 400. Flim, *Omdat Hun Hart Sprak*, 42–4.

14. Cammaert, *Het Verborgen Front*, 411.

15. Ibid. 410–411.

16. Flim, *Omdat Hun Hart Sprak*, 95.

17. De Jong, *Het Koninkrijk* VII, 924–34. C. M. Schulten, *'En verpletterd wordt het juk'; Verzet in Nederland 1940–1945* ('s-Gravenhage: SDU, 1995) 135–6. The group was responsible for the assassination attempt against the leader of the Dutch troops fighting on the Eastern Front, General H. A. Seyffardt on 5 February 1943. The mortally wounded General implicated students as his attackers and the following day, raids took place against universities in Utrecht, Noord-Holland and Zuid-Holland. Flim, *Omdat Hun Hart Sprak*, 39.

18. De Jong, *Het Koninkrijk*, VI, 338. Flim, *Omdat Hun Hart Sprak*, 104, 106.

19. Ibid. Moore, *Victims and Survivors*, 184–5.

20. See Hille de Vries et al., *Een Ophitsend Geschrift. De geschiedenis van een illegaal blad* (Utrecht: Ambo, 1968). De Jong, *Het Koninkrijk* VI, 338.

21. For a full biography, see Gert van Klinken, *Strijdbaar en Omstreden: Een biografie van de calvinistische verzetsvrouw Gezina van der Molen* (Amsterdam: Boom, 2006). Marjan Schwegman, *Het Stille Verzet: vrouwen in illegal organisaties* (Amsterdam: Socialistische Uijgeverij, 1980).

22. Van Klinken, *Strijdbaar en Omstreden*, 95–98. Moore, *Victims and Survivors*, 185.

23. Lydia E. Winkel, *Het Ondergrondse Vrij Nederland* (Baarn: Het Wereldvenster, 1970), 8. De Jong, *Het Koninkrijk* V, 771; VI, 128. The first issue had been in August 1940, but most of the originators had been arrested in early 1941, and van der Molen's recruitment represented an attempted rebuilding of the organization.

24. Flim, *Omdat Hun Hart Sprak*, 108. This document is now in the Verzetsmuseum, Amsterdam.

25. Ibid. 107.

26. She was opposed to other members of the editorial board, not least Henk van Randwijk, whom she regarded as too 'socialist'. She had also been outraged when one of her articles was drastically revised by other members of the editorial group. De Jong, *Het Koninkrijk*, V, 777; VI, 128.

27. USHMM RG50.030.154 Pieter Meerburg, 12 October 1990, 12–13.

28. Hof, *Vrouwen*, 219.

29. Ibid. 221–2.

30. Van Lier was herself the product of a mixed marriage. Flim, *Omdat Hun Hart Sprak*, 66. Hof, *Vrouwen*, 229.

31. Hof, *Vrouwen*, 227–8.

32. Ibid. 214, 235. Flim, *Omdat Hun Hart Sprak*, 67. It was estimated that she helped to save *c.*150 Jewish children.

33. Flim, *Omdat Hun Hart Sprak*, 45–6.

34. Ibid. 46–47.

35. Pontier did continue to shelter some adults, see Flim, *Omdat Hun Hart Sprak*, 96, 102–3. Cammaert, *Het Verborgen Front*, 412.

36. Flim, *Omdat Hun Hart Sprak*, 130. It also retained its former purpose as a day-nursery for a relatively short period from July to October 1942.

37. Ibid. 133–4, cites Semmy Woortman-Glasoog and Jooske de Neve.

38. Ibid. 134–5.

39. Ibid. 137, cites interview with Sieny Kattenburg, 20 August 1990.

40. Ibid. 138, 140–1. Sometimes the nurses had to accompany a group of orphans all the way to Westerbork.

41. Ibid. 141.

42. *Het Grote Gebod*, 8. Flim, *Omdat Hun Hart Sprak*, 145 6. This was one of the few remaining Christian teaching training schools. Others had closed and had transferred their students to Amsterdam. Thus the college had a large student population and was under close scrutiny by the Ministry of Education, not least because this was van Hulst's first year as director.

43. Flim, *Omdat Hun Hart Sprak*, 147.

44. Cammaert, *Het Verborgen Front*, 401, 406. Flim, *Omdat Hun Hart Sprak*, 150–1, 223.

45. Flim, *Omdat Hun Hart Sprak*, 157, cites interview with Johan van Hulst, 31 August 1989.

46. NIOD 471/14g Testimony of Virginie Riwka Oudkerk-Cohen, 18 March 1983. Cammaert, *Het Verborgen* Front, 401. Flim, *Omdat Hun Hart Sprak*, 154.

47. Flim, *Omdat Hun Hart Sprak*, 163–4.

48. Ibid. 132–3, 139, 149.

49. Flim, 148–9. The jenever and schnapps were bought by trading the alcohol that Hester van Lennep's skin care clinic could acquire in large quantities as a cleansing agent.

50. NIOD 251a ES-4 LO District Maastricht, 'Het wegwerken van Franse krijgsgefangenen', 8. This source estimated that some 4,000 escaping French prisoners were helped in the province of Limburg during the occupation. NIOD 251a ES-4 Eugenie Boutet uit Sevenum.

51. Cammaert, *Het Verborgen Front*, 405. Flim, *Omdat Hun Hart Sprak*, 218.

52. NIOD 471/14f Aantekening uit het plakboek van Tienray, 3–4, 7. Cammaert, *Het Verborgen Front*, 405–7.

53. Cammaert, *Het Verborgen Front*, 407. Around 40 of the children were in the 10 to 15 year-old age range, perceived to be the most difficult to place because they were the most likely to forget their new identity and cover story.

54. Flim, *Omdat Hun Hart Sprak*, 222.

55. Ibid. 223.

56. YV M31/2878 Nico Dohmen. Testimonies of Aron Querido January 1983 and Peter Kaufman, 31 January 1983.

57. YV M31/2878 Nico Dohmen. Testimony of Virginie Oudkerk-Cohen, 18 March 1983.

58. NIOD 471/14g Testimony by Peter Kaufmann, 31 January 1983.

59. YV M31/2878 Nico Dohmen. Testimony of Schlomo Kayser, 6 February 1983.

60. For one such case in July 1944 (Oirlo) see, YV M31/2878 Nico Dohmen. Testimony of Hanna Stavi-Prins, 26 January 1983. NIOD 471/14f Aantekening uit het plakboek van Tienray, 8. Cammaert, *Het Verborgen Front*, 408–9.

61. Cammaert, *Het Verborgen Front*, 411. Flim, *Omdat Hun Hart Sprak*, 230. Pontier had provided the identity papers. This protection was particularly good as the Germans were keen to maximize coal production from the Dutch mines and did not therefore attempt to conscript mineworkers for forced labour in Germany or elsewhere in the Netherlands.

62. Flim, *Omdat Hun Hart Sprak*, 236 quotes testimony from Martge van Leeuwen Bockma to Stichting 1940–1945, 14 October 1982.

63. Cammaert, *Het Verborgen Front*, 413.

64. Flim, *Omdat Hun Hart Sprak*, 231.

65. Ibid. 101.

66. Ibid. 174.

67. USHMM CRP RG50.012.072 Riekerk, 29 April 1990. Flim, *Omdat Hun Hart Sprak*, 331, 333–4. Woortman was arrested by the SD on 19 July 1944

and sent to Bergen-Belsen where he died of typhus in March 1945. His wife then took over his work until the liberation.

68. Cammaert, *Het Verborgen Front,* 446, estimates that there were 2,500–3,500 Jews in hiding in the province.

69. Cammaert, *Het Verborgen Front,* 417. Flim, *Omdat Hun Hart Sprak,* 343.

70. Cammaert, *Het Verborgen Front,* 413. Flim, *Omdat Hun Hart Sprak,* 338. Pontier spent six months in solitary confinement in the 'Oranje Hotel' goal in Scheveningen and was released on 17 May 1944.

71. Flim, *Omdat Hun Hart Sprak,* 339–340.

72. NIOD 471/14g Letter from Mia Coelingh, 18 January 1981. Flim, *Omdat Hun Hart Sprak,* 61, 76.

73. Flim, *Omdat Hun Hart Sprak,* 76–7.

74. NIOD 471/14g Letter from Mia Coelingh, 18 January 1981. Flim, *Omdat Hun Hart Sprak,* 79.

75. De Vries, *Verzetswijk,* 5.

76. Stein, *Quiet Heroes,* 57–74.

77. Ibid. 92. The Miedemas subsequently emigrated to Canada when Pieter fell out with the elders of his new parish at Dwingelo. See also USHMM CRP RG50.012.058 Miedema, 6 June 1988.

78. Flim, *Omdat Hun Hart Sprak,* 53, cites his interview with Hetty Voûte, 17 February 1989.

79. Ibid. 202.

80. Ibid. 78–9, cites his interview with Mia Coelingh, 13 August 1990.

81. USHMM CRP RG50.012.0063 Mulder, 18 July 1988.

82. USHMM CRP RG50.012.0049 Labruyere, 1988.

83. USHMM CRP RG50.012.092 Vos, 23 February 1988.

84. USHMM CRP RG50.012.017 DeVries, 2 June 1988.

85. USHMM CRP RG50.012.017 DeVries, 2 June 1988.

86. NIOD LO-LKP, LO-BP3 'Jodenverzorging in Limburg', 3.

87. Flim, *Omdat Hun Hart Sprak,* 226.

88. Ibid. 222.

89. Ibid. 84.

90. Ibid. 341, cites interview with Dick Groenewegen van Wijk, 12 May 1984. The baptismal certificated dated from just after the liberation.

91. Ibid. 60–1.

92. Ibid. 200. When attempts were made to regularize the population register records after the war, Mazirel had some difficulty in convincing the officials that her two children born before the occupation were in fact her own.

93. Ibid. 57.

94. Flim, 60, notes how dangerous the letter was, given that there were four copies and there was explicit mention of hiding Jewish children.

95. Cammaert, *Het Verborgen Front*, 399. De Jong, *Het Koninkrijk* VI, 49.

96. Moore, *Victims and Survivors*, 128. Kempner, *Twee uit Honderdduizend*, 93, 99–100. Of the 694 Dutch and non-Dutch Catholic converts in the Netherlands, 92 were deported to Auschwitz early in August 1942. Many others who had been arrested were released because they were in mixed marriages. Kempner, *Twee uit Honderdduizend*, 105–6.

97. Flim, *Omdat Hun Hart Sprak*, 352–3.

98. J. Michman et al. (eds), *Pinkas: Geschiedenis van de joodse gemeenschap in Nederland* (Ede/Antwerp/Amsterdam, 1992), 218. Joël Fishman, 'De joodse oorlogswezen. Een interview met Gesina van der Molen, voorzitter van de Commissie Oorlogspleegkinderen', in David Barnouw et al. (eds), *Oorlogs-documentatie* VII (1995), 58. Moore, *Victims and Survivors,* 233.

99. Hilbrink, *De Ondergrondse*, 73.

100. USHMM RG50.030.146 Malnik, 5.

101. USHMM RG50.012.0063 Mulder, 4. The woman concerned was described as 'nice' by the daughter of the house and continued to correspond after the war. The problem with such testimonies is that the evidence is, by its very nature, uncorroborated.

102. Brodsky, *A Fragile Identity*, 149.

103. USHMM RG50.030.241 von Halle, 14–20.

104. Hilbrink, *De Ondergrondse*, 86.

105. Ibid.

106. USHMM RG50.012.071 Pritchard, 5.

107. Debórah Dwork, 'Marion van Binsbergen Pritchard's Legacy', in David Scrase, Wolfgang Mieder and Katherine Quimby Johnson, *Making a Difference: Rescue and Assistance during the Holocaust* (Burlington VT: Center for Holocaust Studies at the University of Vermont 2004), 17–18. USHMM RG50.012.071 Pritchard, 5.

108. Flim, *Omdat Hun Hart Sprak*, 342.

109. Hilbrink, *De Ondergrondse*, 77.

110. Ibid.

111. See for example the story of a young girl at a boarding school whose mental health slowly deteriorated. Brodsky, *A Fragile Identity*, 106–8.

CHAPTER 13

1. Steinberg, *La Traque des Juifs* II, 197.

2. De Jong, *Het Koninkrijk* IV, 341.

3. Aalders, *Nazi Looting*, 45.

4. Ibid. 73–4.

5. NIOD HSSpF 111/181a Reports by SS-Sturmbannführer Willi Zoepf (IVB4, The Hague) on meetings with Plümer and Oberregierungsrat Dr Schlüssler, 22 June 1943. Zoepf to Eichmann (RSHA) 20 September 1943.

6. Presser, *Ondergang* I, 441–2.

7. De Jong, *Het Koninkrijk* VI, 274–8.

8. NIOD HSSpF 147/233 Zentralstelle für judische Auswanderung, Zentralstelle to RSHA IVB4 (Berlin), 18 July 1942.

9. Jacob Presser, *Ashes in the Wind*, 347.

10. De Jong, *Het Koninkrijk* VI, 278, note 1.

11. Moore, *Victims and Survivors*, 132. De Jong, *Het Koninkrijk* VI, 276–8.

12. De Jong, *Het Koninkrijk* VI, 276–7.

13. Moore, *Victims and Survivors*, 133.

14. Herzberg, *Kroniek der Jodenvervolging*, 313.

15. De Jong, *Het Koninkrijk* VII, 733.

16. Moore, *Victims and Survivors*, 110.

17. See Yehuda Bauer, *Jews for Sale? Nazi-Jewish negotiations, 1933–1945* (New Haven and London: Yale U.P., 1994), 5–43.

18. Bauer, *Jews for Sale?*, 103.

19. De Jong, *Het Koninkrijk*, VI, 265. Joanne Reilly, *Belsen: The Liberation of a Concentration Camp* (London: Routledge, 1998), 12. Chaya Brasz, *Transport 222. Bergen-Belsen-Palestine, July 1944* (Jerusalem, 1994), 9–10.

20. De Jong, *Het Koninkrijk* VI, 265.

21. Bauer, *Jews for Sale?*, 103—4. Reilly, *Belsen*, 12. The complex at Bergen-Belsen also included a small camp for American Jews, who were not required to work or wear a yellow star. Herzberg, *Kroniek der Jodenvervolging*, 294.

22. Rudolf Hoess, *Commandant of Auschwitz*, 5th ed. (London: Pan, 1982), 183–4. Reilly, *Belsen*, 16

23. Herzberg, *Kroniek der Jodenvervolging*, 290.

24. Ibid. 291.

25. Brasz, *Transport 222*, 11. Miriam and husband, Lieb de Leeuw, were Dutch Zionists who had been in Palestine since the early 1920s. Reilly, *Belsen*, 13–14.

26. Brasz, *Transport 222*, 11–16. Reilly, *Belsen*, 15.

27. Moore, *Victims and Survivors*, 132.

28. De Jong, *Het Koninkrijk* VII, 745, quotes from Herzberg's diary.

29. Ibid. 745.

30. Brasz, *Transport 222*, 17.

31. Reilly, *Belsen*, 16.

32. Moore, *Victims and Survivors*, 132.

33. De Jong, *Het Koninkrijk*, VI, 308.

34. Ibid. 306. Jaap Boas, *Boulevard des Misères: Het verhaal van doorgangskamp Westerbork* (Amsterdam: Nijgh en Van Ditmar, 1988), 49−70. Spanier and his family had been on the SS St Louis and came to the Netherlands as part of the distribution of its passengers in Western Europe. See Gordon Thomas and Max Morgan-Witts, *Voyage of the Damned* (London: Coronet, 1976), 24−7, 302−5.

35. De Jong, *Het Koninkrijk*, VIII, 707−8. Philip Mechanicus, *In depot: dagboek uit Westerbork van Philip Mechanicus* (Amsterdam: Polak en Van Gennep, 1964).

36. Boas, *Boulevard des Misères*, 66−70. Spanier's preferment has been explained by his sharing Düsseldorf as a home town with Gemmeker.

37. In spite of their conduct, none of them was prosecuted by the Dutch authorities. Schlesinger gave evidence at the trial of Gemmeker, but dropped out of sight after 1949 and was rumoured to have immigrated to the United States. Pisk likewise disappeared from view but was reported by a Dutch employee of the camp to have gone to Australia where he died. Details from www.cympm.com [19 March 2008].

38. Paldiel, *Saving the Jews*, 243.

39. Moore, *Victims and Survivors*, 186.

40. Moore, *Victims and Survivors*, 186.

41. See, for example, WL P.IIIh/836 Auschwitz.

42. John David Morley, 'The Nicest SS Man Imaginable', *Times Magazine*, 4 June 1994, 20. Saskia Belleman, 'Saviour or Killer from the Waffen SS', *The Guardian*, 14 December 1993, 12−13. Paldiel, *Saving the Jews*, 240.

43. De Jong, *Het Koninkrijk* VI, 247. Morley, 'The Nicest SS Man Imaginable', 20.

44. Paldiel, *Saving the Jews*, 241.

45. Ibid.

46. Moore, *Victims and Survivors*, 187.

47. Paldiel, *Saving the Jews*, 244.

48. Ibid. 242.

49. Ibid. 243.

50. Aalders, *Nazi Looting*, 212. This was the rate until 10 June 1943, thereafter it was raised to fl.30,000. Herzberg, *Kroniek der Jodenvervolging*, 267. See also the specific scheme to get Jewish diamond merchants to pay for their exemptions. De Jong, *Het Koninkrijk* VI, 286−7.

51. Moore, *Victims and Survivors*, 135. De Jong, *Het Koninkrijk* VI, 268.

52. Aalders, *Nazi Looting*, 214−6.

53. Ibid. 217.

54. Israel Gutman (ed.), *Rechtvaardigen onder de Volkeren: Nederlanders met een Yad Vashem-onderscheiding voor hulp aan joden* (Amsterdam/Antwerpen: Veen/NIOD, 2005), 723. Paldiel, *The Righteous among the Nations*, 353. Moore, *Victims and Survivors*, 119–123.

55. Gutman, *Rechtvaardigen*, 723. Paldiel, *The Righteous*, 355. He was recommended by Nino Kotting, one of the partners in the firm.

56. Paldiel, *The Righteous*, 355.

57. Gutman, *Rechtvaardigen*, 723–4.

58. Paldiel, *The Righteous*, 354.

59. Presser, *Ondergang* II, 54.

60. See Geraldien van Frijtag Drabbe Künzel, 'Zwischen Tätern, Zuschauern und Opfern: Hans Georg Calmeyer und die Judenverfolgung in den besetzten Niederlanden', in Gerhard Hirschfeld and Tobias Jersak, *Karrieren im Nationalsozialismus. Funktionseliten zwischen Mitwirkung und Distanz* (Frankfurt/New York: Campus, 2004).

61. Harry James Cargas, *Voices from the Holocaust* (Lexington: Kentucky University Press, 1993), 71.

62. Paldiel, *The Righteous*, 358–9.

63. R. E. van Galen-Herrmann, 'De Controverse Rond het Ambtelijk Functioneren van Hans Calmeyer tijdens de Bezetting 1940–1945', *Nederlands Juristenblad* 17, 28 April 2006, 943. Paldiel, *The Righteous*, 356, 360. See also, Matthias Middelberg, *Judenrecht, Judenpolitik und der Jurist Hans Calmeyer in den besetzten Niederlanden 1940–1945* (Göttingen: V&R Unipress, 2005). Peter Niebaum, *Ein Gerechter unter den Völkern, Hans Calmeyer in seiner Zeit (1903–1972)* (Osnabrück: Rasch, 2001). Geraldien von Frijtag Drabbe Künzel, 'Gutachten zur Tätigkeit: Hans Calmeyers in den Niederlanden' (Amsterdam: unpublished, 2000).

64. Paldiel, *The Righteous*, 359–360.

65. Van Galen-Herrmann, 'De Controverse', 943.

66. Ibid.

67. Ibid. 944. This idea of functionaries keeping their roles going—especially in 1944—to prevent postings elsewhere has been used to explain the conduct of other leading Nazis in the Netherlands.

68. For the most recent and comprehensive treatment of Calmeyer, see Geraldien van Frijtag Drabbe Künzel, *Het geval Calmeyer* (Amsterdam: Mets en Schilt, 2008).

69. Brodsky, *A Fragile Identity*, 25.

70. Kitson, *The Hunt for Nazi Spies*, 113.

71. NIOD 251a ES-4, Interview with Dick van Veen, 29 August 1947. De Jong, *Het Koninkrijk* VI, 111, 115. Wijbenga, *Bezettingstijd in Friesland*, 318.

72. Liebman, *Né juif*, 69. Steinberg, *La Traque des Juifs* II, 192.

73. Steinberg, *La Traque des Juifs* II, 205.

74. CEGES-SOMA AA1915 Heiber, Dossier 18, Letter from Heiber, 7 May 1946, 3. See also *Leven in de holster van ons land*. MvG DO R497 234.933 Rapport: Actions du groupe Juifs des Partisans Armés, 10 March 1970. Steinberg, *La Traque des Juifs* II, 212–213. For an earlier attempt on his life see Steinberg, *La Traque des Juifs* II, 32. Liebman, *Né juif*, 70–1 notes that he survived this assassination and disappeared at the liberation, being condemned to death *in absentia* by a Belgian tribunal in 1947. See also UHSMM RG50.012.038 Herman, 3.

75. MvG DO R497 237.218 Rapport: Adler, Erich, 14 September 1970.

76. MvG DO R497 234.933 Rapport: Actions du groupe Juifs des Partisans Armés, 10 March 1970. Steinberg, *La Traque des Juifs* II, 195–6, 198.

77. MvG DO R497 237.218 and 234.259 Rapport: Adler, Erich né le 23.1.1897 à Neu-Berum dated 9 January 1970. MvG DO R497 234.933 Actions de groupe Juifs des Partisans Armée, 10 March 1970.

78. Reynders, *Père Bruno Reynders*, 12, 45.

79. Steinberg, *La Traque des Juifs* II, 210. Like Glogowski, he was later targeted by the Pasternak resistance group.

80. Steinberg, *La Traque des Juifs* II, 199. Steinberg makes the point that they are hardly representative, but in a country where 95% of the Jews were foreign nationals or stateless, they may well reflect the wide national base of the community as a whole.

81. Steinberg, *La Traque des Juifs* II, 196.

82. CEGES-SOMA AA1915 Heiber, Dossier 20, Sorokine. Undated memorandum, 'Le cas Sorokine'.

83. For other examples, see CEGES-SOMA AA1915 Heiber, Dossier 18, Letter from Heiber, 7 May 1946, 3 and *Leven in de holster van ons land*.

84. Koos Groen, *Als slachtoffers daders worden. De zaak van de joodse veraadster Ans van Dijk* (Baarn: Ambo, 1994), 22–8.

85. Groen, *Als slachtoffers daders worden*, 37.

86. Groen, *Als slachtoffers daders worden*, 47.

87. De Jong, *Het Koninkrijk*, VI, 351–2. Groen, *Als slachtoffers daders worden*, 83. Testimony of Pieter Schaap in the trial of Anna van Dijk, 24 February 1947.

88. Groen, *Als slachtoffers daders worden*, 86.

89. Ibid. 91–3.

90. De Jong, *Het Koninkrijk*, VI, 352.

91. Groen, *Als slachtoffers daders worden*, 101–2.

92. Ibid. 124.

93. Ibid. 141–8.

94. De Jong, *Het Koninkrijk*, XII, 567–8, 601. Groen, *Als slachtoffers daders worden*, 204, 234. A deathbed conversion to Catholicism proved to no avail. Koos Groen, *Landverraders. Wat deden we met ze?* (Baarn: In de Toren, 1974), 117–118. She was one of 35 Dutch citizens who were sentenced to death and executed after the war. See also, Igor Cornelissen, *Speurtocht naar de (auto)biografie* (Amsterdam: Lubberhuizen, 1993), 98–100. Frank Bovenkerk, 'Het Nederlandse aandeel in de jodenvervolging als criminologisch probleem', in Moerings et al., *Morele kwesties*, 25–6.

95. Groen, *Als slachtoffers daders worden*, 208, 247.

96. De Jong, *Het Koninkrijk* XIII, 113–114. Controversially, Groen argues that she was more involved and had an affair with one of the policemen—something that had to be kept secret because of its contravention of the racial laws. Groen, *Als slachtoffers daders worden*, 106.

97. Groen, *Als slachtoffers daders worden*, 241.

98. De Jong, *Het Koninkrijk*, VII, 425.

99. De Jong, *Het Koninkrijk*, VI, 259.

100. De Jong, *Het Koninkrijk*, VII, 431.

101. De Jong, *Het Koninkrijk*, VII, 436–7.

102. De Jong, *Het Koninkrijk*, XII, 570.

103. Groen, *Als slachtoffers daders worden*, 241. The debate was reignited in 1965 when Jacob Presser chose to portray Weinreb as a scapegoat—a Jewish traitor who somehow exonerated the Dutch who had done so little for their Jewish fellow citizens. De Jong, *Het Koninkrijk*, XII, 571. Boas, *Boulevard des Misères*, 159–161. See also Friedrich Weinreb, *Collaboratie en Verzet, 1940–1945: Een poging tot ontmythologisering*, 3 vols (Amsterdam, 1969).

104. De Jong, *Het Koninkrijk*, XII, 572–3. Daniel Gilthay Veth and A. J. van der Leeuw, *Rapport door het Rijksinstituut voor Oorlogsdocumentatie uitgebracht aan de minister van Justitie inzake de activiteiten van drs. F. Weinreb gedurende de jaren 1940–1945, in het licht van nadere gegevens bezien* ('s-Gravenhage: Staatuitgeverij, 1976). Dick Houwaart, *Weinreb. Een Witboek* (Amsterdam: Meulenhoff, 1975). I. Schöffer, 'Weinreb, een affaire van lange duur', *Tijdschrift voor Geschiedenis* XCV (1982), 196–224. Regina Grüter, *Een Fantasist schrift geschiedenis: de affaires rond Friedrich Wienreb* (Amsterdam: Balans, 1997).

105. Zasloff, *A Rescuer's Story*, 212–213.

106. Kitson, *The Hunt for Nazi Spies*, 23.

107. For an example from inside Nazi Germany see, Peter Wyden, *Stella: One Woman's True Tale of Evil, Betrayal and Survival in Hitler's Germany* (New York: Simon and Schuster, 1992).

CHAPTER 14

1. Lazare, *Le Livre des Justes*, 82–3.

2. Cabanel, 'Des justes', 201. This was used by Philippe Joutard in relation to the Protestants in the Cevennes, but probably owes it origins to Enrico Deaglio, *La Banalita del Bene: Storia di Giorgio Perlasca* (Milan: Feltrinelli, 1991).

3. Snoek, *De Nederlandse Kerken en de Joden*, 67–8.

4. Hilbrink, *De Illegalen*, 73.

5. See, for example, Maxime Steinberg, 'The Judenpolitik in Belgium', in Dan Michman (ed.), *Belgium and the Holocaust* (Jerusalem: Yad Vashem, 1998), 208. Saerens, *Vreemdelingen in een Wereldstad*, 686 et seq.

Glossary

ACI l'Aide Chrétienne aux Israelites

AJB Association des Juifs de Belgique

ASC Amsterdamsch Studenten Corps

CCOJA Comité de Coordination des Œuvres d'Assistance du Grand Paris

CDJ Comité de Défense des Juifs

CDJC Centre de documentation Juine Contemperaine

CEGES–SOMA Centre D'Études et de Documentation Guerre et Sociétés Contemporaines/Studie- en Documentatiecentrum Oorlog en Hedendaagse Maatschappij (Centre for Historical Research and Documentation on War and Contemporary Society, Brussels)

CGD Comité Général de Défense des Juifs

CGQJ Commissariat Générale aux Questions Juives

CIMADE Protestant Comité Inter-Mouvements Auprès d'Evacués

CNT Confederación Nacional del Trabajo

COMASSIS Portuguese Committee of Assistance to Jewish Refugees

CVIA Comite de vigilance des intellectuels antifascistes

DCA Direction de centres d'accueil

DNSAP Danish National Socialist Party

EIF Éclaireurs israëlites de France

ERC Emergency Rescue Committee

FFL Forces Françaises Libres (Free French Forces)

FSC/AFSC Friends Service Committee/American Friends Service Committee

FSJF Fédération des Sociétés Juives de France

FTP Franc-Tireur et Partisans

GTE Groupes de Travailleurs Etrangers

HIAS Hebrew Immigrant Aid Society

HICEM Jewish Migration Organization founded in 1927 with the amalgamation of the HIAS, Jewish Colonization Association and Emigdirect

FI Independence Front *Front Independence* (French) *Onafhankelijksfront* (Flemish)

JDC American Jewish Joint Distribution Committee

JLC Jewish Labor Committee

JOC Jeunesse Ouvrière Chrétienne

KAJ Katholieke Arbeidersjeugd

KBI Katholiek Bureau voor Israël

LKP Landelijke Knokploegen

LO Landelijke Organisatie voor Hulp aan Onderduikers

MI6 British Secret Intelligence Service

MI9 British Military Intelligence Section charged with helping escaping Allied Prisoners of War

MNCR Mouvement Nationale Contre le Racisme

MOE Main d'Oeuvre Étrangère (Belgium)

MOI Main d'Oeuvre Immigrée (France)

MOI-FTP Main d'oeuvre immigrée—Franc-Tireur et Partisans (France)

MVDO Dienst voor de Oorlogsslachtoffers (Belgion Service for war victims)

NIOD Nederlands Instituut voor Oorlogsdocumentatie (Netherlands Institute for War Documentation)

NSB Nationaal-Socialistische Beweging

NSNAP Nederlands Nationaal-Socialistisch Arbeiderspartij (Dutch National Socialist Party)

NV Naamloze Vennootschap

OJC Organisation juive de combat (France)

ONE Oeuvre Nationale de l'Enfance/Nationaal Werk voor Kinderwelzijn (Belgium)

ORT Organization reconstruction travail (France)

OSE Oeuvre de secours aux enfants (France)

PVDE Política de Vigilancia e Defenza do Estado (Portuguese State Security Police)

RSHA Reichssicherheitshauptamt (Reich Security Main Office)

SD Sicherheitsdienst (Security Service)

SDAP Sociaal Democratische Arbeiders Partij

SN Secours Nationale (France)

SNCF Société Nationale des Chemins de fers français

SOBU Speciaal Ontwikkelingsbureau/Speciaal Opdrachtbureau (Philips) Special Commissions Office

SOE Special Operations Executive

SSAE Service Social Internationale d'Aide aux Emigrants

SSE Service Social des Etrangers

STO Service du Travail Obligatoire

UGIF Union Générale des Israélites de France

UJRE Union des Juifs pour la Résistance et l'Entraide

USHMM United States Holocaust Memorial Museum

USC Utrechtsch Studenten Corps

UVSV Utrechtsche Vrouwelijke Studenten Vereeniging

VNV Vlaams Nationaal Verbond (Flemish Nationalist Association)

WIZO Womens International Zionist Organisation

WVHA SS-*Wirtschaftsverwaltungshauptamt* (Economic Administration Central Office)

YMCA Young Men's Christian Association

YV Yad Vashem

List of Works Cited

Aalders, Gerard — *Nazi Looting: The Plunder of Dutch Jewry during the Second World War* (Oxford: Berg, 2004)

Abitbol, Michel — 'The Encounter between French Jewry and the Jews of North Africa: Analysis of a Discourse (1830–1914)' in: Frances Malino and Bernard Wasserstein (eds), *The Jews in Modern France* (Hanover NH: Brandeis U. P., 1985)

Abrahamsen, Samuel — *Norway's Response to the Holocaust: A Historical Perspective* (New York: Holocaust Library, 1991)

—— — 'The Relationship of Church and State during the German Occupation of Norway, 1940–1945; in Jack Fischel and Sanford Pinsker (eds), *Holocaust Studies Annual*, Vol. 2, *The Churches Response to the Holocaust*, (Greenwood FL: Penkevill, 1986)

Adler, Jacques — *The Jews of Paris and the Final Solution: Communal Response and Internal Conflicts, 1940–1944* (New York/London: Oxford University Press, 1987)

Afonso, Rui — 'Le "Wallenberg Portugais": Aristides de Sousa Mendes', *Revue d'Histoire de la Shoah*, 165 (January-April 1999)

Ainsztein, Reuben — *Jewish Resistance in Nazi-Occupied Eastern Europe* (New York: Barnes and Noble, 1975)

Alary, Eric — *La Ligne de Démarcation, 1940–1944* (Paris: Perrin, 2003)

Allen, Robert W. — *Churchill's Guests: Britain and the Belgian Exiles during World War II* (Westport CT: Praeger, 2003)

Amipaz-Silber, Gitta — *Sephardi Jews in Occupied France: Under the Tyrant's Heel, 1940–1944* (Jerusalem: Rubin Mass, 1995)

Amoureux, Henri — *La vie des Français sous l'Occupation* (Paris, 1961)

Aubert, Vilhelm — *The Hidden Society* (New Brunswick NJ: Transaction Books, 1965)

Avni, H. — 'Zionist Underground in Holland and France and the Escape to Spain', in Y. Gutman and E. Zuroff (eds), *Rescue Attempts during the Holocaust* (Jerusalem: Yad Vashem, 1977)

Baldran, Jacqueline and Bochurberg, Claude — *David Rapoport* (Paris: Montorguiel, 1994)

Bank, Jan — 'Protestantism in the Second World War: The Case of The Netherlands and France', in Lieve Gevers and Jan Bank (eds), *Religion under Siege, II, Protestant, Orthodox and Muslim Communities in Occupied Europe (1939–1950)* (Leuven: Peeters, 2007)

Barfod, Jørgen H. and Nielsen, Max — *Escape from Nazi Terror: A Short History of the Jews in Denmark and Norway and the Danish Underground Refugee Service* (Copenhagen: Forlaget for Faglitteratur, 1968)

Barnett, Victoria — *For the Soul of the People: Protestant Protest against Hitler* (New York: Oxford University Press, 1992)

Barnouw, David and van der Stroom, Gerrold — *The Diary of Anne Frank: The Critical Edition* (London: Viking, 1989)

Barot, Madeleine — 'La Cimade: une présence, une communauté, une action', in Emile C. Fabre et al. (eds), *Les Clandestins de Dieu. CIMADE 1939–1945* (Paris: Fayard, 1968)

Bauer, Yehuda — *American Jewry and the Holocaust: The American Jewish Joint Distribution Committee, 1939–1945* (Jerusalem: Hebrew University, 1981)

—— — *Jews for Sale? Nazi-Jewish Negotiations, 1933–1945* (New Haven and London: Yale UP, 1994)

Bekkenkamp, A.   *Leendert Overduin: Het levensverhaal van een pas-tor pimpernel 1900–1976* (Enschede: Van de Berg, 2000)

Benz, Wolfgang (ed.)   *Überleben im Dritten Reich: Juden im Untergrund und ihre Helfer* (München: C. H. Beck, 2003)

Benz, Wolfgang and   *Encyclopedia of the German Resistance to the Nazi*
Pehle, Walter   *Movement* (New York: Continuum, 1997)

Benz, Wolfgang and   *Solidarität und Hilfe für Juden während der NS-Zeit*,
Juliane Wetzel   Vol. 2 (Berlin: Metropol, 1998)
(eds)

Blatt, Joel (ed.)   *The French Defeat of 1940: Reassessments* (Providence RI: Berghahn, 2000)

Blocker, Gay and   *Rescuers: Portraits of Moral Courage in the Holocaust*
Drucker, Malka   (New York: Holmes and Meier, 1992)

Blom, J. C. H.   'The Persecution of the Jews in the Netherlands: A Comparative Western European Perspective', *European History Quarterly*, XIX (1989)

——   *Crisis, Bezetting en Herstel: Tien Studies over Nederland 1930–1950* (Rotterdam: Universitaire, 1989)

——   'Geschiedenis, sociale wetenschappen, bezetting-stijd en jodenvervolging. Een besprekingsartikel', *Bijdragen en Mededelingen betreffende de Geschiedenis der Nederlanden,* CXX (2005)

Blom, J. C. H. and   'Joodse Nederlanders: Nederlandse joden en joden
Cahen, J. J.   in Nederland (1870–1940), in J. C. H. Blom et al. (eds), *Geschiedenis van de Joden in Nederland* (Amsterdam: Balans, 1995)

Blom, J. C. H. et al.   *Geschiedenis van de Joden in Nederland* (Amsterdam:
(eds)   Balans, 1995)

Boas, Jaap   *Boulevard des Misères: Het verhaal van doorgangskamp Westerbork* (Amsterdam: Nijgh en Van Ditmar, 1988)

Boom, Bart van der   *Den Haag in de Tweede Wereldoorlog* (The Hague, SeaPress, 1995)

Boom, Corrie ten   *Gevangene en toch ... Herinneringen uit Scheveningen, Vught en Ravensbrück* (Amsterdam: W. ten Have, 1945)

——   *The Hiding Place* (New York: Chosen Books, 1971)

Bornebroek, A. H.   *De Illegaliteit in Twente* (Hengelo: Witkam, 1985)

Boulet, François   'Les juifs en Isère, Savoie et Haute-Savoie (1940–1944): De la touristophobie aux montagnes-refugies', *Revue d'Histoire de la Shoah*, 172 (May–August 2001)

Bovenkerk, Frank   'Het Nederlandse aandeel in de jodenvervolging als criminologisch probleem', in M. Moerings et al. (eds), *Morele kwesties in het strafrecht* (Deventer: Gouda Quint, 1999)

——   'The Other Side of the Anne Frank Story: The Dutch role in the Persecution of the Jews in World War Two', *Crime, Law and Social Change*, XXXIV (2000)

Ben Braber   *Zelfs als wij zullen verliezen: Joden in Verzet en Illegaliteit 1940–1945* (Amsterdam: Balans, 1990)

——   *Passage naar de vrijheid. Joodse verzet in Nederland, 1940–1945* (Amsterdam: Balans, 1987)

——   'De rol van het joodse verzet in de tweede wereldoorlog', *Terv Herkenning*, XIII (1985)

Brachfeld, Sylvain   *Ze hebben het overleefd* (Brussel: VUB, 1997)

——   *Ils Ont Survecu: Le Sauvetage des Juifs en Belgique Occupée* (Bruxelles: Racine, 2001)

——   'De collaboratie van de politie bij de arrestatie van de Antwerpse joden gedurende de Duits besetting van België (1940–1944), *Bulletin Trimstriel de la Fondation Auschwitz*, LXXXIV (2004)

Brasz, Chaya   *Transport 222: Bergen-Belsen-Palestine, July 1944* (Jerusalem, 1994)

Brasz, Ineke et al. (eds)   *De jeugdalijah van het Pavilioen Loosdrechtse Rade, 1939–1945* (Hilversum: Verloren, 1987)

Breukelaar, John   *Halte Varsseveld: Verhalen over het onderduiken bij de dames Jolink en hun geestverwanten* (Aalten: Fagus, 2005)

Brodsky, Alexandra F   *A Fragile Identity: Survival in Nazi-occupied Belgium* (London/New York: Radcliffe, 1998)

Brostoff, Anita (ed.)   *Flares of Memory: Stories of Childhood during the Holocaust* (Oxford: Oxford University Press, 1998)

Brück, Jean   'L'Aide aux Refractaires, aux Juifs, aux Prisonniers de Guerre', in Emilie Arnoud et al. (eds), *La Résistance dans la Mouvement Jociste (JOC, JOCF, KAJ, VKAJ) pendant la guerre 1940–1945* (Bruxelles, 1985)

Brustin-Berenstein, Tatiana   'The Historiographic Treatment of the Abortive Attempt to Deport the Danish Jews', *Yad Vashem Studies* XVII (1986)

Buskes, J. J.   *Waar Stond de Kerk?* (Amsterdam: De Volkpaedagogische Bibliotheek, 1947)

Caestecker, Frank   *Ongewenste gasten: Joodse vluchtelingen en migranten in de dertiger jaren in België* (Brussel,: VUB 1993)

——   *Alien Policy in Belgium, 1840–1940: The Creation of Guest Workers, Refugees and Illegal Aliens* (New York/Oxford: Berghahn, 2000)

——   'The Reintegration of Jewish Survivors into Belgian Society, 1943–1947', in David Bankier, *The Jews are Coming Back: The Return of the Jews to their Countries of Origin after World War II* (New York/Jerusalem: Berghahn/Yad Vashem, 2005)

Cammaert, A. P. M.   *Het Verborgen Front: Geschiedenis van de georaniseerde illegaliteit in de provincie Limburg tijdens de tweede wereldoorlog*, Vol. 1 (Leeuwarden/Mechelen: Eisma, 1994)

Cammaerts, Emile   *The Prisoner at Laeken* (London: Cresset, 1941)

Cargas, Harry James   *Voices from the Holocaust* (Lexington: Kentucky University Press, 1993)

Caron, Vicki   *Uneasy Asylum: France and the Jewish Refugee Crisis, 1933–1942* (Stanford CA: Stanford University Press, 1999)

——   'French Public Opinion and the "Jewish Question", 1930–1942: The Role of Middle-Class Professional Organisations', in David Bankier and Israel Gutman (eds), *Nazi Europe and the Final Solution* (Jerusalem: Yad Vashem, 2003)

——   'The Path to Vichy: Antisemitism in France in the 1930s', J. B.and Maurice Shapiro Annual Lecture, USHMM, 20 April 2005 (Washington, 2005)

Casutto, E   *The Last Jew in Rotterdam* (Monroeville PA: Whitaker House, 1974)

Cavaglion, Alberto   *Les Juifs de St-Martin-Vésubie, Septembre–Novembre 1943* (Nice: Serre, 1995)

Cesarani, David and Levine, Paul A. (eds)   *'Bystanders' to the Holocaust: A Re-evaluation* (London, 2002)

Citroen, S   *Duet Pathétique: Belevenissen van een Joods Gezin in Oorlogstijd, 1940–1945* (Utrecht: Veen, 1988)

Cohen, Asher   *Persécutions et sauvetages: Juifs et Francais sous l'Occupation et sous Vichy* (Paris: Cerf, 1993)

——   'Rescuing Jews: Jews and Christians in Vichy France', *British Journal of Holocaust Education* III/1 (1994)

Cohen, Maynard M.   *A Stand Against Tyranny: Norway's Physicians and the Nazis* (Detroit: Wayne State, 1997)

Cointet, Michèle   *L'Eglise sous Vichy, 1940–1945* (Paris: Perrin, 1995)

Comte, Madeleine   *Sauvetages et baptêmes; Les religieuses de Notre-Dame de Sion face à la persecutions des juifs en France (1940–1944)* (Paris: l'Harmattan, 2001)

Conway, Martin   *Collaboration in Belgium: Léon Degrelle and the Rexist Movement* (New Haven/London: Yale University Press, 1993)

Cornelissen, Igor   *Speurtocht naar de (auto)biografie* (Amsterdam: Lubberhuizen, 1993)

Croes, Marnix   'The Holocaust in the Netherlands and the Rate of Jewish Survival', *Holocaust and Genocide Studies* XX (2006)

——   'De zesde fase? Holocaust en geschiedschriving', *Bijdragen en Mededelingen betreffende de Geschiedenis der Nederlanden* CXXI (2006), 292–301.

Croes, Marnix and Tammes, Peter   *'Gif laten wij niet voortbestaan': Een onderzoek naar de overlevingskansen van joden in de Nederlandse gemeenten, 1940–1945* (Amsterdam: Aksant, 2004)

Crowe, David   *Oskar Schindler: The Untold Story of His Life, Wartime Activities and the True Story behind the List* (New York: Basic Books, 2004)

Dawidowicz, Lucy   *The War Against the Jews, 1933–1945* (New York: Holt, Reinhard and Winston, 1975)

Deaglio, Enrico   *La Banalita del Bene: Storia di Giorgio Perlasca* (Milan: Feltrinelli, 1991)

De Jong, Louis   *Het Koninkrijk der Nederlanden in de Tweede Wereldoorlog*, 13 vols ('s-Gravenhage: Staatsuitgeverij, 1969–1988)

Dekkers, Frans   *Eindhoven 1933–1945: Kroniek van Nederlands Lichtstad in de schaduw van het Derde Rijk* (Haarlem: Onze Tijd, 1982)

Delleman, Th. (ed.)   *Opdat wij niet vergeten* (Kampen: n.p., 1949)

Delpard, Raphaël   *Les Enfants Cachés* (Paris: JCLattès, 1993)

Delplancq, Thierry and Massange, Catherine   'L'Hospice de Scheut (1943–1944)', *Bijdragen tot de eigentijdse Herinnering/Les Cahiers de la Mémoire contemporaine*, 5 (2003–4)

De Maesschalk, Walter	*Gardes in de oorlog: De Antwerpse politie in WO II* (Antwerpen/Rotterdam: C.de Vries-Brouwers, 2004)
Dequecker, Luc	'Baptism and Conversion of Jews in Belgium', in Michman, *Belgium and the Holocaust, Jews Belgians Germans* (Jerusalem: Yad Vashem, 1998)
Diamond, Hanna	*Fleeing Hitler: France 1940*, (Oxford: Oxford University Press, 2007)
Dien, Ab van	*Opgejaagden: Herinneringen van een joodse onderduiker in het Valther bos* (Valthe: Welzijnswerk, 1982),
Doorslaer, Rudi van	'Jewish Immigration and Communism in Belgium, 1925–1939', in Dan Michman, (ed.) *Belgium and the Holocaust: Jews Belgians Germans* (Jerusalem: Yad Vashem, 1998)
Doorslaer, Rudi van et al. (eds)	*Les Juifs de Belgique. De l'Immigration au Génocide, 1925–1945* (Bruxelles: Centre de Recherches et d'Études Historiques de la Seconde Guerre Mondiale, 1994)
Doorslaer, Rudi van and Schreiber, Jean- Philippe (eds)	*De Curatoren van het Ghetto: De vereniging van de joden in België tijdens de nazi-bezetting* (Brussel: Lannoo, 2004)
Doorslaer, Rudi van et al. (eds)	*Gewillig België: Overheid en Jodenvervolging tijdens de Tweede Wereldoorlog* (Brussel: Meulenhoff/Manteau-SOMA, 2007)
Dost, Jonannes	*Georg Ferdinand Duckwitz in Dänemark* (Bonn: Auswärtiges Amt, 1987)
Douwes, Arnold	*Belevenissen van een verzetsman in de periode 1940–1945* (Heiloo: Stegeman, 2002)
Dratwa, Daniel	'The Zionist Kaleidoscope in Belgium', in Dan Michman, (ed.), *Belgium and the Holocaust Jews Belgians Germans* (Jerusalem: Yad Vashem, 1998), 43–62
Duffy, Peter	*The Bielski Brothers; The True Story of Three Men who Defied the Nazis, Built a Village in the Forest and Saved 1200 Jews* (New York: HarperCollins, 2003)

Dunk, H. W. von der   'The Shock of 1940', *Journal of Contemporary History* II (1967)

Dwork, Debórah   *Children with a Star: Jewish Youth in Nazi Germany* (New Haven CT: Yale University Press, 1991)

——   'Marion van Binsbergen Pritchard's Legacy', in David Scrase, Wolfgang Mieder and Katherine Quimby Johnson, *Making a Difference: Rescue and Assistance during the Holocaust* (Burlington VT: Center for Holocaust Studies at the University of Vermont, 2004)

Emanuel, W.   'Underground in Holland' (Amsterdam: *c*.1979), Mimeograph NIOD

Erlanger, Philippe   *La France sans étoile: Souvenirs de l'avant guerre et du temps de l'occupation* (Paris: Plon, 1974)

Fabre, Emile C. et al. (eds)   *Les Clandestins de Dieu: CIMADE 1939–1945* (Paris: Fayard, 1968), reprinted as *God's Underground* (St Louis MO: Bethany Press, 1970)

Fayol, Pierre   *Les Deux France, 1936–1945* (Paris: Harmattan, 1994)

Fein, Helen   *Accounting for Genocide: National Responses and Jewish Victimization during the Holocaust* (New York: Free Press, 1979)

—— (ed.)   *The Persisting Question: Sociological Perspectives and Social Contents of Modern Antisemitism* (Berlin/New York, 1987)

Ferares, Maurice   *Violinist in het verzet* (Amsterdam: De Bataafsche Leeuw, 1991)

Fermi, Laura   *Illustrious Immigrants: The Intellectual Migration from Europe 1930–1941* (Chicago: University of Chicago Press, 1968)

Ferrand, Gérrard   *Enfants Cachés, Enfants Sauvés: L'Exemple du Loir-et-Cher* (Saint-Cyr-sur-Loire: Sutton, 2005)

Fijalkow, Jacques (ed.)   *Vichy, Les Juifs et les Justes: L'exemple du Tarn* (Toulouse: Privat, 2003)

Fishman, Joel S.   'Jewish War Orphans in the Netherlands; The Guardianship Issue, 1945–1950', *Wiener Library Bulletin*, New Series 30/31 (1973–74),31–6.

——   'The Anneke Beekman Affair and the Dutch News Media', *Jewish Social Studies* XL/1 (Winter 1978)

——   'The War Orphan Controversy in the Netherlands: Majority–Minority Relations', in J. Michman and T. Levie, *Dutch Jewish History* I (Jerusalem, 1984)

——   'De joodse oorlogswezen. Een interview met Gesina van der Molen, voorzitter van de Commissie Oorlogspleegkinderen', in David Barnouw et al. (eds), *Oorlogsdocumentatie* VII (1995)

——   'On Jewish Survival during the Occupation: The Vision of Jacob van Amerongen', *Studia Rosenthaliana* XXXIII/2 (1999)

Fittko, Lisa   *Escape through the Pyrenees* (Evanston IL: Northwestern University Press, 2000)

Flender, Harold   *Rescue in Denmark* (New York: Simon and Schuster, 1963)

Flim, Bert Jan   *Omdat Hun Hart Sprak: Geschiedenis van de georganiseerde hulp aan Joodse kinderen in Nederland*, (Kampen: Kok, 1996)

——   'Opportunities for Dutch Jews to Hide from the Nazis, 1942–1945', in Chaya Brasz and Yosef Kaplan (eds), *Dutch Jews as Perceived by Themselves and by Others: Proceedings of the Eighth International Symposium on the History of the Jews in the Netherlands* (Leiden: Brill, 2001)

Folcher, Gustave *Marching to Captivity: The War Diaries of a French Peasant, 1939–45* (London: Brassey's, 1996)

Foot, M. R. D. *SOE in The Low Countries* (London: St Ermin's Press, 2001)

Foot, M. R. D. and Langley, J. M. *MI9 Escape and Evasion 1939–1945* (London: Bodley Head, 1979)

Ford, Herbert, *Flee the Captor* (London: Pan, 1999)

Fralon, Jose-Alain and Graham, Peter *A Good Man in Evil Times: The Heroic Story of Aristide de Sousa Mendes* (New York: Basic Books, 2001)

Frenck, Jeannine (Levana) 'Righteous Among the Nations in France and Belgium: A Silent Resistance', *Search and Research*, XII (2008), International Institute for Holocaust Research

Friedländer, Saul *The Years of Extermination: Nazi Germany and the Jews 1939–1945* (London: Weidenfeld and Nicholson, 2007)

Frijtag Drabbe Künzel, Geraldien van 'Gutachten zur Tätigkeit. Hans Calmeyers in den Niederlanden' (Amsterdam: unpublished, 2000)

—— 'Zwischen Tätern, Zuschauern und Opfern. Hans Georg Calmeyer und die Judenverfolgung in den besetzten Niederlanden', in Gerhard Hirschfeld and Tobias Jersak, *Karrieren im Nationalsozialismus. Funktionseliten zwischen Mitwirkung und Distanz* (Frankfurt/New York: Campus, 2004)

—— *Het geval Calmeyer* (Amsterdam: Mets en Schilt, 2008)

Froehling-Grunwald, R.and Miriam Visser, 'Frits Philips heeft "al het mogelijke gedaan"', *Nieuw Israelitisch Weekblad*, 12 January 1969

Fry, Varian *Surrender on Demand* (Boulder CO: Johnson Books, 1997)

Galen-Herrmann, R. E. van	'De Controverse Rond het Ambtelijk Functioneren van Hans Calmeyer tijdens de Bezetting 1940–1945', *Nederlands Juristenblad* 17, 28 April 2006
Gans-Premsela, Jenny	*Vluchtweg. Aan de bezetter ontsnapt* (Baarn: Bosch en Koning, 1990)
Garfinkels, Betty	*Les Belges face à la persécution raciale 1940-1944* (Bruxelles: Editions de l'Institut de Sociologie de l'Université Libre de Bruxelles, n.d.)
Gerdes, Uta	*Ökumenische Solidarität mit christlichen und jüdischen Verfolgten. Die CIMADE in Vichy-Frankreich 1940–1944* (Göttingen: Vandenhoeck und Ruprecht, 2005)
Gevers, Lieve	'Catholicism in the Low Countries During the Second World War. Belgium and the Netherlands: a Comparative Approach', in Lieve Gevers and Jan Bank (eds), *Religion under Siege, I: The Roman Catholic Church in Occupied Europe* (1939–1950) (Leuven: Peeters, 2007)
Gevers, Lieve and Bank, Jan (eds)	*Religion under Siege, I: The Roman Catholic Church in Occupied Europe* (1939–1950) (Leuven: Peeters, 2007)
——	*Religion under Siege, II: Protestant, Orthodox and Muslim Communities in Occupied Europe (1939–1950)* (Leuven: Peeters, 2007)
Gies, Miep	*Anne Frank Remembered. The Story of the Woman who Helped to Hide the Frank Family* (New York: Simon and Schuster, 1987)
Gilbert, Martin	*The Righteous: The Unsung Heroes of the Holocaust* (London/New York: Doubleday, 2002)
Gilthay Veth, Daniel and v d Leeuw, A. J.	*Rapport door het Rijksinstituut voor Oorlogsdocumentatie uitgebracht aan de minister van Justitie inzake de activiteiten van drs. F. Weinreb gedurende de jaren 1940–1945, in het licht van nadere gegevens bezien* ('s-Gravenhage: Staatsuitgeverij, 1976)

Glass, James M.   *Jewish Resistance during the Holocaust. Moral Uses of Violence and Will* (Basingstoke: Palgrave, 2004)

Goethem, Herman van   'La convention de La Haye, la collaboration administrative en Belgique et la persecution des Juifs à Anvers, 1940–1942', *Cahiers d'Histoire du Temps Présent* XVII (2006)

Goldenberger, Leo (ed.)   *The Rescue of the Danish Jews: Moral Courage Under Stress* (New York NY: New York University Press, 1987)

Good, Michael   *The Search for Major Plagge: The Nazi Who Saved Jews* (New York: Fordham University Press, 2006)

Gotovitch, José   'Resistance Movements and the "Jewish Question"', in Dan Michman (ed.), *Belgium and the Holocaust: Jews, Belgians, Germans* (Jerusalem: Yad Vashem, 1998)

Gourfinkel, Nina   *L'Autre Patrie* (Paris: Editions du Seuil, 1953)

Graaff, Bob de   *Schakels naar de Vrijheid: Pilotenhulp in Nederland tijdens de Tweede Wereldoorlog* ('s-Gravenhage: SDU, 1995)

Griffioen, Pim and Zeller, Ron   'Jodenvervolging in Nederland en België tijdens de Tweede Werelkoorlog: Een Vergelijkende Analyse', *Ooorlogsdocumentatie '40—'45* VIII (1997)

——   'A comparative analysis of the persecution of the Jews in the Netherlands and Belgium during the second world war', *Netherlands Journal of Social Sciences*, XXXIV (1998)

——   'Anti-Jewish Policy and Organisation of the Deportations in France and the Netherlands, 1940–1944: a comparative study', *Holocaust and Genocide Studies* XX (2006)

Groen, Koos   *Landverraders: Wat deden we met ze?* (Baarn: Inde Toren, 1974)

——   *Als slachtoffers daders worden: De zaak van de joodse veraadster Ans van Dijk* (Baarn: Ambo, 1994)

Grunberg, Albert   *Journal d'un coiffeur juif à Paris sous l'Occupation* (Paris: Les Éditions de l'Atelier, 2001)

Grüter, Regina   *Een Fantasist schrift geschiedenis: de affaires rond Friedrich Wienreb* (Amsterdam: Balans, 1997)

Gutman, Israel   *Resistance: The Warsaw Ghetto Uprising* (Boston: Houghton Mifflin, 1994)

Gutman, Israel, et al. (eds)   *Encyclopedia of the Righteous* (Jerusalem: Yad Vashem, 2003)

Gutman, Israel (ed.)   *The Encyclopedia of the Righteous among the Nations. The Netherlands* (Jerusalem: Yad Vashem, 2004)

——   *Rechtvaardigen onder de Volkeren: Nederlanders met een Yad Vashem-onderscheiding voor hulp aan joden* (Amsterdam/Antwerpen: Veen/NIOD, 2005)

——   *The Encyclopedia of the Righteous among the Nations: Rescuers of Jews during the Holocaust. Europe (Part I) and other Countries* (Jerusalem: Yad Vashem, 2007)

Hæstrup, Jørgen   *Passage to Palestine: Young Jews in Denmark* (Odense: Odense University Press, 1983)

——   'The Danish Jews and the German Occupation', in Leo Goldenberger (ed.), *The Rescue of the Danish Jews: Moral Courage Under Stress* (New York NY: New York University Press, 1987)

Hallie, Philip   *Lest Innocent Blood be Shed* London: Michael Joseph, 1979)

Halls, W. D.   *Politics, Society and Christianity in Vichy France* (Oxford: Berg, 1995)

Hartendorf, Guus   *Noodklokken luiden bij Ten Boom* (Haarlem: Corrie ten Boomhuis, 1994)

Hazan, Katy   *Les Orphelins de la Shoah: Les Maisons de l'Espoir* (Paris: Les Belles Lettres, 2000)

Heijden, Chris van der — *Grijs Verleden: Nederland en de Tweede Wereldoorlog* (Amsterdam: Contact, 2001)

Helman, Albert — *Een doodgewone held: De levensgeschiedenis van Gerrit-Jan van der Veen* (Amsterdam: Der Spieghel, 1946)

Herzberg, Abel J. — *Kroniek der Jodenvervolging 1940–1945* (Amsterdam: Querido, 1985)

Hess, Renate — 'Was Portugal getan hat, hat kein anderes Land getan' in Wolfgang Benz and Juliane Wetzel, *Solidarität und Hilfe für Jüden während der NS-Zeit* (Berlin: Metropol, 1996)

Hilberg, Raul — *The Destruction of the European Jews* (Chicago IL: Quadrangle, 1967)

Hilbrink, Coen — *De Ondergrondse: Illegaliteit in Overijssel* ('s-Gravenhage: SDU, 1988)

—— — *De Illegalen: Illegaliteit in Twente en het aangrenzende Salland 1940–1945* ('s-Gravenhage: SDU, 1989)

Hirschfeld, Gerhard — 'Niederlande', in W. Benz, (ed.), *Dimension der Völkermords. Die Zahl der jüdischen Opfer des Nationalsozialismus* (Munich: Oldenburg, 1991)

Hoess, Rudolf — *Commandant of Auschwitz*, 5th ed. (London: Pan, 1982)

Hof, Jan — *Frits de Zwerver: Twaalf jaar strijd tegen de nazi-terreur* ('s-Gravenhage: Omniboek, 1976)

—— — *Vrouwen in het Verzet* (Baarn: La Rivière en Voorhoeve, 1995)

Hoffmann, Christhard — 'Fluchthilfe als Widerstand: Verfolgung und Retuung der Juden in Norwegen', in Wolfgang Benz and Juliane Wetzel (eds), *Solidarität und Hilfe für Juden während der NS-Zeit, Vol. 2* (Berlin: Metropol, 1998)

Hofke, Els — *Vrouw in Verzet: Miet Pauw en de bezetting in Baarle* (Baarle-Nassau: De Jong, 1989)

Hondius, Dienke — *Return: Holocaust Survivors and Dutch Antisemitism* (Westport CT: Praeger, 2003)

Houwaart, Dick — *Weinreb. Een Witboek* (Amsterdam: Meulenhoff, 1975)

Hovanissian, Richard G. — 'Intervention and Shades of Altruism during the Armenian Genocide', in Richard G. Hovanissian (ed.), *The Armenian Genocide: History, Politics, Ethics* (New York: St Martin's Press, 1992)

Hovingh, G. C. — *Johannes Post. Exponent van het verzet* (Kampen: Kok, 1995)

Howarth, David — *The Shetland Bus* (Shetland: Shetland Times, 1998)

Hulst, J. W.van — *Wat aan Westerbork voorafging* (Amsterdam: Blaak, 2000)

Huneke, Douglas — 'A Study of Christians who saved Jews during the Nazi Era', *Humboldt Journal of Social Relations* IX/1 (1981–82)

Hyman, Paula E. — *From Dreyfus to Vichy: The Remaking of French Jewry, 1906–1939* (New York, 1979)

Inghelram, Miek — 'Joodse Kinderen Opgevangen in Een Katholiek Milieu tijdens de Tweede Wereldoorlog. Belgische Situatie, 1942–1945' (Licentiaat, Katholieke Universiteit Leuven, 1992)

Instituto Diplomatico — *Spared Lives: The Actions of Three Portuguese Diplomats in World War II/Vidas Poupadas: A acção de três diplomatas portugueses na Guerra Mundial II* (Lisbon: Ministério dos Negócios Etrangeiros, 2000)

Isenberg, Sheila — *A Hero of Our Own: The Story of Varian Fry* (New York: Random House, 2001)

Jackman, Jarrell C. and Borden, Carla M. — *The Muses Flee Hitler: Cultural Transfer and Adaptation* (Washington DC: Smithsonian Institute, 1983)

Jackson, Julian   *The Fall of France: The Nazi Invasion of 1940* (Oxford: Oxford University Press, 2003)

Jacquemart, C   'Les Justes et les Sauveurs de l'Holocaust au regard de l'opinion publique belge' (Magister Thesis, Université de Bruxelles Libre, 1996)

Jensen, Mette Bastholm & Jensen, Steven L.B.   *Denmark and the Holocaust* (Copenhagen: Institute for International Studies, 2003)

Joly, Françoise et al.   'Les camps d'internement en France de septembre 1939 à mai 1940', in Gilbert Badia et al. (eds), *Barbelés de l'exil: Etudes sur l'émigration allemande et autrichienne (1938–1940)* (Grenoble, 1979)

Jones, W. Glyn   *Denmark: A Modern History* (Beckenham: Croome Helm, 1986)

Kar, Jac. van der   *Joods Verzet: Terugblik op de Periode Rond de Tweede Wereldoorlog* (Amsterdam: Stadsdrukkerij, 1981)

Keith, Janet   *A Friend Among Enemies: The Incredible Story of Arie Van Mansum in the Holocaust* (Richmond Hill: Fitzhenry and Whiteside, 1991)

Kempner, Robert M. W.   *Twee uit Honderdduizend: Anne Frank en Edith Stein* (Bilthoven: H. Nelisen,1969)

Kersaudy, François   *Norway 1940* (London: Arrow, 1991)

Kévorkian, Raymond   'L'opposition de fonctionnaires ottomans au génocide des Arméniens', in Semelin et al. (eds), *La Résistance aux genocides* (Paris: Sciences Po, 2008)

———   'Pour une typologie des 'Justes' dans l'Empire ottoman face au genocide des Arméniens', Conference paper, *Si può sempre dire un sì o un no: I Giusti contro I genocidi degli Armeni e degli Ebrei* (University of Padova, 30 November 2000)

Keyes, Roger   *Outrageous Fortune: The Tragedy of Leopold III of the Belgians, 1901–1941* (London: Secker and Warburg, 1984)

Kierszencweig, Gabriel   *Exode de Juifs de Charleroi à Jauche* (n.p., n.d.)

Kieval, Hillel J.   'From Social Work to Resistance: Relief and Rescue of Jewish Children in Vichy France' (BA Harvard University, 1973)

Kirchhoff, Hans   'SS-*Gruppenführer* Werner Best and the Action Against the Danish Jews—October 1943', *Yad Vashem Studies* XXIV (1994)

——   'Denmark', in Bob Moore (ed.), *Resistance in Western Europe* (Oxford: Berg, 2000)

Kitson, Simon   *The Hunt for Nazi Spies: Fighting Espionage in Vichy France* (Chicago: University of Chicago Press, 2007)

Klein, W. C. and Grient Dreux, P.de (eds)   *Pittige verhalen uit onveilige tijden: Scetsen van illegale werkers, hongerlijders enz. uit alle rangen en standen* ('s-Gravenhage: van Stockum, 1947)

Klein, P. W. and van de Kamp, Justus   *Het Philips-kommando in Kamp Vught* (Amsterdam: Contact, 2003)

Klempner, Mark   *The Heart Has Reasons: Holocaust Rescuers and their Stories of Courage* (Cleveland OH: Pilgrim Press, 2006)

Kless, Shlomo   'The Rescue of Jewish Children in Belgium during the Holocaust', *Holocaust and Genocide Studies*, III/3 (1988)

Klinken, Gert van   *Strijdbaar en Omstreden: Een biografie van de calvinistische verzetsvrouw Gezina van der Molen* (Amsterdam: Boom, 2006)

——   'Dutch Jews as Perceived by Dutch Protestants, 1860–1960', in Chaya Brasz and Yosef Kaplan (eds), *Dutch Jews as perceived by themselves and by others* (Leiden: Brill, 2001)

Klugman, David   *The Conspiracy of the Righteous: The Silence of the Village of Prélenfrey-du-Guâ Saved Jewish Children and Adults in 1944* (Nîmes: C. Lacour, 1994)

Knoop, Hans   *De Joodsche Raad: Het Drama van Abraham Asscher en David Cohen* (Amsterdam/Brussel: Elsevier, 1983)

Konopnicki, David   'Le Reseau Abadi: Histoire d'un réseau de sauvetage d'enfants dans les Alpes-Maritimes Durant la Seconde Guerre Mondiale' (Université Pierre Mendes-France, Grenoble, 2001)

Kossmann, E. H.   *The Low Countries 1780–1940* (Oxford: Clarendon, 1978)

Kuipers, Eppo   *Er was zoveel werk nog te doen ... Tante Riek en Oom Piet in de jaren '40—'45*, (Winterswijk: Het Museum, 1988)

Kulok, Jan Sigurd   'Trait d'Union: the history of the French relief organisation *Secours national/Entr'aide française* under the Third Republic, the Vichy regime and the early Fourth Republic, 1939–1949' (Unpublished Oxford DPhil, 2002)

Lammers, Cornelis J. 'Persecution in the Netherlands during World War Two: An Introduction', *The Netherlands' Journal of Social Sciences* XXXIV/2 (1998)

Lampe, David   *The Savage Canary: The Story of Resistance in Denmark* (London: Cassell, 1957)

Lazare, Lucien   *La Résistance Juive en France* (Paris: Stock, 1987)

———   *L'Abbé Glasberg* (Paris: Le Cerf, 1990)

———   *Le Livre des Justes: Histoire du sauvetage des juifs par des non-juifs en France, 1940–1944* (Paris: JC Lattès, 1995)

———   *Rescue as Resistance: How Jewish Organisations Fought the Holocaust in France* (New York: Columbia University Press, 1996)

———   *Dictionnaire des Justes de France* (Jerusalem/Paris: Yad Vashem/Fayard, 2003)

Leclef, E.   *Le Cardinal van Roey et l'occupation allemande en Belgique* (Bruxelles: Goemaere, 1945)

Le Douairon,
Béatrice
'Le Comité "Rue Amelot", 1940–1944 à Paris: Assistance aux Juifs et Sauvetage des Enfants' (Maitrise, Paris 1—Sorbonne, 1994)

Leeuw, A. J.van der
'Meer slachtoffers dan elders in West-Europa', *Nieuw Israëlitisch Weekblad*, 15 November 1985.

Lemalet, Martine (ed.)
Au secours des enfants du siècle (Paris: Nil, 1993)

Léons, Max and Douwes, Arnold
Mitswa en christenplicht: Bescheiden helden uit de illegaliteit ('s-Gravenhage: BZZTôH, 2000)

Levenstein, Aaron
Escape to Freedom: The Story of the International Rescue Committee (Westport CT: Greenwood,1983)

Levin, D.
'The Fighting Leadership of the Judenräte in the Small Communities of Poland', in Michael Marrus (ed.), *Jewish Resistance to the Holocaust* (London Meckler, 1989)

Lévy, Claude and Tillard, Paul
La Grande rafle du Vel d'Hiv (Paris: Laffont, 1967)

Levy, Denise
'Les EI et la Sixième en Zone Sud pendant la guerre', *Revue d'histoire de la Shoah*, No.161, Sept–Dec 1997

Lewin, Abraham
A Cup of Tears: A Diary of the Warsaw Ghetto, ed. Anthony Polonsky (Oxford: Blackwell, 1988)

Liebman, Marcel
Né juif. Une famille juive pendant la guerre (Paris/Gembloux: Duculot, 1977)

Liempt, Ad van
Hitler's Bounty Hunters: The Betrayal of the Jews (Oxford: Berg, 2005)

——
Kopgeld. Nederlandse premiejagers op zoek naar joden 1943 (Amsterdam: Balans, 2002)

Lindeman, Yehudi
'All or Nothing: The Rescue Mission of Joop Westerweel', in David Scrase, Wolfgang Mieder and Katherine Quimby Johnson, *Making a Difference: Rescue and Assistance during the Holocaust* (Burlington VT: Center for Holocaust Studies at the University of Vermont 2004)

Lisser, Meijer   'Boekhouden 1940–1943' (Alkmaar: Falstaff, 2008)

Loebl, Susanne   At the Mercy of Strangers: Growing up on the edge of the Holocaust (Pacifica CA: Pacifica Press, 1997)

Loeffler, Martha   Boats in the Night (Blair NE: Lur, 2000)

Loinger, Georges   'Les circuits clandestins: l'exemple du réseau Garel', in Association pour la recherché et la sauvetage de la vérité historique sur la résistance en Creuse, Le Sauvetage des Enfants Juifs de France (Guéret, 1996)

Lombard, L.   L'heroïque cure de Comblain-au-Pont (Liège, n.d.)

London, Perry   'The Rescuers: Motivational Hypotheses About Christians Who Saved Jews from the Nazis', in J. Macauley and L. Berkowitz, (eds), Altruism and Helping Behavior (New York: Academic Press, 1970)

Lowrie, Donald A.   The Hunted Children (New York: W. W. Norton, 1963)

Lund, Sigrid   Always on the Way (London: 2000)
Helliesen

Luyten, Dirk (ed.)   Penalization of economic collaboration in Western Europe after the Second World War (Brussels: VUB, 1996)

McCabe, Cynthia   ' "Wanted by the Gestapo: Saved by America" '
Jaffee   —Varian Fry and the Emergency Rescue Committee', in Jarrell C. Jackman and Carla M. Borden, The Muses Flee Hitler: Cultural Transfer and Adaptation (Washington DC: Smithsonian Institute, 1983)

McPhail, Helen   The Long Silence: Civilian Life under the German Occupation of Northern France, 1914–1918 (London/New York: I. B.Taurus, 2001)

Maerten, Fabrice   Entre la peste et le cholera: Vie et attitude des catholiques et al(eds)   belges sous l'occupation (Gerpinnes, 1999)

Marino, Andy | *A Quiet American: The Secret War of Varian Fry* (New York: St Martin's, 2000)

Marks, Sally | *Innocent Abroad. Belgium at the Paris Peace Conference of 1919* (Chapel Hill NC: University of North Carolina Press, 1981)

Marrus, Michael R. and Paxton, Robert O. | *Vichy France and the Jews* (Stanford CA: Stanford University Press, 1995)

—— | 'The Nazis and the Jews in Occupied Western Europe 1940–1944', *Journal of Modern History* LIV (1982)

Matteazzi, Florence | 'L'attitude du clergé face à la *Shoa* dans le diocese de Liège', in Maerten et al. (eds), *Entre la peste et le cholera: Vie et attitude des catholiques belges sous l'occupation* (Gerpinnes, 1999)

Maxwell, Elisabeth | 'The Rescue of Jews in France and Belgium During the Holocaust', *Journal of Holocaust Education*, VII/1–2 (1998)

Mechanicus, Philip | *In depot: dagboek uit Westerbork van Philip Mechanicus* (Amsterdam: Polak en Van Gennep, 1964)

Meershoek, Guus | *Dienaren van het Gezag: De Amsterdamse Politie tijdens de Bezetting* (Amsterdam: van Gennep, 1999).

—— | 'De Amsterdamse hoofdcommissaris en de deportatie van de joden', *Oorlogsdocumentatie '40—'45 Derde Jaarboek van het Rijksinstituut voor Oorlogsdocumentatie* (Zutphen: Walburg Pers, 1992)

Meihuizen, Joggli | *Noodzakelijk kwaad: de bestraffing van economische collaboratie in Nederland na de Tweede Wereldoorlog* (Amsterdam: Boom, 2003)

Ménager, Camille | 'Le Sauvetage des Juifs à Paris: Histoire et Mémoire' (Institut d'Études Politiques de Paris, 2005)

Mendelsohn, Oskar   *The Norwegian Rescue of Jews* (New York: Thanks to Scandinavia, n.d.)

——   *The Persecution of the Norwegian Jews in WWII* (Oslo: Norges Hjemmefrontmuseum, 1991)

Meschman, Beatrice   *Never to be forgotten: A Young Girl's Holocaust Memoir* (Hoboken NJ: KTAV, 1997)

Meulenbelt, J.   'Bezetting en Verzet', in J. J.Bolhuis et al. (eds), *Onderdrukking en Verzet: Nederland in Oorlogstijd*, III (Arnhem: van Loghum Slaterus 1949–53)

——   *De duitse tijd: Vijf jaar vaderlandse geschiedenis* (Amsterdam: J. H.de Bussy, 1965)

Meyers, Odette   *Doors to Madame Marie* (Washington: University of Washington, 1998)

Michman, Dan (ed.) *Belgium and the Holocaust: Jews, Belgians, Germans* (Jerusalem: Yad Vashem, 1998)

——   *The Encyclopedia of the Righteous Among the Nations. Rescue of Jews during the Holocaust: Belgium* (Jerusalem: Yad Vashem, 2005)

——   'Why Did So Many of the Jews in Antwerp Perish in the Holocaust?' *Yad Vashem Studies* XXX (2002)

Michman, Jozef   'The Controversial Stand of the Joodse Raad in the Netherlands. Lodewijk E. Visser's Struggle', *Yad Vashem Studies*, X (1974)

——   'The Problems of the Jewish War Orphans in Holland', *She'erit Hapletah* (Jerusalem 1990)

Michman, Jozef   *Pinkas. Geschiedenis van de joodse gemeenschap in*
et al (eds)   *Nederland* (Ede/Antwerp/Amsterdam, 1992)

Michman, Jozef and *The Encyclopedia of the Righteous Among the Nations:*
Flim, Bert-Jan (eds) *Rescuers of Jews during the Holocaust. The Netherlands*, 2 vols (Jerusalem: Yad Vashem, 2004)

Middelberg, Matthias   *Judenrecht, Judenpolitik und der Jurist Hans Calmeyer in den besetzten Niederlanden 1940–1945* (Göttingen: V&R Unipress, 2005)

Milgram, Avraham   'Portugal, The Consuls, and the Jewish Refugees, 1938–1941', *Yad Vashem Studies* XXVII (1999)

Moeyes, Paul   *Buiten Schot: Nederland tijdens de Eerste Wereldoorlog, 1914–1918* (Amsterdam: Arbeiderspers, 2001)

Mogensen, Michael   'October 1943—The Rescue of the Danish Jews', in Jensen and Jensen, *Denmark and the Holocaust* (Copenhagen: Institute for International Studies, 2003)

Moland, Arnfinn   *Over grensen? Hjemmefrontens likvidasjoner under den tyske okkupasjonen av Norge 1940-1945* (Oslo, 1999)

———   'Norway', in Bob Moore (ed.), *Resistance in Western Europe* (Oxford: Berg, 2000)

———   'The Norwegian Holocaust and the Resistance'. Text courtesy of the author

Molette, Charles   *Prêtres, Religieux et Religieuses dans la Résistance au Nazisme, 1940–1945* (Paris: Fayard, 1995)

Monroe, Kirsten R.   *The Hand of Compassion: Portraits of Moral Choice During the Holocaust* (Princeton NJ: Princeton University Press, 2004)

———   *The Heart of Altuism: Perception of a Common Humanity* (Princeton NJ: Princeton University Press, 1996)

Monroe, Kirsten et al.   'Altuism and the Theory of Rational Action', *Ethics* CI (1990)

Moore, Bob   *Refugees from Nazi Germany in the Netherlands, 1933–1940* (Nijhoff: Dordrecht, 1986)

———   *Victims and Survivors: The Nazi Persecution of the Jews in the Netherlands, 1940–1945* (London: Arnold, 1997)

Moore, Bob   'Nazi Masters and Accommodating Dutch Bureaucrats: Working towards the Führer in the Occupied Netherlands, 1940–1945', in Tim Kirk and Tony Mc Elligott,(eds), *Working Towards the Führer* (Manchester: Manchester University Press 2003)

——   'The Rescue of Jews in Nazi-Occupied Belgium, France and the Netherlands', *Australian Journal of Politics and History* L/3 (2004)

——   ' "Goed en Fout" or "Grijs Verleden": Competing Perspectives on the History of the Netherlands under German Occupation', *Dutch Crossing* XXVII (2006)

Moszkiewicz, Helene   *Inside the Gestapo: A Jewish Woman's Secret War* (New York: Dell, 1985)

Nederlands-Israëlitisch Kerkgenootschap and Portugees-Israëlitisch Kerkgenootschap,   *De Verdwijning van Anneke Beekman en Rebecca Meljado: Witboek* (Amsterdam, 1954)

Nicault, Catherine   'L'Acceuil des juifs d'Europe Centrale par le communauté juive français (1933–1939) in IHTP/CNRS, *Réfugiés et immigrés d'Europe Centrale dans le mouvement anti-fasciste et la résistance en France (1933–1945)*, Mimeogr. (Paris: Université de Paris VIII, 17–18 October 1986)

Nicosia, Francis R. (ed.)   *Archives of the Holocaust: Vol. 4 Central Zionist Archives 1939–1945* (New York: Garland, 1990)

Nidam-Orvieto, Eliot   'Catholic Religious and the Hiding of Jewish Children within their Convents and Institutions in France' (MA, Hebrew University of Jerusalem, 2002)

Niebaum, Peter   *Ein Gerechter unter den Völkern: Hans Calmeyer in seiner Zeit (1903–1972)* (Osnabrück: Rasch, 2001)

Ofer, Dalia   *Escaping the Holocaust* (New York: Oxford University Press, 1990)

Oliner, Pearl M.   *Saving the Forsaken: Religious Culture and the Rescue of Jews in Nazi Europe* (New Haven CT: Yale University Press, 2004)

Oliner, Samuel P. and   *The Altruistic Personality: Rescuers of Jews in Nazi*
Oliner, Pearl M.   *Europe* (New York: Free Press, 1988)

Oliner, Samuel P.   'The Unsung Heroes in Nazi-Occupied Europe: The Antidote for Evil', *Nationalities Papers* XII/1 (1984)

——   'Heroic Altruism. Heroic and Moral Behaviour in a Variety of Settings', in John K. Roth and Elisabeth Maxwell (eds), *Remembering for the Future. Vol. 2, The Holocaust in an Age of Genocide* (Basingstoke: Palgrave, 2001)

Ommeren, Anita van   '*Die man moeten blijven leven': Gerrit Jan van der*
and Scherphuis,   *Veen in het verzet* (Amsterdam: Sijthoff, 1988)
Ageeth

Ottosen, Kristian   *I slik en natt* (Oslo: Aschehoug, 1994)

Ousby, Ian   *Occupation: The Ordeal of France 1940–1944* (New York: St Martin's, 1998)

Paldiel, Mordecai   *The Path of the Righteous: Gentile Rescuers of the Jews during the Holocaust* (Hoboken NJ: KTAV, 1993)

——   *Sheltering the Jews: Stories of Holocaust Rescuers* (Minneapolis MN: Fortress Press, 1996)

——   *Saving the Jews: Amazing Stories of Men and Women Who Defied the 'Final Solution'* (Rockville MD: Schreiber, 2000)

——   'To the Righteous among the Nations Who Risked Their Lives to Rescue Jews', *Yad Vashem Studies* XIX (1988)

——   'The Face of the Other: Reflections on the Motivations of Gentile Rescuers of Jews', in Roth and Maxwell (eds), *Remembering for the Future. Vol. 2, The Holocaust in an Age of Genocide* (Basingstoke: Palgrave, 2001)

Panicacci, Jean-Louis   'Les juifs et la Question Juive dans les Alpes-Maritimes de 1939 à 1945' *Bulletin Trimestral ADAM* (1983)

Papeleux, Leon   'Un Liégeois qui sauva des centaines de Juifs (1940–1944)', *La Vie Wallonie* (1980)

——   'Le Réseau Van Den Berg', *La Vie Wallonie* (1981)

Perrault, Gilles   'Suzanne Spaak, du sauvetage d'enfants à l'Orchestre Rouge de Trepper', in *La Lettre des résistants et déportés juifs* No. 46, December 1999

Peterson, Walter F.   *The Berlin Liberal Press in Exile: A History of the Pariser Tageblatt—Pariser Tageszeitung* (Tübingen: Niemeyer, 1987)

Philips, Frits   *Vijfenveertig Jaar met Philips* (Rotterdam, 1976)

Plantinga, Sierk   'Joseph Willem Kolkman (1896–1944) en de Engelandvaarders: De hulp aan Nederlandse vluchtelingen in Vichy-Frankrijk', *Oorlogsdocumentatie IX* (1998)

Poels, Bert   *Mémoires; Vriend en Vijand* (Venlo: Van Spijk, 1977)

Poley, Han   *Return to the Hiding Place* (Elgin IL: LifeJourney Books, 1993)

Poliakov, Leon   *L'Auberge des musicians* (Paris: Mazarine, 1981)

Poliakov, Leon and Sabille, Jacques   *Jews under the Italian Occupation* (Paris: Éditions du Centre, 1955)

Poujol, Jacques   *Protestants dans la France en guerre 1939–1945* (Paris: Les Éditions de Paris, 2000)

Pouplain, Jean-Marie   *Les Enfants Cachés de la 'Résistance'* (La Crèche: Geste, 1998)

Poznanski, Renée — *Les Juifs en France pendant la Seconde Guerre Mondiale* (Paris: Hachette, 1994)

—— — 'De l'action philanthropique à la résistance humanitaire', in Martine Lemalet (ed.), *Au secours des enfants du siècle* (Paris: Nil, 1993)

Presser, Jacques — *Ondergang: De Vervolging en verdelging van het Nederlandse jodendom, 1940–1945* ('s-Gravenhage: Staatsuitgeverij, 1977)

—— — *Ashes in the Wind: The Destruction of Dutch Jewry* (London: Souvenir, 1968)

Rajsfus, Maurice — *Sois juif et tais-toi! 1930–1940: Les français 'israélites' face au nazisme* (Paris, 1981)

Ravine, Jacques — *La Résistance Organisée des Juifs en France, 1940–1944* (Paris: Julliard, 1973)

Rayski, Adam — *The Choice of the Jews under Vichy: Between Submission and Resistance* (Notre Dame IN: University of Notre Dame Press, 2005)

Reilly, Joanne — *Belsen: The Liberation of a Concentration Camp* (London: Routledge, 1998)

Reuter, Frits — *Communistische Partij van Nederland in oorlogstijd: Herrineringen* (Amsterdam: van Gennep, 1978)

Reymmenants, Geraldine — ' "La Bergère d'un immense troupeau d'âmes": Betsie Hollants' leven n dienst van katholieken, joden en vrouwen', *Brood en Rozen. Tijdschrift voor de Geschiedenis van Sociale Bewegingen* (2003/3)

Reynders, Michel — *Père Bruno Reynders: Héros de la Résistance* (Bruxelles: Carrefours de la Cité, 1992); *Resistance: Père Bruno Reynders. Juste des Nations* (Brussels: Les Carrefours de la Cité, 1993)

Richardot, J. P. — *Le peuple protestant français aujourd'hui* (Paris: Laffont, 1980)

Riessen, Hendrik van et al. (eds) — *Het Grote Gebod: gedenkboek van het verzet in LO en LKP* (Kampen: Kok, 1951)

Ringelblum,
Emmanuel

Notes from the Warsaw Ghetto: The Journal of Emmanuel Ringelblum, ed. Jacob Sloan (New York: McGraw Hill 1958)

Roegholt, Richter
and Zwaan, Jacob

Het verzet 1940–1945 (Weesp: Unieboek, 1985)

Rohrlich, Ruby (ed.)

Resisting the Holocaust (Oxford: Berg, 1998)

Romijn, Peter

Burgemeesters in Oorlogstijd. Besturen onder Duitse bezetting (Amsterdam: Balans, 2006)

Roseman, Mark

The Past in Hiding (London: Allen Lane, 2000)

Rosengart, Laurence

'Les maisons de l'OSE: parcours d'une enfance fragmentée', in Martine Lemalet (ed.), *Au secours des enfants du siècle* (Paris: Nil, 1993)

Rosengarten, Israel J.

Survival: The Story of a Sixteen-Year-Old Jewish Boy (Syracuse NY: Syracuse University Press, 1999)

Roth, John K. and
Maxwell, E. (eds)

Remembering for the Future: The Holocaust in an Age of Genocide, Vol. 2 (Basingstoke: Palgrave, 2001)

Rozenblum, Thierry

'Une cité si ardente: L'administration communale de Liège et la persécution des Juifs, 1940–1942', *Revue d'Histoire de le Shoah*, no. 179 (septembre–décembre 2003)

Rousseau, Jean

Des enfants juifs en Vendée: Chavagnes 1942–1944 (La Roche-sur-Yon: Centre Vendéen de recherché historique, 2004)

Rousso, Henry

The Vichy Syndrome: History and Memory in France since 1944 (Cambridge MS: Harvard University Press, 1991)

Rünitz, Lone

'The Politics of Asylum in Denmark in the wake of the *Kristallnacht*—A Case Study', in Mette Bastholm Jensen and Steven L. B.Jensen (eds), *Denmark and the Holocaust* (Copenhagen: Institute for International Studies—Department for Holocaust and Genocide Studies, 2003)

Saerens, Lieven   *Vreemdelingen in een Wereldstad: Een geschiedenis van Antwerpen en zijn joodse bevolking (1880–1940)* (Tielt: Lannoo, 2000)

——   'The attitude of the Belgian Catholic Church regarding the Persecution of the Jews' in J. Th. M. Bank and Lieve Gevers (eds), *Churches and Religion in Occupied Europe. Politics and Theology.* (n.d.).

——   'Het Katholiek Bureau voor Israel (1936–1938), *Onze Alma Mater* XL/1 (1986)

——   'Die Hilfe für Juden in Belgien', in Wolfgang Benz and Juliane Wetzel, (eds), *Solidarität und Hilfe für Juden während der NS-Zeit, Vol. 2* (Berlin: Metropol, 1998)

——   'Antwerp's Attitude to the Jews from 1914–1940 and Its Implications for the period of the Occupation', in Dan Michman (ed.), *Belgium and the Holocaust: Jews Belgians Germans* (Jerusalem: Yad Vashem, 1998)

——   'The Attitude of the Belgian Roman Catholic Clergy Towards the Jews Prior to the Occupation', in Dan Michman (ed.), *Belgium and the Holocaust: Jews Belgians Germans* (Jerusalem: Yad Vashem, 1998),

——   'L'aide des catholiques dans l'archevêché de Malines', in Fabrice Maerten et al. (eds), *Entre la peste et le cholera: Vie et attitude des catholiques belges sous l'occupation* (Gerpinnes, 1999)

——   'De jodenvervolging in België in cijfers', *Cahiers d'Histoire du temps Présent* XVII (2006)

——   'The General Attitude of the Protestant Churches in Belgium Regarding the Jews from the End of the 19th Century to the Second World War', in Lieve Gevers and Jan Bank (eds), *Religion under Siege, II: Protestant, Orthodox and Muslim Communities in Occupied Europe (1939–1950)* (Leuven: Peeters, 2007)

Sauvage, Pierre 'Varian Fry in Marseille', in John K. Roth and Elisabeth Maxwell (eds), *Remembering for the Future: The Holocaust in an Age of Genocide*, Vol. 2 (Basingstoke: Palgrave, 2001)

Schenkel, Marjolein J. *De Twentse Paradox: De lotgevallen van de joodse bevolking van Hengelo en Enschede tijdens de Tweede Wereldoorlog* (Zutphen: Walburg Pers, 2003)

Schindler, Emilie *Where Light and Shadows Meet: A Memoir* (New York: W.W.Norton,1997)

Schmidt, Ephraïm *Geschiedenis van de Joden in Antwerpen* (Antwerpen/Rotterdam: De Vries-Brouwers,1994)

Schmitt, Hans A. *Quakers and Nazis: Inner Light and Outside Darkness* (Columbia MO: University of Missouri Press, 1997)

Schöffer, Ivo 'Weinreb, een affaire van lange duur', *Tijdschrift voor Geschiedenis* XCV (1982)

Schor, Ralph *Monseigneur Paul Rémond, un évêque dans le siècle* (Nice: Serre, 1984)

Schrieber, Marion *The Twentieth Train: The True Story of the Ambush of the Death Train to Auschwitz* (New York: Grove, 2003)

Schulten, C.M. *"En verpletterd wordt het juk": Verzet in Nederland 1940–1945* ('s-Gravenhage: SDU, 1995)

Schulten, J. W. M. *De geschiedenis van de Ordedienst: Mythe en werkelijkheid van een verzetsorganisatie* ('s-Gravenhage: SDU, 1998)

Schwegman, Marjan *Het Stille Verzet: vrouwen in illegal organisaties* (Amsterdam: Socialistische Uijgeverij, 1980)

Scrase, David et al.
(eds)
Making a Difference: Rescue and Assistance during the Holocaust (Burlington VT: Center for Holocaust Studies at the University of Vermont 2004)

Semelin, Jacques
et al. (eds)
La Résistance aux genocides. De la pluralité des actes de sauvetage (Paris: Sciences Po, 2008)

Sijes, Ben
Studies over Jodenvervolging (Assen: Van Gorcum, 1974)

Sim, Kevin
Women of Courage (London: Corgi, 1983),

Smedts, Mathieu
Waarheid en leugen in het verzet (Maasbree: Corrie Zelen, 1978)

Smilovitsky, L.
'Righteous Gentiles, The Partisans and Jewish Survival in Belorussia 1941–44', *Holocaust and Genocide Studies* XI/3 (1997)

Snoek, J. M.
De Nederlandse Kerken en de Joden 1940–1945 (Kampen: Kok, 1990)

Stam, Cor van
Wacht binnen de dijken: Verzet in en om de Harlemmermeer (Haarlem: De Toorts, 1986)

Stegeman, H. B. J.
and Vorstveld, J. P.
Het Joodse werkdorp in de Wieringermeer 1934–1941 (Zutphen: Walburg Pers, 1983)

Stein, André
Quiet Heroes: True Stories of the Rescue of Jews by Christians in Nazi-occupied Holland (Toronto: Lester and Orpen Dennys, 1988)

Steinberg, Lucien
Le Comité de Défense des Juifs en Belgique, 1942–1944 (Bruxelles: Editions de l'Université de Bruxelles, 1973)

——
'Un aspect peu connu de la résistance juive: le sauvetage à main armée', *Le Monde Juif* LII (1968)

Steinberg, Maxime
Dossier Brussel-Auschwitz: De SS politie en het uitroeien van de Joden (Brussels: Steuncomité bij de burgelijke partij in het process tegen de SS-officieren, 1981)

Steinberg, Maxime — *L'Etoile et le Fusil: 1942 Les Cent Jours de la Déportation* (Bruxelles: Vie Ouvriere, 1984)

—— *L'Etoile et le Fusil: La Traque des Juifs*, I (Bruxelles: Vie Ouvriere, 1986)

—— *La Persécution des Juifs en Belgique, 1940–1945: Questions à l'histoire* (Bruxelles: Complexe, 2004)

—— 'The Trap of Legality: The Association of the Jews of Belgium', in Y. Gutman and C. J. Haft (eds), *Patterns of Jewish Leadership in Nazi Europe, 1933–1945. Proceedings of the Third International Historical Conference* (Jerusalem: Yad Vashem, 1979)

—— 'The Jews in the Years 1940–1944: Three Strategies for Coping with a Tragedy', in Michman (ed.), *Belgium and the Holocaust:Jews Belgians Germans* (Jerusalem: Yad Vashem, 1998)

Stichting Geschiedschrijving Philips-Kommando, — *Licht in het Donke:. Het Philips-Kommando in Kamp Vught* (Vught: Stichting Nationaal Monument Kamp Vught, n.d.)

Stille, Alexander — *Benevolence and Betrayal: Five Italian Jewish Families under Fascism* (London: Penguin, 1993)

Stokker, Kathleen — *Folklore Fights the Nazis. Humor in Occupied Norway 1940–1945* (London: Associated University Presses, 1995)

Stokman, S. — *Het verzet van de Nederlandsche Bisschoppen tegen Nationaal-Socialisme en Duitse Tyrannie* (Utrecht: Het Spectrum, 1945)

Stolz, Gerd — '1943—Georg Ferdinand Duckwitz und die Rettung der Juden aus Dänemark', *Grenzfriedenshefte* I (1993)

Stræde, Therkel — *October 1943: The Rescue of the Danish Jews from Annihilation* (Copenhagen: Danish Ministry of Foreign Affairs, 1993)

Strauss, Herbert A.   'Jewish Emigration from Germany: Nazi Policies and Jewish Responses', *Leo Baeck Institute
Yearbook*, XV (1980), 318–61 and XXVI (1981)

Suchon, Sandrine   'Dieulefit 1940–1944: Résistance et Liberté'
(Grenoble, 1989)

Suhl, Yuri   *They Fought Back: The Story of Jewish Resistance
in Nazi Europe* (New York: Schocken, 1975)

Sutters, Jack (ed.)   *Archives of the Holocaust. Vol. 2 Pt. 2 American
Friends Service Committee, Philadephia 1940–1945*
(New York: Garland, 1990)

Tec, Nechama   *When Light Pierced the Darkness: Christian Rescue of Jews in Nazi-Occupied Poland* (New
York/Oxford: Oxford University Press, 1986)

——   *Defiance: The Bielski Partisans* (Oxford: Oxford
University Press, 1993)

——   'Helping Behaviour and Rescue During the
Holocaust', in Peter Hayes (ed.), *Lessons and
Legacies: The Memory of the Holocaust in a
Changing World* (Evanston IL: Northwestern
University Press, 1991)

Teitelbaum-Hirsch,   *Enfants cachés: Les larmes sous le masque* (Brux-
Viviane   elles: Labor, 1994)

Thomas, Gordon and   *Voyage of the Damned* (London: Coronet,
Morgan-Witts, Max   1976)

Thyange, Geneviève   'L'Abbé Joseph André et l'Aide aux Juifs à
Namur', in Maerten et al. (eds), *Entre la peste et
le choléra: Vie et attitude des catholiques belges sous
l'occupation* (Gerpinnes, 1999)

Touw, H. C.   *Het verzet der Hervormde Kerk* (Den Haag: Boekcentrum, 1946)

Tricht, Coen van   *Onderduikers en Knokploegen. Het verzet van de
Landelijke Organisatie voor Hulp aan Onderduikers*

	en de Landelijke Knokploegen (Amsterdam: De Bataafsche Leeuw, 1991)
Trunk, Isiah	'Attitudes of the Judenrats to the Problem of Armed Resistance against the Nazis', in Y. Gutman and L. Rothkirchen (eds), *The Catastrophe of European Jewry* (Jerusalem: Yad Vashem, 1976)
Turksma, Bep	*Vraag me niet waarom* (Baarn: Het Wereldvenster, 1971)
Ulstein, Ragnar	'The Rescue of c.1000 Jews in Norway during the Second World War' (1985)
Üngör, Ugur Ümit	'Stratégies de survie au cours du genocide des Arméniens', in Semelin et al(eds), *La Résistance aux genocides*, (Paris: Sciences Po, 2008)
Valentin, Hugo	'Rescue and Relief Activities on behalf of Jewish Victims of Nazism in Scandinavia' *YIVO Annual of Jewish Social Science* VIII (1953)
Varese, Frederico and Yaish, Meir	'The Importance of Being Asked: The Rescue of Jews in Nazi Europe', *Rationality and Society*, XII (2000)
——	'Resolute Heroes: The Rescue of Jews During the Nazi Occupation of Europe', *Archives Européenes de Sociologie*, XLVI (2005)
Vergara, Paul	*Le Pasteur Paul Vergara* (Nancy: Berger-Levrault, 1966)
Verheij, Elma	*Om het Joodse Kind* (Amsterdam: Nijgh en van Ditmar, 1991)
Velaers, Jan and Goethem, Hermann von	*Leopold III. de Koning, het Land, de Oorlog* (Tielt, 1994)
Vilhjámsson, Vilhjálmur Örn	*Medaljens Bagside: Joediske flygtningskaebner i Danmark 1933–1945* (Copenhagen: Forlaget Vandkunsten, 2005).

Vilhjámsson, Vilhjálmur Örn and Blüdnikow, Bent
'Rescue, Expulsion and Collaboration. Denmark's Difficulties with its World War II Past', *Jewish Political Studies Review* XVIII/3–4 (2006)

Visser, Frank
De pensionhoudster en de onderduiker (Baarn: Bosch en Keuning, 1980)

Volder, Jan de and Wouters, Lieve
Van binnen weent mijn hart. De vervolging van de Antwerpse joden (Brussels: Standaard, 1999)

Vries, Geale de
Verzetswijk (Leeuwarden, 1968)

Vries, Hille de et al,
Een Ophitsend Geschrift: De geschiedenis van een illegaal blad (Utrecht: Ambo, 1968)

Vromen, Suzanne
Hidden Children of the Holocaust: Belgian Nuns and their Daring Rescue of Young Jews from the Nazis (New York: Oxford, 2008)

Weber, Eugen
'Reflections on the Jews in France', in Frances Malino and Bernard Wasserstein (eds), *The Jews in Modern France* (Hanover NH: Brandeis University Press, 1985)

Webster, Paul
Pétain's Crime: The Full Story of French Collaboration in the Holocaust (London: Macmillan, 1990)

Weidner, Jean H.
'De Weg naar de Vrijheid', in J. J. Bolhuis et al. (eds), *Onderdrukking en Verzet: Nederland in Oorlogstijd*, III (Arnhem: van Loghum Slaterus 1949–53)

Weinberg, David H.
A Community on Trial: The Jews of Paris in the 1930s (New York, 1994)

Weinreb, Friedrich
Collaboratie en Verzet, 1940–1945: Een poging tot ontmythologisering, 3 vols (Amsterdam, 1969)

Weiss, Hermann
'Die Rettung der Juden in Dänemark während der deutschen Besetzung 1940–1945', in Wolfgang Benz and Juliane Wetzel (eds), *Solidarität und Hilfe für Juden während der NS-Zeit*, Vol. 2 (Berlin: Metropol, 1998)

Werner, Emmy E.   *A Conspiracy of Decency: The Rescue of Danish Jews during World War II* (Boulder CO: Westview, 2002)

Westerweel, W.   *Verzet zonder geweld: Ter herinneringen van Joop Westerweel* (n.p., n.d.), mimeograph NIOD

Wiegman, T.   'Ds Overduin helpt onderduikers', *Sliepsteen* III (Autumn, 1985), 7; IV (Winter 1985); V (1986)

Wielek, H.   *De Oorlog die Hitler Won* (Amsterdam: Amsterdam Boek- en Courantmaatschappij, 1947)

Wijbenga, P.   *Bezettingstijd in Friesland*, Vol. I (Leeuwarden: De Tille, 1995)

Wijngaert, Mark van den   'Les Catholiques Belges et les Juifs durant l'occupation Allemande 1940–1944', in Rudi van Doorslaer et al. (eds), *Les Juifs de Belgique: De l'Immigration au Génocide, 1925–1945* (Brussels: Centre de Recherches et d'Études Historiques de la Seconde Guerre Mondiale, 1994)

――――   'The Belgian Catholics and the Jews During the German Occupation 1940–1944', in Dan Michman (ed.), *Belgium and the Holocaust: Jews Belgians Germans* (Jerusalem: Yad Vashem, 1998)

Wijsmuller-Meijer, Truus   *Geen Tijd voor Tranen* (Amsterdam: n.p., 1961)

Wilson, Roger C.   *Quaker Relief: An account of the relief work of the Society of Friends* (London: Allen and Unwin, 1952)

Winkel, Lydia E.   *Het Ondergrondse Vrij Nederland* (Baarn: Het Wereldvenster, 1970)

Wolf, H.   *De Gespijkerde God* (Nijmegen: SUN, 1995)

Wright, Myrtle   *Norwegian Diary 1940–1945* (London: Friends Peace International Relations Committee, 1974)

Wyden, Peter   *Stella: One Woman's True Tale of Evil, Betrayal and Survival in Hitler's Germany* (New York: Simon and Schuster, 1992).

Wyman, David S.   *Paper Walls: America and the Refugee Crisis 1938–1941* (Amherst MA: University of Massuchusetts, 1968)

Yagil, Limore   *Chrétiens et Juifs sous Vichy (1940–1944) Sauvetage et Désobéissance Civile* (Paris: Éditions du Cerf, 2005)

Yahil, Leni   *The Rescue of Danish Jewry: Test of a Democracy* (Philadelphia: Jewish Publication Society, 1969)

——   'Methods of Persecution: A Comparison of the Final Solution in Holland and Denmark', *Scripta Hierosolymitana*, XIII (1972)

Zasloff, Tela   *A Rescuer's Story: Pastor Pierre-Charles Toureille in Vichy France* (Madison WI: University of Wisconsin Press, 2003)

Zee, Nanda van der   *Om erger te voorkomen* (Amsterdam: Meulenhoff, 1997)

Zeitoun, Sabine   'L'OSE au secours des enfants juifs', in Association pour la recherché et la sauvetage de la vérité historique sur la résistance en Creuse, *Le Sauvetage des Enfants Juifs de France* (Guéret, 1996)

Zuccotti, Susan   *The Italians and the Holocaust: Persecution, Rescue and Survival* (London: Peter Halban, 1987)

Zucker, Bat-Ami   *In Search of Refuge. Jews and US Consuls in Nazi Germany 1933–1941* (London: Vallentine Mitchell, 2001)

Index